FAVORITE RECIPES® OF LUTHERAN LADIES
Traditional Meats

INCLUDING SEAFOOD and POULTRY

Favorite Recipes of Lutheran Ladies © MCMLXVI

P. O. Box 3376

Montgomery, Alabama 36109

INTRODUCTION

Lutheran homemakers are tops when it comes to cooking. These homemakers are well informed about nutrition and concerned with preparing wholesome, nutritious meals for their families. Lutheran cooks are known for serving delicious food. Any guest is always welcome in a Lutheran home and will find the table set with food to satisfy all tastes.

Many meat favorites of Lutheran homemakers can be found in this unusual collection. These recipes were home-tested before being submitted and were found to be successful for family meals. They made a hit at church suppers, birthday dinners and other special occasions. One popular Christmas event with Lutherans is to have a church dinner, a "progressive" meal for the young people, with each course served at a different home.

These meat favorites come from Lutheran homemakers all over the United States and Canada. Some may be familiar to you. Others may be new and different from any you have ever tried. Each recipe is endorsed by the homemaker whose name appears under the recipe.

We hope you will enjoy this collection of meat, seafood and poultry recipes and will share it with others.

St. Paul Lutheran Ladies Aid Society

COOKBOOK COMMITTEE

Mrs. Phoebe Bylsma, Chairman

Mrs. Arlene Hintz   Mrs. Mary Price

Mrs. Nora Zielinski

TABLE OF CONTENTS

ACKNOWLEDGMENTS

We wish to thank the many Lutheran women who submitted their favorite recipes for inclusion in this book. We regret that lack of space made it impossible for us to include all of them.

We wish also to express our appreciation for the use of photographs supplied us by the following: Covers — Accent International (recipe on page 38); Inside Front Cover — Evaporated Milk Association (recipe on page 247); Inside Back Cover — McIlhenny Company, Tabasco (recipe on page 61.)

Title and order blank page photographs were supplied by the following: National Fisheries Institute; United Fresh Fruit and Vegetable Association; McIlhenny Company (Tabasco); National Canners Association; California Raisin Advisory Board; American Lamb Council; Florida Citrus Commission; International Packers Limited; and Accent International.

ABBREVIATIONS USED IN THIS BOOK

Cup ....c.
Tablespoon ....tbsp.
Teaspoon ....tsp.
Pound ....lb.
Ounce ....oz.
Gallon ....gal.

Large ....lge.
Package ....pkg.
Square ....sq.
Dozen ....doz.
Pint ....pt.
Quart ....qt.

IN MEASURING, REMEMBER . . .

3 tsp. = 1 tbsp.

2 tbsp. = ⅛ c.

4 tbsp. = ¼ c.

8 tbsp. = ½ c.

16 tbsp. = 1 c.

5 tbsp. + 1 tsp. = ⅓ c.

12 tbsp. = ¾ c.

4 oz. = ½ c.

8 oz. = 1 c.

16 oz. = 1 lb.

1 oz. = 2 tbsp. fat or liquid

2 c. fat = 1 lb.

2 c. = 1 pt.

2 c. sugar = 1 lb.

⅝ c. = ½ c. + 2 tbsp.

⅞ c. = ¾ c. + 2 tbsp.

1 lb. butter = 2 c. or 4 sticks

2 pts. = 1 qt.

1 qt. = 4 c.

A few grains = less than ⅛ tsp.

Pinch = as much as can be taken between tip of finger and thumb

Speck = less than ⅛ tsp.

OVEN TEMPERATURES

Temperature (°F.)	Term
250-300	Slow
325	Moderately slow
350	Moderate
375	Moderately quick
400	Moderately hot
425-450	Hot
475-500	Extremely hot

MEAT IN THE MENU

Menus are usually planned around the meat which is to be served at the meal. It acts as the foundation for the meal and is most often the main dish. Meat contains many essential nutrients and is therefore an important part of a meal.

The homemaker will find a wide variety of meats at the market and will need to be able to make a wise choice. Because meat is relatively expensive, it is important that the homemaker know how to buy, store, and cook meat.

GUIDES TO MEAT BUYING

There are three basic things to look for when buying meat. These are the Government Inspection Stamp, the Meat Grade and Brand Name Stamp, and the appearance of the meat.

1. Government Inspection Stamp — This stamp guarantees the consumer that the meat is from a healthy animal which has passed federal inspection standards.

2. Meat Grade and Brand Name Stamp — This is the grade or brand name of the individual packer and grade names of the U.S. Department of Agriculture. The grade put on by the individual packer varies with each company. The government has only one manner of grading meat. Their grades are U.S. Prime, U.S. Choice, U.S. Good, U.S. Standard, U.S. Commercial and U.S. Utility.

3. Appearance — Meat of high quality has well marbleized lean, fine grained texture and a color typical of the particular meat.

AGING OF MEAT

The main purpose of aging meat is to develop additional tenderness and flavor. During the process of aging, the meat is kept at about 36°F. for three to six weeks. Ribs and loin of beef and mutton are usually aged. Veal and pork are not improved at all by aging. Meat which is suitable for aging is meat with a fairly thick covering of fat. This layer of fat protects the meat against discoloration and excessive drying. Only the higher grades of beef and mutton have a covering of fat which is thick enough to allow aging.

CUT OF MEAT	SERVINGS PER LB.	.29	.39	.49	.59	.69	.79	.89	.99	1.09	1.19
BEEF											
T-bone, rib, porterhouse steaks	2					.35	.40	.45	.50	.55	.60
Sirloin steak	2½					.29	.32	.36	.40	.44	
Sirloin tip	3					.23	.27	.30	.33	.36	.40
Standing rib roast	2				.30	.35	.40	.45	.50		
Boneless rump roast	3				.20	.23	.26	.30	.33		
Round steak	3½				.17	.20	.22	.25	.28		
Boneless beef stew	4				.15	.17	.20	.22			
Chuck roast	2		.20	.25	.30	.35	.40				
Ground beef	4		.10	.12	.15	.17					
Short ribs	2		.20	.25	.30	.35					
Brisket	1½		.26	.33	.37	.46					
Liver	5		.08	.10	.12	.14	.16	.18			
Heart	4		.10	.12	.15	.17					
Tongue	4		.10	.12	.15	.17					
PORK											
Chops	4				.15	.17	.20	.22	.25		
Spareribs	1⅓		.30	.36	.45	.52					
Loin roast	2½			.20	.24	.28					
Shoulder roast	3	.10	.13	.16	.20	.23					
Boneless Boston butt	4		.10	.12	.15	.17					
Shoulder steak	3		.13	.16	.20	.23					
Ham											
Cured — whole	3		.13	.16	.20	.23	.26				
Cured — portions	2½	.12	.16	.20	.24						
Cured — center slice	4			.12	.15	.17	.20				
Cooked — whole	4			.12	.15	.17	.20				
Cooked — portions	3		.13	.16	.20	.23					
Cooked — boneless or canned	5				.12	.14	.16	.18	.20		
Sausage	4	.07	.10	.12	.15						
Bacon — 2 slices per person	8					.09	.10	.11	.12		

STORING MEAT

FRESH MEAT

Should be stored either wrapped or loosely wrapped in the coldest part of the refrigerator. A partial drying on the surface of the meat increases its keeping quality. A moisture-vapor-proof wrapper is not needed for storing fresh meat but is used in freezing meat. Do not store meat in the market wrapping paper. This paper should be removed if the meat is not to be used the day it is purchased.

PROCESSED MEAT

Cured meats and ready-to-serve meats should be stored in the coldest part of the refrigerator. These meats should not be kept for long periods of time (ready-to-serve meats not over one week, cured meats not over one to two weeks). Processed meats should not be frozen. The salt in these meats favors rancidity.

COOKED MEAT

Should be cooled quickly and stored in the refrigerator. It should be covered or wrapped.

FROZEN MEAT

Should be stored in freezer with the temperature 0°F or below. It must be properly wrapped for freezing. Below is a listing of the various lengths of time meat can be kept safely frozen.

MEAT STORAGE CHART

MEAT	MAXIMUM STORAGE TIME*
Beef	6 to 12 months
Lamb and veal	6 to 9 months
Ground beef, veal and lamb	3 to 4 months
Pork	3 to 6 months
Ground pork	1 to 3 months
Variety meats	3 to 4 months

*This range in maximum storage time reflects differences in recommendations of various authorities using meat from different sources.

HERB, SPICE AND SEASONING CHART

Herbs, spices and seasonings must be used sparingly to enhance, not overpower the flavor of meats, seafood or poultry. The general rule as to quantity is ¼ teaspoon of herbs, spices or seasonings per pound for meats, seafood and poultry, or according to individual taste.

HERB OR SPICE	USE IN
ALLSPICE	Meat ball appetizers, oyster stew, beef stew, pot roast, ham, lamb, oysters
BASIL	Crab spread, turtle soup, lamb liver, meat loaf, heart, venison, bluefish, halibut, mackerel, goose, duck, turkey
BAY LEAF	Beef soup, fish chowders, veal liver, spareribs, beef stew, lamb goulash, pickled fish, shrimp, crab, boiled chicken, seafood casseroles
CARAWAY SEED	Roast pork, kidney, sauerbraten, tuna casseroles, roast goose
CELERY (salt, seeds, flakes)	Ham spread, oyster stew, bouillon, meat loaf, meat stews, pot roasts, codfish, chicken pie or croquettes, tuna salads
CLOVES	Beef soup, ham, pork roasts, boiled tongue, baked fish, chicken a la king, roasted chicken
CURRY POWDER	Clam chowder, chicken soup, lamb, veal, shrimp, baked fish, chicken hash
GARLIC (liquid, salt, powder)	Clam dip, barbecue sauce, steaks, stews, Italian and French meat dishes, chicken, fish
GINGER	Boiled beef, lamb, veal, sauted or baked chicken, Cornish hen, squab
MARJORAM	Oyster stew, pot roasts, stews, lamb, creamed crab, scallops, broiled fish, chicken or seafood salads
MUSTARD	Meat dips, ham sauces, beef-onion soup, pickled meat, ham, kidney, seafood casseroles
NUTMEG	Chopped oyster appetizers, cream of chicken soup, Salisbury steak, meat loaf, chicken
OREGANO	Meat sauces, beef, pork, veal, lamb, Swiss steak, seafood stuffing, fried chicken, seafood salads
ROSEMARY	Turtle, chicken or meat soups, kidney, veal stews, lamb, creamed shellfish, chicken fricassee
SAFFRON	Poultry stuffing, chicken soup stock, lamb, veal, sausage, halibut, sole, chicken, seafood salads
SAGE	Meat sauces and gravies, baked fish stuffing, consomme, chowders, cold roast beef, stews, pork dishes, baked fish, duck
SAVORY	Chicken and fish sauces, liver pastes, fish chowders, hamburgers, lamb roasts, veal, pork, baked or broiled fish
TARRAGON	Meat sauces, meat canape mixtures, veal, sweetbreads, creamed seafood, turkey, game, chicken, chicken salads
THYME	Sauces for meats, chowders, oyster stew

CALORIE CHART

Food	Amount	Calories
Bacon, broiled or fried crisp	2 slices	95
Beef, trimmed to retail basis, cooked:		
Cuts braised, simmered or pot-roasted:		
Lean and fat	3 oz.	245
Lean only	2.5 oz.	140
Hamburger, broiled:		
Market ground	3 oz.	245
Ground lean	3 oz.	185
Roast, oven-cooked, no liquid added:		
Relatively fat, such as rib:		
Lean and fat	3 oz.	390
Lean only	1.8 oz.	120
Relatively lean, such as round:		
Lean and fat	3 oz.	220
Lean only	2.5 oz.	130
Steak, broiled:		
Relatively fat, such as sirloin:		
Lean and fat	3 oz.	330
Lean only	2 oz.	115
Relatively lean, such as round:		
Lean and fat	3 oz.	220
Lean only	2 oz.	130
Beef, canned:		
Corned beef	3 oz.	180
Corned beef hash	3 oz.	120
Beef, dried or chipped	2 oz.	115
Beef and vegetable stew	1 c.	185
Beef pot pie, baked, about 8 oz. before baking	1 pie	460
Chicken, cooked:		
Flesh and skin, broiled, no bone	3 oz.	185
Breast, fried, with bone	½ breast	215
Leg, fried (thigh and drumstick) with bone	4.3 oz.	245
Chicken, canned, boneless	3 oz.	170
Chile con carne, canned:		
With beans	1 c.	335
Without beans	1 c.	510
Heart, beef, trimmed of fat, braised	3 oz.	160
Lamb, trimmed to retail basis, cooked:		
Chop, thick, with bone, broiled		
Lean and fat	4 oz.	405
Lean only	2.6 oz.	140
Leg, roasted:		
Lean and fat	3 oz.	235
Lean only	2.5 oz.	130
Shoulder, roasted:		
Lean and fat	3 oz.	285
Lean only	2.3 oz.	130

CALORIE CHART (Continued)

Food	Amount	Calories
Liver, beef, fried	2 oz.	120
Pork, cured, cooked:		
Ham, smoked, lean and fat	3 oz.	290
Luncheon meat:		
Cooked ham, sliced	2 oz.	170
Canned, spiced or unspiced	2 oz.	165
Pork, fresh, trimmed to retail basis, cooked:		
Chop, thick with bone:		
Lean and fat	2.3 oz.	260
Lean only	1.7 oz.	130
Roast, oven-cooked, no liquid added:		
Lean and fat	3 oz.	310
Lean only	2.4 oz.	175
Cuts, simmered:		
Lean and fat	3 oz.	320
Lean only	2.2 oz.	135
Poultry pot pie, about 8 oz.	1 pie	485
Sausage:		
Bologna, slice 4.1x0.1"	8 slices	690
Frankfurter, cooked	1 frank	155
Pork, bulk, canned	4 oz.	340
Tongue, beef, simmered	3 oz.	205
Veal, cooked:		
Cutlet, broiled, no bone	3 oz.	185
Roast, med. fat, medium done, lean and fat	3 oz.	305
Fish and Shellfish:		
Bluefish, baked or boiled	3 oz.	135
Clams:		
Raw, meat only	3 oz.	70
Canned, solids and liquids	3 oz.	45
Crabmeat, canned or cooked	3 oz.	90
Fish sticks, breaded, cooked, frozen	8-oz. pkg.	400
Haddock, fried	3 oz.	135
Mackerel:		
Broiled, Atlantic	3 oz.	200
Canned, Pacific, solids and liquids	3 oz.	155
Ocean perch, breaded, fried	3 oz.	195
Oysters, meat only, raw	1 c.	160
Oyster stew, 1 part oysters, 3 parts milk	1 c.	200
Salmon, pink, canned	3 oz.	120
Sardines, Atlantic type, canned in oil, drained	3 oz.	180
Shad, baked	3 oz.	170
Shrimp, canned, meat only	3 oz.	110
Swordfish, broiled with butter or oleo	3 oz.	150
Tuna, canned in oil, drained	3 oz.	170

HOW TO COOK FRESH MEAT

The method used for cooking meat is determined by the tenderness of the meat. This will vary with the cut of meat. Any cut can be tender and palatable when the appropriate method of cooking is used.

Tender cuts are best when dry heat is used for cooking. Methods of dry heat cookery are roasting, broiling, panfrying and panbroiling.

Less tender cuts can be made tender by cooking with moist heat. Steam is created in the moist heat method and this softens the connective tissue in the meat.

Meat should be cooked at a low temperature to have a tender, flavorful and juicy product. A moderate temperature will give you best results. How the meat is cooked will also determine how easily it carves.

SIX BASIC METHODS OF MEAT COOKERY

Roasting

Any tender cut of beef, veal, pork, or lamb may be roasted. The steps in this method of cooking are as follows:

1. Season with salt and pepper, if desired. It matters little whether a roast is salted before or during cooking because when it is done, the salt has penetrated only to a depth of about half an inch.

2. Place meat, fat-side up, on rack in open shallow roasting pan. The rack holds the roast out of the drippings; with the fat on top, the roast will do its own basting.

3. Insert a meat thermometer so that its bulb is in the center of the largest muscle. The bulb should not touch bone or rest in fat.

4. Add no water and do not cover. Roasting is a dry heat method of cooking, and if the pan is covered or water added, the meat will become a pot roast.

5. Roast in a slow oven — 300°F. to 350°F. The oven may be started just as the roast is put in.

6. Roast to the desired degree of doneness. There will be no overcooking nor undercooking if a meat thermometer is used.

Broiling

Tender beef steaks, lamb or mutton chops, sliced ham or bacon, and ground beef or lamb are suitable for broiling. Fresh pork and veal are seldom broiled. Steaks and chops should be cut at least 1-inch thick for best broiling, a slice of ham at least ½-inch thick. These steps show how to broil:

1. Turn the oven regulator to "Broil". The broiler may be preheated or not, as desired. With some broilers thick steaks or chops may be cooked without preheating the broiler.

2. Place meat on rack of broiler pan, 2 to 3 inches from the heat. Steaks or chops 1½ to 2 inches thick should be at least 3 inches from the heat; those 1 inch or less in thickness, about 2 inches.

3. Broil until top side is brown. The meat should be approximately half done by the time it is browned on top.

4. Season the top side with salt and pepper. For a slice of ham or bacon this step would be omitted. Steaks and chops brown better if browned before salting.

5. Turn and brown the other side. For determining accurately the degree of doneness, a meat thermometer may be used.

6. Season and serve at once. To keep broiled meats hot, the plate should be heated.

Panbroiling

The same tender cuts suitable for broiling may be panbroiled or griddle-broiled. When cuts are very thin, panbroiling or griddle-broiling may even be preferred. Panbroiling is also a convenient method for a small steak or a few chops. Follow these steps, whether panbroiling or griddle-broiling:

1. Place meat in heavy frying pan or on griddle. Cook slowly. The pan or griddle need not be sizzling hot nor is it necessary to preheat it. The meat merely starts cooking more quickly if it is warm or hot at the beginning.

2. Do not add fat or water. Do not cover. Most meat cuts have enough fat to prevent their sticking; if fat is added they will be fried.

3. Turn occasionally. Since the meat is in contact with the hot metal of the pan or griddle, turning more than once is essential for even cooking.

4. Pour off or remove fat as it accumulates. If fat is, permitted to collect, the meat will fry instead of panbroil or griddle-broil.

5. Brown meat on both sides. It does not need to be seared or browned quickly at the beginning — searing does not hold in meat juices — a gradual browning is better.

6. Do not overcook. Season and serve at once.

Frying

Tender meat or that made tender by pounding, scoring, cubing, or grinding, and left-over meat may be fried. When a small amount of fat is added or allowed to accumulate during cooking, the method is called frying, panfrying or sauteing. When the meat is immersed in fat, it is called deep-fat frying.

To Panfry:

1. Use a heavy frying pan. Cooking in a heavy pan will give more even and uniform cooking.

2. Brown meat on both sides in a small amount of fat.

3. Season with salt and pepper. If the meat is cooked with a coating, the seasoning may be added to the coating ingredients.

4. Do not cover the meat.

5. Cook at moderate temperature until done, turning occasionally. Do not allow the fat to smoke. A temperature this high is too hot for the meat.

To Deep-Fat Fry:

1. Use a deep kettle and a frying basket. There should be enough fat to completely cover the meat.

2. Heat fat to frying temperature. The temperature for deep-fat frying will range from 300°F. to 350°F.

3. Using the basket, lower a few uniform pieces of meat at a time, gradually, into the hot fat.

4. Brown meat and cook it through.

5. When done, drain fat from meat into kettle before removing meat from basket.

6. Strain fat through cloth and cool. Cover and store in refrigerator.

Braising

Less tender cuts of meat are cooked by braising. Some tender cuts also are best if braised. These include pork chops, steaks and cutlets; veal chops, steaks and cutlets; and pork liver. Steps in braising are as follows:

1. Brown meat slowly on all sides in heavy utensil. To intensify the browning, the meat may be dredged with flour.

2. Season with salt, pepper, herbs, spices and vegetables.

3. Add a small amount of liquid to less tender cuts. Liquid is not necessary in braising tender cuts.

4. Cover tightly.

5. Cook at low temperature until tender.

6. Make sauce or gravy from the liquid in the pan.

Cooking In Liquid

Large cuts and stews are cooked in liquid. This is another method of cooking less tender cuts. The steps involved in this method are as follows:

Large Cuts:

1. Brown meat on all sides, if desired.

2. Cover the meat with water or stock.

3. Season well with salt, pepper, herbs, spices, and vegetables as desired.

4. Cover kettle and simmer until tender.

5. If the meat is to be served cold, let it cool, and then chill in the stock in which it was cooked.

6. If vegetables are to be cooked with the meat, as in "boiled" dinners, add them whole or in large pieces, just long enough before the meat is tender to cook them.

Stews:

1. Cut meat into uniform pieces, usually 1 to 2-inch cubes.

2. If a brown stew is desired, brown meat cubes on all sides.

3. Add just enough water, vegetable juices or soup stock to cover he meat.

4. Season with salt, pepper, herbs, and spices.

5. Cover kettle closely and simmer until meat is tender.

6. Add vegetables to the meat at the proper time so as not to overcook them.

7. When done, remove meat and vegetables to a pan, platter or casserole and keep hot.

8. Thicken the stock with flour made into a paste, using a small amount of cold water or stock.

9. Pour hot gravy over the meat and vegetables or serve separately in a sauce boat.

10. If desired, make meat pie from the stew.

COOKING FROZEN MEAT

Frozen meats may be cooked from frozen, partially thawed, or completely thawed state. If properly cooked, there is no difference in flavor or in amount of shrinkage.

Thawing may be done in the refrigerator or at room temperature. The meat should be left in the original wrapper and after thawing should be put into the refrigerator and not allowed to remain out. Cooking methods for frozen meat are the same as for fresh. Additional time should be allowed for cooking when cooking meat from the frozen state.

BEEF

Beef of high quality has a covering of evenly distributed, firm fat over the exterior. The lean is bright, uniform and well-marbled with creamy white fat. It is firm, velvety in appearance and fine grained.

Tenderness of the beef will vary with the cut and also the grade. In choosing a cut it is necessary to keep in mind the cooking method required for that cut of beef. Most cuts of Prime and Choice grades can be cooked with dry heat. Beef which has been properly aged will be tender.

Ground beef is made from trimmings of high grade beef mixed with meat from older beef. The high grade beef gives tenderness and the older beef adds a well-developed flavor. There is as much nutritive value in ground beef as there is in steak.

TIME-TABLE FOR COOKING MEAT

CUT	ROASTED AT 300°F. OVEN TEMPERATURE		BROILED		BRAISED	COOKED IN LIQUID
	Meat Thermometer Reading	Time	Meat Thermometer Reading	Total Time	Total Time	Total Time
Standing Ribs	Degrees F. 140 (rare)	Minutes per lb. 18 to 20	Degrees F. Minutes		Hours	Hours
Standing Ribs	160 (medium)	22 to 25				
Standing Ribs	170 (well)	27 to 30				
Rolled Ribs	Same as above	Add 10 to 15				
Blade, 3rd to 5th Rib (high quality only)	150-170	25 to 30				
Rump (high quality only)	150-170	25 to 30				
Tenderloin	140-170	20 to 25				
Beef Loaf	160-170	25 to 30				
Steaks (1 inch)			140 (rare) 160 (med.)	15 to 20 20 to 30		
Steaks (1½ inch)			140 (rare) 160 (med.)	25 to 35 35 to 50		
Steaks (2 inch)			140 (rare) 160 (med.)	30 to 40 50 to 70		
Beef Patties (1 inch)			140 (rare) 160 (med.)	12 to 15 18 to 20		
Pot-Roasts						
Arm or Blade					3 to 4	
Rump					3 to 4	
Swiss Steak					2 to 3	
Corned Beef						3½ to 5
Fresh Beef					3 to 4	3 to 4
Stew						2 to 3

BEEF CHART

RETAIL CUTS OF BEEF — WHERE THEY COME FROM AND HOW TO COOK THEM

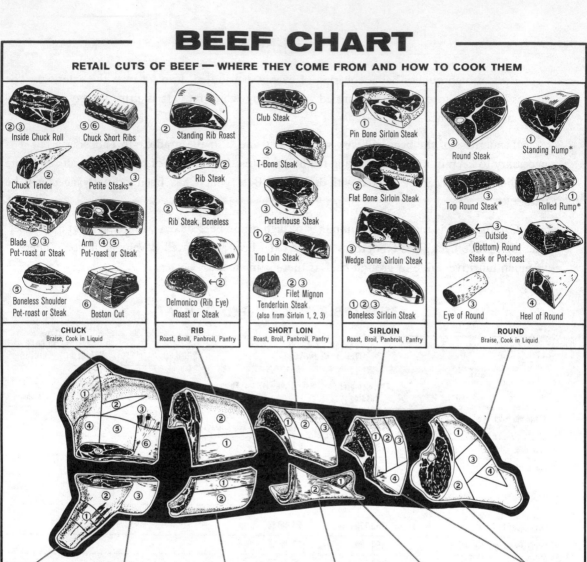

CHUCK
Braise, Cook in Liquid

- ② ③ Inside Chuck Roll
- ⑤ ⑥ Chuck Short Ribs
- ② Chuck Tender
- ③ Petite Steaks*
- Blade ② ③ Pot-roast or Steak
- Arm ④ ⑤ Pot-roast or Steak
- ⑤ Boneless Shoulder Pot-roast or Steak
- ⑥ Boston Cut

RIB
Roast, Broil, Panbroil, Panfry

- ② Standing Rib Roast
- ② Rib Steak
- ② Rib Steak, Boneless
- ② Delmonico (Rib Eye) Roast or Steak

SHORT LOIN
Roast, Broil, Panbroil, Panfry

- ① Club Steak
- ② T-Bone Steak
- ③ Porterhouse Steak
- ① ② ③ Top Loin Steak
- ② ③ Filet Mignon Tenderloin Steak (also from Sirloin 1, 2, 3)

SIRLOIN
Roast, Broil, Panbroil, Panfry

- ① Pin Bone Sirloin Steak
- ② Flat Bone Sirloin Steak
- ③ Wedge Bone Sirloin Steak
- ① ② ③ Boneless Sirloin Steak

ROUND
Braise, Cook in Liquid

- ③ Round Steak
- ① Standing Rump*
- ③ Top Round Steak*
- ① Rolled Rump*
- ③ Outside (Bottom) Round Steak or Pot-roast
- Eye of Round
- ④ Heel of Round

FORE SHANK
Braise, Cook in Liquid

- ① Shank Cross Cuts

- ① ② Beef for Stew (also from other cuts)

BRISKET
Braise, Cook in Liquid

- ③ Fresh Brisket
- ③ Corned Brisket

SHORT PLATE
Braise, Cook in Liquid

- ① Short Ribs
- ① ② Skirt Steak Fillets*
- ① ② Rolled Plate
- ① ② Plate Beef

GROUND BEEF
Roast, Broil, Panbroil, Panfry

Ground Beef (Flank, Short Plate, Shank, Brisket, Rib, Chuck, Loin, Round)

Beef Patties

FLANK STEAK
Braise, Cook in Liquid

- ① Flank Steak*
- ① Flank Steak Fillets*

TIP (KNUCKLE)
Braise, Cook in Liquid

- ④ ② Tip Steak*
- ④ ② Sirloin Tip*
- ④ ② Cube Steak*

* May be Roasted, Broiled, Panbroiled or Panfried from high quality beef.

NLS&MB

NATIONAL LIVE STOCK AND MEAT BOARD

SELECTION OF BEEF CUTS

Wholesale	Retail Cuts	Characteristics	Cooking Methods
Round (and rump)	Round steak (full cut)	Round or oval shape with small round bone. One large muscle, three smaller ones.	Braise
	Top round steak or pot roast	Most tender portion of round. Is one large muscle.	Braise; roast; panfry
	Bottom round steak or pot roast	Less tender than top round. Distinguished from top round by having two muscles.	Braise
	Tip roast or steak	Triangular cut; roast may contain kneecap. Steaks are boneless.	Braise; roast; broil; panbroil; panfry
	Standing rump	Triangular shape; contains portions of aitch bone and tail bone. Knuckle end of leg (round) bone usually removed.	Braise; roast (high quality)
	Rolled rump	Boneless roll.	Braise; roast (high quality)
	Heel of round	Boneless wedge-shaped cut from lower part of round. Weighs 4 to 8 pounds. Has very little fat and is least tender cut of round.	Braise; cook in liquid
	Hind shank	Boney, considerable connective tissue, rich in extractives.	Cook in liquid (soup)
Sirloin	Sirloin steak	Contains portions of back bone and hip bone. Wide variation in bone and muscle structure of the various steaks.	Broil; panbroil; panfry
	Pinbone sirloin steak	Lies next to the porterhouse. Contains pin bone which is the forward end of hip bone.	Broil; panbroil; panfry
	Boneless sirloin steak	Any boneless steak from the sirloin.	Broil; panbroil; panfry
Short loin	Porterhouse steak	Largest steak in short loin. Loin strip and tenderloin muscles. T-shaped bone. Tenderloin larger in porterhouse than in other short loin steaks.	Broil; panbroil; panfry
	T-bone steak	Same as porterhouse except tenderloin is smaller. T-bone and porterhouse used more or less interchangeably.	Broil; panbroil; panfry
	Club (Delmonico) steak	Triangular-shaped; smallest steak in short loin. Tenderloin has practically disappeared.	Broil; panbroil; panfry
	Tenderloin roast or steak	Boneless tapering muscle. Most tender cut of beef.	Roast; broil; panbroil; panfry
Flank	Flank steak	Oval-shaped boneless steak — usually weighing ¾ to 1½ pounds. Muscles run lengthwise; usually scored to shorten muscle fibers. Less tender cut.	Braise
	Flank steak fillets	Sections of flank steak rolled and fastened with skewers.	Braise
	Flank meat	Boneless. Coarse fibers. May be rolled, cut in stew or ground.	Braise; cook in liquid
Rib	Standing rib roast (short cut)	Contains two or more ribs from which short ribs and chine bone have been removed. Comparable to rib roast served in restaurants.	Roast
	Rolled rib roast	Boneless roll. Outer cover of roll consists largely of thin plate meat wrapped around rib eye.	Roast
	Rib steak	Contains rib eye and may contain rib bone.	Broil; panbroil; panfry
	Short ribs	Cut from ends of ribs; layers of lean and fat.	Braise; cook in liquid
Short plate	Plate boiling beef	Cut across plate parallel with ribs.	Braise; cook in liquid
	Rolled plate	When rolled the absence of the rib eye distinguishes this cut from rolled rib.	Braise; cook in liquid
	Short ribs	Cut from ends of ribs; layers of lean and fat.	Braise; cook in liquid
Square-cut chuck	Arm pot roast of steak	Has a round bone and cross sections of three to five ribs. A small round muscle near the round bone is surrounded by connective tissue.	Braise
	Blade pot roast or steak	Pot roast contains portions of rib and blade bones. Steaks cut between ribs will not contain rib bone.	Braise
	Boneless chuck	Any part of the square-cut chuck except the neck from which the bones have been removed.	Braise
	Boneless neck	Any part of the neck without the neck bone.	Braise; cook in liquid
	English (Boston) cut	A rectangular piece cut across two or three chuck ribs.	Braise
Brisket	Brisket	Layers of lean and fat. Presence of breast bone sure indication that cut is from the brisket.	Braise; cook in liquid
	Boneless brisket	Same as above with ribs and breast bone removed.	Braise; cook in liquid
Fore shank	Shank knuckle	Knuckle or upper end of fore shank.	Cook in liquid; braise
	Shank cross cuts	Small pieces cut across shank bone.	Braise; cook in liquid

17

CARVING INSTRUCTIONS FOR BEEF

STANDING RIB ROAST

Place the roast on a platter with the largest end down. If necessary cut wedge-shaped slice from the large end so the roast will have a solid base. Insert the fork between the two top ribs. Carve across the roast from the fat side to rib bone.

Cut along the rib bone to loosen the slice. Keep close to the bone in order to have as large a serving as possible.

Slide the knife under the slice and place on the side of the platter or on a heated platter.

PORTERHOUSE STEAK

Holding the steak with the fork, cut closely around the bone. Remove bone, and place to side of platter.

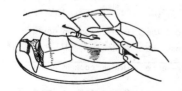

With fork firmly holding the tenderloin, cut across width of steak. Each serving will include both top loin and tenderloin.

BEEF BLADE POT ROAST

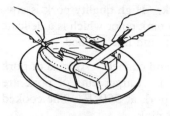

Holding roast firmly with fork, cut between muscles and around bones.   Remove solid sections of roast one at a time.

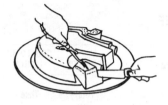

Turn section just removed on side so as to be able to make slices across the grain.

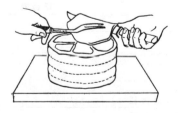

Carve slices which are about ¼-inch thick.

ROLLED RIB ROAST

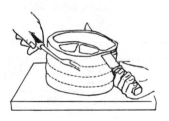

Do not remove the cords from the roast before carving. Insert the fork into the left side of the roast about one or two inches below the top.   Start slicing across the meat grain from the right side toward the fork.

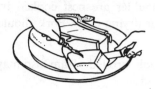

Make the first slice fairly thick to get a level surface. Use the knife and fork to lift each slice to the side of the platter.   Move the fork lower in the meat for each slice and sever the cords as they are reached.

PORK

Pork has a very desirable flavor due largely to the fat of pork. High quality pork is covered with a layer of rather firm, white fat. The lean has a grayish pink color which is a delicate rose color in older animals. It is well-marbled with fat and is firm and fine grained.

Pork is sold in many forms — fresh cured, smoked, pickled and canned. All cuts of pork are tender, therefore, dry heat methods of cooking may be applied. Larger cuts of pork are usually best roasted. Cured pork is roasted at 300°F and fresh pork at 350°F. The cooked lean of fresh pork should be grayish white without even a tinge of pink.

Cuts of pork such as — chops, cutlets, sliced fresh ham or shoulder are best cooked by braising. Braising allows these cuts to be cooked well done without drying out. Pork should always be cooked well done.

Sliced cured ham and bacon may be broiled, panbroiled or griddle-broiled. Ham also may be panfried and bacon may be panfried, deep-fat fried or oven cooked.

TIME-TABLE FOR COOKING BEEF

CUT	ROASTED AT 300°-350°F. OVEN TEMPERATURE		BROILED		BRAISED	COOKED IN LIQUID
	Meat Thermometer Reading	Time	Meat Thermometer Reading	Total Time	Total Time	Time
	Degrees F.	Minutes per lb.	Degrees F.	Minutes	Hours	Minutes per lb.
FRESH						
Loin						
Center	185	35 to 40	Fresh pork is never broiled			
Whole	185	15 to 20				
Ends	185	45 to 50				
Shoulder						
Rolled	185	40 to 45				
Cushion	185	35 to 40				
Boston Butt	185	45 to 50				
Leg or Ham	185	30 to 35				
Chops					¾ to 1	
Steaks					¾ to 1	
Spareribs		30 to 35			1½	30
Pork and Ham Loaf		30 to 35				
SMOKED						
Ham						
Large	160	15 to 18				18 to 20
Medium	160	18 to 22				
Small	160	22 to 25				
Half	160	25 to 30				25
Ham Loaf	160	30 to 35				
Ham Slice (½ inch)			160 to 170	10 to 12		
(1 inch)			160 to 170	16 to 20		
Picnic	170	35				35 to 45
Shoulder Butt	170	35			4 to 5	
Bacon						

PORK CHART

RETAIL CUTS OF PORK — WHERE THEY COME FROM AND HOW TO COOK THEM

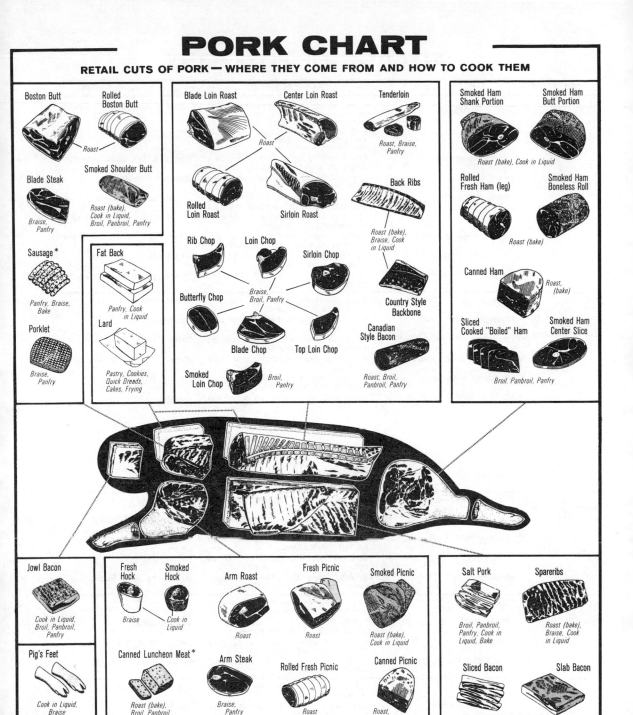

Boston Butt

Rolled Boston Butt
Roast

Blade Steak
Braise, Panfry

Sausage*
Panfry, Braise, Bake

Porklet
Braise, Panfry

Smoked Shoulder Butt
Roast (bake), Cook in Liquid, Broil, Panbroil, Panfry

Fat Back
Panfry, Cook in Liquid

Lard
Pastry, Cookies, Quick Breads, Cakes, Frying

Blade Loin Roast

Center Loin Roast
Roast

Rolled Loin Roast

Sirloin Roast

Tenderloin
Roast, Braise, Panfry

Back Ribs
Roast (bake), Braise, Cook in Liquid

Rib Chop

Loin Chop

Sirloin Chop

Butterfly Chop

Blade Chop

Top Loin Chop
Braise, Broil, Panfry

Smoked Loin Chop
Broil, Pantry

Country Style Backbone

Canadian Style Bacon
Roast, Broil, Panbroil, Panfry

Smoked Ham Shank Portion

Smoked Ham Butt Portion
Roast (bake), Cook in Liquid

Rolled Fresh Ham (leg)

Smoked Ham Boneless Roll
Roast (bake)

Canned Ham
Roast, (bake)

Sliced Cooked "Boiled" Ham

Smoked Ham Center Slice
Broil, Panbroil, Panfry

Jowl Bacon
Cook in Liquid, Broil, Panbroil, Panfry

Pig's Feet
Cook in Liquid, Braise

Fresh Hock

Smoked Hock
Braise *Cook in Liquid*

Canned Luncheon Meat*
Roast (bake), Broil, Panbroil

Arm Roast
Roast

Arm Steak
Braise, Panfry

Fresh Picnic
Roast

Rolled Fresh Picnic
Roast

Smoked Picnic
Roast (bake), Cook in Liquid

Canned Picnic
Roast, (bake)

Salt Pork
Broil, Panbroil, Panfry, Cook in Liquid, Bake

Spareribs
Roast (bake), Braise, Cook in Liquid

Sliced Bacon

Slab Bacon
Broil, Panbroil, Panfry, Bake

*These items may come from several areas of the pork side.

RLS&MB

NATIONAL LIVE STOCK AND MEAT BOARD

SELECTION OF PORK CUTS

WHOLESALE	RETAIL CUTS	CHARACTERISTICS	COOKING METHODS
Ham — Fresh, pickled, or smoked	Ham, whole	Corresponds to beef round with tail bone and portion of backbone removed. Outer skin or rind is left on the regular ham but it is removed, with excess fat, from the skinned ham.	Roast (bake); cook in liquid
	Ham, shank half	Lower half of ham. Includes shank and half of center section.	Roast (bake); cook in liquid
	Ham shank	Cone-shaped, rind-covered piece containing shank bones.	Cook in liquid
	Ham, butt half	Upper half of ham. Includes butt and half of center section.	Roast (bake); cook in liquid
	Ham butt	Same as above minus most of center section.	Roast (bake); cook in liquid
	Ham, center baking piece	Center section of ham. Both cut surfaces look like center slices.	Roast (bake); cook in liquid
	Ham, center slice	Oval-shape, small round bone, four separate muscles.	Broil; panbroil; panfry
	Ham, boneless	Boneless roll. Fresh, pickled or smoked.	Roast (bake); cook in liquid
Loin — Also tenderloin, boneless back strip, and Canadian-style bacon	Tenderloin	Long tapering round muscle. Weighs ½ to 1 pound.	Roast; braise
	Frenched tenderloin	Piece cut from tenderloin and flattened.	Braise; panfry
	Boneless loin roast	Boneless back strip. Two pieces sometimes tied together.	Roast
	Canadian-style bacon	Boneless back strip, cured and smoked.	Roast; broil; panbroil; panfry
	Butterfly chop	Double chop, hinged together, cut from boneless loin strip.	Braise; panfry
	Sirloin roast	Ham end of loin containing hip bone.	Roast
	Blade loin roast	Shoulder end of loin containing rib bones and blade bone.	Roast
	Loin chop	T-shaped bone and two muscles (back strip and tenderloin).	Braise; panfry
	Rib chop	Alternate chops have rib bone. May be "frenched"	Braise; panfry
	Crown roast	Rib sections "frenched" and formed in shape of crown.	Roast
Picnic shoulder Fresh, pickled or smoked	Picnic shoulder	Includes arm and shank sections of shoulder.	Roast; cook in liquid
	Rolled picnic shoulder	Boneless roll. Fresh, pickled or smoked.	Roast; cook in liquid
	Cushion picnic shoulder	Arm section of fresh picnic with pocket for stuffing.	Roast
	Arm steak	Oval at one end, squared off at other. Small round bone.	Braise; panfry
	Pork hock	Round, tapering, skin-covered piece containing shank bones.	Braise; cook in liquid
Boston butt Also smoked shoulder butt	Boston butt	Upper half of shoulder. Contains part of blade bone.	Roast
	Blade steak	Cut from Boston butt. Most steaks have section of blade bone.	Braise; panfry
	Smoked shoulder butt	Eye of Boston butt. Cured and smoked boneless roll.	Roast; cook in liquid
	Small shoulder butt slices	Round boneless slices. Lean and fat intermixed.	Broil; panbroil; panfry
Side (belly) Fresh, salt, pickled or smoked	Fresh side pork	Usually sliced. Alternating layers of lean and fat.	Braise; panfry
	Pickled side pork	Same as above but cured in sweet pickle solution.	Braise; panfry
	Salt side pork	Same as above but cured with dry salt.	Panfry; cook in liquid
	Sliced bacon	Same as above but cured, dry or in pickle, then smoked.	Broil; panbroil; panfry
Spareribs	Spareribs	Ribs and breastbone which have been removed from the bacon strip.	Roast; braise; cook in liquid
Jowl	Jowl bacon square	Jowl, trimmed square, then cured and smoked. High percentage of fat. May be sliced.	Cook in liquid; broil; panbroil; panfry
Feet	Pig's feet, fresh	Contains bones and tendons of foot and ankle. Little lean meat.	Cook in liquid
	Pig's feet, pickled	Pickled, cook and ready to eat.	No cooking necessary

CARVING INSTRUCTIONS FOR PORK

PORK LOIN ROAST

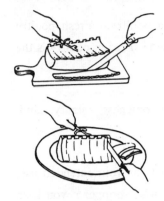

Remove back bone from roast before bringing to table. The retailer can saw the backbone free from ribs at the meat counter.

Insert fork in top of roast and make slices by cutting close to bone.   Every other slice will contain a rib.

PICNIC SHOULDER

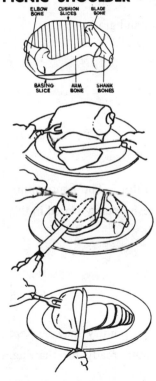

This diagram shows how to carve attractive servings from a pork picnic shoulder.

Place on platter with fat-side up and shank to carver's right.   Remove slice from side opposite elbow bone.

Cut down to arm bone and then turn knife and cut along arm bone.   This will be the boneless arm meat in one piece.

Place boneless arm meat on platter and carve by making perpendicular slices from top side of meat down to platter.

SHANK HALF OF HAM

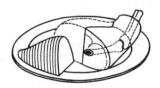

Remove boneless cushion section.   Place on carving board and make perpendicular slices.   Separate remaining section from the shank by cutting through the joint; remove bone, turn and slice.

POULTRY

When shopping for poultry there are several points to remember.

—Make your choice according to when you intend to use the poultry. Fresh poultry should be used within one to two days after it is purchased. Frozen poultry is the best choice if you intend to use it at a later date.

—Read the label carefully. It should inform you as to wholesomeness, quality, kind, weight, and price.

—Know what kind (whole or cut-up) and weight you will need for your intended use. If your family prefers white to dark meat, you will be a wise shopper if you keep this in mind.

—Check the label for brand name, Government inspection stamp and grade.

STORING POULTRY

Fresh, Uncooked

Wrap loosely in waxed paper and store in coldest part of refrigerator. The temperature should be as low as possible without actually freezing the poultry. Fresh poultry stored in this manner may be kept for one to three days.

Frozen, Uncooked

Wrap in moisture, vapor-proof paper and store in freezer. Frozen poultry may be kept in the freezer until ready to use. Do not remove from the freezer until ready for thawing. Stewing hens may be cooked without thawing.

Cooked

Poultry which has been cooked should be served promptly. If you have any left-over cooked poultry, be sure to refrigerate it as soon as possible.

FISH AND SHELLFISH

Fish and shellfish can be found on the market in several different forms.

Market Forms of Fish

WHOLE OR ROUND — as they come from the water. In preparing for cooking they must be scaled, entrails, heads, fins and tails removed. Small fish may be cooked without removing the fins and tails.

DRAWN — fish that has been eviscerated. It has been scaled and fins and tail have been removed.

DRESSED OR PAN-DRESSED — ready to cook as purchased. The entrails and scales have been removed. Usually the head, fins and tail have been removed also.

STEAKS — fish has been dressed and cross-section cuts have been made which are usually three quarters of an inch thick.

FILLETS — side cuts of fish. These lengthwise pieces are practically boneless and have very little waste.

STICKS — elongated pieces of fish cut from fillets and steaks.

In buying fresh fish you will want to consider all points which are characteristic of fresh fish.

Flesh..........should be firm and elastic. It should not be separating from the bones.

Odor..........should have a mild and fresh odor. Any fish which has a "fishy odor" should not be purchased.

Eyes..........fresh fish have bright and clear eyes. Protruding eyes are also characteristic of fresh fish.

Gills..........should be red and free of slime. The older the fish the less color it will have. The gills will gradually turn to a pink, then gray and finally brownish or greenish.

Skin..........should be shiny and color should not be faded.

AMOUNT TO BUY

FRESH OR FROZEN FISH	AMOUNT PER PERSON
Fillets, steaks, or sticks	⅓ pound
Dressed fish	½ pound
Whole or round fish	1 pound

Market Forms of Shellfish

IN SHELL — If bought in the shell, hard and soft blue crabs, clams, lobsters and oysters should be alive. Lobsters and crabs can be cooked in the shell before marketing.

SHUCKED — Meat from clams, oysters and scallops has been removed from the shell.

HEADLESS — Usually refers to shrimp and lobster which have their heads removed before marketing.

COOKED MEAT — Shellfish which have been cooked and the edible portion has been removed.

SHELLFISH	To Serve 6	To Serve 100
Crabs:		
Hard		
Live	6 to 12 lbs. (18 to 36 crabs)	90 to 100 lbs.
Cooked Meat	1 lb.	15 lbs.
Dungeness, cooked	4 to 6 lbs. (3 to 6 crabs)	50 lbs.
Lobsters:		
Live	4 to 6 lbs.	75 to 100 lbs.
Cooked Meat	¾ lb.	12 lbs.
Oysters and Clams:		
In Shell	3 dozen	2½ bushels
Shucked	1 quart	3½ gallons
Scallops	1 lb.	15 lbs.
Shrimp:		
Headless, fresh or frozen	1½ lbs.	24 to 30 lbs.
Cooked Meat	¾ lb.	12 to 15 lbs.

LAMB

Lamb of high quality has a covering of clear, white, brittle fat. The lean is pinkish red in color and has a fine-grained, velvety appearing texture. Over this exterior covering of fat is a thin, paper-like covering called the "fell". It does not affect the flavor unless the lamb has been aged for some time.

Most cuts of lamb are tender and can be cooked using dry heat. Stew may be made from the neck, shanks and breast. These pieces may also be braised.

Lamb should be cooked medium to well done. If slightly pink on the inside there will be less shrinkage and the meat will be very juicy and delicious. Lamb should be served hot or cold, never lukewarm.

TIME-TABLE FOR COOKING LAMB

CUT	ROASTED AT 300°F. OVEN TEMPERATURE		BROILED		BRAISED	COOKED IN LIQUID
	Meat Thermometer Reading	Time	Meat Thermometer Reading	Time	Total Time	Time
	Degrees F. 175 to 180	Minutes per lb. 30 to 35	Degrees F.	Minutes	Hours	Hours
Leg						
Shoulder Whole	175 to 180	30 to 35				
Rolled	175 to 180	40 to 45				
Cushion	175 to 180	30 to 35				
Breast Stuffed					1½ to 2	
Rolled	175 to 180	30 to 35			1½ to 2	
Lamb Loaf	175 to 180	30 to 35				
Chops (1 inch)	175 to 180	30 to 35	170	12		
Chops (1½ inch)			170	18		
Chops (2 inch)			170	22		
Lamb Patties (1 inch)				15 to 18		
Neck Slices					1	
Shanks					1½	
Stew						1½ to 2

LAMB CHART

RETAIL CUTS OF LAMB — WHERE THEY COME FROM AND HOW TO COOK THEM

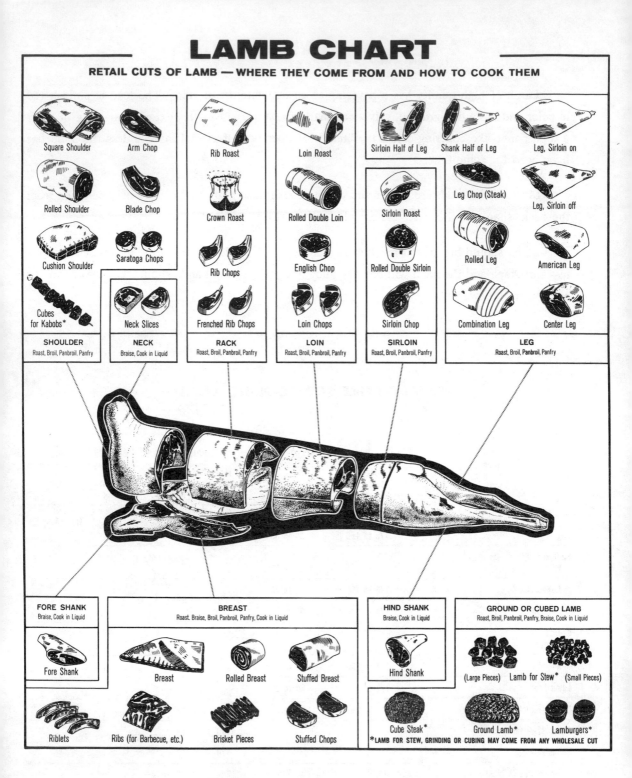

SHOULDER
Roast, Broil, Panbroil. Panfry

Square Shoulder • Arm Chop • Rolled Shoulder • Blade Chop • Cushion Shoulder • Saratoga Chops • Cubes for Kabobs*

NECK
Braise, Cook in Liquid

Neck Slices

RACK
Roast, Broil, Panbroil, Panfry

Rib Roast • Crown Roast • Rib Chops • Frenched Rib Chops

LOIN
Roast, Broil, Panbroil, Panfry

Loin Roast • Rolled Double Loin • English Chop • Loin Chops

SIRLOIN
Roast, Broil, Panbroil, Panfry

Sirloin Roast • Rolled Double Sirloin • Sirloin Chop

LEG
Roast, Broil, Panbroil, Panfry

Sirloin Half of Leg • Shank Half of Leg • Leg, Sirloin on • Leg Chop (Steak) • Leg, Sirloin off • Rolled Leg • American Leg • Combination Leg • Center Leg

FORE SHANK
Braise, Cook in Liquid

Fore Shank • Riblets

BREAST
Roast. Braise, Broil, Panbroil, Panfry, Cook in Liquid

Breast • Rolled Breast • Stuffed Breast • Ribs (for Barbecue, etc.) • Brisket Pieces • Stuffed Chops

HIND SHANK
Braise, Cook in Liquid

Hind Shank

GROUND OR CUBED LAMB
Roast, Broil, Panbroil, Panfry, Braise, Cook in Liquid

(Large Pieces) Lamb for Stew* (Small Pieces) • Cube Steak* • Ground Lamb* • Lamburgers*

*LAMB FOR STEW, GRINDING OR CUBING MAY COME FROM ANY WHOLESALE CUT

NATIONAL LIVE STOCK AND MEAT BOARD

SELECTION OF LAMB CUTS

Wholesale	Retail Cuts	Characteristics	Cooking Methods
Leg	Frenched leg	Shank bone is "frenched" which means the bone is removed to expose 1 inch or more of lower end of shank bone.	Roast
	American leg	Shank meat is removed at stifle joint. Shank meat is tucked into pocket under fell and pinned into place.	Roast
	Half of leg	Either the shank or loin half.	Roast
	Leg chops (steaks)	May contain cross section of back bone and aitch bone. Center cut steaks look like miniature beef round steaks.	Broil; panbroil; panfry
	Sirloin chops	Corresponds to beef sirloin steaks. Pinbone chops have considerable bone.	Broil; panbroil; panfry
	Boneless sirloin roast	Small boneless roll weighing from 2 to 3½ pounds.	Roast
Loin	Loin roast	Corresponds to beef short loin. Can be the unsplit loin but is usually one side of the split loin.	Roast
	Rolled loin roast	Boned and rolled loin.	Roast
	Loin chops	Contain T-shaped bones; correspond to porterhouse, T-bone and club beef steaks.	Broil; panbroil; panfry
	English chops	Cut across unsplit loin. Back bone removed and boneless chop skewered into shape.	Broil; panbroil; panfry
Rack	Rib (rack) roast	Contains rib bones and rib eye muscle.	Roast
	Crown roast	Ribs are "frenched" — meat is removed from rib ends, then two or more rib sections are shaped and tied into a crown.	Roast
	Rib chops	Contain rib bone and rib eye muscle.	Broil; panbroil; panfry
	Frenched chops	Same as rib chops except meat is removed from ends of ribs.	Broil; panbroil; panfry
Shoulder	Square cut shoulder	Thickest part of fore-quarter, with shank, breast, rib (rack), and neck removed.	Roast
	Cushion shoulder	Boned and left flat. Sewed on two sides. One side may be left open for stuffing, then skewered or sewed.	Roast
	Rolled shoulder	Boneless roll made from square cut shoulder.	Roast
	Boneless shoulder chops	Cut from boneless rolled shoulder.	Broil; panbroil; panfry; braise
	Mock duck	Made from outside of shoulder. Shaped like a duck.	Roast
	Arm chops	Contain small round bone and usually the cross sections of four or five rib bones.	Broil; panbroil; panfry; braise
	Blade chops	Contain portions of rib, back and blade bones.	Broil; panbroil; panfry; braise
	Saratoga chops	Boneless chops made from inside shoulder muscle.	Broil; panbroil; panfry; braise
	Neck slices	Round slice with neck vertebrae in center.	Braise; cook in liquid
Breast	Breast	Corresponds to veal breast and to short plate and brisket of beef. Narrow strip of meat containing breast bone and ends of 12 ribs.	Roast; braise; cook in liquid
	Breast with pocket	Same as above but with pocket between ribs and lean.	Roast; braise
	Rolled breast	Small boneless roll. Alternating layers of lean and fat.	Roast; braise
	Riblets	Breast bone removed and breast cut between ribs. Each small piece contains part of a rib bone.	Braise; cook in liquid
Shank	Shank	Contains shank and elbow bones.	Braise; cook in liquid
Ground Lamb	Loaf	Usually made from flank, breast, shank and neck. May be straight ground lamb or combined with varying amounts of beef, pork or veal.	Roast (bake)
	Patties	Ground lamb formed into patties. May be encircled with sliced bacon.	Broil; panbroil; panfry

CARVING INSTRUCTIONS FOR LAMB

ROAST LEG OF LAMB

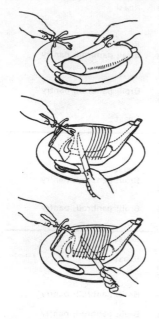

Place roast on platter, shank to the carver's right. With the tip section on the near side, remove two or three slices to form a base.

With the roast resting on the base, make slices perpendicular to the leg bone. Begin slices at the shank end.

Loosen slices by cutting under them. Remove and place on a platter.

CUSHION LAMB SHOULDER

All that is necessary of this boneless cut is to slice the desired thickness through the meat and the stuffing.

CROWN ROAST OF LAMB

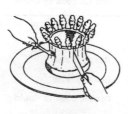

Insert fork so as to get a firm hold. Begin carving at one of the two ends where ribs are tied together.

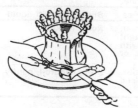

Make slices down between the ribs. Lift the slices on the knife blade to the platter. (Use fork to steady the slice.)

Beef and Veal Favorites

RECIPE FOR BRAISED STEAK AND ONIONS ON PAGE 42

BARBECUED BEEF CHUCK ROAST

1 3 ½ to 4-lb. chuck roast
Meat tenderizer
Seasoned salt
Hickory flavored barbecue sauce

Sprinkle roast with meat tenderizer; let stand for a few minutes. Sprinkle with seasoned salt on all sides. Place meat on foil. Cover top and sides of meat with barbecue sauce. Wrap meat in foil, sealing completely. Place in roasting pan. Cover; bake at 350 degrees for 1 hour and 30 minutes. NOTE: May be cooked on outdoor grill for 1 hour on each side. Yield: 8 servings.

Mrs. Clayton Hustad, Pres.
First Lutheran Church LWML
Gainesville, Florida

BARBECUED BEEF KABOBS

½ c. olive or salad oil
1 tsp. salt
½ tsp. pepper
½ tsp. rosemary or oregano
1 lb. tender lean beef, cut into 1 ½-in. cubes
2 lge. onions, cut into wedges
2 tomatoes, cut into wedges
8 ripe olives, pitted

Combine oil and seasonings; add meat. Let stand for s e v e r a l hours. Place meat, vegetables and olives on four skewers. Broil over charcoal for 12 minutes, turning to brown evenly. Yield: 4 servings.

Mrs. Marlowe Erickson
Zion Lutheran Church
Donnybrook, North Dakota

CHARCOAL-BROILED CHUCK ROAST

1 3 to 4-lb. chuck roast
½ c. salad oil
¼ c. vinegar
Meat tenderizer
Salt and pepper to taste

Marinate meat in mixture of salad oil and vinegar for 3 to 4 hours, turning once. Remove meat from marinade; drain. Make holes in both sides of roast; sprinkle with meat tenderizer, following directions on label. Season with salt and pepper. Cook over hot coals; browning quickly on both sides. Raise rack 3 inches from coals. Cook meat for 10 to 15 minutes on each side or until done. Yield: 6 servings.

Mrs. Thomas E. Fricke, Pres.
St. Michael Women's Guild
Kalamazoo, Michigan

CHARCOALED CHUCK ROAST

3 lb. economy beef roast
Instant unseasoned meat tenderizer
Seasonings to taste

Sprinkle roast with tenderizer; pierce meat with long-tined fork on both sides. Season to taste. Let stand for 30 minutes. Place on charcoal grill. Broil over medium coals for 12 to 15 minutes on each side. Slice in thin strips to serve. Yield: 6 servings.

Mrs. W. A. Pittack, Past Pres.
Omaha Bethany Library Guild
Omaha, Nebraska

GRILLED CHUCK ROAST

1 3 to 4-lb. chuck roast
1 clove of garlic
1 tbsp. brown sugar
½ tsp. ground ginger
½ tsp. coarsely ground black pepper
1 tbsp. cooking oil
2 tbsp. water
¼ c. soy sauce
½ tsp. monosodium glutamate

Sprinkle meat tenderizer on each side of roast; pierce deeply with a fork. Let set at room temperature for 1 hour. Cut into 1 1/2-inch cubes. Mash garlic with sugar to a fine pulp; mix with remaining ingredients in a shallow dish; add meat. Marinate for 1 hour and 30 minutes to 2 hours, turning occasionally; drain. Place on the charcoal grill; cook on each side for 10 minutes, brushing often with marinade. Yield: 4-6 servings.

Mrs. Jack Riech, VP
Our Good Shepherd LWML
Roanoke, Virginia

KABOBS

1 1 ½-lb. sirloin steak or top round, cut into 1 ½-in. cubes
Meat tenderizer
2 green peppers, cubed
1 12-oz. can whole onions
1 lb. fresh mushrooms
½ c. butter or margarine
3 tbsp. soy sauce

Sprinkle meat with meat tenderizer. Alternate meat, green pepper, onions and mushrooms on skewers. Melt butter; add soy sauce. Brush kabobs with mixture. Cook over medium hot coals for 10 to 20 minutes, basting with sauce several times. Yield: 4 servings.

Mrs. Donald Sweeney, Sec.
Hope Dorcas Soc.
Aurora, Illinois

SHISH KABOB

2 tbsp. oil
½ c. white wine
1 tbsp. vinegar
1 bay leaf, crushed
2 tbsp. chopped onion
½ tsp. celery salt
½ tsp. seasoned salt

(Continued on next page)

½ tsp. salt
½ tsp. pepper
1 tsp. monosodium glutamate
2 to 3 lb. lean stew meat or chuck roast, cubed
Onion strips
Green pepper strips
Pineapple chunks
Cherry tomatoes

Combine oil, wine, vinegar, bay leaf, onion, celery salt, seasoned salt, salt, pepper and monosodium glutamate; add meat. Cover; refrigerate for 12 to 24 hours. Place meat alternately with strips of onion, green pepper strips, pineapple chunks and cherry tomatoes on a skewer. Place over hot fire until done on one side; turn and cook on other side. Yield: 6 servings.

Mrs. Reijer Groenveld, Pres.
Good Shepherd LCW
Concord, California

WESTERN STEAK BARBECUE

1 4-lb. chuck or round pot roast, 1-in. thick
Unseasoned meat tenderizer
½ c. minced onion
½ c. margarine
⅓ c. lemon juice
1 tbsp. catsup
1 tbsp. Worcestershire sauce
1 tbsp. horseradish
½ tsp. salt
¼ tsp. pepper
1 lge. clove of garlic, minced

Prepare steak with tenderizer according to package directions. Saute onion in margarine until limp; stir in remaining ingredients. Pour sauce over steak. Marinate at room temperature for 1 hour, turning once. Cook steak over hot coals until done, basting with remaining marinade. Yield: 6 servings.

Mrs. Arthur C. Dallman
St. Paul's LWML
Buffalo, New York

BARBECUED BRISKET OF BEEF

5 to 6-lb. brisket of beef
2 tsp. salt
Pepper to taste
2 med. onions, chopped
4 tbsp. margarine
1½ c. water
½ c. lemon juice
4 tbsp. vinegar
3 tbsp. dry mustard
2 c. catsup
4 tbsp. brown sugar
6 tbsp. Worcestershire sauce

Season meat with salt and pepper. Place in greased baking pan; cover with foil. Bake at 275 degrees for 5 hours. Saute onions in margarine until golden. Add remaining ingredients; simmer for 30 minutes. Remove meat to cutting board;

slice thin. Place in barbecue sauce; cover. Heat for 15 minutes. Yield: 10 servings.

Mrs. Charlyne Ohlemacher
Calvary LWML
Charleston, South Carolina

BARBECUED POT ROAST

2 tbsp flour
2 tsp. salt
¼ tsp. pepper
1 3 to 4-lb. beef arm or blade pot roast
2 tbsp. lard or drippings
½ tsp. caraway seed
1 med. onion, sliced
1 bay leaf
2 tbsp. vinegar
¼ c. water

Combine flour, salt and pepper. Dredge meat in seasoned flour. Brown in lard over medium heat. Pour off drippings. Sprinkle with caraway seed; top with onion slices. Add bay leaf, vinegar and water. Cover; simmer for 3 hours or until meat is tender. Remove meat; discard bay leaf. Thicken liquid with remaining seasoned flour, if desired. NOTE: Meat may be browned in electric fry pay an 360 degrees and cooked at 300 degrees for 2 to 3 hours.

Mrs. Earl B. Spokely, Pres.
Benton LCW
Hartford, South Dakota

BEEF ROAST

1 6-lb. roast
Salt and pepper to taste
1 lge. onion, chopped
1 lge. green pepper, chopped
5 stalks celery, chopped
1 bottle catsup
2 bottles beer

Place roast in pan; cover with remaining ingredients, reserving 1 bottle beer. Cover and bake at 350 degrees until tender. Add remaining beer. Thicken liquid for gravy. Yield: 6-8 servings.

Frieda Baecht, Pres.
St. Matthew Dorcas Soc.
Golden Eagle, Illinois

BEEF ROAST WITH GRAVY

Butter (opt.)
1 roast
1 pkg. dry onion soup mix
1 can cream of mushroom soup
½ soup can water (opt.)
2 to 3 tbsp. steak sauce (opt.)

Spread roast with butter. Place roast on heavy foil. Spread onion soup over roast, add mushroom soup, water and steak sauce. Wrap loosely in foil. Place roast on cookie sheet. Bake at 300 to 350 degrees to desired doneness. NOTE:

(Continued on next page)

Roast may be baked in Dutch oven instead of foil. Salt and pepper to taste may be added, if desired.

Mrs. Daniel T. Wagoner, Pres.
St. Ansgar ALCW
Fullerton, North Dakota
Mrs. Isla Mae Fear, Pres.
St. Paul's Mary Martha Guild
Lupton, Michigan
Ruth Borcherding, Pres.
Trinity LWML
Iuka, Illinois
Mrs. Ida Missal, Chmn.
Zion Ladies Aid
Wenona, Illinois
Mrs. Ken Baier, Pres.
St. John's Concordia Soc.
Millbank, Ontario, Canada
Mrs. L. B. Haloerson
Swede Home LCW
Minneota, Minnesota
Mrs. LaRoux Cochran, Pres.
ULCW
Clairton, Pennsylvania
Mrs. John Sodnak
Christ the King ALCW
Moorehead, Minnesota
Mrs. Harlan Twedt, Pres.
Bethany LCW
McCallsburg, Iowa
Florence E. Spangler, Sec.
St. Peter's LCW
Amanda, Ohio
Marge Hanke, Pres.
Our Father's Ladies Guild
Milwaukee, Wisconsin

BRAISED POT ROAST

2 tbsp. flour
2 tsp. salt
¼ tsp. pepper
1 3 to 4-lb. beef blade or arm roast, cut 2-in. thick
2 tbsp. fat or oil
1 med. onion, sliced
3 peppercorns
1 sm. bay leaf
1 c. water

Combine flour, salt and pepper; rub into meat. Brown meat on one side in fat in s k i l l e t. Add onion, peppercorns and bay leaf. Turn meat; brown. Place meat on low rack in roaster; add water. Cover; cook slowly for 2 hours. Add water as needed to keep 1/2 to 1 inch in pan. Yield: 6-8 servings.

Mrs. Chris F. Holtzman, Pres.
St. Paul LWML
Ridgeway, North Carolina

BRISKET OF BEEF

1 5 to 6-lb. brisket
1 tbsp. meat tenderizer
2 to 4 tbsp. liquid smoke
2 tsp. salt
½ tsp. pepper
1 tsp. celery salt
1 tsp. onion salt
1 tsp. garlic salt

1 tsp. paprika
½ tsp. nutmeg
¼ c. brown sugar

Place meat on large sheet heavy foil. Sprinkle meat generously with tenderizer, liquid smoke, salt and pepper. Let stand for 2 to 3 hours. Sprinkle with other ingredients. Wrap meat tightly in foil. Bake at 300 degrees for 2 hours. Uncover or loosen foil. Bake at 200 degrees for 5 to 6 hours or until tender. May be served immediately or cooled; sliced and reheated at 200 degrees for 1 hour. NOTE: Amount of seasonings may be varied according to individual taste. Yield: 12 servings.

Mrs. June Wilson, Pres.
Hope Ruth Guild
Shawnee Mission, Kansas

BURGUNDY POT ROAST

1 box dry onion soup mix
1 4 to 5-lb. chuck roast
1 can mushrooms
1 c. Burgundy wine

Place large piece of foil in pan. Sprinkle 1 package onion soup on foil. Place roast on soup; sprinkle remaining soup on roast. Top with mushrooms. Pour wine over meat. Seal with foil. Bake at 300 degrees for 4 hours. Yield: 8 servings.

Mrs. A. S. Willumsen, Pres.
Grace LCW
Oak Ridge, Tennessee

COFFEE-FLAVORED POT ROAST

1 pkg. instant meat marinade
⅔ c. cold coffee
1 med. clove of garlic, minced or pressed
¼ tsp. sweet basil
1 3 to 4-lb. beef pot roast
1 10 ½-oz. cream of mushroom soup
1 lge. onion, sliced

Pour marinade into Dutch oven; blend in coffee, garlic and basil. Place meat in mixture. Pierce surfaces of meat deeply and thoroughly with fork. Marinate for 15 minutes, turning several times. Add soup and onion. Cook, turning meat once, until liquid begins to bubble; reduce heat. Cover; simmer for 2 hours to 2 hours and 30 minutes. Remove meat from gravy to hot platter. Thicken gravy, if desired. Slice meat; serve gravy separately. Yield: 6-8 servings.

Mrs. Walter Senechal
Grace LWML
Banning, California

DIFFERENT WAY TO SERVE BEEF

2 tbsp. brown sugar
3 tsp. salt
¼ tsp. pepper
¼ c. flour
1 3-lb. rolled roast

(Continued on next page)

¼ c. shortening
1 c. hot water
1 c. chili sauce

Mix brown sugar, salt, pepper and 2 tablespoonfuls flour; pound into both sides of meat. Brown meat in hot shortening. Remove meat. Add water to pan drippings; thicken with remaining flour. Add chili sauce and meat. Cover; simmer for 2 hours and 30 minutes. Yield: 8 servings.

Mrs. R. E. Claiborne, Pres.
Mt. Olives LCW
Phoenix, Arizona

FAMILY POT ROAST

1 3 to 4-lb. beef blade or arm pot roast
3 tbsp. lard or drippings
1 tbsp. dry mustard
2 tbsp. brown sugar
2 tsp. salt
¼ tsp. pepper
¼ c. lemon juice
¼ c. water
1 med. onion, sliced

Brown meat in lard; drain. Combine mustard with brown sugar, salt, pepper, lemon juice and water. Add with onion to meat. Cover; simmer for 2 hours and 30 minutes to 3 hours or until tender. Remove meat; thicken gravy, if desired. Yield: 6-8 servings.

Mrs. Caroline Roux
First Trinity Ladies Aid
Washington, District of Columbia

FOIL-BAKED ROAST BEEF

1 3 to 5-lb. chuck roast
½ pkg. dry mushroom soup mix
½ pkg. dry onion soup mix
4 tbsp. water

Place roast on large heavy piece of foil. Mix soup mixes; sprinkle over roast. Drizzle water over the soup; seal tightly. Place in large roaster. Bake at 250 degrees for at least 5 hours. If desired, thicken liquid for gravy. NOTE: One 1-ounce can mushrooms plus water to make 4 tablespoonfuls liquid may be used for water.

Mrs. George Kobilan, Pres.
St. Paul Evangelical LCW
Calhan, Colorado

GARDEN ROAST

⅓ tsp. celery seed
½ c. flour
2 tbsp. salt
2 tbsp. sugar
2 tsp. pepper
2 tsp. dry mustard
Butter
1 3-lb. rump roast
1 can tomato soup
1 lge. can tomatoes, strained

Make paste of dry ingredients, small amount of butter and water. Spread over meat. Brown; cover with soup and tomatoes. Bake at 350 degrees for several hours, basting often. Small potatoes may be added the last hour of cooking, if desired. Strain liquid for gravy.

Mrs. James D. Young, English Dist. Dir. LWML
Trinity Ladies Aid
Pittsburgh, Pennsylvania

MONTANA COWBELLES SLOW AND EASY ROAST BEEF

2 tsp. salt
½ tsp. pepper
1 5-lb. beef roast

Salt and pepper roast. Place in roasting pan. Roast at 150 degrees for rare meat or 180 degrees for well done. Cook for 6 to 7 hours or until done.

Mrs. Wraal S. Arthun, Pres.
Immanuel LCW
Absarokee, Montana

MUSHROOM POT ROAST

1 3 to 4-lb. pot roast
Flour
Fat
Salt and pepper
2 onions, sliced
¼ c. catsup
⅓ c. cooking Sherry (opt.)
1 clove of garlic, minced or ¼ tsp. garlic salt (opt.)
¼ to ½ tsp. dry mustard
⅛ to ¼ tsp. rosemary
⅛ to ¼ tsp. thyme
1 bay leaf (opt.)
¼ tsp. marjoram (opt.)
1 6-oz. can broiled sliced mushrooms

Trim off excess fat from meat; dredge in enough flour to cover. Brown slowly on all sides in a small amount of fat. Season generously with salt and pepper; add onions. Mix 1/2 to 1 1/2 cup water and remaining ingredients except mushrooms. Add to meat. Cover. Cook slowly for 2 hours and 30 minutes or until done. Add mushrooms and liquid; heat. Remove meat to warm platter. Skim fat from stock. Blend 1 tablespoonful flour and 1/4 cup cold water; gradually stir into stock. Cook, stirring, until sauce thickens. Season to taste. Serve over meat. Yield: 6-8 servings.

Mrs. O. J. Peterson, Pres.
Trinity Evangelical LCW
Rice Lake, Wisconsin
Eleanor Brumbaugh, Sec.
Trinity LCW
Boulder, Colorado

PASTRAMI BEEF

4 cloves of garlic
3 tbsp. kosher salt
2 tbsp. pepper
1 tsp. ground cloves
1 6-lb. lean beef rump

Combine seasonings; rub well into beef. Let stand for 1 hour. Place beef in roaster on rack. Pour a small amount of water into roaster. Cover and bake at 325 degrees for 40 minutes per pound. Yield: 12 servings.

Mrs. Rosalie Collins, Past Pres.
Peace Tabitha Circle
Cordell, Oklahoma

PEKING BEEF ROAST

1 2 to 5-lb. chuck roast
1 onion, slivered
1 clove of garlic, slivered
3 tbsp. oil
1 c. vinegar
2 c. black coffee
2 c. water
Salt and pepper to taste

Cut slits completely through meat; insert slivers of onion and garlic into slits. Place beef in a bowl; pour vinegar over meat. Refrigerate for 24 to 48 hours. Discard vinegar solution; brown meat in oil in a heavy pot until nearly burned on both sides. Pour coffee and water over roast. Cover; cook slowly for 3 to 6 hours. Season with salt and pepper.

Mrs. J. L. Mills, Pres.
Good Shepherd LCW
Brevard, North Carolina

BEEF POT ROAST

1 pot roast
Margarine
1 onion, sliced
1 No. 2 can tomatoes
Pepper and salt

Brown beef on both sides in margarine. Add onion, tomatoes, pepper and salt. Cover; simmer for 2 hours. Yield: 10 servings.

Mrs. John Herer, Pres.
Trinity Church ALCW
Oconton, Wisconsin

POT ROAST

1 4-lb. chuck roast
Bacon strips
Halved stuffed green olives
Salt and pepper
Flour
1 onion
1 bay leaf

Cut slits in roast; lay bacon strips and olives in slits. Secure with small skewers. Sprinkle with salt and pepper; roll in flour. Brown meat on all sides. Add a small amount of water, onion and bay leaf. Simmer for 2 hours. Thicken drippings with flour. Yield: 8 servings.

Mrs. Eugenia Tomaselli
Redeemer Ladies Guild
Stuart, Florida

POT ROAST

1 4 to 5-lb. chuck or shoulder roast
1 tbsp. shortening
2 lge. onions, sliced
1 clove of garlic, minced
2 7-oz. bottles 7-Up
2 bay leaves
2 tbsp. vinegar
1 tbsp. brown sugar
1 tsp. salt
3 tbsp. catsup
½ c. raisins

Brown meat in shortening. Add onions; cook until brown. Add garlic, 7-Up and bay leaves. Cook, covered, at 250 to 275 degrees for 2 hours. Add remaining ingredients; cook for 30 minutes to 1 hour longer or until tender. Yield: 8-10 servings.

Mrs. James D. Hruska, Treas.
Eternal Trinity LWML
Milton, Florida

POT ROAST BEEF

1 4 to 6-lb. beef roast
2 tsp. salt
½ tsp. pepper
1 c. flour
3 tbsp. beef fat or 2 1-in. cubes salt pork
½ c. water

Rub meat with salt, pepper and flour. Brown on all sides in fat in deep iron skillet. Place on rack in pan; add water. Cover. Simmer, turning occasionally, for 3 hours or until tender. NOTE: Vegetables may be added the last hour of cooking. Yield: 6 servings.

Mrs. Robie Dorey, Pres.
St. Mark Ladies Aid
Mahone Bay, Nova Scotia, Canada

ROAST BEEF

1 2 ½ to 3-lb. beef roast
Salt
Flour
1 can cream of mushroom soup
½ soup can water
4 med. potatoes, cut into large pieces
1 med. onion, chopped
4 carrots, sliced

Sprinkle roast with salt; dredge in flour. Brown in a small amount of fat. Place in roasting pan;

(Continued on next page)

cover with soup and water. Cover; bake at 350 degrees for 1 hour and 30 minutes. Add potatoes, onion and carrots. Cook for 45 minutes to 1 hour longer.

Mrs. Marilyn Belsky
St. Paul Lutheran Church for the Deaf
Ladies Guild
Flint, Michigan

RUMP ROAST

1 6-lb. rump roast
1 tsp. salt
¼ tsp. pepper
1 lge. onion, finely chopped
1 clove of garlic, finely chopped
1 c. water

Brown meat on both sides; add salt, pepper, onion, garlic and water. Cover; bake in preheated 450 degree oven for 15 minutes. Reduce temperature to 250 degrees; let simmer for 3 hours to 3 hours and 30 minutes or until tender, basting often. Yield: 8-10 servings.

Mrs. A. Ehrsam
Mount Calvary Ladies Guild
Pittsburgh, Pennsylvania

BEST SAUERBRATEN

1 6 to 8-lb. boneless rolled rump roast
Vinegar
Water
1 tbsp. salt
10 peppercorns
2 tbsp. sugar
2 lge. onions, diced
1 tbsp. pickling spices
3 bay leaves
½ c. flour
6 gingersnaps, mashed

Place meat in earthern crock. Cover with equal parts of vinegar and water. Add salt, peppercorns, sugar, onions, pickling spices and bay leaves. Marinate for two days. Cook meat with 3 cups marinade in pressure cooker for 45 minutes or until tender. Remove meat; slice. Reserve marinade. Brown flour in skillet. Add reserved marinade a little at a time; add gingersnaps. Cook until of desired thickness. Pour over meat; serve. Yield: 12 servings.

Mrs. Adelbert E. Joost, Treas.
St. John's Ladies Aid Soc.
Columbus, Ohio

QUICK SAUERBRATEN

1 4 to 5-lb. chuck, round or rump roast
¼ c. oil
½ c. chopped onion
2 tsp. salt
2 tbsp. mixed pickling spices
1 c. red wine vinegar
3 c. water
½ c. brown sugar
12 gingersnaps, crumbled

Brown roast slowly on all sides in oil in heavy kettle. Pour off excess oil. Add remaining ingredients except gingersnaps. Simmer for 3 to 4 hours or until meat is tender. Remove meat; keep warm. Strain liquid, reserving 4 cups. Add reserved liquid and gingersnaps. Cook, stirring until smooth and slightly thickened. Cook for 5 minutes longer, stirring frequently.

Mrs. W. Schmoll, Sec.
St. Trinity Ladies Aid
St. Louis, Missouri

EASY SAUERBRATEN

1 c. vinegar
3 c. water
1 med. onion, sliced
3 tbsp. whole mixed spices
1 tbsp. salt
1 carrot, sliced
1 4-lb. beef roast
2 ½ tbsp. shortening
¼ c. sugar
⅓ c. flour
2 to 4 gingersnaps, crushed
½ c. red wine

Mix vinegar, water, onion, spices, salt and carrot. Place meat in a glass, enamel or earthenware bowl. Pour vinegar mixture over meat. Refrigerate for three or four days, turning over several times. Drain meat, saving remaining brine for gravy. Wipe meat dry. Sear meat in heavy pan in shortening on both sides. Add part of marinade. Cover; roast at 300 degrees for 2 hours, basting meat occasionally. Sprinkle sugar over meat. Roast for 5 to 10 minutes longer, turning meat while roasting until sugar is dissolved. Thicken remaining marinade with flour and gingersnaps. Mix well; pour over meat. Roast meat for 30 minutes longer or until gravy is creamy and thick. Remove meat. Stir wine into gravy and strain. NOTE: If desired, roast may be cooked on top of stove. If so, cook for 1 hour or until done. Yield: 6-8 servings.

Mrs. Herbert Malueg, VP
Immanuel Ladies Aid
Caroline, Wisconsin
Mrs. Harold O. Bomhoff
St. Paul's ALCW
Baytown, Texas

SAUERBRATEN

1 3 to 4-lb. pot roast
Bacon strips
Dash of pepper
Dash of nutmeg
2 tsp. salt
1 med. onion, sliced
1 bay leaf
2 tbsp. chopped parsley
¾ c. vinegar
¾ c. water
¼ c. sugar
2 tbsp. butter or bacon drippings
2 tbsp. flour
¼ c. evaporated milk or cream
½ c. seedless raisins

(Continued on next page)

Cut slits in roast; insert bacon in strips. Rub meat with pepper, nutmeg and salt. Place in crock or enamel dish. Add onion, bay leaf and parsley. Heat vinegar, water and sugar to boiling; pour over meat. Cover; refrigerate overnight. Drain meat, reserving mixture; brown meat in butter in heavy skillet. Add 1/2 cup vinegar mixture. Cover; simmer for 3 hours or until tender, adding additional vinegar mixture if needed. Remove meat; blend flour with milk and remaining vinegar mixture. Add raisins; cook, stirring until gravy is thick. Serve over meat. Yield: 5-7 servings.

Mrs. Vera Hoehne
Emmanuel Lutheran Church
Nashville, Tennessee

SAUERBRATEN

2 c. Sauterne wine
1 lge. onion, chopped
6 cloves
2 bay leaves
Salt and pepper
1 3-lb. pot roast

Combine all ingredients except meat. Pour over meat; marinate overnight. Drain; brown meat on both sides. Add marinade. Cover; bake at 300 degrees for 3 hours. Yield: 6 servings.

Mrs. Richard Lensman, Mission Chmn.
Zion Ladies Aid
St. Ignatius, Montana

SAUERBRATEN POT ROAST

1 sm. onion
1 tbsp. oil
2 c. water
2 c. vinegar
1 c. raisins
2 tbsp. brown sugar
½ tsp. pepper
2 tsp. salt
½ tsp. celery salt
¼ tsp. ginger
18 whole cloves
1 bay leaf, crushed
4 lb. beef
¼ c. fat
1 c. gingersnaps

Cook onion in oil until tender. Add all ingredients except beef, fat and gingersnaps. Cool. Place meat in bowl. Pour on marinade. Refrigerate for 48 hours. Brown meat in fat. Add 1 1/2 cups strained marinade. Cook for 2 hours and 30 minutes or until done. Remove meat. Add 3/4 cup water and gingersnaps; cook until thick. Yield: 6 servings.

Mrs. Frank Westfall, Sr.
Gallupville Evangelical LCW
Gallupville, New York

SAUERBRATEN WITH PRUNES

3 c. water
½ lge. onion, sliced
½ c. apple cider vinegar
1 ½ tsp. salt
¼ tsp. pepper
1 bay leaf
4 ½ lb. rump or chuck beef
12 lge. dried prunes
4 to 6 sm. gingersnaps
1 c. sour cream (opt.)

Combine water, onion, vinegar, salt, pepper and bay leaf in a large glass, enamel or stone bowl; add beef to mixture. Refrigerate for eight days, turning meat each day. Remove meat and place in roaster with one-fourth of liquid. Remove stones from prunes; place in roaster with onion. Remove bay leaf. Bake, uncovered, at 350 degrees, turning meat once. Add additional liquid if needed. Add gingersnaps. Remove meat. Place liquid in a blender or through a sieve. Return to roaster with meat. Reheat, adding sour cream, if desired. Serve with potato dumplings. Yield: 8-9 servings.

Mrs. Ida Flier
Rainbow Lakes Ladies Guild
Dunnellon, Florida

SAUERBRATEN

1 5-lb. boneless bottom round, chuck or rump pot roast
1 tbsp. Accent
1 tbsp. salt
2 tbsp. sugar
6 peppercorns
2 onions, sliced
2 carrots, pared and sliced
3 bay leaves
1 stalk celery, chopped
6 whole cloves
1 ½ c. red wine vinegar
1 ½ c. water
2 tbsp. flour
4 tbsp. butter or margarine
½ c. gingersnap crumbs

Place meat in earthenware, glass or enamel bowl; add Accent, salt, sugar, peppercorns, onions, carrots, bay leaves, celery, cloves, red wine vinegar and water. Cover and marinate in refrigerator two to four days, turning once each day. Remove meat from marinade; pat dry. Strain marinade; reserve marinade and vegetables. Roll meat in flour. Heat butter in a deep kettle; add meat and brown for about 15 to 20 minutes. Add strained vegetables to 2 cups of the marinade; add to kettle. Cover tightly. Cook over low heat for 3 hours and 30 minutes to 4 hours or until meat is tender, adding a small amount additional marinade when necessary. Remove meat to heated platter. Strain vegatables from marinade, if necessary, adding enough reserved marinade to make 2 cups. Return to kettle; blend in gingersnap crumbs. Cook, stirring constantly, until slightly thickened. Yield: 12-14 servings.

Photograph for this recipe on front cover.

SPICY SAUERBRATEN

4 lb. bottom round beef
1 c. vinegar
2 c. water
2 bay leaves
1 tsp. mixed spices
2 tbsp. flour
2 tsp. salt
Pepper to taste
2 lge. onions
Browned flour

Place meat, vinegar, water, bay leaves and spices in earthen crock; let stand in cool place for two or three days. Baste frequently; turn over once a day. Drain meat, reserving liquid. Sprinkle with flour, salt and pepper. Brown in hot fat on all sides; add marinade and onions. Cover; cook slowly for 1 hour and 30 minutes or until tender. Remove meat; strain liquid. Thicken with browned flour. Slice meat; add to gravy. Yield: 6-8 servings.

Mrs. John Jost, Sr.
Trinity Lutheran Church
Fredericktown, Missouri

SMOTHERED BEEF

1 3-lb. beef rump roast
Seasoned flour
3 tbsp. fat
3 lge. onions, sliced
2 tbsp. mild mustard
1 tsp. celery seed
1 can tomato soup

Dredge meat with flour; brown in fat in heavy pan. Remove meat. Brown onions in same fat; add mustard, celery seed and soup. Pour over meat. Cover and simmer for 3 to 4 hours or until tender. Yield: 8 servings.

Mrs. Wayne Roock, VP
St. Stephen LCW
Warren, Michigan

SPICED YORK POT ROAST

1 5-lb. roast
Salt and pepper
1 med. onion, thinly sliced
1 carrot, thinly sliced
1 sm. piece horseradish root, scraped
Celery tops
1 tsp. peppercorns
3 bay leaves
Red wine vinegar
Shortening
1 c. sour cream (opt.)
1 egg, beaten

Rub meat with salt and pepper; place in crock. Add onion, carrot, horseradish, celery tops, peppercorn and bay leaves. Cover with mixture of vinegar and water, using an equal amount of each. Place in cold place; marinate for two to three days. Drain and dry meat. Brown in skillet in melted shortening. Place in roasting pan; add a small amount of the strained, spiced vinegar water. Cover tightly and bake at 350 degrees until meat is tender, about 3 hours. Remove meat. Simmer pan juices until reduced to one-half. Slowly add mixture of sour cream and egg. Cook over very low heat, stirring constantly. Yield: 10-12 servings.

Mrs. Louis R. Winemiller, Pres.
Keller Memorial LCW
Hyattsville, Maryland

STUFFED AND ROLLED RIB ROAST

¼ c. chopped onion
1 clove of garlic, minced
1 tbsp. brown sugar
1 tsp. salt
Dash of pepper
1 tsp. mustard
¼ c. water
1 tsp. Worcestershire sauce
1 c. soft bread crumbs
1 3 to 4-lb. rolled rib roast
1 3-oz. can sliced broiled mushrooms, drained
2 tbsp. chopped stuffed green olives
½ c. shredded sharp American cheese

Combine onion, garlic, brown sugar, salt, pepper, mustard, water, Worcestershire sauce and bread crumbs. Unroll roast; spread with bread mixture. Sprinkle with mushrooms, olives and cheese. Roll roast and tie securely; fasten ends with skewers. Place on rack in shallow baking pan. Bake at 325 degrees for desired doneness. Yield: 9-12 servings.

Mrs. Kenneth Lloyd, Pres.
Prince of Peace LCW
Latrobe, Pennsylvania

SWEET-SOUR POT ROAST

1 3½-lb. beef pot roast, cut 2-in. thick
2 tbsp. fat
1 med. onion, chopped
1 bay leaf
1 tsp. salt
1 tbsp. brown sugar
2 tbsp. vinegar
3 tbsp. catsup
⅓ c. raisins
1 tbsp. cornstarch

(Continued on next page)

Brown meat on both sides in fat in heavy kettle. Add onion, bay leaf, salt and 3/4 cup water. Cover; simmer for 1 hour. Mix brown sugar with vinegar, catsup and raisins. Add to meat mixture. Cover; simmer for 1 hour or until fork tender. Place roast on hot platter. Skim off excess fat from broth, reserving 2 tablespoonfuls fat. Mix 1/2 cup cold water with cornstarch until smooth. Add to broth, stirring until gravy is clear and thickened. Serve over roast. Yield: 6-8 servings.

Mrs. Julius Kluksdahl, Pres.
Zion LCW
Driscoll, North Dakota

TEXAS BARBECUE

1 4-lb. roast or shortribs
Salt and pepper
¼ c. water
5 bay leaves
3 whole cloves
½ c. finely chopped onion
2 tbsp. brown sugar
2 tbsp. hot sauce
½ tbsp. mustard
¼ c. lemon juice
½ c. chopped celery
3 tbsp. Worcestershire sauce
1 c. catsup
2 tbsp. vinegar

Cook roast as desired, using salt and pepper. Combine remaining ingredients; cook for 10 minutes. Cut roast into slices or into 2-inch chunks. Pour sauce over meat. Simmer for at least 2 hours. Serve with sauce over meat. Yield: 8 servings.

Mrs. Jewel Ward, Pres.
Faith LCW
Spearman, Texas

UNCORNED BRISKET OF BEEF

1 4 to 5-lb. beef brisket

Bake meat at 325 degrees for 3 to 4 hours. Remove from pan. Slice thinly, cutting across grain; place in casserole. Make gravy from drippings in pan. Pour gravy over meat. Cover and bake for 2 hours. Yield: 12 servings.

Dorothy W. Howland, Pres.
Grace Guild
Akron, Ohio

BARBECUED SHORT RIBS

3 to 3 ½ lb. beef short ribs
2 tbsp. oil (opt.)
1 onion, finely chopped
1 clove of garlic, mashed (opt.)
¼ c. vinegar
2 tbsp. sugar

1 c. catsup
½ c. water
1 to 3 tbsp. Worcestershire sauce
1 tsp. prepared mustard
½ c. sliced celery
1 to 2 tsp. salt

Brown short ribs in their own fat, adding more fat if needed. When partially browned, add onion and garlic. Pour off drippings. Add remaining ingredients. Cover; simmer for 1 hour and 30 minutes or until ribs are tender. Serve with cooked noodles. NOTE: Ribs may be baked at 325 degrees for 1 hour and 30 minutes to 2 hours. Yield: 5-6 servings.

Mrs. Betty Erickson, Contact Chmn.
First Lutheran Church Phebian Soc.
Reseda, California
Mrs. Lawrence Berg, Pres.
Faith ALCW
Zahl, North Dakota

BRAISED SHORT RIBS

4 lb. beef short ribs
Seasoned flour
½ tsp. onion salt
½ tsp. marjoram
¼ tsp. thyme
¼ tsp. rosemary
½ c. water

Cut ribs into serving pieces; roll in seasoned flour. Brown on all sides in small amount of hot fat in a Dutch oven. Drain off all except 3 tablespoonfuls of fat; add seasonings and water. Cover; simmer for 2 or 3 hours, adding liquid if necessary. Remove meat; thicken liquid for gravy. Serve with ribs. Yield: 6-8 servings.

Mrs. John Hershberger
King of Kings LCW
Oceanside, California

SPICY SHORT RIBS

2 lb. short ribs
Flour
Fat
½ c. sliced onion
1 c. chili sauce
½ tsp. salt
½ tsp. garlic salt
¼ tsp. pepper
Dash of Tabasco sauce
1 tbsp. Worcestershire sauce

Cut short ribs into serving pieces; roll in flour. Brown slowly in fat in electric skillet. Combine remaining ingredients; pour over short ribs. Cover; simmer for 1 hour and 30 minutes or until tender.

Mrs. Betty Welsh
Bethany Ladies Guild
Lompoc, California

BAKED POTATOES AND STEAK

1 lb. round steak, thinly cut
5 med. baking potatoes, pared
1 tsp. salt
⅓ c. flour
1 tbsp. fat

Pound steak with edge of heavy saucer or meat pounder; cut into pieces the proper size to wrap around potatoes. Rub a small amount of salt on potatoes; wrap the pieces of steak around potatoes fastening with toothpicks. Roll in mixture of flour and remaining salt; brown in hot fat. Place in a greased casserole. Cover; bake at 325 degrees for 1 hour and 20 minutes or until potatoes are tender, adding small amount of water as needed to prevent drying of steak. If desired, catsup may be put over meat a few minutes before serving. Yield: 5 servings.

Mrs. Walter Butson, Pres.
St. John's Women's Soc.
Mazomanie, Wisconsin

BAKED SIRLOIN

1 clove of garlic
1 slice sirloin steak, 1 ½-in. thick
1 stick butter
1 14-oz. bottle catsup

Cut garlic into small slivers; press into meat. Let stand for 20 minutes. Melt butter; mix with catsup. Pour over meat in shallow pan. Bake at 350 degrees for 20 to 25 minutes per pound.

Isobel L. Tierney
Prince of Peace Dorcas Guild
Ozark, Alabama

BARBECUED ROUND STEAK

2 lb. round steak
½ c. flour
1 ½ tsp. salt
¼ tsp. pepper
Shortening
1 c. chopped onions
2 tbsp. vinegar
3 tbsp. brown sugar
2 tbsp. Worcestershire sauce
¾ c. chili sauce
¼ c. water
¼ tsp. chili powder

Cut steak into 2 1/2 x 2-inch pieces. Roll steak pieces in flour seasoned with salt and pepper. Fry in shortening until brown. Place in baking pan. Mix remaining ingredients; pour over steak. Bake, covered, at 325 degrees for 1 hour.

Mrs. Carl A. Holm, Pres.
Oscar Lake Evangelical Ladies Aid
Farwell, Minnesota

BARBECUED ROUND STEAK

2 onions, chopped
½ c. catsup
1 tbsp. vinegar
1 tbsp. brown sugar
1 c. water
¼ tsp. Tabasco sauce
⅛ tsp. chili powder
2 lb. steak

Combine all ingredients except steak. Pour sauce over steak. Bake at 325 to 350 degrees for 2 hours. Yield: 6 servings.

Mrs. John H. Lettow
Immanuel Ladies Aid
Iowa Falls, Iowa

BARBECUED STEAK

¾ c. flour
1 tsp. salt
¼ tsp. pepper
1 ½ lb. round steak, cut into serving pieces
2 tbsp. lard
2 tbsp. vinegar
2 tbsp. brown sugar
2 tbsp. Worcestershire sauce
¾ c. chili sauce
¼ c. water
¼ tsp. chili powder

Combine flour with salt and pepper. Pound seasoned flour into meat. Brown slowly in lard. Place in baking dish. Combine remaining ingredients; pour over meat. Cover; bake at 325 degrees for 1 hour. Uncover the last 15 minutes of cooking. Yield: 4-5 servings.

Mrs. Velma Wiethorn, Chmn.
Zion Women of the Church
McGregor, Texas

OVEN-BARBECUED ROUND STEAK

Flour
1 ¼ tsp. salt
Pepper
1 ½ to 2 lb. round steak
2 tbsp. oil
2 8-oz. tomato sauce
1 tbsp. sugar
1 tbsp. vinegar
1 tbsp. Worcestershire sauce
Dash of Tabasco sauce
1 med. onion, sliced

Mix flour, 1 teaspoonful salt and 1/4 teaspoonful pepper; rub into meat. Brown meat slowly in oil in Dutch oven or oven-proof skillet. Combine tomato sauce, sugar, 1/4 teaspoonful salt, pepper to taste, vinegar, Worcestershire sauce and Tabasco sauce. Pour over steak; simmer, uncovered, for 5 minutes. Add onion slices; cover. Bake at 350 degrees for 1 hour or until meat is fork tender. Yield: 4 servings.

Mrs. Darrell Atchison, Pres.
Martin Luther LCW
Lee's Summit, Missouri

BEEF PIE

1 round steak, ¼-in. thick
Shortening
Salt and pepper
Onion slices
Potatoes, sliced ¼-in. thick

Cut steak into serving pieces; brown well in shortening. Season both sides with salt and pepper. Transfer meat to casserole. Add additional shortening to drippings in skillet; add enough flour and water for medium to thin gravy. Add salt and pepper to taste. Place onion and raw potatoes on top of meat in casserole; cover with gravy. Bake, covered, at 350 degrees for 1 hour and 30 minutes. Add additional water, if necessary to keep ingredients covered with gravy.

Mrs. Florence Barickman, Pres.
Zion LCW
Streator, Illinois

BORDER-TOWN STEAK

1 lge. round steak, 1-in. thick
½ c. wine vinegar
1 9-oz. can tomato sauce
½ c. vegetable oil
1 clove of garlic, crushed
2 tbsp. Worcestershire sauce
2 tsp. chili powder
1 tsp. instant minced onion or 1 tbsp. finely
   minced fresh onion

Prick both sides of meat thoroughly with fork. Combine remaining ingredients; pour over steak in shallow dish. Marinate in refrigerator overnight or for several hours. Broil steak; baste with marinade until done. Yield: 4 servings.

Mrs. Walter Snyder, Prgm. Chmn.
Zion Women's League
Pittsburg, Kansas

BRAISED STEAK AND ONIONS

1 ½ lb. round steak, 1-in. thick
1 ½ tsp. salt
¼ tsp. pepper
⅓ c. plus 2 tbsp. flour
3 tbsp. shortening
2 c. onion rings

Pound meat on both sides with edge of heavy saucer; cut meat into serving pieces. Mix salt and pepper; rub one-half of mixture into both sides of meat. Blend remaining salt and pepper with 1/3 cup flour; sprinkle over both sides of meat. Brown both sides in hot shortening. Add hot water to 1/2-inch depth. Cover and cook for 30 minutes or until meat is tender. Add onion rings 15 minutes before end of cooking time. Place meat on hot platter; cover with onions. Stir remaining flour into pan drippings. Cook for 1 to 2 minutes. Pour over steak and onions. Serve at once. Yield: 6 servings.

Photograph for this recipe on page 31.

CHICKEN-FRIED ROUND STEAK

1 ½ to 2 lb. round steak, ½-in. thick
2 eggs, beaten
2 tbsp. milk
1 c. fine cracker crumbs
¼ c. fat
Salt and pepper

Pound steak thoroughly with sharp meat pounder. Dip into eggs mixed with milk, then into crumbs. Brown on both sides in hot fat. Season. Cover; cook over very low heat for 45 minutes to 1 hour. Yield: 6 servings.

Mrs. Leonard Gaul, Pres.
Christ Lutheran Church Ladies Aid
Troy, Kansas

CONTINENTAL STEAK

½ c. fat
2 onions, thinly sliced
2 lb. chuck or round steak
1 tsp. salt
¼ tsp. pepper
1 clove of garlic, mashed
½ lb. fresh mushrooms, sliced
1 green pepper, thinly sliced
1 8-oz. can tomato sauce
1 c. water

Melt fat in heavy skillet; add onions and cook until golden brown. Remove onions. Rub meat with salt, pepper and garlic. Sear meat on both sides. Add onions, mushrooms, green pepper and tomato sauce. Cook for 15 minutes; add water. Simmer over low heat for 1 hour and 30 minutes or until meat is tender and sauce has thickened. Serve hot with parsley butter potato balls.

Lydia Grossman
Bethlehem Lutheran Church
Bristol, Connecuticut

DEVILED STEAK

1 tbsp. chopped onion
2 tbsp. butter, melted
1 lb. round steak
3 tbsp. flour
¾ tsp. salt
¼ tsp. pepper
¼ tsp. paprika
¾ tsp. dry mustard
1 tbsp. vinegar
2 c. water

Cook onion in butter in heavy skillet until lightly browned. Add steak which has been dredged in 2 tablespoonfuls flour. Brown on both sides; season with salt, pepper and paprika. Place on hot plate. Mix mustard with 1 tablespoonful flour and vinegar to a smooth paste; add with water to frying pan, stirring until thickened. Add meat; cover. Simmer for 1 hour. Yield: 4-6 servings.

Mrs. Helena Lawrason, Pres.
Emmanuel LCW
Czar, Alberta, Canada

CREAM OF MUSHROOM STEAK

2 lb. round steak
Meat tenderizer
Flour
3 tbsp. shortening
Salt and pepper
1 can cream of mushroom soup
½ soup can water

Sprinkle steak with tenderized and flour. Brown in shortening. Season to taste; place in casserole. Cover with soup and water. Cover; bake at 350 degrees for 1 hour.

Mrs. Glenn Bengtson, Pres.
Odebalt Immanuel Ladies Aid
Wall Lake, Iowa

DEVON STEAKS

3 lb. round steak, 1-in. thick
1 clove of garlic, cut
½ c. flour
2 ½ tsp. salt
1 tbsp. paprika
1 c. sliced onions
1 c. sliced mushrooms
¼ c. fat
½ c. hot water
1 c. sour cream

Cut meat into eight pieces. Rub with garlic. Mix flour, salt and paprika; pound into meat. Brown onions and mushrooms in fat; add meat and brown. Add water; cover. Cook over low heat for 40 to 45 minutes. Add more water if necessary. Pour sour cream over meat; simmer for 10 minutes. Yield: 8 servings.

Mrs. Anton Levine, VP
Immanuel Ladies Aid
South Range, Wisconsin

EIGHT-HOUR STEAK

1 lge. round steak
1 can cream of mushroom soup, undiluted
1 pkg. dry onion soup mix

Place steak in pan. Pour soup over steak. Sprinkle with soup mix. Cover; bake at 200 degrees for 8 hours.

Mrs. Susan Dewsnup, Sunday School Teacher
Peace Lutheran Church
Sacto, California

FLAVORSOME FLANK STEAK

1 c. oil
1 clove of garlic or ¼ tsp. garlic salt
1 tbsp. soy sauce
Salt and pepper to taste
1 ½ lb. flank steak

Thoroughly mix all ingredients except steak in jar. Marinate steak for 6 to 24 hours. Drain;

broil for 6 minutes on each side. Carve into thin slices. Serve on hot platter. Yield: 4-6 servings.

Arline Langebartels, Chmn.
Trinity LCW
Park Forest, Illinois

OVEN STEAK DISH

1 round steak
Potatoes
Carrots
2 med. onions, sliced
4 or 5 ½-in. slices green pepper

Place steak in bottom of a 9 x 13-inch baking dish or pan; place potatoes and carrots around steak. Lay onions and pepper slices on top of steak; season to taste. Cover pan with aluminum foil; close edges airtight over edge of pan. Bake at 375 degrees for 1 hour and 30 minutes or until done.

Mrs. Leota M. Joy
Trinity Women's Guild
Cumberland, Maryland

QUICK SWISS STEAK WITH MUSHROOM GRAVY

3 lb. round steak
1 envelope dry onion soup mix
2 cans cream of mushroom soup
1 ½ soup cans water
1 can mushrooms

Place unseasoned steak in roaster casserole. Sprinkle onion soup mix evenly over steak. Dilute soup with water; add mushrooms. Bring to a boil. Spoon gently over onion soup mix. Cover; bake at 350 degrees for 2 hours. Remove cover; bake for 30 to 40 minutes or until meat and gravy are brown. Yield: 6 servings.

Gertrude Schneider, Pres.
St. John's Guild
South Euclid, Ohio

ROAST WITH WINE, OLIVES AND MUSHROOMS

1 4 to 5-lb. roast, cut into steaks
Seasoned flour
½ c. olive oil
½ c. Claret wine
½ c. tomato juice
Juice of 1 lemon
Juice of 1 orange
2 bay leaves
2 tbsp. currant jelly
1 c. pitted ripe olives, sliced
1 med. bottle stuffed green olives
2 cans mushrooms
1 can pimento
Finely chopped parsley

Soak meat overnight in cold water; wash and dry. Roll in seasoned flour; brown in hot olive oil. Mix wine with tomato juice, lemon juice, orange juice, bay leaves and jelly. Pour over meat in

43

(Continued on next page)

baking pan. Bake at 350 degrees for 2 hours or until tender. Add olives, mushrooms, pimento and parsley. If sauce is too thick, add additional water. Yield: 9 servings.

Mrs. O. W. Strange, Sec.-Treas.
Zion Guild
Douglas, Wyoming

ROUND STEAK

Salt and pepper
Flour
1 lge. round steak
1 onion, chopped
1 green pepper, chopped

Combine salt, pepper and flour. Pound into steak. Brown meat in a small amount of hot fat on both sides; turn heat low. Cover steak with onion and pepper; add a small amount of water. Simmer, covered, for 1 hour. Yield: 4-6 servings.

Mrs. John W. Staples, Pres.
St. Marks Ladies Aid LWML
Pacific, Missouri

ROUND STEAK

1 round steak
Salt and pepper
1 egg, slightly beaten
Milk or water
1 c. cracker crumbs
Vegetable shortening

Pound steak well. Season; cut into serving pieces. Dip into egg mixed with milk. Roll in cracker crumbs. Brown in skillet in 1/4-inch shortening. Bake at 250 to 300 degrees until tender.

Mrs. Rudy Lynn, Sec.
St. John's Ladies Aid
Unity, Wisconsin

ROUND STEAK WITH DRESSING

3 c. dry bread crumbs
1 sm. onion, finely chopped
2 tbsp. butter, melted
¾ c. water
Salt and pepper to taste
Dash of sage
1 2-lb. round steak, ½-in. thick

Combine all ingredients except meat. Pound steak; spread dressing on one-half of steak. Fold the remaining half over dressing. Sew or skewer edges. Dredge with 4 tablespoonfuls flour; and brown in small amount of fat. Place in medium baking dish; add additional water or tomato juice. Cover; bake at 350 degrees for 2 hours. Yield: 5 servings.

Mrs. A. F. Bergt, Pres.
First Trinity Ladies Aid Soc.
Wisner, Nebraska

SKILLET-BROILED STEAK WITH PAN GRAVY

1 to 2 tbsp. cooking oil
Fillet mignon, sirloin or T-bone steak
Monosodium glutamate
Salt and pepper
¼ to ½ c. water

Set electric skillet at hottest temperature. Heat oil in skillet; season steaks with monosodium glutamate, salt and pepper to taste. Place steaks in skillet. Cover; sear on both sides. Cook for 5 to 10 minutes on each side. Disconnect cord. Remove steaks to plates or platter. Pour all grease from skillet; immediately add water. Cover for 1 minute; remove all liquid from skillet. Spoon about 1 teaspoonful on each steak and remainder into a small bowl.

Mrs. James Oney, Pres.
Kent Memorial LCW
Sunrise Beach, Missouri

SMOTHERED STEAK

1 ½ lb. round or sirloin steak
Salt and pepper
Flour
Fat
1 can cream of mushroom soup
1 tsp. Worcestershire sauce

Cut steak into serving pieces; sprinkle with salt and pepper. Dip into flour. Fry in a small amount fat in skillet until brown on both sides. Add soup and Worcestershire sauce. Bake at 350 degrees until steak is tender. Yield: 4 servings.

Mrs. Norman Braner, Chmn.
Good Shepherd Ladies Guild
Rochester, Illinois

STEAK WITH MUSHROOM SAUCE

3 lb. Swiss or round steak
Flour
2 to 3 tsp. salt
¼ tsp. pepper
Seasoned salt
Shortening
1 10 ½-oz. can cream of mushroom soup
½ c. water

Pound steak well; roll in flour. Sprinkle with salt, pepper and seasoned salt. Brown in shortening in roaster or covered pan. Cover with soup; add water. Cover tightly and bake at 250 degrees for 2 hours and 30 minutes or until tender. Yield: 10-12 servings.

Lillie Studt, Pres.
St. Paul's Ladies' Aid
Glasco, Kansas

STEAK IN SOUR CREAM

3 lb. round steak, 2-in. thick
Flour
Salt and pepper
Fat
2 onions, sliced
½ c. water
½ c. sour cream
2 tbsp. grated cheese
¾ tsp. paprika

Roll steak in flour; season with salt and pepper to taste. Brown on both sides in hot fat. Add remaining ingredients; cover pan closely. Simmer for 2 hours and 30 minutes or until meat is tender. Yield: 6-8 servings.

Mrs. Everett Wetzler, Sec.
Mt. Olive LWML
Norfolk, Nebraska

STEAK SUPREME

2 lb. round steak
Seasoned flour
2 to 3 tbsp. fat
1 can cream of mushroom soup
1 soup can water
1 med. onion, chopped
1 sm. can mushrooms

Pound steak, with seasoned flour. Cut into serving pieces. Brown in heated fat. Heat soup with water, onion and mushrooms, pour over steak. Place in roaster. Cover and bake at 325 degrees for 2 hours. Add more liquid and salt, if necessary. Yield: 4 servings.

Mrs. Gerald Cook, Pres.
Trinity LCW
Waupaca, Wisconsin

BEEF STROGANOFF

1 ½ lb. round steak, cut into serving pieces
¼ c. flour
¼ c. cooking oil
1 sm. onion, diced
1 can beef consomme
1 tsp. seasoned salt
⅛ tsp. cloves
⅛ tsp. thyme
1 tsp. paprika
1 sm. can mushroom pieces
½ to 1 c. sour cream

Turn steak in flour; brown in oil. Remove from oil; place on plate. Brown onion in fat; add consomme, seasoned salt and spices. Heat; add mushrooms. Place meat in skillet or pour seasoned broth over meat in casserole. Simmer or bake at 325 to 350 degrees for 2 hours and 30 minutes. Just before serving, add sour cream to gravy; pour over meat on serving dish. Yield: 4 servings.

Mrs. C. H. L. Stehl, VP
Our Savior Tabitha Soc.
Norfolk, Nebraska

BEEF STROGANOFF

Salt and pepper
Flour
2 lb. round steak
Butter
1 ½ c. water
1 can mushroom stems and pieces
1 can chicken with rice soup

Pound salt, pepper and flour into steak on both sides. Cut into serving pieces; brown in buttered fry pan. Add water, mushrooms and soup to steak. Cook for 1 hour and 30 minutes or until steak is tender. Add additional water if needed. Serve over rice or potatoes. Yield: 5-6 servings.

Mrs. John Oppliger
St. John Lutheran Church
Lake Charles, Louisiana

BEEF ROLL

1 ½ lb. round steak, ½-in. thick
Instant meat tenderizer
2 hard-cooked eggs, chopped
3 slices bacon, diced and fried
⅓ c. chopped pimento, stuffed green olives
1 tbsp. chopped parsley
1 tbsp. capers
¼ tsp. pepper
3 tbsp. melted fat
1 tsp. paprika
Salt to taste

Sprinkle meat with meat tenderizer, following label directions. Combine eggs, bacon, olives, parsley, capers and pepper; spread on steak. Roll up as for jelly roll; fasten with string. Brown in hot fat. Sprinkle with paprika and salt. Add enough water to cover bottom of pan. Cover; simmer for 1 hour and 15 minutes, adding additional water if necessary. Yield: 4 servings.

Mrs. E. L. Albrecht, Pres.
St. Martin LWML
Anamoose, North Dakota

BEEF ROLL-UPS

1 round steak
1 tbsp. flour
Salt and pepper to taste
1 tbsp. mustard
1 tbsp. onion flakes
2 tbsp. salad oil
1 can beef broth

Remove bone from steak; sprinkle with flour, salt and pepper. Tenderize steak by pounding with a plate; spread steak with mustard. Sprinkle with onion flakes. Roll as for cinnamon roll; cut into 1/2-inch slices. Insert a toothpick in each roll; brown on both sides in oil. Pour beef broth over rolls. Simmer for 1 hour or until tender. Yield: 6-8 servings.

Mrs. Lloyd Lorensen, Pastor's Wife
Atonement WMS
Colorado Springs, Colorado

FIX AHEAD BEEF ROLLS

2 lb. round steak, ½-in. thick
Long thin slices sweet pickle
Onion, sliced
3 sliced bacon
3 tbsp. flour
1 tsp. salt
¼ tsp. pepper
1 tbsp. fat
1 pt. sour cream
Paprika

Divide steak into six pieces the size and shape of hand. Across center of each steak, lay a pickle slice, one or two onion slices and one-half slice of bacon. Roll up; fold ends. Tie securely with cord in several places. Place rolls in baking dish; cover tightly and re-frigerate or freeze overnight. Flour each roll; sprinkle with salt and pepper. Brown steak in hot fat. Place browned rolls on baking dish; add 1/2-inch depth of water. Cover tightly. Bake at 350 degrees for 1 hour. Bake longer if meat was frozen. When done, meat should be fork tender. Place meat rolls on platter; remove cord. Pour off part of fat; stir sour cream into remaining drippings. Stir over low heat so cream will not curdle. Sprinkle with paprika. Yield: 6 servings.

Mrs. Paul O. Bug, Pres.
Spring Lake Ladies Aid
Douglas, North Dakota

PIGGIES IN THE BLANKET

2 lb. round steak, ¼-in. thick
1 tsp. salt
Dash of pepper
1 med. onion, chopped
4 slices bacon, diced
Bacon drippings or butter

Pound steak; sprinkle with salt and pepper. Cut steak into 4 x 6-inch pieces. Place small amount of onion and bacon on each pieces of steak. Roll up steak; fasten ends with tooth-picks. Brown in bacon drippings. Add a small amount of water. Cover; cook on low heat for 45 minutes or until tender. Yield: 8 servings.

Mrs. Agnes E. Schmidt, Pres.
LWML
Woodburn, Indiana

ROLLED STEAK

1 round steak
Salt and pepper to taste
Bacon slices
Onion slices

Cut steak into serving pieces, 3 to 4 inches wide and 7 to 8 inches long; season with salt and pepper. Lay a bacon slice on each piece; top with onion slices. Roll up like a jelly roll. Pin rolls with toothpicks. Place rolls in roasting pan. Bake, covered, at 350 degrees until done.

Mrs. Paul Junas, Pres.
St. John's Lydia Soc.
Hazelton, Pennsylvania

ROLLED STEAK

6 thin slices steak
Salt
Pinch of pepper
Mustard
6 slices bacon
1 med. onion, diced
1 tbsp. flour
1 tbsp. lard
2 c. boiling water
Mushrooms (opt.)

Pound steak. Sprinkle with salt and pepper; spread with mustard. Place one bacon and onion slice on each strip of meat. Roll; fasten with toothpick. Sprinkle with flour; fry in lard until brown. Add water; stew until well done. Make gravy; add mushrooms.

Mrs. O. Frank
Our Savior LCW
Slay Lakes, Alberta, Canada

ROULADEN

2 slices round steak, very thinly sliced
Salt and pepper
Nutmeg
1 med. onion, chopped
1 lb. bacon, chopped
2 tbsp. shortening
Cornstarch

Season steak with salt, pepper and nutmeg; spread mixture of onion and bacon on steak. Cut steak into individual servings; roll and tie. Brown meat in shortening. Remove meat from pan. Make a generous amount of gravy, using the cornstarch for thickening. Return meat to gravy. Simmer for 2 hours. Yield: 4-6 servings.

Mrs. Leonard Givens, Treas.
Church of Our Redeemer LCW
Omaha, Nebraska

ROULADEN

6 slices top round steak, ¼-in. thick
Salt
6 slices bacon
6 onion slices
6 slices dill pickle
3 tbsp. butter
2 bay leaves
Pinch of thyme
Flour

Cut steak into 3-inch widths and long enough to roll. Sprinkle with salt. Place a slice of bacon, onion and dill pickle on each slice. Roll and fasten with toothpicks. Partially melt butter in a Dutch oven; add bay leaves and thyme. Brown Rouladens on all sides. Add just enough water to cover. Simmer for 2 hours and 30 minutes to 3 hours. Thicken with flour. Serve with creamed cauliflower.

Leora Balash
Trinity Ladies Aid
Blackduck, Minnesota

ROULADEN

8 slices bacon
2 lb. thinly sliced round steak
4 tbsp. fat
1 tsp. salt
¼ tsp. pepper
1 onion, chopped
2 c. water

Fry bacon. Brown steak in fat; cut into 3 x 4-inch pieces. Season with salt and pepper. Place onion and bacon pieces on each strip of meat; roll, fastening with toothpick. Place in baking dish; add water. Cover; bake at 325 degrees for 2 hours. Yield: 6-8 servings.

Mrs. Richard Claybaker, Chmn.
First Lutheran Church Altar Guild
Plattsmouth, Nebraska

ROUND STEAK ROLL-UPS

6 pieces round steak
Salt and pepper to taste
3 onions, sliced
6 sm. carrots, quartered
4 med. potatoes, quartered
1 can cream of mushroom soup
1 can warm water

Season steak with salt and pepper; roll up and secure with toothpicks. Brown steak; place in heavy roaster or Dutch oven. Add onions, carrots and potatoes. Combine soup and water; pour over steak and vegetables. Bake at 300 degrees for 2 hours and 30 minutes to 3 hours. Yield: 6 servings.

Mrs. Vera Niermeier, Pres.
First Lutheran Church Ladies Aid.
Plainville, Kansas

STEAK ROLL

1 1¼-lb. round steak, cut ¼-in. thick
¼ c. chopped onion
¼ c. bacon fat or corn oil
1 qt. (packed) soft bread crumbs
1 bouillon cube
1¼ c. boiling water
½ tsp. sage
2 tsp. crushed dried celery leaves or ¼ c.
    fresh celery, finely chopped
1 egg, beaten
Salt and pepper to taste

Wipe steak thoroughly with damp cloth; pound all over vigorously with edge of heavy saucer. Saute onion in fat until yellow; add to bread crumbs. Dissolve bouillon in water. Combine crumb mixture lightly with bouillon and remaining ingredients. If crumbs are too dry, more liquid may be added. Spread dressing over steak; roll up like a jelly roll. Secure by tying ends and center with string. Brown on all sides in a small amount additional fat in a skillet; add 1/2 cup additional hot water. Cover tightly. Bake at 325 degrees for 1 hour or until meat is very tender. Remove meat roll to hot

platter; remove string and keep hot. Make gravy from drippings in skillet, if desired. Yield: 5 servings.

Mrs. Hazel E. Gonder, Pres.
Moxham LCW
Johnstown, Pennsylvania

STEAK ROLL-UPS

½ c. uncooked long grained rice
¼ tsp. thyme
¼ tsp. crushed marjoram
¼ c. sliced green onion
¼ c. chopped green pepper
2 tbsp. chopped pimento
1 3-oz. can broiled chopped mushrooms,
    drained
2 tbsp. butter
2 lb. round steak, ½-in. thick
2 tbsp. fat
¼ c. dry onion soup mix
Water
2 tbsp. flour

Cook rice until tender; stir in seasonings, green onion, green pepper, pimento, mushrooms and butter. Cut steak into six pieces and pound. Spread steaks with rice mixture; roll up. Fasten with picks; brown in hot fat. Add soup and 1 cup water. Cover; simmer 1 hour and 30 minutes. Remove meat; add water to pan drippings to make 1 cup. Combine flour with 1/2 cup water; stir into liquid. Cook and stir until thick. Serve with meat. Yield: 4-6 servings.

Jackie Lieschner
Peace LCW
Plevna, Montana

STUFFED BEEF ROLL

1 2½ to 3-lb. full cut round steak
Meat tenderizer
Paprika
1 lge. jar pimento
1 lge. onion, thinly sliced
Salt and pepper
8 to 12 stuffed olives
Flour
1 c. red wine
1 c. water
8 sm. onions, boiling size
1 lge. can whole mushrooms

Sprinkle meat with tenderizer and lots of paprika. Cover steak with layers of pimento and sliced onion. Add salt and pepper to taste. Place row of olives on one end of meat and roll like jelly roll, starting with olive end. Tie securely. Sprinkle lightly with flour; brown in Dutch oven. Add wine, water, small onions and mushrooms and liquid. Bake, uncovered, at 350 degrees for 2 hours and 30 minutes to 3 hours or until well done. Add more water while baking if needed. To serve, slice into rounds with natural gravy. Yield: 4-6 servings.

Mrs. Nathan C. Reeder, Pres.
Advent Dorcas and Lydia Circle
Dallas, Texas

STUFFED BEEF TENDERLOIN

½ sm. onion, chopped
1 4-oz. can mushrooms
¼ c. butter or margarine
1 ½ c. soft bread crumbs
½ c. diced celery
Salt and pepper
1 3-lb. beef tenderloin, split and flattened
4 slices bacon

Brown onion and mushrooms lightly in butter. Add bread crumbs, celery and enough hot water to moisten. Season; spread over one-half the meat. Top with second half; secure edges. Season; top with bacon slices. Bake, uncovered, at 350 degrees for 1 hour. Yield: 6-8 servings.

Mrs. Arthur Ramse, Miss'y Wife
Tokio Lutheran Mission
Tokio, North Dakota

STUFFED FLANK STEAK

Fat
½ c. chopped celery
½ tbsp. parsley
1 tbsp. chopped onion
2 c. bread crumbs
1 tsp. savory seasoning
Salt and pepper to taste
1 1 ½-lb. flank steak

Melt 1/4 cup fat in fry pan; add celery, parsley and onion. Cook for a few minutes. Place crumbs in a bowl; add celery mixture and seasonings. Mix lightly but well. Spread stuffing over steak; roll steak like a jelly roll. Tie securely in several places with string; brown meat on all sides in 2 tablespoonfuls fat in a heavy pan on surface unit. Slip a rack under meat in pan; cover pan closely. Bake at 350 degrees for 1 hour and 30 minutes. To carve meat, start slicing at end of roll, cutting across grain so that each serving is a round slice with stuffing in center. Make gravy with drippings, if desired. Yield: 6-8 servings.

Mrs. Dora Larson
Knife River Ladies Aid
Stanley, North Dakota

STUFFED ROUND STEAK

1 ½ lb. round steak
Salt and pepper to taste
3 or 4 slices dry bread, crumbled
¾ c. milk
¼ lb. hamburger
1 egg, beaten
1 tbsp. melted butter
1 tbsp. dry onion soup mix
Barbecue sauce or catsup
2 tbsp. diced onion

Season steak with salt and pepper on both sides. Combine bread crumbs, milk, hamburger, egg, butter, dry soup mix, dash of pepper and salt to taste. Spread mixture on steak; roll up and tie with string. Place on 9 x 13-inch cake pan.

Baste top with small amount of barbecue sauce or catsup; sprinkle with onion. Bake at 350 degrees for 1 hour. Yield: 6-8 servings.

Mrs. Jean Lueders, Pres.
Nicolai Ladies Aid
Canby, Minnesota

STUFFED ROUND STEAK

1 round steak, cut thin
Chopped bacon
Chopped onion
Flour
Salt and pepper
1 bouillon cube

Pound steak until very thin. Cut into 3 x 4-inch pieces. Place small amounts of bacon and onion on steak. Roll each piece; secure with skewers or toothpicks. Dredge in flour; brown. Add salt and pepper. Dissolve bouillon cube in a small amount of water; pour over steak. Bake, covered, at 325 degrees for 2 hours and 30 minutes to 3 hours.

Mary Lou Strandberg, Pres.
Emmanual LCW
Dayton, Iowa

STUFFED STEAK ROLL

1 onion, grated
1 clove of garlic, minced
¼ c. butter or margarine
3 c. dry coarse bread crumbs
½ c. diced celery
½ c. chopped carrots
1 tbsp. chopped parsley
1 tsp. salt
¼ tsp. basil
¼ tsp. thyme
⅛ tsp. nutmeg
1 ½ lb. thinly sliced round steak
½ c. mixed vegetable juice

Saute onion and garlic in butter. Combine all ingredients except steak and vegetable juice. Spread over round steak. Roll like jelly roll; tie with clean string. Brown in little hot fat in large heavy kettle. Add juice; cover. Bake at 350 degrees for 30 minutes. Bake, uncovered, for 30 minutes longer or until meat is tender. Yield: 4-6 servings.

Mrs. Betty Krumland, Pres.
United Women of Redeemer
Spokane, Washington

DELICIOUS SWISS STEAK

2 cans cream of mushroom soup
1 lge. can tomato juice
Salt and pepper to taste
12 steaks
½ c. flour
4 tbsp. lard or shortening
12 onion slices

(Continued on next page)

Stir cream of mushroom soup into tomato juice; set aside. Salt and pepper steaks; dip into flour. Brown in lard or shortening. Pour soup mixture over steaks; add onions. Bake at 375 degrees for 1 hour and 30 minutes, stirring steaks loose from bottom of pan occasionally.

Mrs. Ethel Freeman, Pres.
Christ Lutheran Church ALCW
Genoa, Colorado

INDIVIDUAL SWISS STEAKS

2 lb. beef round steak, ¾-in. thick
1 ½ to 2 tsp. salt
⅛ to ¼ tsp. pepper
3 tbsp. flour
3 tbsp. lard
1 onion, sliced
1 No. 303 can tomatoes

Cut steak into individual servings; dredge with seasoned flour. Brown in hot fat. Pour off drippings. Add onion and tomatoes. Cover and cook slowly for 2 hours or until tender. Thicken liquid for gravy; season to taste. Yield: 6 servings.

Mrs. Emil Radtke, Pres.
Ebenezer ALCW
Albany, Minnesota
Mrs. A. H. Williams
St. Timothy Ladies Aid Soc.
Selma, Alabama

OVEN SWISS STEAK

2 lb. round steak
Salt and pepper to taste
4 tbsp. flour
1 tbsp. seasoning salt
Oil
1 No. 303 can whole tomatoes
1 8-oz. can tomato sauce
1 c. water
1 lge. bay leaf
1 lge. onion, cut into rings

Cut steak into serving pieces; salt and pepper to taste. Mix flour with seasoning salt; dust steak. Place oil in 13 x 9 x 2-inch pan; add steak to pan. Brown steak on both sides in preheated 450 degree oven. Add tomatoes, tomato sauce, water and bay leaf. Arrange onion on top of steak. Cover pan with aluminum foil. Bake at 350 degrees for 1 hour and 30 minutes. Serve with fluffy rice.

Mrs. David Joeckel Pastor's Wife
Holy Trinity LWML
Hacienda Heights, California

SWISS STEAK

1 ½ lb. round steak
2 tsp. salt
½ tsp. pepper
2 tbsp. flour

4 tbsp. cooking oil
1 onion, chopped
1 green pepper, sliced
1 can tomatoes

Season steak with salt and pepper; pound in flour. Brown in hot fat; add onion and green pepper. Saute until brown; add tomatoes. Cover; bake at 350 degrees for 1 hour and 30 minutes. Yield: 6 servings.

Mrs. Hattie Goforth
Mt. Olive Evangelical Ladies Aid Soc.
Newton, North Carolina

SWISS STEAKS

6 lb. steak
1 c. flour
1 carrot, chopped
½ green pepper, chopped
½ c. finely chopped celery
1 ½ 1-lb. 12-oz. cans tomatoes
1 ½ tbsp. salt
3 bay leaves
Dash of pepper

Cut steak into serving pieces. Pound flour into steak. Brown meat in a small amount fat. Place in shallow roasting pan. Combine remaining flour, vegetables, water and seasonings with drippings. Heat; stir until thickened. Pour over meat. Bake at 325 degrees for 2 hours and 30 minutes. Yield: 18 servings.

Mrs. John Riekena, Jr., Pres.
St. Peter's LCW
Bartonville, Illinois

SWISS STEAK AND CARROTS

⅓ c. diced suet
2 lb. swiss steak, ¾-in. thick
1 ½ tsp. salt
⅛ tsp. pepper
½ c. sliced onion
1 c. sliced carrots
½ c. diced celery
2 c. tomato juice
¾ c. water
¼ c. diced green pepper
⅛ tsp. monosodium glutamate
½ c. mushrooms

Render suet in medium iron skillet. Cut meat into servings. Pound in flour, salt and pepper. Reserve remaining flour mixture for gravy. Brown meat in suet drippings. Add onion, carrots and celery. Cover; cook slowly for 30 minutes. Add tomato juice and water; cook for 45 minutes. Add green pepper, monosodium glutamate, mushrooms and reserved flour mixture. Cook, uncovered, for 15 minutes, stirring occasionally. Serve on platter with gravy. Yield: 4-5 servings.

Mrs. Herman W. Schade, Past Treas.
Our Savior LWML
Aurora, Illinois

SWISS STEAK SPECIAL

2 tbsp. flour
1 tsp. salt
¼ tsp. pepper
2 lb. round steak, 1-in. thick
½ c. finely chopped onion
½ c. finely chopped celery
½ c. finely chopped green pepper
1 c. canned tomatoes

Combine flour and seasonings; pound mixture thoroughly into steak. Cut steak into serving pieces. Brown steak well in fat. Mix vegetables; place over meat. Cover and simmer for 1 hour to 1 hour and 30 minutes. Thicken sauce as desired. Yield: 6 servings.

Mrs. Richard Saloga, Sec.
Trinity Ladies Aid
Sarcoxie, Missouri

SWISS STEAK SPECIAL

½ c. flour
1 ½ tsp. salt
¼ tsp. pepper
4 lb. round steak, 2-in thick
1 med. onion, chopped
4 tbsp. fat
1 c. steamed tomatoes
½ c. diced celery
½ c. water

Combine flour, salt and pepper. Pound steak; brush flour mixture into meat. Lightly brown onion in fat; remove from pan. Brown meat well on both sides. Place in Dutch oven or roaster. Add onion, 1 cup or more tomatoes, celery and water. Cover tightly; bake at 350 degrees for 2 hours and 30 minutes. If desired, add 12 medium carrots. Garnish with parsley. Yield: 12 servings.

Mrs. Henry Gumz, Pres.
St. Peter's LWML and Sewing Circle
Dorchester, Wisconsin

SWISS STEAK SUPREME

½ c. flour
2 tsp. salt
½ tsp. pepper
2 lb. round or chuck steak, 1 ½-in. thick
1 sm. onion, chopped
3 tbsp. fat
1 c. canned tomatoes

Mix flour, salt and pepper. Thoroughly pound into steak. Brown meat and onion in hot fat; add tomatoes. Cover; cook over low heat or bake at 350 degrees for 1 hour and 30 minutes or until tender. Yield: 6 servings.

Mrs. Paul Kittelson
Ellsborough ALCW
Balaton, Minnesota

SWISS STEAK AND VEGETABLES

½ c. flour
2 tsp. salt
¼ tsp. pepper
1 lge. round steak, 1 ½-in. thick
½ c. onion rings
¼ c. shortening
1 8-oz. can tomato sauce
1 c. pizza sauce
1 c. finely diced celery
1 green pepper, finely diced
1 c. chili sauce
1 sm. can peas
1 sm. can whole kernel corn

Combine flour, salt and pepper; pound into meat. Brown onion in hot fat in large skillet. Remove; add meat and brown. Place onion on top of meat; add remaining ingredients. Simmer, covered, for 1 hour and 30 minutes or until fork tender. Yield: 6 servings.

Ida Rohlfing, Treas.
St. John's Mission Soc.
Red Bud, Illinois

TANGY SWISS STEAK

2 lb. round steak, 1 ½ to 2-in. thick
Flour
3 tbsp. shortening
½ tsp. salt
½ tsp. pepper
⅓ c. minced onion
⅓ c. minced celery
½ clove of garlic, chopped
1 can tomato soup, undiluted
2 tbsp. brown sugar
2 tbsp. Worcestershire sauce
2 tsp. lemon juice
2 tsp. prepared mustard
Dash of Tabasco sauce

Make several cuts in edge of meat. Pound in flour. Brown in shortening on both sides. Add salt, pepper, onion, celery and garlic. Simmer for a few minutes. Combine remaining ingredients. Pour over meat. Simmer for 1 hour and 30 minutes or until tender. Add water if needed. NOTE: May be baked in casserole at 325 to 350 degrees until done. Yield: 6 servings.

Mrs. Eugene Meierhoefer, Pres.
Atonement LWML
Columbus, Ohio

WESTERN STEAK

2 lb. round steak, 1-in. thick
1 ½ tsp. salt
Pepper to taste
Monosodium glutamate to taste
2 lge. onions, sliced and separated into rings
1 lge. green pepper, sliced
1 No. 303 can or 1 pkg. frozen green beans
1 No. 303 can plum tomatoes

Brown steak in small amount of fat; add salt, pepper and monosodium glutamate. Place onions

(Continued on next page)

and green pepper in layers over meat. Add green beans and tomatoes. Cover; simmer for 1 hour or until meat is tender.

Mrs. Carl Arnold, Treas.
Bethany Ladies Guild
Lompoc, California

YANKEE CHEDDAR STEAK

1 lb. round steak, ½-in. thick
¼ c. flour
1 tsp. salt
¼ tsp. pepper
1 med. onion, thinly sliced
Oil
1 8-oz. can tomato sauce
1 tsp. garlic salt
1 c. shredded Cracker Barrel sharp natural
   Cheddar cheese

Cut steak into serving pieces. Combine flour, salt and pepper; pound into steak. Brown in oil; place in shallow baking dish. Cover with onion slices; pour mixture of tomato sauce and garlic salt over steak. Bake at 350 degrees for 40 minutes. Sprinkle with cheese; bake until cheese melts. Yield: 4 servings.

Mrs. Nora Zielinski
St. Paul Ladies Guild
Montgomery, Alabama

BARBECUE

1 ½ lb. stew beef, cubed
¾ c. water
2 med. onions, sliced
3 tbsp. vinegar
2 tbsp. Worcestershire sauce
1 tsp. salt
1 tsp. paprika
¼ tsp. pepper
1 tsp. chili powder
¾ c. catsup

Cook beef in water in pressure saucepan for 30 minutes. Add remaining ingredients to cooked meat and liquid. Simmer until part of liquid is reduced and meat is tender. Heat and serve on buns. Yield: 12 servings.

Mrs. R. H. Bokenkamp, Past Pres.
Redeemer Ladies Guild
Charleston, West Virginia

BEEF BROWNIES

2 lb. round steak, 1-in. thick
4 c. bread crumbs
½ tsp. sage
1 tsp. salt
Dash of pepper
1 egg, beaten
1 tbsp. onion
½ c. plus 3 tbsp. melted butter

Pound steak; cut into 2 x 6-inch strips. Combine remaining ingredients except 3 tablespoonfuls butter; spread on strips of meat. Roll up and pin with round toothpicks. Brown in remaining butter. Add enough water to almost cover. Simmer for 1 hour and 30 minutes or until tender. Yield: 6 servings.

Mrs. Walter Rabe, Pres.
St. Paul's Ladies Aid Soc.
Ricketts, Iowa

BEEF INTERNATIONAL

Flour
2 lb. round steak
4 tbsp. butter or margarine
2 med. onions, thinly sliced
½ c. water
1 10 ½-oz. can cream of celery soup
1 3-oz. can sliced mushrooms, drained
½ c. salad dressing
Salt and pepper to taste

Flour steak; cut into thin slices. Brown in butter on both sides. Add onions, water and celery soup; simmer in electric skillet for 1 hour or until tender. Add mushrooms, salad dressing, salt and pepper. Simmer for 10 minutes. Serve over wide cooked noodles. Yield: 12 servings.

Mrs. Graydon Bordner, Chmn.
St. Johns Circle No. 4
New Washington, Ohio

BEEF SAMOVAR

1 ½ lb. round steak, cut into ¾-in. strips
Flour
2 tbsp. fat
½ c. chopped onions
1 clove of garlic, minced
1 6-oz. can broiled mushrooms, sliced
1 c. sour cream
1 10 ½-oz. can tomato soup
1 tbsp. Worcestershire sauce
6 to 8 drops of Tabasco sauce
½ tsp. salt
⅛ tsp. pepper
1 pkg. noodles, cooked

Dip meat into flour; brown in hot fat. Add onions, garlic and mushrooms. Combine remaining ingredients except noodles; pour over meat. Simmer for 1 hour. Serve over noodles; sprinkle with Parmesan cheese, if desired. Yield: 4 servings.

Mrs. Charles Winemiller
Christ the King Lutheran Church Guild
Lincoln Park, Michigan

BEEF TIPS

1 can cream of chicken soup
1 can beef broth or bouillon
1 ½ lb. stew meat, cubed

51

(Continued on next page)

Mix soup and broth; add meat. Place in casserole. Bake, covered, at 350 degrees for 2 hours. Yield: 6 servings.

Mrs. Michael Polovitz, Pres.
Redeemer LWML
Grand Forks, North Dakota

BEEF PAPRIKA

1 c. sliced onions
3 tbsp. shortening
1 ½ lb. beef, cubed
¼ c. flour
3 c. hot water
2 tsp. vinegar
½ tsp. salt
1 tbsp. paprika
⅛ tsp. pepper
2 tbsp. evaported milk or cream

Saute onions in shortening. Remove onions; add beef to pan. Sear until brown. Add onions; sprinkle with flour. Immediately add hot water and stir. Add vinegar, salt, paprika and pepper. Simmer for 1 hour. Add evaporated milk. Serve in noodle ring or with mashed potatoes. Yield: 8 servings.

Mrs. Aidle Meller, Pres.
Balfour LCW
Balfour, North Dakota

BENOITS BEEF AND BARLEY

¾ c. chopped onion
1 c. pearled barley
1 tbsp. butter
4 c. water
2 lb. round or sirloin steak
⅓ c. fine bread crumbs
1 tbsp. sesame seed
1 ½ tsp. salt
1 tsp. paprika
2 tbsp. shortening
1 4-oz. can button mushrooms, undrained
1 can pimento, chopped
1 tsp. Worcestershire sauce

Saute onion and barley in butter; add 2 cups water and simmer for 15 minutes. Cut steak into 2-inch strips; roll in mixture of crumbs, seasame seed, 1 teaspoonful salt and paprika. Brown in shortening. Combine barley mixture with soup, mushrooms, remaining salt, pimento, Worcestershire sauce and remaining water. Add browned steak; pour into 3-quart casserole. Cover; bake at 325 degrees for 1 hour and 30 minutes. Uncover; bake for 30 minutes longer. Yield: 8-10 servings.

Mrs. Victor Anderson
Salem LCW
St. Cloud, Minnesota

BRAISED BEEF WITH MUSHROOMS

1 4-oz. can sliced mushrooms
1 ½ lb. stew beef, cut into 1-in. cubes
1 clove of garlic
¾ c. sliced onions
3 tbsp. shortening
1 bouillon cube
1 c. hot water
1 can tomato sauce
2 tsp. sugar
2 tsp. Worcestershire sauce
1 tsp. basil or oregano
1 tsp. salt
⅛ tsp. pepper

Drain mushrooms; reserve liquid. Brown meat, garlic, onions and mushrooms in hot shortening in Dutch oven or heavy skillet. Dissolve bouillon in water; add to meat with mushroom liquid and remaining ingredients. Bake, covered, 300 degrees for 2 hours and 30 minutes to 3 hours. Add additional water if necessary. Thicken liquid if desired and serve over hot noodles, spaghetti or mashed potatoes.

Mrs. John W. Crane, Pres.
Zion Women's League
Anaheim, California

BRAISED MEAT CUBES

2 lb. beef chuck
1 tbsp. shortening
1 8-oz. can tomato sauce
1 c. water
1 med. onion, chopped
1 sm. clove of garlic, minced
1 tsp. salt
½ tsp. sugar
¼ tsp. dry mustard
⅛ tsp. pepper
4 c. hot mashed potatoes
1 tbsp. chopped parsley

Trim excess fat from meat; cut into 1-inch cubes. Brown meat on all sides in hot shortening in 10-inch skillet or Dutch oven. Add tomato sauce, water, onion, garlic, salt, sugar, mustard and pepper. Stir well. Cover and simmer, stirring occasionally, for 1 hour and 30 minutes to 2 hours or until fork tender. Skim off fat. Arrange mashed potatoes in ring on heated platter; sprinkle with parsley. Spoon beef and gravy into center of potato ring. Yield: 6 servings.

Helen Borecki, Treas.
St. Peter's LWML
Medford, Oregon

BURGUNDY BEEF

1 ½ lb. round steak, cut into 1-in. cubes
Seasoned flour
3 strips bacon
½ c. water
1 bouillon cube
½ c. dry red wine
½ tsp. salt
1 med. onion, sliced
3 carrots, sliced or diced
2 whole cloves
1 bay leaf
½ lb. fresh mushrooms, sliced or canned
Butter

(Continued on next page)

Sprinkle meat with seasoned flour. Brown bacon in skillet; remove. Brown steak in bacon fat. Add water, bouillon cube, wine and salt. Bring to a boil; transfer to 1 1/2 or 2-quart casserole. Add onion, carrots, spices and diced bacon. Cover and bake at 300 degrees for 2 hours. Cook fresh mushrooms in butter until limp; add to casserole the last 15 minutes of baking Serve with buttered noodles. Yield: 5-6 servings.

Mrs. Raymond Quale, Pres.
Marin LCW
Mill Valley, California

BURGUNDY BEEF

1 clove of garlic
3 med. onions, thinly sliced
4 tbsp. butter
2 lb. beef round, cubed
2 8-oz. cans beef gravy
Salt and pepper to taste
¼ tsp. marjoram
¼ tsp. oregano
½ c. Burgundy
½ pt. sour cream

Brown garlic and onions in butter; discard garlic. Remove onions from pan. Brown meat in same pan; beef gravy, salt, pepper and onions. Simmer for 1 hour or until beef is tender. Add marjoram, oregano and wine. Simmer for 15 minutes longer. Stir in sour cream. Serve over rice or noodles, if desired. Yield: 6 servings.

Mrs. Betty Broom Baugh, Pres.
Zion LCW
Pevely, Missouri

CHINESE BEEF

1 lb. round steak
2 tbsp. oil
1 clove of garlic, crushed
3 med. onions, cut into wedges
1 green pepper, cut into strips
2 or 3 pieces celery, cut diagonally
2 tbsp. cornstarch
1 tbsp. sugar
1 tsp. salt
3 tbsp. soy sauce
1 c. water

Cut steak diagonally across grain into bite-sized pieces. Heat oil in large heavy skillet. Brown garlic; remove from skillet. Reduce heat and brown meat. Add onion wedges while browning; add green pepper and celery. Blend cornstarch, sugar, salt, soy sauce and water in small bowl. Push meat to sides of skillet; add sauce, stirring constantly. Cook until thickened; mix all ingredients. Serve on fluffy rice. Yield: 4-5 servings.

Eileen Sryberg
Trinity LWML
Santa Susana, California

CHINESE BEEF

1 lge. flank steak
2 tbsp. olive or salad oil
1 sm. clove of garlic, minced
1 tsp. salt
¼ tsp. ginger
¼ c. soy sauce
½ tsp. sugar
2 lge. or 3 sm. ripe tomatoes, quartered
2 green peppers, coarsely chopped
1 can bean sprouts, drained
¼ c. water
1 tbsp. cornstarch

Cut steak into thin strips across grain. Heat oil in skillet; add beef, garlic, salt and ginger. Fry until brown. Add soy sauce and sugar; cover tightly. Cook slowly for 5 minutes. Toss in tomatoes, peppers and bean sprouts. Bring to a boil; cover and cook for 7 minutes. Make a smooth paste of water and cornstarch; add to beef. Heat until slightly thickened. Serve over rice. Yield: 6 servings.

Mrs. Donald Meinhold, Pres.
St. Mark LCW
Morristown, New Jersey

CHUCK WAGON CASSEROLE

2 c. cooked beef, cubed
1 1-lb. can whole kernel corn, drained
1 10 ½-oz. can tomato soup
1 c. shredded Cheddar cheese
1 tbsp. instant minced onion
1 tsp. chili powder
1 can refrigerator biscuits
2 tbsp. melted butter
¼ c. yellow corn meal

Mix all ingredients except biscuits, butter and corn meal. Place in shallow 2 1/2-quart casserole. Bake at 400 degrees for 10 minutes. Dip biscuits into melted butter, then into corn meal. Arrange on casserole. Bake for 20 to 25 minutes longer or until biscuits are golden brown. Yield: 4-6 servings.

Mrs. Harold Lee Howdyshell, Group Leader II
Mt. Tabor LCW
Staunton, Virginia

COMPANY DELIGHT

1 ½ lb. cubed round steak
⅓ c. margarine
2 lge. onions, diced
1 can tomato soup
1 can water
2 tbsp. Worcestershire sauce
½ lb. cheese, grated
1 tsp. (heaping) sugar
1 c. mushrooms
2 c. elbow spaghetti, cooked
1 c. salted nuts

Brown steak in margarine; add onions. Add tomato soup, water, Worcestershire sauce, one-half the cheese, sugar and undrained mushrooms.

53

(Continued on next page)

Simmer for 30 minutes. Combine meat mixture and spaghetti; pour into buttered 11 x 9 x 2-inch pan or casserole. Sprinkle remaining cheese on top; sprinkle salted nuts over cheese. Bake at 350 degrees for 45 minutes. Yield: 8 servings.

Mrs. Jack Peterson, Pres.
Immanuel LWML
Alliance, Nebraska

MOCK SUKIYAKI

1 lb. thinly sliced round steak
2 tbsp. salad oil
1 ½ c. sliced celery
1 med. green pepper, sliced
1 lge. onion, thinly sliced
1 ½ c. fresh mushrooms or 1 6-oz. can
    mushrooms, drained
½ c. green onions, cut into 1-in. pieces
1 10 ½-oz. can beef broth
1 tbsp. soy sauce
¼ c. water
2 tbsp. cornstarch
4 c. hot cooked rice

Brown meat in salad oil; add vegetables, beef broth and soy sauce. Cover. Cook over low heat for 10 minutes or until vegetables are tender. Stir often. Combine water and cornstarch; add to meat mixture. Stir until thickened. Serve over hot rice. Yield: 4-6 servings.

Mrs. Fred Miller, Pastor's Wife
Trinity First Ladies Aid
Minneapolis, Minnesota

PASTIES

¼ lb. beef, cut into small cubes
¾ c. finely diced potatoes
⅓ c. finely chopped onion
½ tsp. salt
Dash of pepper
1 recipe pastry for two-crust pie
Milk

Combine beef, potatoes, onion, salt and pepper. Divide pastry in half; roll into 10-inch squares. Cut each square into quarters. Place about 3 tablespoonfuls of meat mixture on each square of pastry. Moisten edges and fold. Pinch edges and cut slits for steam. Brush tops with milk. Bake at 425 degrees for 35 to 40 minutes. Yield: 4 servings.

Louise G. Hamor
Christ Evangelical Lutheran Church
Lancaster, Pennsylvania

PASTIES

4 lge. or 6 med. potatoes, cubed
2 med. onions, finely cut
2 tbsp. chopped or ground suet
1 ½ lb. round steak, cubed or coarsely
    ground
1 tsp. salt

2 ½ c. flour
1 tsp. baking powder
⅔ c. lard
6 tbsp. cold water
4 tsp. butter

Combine potatoes, onions, suet, steak and salt. Sift flour and baking powder; cut in lard. Add cold water; mix lightly. Divide dough into four portions, roll out each as for pie crust. Place 1 cup meat mixture and 1 teaspoonful butter on one-half of each round. Fold remaining crust over filling; seal edges. Bake at 400 degrees for 1 hour. Yield: 4 servings.

Mrs. Eugene Filby, Chmn.
Messiah LCW
Duluth, Minnesota

ROUND STEAK SAUERBRATEN

1 ½ lb. round steak
1 tbsp. fat
1 envelope brown gravy mix
2 c. water
1 tbsp. instant minced onion
2 tbsp. white wine vinegar
2 tbsp. brown sugar
½ tsp. salt
¼ tsp. pepper
½ tsp. ginger
1 tsp. Worcestershire sauce
1 bay leaf
Hot buttered noodles

Cut meat in 1-inch squares. Brown in hot fat. Remove meat from skillet; add gravy mix and water. Bring to boiling, stirring constantly. Stir in remaining ingredients except noodles. Return meat to skillet; cover and simmer for 1 hour and 30 minutes, stirring occasionally. Remove bay leaf. Serve meat over hot buttered noodles. Yield: 5-6 servings.

Mrs. Weida Beth, Treas.
St. John's Evangelical Ladies Aid
Algonquin, Illinois

SAILOR'S BEEF

2 tbsp. butter or margarine
1 med. onion, sliced
2 lb. round steak, cut into ½-in. thick slices
3 c. thinly sliced potatoes
1 bottle or 11-oz. can beer
1 tsp. salt
¼ tsp. pepper
½ tsp. thyme

Melt butter in skillet. Cook onion in butter until light brown. Remove onion from pan. Pound meat; cut into 1/2-inch strips. Brown meat in skillet. Alternate layers of meat, onion and potatoes in 2-quart casserole. Pour beer into skillet in which meat was browned; add seasonings and stir. Pour into casserole. Cover and bake at 350 degrees for 1 hour. Yield: 6 servings.

Clara S. Lehmberg
St. John's Martha Soc.
Bakersfield, California

SIRLOIN TIPS JARDINIERE

2 lb. sirloin tip, cubed
4 tbsp. flour
2 tbsp. salad oil
Salt and pepper to taste
Monosodium glutamate to taste
½ c. chopped onion
½ c. chopped carrots
½ c. chopped celery
½ tsp. chopped garlic
1 tsp. paprika
¼ tsp. cumin
¼ tsp Italian seasoning
¼ c. water
2 4-oz. cans sliced mushrooms

Roll beef in flour; brown in skillet in the oil. Season with salt, pepper and monosodium glutamate. Scatter onion, carrots, celery and garlic over meat; add paprika, cumin, Italian seasoning, water and mushrooms. Cover; simmer for 45 minutes or until tender. Serve over hot noodles or rice, if desired. Yield: 6 servings.

Mrs. Al Meisner, Pres.
First Lutheran Church LCW
South Sioux City, Nebraska

SKILLET DINNER

½ lb. lean beef, cut into thin strips
2 tbsp. oil
½ c. finely chopped onion
1 green pepper, sliced
1 c. chopped celery
1 c. canned or cooked green beans
4 tsp. cornstarch
1 tbsp. soy sauce
¾ c. water
4 oz. sliced mushrooms

Brown beef in oil. Add onion and green pepper; cook for 3 minutes. Add celery and green beans; cook for 5 minutes. Combine cornstarch, soy sauce and water; add to skillet. Stir in mushrooms. Cook 10 minutes longer until liquid is clear. Serve over rice, if desired. Yield: 4-6 servings.

Mrs. Donald J. Richow, Pres.
St. Timothy's LCW
Minneapolis, Minnesota

BEEF OR CHICKEN STROGANOFF

2 lb. beef or chicken, cubed
Flour
4 tbsp. butter
6 med. onions, chopped
2 c. meat broth
8 oz. mushrooms
½ pt. sour cream
1 tsp. salt (opt.)
½ tsp. pepper (opt.)

Dredge meat in flour; brown in butter. Add onions and broth. Simmer for 1 hour and 30 minutes to 2 hours or until meat is tender. Add mushrooms. Turn heat to low. Slowly add sour cream and seasonings. Heat for 10 to 15 minutes. Serve on

rice, noodles, mashed potatoes or biscuits, if desired. Yield: 4 servings.

Mrs. Mary M. Sheets, Pres.
St. Mary's Pine LCW
Quicksburg, Virginia

BEEF STROGANOFF

2 lb. steak, cut into small pieces
½ c. seasoned flour
5 tbsp. butter or margarine
1 med. onion, diced
½ tsp. paprika
2 tbsp. flour
2 beef bouillon cubed
1 c. boiling water
1 can cream of mushroom soup
½ c. sour cream
1 tsp. Worcestershire sauce
Salt and pepper to taste

Roll steak in seasoned flour. Brown meat in butter. Remove meat from skillet. Saute onions in remaining butter; sprinkle with paprika and flour. Dissolve bouillon in boiling water; pour into skillet with soup, stirring constantly. Cook until thickened. Blend in sour cream. Return meat to skillet; add Worcestershire sauce and salt and pepper. Heat thoroughly. Serve on rice or noodles, if desired. Yield: 6 servings.

Mrs. Marla Carlson, Pres.
Advent LCW
Arvada, Colorado

CANADIAN BEEF STROGANOFF

2 lb. round steak
1 tsp. meat tenderizer
Flour
1 tsp. salt
¼ tsp. pepper
1 tsp. paprika
¼ c. salad oil
1 10-oz. can mushrooms
2 lge. onions, sliced
¼ tsp. garlic powder
1 c. water
1 tbsp. Worcestershire sauce
1 c. sour cream
3 c. cooked noodles

Cut steak into 1/2-inch wide strips. Sprinkle with tenderizer; let stand for 20 minutes. Mix 1/3 cup flour, salt, pepper and paprika in bag; add meat strips and shake well. Brown meat on all sides in hot oil; add mushrooms, onions, garlic powder, water and Worcestershire sauce. Simmer, covered, for 4 minutes or until meat is tender. Blend 1 tablespoonful flour with sour cream; blend into meat mixture, stirring until smooth. Cook over low heat, stirring until gravy thickens. Serve over noodles. Yield: 6-8 servings.

Mrs. Mona D. Wagner, Sec.
North Southey Zion LWML
Southey, Saskatchewan, Canada

BEEF STROGANOFF

3 ½ lb. round or tenderloin, cut ½-in. thick
2 tsp. salt
1 ½ tsp. pepper
½ c. butter
¼ c. grated onion
3 tbsp. flour
¼ tsp. dry mustard
2 c. water
2 beef bouillon cubes
½ can cream of mushroom soup
⅓ c. sour cream

Cut beef into 2-inch long strips; salt and pepper meat. Let stand for 1 hour. Heat 1/4 cup butter in heavy skillet; add beef. Cook on low heat until well browned; add onion. Melt remaining butter in saucepan; add flour and mustard. Stir until mixture is brown; add water, bouillon cubes and soup, stirring until smooth and thick. Add beef and sour cream; cover. Cook slowly until tender. Yield: 8 servings.

Mrs. Raymond Koterba, Pres.
Highland Ladies Aid
Outlook, Montana

BEEF STROGANOFF

2 lb. round steak
¼ c. flour
½ c. chopped onion
6 tbsp. butter
1 ½ tsp. salt
⅛ tsp. pepper
½ c. water
1 can cream of mushroom soup
1 4-oz. can mushrooms, drained
1 c. sour cream

Cut meat into 1/2 x 2-inch pieces; dredge in flour. Brown with onion in butter; add seasonings and water. Cover and simmer gently until almost tender, 45 minutes to 1 hour, stirring occasionally. Add soup and mushrooms; stir to mix. Cook gently until beef is tender, about 30 minutes. Heat until piping hot; stir in sour cream. Serve over noodles or cooked rice, if desired. Yield: 10 servings.

Mrs. Otto F. Marx, VP
St. Paul's Ladies Aid Soc.
Rushville, Nebraska

DIFFERENT BEEF STROGANOFF

1 ½ to 2 lb. round or flank steak
2 tbsp. butter
2 4-oz. cans mushrooms
1 lge. onion, sliced
Flour
1 tbsp. horseradish
1 tsp. thick condiment sauce
1 ¼ tsp. salt
⅛ tsp. pepper
½ c. water
1 c. sour cream

Slice meat across grain into 1-inch strips. Melt butter; saute mushrooms and onion slices for 5 minutes. Remove from pan. Roll meat strips in flour; brown on all sides in same butter. Place onion mixture on top of meat. Add horseradish, condiment sauce, salt, pepper and water. Cover and simmer for 2 hours or until meat is tender. Add sour cream just before serving. Serve over rice, if desired. Yield: 6 servings.

Mrs. Olaf A. Langehough, Pastor's Wife
Messiah LCW
Vancouver, Washington

DILLY BEEF STROGANOFF

2 lb. sirloin steak, cut ½-in. thick
4 tbsp. butter
¼ c. chopped onion
1 med. clove of garlic, crushed
3 tbsp. flour
Dash of pepper
1 10 ½-oz. can beef bouillon
1 10 ½-oz. can cream of mushroom soup
¼ tsp. dill weed
1 6-oz. can mushrooms, drained
½ c. sour cream
Salt to taste

Trim fat from meat; cut meat crosswise into 1/2 x 2-inch strips. Melt 2 tablespoonfuls butter in large skillet; add enough beef strips to cover skillet. Brown quickly on both sides; remove. Brown remaining beef strips. Set meat aside. Add remaining 2 tablespoonfuls butter to skillet; cook onion and garlic until tender. Blend in flour and pepper. Add bouillon, mushroom soup and dill weed. Stir until smooth; add meat and mushrooms. Heat through. Stir in sour cream; salt to taste. Serve over rice. Yield: 6 servings.

Mrs. Alvin Lemke, Pres.
Trinity LCW
Bruning, Nebraska

FIFTEEN-MINUTE STROGANOFF

1 lb. round steak, ¼-in. thick
⅔ c. water
1 3 or 4-oz. can sliced mushrooms
1 envelope dry onion soup mix
1 c. sour cream
2 tbsp. flour

Trim fat from meat and reserve. Cut meat diagonally across grain into very thin strips. Heat trimmings in skillet until there is 3 tablespoonfuls melted fat, adding butter, if necessary. Remove trimmings. Brown meat; add water and mushrooms. Stir in soup mix. Bring to a boil. Blend sour cream and flour; add to hot mixture. Cook and stir until mixture thickens. Serve over noodles or rice, if desired. Yield: 5 servings.

Mrs. Madeleine Docherty, Pres.
St. John's LCW
Englewood, New Jersey
Mrs. Rosena Novotany, Pres.
LWML
Claflin, Kansas

EASY STROGANOFF

1 lb. round steak, cut into thin strips
½ c. chopped onion
2 tbsp. butter or margarine
1 10½-oz. can cream of mushroom soup
¼ c. water
½ c. sour cream
½ tsp. paprika
2 c. cooked noodles

Brown steak and onion in butter in frying pan; stir in soup, water, sour cream and paprika. Cover and simmer for 45 minutes or until meat is tender, stirring often. Serve over noodles. Yield: 4 servings.

Mrs. Irvin D. Westerberg
Messiah LWML
Valdosta, Georgia

QUICK BEEF STROGANOFF

2 ½ lb. beef, cubed
Butter
5 oz. onions, minced
½ clove of garlic, minced
1 ½ tsp. paprika
Dash of pepper
1 can cream of mushroom soup
4 oz. water
Cooked noodles
4 oz. sour cream

Saute meat in butter; add onions; garlic, paprika and pepper. Stir in soup, blending until smooth; blend in water. Cover and simmer for 1 hour. Serve over mixture of noodles and sour cream. Yield: 6 servings.

Mrs. Hugh McKindley
Mt. Calvary Ladies Aid
Cahokia, Illinois

STEAK STROGANOFF

1 lb. steak, cut into ¾-in. pieces
Flour
2 tbsp. fat
¼ to ½ c. chopped onion
1 clove of garlic, minced
1 6-oz. can broiled mushrooms, quartered
1 10½-oz. can tomato soup
1 tbsp. Worcestershire sauce
6 to 8 drops of Tabasco sauce
½ tsp. salt
⅛ tsp. pepper
1 c. sour cream
Cooked rice or spaghetti

Dip meat into flour; brown in hot fat. Add onion, garlic and mushrooms. Combine remaining ingredients except rice; add to meat. Simmer until tender, about 1 hour. Serve over fluffy rice. Yield: 4-6 servings.

Mrs. Edna Mall
Redeemer LCW
El Monte, California
Mrs. Walter Schauer, Pres.
Spencer Trinity Lutheran Church Ladies Aid
Spencer, Wisconsin

STEAK STROGANOFF

1 ½ lb. sirloin or round steak
1 clove of garlic, cut (opt.)
3 tbsp. flour
1 ¾ tsp. salt
¼ tsp. pepper
1 tsp. paprika
¼ c. shortening
½ c. finely cut onion
1 can consomme
½ c. water
1 lb. fresh or 1 lge. can mushrooms, sliced
½ c. sour cream
2 tbsp. finely cut chives or parsley

Rub both sides of meat with garlic. Cut meat into 1 1/2 x 1-inch strips. Mix flour, salt, pepper and paprika; add meat strips and toss lightly until strips are well coated. Reserve remaining mixture. Heat shortening in skillet; add meat and brown well. Add onion; cook for 5 minutes. Add remaining flour mixture, consomme, water and mushrooms. Cover and cook slowly for 1 hour and 30 minutes. Add sour cream and chives just before serving. Serve with noodles, rice or mashed potatoes, if desired. Yield: 4-5 servings.

Mrs. Elaine Christensen
Pella LCW
Omaha, Nebraska

STROGANOFF

2 lb. lean round or chuck, cut into ½-in. cubes
½ c. butter, melted
1 lb. fresh mushrooms, sliced
2 lb. onions, chopped
1 6-oz. can tomato paste
2 tsp. salt
¼ tsp. pepper
1 tbsp. Worcestershire sauce
1 tbsp. cornstarch
2 tbsp. cold water
1 c. sour cream

Brown meat in butter over low heat. Add mushrooms and onions. Cook for 5 minutes. Stir in tomato paste, salt, pepper and Worcestershire sauce. Cover; simmer for 1 hour or until meat is tender. Mix cornstarch with water until smooth. Stir into meat mixture. Cover; simmer for 10 minutes, stirring frequently. Blend in sour cream, just before serving. Yield: 4-6 servings.

Mrs. Ruth Brake, Pres.
St. Thomas Evangelical LCW
Saint Thomas, Pennsylvania

STROGANOFF

1 lb. sirloin tip, cut into ⅛-in. strips
4 tbsp. flour
½ tsp. salt
4 tbsp. butter
1 c. sliced mushrooms
½ c. chopped onion
1 clove of garlic, minced
1 can beef stock
1 c. sour cream
2 tbsp. cooking Sherry

(Continued on next page)

Dredge meat in 1 tablespoonful flour and salt. Brown in 10-inch skillet in 2 tablespoonfuls butter. Add mushrooms, onion and garlic. Cook for 4 minutes. Remove meat mixture; add 2 tablespoonfuls butter to pan drippings. Blend in 3 tablespoonfuls flour. Slowly add beef stock, stirring constantly, until thickened. Add meat mixture; cook for 1 hour and 30 minutes or until tender. Add sour cream and cooking Sherry just before serving. Heat; serve over rice or noodles. Yield: 6 servings.

> Mrs. Willard Heilmann, Pres.
> Our Saviour Women's Guild LCW
> Evansville, Indiana

STROGANOFF

2 lb. round steak, cubed
1 can onion soup
1 can cream of mushroom soup
1 can milk
1 c. bread crumbs

Place steak in casserole. Add soups and milk. Bake at 350 degrees for 2 hours. Sprinkle with bread crumbs last 30 minutes of baking. Yield: 6 servings.

> Mrs. Fred Sprecher, Pres.
> St. Paul's Ladies Aid
> Walnut Shade, Missouri

STROGANOFF

1 ½ lb. thick sirloin steak, cubed
½ tsp. salt
⅛ tsp. pepper
½ tsp. paprika
1 sm. onion, chopped
⅓ c. mushrooms
¼ c. butter, melted
1 c. bouillon
1 sm. bay leaf
1 tsp. Worcestershire sauce
Cooked white or brown rice
2 c. sour cream

Season steak with salt, pepper and paprika. Brown onions and mushrooms in butter. Add bouillon and bay leaf; simmer for 15 minutes. Add Worcestershire sauce; simmer until meat is tender. Place meat over rice on serving plate. Add sour cream to sauce in pan. Cook over low heat, stirring constantly. Pour over rice and meat. Serve at once. Yield: 6-8 servings.

> Mrs. Elmer Holk, Pres.
> First Lutheran Church LCW
> Camarillo, California

STROGANOFF

1 lb. trimmed beef tenderloin, sliced
   ¼-in. thick
¼ c. butter or margarine
½ c. chopped onion
1 can beef broth

1 c. sour cream
2 ½ tbsp. flour
½ tsp. salt
Dash of pepper

Brown meat in hot butter. Add onion; cook until tender, but not brown. Add broth; bring to a boil. Blend sour cream and flour; stir into broth until mixture thickens. Add salt and pepper to taste. Serve over rice or buttered noodles. Yield: 4-5 servings.

> Mrs. Carl Roehm, Pres.
> Trinity Ladies Aux.
> Baton Rouge, Louisiana

STROGANOFF

1 lb. sirloin steak, cut 1-in. thick
1 pkg. onion soup mix
1 c. water
1 3-oz. can mushrooms
Butter
1 c. sour cream
2 tbsp. flour

Trim fat from meat and fry out. Reserve fat. Cut meat across grain into 1/4-inch wide strips. Brown in fat; add soup mix and water. Add additional water if needed while cooking. Cook for 1 hour to 1 hour and 30 minutes or until tender. Drain mushrooms, reserving liquid. Brown mushrooms in a small amount butter; add mushrooms and liquid to meat. Blend sour cream with flour; mix well. Add to meat mixture very slowly just before serving. Serve over egg noodles or rice. Yield: 4 servings.

> Mable M. Corbat
> Holy Cross Ladies Aid
> Onaway, Michigan

TEXAS BEEF STROGANOFF

3 cans mushrooms
2 lge. onions, chopped
Butter
3 c. beef broth or bouillon
3 tbsp. Worcestershire sauce
3 ½ lb. round steak, cubed
Salt and pepper
Flour
1 pt. sour cream

Saute mushrooms and onions separately in butter. Mix; add beef broth and Worcestershire sauce. Add steak which has been cubed, seasoned, floured and browned. Simmer for 1 hour and 30 minutes or longer. Add sour cream; heat almost to boiling. Serve over hot rice. Yield: 8 servings.

> Mrs. Darrel Reynolds, Pres.
> St. Johns Ladies Aid
> Dumas, Texas

SUKIYAKI

1 lb. sirloin steak, cut into 1-in. cubes
½ c. water
Salt to taste
½ c. soya sauce
¼ c. sugar
1 bunch green onions

Brown meat in deep fat for 2 to 3 minutes. Add water, salt, soya sauce and sugar. Add onions. Cook for a few minutes or until done. Serve on rice. Yield: 6 servings.

Mrs. Einar Lasko, Pres.
St. Paul's Ladies Aid
Iron River, Michigan

SWISS STEAK

1 2-lb. round steak
1 ½ c. flour
1 ½ tsp. salt
⅛ tsp. pepper
1 sm. onion, chopped
2 tbsp. shortening
¼ c. chopped green pepper
1 c. stewed or canned tomatoes
1 c. boiling water

Wipe meat with clean damp cloth; cut into 2-inch squares. Mix flour with salt and pepper. Pound into meat. Brown onion and meat in shortening; add green pepper, tomatoes and water. Cover; cook slowly for 2 hours or until meat is tender. Yield: 6 servings.

Mrs. Dorothea Jasper, Pres.
Christ Lutheran Church LCW
Beaver Falls, Pennsylvania

TERIYAKI STICKS

1 ½ c. soy sauce
½ c. cooking oil
1 c. vinegar
1 c. water
1 c. brown sugar
1 tsp. salt
5 cloves of garlic, chopped
1 lge. onion, chopped
⅓ c. chopped fresh ginger root
3 lb. boneless beef roast or round steak

Mix liquids, brown sugar and salt with remaining ingredients except meat in deep bowl. Slice meat into 1-inch strips that are 1/8-inch thick. Skewer meat strips accordian-style on bamboo sticks, using 4-inches of meat per stick. Marinate in sauce for 4 hours or overnight. Broil over white coals for 15 minutes, turning often. Yield: 10 servings.

Carolyn Fenning, Sec.
St. John's LCW
Stacy, Minnesota

BEEF CASSEROLE

2 c. macaroni
2 c. chopped beef
1 c. cream of mushroom soup
½ c. milk
½ tsp. salt
Few grains of pepper
2 c. grated cheese

Cook macaroni in boiling salted water; drain. Pour into buttered casserole. Add meat. Heat soup and milk. Add seasonings. Pour over meat; top with c h e e s e. Bake at 350 d e g r e e s for 30 minutes.

Mrs. Doris Freeman, Rep.
Ascension Guild LWML
Littleton, Colorado

BEEF AND EGGPLANT CASSEROLE

2 med. onions, chopped
¼ c. butter or margarine
1 lb. chuck, chopped
1 8-oz. can tomato sauce
1 c. hot water
2 tbsp. salt
⅛ tsp. pepper
1 tsp. sugar
2 sm. eggplants, peeled and sliced
4 tbsp. salad oil

Fry onions slowly in butter until golden brown. Add beef, tomato sauce, water, salt, pepper and sugar. Simmer for 15 minutes. Fry eggplants quickly in oil. Place eggplants and meat mixture in layers in 1-quart casserole, ending with meat. Bake at 325 degrees for 1 hour. Yield: 4 servings.

Mrs. Martha McGee
St. John's Lutheran Church
Iota, Louisiana

BEEF PIE

3 to 4 c. diced potatoes
1 pkg. frozen peas
2 cubed left-over roast beef
1 c. gravy
Seasonings to taste
2 c. flour
2 ½ tsp. baking powder
1 tsp. salt
¼ c. shortening
1 c. milk

Cook potatoes in a small amount water; when almost done, add peas. Cook for a few minutes longer. Add meat and gravy. Heat until mixture begins to boil. Place in a 2 or 3-quart baking pan or skillet. Season to taste. Sift flour with baking powder and salt; finely cut in shortening. Stir in milk. Drop from spoon over meat and vegetables. Bake at 425 degrees for 25 minutes. Yield: 6 servings.

Mrs. Richard Totton, Pres.
St. John's LWML
Norris, South Dakota

BEEF-NOODLE CASSEROLE

2 c. cubed left-over roast beef
½ to 1 c. chopped onions
2 tbsp. butter
1 can cream of mushroom soup
1 tsp. salt
⅛ tsp. pepper
¼ tsp. marjoram
2 c. cooked noodles
1 c. corn flakes

Place all ingredients in casserole. Bake at 350 degrees for 20 to 25 minutes. Yield: 6 servings.

Mrs. Gilbert Wilkens
St. Peter's English Lutheran Church
Newell, Iowa

BIRD IN THE NEST

1 sm. onion, chopped
Butter
1 lb. chopped lean beef
Salt and pepper to taste
1 8-oz. pkg. macaroni, cooked
1 can tomatoes or tomato soup
Bread crumbs

Saute onion in butter; add beef, salt and pepper. Brown lightly. Arrange macaroni in large buttered casserole, leaving a hole in center. Place meat in center of macaroni; pour tomatoes over top. Sprinkle with bread crumbs; dot with butter. Bake at 375 degrees for 30 minutes. Yield: 6-8 servings.

Mrs. John Kaiser, Cor. Sec.
Christ Lutheran Church LCW
New Hyde Park, New York

LONG ISLAND SWEET-SOUR BEEF

1 to 2 c. cubed left-over roast beef
2 lge. onions, sliced lengthwise
1 clove of garlic
Oil
1 tbsp. cornstarch
1 c. water
1 tbsp. vinegar
2 tbsp. soy sauce
2 tbsp. brown sugar
1 or 2 green peppers, cut into 1-in. cubes
1 tsp. monosodium glutamate

Heat heavy covered skillet until hot; remove from heat. Place meat, onions, garlic and oil in skillet; steam for 30 minutes. Mix cornstarch and water; add to meat. Add remaining ingredients; return to heat. Cook slowly for 20 minutes or until peppers are cooked. Serve with rice or noodles. Yield: 2-4 servings.

Lorraine Keller, Stewardship Sec.
Oceanside Evening Circle
Baldwin, New York

PASTIE

1 recipe pastry for two-crust pie
¾ c. sliced potatoes
5 oz. finely cut beef
1 med. onion, finely chopped
1 tbsp. finely cut rutabaga (opt.)
¼ tsp. salt
Dash of pepper
Suet (opt.)

Roll pie crust to size and shape of a dinner plate; place potatoes on upper half of pastry. Add pieces of meat to cover potatoes. Place onion over meat and potatoes. Lay rutabaga on potatoes. Season with salt and pepper; add suet, if desired. Moisten all edges of pastry circle with fingers dipped in cold water. Turn lower half up over pastry mixture to meet moistened edge of top of circle. Shape into an oblong. Crimp edges carefully. Raise the joined edges up; fold edges over the side of pastry until all the edge is curled over the wall of the pastry. Be sure crust is sealed tightly to prevent juice from escaping. Place in baking pan. Bake at 400 degrees for 15 minutes. Reduce heat to 350 degrees and bake for 45 minutes longer.

Mrs. Peggy Johnson, Pres.
Zion Guild
Chatham, Michigan

PRESSED BEEF

4 lb. beef shank
6 whole cloves
1 med. onion, sliced
1 stick cinnamon
2 tsp. salt
¼ tsp. pepper
1 tbsp. sage

Cover shanks with water; add cloves, onion, cinnamon, salt and pepper. Cook for 3 to 4 hours or until meat is tender. Remove meat from bones; chop finely. Pack into 5 x 9-inch loaf pan. Strain liquid; add sage. Cook down to 1 cup. Pour over meat. Chill until firm. Serve in thin slices. Yield: 10-12 servings.

Mrs. Owen Myhre, Pres.
Waterloo Ridge LCW
Dorchester, Iowa

SOUP KETTLE SUPPER

8 strips bacon
1 c. diced cooked beef or ham
1 can whole tomatoes, diced
1 can mixed vegetables
1 ⅓ c. instant rice

Fry bacon until crisp in large pan or kettle. Leave 2 tablespoonfuls drippings in pan; add crumbled bacon, beef, tomatoes, vegetables and rice. Bring to a boil; simmer for a few minutes. Yield: 4 servings.

Mrs. Robert Fuller, Pres.
Our Saviour LWML
Butler, Alabama

VEAL CHOPS, CALIFORNIA-STYLE

4 veal chops, 1-in. thick
Salt and pepper
¼ c. flour
¼ c. bacon drippings
3 tbsp. butter
¼ c. chopped onion
¼ c. chopped celery
¼ c. chopped parsley
3 c. bread crumbs
⅛ tsp. dried marjoram or thyme
¾ c. coarsely chopped walnuts
1 bouillon cube
¾ c. hot water
¼ c. cream

Sprinkle chops with salt and pepper. Roll in flour; brown on both sides in bacon drippings in skillet. Arrange chops in single layer in casserole. Place butter, onion, celery and parsley in skillet. Simmer for 5 minutes. Add crumbs, marjoram and walnuts, stirring until well mixed. Heap on chops. Dissolve bouillon cube in hot water; pour around chops, not moistening crumbs. Cover; bake at 350 degrees for 45 minutes or until chops are tender. Pour cream around chops. Cover; bake for 10 minutes longer. Yield: 4 servings.

Mrs. Joseph A. Raymond, Pres.
St. Peter's Mary and Martha Altar Guild
Uniontown, Pennsylvania

OSSOBUCO MILANESE STYLE

3 tbsp. cooking oil
1 clove of garlic, chopped
4 veal shanks, 4-In. long with meat
3 tbsp. flour
½ tsp. Accent
½ c. dry white wine
1 c. water
¼ tsp. Tabasco sauce
6 strips lemon peel
3 anchovy fillets, chopped
¼ c. chopped parsley
1 12-oz. box bow-shaped pasta, cooked

Heat oil in skillet. Add garlic and saute. Roll veal shanks in flour and Accent. Add veal to skillet and saute until browned, turning occasionally. Pour wine and water over all; stir in Tabasco sauce. Cover skillet and continue cooking for about 1 hour. Add more water, if necessary. During last 5 minutes of cooking, add lemon peel and anchovy. Remove veal to serving plate; sprinkle with parsley. Surround with pasta; pour gravy over all. NOTE: One-half cup veal or chicken broth may substituted for wine. Yield: 4 servings. ings.

Photograph for this recipe on inside back cover.

BREADED VEAL CUTLET

1 2-lb. veal steak, 1-in. thick
½ c. buttermilk
½ c. fine dry bread crumbs
2 tbsp. fat or salad oil
1 c. tomato juice

Dip meat into buttermilk; coat with crumbs. Chill for several hours. Brown meat on both sides in fat. Add tomato juice. Cover; simmer for 1 hour or until tender. Add additional tomato juice, if needed. Yield: 6 servings.

Mrs. Mary Ellen Maunula, Pres.
Our Saviour LWML
Dryden, Ontario, Canada

BREADED VEAL CUTLETS

2 tsp. prepared mustard
1 tsp. salt
Dash of pepper
1 tbsp. butter
6 veal cutlets, ½-in. thick
1 c. fine bread crumbs
2 eggs, slightly beaten
Fat

Mix mustard, salt, pepper and butter; rub into cutlets. Dip into bread crumbs; dip into eggs and again into crumbs. Fry for 15 minutes on each side in fat. Yield: 6 servings.

Mrs. Margaret McCallum, Pres.
St. Matthew LWML
Chicago, Illinois

SUNDAY BEST VEAL

1 egg
1 ½ lb. veal cutlet, ½-in. thick
Fine bread crumbs
1 onion, sliced
Fat
1 ½ tsp. paprika
1 ½ tsp. salt
⅛ tsp. pepper
1 c. water
1 c. sour cream
½ c. blanched almonds, sliced
2 tbsp. butter
1 6-oz. pkg. noodles, cooked

Beat egg slightly with 1 tablespoonful water. Cut veal into serving pieces; dip into crumbs. Dip into egg; roll in crumbs again. Cook onion in hot fat until yellow; remove from pan. Brown veal quickly on each side. Reduce heat; add paprika, salt, pepper and onion to meat. Pour water over all. Cover and simmer until veal is tender and water almost evaporated. Add sour cream to pan, mixing with meat liquid for gravy; spoon gravy over meat while heating. Brown almonds lightly in melted butter in separate skillet; fold in noodles. Heat thoroughly. Arrange veal on platter; surround with noodles. Yield: 6 servings.

Mathilde Thomsen
St. Ansgar's Lutheran Church Ladies Aid
Parlier, California

VEAL BIRDS

1 ⅓ c. crumbled corn bread and bread crumbs
½ sm. onion, diced
Chicken broth or water

61

(Continued on next page)

4 thinly sliced cubed veal cutlets
Salt and pepper to taste
½ c. flour
2 tbsp. melted shortening
½ c. white wine
1 6-oz. can mushroom gravy

Mix bread crumbs with onion; add enough broth to moisten. Sprinkle veal cutlets with salt and pepper. Place 1/3 cup corn bread dressing in center of each cutlet; roll each like a jelly roll, securing each with a toothpick. Roll each veal bird in flour; brown on all sides in shortening. Remove birds from skillet; place in shallow baking dish. Pour wine over birds. Bake, uncovered, at 350 degrees for 45 minutes or until tender. Turn occasionally to allow wine to saturate meat. When ready to serve, pour mushroom gravy over veal birds and return to oven for ten minutes longer. Yield: 4 servings.

Dorothy Malcom, Pres.
Peach LWML
Decatur, Georgia

VEAL CUTLET PARMESAN

6 to 8 veal cutlets
Salt to taste
1 egg, beaten
Bread crumbs
⅓ c. Parmesan cheese
Fat
1 ½ c. canned tomato sauce
½ tsp. oregano
Dash of garlic salt
6 to 8 slices Mozzarella cheese

Sprinkle cutlets lightly with salt. Dip into egg, then into bread crumbs mixed with Parmesan cheese. Brown in hot fat; place in buttered baking dish. Heat tomato sauce with oregano and garlic salt. Pour over cutlets. Cover and bake at 350 degrees for 30 to 35 minutes. Uncover and place 1 slice of Mozzarella cheese on each cutlet. Return to oven and bake for 5 to 8 minutes or until cheese melts. Yield: 6-8 servings.

Mary Louise Morgan
Resurrection LCW
Cocoa Beach, Florida

VEAL PARMESAN

1 lb. thin veal cutlets
1 egg, beaten
½ c. bread crumbs
2 tbsp. shortening
1 can tomato sauce
¼ c. water
¼ c. chopped onion
1 clove of garlic, minced
Dash of thyme
4 oz. Mozzarella cheese, thinly sliced
¼ to ½ c. Parmesan cheese

Dip cutlets into egg, then into bread crumbs. Brown in shortening. Add tomato sauce and

water; add onion, garlic and thyme. Cook over low heat for 30 to 45 minutes or until tender, stirring occasionally. Top with Mozzarella slices; sprinkle with Parmesan. Broil until cheese melts. Yield: 4 servings.

Mrs. David T. Hinkley, Pres.
St. Paul's LCW
Roanoke, Virginia
Mrs. T. Marshall Freed, Pres.
Bethany-Trinity Ladies Aid Soc.
Waynesboro, Virginia

VEAL PARMESAN

4 pieces veal cutlet
½ c. seasoned flour
2 eggs, beaten and seasoned
Oil or shortening
1 can Italian tomato sauce
4 slices Mozzarella cheese

Dredge veal in flour that has been seasoned with salt and pepper; dip into egg. Dip veal into flour again. Brown in oil in hot skillet. Place in flat pan. Pour tomato sauce over the meat. Place a piece of cheese on each piece of meat. Bake, uncovered, at 350 degrees for 45 minutes. Yield: 4 servings.

Mrs. Arthur M. Hast, Pres.
Our Savior's LCW
Sherman Oaks, California

VEAL ROLLS

¼ c. melted butter
2 tbsp. grated onion
2 to 3 c. soft bread crumbs
¼ tsp. salt
⅛ tsp. pepper
½ tsp. poultry seasoning
1 tsp. minced celery leaves
1 tbsp. chopped parsley
1 ½ to 2 lb. veal cutlets, ¼-in. thick
Flour
3 tbsp. fat
1 ¼ c. hot water

Combine butter, onion, crumbs, salt, pepper, poultry seasoning, celery and parsley; mix well. Cut veal into serving pieces; pound until thin. Arrange stuffing in center of each piece, spreading lengthwise. Roll up; tie with string. Roll in flour. Preheat electic fry pan; add fat. Brown rolls well on all sides. Add water. Simmer, covered, at 200 degrees until tender. Remove meat; cut string. Prepare gravy, if desired. Pour over rolls. Garnish with parsley or tomato wedges.

Mrs. Clifford Hansen, Pres.
Trondhjem Ladies Aid
Irene, South Dakota
Mrs. Anne Bartoli, Pres.
Christ Lutheran Chruch LCW
Sudbury, Ontario, Canada

MARINATED ROAST VEAL

1 tsp. dry parsley flakes
1 tsp. dried thyme
1 tsp. salt
4 tsp. chopped scallions
1 3-oz. can sliced mushrooms, drained
3 tbsp. salad oil
1 bay leaf, crushed
¼ tsp. pepper
Pinch of nutmeg
1 tbsp. Kitchen Bouquet
1 2½-lb. loin veal roast
1 tbsp. butter
1 tbsp. flour
1 tbsp. vinegar

Combine parsley flakes, thyme and salt; add scallions, mushrooms, salad oil and seasonings. Add veal and cover. Refrigerate for 24 hours, turning occasionally. Wrap veal and herb mixture in heavy foil. Bake at 350 degrees for 2 hours and 15 minutes or until tender. Unwrap. Scrape off herbs, reserving juices. Melt butter in saucepan. Stir in flour, vinegar and herbs with juices. Bring to a boil, stirring constantly. Slice meat thinly. Serve sauce with meat. Yield: 6-8 servings.

Mrs. Douglas W. MacLeod, Pres.
Immanuel LCW
Oxford, Connecuit

SAVORY VEAL POT ROAST

3 lb. boneless rolled veal roast
2 tbsp. melted shortening
1 envelope onion soup mix
1 8-oz. can tomato sauce
1½ c. water
4 carrots, cut ½-in. thick
2 stalks celery, chopped
1 8-oz. pkg. medium egg noodles, cooked

Brown roast well on all sides in shortening. Combine soup mix, tomato sauce and water; add to roast. Cover and simmer for 1 hour, turning occasionally. Add carrots and celery. Cover and simmer for 30 minutes or until tender; add water if needed. Serve over noodles. Yield: 6-8 servings.

Mrs. C. W. Oletzke, Pres.
St. Peter's Mission Circle
St. Paul, Minnesota

SPICY VEAL POT ROAST

1 tbsp. dry mustard
1 tsp. poultry seasoning
1 tbsp. brown sugar
1 tbsp. salt
1 tsp. pepper
1 5-lb. rump roast of veal with bone
3 tbsp. lard
½ c. chopped onion
2 tbsp. vinegar

Mix all seasonings; rub into roast. Brown roast very slowly in lard. Add onion and vinegar. Cover

tightly. Simmer over low heat for 2 hours and 30 minutes. Makes its own gravy.

Mrs. Virgie Seebo, Chmn.
St. Paul's Evangelical Martha Guild
Glen Burnie, Maryland

SCALLOPINI

1 1½-lb. veal steak, ½-in. thick
1 tsp. salt
1 tsp. paprika
½ c. salad oil
¼ c. lemon juice
1 clove of garlic, split
1 tsp. prepared mustard
¼ tsp. nutmeg
½ tsp. sugar
¼ c. flour
¼ c. fat
1 med. onion, thinly sliced
1 green pepper, cut into strips
1 can chicken bouillon
¼ lb. mushrooms, sliced
1 tbsp. butter or margarine
6 pimento stuffed olives, sliced

Cut veal into serving pieces. Combine salt, paprika, oil, lemon juice, garlic, mustard, nutmeg and sugar. Beat well or shake in a bottle to combine thoroughly. Place veal flat in a baking pan; pour sauce over veal. Turn to coat with sauce. Let stand for 15 minutes. Remove garlic. Remove veal from sauce. Dip into flour. Brown in hot fat in a skillet; add onion and green pepper. Combine chicken bouillon with remaining sauce; pour over veal. Cover; cook slowly for 40 minutes or until tender. Brown mushrooms lightly in butter; add mushrooms and olives to veal. Stir and dip sauce over veal. Cook for 5 minutes longer. Yield: 6 servings.

Mrs. Fred Robertson
Trinity LCW
Fort Bragg, California

SCALLOPINI

1½ lb. veal, thinly sliced
1¼ tsp. salt
1 tbsp. paprika
¼ c. salad oil
2 tbsp. lemon juice
1 clove of garlic, chopped
1 tsp. prepared mustard
¼ tsp. nutmeg
½ tsp. sugar
½ c. flour
⅓ c. shortening
1 c. onions
1 4-oz. can mushrooms
1 or 2 cans chicken broth

Cut veal into small serving pieces. Combine salt, paprika, salad oil, lemon juice, garlic, mustard, nutmeg and sugar. Coat veal with mixture; let set for 15 minutes. Remove garlic; roll veal in flour. Brown in shortening. Add onion,

(Continued on next page)

mushrooms, broth and r e m a i n i n g marinade. Cook slowly for 50 minutes. Yield: 3 servings.

Mrs. Esther Strieter, Pres.
Trinity LWML
Lisle, Illinois

VEAL SCALLOPINI

2 lb. veal cutlets, thinly sliced
2 tbsp. flour
1 ¼ tsp. salt
1 ¼ tsp. pepper
1 clove of garlic, chopped
¼ c. butter
2 tbsp. salad oil
½ lb. mushrooms, thinly sliced
½ c. water
1 c. Marsala or Sherry wine

Pound cutlets until very thin; sprinkle lightly with a mixture of flour, 1/4 teaspoonful salt and pepper. Brown garlic in 3 tablespoonfuls butter and salad oil. Remove garlic; add cutlets to the hot fat. Cook quickly until browned on all sides. Place cutlets in a shallow baking dish. Melt remaining butter in skillet; add mushrooms and saute until golden. Add water, remaining salt and wine. Bring to a boil; simmer for 2 minutes. Pour mushroom sauce over veal. Cover; bake at 350 degrees for 30 minutes or until veal is tender; basting twice during baking. Yield: 8 servings.

Mrs. B. L. Wellman
Concordia Miss'y League
Worcester, Massachusetts

VEAL SCALLOPINI

8 veal cutlets, cut into 4 x 3-in. cubes
5 tbsp. fine bread crumbs
5 tbsp. grated Parmesan cheese
Dash of salt
1 lge. egg, slightly beaten
3 tbsp. olive oil
1 8-oz. can tomato sauce

Pound veal, paper thin. Mix b r e a d crumbs, cheese and salt. Dip veal into egg and then into crumbs. Cook in hot oil until well browned on both sides. Place in baking pan; pour tomato sauce over meat. Cover; bake at 350 degrees for 1 hour. Yield: 8 servings.

Mrs. Robert Haner, Pres.
Emmanuel LCW
Warren, Ohio

BRAISED VEAL STEAK WITH MUSHROOMS

2 lb. veal steak, cut 1-in. thick
1 egg, slightly beaten
2 tbsp. milk
2 c. crushed cereal flakes
4 tbsp. fat
1 sm. can mushrooms

Cut veal into serving pieces. Combine egg and milk. Dip steak into egg mixture. Roll steak in cereal flakes. Brown in fat. Cover with mushrooms and m u s h r o o m liquid. Cover tightly. Simmer for 45 minutes or until tender. Thicken liquid for gravy. Serve with veal steak. Bake at 300 degrees for 45 minutes. Yield: 4 servings.

Mrs. Alice N. F. McDonald
Trinity Ladies Aid
Greeley, Colorado

PEPPERY SCHNITZEL

1 ½ lb. thin veal steak
½ c. chopped onion
1 clove of garlic, minced
Vegetable shortening
¼ c. flour
1 ½ tsp. salt
¼ tsp. pepper
1 c. sour cream
⅓ c. beef consomme
1 tbsp. paprika
3 drops of hot pepper sauce
1 2 ½-oz. jar sliced mushrooms, drained
⅓ c. chopped green pepper
1 8 ½-oz. can sweet peas, drained
1 8-oz. can sliced carrots, drained

Pound veal to 1/8-inch thickness. Saute onion and garlic in shortening until tender; remove from pan. Mix flour with salt and pepper. Dip meat into seasoned flour; brown on both sides in shortening. Add onion and garlic. Cover; cook slowly for 25 minutes or until meat is tender. Combine sour cream, consomme, paprika and pepper sauce; pour over meat, stirring to coat. Add mushrooms and v e g e t a b l e s. Cover; simmer until heated through. Serve with parsley and buttered noodles. Yield: 6 servings.

Ruth E. Lundberg, Pres.
St. Mathew's LCW
Burbank, California

ROLL-UPS

3 c. cubed bread
3 tbsp. butter, melted
2 ½ tbsp. chopped onion
Salt and pepper
2 tsp. water
2 ½ lb. veal round steak or arm steak
Fat

Mix bread with melted butter; add onion, 3/4 teaspoonful salt, pepper to taste and water. Mix well. Pound or tenderize steak; lay flat. Rub salt and pepper into meat. Pat stuffing onto meat; roll up and fasten with toothpicks or small metal skewers. Brown in hot fat; add 1/3 cup hot water. Cover tightly. Cook slowly for 1 hour. Yield: 5 servings.

Mrs. Bill Wagnusson
Zion LWML
Munich, North Dakota

VEAL BIRDS

1 tbsp. butter
1 c. milk
6 slices dry bread, toasted and cubed
½ c. chopped celery
1 tbsp. minced parsley
1 onion, minced
½ tsp. poultry seasoning
Salt and pepper
1 egg
3 veal steaks, thinly sliced
Bacon drippings
1 can cream of mushroom soup
1 soup can milk
1 soup can water

Heat butter in milk; place in bowl. Add bread cubes, celery, parsley, onion, poultry seasonings, 1 teaspoonful salt, 1/8 teaspoonful pepper and egg. Mix well. Cut steaks into 2 x 4-inch pieces; sprinkle with salt and pepper. Place 1 rounded tablespoonful dressing mixture on each piece of veal. Roll meat and fasten with a toothpick. Brown in drippings; place in baking dish. Sprinkle with salt and pepper. Mix mushroom soup with milk and water; pour over veal. Bake, covered, at 350 degrees for 1 hour.

Mrs. Hulda Pansa, Pres.
St. Paul's LWML
Beecher, Illinois

VEAL BIRDS

½ c. chopped celery
½ clove of garlic, finely minced
½ c. chopped onion
¾ c. butter
1 c. raisins
3 c. dry bread cubes
4 slices crisp cooked bacon, crumbled
¼ tsp. rosemary
1 tbsp. salt
¾ tsp. pepper
2 tbsp. chopped parsley
2 bouillon cubes
2 ½ c. hot water
3 lb. boneless veal steaks or cutlets, thinly sliced
½ c. flour

Saute celery, garlic and onion in 1/4 cup butter; add raisins, bread cubes, bacon, rosemary, 1/2 teaspoonful salt, 1/2 teaspoonful pepper and parsley. Mix well. Dissolve bouillon cubes in hot water; add 1 cup bouillon to bread mixture. Cut veal into serving pieces. Place 1 rounded tablespoonful stuffing on each veal slice. Roll slices; fasten securely with toothpicks. Mix flour with remaining salt and pepper; dredge veal birds in mixture. Brown on all sides in remaining butter. Add remaining bouillon. Cover tightly; simmer gently for 1 hour or until meat is tender, adding water if necessary. Yield: 8 servings.

Mrs. Carl Hankey, Pres.
St. Lukes LWML
Rensselaer, Indiana

VEAL BIRDS

1 lb. veal steak
Flour
Salt and pepper
1 med. onion, finely chopped
1 clove of garlic, finely chopped
4 tbsp. shortening
6 sprigs parsley, chopped
3 c. rye bread crumbs
1 egg, slightly beaten
1 10 ½-oz. can consomme
½ tsp. monosodium glutamate
½ tsp. caraway seed

Pound meat thin and flat as for scallopini. Cut into eight 4 x 6-inch uniform pieces. Coat meat with flour; sprinkle with salt and pepper. Brown onion and garlic slightly in 2 tablespoonfuls shortening in skillet. Scoop vegetables from fat; mix with parsley, bread crumbs, egg, 1/2 cup consomme and remaining ingredients. Mix well. Place a heaping tablespoonful stuffing on each piece of meat; bring sides of meat together over stuffing and fasten with a toothpick. Heat remaining shortening in same skillet; brown meat on all sides. Pour remaining consomme over meat; cover and cook over a low heat for 30 minutes. Yield: 4 servings.

Mrs. Alice Koepke, Parish Sec.
Faith Ladies Aid
Milwaukee, Wisconsin

VEAL BIRDS

1 ½ lb. veal steak
4 c. dry bread cubes
3 tbsp. chopped onion
1 tsp. salt
¼ tsp. pepper
Sage to taste
¼ tsp. poultry seasoning
⅛ c. melted butter
Bacon slices (opt.)
Hot water or stock

Cut veal into 3 x 5-inch pieces. Mix bread cubes with onion, seasonings and butter; spread mixture on veal pieces. Roll up and fasten with toothpicks. Wrap each roll with a bacon slice, if desired. Brown rolls in hot fat; add a small amount hot water or stock. Cover tightly. Bake at 350 degrees for 1 hour and 30 minutes. Yield: 6 servings.

Mrs. Paul Bohlken, Pres.
Good Shepherd LCW
Wichita, Kansas

VEAL PARMIGIANO

3 cloves of garlic, finely minced
1 onion, minced
6 tbsp. olive oil or salad oil
1 No. 2 can tomatoes
1 ¼ tsp. salt
¼ tsp. pepper
1 8-oz. can tomato sauce
¼ tsp. dried thyme
¼ c. packaged dried bread crumbs
½ to ⅔ c. grated Parmesan cheese

(Continued on next page)

1 lb. thin veal steak, cut into 8 pieces
1 egg, well beaten
½ lb. Mozzarella or Munster cheese, thinly
    sliced

Saute garlic and onion in 3 tablespoonfuls hot oil until golden. Add tomatoes, salt and pepper; break up tomatoes with spoon. Simmer, uncovered, for 10 minutes. Add tomato sauce and thyme; simmer, uncovered, for 20 minutes. Combine crumbs with 1/4 cup Parmesan cheese. Dip each veal piece into egg, then into crumbs. Saute in remaining hot oil until golden brown on both sides, turning once. Set slices side by side into 12 x 8-inch baking dish. Pour two-thirds of tomato mixture over veal, straining it if desired. Arrange Mozzarella on top; spoon remaining tomato mixture. Sprinkle with remaining Parmesan cheese. Bake, uncovered, at 350 degrees for 40 minutes. Yield: 4 servings.

Mrs. Lou Lundstrom, Pres.
Augustana Evangelical LCW
East Elmhurst, New York

VEAL WITH SOUR CREAM GRAVY

1 ½ to 2 lb. veal steak, cut into pieces
2 tbsp. fat
2 tbsp. Worcestershire sauce
¼ tsp. salt
1 clove of garlic, minced
1 c. sour cream
2 tsp. flour
1 ½ tsp. paprika
1 tbsp. cooking Sherry

Brown meat in hot fat; add Worcestershire sauce, salt and garlic. Cook gently until tender. Combine sour cream, flour and paprika; stir into drippings. Cook and stir just until thick; add Sherry. Serve over boiled rice. Yield: 6-8 servings.

Mrs. Ray Juedes
St. Lukes LWML
Mesa, Arizona

AFRICAN CHOW MEIN

1 to 1 ½ lb. veal, chopped
1 or 2 med. onions, chopped
Seasonings to taste
1 c. uncooked rice
2 c. chopped celery
1 can mushrooms, drained
2 cans cream of mushroom soup
2 cans cream of chicken soup
2 c. water
¼ lb. cashews or a few almonds
Chow mein noodles (opt.)

Brown veal and onions; season to taste. Mix all ingredients except noodles. Pour into large greased baking dish. Bake at 350 degrees for 1 hour and 30 minutes to 2 hours, adding more water, if needed. Sprinkle chow mein noodles over top just before serving. NOTE: If desired, 2 cans chicken-rice soup may be substituted for either the cream of chicken or cream of mushroom soup. Yield: 15 servings.

Mrs. Fred Schaub, Pres.
Round Prairie ALCW
Glenville, Minnesota
Mrs. Paul Nuss, Pres.
Bethel Lutheran Church
Gary, Indiana

CALIFORNIA CASSEROLE

2 lb. veal round steak, cut into 2-in. pieces
⅓ c. flour
1 tsp. paprika
¼ c. shortening
½ tsp. salt
⅛ tsp. pepper
2 ¾ c. water
1 can cream of chicken soup
1 ¾ c. small cooked onions

Coat steak with flour and paprika; brown in shortening. Add salt, pepper and 1 cup water; cover and simmer for 30 minutes or until tender. Place meat in 3-quart casserole. Heat soup in skillet used for browning meat. Gradually blend in 1 3/4 cups water; bring to a boil, stirring constantly. Combine with meat and gravy; add onions.

BUTTER CRUMB DUMPLINGS:

2 c. flour
4 tsp. baking powder
½ tsp. salt
1 tsp. poultry seasoning
1 tsp. celery seed
1 tsp. onion flakes
1 tsp. poppy seed (opt.)
¼ c. salad oil
1 c. milk
¼ c. melted butter
1 c. bread crumbs
1 can cream of chicken soup
1 c. sour cream

Sift flour with baking powder, salt and poultry seasoning. Add celery seed, onion flakes and poppy seed. Add oil and milk, stirring until moistened. Drop rounded tablespoonfuls dough into mixture of butter and crumbs. Coat well with crumbs. Top meat with dumplings. Bake, uncovered, at 425 degrees for 20 to 25 minutes or until deep golden brown. Heat soup and sour cream to boiling. Serve with casserole. Yield: 8 servings.

Mrs. Gertrude Hoffman
Salem Lutheran Church
Whittier, California

CUBED VEAL IN SOUR CREAM

1 ½ lb. boneless veal, cubed
1 ½ tbsp. butter
1 tbsp. chopped onion
½ lb. mushrooms, sliced
1 tbsp. flour

(Continued on next page)

3 tbsp. water or meat stock
¾ c. sour cream
⅛ tsp. pepper
½ tsp. salt

Brown veal in butter; remove the meat to an oven-proof baking dish. Saute onion and mushroom in remaining butter; remove from heat. Stir in flour, water or stock, sour cream, pepper and salt. Pour over veal. Bake at 350 degrees for 1 hour. Yield: 3 servings.

Margaret I. Fiedler
Holy Ghost Ladies Aid Soc.
Monroe, Michigan

SWISS VEAL SAUTE

2 lb. top round leg of veal, ¼-in. thick
1 med. onion, diced
4 oz. butter
½ lb. fresh mushrooms
½ pt. white wine
1 qt. brown gravy
1 tsp. salt
Dash of pepper
Egg noodles
Nutmeg

Cut veal into 1-inch cubes. Saute with onion and butter in skillet until light golden brown. Add mushrooms and wine. Simmer for 3 to 4 minutes. Add gravy and simmer for 5 minutes longer. Season. Serve with hot buttered egg noodles sprinkled lightly with nutmeg. Yield: 6 servings.

Mrs. Audrey Jagels
Lutheran Church of The Reformation
Women's Guild
Affton, Missouri

VEAL AMANDINE

3 lb. stewing veal, cut into 1-in. cubes
Flour
1 tsp. salt
⅛ tsp. pepper
2 tbsp. butter
1 c. chopped onions
1 can cream of mushroom soup
1¼ c. milk
⅛ tsp. instant minced garlic
Pinch of thyme
Pinch of marjoram
1 c. slivered almonds

Dredge veal in flour seasoned with salt and pepper. Saute in butter until golden brown on all sides. Add onions; cook until golden and tender. Place meat and onions into 2 1/2-quart casserole. Heat soup and milk in skillet until blended. Add garlic, thyme and marjoram; additional salt and pepper may be added to taste. Stir in almonds; pour over meat. Bake at 350 degrees for 45 minutes. Yield: 6 servings.

Janet Price, Pres.
Pilgrim Women's Guild
Lakewood, Ohio

VEAL A LA STROGANOFF

1½ lb. boneless veal, cut into 1-in. pieces
3 tbsp. flour
1½ tsp. salt
¾ tsp. paprika
1 clove of garlic, minced
3 tbsp. margarine
2 tbsp. tomato paste
½ tsp. Worcestershire sauce
¼ tsp. dry mustard
1 7-oz. bottle lemon or lime carbonated beverage
1 c. thick sour cream
4 to 6-oz. noodles, cooked

Coat veal with mixture of flour, salt and paprika. Saute garlic in margarine for 2 minutes, stirring. Stir a mixture of tomato paste, Worcestershire sauce and dry mustard into skillet. Blend in lemon beverage. Cover and cook over low heat for 1 hour or until veal is tender, stirring occasionally. Remove skillet from heat; stir in sour cream in very small amounts. Return to heat; cook, stirring constantly, for 1 to 2 minutes to heat thoroughly. Do not boil. Serve over cooked noodles. Yield: 6 servings.

Mrs. Gladys Sehaldach, Cor. Sec.
Trinity Women's League
Fort Pierce, Florida

VEAL BIRD SHISH KABOBS

1 c. bread crumbs
2 tbsp. Parmesan cheese
1 tsp. chopped parsley
½ tsp. salt
¼ tsp. pepper
4 tbsp. spaghetti sauce
1 lb. veal steak, cut into 2-in. squares
Bay leaves
Juice of 1 lemon
3 tbsp. salad oil
1 tsp. oregano
Pinch of salt and pepper

Mix bread crumbs, cheese, parsley, salt, pepper and spaghetti sauce. Place 1 teaspoonful of crumb mixture on each veal square; roll to make veal bird. Alternate birds and bay leaves on skewer. Combine remaining ingredients. Broil veal birds, turning and basting frequently with sauce for 20 to 30 minutes. Yield: 6-8 servings.

Mrs. Robert Locker, Pres.
Good Hope LCW
Zoarville, Ohio

VEAL CHOP SUEY

1 lb. veal rump or shoulder
¼ c. flour
2 tbsp. fat
1½ c. plus 2 tbsp. hot water
1 c. diced celery
½ c. chopped green pepper
½ c. chopped onion
1 tsp. salt
Dash of pepper
1½ tsp. soy sauce
1 bouillon cube

(Continued on next page)

Cut veal into 1/2-inch cubes; dredge in flour. Brown in hot fat. Add 2 tablespoonfuls water; simmer until meat is tender, adding additional hot water if necessary. Add celery, green pepper, onion, salt, pepper and soy sauce. Dissolve bouillon cube in remaining water; add to veal. Cook slowly until vegetables are tender. NOTE: Liquid may be thickened by blending 1 tablespoonful flour with 1 1/2 tablespoonfuls water and adding to liquid. Simmer until thickened. Yield: 6 servings.

Mrs. Ruth Hartenberger
Grace Ladies Guild
Victoria, Texas

VEAL DELIGHT

1 lb. sliced veal
2 tbsp. butter
1 med. onion, thinly sliced
2 tbsp. chopped celery
2 tbsp. chopped green pepper
1 clove of garlic, minced
1 bay leaf
1 10 ¾-oz. can beef gravy
¼ c. sour cream
Buttered cooked noodles

Brown veal in butter. Add onion, celery, green pepper, garlic, bay leaf and beef gravy. Simmer, covered, for 30 minutes. Stir in sour cream, just before serving. Serve with buttered noodles. Yield: 4 servings.

Mrs. Alfred Jander
Trinity Evening Guild
Riesel, Texas

VEAL FRICASSE

1 ½ lb. veal round steak
3 tbsp. butter
1 ½ c. hot water
3 tbsp. flour
1 tsp. lemon juice
¼ tsp. pepper
1 tsp. onion juice
1 tsp. salt
1 c. canned mushrooms
1 c. cream or evaporated milk

Cut veal into 1-inch pieces. Brown in butter. Add water. Cover; cook until tender. Mix flour with a small amount of water for smooth paste; add with lemon juice, pepper, onion juice and salt. Add mushrooms; cook for a few minutes longer. Add cream; keep hot until serving time. Yield: 4-6 servings.

Mrs. Paul N. Carlson, Pres.
Bethlehem Women's Guild
Gary, Indiana

VEAL HOT DISH

1 lb. veal shoulder
1 onion, chopped

2 c. diced celery
1 can cream of chicken
1 can cream of mushroom soup
2 soup cans water
¾ c. uncooked rice
2 to 3 tbsp. soy sauce

Cut veal into small pieces; brown with onion and celery. Add all remaining ingredients. Place in baking dish. Bake at 350 degrees for 1 hour and 30 minutes to 2 hours. Yield: 12 servings.

Helen T. Benson, Pres.
Bethlehem ALCW Serv. Guild
Wright, Minnesota

VEAL-NOODLE CASSEROLE

1 8-oz. can mushroom stems and pieces
2 lb. veal shoulder, cut into 1-in. cubes
1 med. onion, chopped
½ clove of garlic, chopped
4 tbsp. bacon drippings
5 tbsp. flour
1 c. dry white table wine
1 ½ c. water
1 tsp. Worcestershire sauce
½ tsp. paprika
Salt and pepper to taste
¾ lb. wide noodles
1 c. sour cream
Grated Parmesan cheese

Drain mushrooms, reserving liquid. Cook veal, onion and garlic in bacon drippings, stirring frequently, until meat is no longer pink. Stir in flour; add wine, water and mushroom liquid. Cook, stirring constantly, until sauce boils and thickens. Add Worcestershire sauce, paprika, salt and pepper. Cover; simmer for 45 minutes or until veal is tender, stirring frequently. Cook noodles in water until tender; drain. Combine veal, sauce, noodles, mushrooms and sour cream. Add additional salt and pepper, if desired. Turn into greased casserole; sprinkle with cheese. Bake at 350 degrees for 30 or 40 minutes. Yield: 8 servings.

Mrs. Arnold Davis, Pres.
St. James Evangelical Ladies Aid
Newman, California

VEAL-NOODLE CASSEROLE

1 lb. veal or round steak, cut into 1-in. cubes
Flour
Salt and pepper
Paprika
1 lge. onion, diced
2 c. water
1 pkg. noodles, cooked and drained
1 c. sour cream
Buttered bread crumbs

Roll veal cubes in flour seasoned with salt, pepper and paprika. Brown in skillet with onion. Add water; simmer until done. Combine veal, noodles and sour cream; put into baking dish.

(Continued on next page)

Top with bread crumbs. Bake at 325 degrees for 30 to 40 minutes. Yield: 8 servings.

Mrs. John Weber, Pres.
St. Peter's LWML
Hannover, North Dakota

VEAL PAPRIKA

2 lb. veal chunks
1 tbsp. fat
½ c. chopped onion
1 clove of garlic
1 c. water
¾ c. tomatoes
1 tsp. salt
½ tsp. pepper
1 tbsp. paprika
½ c. sour cream

Saute meat well in fat. Add onion and garlic; brown. Add water, tomatoes and seasonings; simmer for 1 hour. Just before serving, add sour cream and stir. Yield: 4 servings.

Mrs. Harold Lucas, Pres.
St. Martins LCW
Malvern, Ohio

VEAL PAPRIKA

2 c. chopped onions
3 tbsp. butter or margarine
1 tbsp. paprika
2 lb. boned veal shoulder, cut into 1-in. cubes
1 ¼ tsp. salt
1 ½ c. water
1 ½ tbsp. flour
½ c. sour cream

Saute onions in hot butter in a Dutch oven until golden; stir in paprika. Add veal sprinkled with salt; saute until golden. Simmer, covered, for 30 minutes, stirring occasionally. Add water; cover and simmer for 45 minutes or until veal is almost tender. Combine flour with a few tablespoonfuls gravy from Dutch oven; stir back into gravy. Simmer until thickened, stirring occasionally. Just before serving, stir in sour cream. Heat, but do not boil. Yield: 6 servings.

Mrs. Charles H. Harbaugh, Sec.-Treas.
Fremont Lutheran Church
Winchester, Virginia

VEAL PAPRIKA

2 lb. boned veal shoulder, cubed
¼ c. flour
½ tsp. salt
Dash of pepper
¼ c. margarine or butter
1 ½ c. water
1 chicken bouillon cube
1 tbsp. paprika
1 pkg. sour cream sauce mix

Coat veal with mixture of flour, salt and pepper; brown in margarine. Add remaining ingredients.

Bring to a boil; reduce heat. Cover pan; simmer for 1 hour or until meat is tender. Serve hot over buttered noodles. Yield: 6-8 servings.

Mrs. Dorothy Kolarik, Pres.
Martin Luther Ladies Aid
Muskegon Heights, Michigan

VEAL PAPRIKA

6 slices bacon, cut into 1-in. slices
3 lb. boneless veal, cut into 1 ½-in. pieces
⅔ c. chopped onions
1 ½ tsp. salt
1 tbsp. paprika
4 c. chicken broth
½ c. Sherry wine
1 c. sour cream
Sliced almonds

Fry bacon until crisp; remove from skillet. Brown veal in bacon fat. Add onions; cook until onions are golden. Add all ingredients except sour cream and almonds. Cover and simmer for 1 hour and 30 minutes or until tender. Thicken sauce; add sour cream. Pour into serving casserole or dish. Top with bacon curls and almonds. Yield: 6-8 servings.

Mrs. Walter E. Fadden, Pres.
St. Paul's LCW
Santa Monica, California

VEAL RAGOUT MARENGO

2 lb. veal shoulder, cubed
2 tbsp. vegetable oil
1 ½ c. finely chopped onions
1 clove of garlic, mashed
2 c. beef broth
1 tsp. leaf thyme, crumbled
1 bay leaf
2 c. peeled chopped tomatoes
1 tsp. salt
¼ tsp. pepper
2 tbsp. diced pimento
1 6-oz. can sliced mushrooms, undrained

Brown veal on all sides in oil in heavy kettle or Dutch oven. Remove veal; saute onions and garlic in remaining oil until soft. Add beef broth, thyme and bay leaf; simmer until liquid is reduced to one-half its original volume. Add tomatoes, salt, pepper and browned veal. Cover; simmer for 1 hour and 45 minutes to 2 hours or until veal is tender. Add pimento and mushrooms. Add additional salt and pepper, if desired. Heat through. Remove bay leaf. Thicken gravy with flour that has been mixed to a smooth paste with cold water, if desired. Yield: 8 servings.

Loretta Ohl, Pres.
Trinity LCW
Philadelphia, Pennsylvania

VEAL PAPRIKASH

3 onions, chopped
Butter
1 ½ tsp. paprika
1 tsp. salt
2 lb. veal shank, cubed
1 c. sour milk
2 tbsp. flour

Brown onions in butter until soft. Add paprika, salt, veal and water to cover within 1/2-inch of the top of the meat. Cook, covered, for 1 hour and 30 minutes or until tender. Add sour milk and a paste made by mixing flour and water. Simmer for 10 minutes longer. Serve with noodles, rice or mashed potatoes. Yield: 6 servings.

Mrs. Tony Kumpula, Pres.
Zion LCW
Fairport Harbor, Ohio

VEAL IN SOUR CREAM

2 lb. boneless veal, cut into 2-in. pieces
1 sm. onion, finely chopped
3 tbsp. shortening
1 tbsp. salt
5 to 6 tbsp. flour
1 egg
1 c. sour cream

Saute meat and onion in shortening for about 10 minutes or until lightly browned. Add enough water to cover meat; add salt. Cover and cook slowly for 1 hour and 15 minutes or until soft. Add a little water during cooking time, as it cooks down. Thicken gravy with the flour mixed with a small amount of water; gravy must be very thick. Remove from heat. Add egg to sour cream; mix well. Add a little hot gravy to the sour cream; add sour cream mixture to the gravy and meat. NOTE: If reheating, heat slowly and do not boil. Yield: 4-5 servings.

Mrs. P. Rieger
St. Johns LWML
Yonkers, New York

SPANISH FLUFF

2 c. ground veal or beef
1 onion, diced
Salt and pepper
1 c. cooked rice
2 c. diced celery
1 sm. can peas
1 sm. can diced mushrooms
1 can Spanish tomato sauce

Fry meat and onion until brown; season with salt and pepper to taste. Add all remaining ingredients; simmer for 10 minutes. Serve with noodles, garnished with bread crumbs. Yield: 10 servings.

Mrs. A. J. Flemmer, Treas.
Concordia Women's Guild
Maplewood, Missouri

STUFFED VEAL BREAST

4 ½ lb. veal breast, boned
Butter
1 to 2 c. grated carrots
1 tbsp. chopped parsley
1 tbsp. lemon juice
1 egg, slightly beaten
Salt
Sugar
1 to 1 ½ c. beef broth
Flour or cornstarch
2 tbsp. light cream

Wipe meat with clean cloth; pound well. Melt 1 stick butter; add carrots, parsley, lemon juice, egg and small amount of salt and sugar. Mix well. Spread mixture inside veal breast. Roll; stitch edge and ends with string or skewer. Place meat in roasting pan or baking dish; baste with butter. Brown for 15 to 20 minutes in preheated 250 degree oven. Add beef broth or water. Cook, uncovered, basting occasionally with liquid for 1 hour or until done. Remove string or skewers; slice meat and arrange on platter. Add flour paste to liquid; bring to a boil. Add cream and butter, if desired. Serve with boiled potatoes. Yield: 4-5 servings.

Mrs. Juta Mitt, Chmn.
Estonian Evangelical Women's Soc.
Chicago, Illinois

VEAL IN SOUR CREAM

1 ½ to 2 lb. veal
¼ c. butter or margarine
1 tsp. salt
1 tbsp. flour
1 c. water
1 c. sour cream

Wipe the veal with damp cloth. Cut into serving pieces. Combine salt and flour. Dip meat into seasoned flour. Saute on both sides in butter in frying pan. Pour mixture of water and sour cream over meat. Cover; simmer for 1 hour. Yield: 4-6 servings.

Margaret H. Strailman, Pres.
Bethany LCW
Brunswick, Maryland

VEAL SUPREME

2 lb. ground veal
¼ c. instant tapioca
1 pt. milk
1 green pepper, chopped
1 onion, chopped
1 tsp. seasoned salt
1 can cream of mushroom soup

Combine all ingredients except soup; mix well. Place mixture in a flat 9 x 13-inch glass casserole; top with soup. Bake at 375 degrees for 2 hours. Yield: 10-12 servings.

Mrs. Frank McClain, Sec. of Education
Zion LCW
Lima, Ohio

Ground Beef Favorites

RECIPE FOR KOFTAS ON PAGE 74

AUNT KATE'S HAMBURGER STEW

1 lb. ground beef
4 or 5 med. potatoes, quartered
6 med. onions, halved
Salt and pepper to taste
1 10 ½-oz. can tomato soup

Shape hamburger into balls; place in large baking dish with potatoes, onions, salt and pepper. Pour soup over all. Bake at 350 degrees for 1 hour. Yield: 4-5 servings.

Althea Steinhauer, Pres.
St. John's Ladies Aid
Dover, Delaware

BARBECUED MEAT BALLS

1 c. soft bread crumbs
½ c. milk
1 lb. ground beef
1 tsp. salt
Pepper to taste
1 ½ tbsp. Worcestershire sauce
¼ c. vinegar
1 tbsp. sugar
½ c. catsup
½ c. water
½ c. chopped green pepper
½ c. chopped onion

Moisten bread crumbs with milk. Combine with ground beef, salt and pepper. Shape into balls. Place in baking dish. Combine remaining ingredients; pour around meat balls. Bake at 375 degrees for 45 minutes. Yield: 6 servings.

Mrs. J. Cletus Travis
Mt. Olive Ladies Aid
Conover, North Carolina
Mrs. Stuert Erickson, Pres.
First Lutheran Church Ladies Soc.
Hot Springs, Arkansas

BEEF BALLS

1 ½ lb. beef shank
⅓ c. bread crumbs
Salt and pepper
1 tsp. lemon juice
Nutmeg
1 egg, beaten
2 tbsp. flour
3 tbsp. soft fat
1 c. stock

Put meat through chopper twice. Add crumbs, salt, pepper, lemon juice, nutmeg and egg. Shape meat into balls. Let stand for 30 minutes. Roll balls in flour; brown in fat in frying pan. Remove meat balls; add flour and stock to fat. Season well. Return meat balls to frying pan. Simmer for 1 hour and 30 minutes. Yield: 4 servings.

Lillian Bovee
St. Lukes Ladies Aid
Big Falls, Wisconsin

BEEF BALLS STROGANOFF

1 lb. ground beef
½ c. milk
½ c. dried bread crumbs
Salt
Pepper
1 tbsp. minced fresh parsley
3 tbsp. butter or margarine
1 med. onion, finely diced
½ green pepper, finely diced
¼ lb. mushrooms, sliced
½ tsp. paprika
2 tbsp. flour
1 c. beef stock
½ c. sour cream
1 tsp. Worcestershire sauce

Combine ground beef, milk, bread crumbs, 1 teaspoonful salt, 1/8 teaspoonful pepper and parsley. Blend well; shape into 1-inch balls. Melt butter to sizzling in large deep skillet; brown balls well on all sides. Remove meat from pan; place onion, green pepper and mushrooms in skillet. Saute; sprinkle with paprika and flour. Pour in beef stock, stirring constantly; cook until thickened. Blend in sour cream; return beef balls to fry pan. Add Worcestershire sauce, salt and pepper. Heat thoroughly, but gently. Serve with buttered noodles or rice. NOTE: Two beef bouillon cubes dissolved in 1 cup boiling water may be substituted for beef stock. Yield: 4-5 servings.

Mrs. Donald Unruh, VP
Trinity LCW
Fremont, Ohio

CREOLE MEAT BALLS AND NOODLES

½ lb. hamburger
1 egg, slightly beaten
⅓ c. dry bread crumbs
½ tsp. salt
⅛ tsp. pepper
2 tbsp. cooking fat
¼ c. chopped onion
¼ c. chopped celery
2 ½ c. canned tomatoes
1 tbsp. Worcestershire sauce
1 tbsp. sugar
1 tsp. salt
¼ tsp. pepper
3 tbsp. butter
3 tbsp. flour
6 oz. raw wide noodles, cooked

Combine hamburger, egg, bread crumbs and seasonings; shape into balls. Brown in cooking fat in large skillet. Add remaining ingredients except butter, flour and noodles. Cover; simmer for 30 minutes. Blend flour with butter; stir into meat ball mixture. Cook until thick, stirring constantly. Serve over noodles. Yield: 4 servings.

Mrs. Herbert Galle, Pres.
Timothy LWML
Council Bluffs, Iowa

CAROLERS' WARM-UP

3 lb. ground beef
2 eggs, beaten
1 ½ c. quick cooking oats
⅓ c. minced onion
1 ½ tsp. basil
2 tsp. oregano
2 tsp. salt
½ tsp. pepper
6 c. water
2 10 ½-oz. cans tomato soup
2 8-oz. cans tomato sauce
2 beef bouillon cubes
1 bay leaf
1 4-oz. pkg. uncooked thin egg noodles

Combine ground beef, eggs, oats, onion and seasonings except bay leaf in large bowl. Mix well; shape into 48 meat balls. Combine water, soup, tomato sauce, bouillon cubes and bay leaf. Bring to a boil; add meat balls. Cover and simmer for 30 minutes, stirring occasionally. Remove bay leaf. Add noodles; simmer, uncovered, for 15 minutes. Yield: 12 servings.

Mrs. William Bendorf
St. John's LWML
Wilcox, Nebraska

HAMBURGER CHOP SUEY

1 ½ lb. hamburger
Salt and pepper to taste
2 med. onions, diced
3 c. chopped celery
1 lge. can chop suey vegetables with mushrooms
2 tsp. cornstarch

Shape hamburger into small balls the size of marbles; add salt and pepper. Brown; add onions and celery. Cook until done. Add chop suey vegetables; thicken with cornstarch. Serve over rice. Yield: 6 servings.

Mrs. William Keller, Pres.
Bethel Ladies Aid
Prentice, Wisconsin

HAMBURGER AND RICE MEAT BALLS

1 lb. hamburger
½ c. cracker crumbs
1 egg
1 sm. onion, chopped
½ tsp. salt
Dash of pepper
½ tsp. paprika
1 10 ¾-oz. can tomato soup
1 8-oz. can tomato sauce
½ c. hot water
¼ c. uncooked rice

Mix hamburger with cracker crumbs, egg, onion, salt, pepper and paprika. Shape into balls; brown in frying pan. Mix soup with tomato sauce, water and rice; pour over meat balls. Cover and simmer for 1 hour. Yield: 5-6 servings.

Mrs. William Yudes, Jr.
Zion Evangelical Ladies Aid
Oconto, Wisconsin

HAWAIIAN MEAT BALLS

1 ½ lb. ground beef
⅔ c. cracker crumbs
½ c. chopped onion
⅔ c. evaporated milk
1 tsp. seasoned salt
⅓ c. flour
3 tbsp. shortening

Combine all ingredients except flour and shortening; mix lightly but thoroughly. Shape into 30 balls. Roll in flour; brown in shortening. Drain off excess fat.

SWEET-SOUR SAUCE:

1 13 ½-oz. can pineapple chunks
2 tbsp. cornstarch
½ c. vinegar
2 tbsp. soy sauce
2 tbsp. lemon juice
½ c. brown sugar
1 c. coarsely chopped green pepper
1 tbsp. chopped pimento

Drain pineapple; reserve syrup. Add enough water to make 1 cup liquid. Blend pineapple liquid and cornstarch until smooth. Stir in vinegar, soy sauce, lemon juice and brown sugar; cook until thickened and clear. Add pineapple, green pepper and pimento; mix well. Cover; simmer over low heat for 15 minutes. Pour over meat balls. Cover; simmer for 15 minutes. Yield: 6 servings.

Mrs. Helen Wetzel, Pres.
Mount Zion Eventide Guild
Minneapolis, Minnesota

ITALIAN SPAGHETTI WITH BREAD BALLS

1 lb. ground beef
2 c. grated Romano cheese
5 eggs
1 ½ tsp. salt
¾ tsp. pepper
½ c. fat
1 c. bread crumbs

Mix beef, 1 cup Romano cheese, 3 eggs, 1 teaspoonful salt and 1/2 teaspoonful pepper thoroughly. Roll into balls 1-inch in diameter. Fry slowly in fat until brown. Mix remaining ingredients throughly. Roll into balls 1/2-inch in diameter. Fry in same fat as meat balls until brown.

SAUCE:

3 6-oz. cans tomato paste
5 c. water
1 med. onion, finely chopped
2 med. cloves of garlic, grated
1 ½ tsp. salt
½ tsp. pepper
Cooked spaghetti
Grated Romano cheese

Combine all ingredients except spaghetti and cheese. Add meat balls and bread balls to sauce;

(Continued on next page)

simmer for 1 hour. Toss 1 cup sauce into spaghetti. Pour onto platter; arrange balls on top. Sprinkle with Romano cheese. Garnish with parsley. Yield: 6-8 servings.

Mrs. Floyd H. Pretz
Grace Lutheran Church
Orange, Texas

ITALIAN SPAGHETTI SAUCE
SAUCE:

¾ c. chopped onions
1 tsp. garlic salt
3 tbsp. fat
2 1-lb. cans tomatoes
2 6-oz. cans tomato paste
1 c. water
1 tbsp. sugar
1 ½ tsp. salt
½ tsp. pepper
1 bay leaf
1 ½ tsp. crushed oregano

Cook onions with garlic salt in hot fat until tender, but not brown. Combine and add remaining ingredients. Simmer, uncovered, for 45 minutes; remove bay leaf.

MEAT BALLS:

1 lb. ground beef
1 c. dry bread crumbs
½ c. grated Parmesan cheese
1 tbsp. chopped parsley
1 tsp. garlic salt
½ c. milk
2 eggs, beaten
½ tsp. salt
Dash of pepper
2 tbsp. fat

Combine all ingredients except fat; shape into meat balls. Brown in fat. Drop into simmering sauce. Cook for 15 minutes. Yield: 4 servings.

Mrs. Eugene Lange
Trinity Women's Guild
Champaign, Illinois

JAPANESE MEAT BALLS

¼ c. cornstarch
1 ¼ c. water
2 lb. ground beef
¼ c. soy sauce
1 tbsp. sugar
1 tsp. monosodium glutamate
1 sm. piece ginger, crushed

Blend cornstarch with 1/4 cup water; combine with meat. Shape meat into walnut-sized balls. Place in saucepan. Combine remaining water, soy sauce, sugar, monosodium glutamate and ginger. Add to meat balls. Simmer for 15 minutes. Yield: 6 servings.

Mrs. Alice Kastens
Christ Lutheran Church Mary Martha Soc.
Hilo, Hawaii

KOFTAS

1 med. onion, minced
1 med. sweet red pepper, minced
1 clove of garlic, minced
2 tbsp. ground coriander
2 tsp. salt
½ tsp. cinnamon
¼ tsp. ground cloves
¼ tsp. ground cardamom
½ tsp. chili powder
½ tsp. Tabasco sauce
1 lb. ground chuck
4 tbsp. butter or margarine

Combine onion, red pepper, garlic, coriander, salt, cinnamon, cloves, cardamom, chili powder and Tabasco sauce; mix well. Add meat and mix thoroughly. Form into 1-inch balls. Brown quickly in melted butter, shaking pan to prevent sticking. Yield: 4 servings.

Photograph for this recipe on page 71.

LOW CALORIE-HIGH PROTEIN MEAT BALLS
MEAT LOAF:

1 lb. lean ground beef
¼ c. finely chopped onion
2 to 3 c. powdered milk
1 c. drained tomatoes
2 slices bread, crumbled
1 tsp. salt
⅛ tsp. pepper
⅛ tsp. dry mustard
⅛ tsp. celery salt
1 ¼ tsp. garlic salt
2 tsp. Worcestershire sauce

Combine all ingredients; shape into balls. Roll balls lightly in flour. Brown in small amount of shortening. Place in casserole; top with heated sauce. Bake at 350 degrees for 30 minutes.

SAUCE:

1 can cream of mushroom soup
1 tsp. Worcestershire sauce
½ tsp. beef extract
½ c. tomato juice

Combine all ingredients; heat. Pour over meat balls. Yield: 6 servings.

Mrs. August Spitzer, Pres.
St. Paul's Ladies Aid
Kensal, North Dakota

MEAT BALLS

3 slices white bread
1 lb. ground chuck
1 tbsp. Parmesan cheese
1 tbsp. fresh or dried chopped parsley
Salt and pepper
½ c. chopped onion
1 can tomato sauce
1 can tomato juice
1 tsp. sugar
¼ tsp. soda
¼ tsp. Italian Herb seasoning

(Continued on next page)

Dampen bread with cold water; squeeze out and fluff with fork. Mix bread, chuck, cheese, parsley, salt and pepper; form into small balls 1 1/2-inch in diameter. Refrigerate for 1 hour or more. Brown onion in fat. Add remaining ingredients. Yield: 10 servings.

Mrs. Owen Reel, Education Chmn.
First Lutheran Church LCW
Kettering, Ohio

MEAT BALLS

1 c. milk
¼ c. dry bread crumbs
1 lb. round steak, ground
1 egg, well beaten
3 tbsp. chopped onion
1 tsp. salt
½ tsp. monosodium glutamate
¼ tsp. nutmeg
½ tsp. pepper
5 tbsp. butter
1 bouillon cube
2 c. water
1 lge. onion, sliced
1 tbsp. sugar

Pour milk over bread crumbs; stir until blended. Add meat, egg, chopped onion, salt, monosodium glutamate, nutmeg and pepper; mix lightly until thoroughly blended. Shape mixture into small meat balls. Melt 3 tablespoonfuls butter in large fry pan. Add meat balls; cook over medium heat until well browned. Dissolve bouillon cube in water. Fry sliced onion in remaining butter. Remove onion; add sugar. Heat until sugar is melted. Add bouillon gradually. Pour over meat balls; cover with onion slices. Cover; bake at 325 degrees for 1 hour. Add additional water, if necessary. Yield: 6 servings.

Mrs. Bernard Hultquist, Pres.
Swedesburg LCW
Mt. Pleasant, Iowa

MEAT BALLS "SOUPREME"

1 can cream of vegetable soup
½ soup can water
1 lb. ground beef
1 egg
¼ tsp. salt
2 tbsp. fine dry bread crumbs
2 tbsp. chopped onion
1 tbsp. chopped parsley
Dash of pepper

Blend soup and water. Combine 1/4 cup of soup mixture with remaining ingredients. Shape into 12 meat balls; brown meat balls in skillet in small amount of shortening. Add remaining soup mixture. Cover. Simmer for 20 minutes, stirring occasionally. NOTE: If sauce is thin, remove cover and cook a few minutes longer. Yield: 6 servings.

Mrs. A. Dannenhoffer, Pres.
Redeemer Ladies Aid Soc.
Glendale, New York

MEAT BALLS

1 to 1 ½ lb. hamburger
½ c. uncooked rice
1 egg (opt.)
1 to 4 tbsp. minced onion or 1 sm. onion, chopped
½ to 1 tsp. salt
⅛ to ¼ tsp. pepper
1 can tomato soup
½ to 1 c. hot water

Combine hamburger, rice, egg, onion, salt and pepper; form into balls. Place in 1-quart casserole. Dilute tomato soup with water; pour over meat balls. Bake at 350 degree for 1 hour. Serve with baked potatoes, if desired. NOTE: If desired, meat balls may be cooked in pressure cooker at 15 pounds pressure for 10 minutes. Yield: 4 servings.

Mrs. Mary S. Butler
Grace Miss'y Soc.
Sugar City, Colorado
Mrs. Marvin Bauer, VP
St. Peter's English Lutheran Church
Newell, Iowa
Mrs. Richard Hamann
St. Paul's Ladies Aid Soc.
Correctionville, Iowa
Mrs. O. Hellwege
Redeemer Ladies Aid
Marshall, Missouri

MEAT BALLS WITH SPAGHETTI

SAUCE:

1 med. onion, finely chopped
3 tbsp. fat
1 No. 2 can tomatoes
2 6-oz. cans tomato paste
2 c. water
1 tsp. salt
½ tsp. pepper
1 tbsp. sugar
1 bay leaf

Brown onion in hot fat; add tomatoes, tomato paste, water and seasonings. Cook slowly for 1 hour.

MEAT BALLS:

1 lb. ground beef
1 c. fine dry bread crumbs
¼ tsp. dried parsley or 1 sprig fresh parsley, chopped
¼ tsp. garlic salt or 1 clove of garlic, minced
½ c. milk
2 eggs, well beaten
Salt and pepper to taste

Combine all ingredients; mix thoroughly. Form into small balls; brown in small amount hot fat. Add to sauce; cook over low heat for 15 minutes.

SPAGHETTI:

1 8-oz. pkg. spaghetti, cooked
½ c. grated American cheese
Fresh parsley

(Continued on next page)

Place spaghetti on platter. Place meat balls on top of spaghetti. Spoon enough of remaining sauce to cover generously. Sprinkle with grated cheese; garnish with fresh parsley. Yield: 6 servings.

Mrs. Ernest A. Bolland, Pres.
St. Paul's LWML
Bishop, Texas

MEAT BALLS IN SOUR CREAM

4 slices bread, crumbled
½ c. milk
1 ½ lb. ground beef
7 green onions, thinly sliced
1 ½ tsp. salt
Pepper to taste
Bacon drippings
1 c. sour cream
Paprika to taste

Combine bread and milk; let stand for 10 minutes. Add meat, onions, salt and pepper; form into balls. Brown balls in bacon drippings. Place in casserole; cover with sour cream. Sprinkle generously with paprika. Cover; bake at 350 degrees for about 45 minutes. NOTE: One cup sweet cream mixed with 1 tablespoonful lemon juice or vinegar may be substituted for sour cream. Yield: 6 servings.

Mrs. James Wesner, Pres.
Ascension LCW
Indian Harbor Beach, Florida
Barbara Schlegelmilch, Pres.
Faith Ladies Guild
Merritt Island, Florida

MEAT BALLS IN TOMATO JUICE

1 lb. hamburger
1 c. bread crumbs
1 or 2 eggs
¾ tsp. salt
Dash of onion or garlic salt
⅛ tsp. pepper
¼ tsp. milk
1 pt. tomato juice
1 lge. onion, minced

Combine all ingredients except tomato juice and onion; shape into eight balls. Brown in large skillet. Add tomato juice and onion. Simmer for 1 hour. Yield: 4 servings.

Mrs. A. Sheiberg
Bardo Lutheran Church
Kingman, Alberta, Canada

MEAT BALLS AND TOMATO SAUCE

1 lb. ground beef
1 ½ tsp. salt
⅛ tsp. pepper
1 egg
¼ c. oats
1 c. American cheese cubes, ¼-in. thick
4 drops of liquid smoke
1 c. cooked or canned tomatoes
1 c. drained whole kernel corn

2 tbsp. flour
2 tbsp. chopped onion
2 tbsp. chopped green pepper
2 tbsp. chopped celery
2 tbsp. barbecue sauce
1 tsp. sugar

Combine ground beef, salt, pepper, egg, oats, cheese and liquid smoke. Form into 18 small meat balls. Combine remaining ingredients; mix well.

PASTRY:

1 ½ c. flour
¾ tsp. salt
½ c. shortening
4 drops of liquid smoke
5 tbsp. cold water

Combine flour and salt in mixing bowl; cut in shortening until mixture is the size of small peas. Add liquid smoke to water; sprinkle a little at a time over flour-shortening mixture, tossing and stirring with a fork. Add water; mix enough to hold together. Shape into two balls, one twice as large as the other. Flatten balls to 1/2-inch thickness; smooth edges. Roll out larger ball on floured surface to a circle 1 1/2-inches larger than inverted 9-inch pie pan. Fit into pan. Fold edge to form a standing rim; flute. Place meat balls in pastry-lined pan. Top with sauce. Roll out remaining pastry. Cut into 3-inch rings. Place around edge of pie. Bake at 425 degrees for 10 minutes, reduce temperature to 375 degrees. Bake for 35 to 45 minutes or until crust is golden brown. Let stand for 5 to 10 minutes before serving. Yield: 6 servings.

Mrs. Alvin Moore
Good Shepherd Lutheran Church
Spencer, Oklahoma

MUSHROOM MEAT BALLS

1 can cream of mushroom soup
1 lb. ground beef
2 tbsp. minced onion
1 egg
½ c. bread crumbs
1 tbsp. minced parsley
1 tbsp. shortening
½ c. milk

Combine 1/4 cup soup with beef, onion, egg, bread crumbs and parsley; shape into balls. Brown in shortening. Blend remaining soup with milk; pour over meat balls. Cook over low heat for 10 to 15 minutes, stirring occasionally. Yield: 6 servings.

Anita Littledale, Treas.
Grace LCW Guild
Streamwood, Illinois

PINEAPPLE MEAT BALLS

MEAT BALLS:

¼ c. milk
1 slice bread, crumbled

76

(Continued on next page)

1 lb. hamburger
1 lb. ground round
1 egg
2 tsp. salt
⅛ tsp. pepper
⅛ tsp. garlic salt
Oil

Pour milk over bread to soften; add meats, egg, salt, pepper and garlic salt. Mix well; form into walnut-sized balls. Brown in hot oil, shaking pan frequently so balls will keep their shape.

PINEAPPLE SAUCE:

1 No. 2 can pineapple chunks, undrained
½ c. chopped green pepper
¼ c. wine vinegar
½ c. sugar
2 tbsp. soy sauce
½ tsp. salt
1 tsp. monosodium glutamate
2 tbsp. cornstarch
1 can beef consomme

Combine all ingredients except consomme, pineapple and cornstarch; simmer for 15 minutes. Moisten cornstarch with a small amount of water; stir into boiling liquid. Simmer and stir until sauce is clear and thickened. Add meat balls; simmer for 10 to 15 minutes until flavors are blended. Serve with fluffy white rice, noodles or mashed potatoes, if desired.

Mrs. Ray Toltzman
St. John's Lutheran Church
Spencer, Wisconsin

PORCUPINE MEAT BALLS

1 lb. ground beef
1 c. uncooked rice
1 tsp. salt
¼ tsp. pepper
½ med. onion, thinly sliced
½ green pepper, thinly sliced
1 tbsp. fat
2 ½ c. tomato juice

Mix ground beef, rice, salt and pepper. Form into small balls, about 1 1/2-inches in diameter; place in a covered baking dish. Saute onion and green pepper in fat. Top meat mixture with onion, green pepper and tomato juice. Bake in 350 degree oven for 1 hour to 1 hour and 30 minutes. Serve with additional tomato sauce, if desired.

Mrs. Eldore Messerschmidt
St. John's Lutheran Church
Ladysmith, Wisconsin

PORCUPINE MEAT BALLS

½ c. uncooked rice
1 ½ lb. ground beef
⅛ tsp. pepper
1 tsp. salt
1 No. 303 can tomato juice
1 c. hot water
1 tbsp. minced green onion
2 tbsp. chopped green pepper

Mix rice, meat and seasoning; form into meat balls. Combine tomato juice, water, onion and green pepper in pan; bring to a boil. Drop in meat balls. Bake at 350 degrees for 1 hour. Serve covered with sauce; garnish with parsley. Yield: 6 servings.

Mrs. Martin Henrichs, Pres.
St. Peter's LWML
Humbolt, Kansas

SOUPER MEAT BALLS

1 can cream of mushroom soup
1 lb. ground chuck
1 egg
½ c. corn flakes, slightly crushed
1 sm. onion, minced
Salt and pepper to taste
2 tbsp. margarine

Warm soup in saucepan over very low heat. Combine all remaining ingredients except margarine; mix well. Form into eight meat balls. Brown balls on all sides in margarine in skillet. Place balls carefully into warmed soup; simmer slowly for 30 minutes. Yield: 4 servings.

Mrs. Charles Buesser, Pres.
Beautiful Savior LWML
Tempe, Arizona

SPAGHETTI AND MEAT BALLS

1 lb. ground beef
½ c. fine dry bread crumbs
¼ c. grated American cheese
1 tbsp. chopped parsley
1 clove of garlic, minced
½ c. milk
2 eggs, beaten
Salt and pepper
Shortening
1 med. onion, chopped
2 ½ c. tomatoes
2 c. water
1 8-oz. can tomato sauce
1 bay leaf
1 tbsp. sugar
1 8-oz. pkg. spaghetti

Combine meat, crumbs, cheese, parsley, garlic, milk, eggs, 1 teaspoonful salt and 1/2 teaspoonful pepper. Mix thoroughly; form into small balls. Brown in hot shortening; add onion. Cook until golden brown. Add remaining ingredients except spaghetti; blend. Cover; simmer for 1 hour and 30 minutes. Cook spaghetti in boiling salted water until tender; drain. Arrange on hot platter. Pour meat balls and sauce over spaghetti. Yield: 6 servings.

Mrs. Lee Warmke
Welcome Lutheran
Bleiblerville, Texas

SPAGHETTI AND MEAT BALLS A LA PHURNE
SAUCE:

1 lge. can tomato puree
1 clove of garlic, finely chopped
2 tbsp. chopped parsley
2 or 3 stalks celery, chopped

Combine all ingredients; simmer to blend flavors.

MEAT BALLS:

1 lb. ground beef
4 slices bread, slightly soaked
3 eggs
3 tsp. salt
Dash of pepper
2 tbsp. Parmesan cheese
2 tbsp. chopped parsley
Salad oil

Mix all ingredients except oil; shape into meat balls and fry in oil. Grate dry bread into mixture if too moist. Drop the meat balls into simmering sauce. Simmer for 15 minutes. Yield: 6 servings.

Mrs. Francis Langland, Pres.
Redeemer LWML
Wichita, Kansas

SPICED MEAT BALLS

1 lb. ground meat
1 egg, beaten
1 can tomato paste
Salt and pepper to taste
½ c. chopped onion
½ c. chopped green pepper
½ c. shortening
½ tsp. ginger
½ tsp. cloves
1 tsp. cinnamon
1 c. sugar
1 ½ c. water

Combine meat, egg, tomato paste, salt, pepper, onion and green pepper; roll into balls. Brown in shortening. Combine ginger, cloves, cinnamon, sugar and water. Cook until mixture forms a thin syrup; pour over meat balls. Simmer over low heat for 1 hour or bake at 275 degrees for 1 hour. Yield: 4 servings.

Martha Constien
St. John's Ladies Aid
Hinton, Oklahoma

SWEET AND SOUR MEAT BALLS

1 slice bread
½ c. milk
2 lb. ground beef
1 egg
1 ½ tsp. salt
½ tsp. garlic salt
Pepper to taste
2 tbsp. cornstarch
½ c. sugar
1 tsp. monosodium glutamate

1 can beef bouillon
¼ c. wine vinegar
2 tbsp. soy sauce
1 can pineapple chunks

Soak bread in milk; add meat, egg, 1 teaspoonful salt, garlic salt and pepper. Mix well; form into small balls. Brown until done. Combine remaining ingredients except pineapple; cook until thick and clear. Add meat balls; simmer for 30 minutes. Add pineapple, just before serving. Serve with rice. Yield: 6 servings.

Mrs. Eugene Sailer, Treas.
Redeemer LCW
Great Falls, Montana

SWEDISH MEAT BALLS

1 lb. ground beef
1 c. bread crumbs
1 egg, beaten
½ c. milk
1 tbsp. chopped onion
1 tbsp. catsup
½ tsp. mustard
½ tsp. salt
Margarine
1 tbsp. flour
1 can cream of mushroom soup

Combine ground beef, bread crumbs, egg, milk, onion, catsup, mustard and salt. Mix well; form into small balls. Brown in margarine in frying pan. Place meat balls in casserole. Stir in flour and enough liquid to make a thin gravy. Add soup, stirring until smooth and hot. Pour over meat balls. Bake in preheated 375 degree oven for 45 minutes. Yield: 6 servings.

Olive Martin
St. John's LWML
West Branch, Michigan

SWEDISH MEAT BALLS

1 lb. lean beef
½ lb. lean pork
1 med. onion, minced
Butter
1 c. bread crumbs
1 c. milk
1 tsp. sugar
1 egg

Grind beef with pork very fine. Fry onion in butter until brown. Soak bread crumbs in milk; mix with all ingredients. Form into small meatballs; fry in skillet for 20 minutes, turning occasionally to prevent burning.

Mrs. Alice Wallhausen
Calvary Tabitha Soc.
Monroeville, Pennsylvania

SWEDISH MEAT BALLS

80 lb. hamburger
10 qt. half and half or cream

(Continued on next page)

6 boxes cornstarch
8 lge. onions, diced or grated
Salt and pepper to taste
Shortening
Butter
Kitchen Bouquet

Combine all ingredients except shortening, butter and Kitchen Bouquet. Mix well; form into balls the size of walnuts. Brown in part butter and part shortening. Remove from pan; make gravy, using Kitchen Bouquet. Simmer or bake at 325 to 350 degrees for 1 hour.

Mrs. Dick Kroeze
Ezekiel Lutheran Church
Beldenville, Wisconsin

SWEDISH MEAT BALLS

2 lb. hamburger
¼ c. catsup
2 tsp. salt
¼ tsp. pepper
½ c. bread crumbs
1 ¼ c. instant dry milk
2 eggs
½ c. chopped onion

Mix all ingredients; shape into balls. Place in a casserole. Bake at 325 degrees for 45 minutes. Yield: 8 servings.

Mrs. Vern Esterly, Treas.
Bethlehem Ladies Aid
Herman, Minnesota

SWEDISH MEAT BALLS

2 lb. hamburger
2 tsp. salt
1 tbsp. onion
Pepper to taste
2 eggs, beaten
Bread
1 c. milk
1 can beef broth
¾ soup can water
1 tbsp. flour

Mix hamburger, salt, onion, pepper and beaten eggs. Place enough stale bread in milk to soak up all of milk; add to meat mixture. Shape into balls; brown lightly on both sides. Place in casserole. Pour beef broth and water in skillet; thicken with flour. Pour over meat balls. Cover; bake at 350 degrees for 1 hour. Yield: 12 servings.

Esther E. Peterson, Pres.
Zion Clyde LCW
Clifton, Kansas

SWEDISH MEAT BALLS IN BURGUNDY

¾ lb. chuck, ground
¾ c. packaged dried bread crumbs or finely
    crushed corn flakes
1 sm. onion, minced
¾ tsp. cornstarch
Dash of allspice

1 egg, beaten
¾ c. light cream
1 ¼ tsp. salt
¼ c. fat or salad oil
3 tbsp. flour
2 c. water
1 c. Burgundy
2 beef bouillon cubes
⅛ tsp. pepper
1 ½ tsp. sugar
Bottled gravy sauce

Combine chuck, crumbs, onion, cornstarch, allspice, egg, cream and 3/4 teaspoonful salt; shape into 24 to 26 balls. Drop meat balls, a few at a time, into hot fat in skillet. Brown well on all sides; remove to plate. Stir flour into remaining fat in skillet; stir in water, Burgundy, bouillon cubes, 1/2 teaspoonful salt, pepper, sugar and gravy sauce. Cook, stirring until smooth. Arrange meat balls in sauce, simmer, covered, for 30 minutes. Cool; refrigerate. Just before serving, reheat meat balls in sauce. Serve with mashed potatoes, fluffy rice or buttered noodles. Yield: 6 servings.

Mrs. Daniel Coker, Christian Serv. Chmn.
St. Paul's Lutheran Church
Falls Church, Virginia

BEEF CHOP SUEY

1 lb. ground beef
¼ c. butter
1 c. chopped celery
1 tsp. salt
1 can tomato soup
1 med. onion, minced
¼ lb. mushrooms or canned mushrooms

Brown meat in butter. Place in casserole with remaining ingredients. Bake at 400 degrees for 30 minutes. Yield: 5 servings.

Mrs. William Dick, VP
Faith English Dorcas Soc.
Crook, Colorado

BOBOTIE

1 slice white bread
1 c. milk
1 onion, chopped
2 tbsp. butter
1 lb. ground beef
2 or 3 tsp. curry powder
1 tsp. sugar
2 tsp. salt
½ tsp. pepper
Juice of 1 lemon
2 tsp. Angostura bitters
12 blanched almonds, finely chopped
2 eggs

Soak bread in a little of the milk and squeeze dry, reserving milk. Saute onion in butter. Add meat; brown lightly. Remove from heat. Add curry powder, sugar, salt, pepper, lemon juice and Angostura bitters. Add bread and almonds; mix thoroughly. Pour into buttered casserole. Beat

79

(Continued on next page)

eggs with milk, including milk squeezed from bread; pour over meat mixture in dish. Bake at 350 degrees until egg mixture has set into a custard, about 20 minutes. Knife inserted into center of dish will come clean when Bobotie is done. Serve with rice and curry condiments. Yield: 4-6 servings.

Mrs. M. B. Casey, Pres.
University Hills Ruth Guild
Denver, Colorado

EASY STROGANOFF

1 ½ lb. ground beef
2 tbsp. instant minced onion or ⅓ c. finely chopped onion
1 to 2 tbsp. parsley flakes
¼ tsp. garlic powder
¼ to ½ tsp. pepper
1 tsp. salt
⅔ c. mushrooms
1 10 ½-oz. can vegetable soup
1 c. sour cream
½ c. milk

Brown beef with onion; add parsley and garlic powder. Stir in pepper, salt, mushrooms and soup. Simmer for 15 minutes. Blend in sour cream and milk; heat thoroughly. Place in a 2 1/2-quart casserole.

BISCUIT TOPPING:

1 ½ c. sifted flour
2 tsp. baking powder
1 tsp. paprika
½ tsp. salt
½ tsp. celery seed
½ tsp. pepper
¼ c. shortening
¾ c. milk
1 tsp. poppy seed

Sift flour with baking powder, paprika, salt, celery seed and pepper; cut in shortening until particles are fine. Add milk; stir only until dry particles are moistened. Drop by tablespoonfuls onto meat mixture. Sprinkle with poppy seed. Bake at 475 degrees for 15 to 20 minutes. NOTE: Plain biscuits may be used instead of herb biscuits. Yield: 8 servings.

Mrs. Herbert Haer
Grace LWML
Knoxville, Tennessee
Mrs. Bradford D. Rodman
Lord Jesus Evangelical Lutheran Church
Chicago, Illinois

HAMBURGER CASSEROLE

1 ½ lb. ground beef
1 can mushrooms
1 c. diced celery
1 onion, chopped
1 can of cream of chicken soup
1 can cream of mushroom soup
1 can chow mein noodles

Combine all ingredients except noodles; pour into casserole. Top with noodles. Bake at 350 degrees for 30 minutes. Yield: 12 servings.

Mrs. Doris L. Kuhlmann, VP
St. John's Ladies Aid
Charter Oak, Iowa

GROUND BEEF CASSEROLE

2 to 4 c. bread stuffing, as for fowl
1 lb. ground beef
1 tsp. salt
Dash of pepper
1 can cream of mushroom soup
1 can evaporated milk

Place one-half of bread stuffing in a buttered baking dish. Add a layer of meat seasoned with salt and pepper. Mix soup and milk; heat. Pour one-half of mixture into casserole. Repeat layers. Bake at 350 degrees for 1 hour. Yield: 2-4 servings.

Mrs. Harold Smith, Pres.
Mt. Zion and St. Mark's LCW
Rohrersville, Maryland

JAMBALAYA

1 onion, chopped
1 ½ lb. ground meat
1 can vegetable soup
½ can cream of mushroom soup
½ can cream of chicken soup
1 can chow mein noodles

Brown onion and meat; add soups and one-half of noodles. Place in 9 x 13-inch baking dish; top with remaining noodles. Bake at 350 degrees for 30 to 40 minutes. Yield: 6 servings.

Mrs. Russell Holmbeck, Pres.
First Lutheran Church LCW Naomi Soc.
Granville, Illinois

BEEF CASSEROLE

1 ½ lb. ground beef
1 onion, chopped
Salt to taste
1 can tomato soup
1 can cream of mushroom soup
½ lb. macaroni
¼ lb. cheese, sliced

Brown ground beef; add onion and salt. Continue cooking meat for a few minutes longer or until onion is partially transparent. Add undiluted soups to meat. Cook macaroni in boiling salted water; drain. Add to meat and soup mixture. Mix well. Place mixture in casserole; top with slices of cheese. Bake at 350 degrees for 30 minutes.

Mrs. A. W. Truett
Holy Cross Ladies Guild
Mobile, Alabama

HAMBURGER CASSEROLE

1 8-oz. pkg. elbow macaroni
1 lb. hamburger
2 med. onions, finely chopped
1 ½ tsp. salt
1 pt. tomatoes
1 can tomato soup
½ c. shredded cheese
Bread crumbs

Cook macaroni and drain. Brown hamburger with onions; add salt, tomatoes and tomato soup. Add macaroni and three-fourths of grated cheese. Place in a greased casserole; sprinkle bread crumbs and remaining cheese over top. Bake at 350 degrees until bubbly. Yield: 6 servings.

Mrs. Tana Saylor
Trinity Women's Guild
Urbana, Illinois

ITALIAN DELIGHT

1 ½ lb. hamburger
1 c. diced carrots
1 c. diced celery
1 onion, chopped
1 green pepper, diced
2 c. cooked macaroni
2 cans tomato sauce
Salt and pepper

Saute hamburger and vegetables until browned; season with salt and pepper. Add all remaining ingredients. Place in a greased casserole. Bake at 350 degrees for 45 minutes. Yield: 6-8 servings.

Mrs. Gertrude Kloth, Pres.
Messiah Ladies Circle
Santa Cruz, California

QUICK CASSEROLE

1 lb. ground beef
1 onion, chopped
1 sm. pkg. macaroni or noodles
1 can corn
1 can tomatoes
Sliced cheese
Salt and pepper to taste

Brown beef and onion. Alternate layers of macaroni, corn, meat mixture and tomatoes in a casserole, placing slices of cheese between each layer. Season. Bake at 250 to 300 degrees for 1 hour. Yield: 14 servings.

Anna Mae Rohmann
St. Mark's Ladies Guild
Flint, Michigan

SMASH-UP IN THE VALLEY

1 onion, finely cut
2 tbsp. shortening
1 lb. hamburger or left-over meat
1 No. 2 can tomatoes
1 can vegetable soup

Box macaroni and cheese dinner
Salt and pepper to taste
½ c. bread crumbs

Saute onion in shortening; brown hamburger in same pan. Add tomatoes and soup. Cook the macaroni dinner according to directions on box, reserving the grated cheese. Add to meat mixture; add salt and pepper. Add one-half the cheese. Pour into well greased baking dish. Top with bread crumbs and remaining cheese. Bake at 375 degrees for 30 minutes. Yield: 6-8 servings.

Mrs. Inez Pape, Pres.
St. Paul's Ladies Aid
Wautoma, Wisconsin

YANKEE DOODLE GOULASH

Diced onions
Margarine
1 lb. hamburger
1 c. raw elbow macaroni, cooked
1 can cream of chicken soup
½ c. water
1 can or 4 fresh tomatoes or ½ c. catsup
Buttered bread crumbs

Brown onions in margarine in skillet; add hamburger and brown thoroughly. Combine onions, hamburger, macaroni, soup, water and tomatoes. Place in casserole. Cover with buttered bread crumbs. Bake at 350 degrees for 1 hour. Yield: 6 servings.

Mrs. Hildegarde M. Snow
Concordia LWML
Shrewsbury, Massachusetts

MOCK DUCK

DRESSING:

4 c. bread crumbs
¾ tsp. sage
½ tsp. salt
Dash of pepper
1 med. onion, chopped
4 tbsp. melted butter

Combine all ingredients; mix well.

BEEF MIXTURE:

2 lb. ground beef
1 c. oats
2 tsp. salt
½ tsp. pepper
2 c. milk
1 can tomato soup

Mix all ingredients except soup. Place one-half the mixture into 8-cup casserole. Place dressing over meat mixture; cover with remaining meat mixture. Bake at 325 degrees for 1 hour and 30 minutes. Remove from oven and cover with tomato soup. Bake for 10 minutes longer. Yield: 6-8 servings.

Mrs. Dennis Peterson, Pres.
Bethlehem LCW
Midale, Saskatchewan, Canada

BEEF CASSEROLE

1 lb. hamburger
1 onion, chopped
Butter
1 pkg. noodles Romanoff
1 can cream of mushroom soup
Crushed Wheaties or potato chips (opt.)

Brown hamburger. Brown onion in a small amount of butter; mix with hamburger. Prepare noodles according to package directions. Alternate layers of meat mixture and noodles in a greased casserole. Pour soup over all. Milk may be added if it seems a little dry. Top with Wheaties. Bake at 350 degrees for 30 to 40 minutes. Yield: 4-6 servings.

Joyce Hansen, Chmn.
Christ Ladies Friendship Soc.
Bouton, Iowa

CASHEW-BEEF BAKE

1 lb. ground beef
1 c. chopped onions
1 c. diced celery
3 tbsp. butter
1 8-oz. pkg. egg noodles
1 can cream of chicken soup
1 can cream of mushroom soup
1 c. milk
1 tsp. salt
¼ tsp. pepper
1 c. salted cashew nuts (opt.)

Brown meat, onions and celery in butter in heavy skillet. Cook noodles; drain. Layer with meat mixture in greased 2-quart casserole. Combine soups, milk and seasonings; pour over casserole. Bake, covered, at 325 degrees for 1 hour. Uncover; sprinkle with nuts. Bake for 10 minutes. Yield: 6-8 servings.

Mrs. Francis I. Root
Lutheran LCW
Rochester, New York
Mrs. Tom Soulek, Pres.
East Lake Andes ALCW
Wagner, South Dakota
Mrs. Gerald Buckentin
Emanuel Ladies Aid
Hamburg, Minnesota

CHILI TOPANGA

4 lb. ground beef
3 onions, chopped
Bacon grease
Salt and pepper to taste
2 12-oz. pkg. noodles

4 12-oz. cans whole kernel corn
5 sm. cans tomato sauce
4 cans cream of mushroom soup
6 to 8 tsp. chili powder
3 to 4 oz. grated American cheese

Brown meat and onions in bacon grease with salt and pepper to taste. Cook noodles according to package directions. Add undrained corn, tomato sauce, soup and chili powder. Bake at 350 degrees for 1 hour. Sprinkle with cheese during the last 30 minutes of baking. Yield: 24 servings.

Marian Hiller, Sec.
Trinity Women's Soc.
Palo Alto, California

COMPANY BEEF CASSEROLE

1 ½ lb. ground beef
¼ c. chopped onion
1 tbsp. fat
¼ c. grated Parmesan cheese
1 tsp. salt
⅛ tsp. pepper
¼ tsp. ground oregano
2 cans tomato soup
3 c. cooked white noodles
½ c. sliced stuffed olives
Crushed barbecue or plain potato chips

Brown ground beef and onion in fat; pour off excess fat. Combine cheese, salt, pepper, oregano and 1 can soup. Combine noodles, olives and remaining soup. Place one-half of noodle mixture in a baking dish; top with one-half meat mixture. Repeat layers. Top with crushed potato chips. Bake at 350 degrees for 30 to 35 minutes or until lightly browned. Yield: 6-8 servings.

Mrs. Erwin Moldenhauer
St. Paul's Dorcas Soc.
Holstein, Nebraska

COMPANY CASSEROLE

1 5 to 8-oz. pkg. medium noodles
2 tbsp. butter
1 ½ lb. ground beef
1 tsp. salt
Pepper to taste
¼ tsp. garlic salt
1 8-oz. can tomato sauce
1 c. creamy cottage cheese
1 c. sour cream
2 to 6 green onions, chopped
¾ c. sharp American cheese, grated

Cook noodles until tender in boiling salted water; drain. Rinse with cold water. Melt butter in skillet; add meat. Cook, stirring, until meat has lost red color; add salt, pepper, garlic salt and tomato sauce. Simmer gently for 5 minutes. Remove from heat. Combine cottage cheese, sour cream, onions and noodles. Alternate layers of noodles and meat mixture in a 3-quart casserole; top with grated cheese. Bake at 350 degrees

(Continued on next page)

for 30 minutes or until brown on top. Yield: 8-10 servings.

Mrs. Walter Johanning
Holy Cross Ladies Aid
Renault, Illinois
Mrs. Adolph H. Prange
Holy Cross Ladies Aid
Prairie DuRocher, Illinois
Mrs. Paul Schwein
Trinity Ladies Aid
Russell, Kansas

EASY CASSEROLE

4 c. cooked fine noodles
1 c. cottage cheese
1 8-oz. pkg. cream cheese
¼ c. sour cream
1 sm. onion, chopped
1 lb. ground chuck
1 can tomato sauce

Place noodles in greased casserole; mix cottage cheese with cream cheese, sour cream and onion. Place cheese mixture over noodles. Spread with meat; top with tomato sauce. Heat through in oven.

Mrs. E. A. Silsby, Pres.
Rogate Ladies Guild
Largo, Florida

FOR THE CROWD CASSEROLE

1 ½ lb. ground beef
1 c. chopped onions
1 12-oz. can peas or whole kernel corn
1 can cream of chicken soup
1 can cream of mushroom soup
1 c. sour cream
¼ c. chopped pimento
¾ tsp. salt
½ tsp. monosodium glutamate
¼ tsp. pepper
4 to 6 oz. medium wide noodles
1 c. buttered soft bread crumbs

Brown meat; add onions and cook until tender but not brown. Add peas, soups, sour cream, pimento, salt, monosodium glutamate and pepper. Mix well. Cook and drain noodles; stir into mixture. Pour into 2-quart casserole. Sprinkle crumbs over top. Bake at 350 degrees for 30 minutes to 1 hour. Yield: 8-12 servings.

Loretta V. Dixon, Pres.
Zion Ladies Aid
McHenry, Illinois
Mrs. Lester E. Salka, Pres.
St. John's Ladies Aid Soc.
Meriden, Connecticut
Mrs. Martha Estock, Pres.
St. Mark's Ladies Aid Soc.
Cleveland, Ohio
Francis R. Lindahl, VP
Park View ALCW
Skokie, Illinois

GROUND MEAT HOT DISH

1 8-oz. pkg. noodles,
1 can cream of chicken soup
1 can cream of mushroom soup
1 lb. ground beef
1 c. chopped onions
1 c. chopped celery
1 ¼ c. milk
1 tsp. salt

Mix all ingredients in bowl. Pour into greased casserole. Bake at 275 degrees for 2 hours. Yield: 8 servings.

Mrs. Armas Abrahamson
First Lutheran Church Ladies Aid
Grand Marais, Michigan

HAMBURGER-NOODLE CASSEROLE

1 lb. hamburger
1 c. finely chopped celery
1 onion, finely chopped
1 can chicken-rice soup
1 can cream of mushroom soup
1 soup can water
1 sm. can chow mein noodles

Brown hamburger, celery and onion; add soups and water. Pour into a 8 x 12-inch or 9 x 9-inch baking dish; cover. Bake at 350 degrees for 30 minutes. Uncover; add noodles. Bake, uncovered, for 30 minutes longer. If desired, sprinkle each serving with additional noodles. Yield: 6-8 servings.

Mrs. Pete Mazelin
Trinity Ladies Aid
Ligonier, Indiana

HAMBURGER-NOODLE CASSEROLE

1 tbsp. shortening
1 lb. ground beef
½ tsp. salt
⅛ tsp. pepper
1 c. catsup
2 8-oz. cans tomato sauce
½ lb. narrow noodles, cooked and drained
½ lb. grated Cheddar cheese

Heat shortening in heavy skillet; add meat. Saute until lightly browned; add salt, pepper, catsup and tomato sauce, blending well. Stir in cooked noodles. Spoon mixture into lightly buttered 2 1/2-quart baking dish or casserole. Sprinkle top with grated cheese. Bake at 350 degrees for 25 to 30 minutes or until bubbly and cheese melts. Yield: 4 servings.

Mrs. Joyce Anderson
Our Savior Ladies Guild
Centereach, New York

HEAVENLY HASH

1 lb. hamburger
1 med. onion, chopped
½ c. wide noodles, cooked
1 15-oz. can whole kernel corn

(Continued on next page)

½ tsp. salt
1 20-oz. can tomatoes
1 10-oz. can vegetable soup
⅛ tsp. pepper
½ c. crushed crackers

Fry meat and onions; remove from heat. Place in roaster; add remaining ingredients except cracker crumbs. Mix well. Cover with cracker crumbs. Bake at 375 degrees for 1 hour. Yield: 6 servings.

Mrs. Aron Scansen, Pres.
South Immanuel LCW
Cadillac, Saskatchewan, Canada

HOT DISH DELICIOUS

1 sm. onion, chopped
1 c. chopped celery
3 tbsp. chopped green pepper
Butter
1 lb. ground beef
1 tsp. salt
Pepper to taste
½ c. milk
¼ c. mayonnaise
1 can cream of mushroom soup
1 can cream of chicken soup
1 4-oz. pkg. noodles
Cracker crumbs

Brown onion, celery and green pepper in a small amount of butter. Add ground beef and seasonings; brown beef. Blend milk and mayonnaise. Add soups and mayonnaise mixture to ground beef mixture. Cook noodles according to package directions; chop slightly. Combine noodles and meat mixture; place in greased casserole. Top with cracker crumbs. Bake at 350 degrees for one hour.

Mrs. Robert E. Till
Mt. Calvary Lutheran Church
Watonga, Oklahoma

JOHN BEN GETTY

3 tbsp. butter
1 ½ lb. hamburger
2 med. onions, minced
1 green pepper, minced
1 7-oz. pkg. noodles, cooked
1 can peas
1 can tomato soup
1 can cream of mushroom soup
Salt and pepper to taste
Grated cheese

Melt butter in skillet. Cook hamburger, onion and pepper in butter until done, but not brown. Add noodles and peas; stir well. Add soups, salt and pepper. Place in casserole. Bake at 350 degrees for 45 minutes. Sprinkle with cheese. Bake for 10 minutes longer. Yield: 12 servings.

Mrs. Hertha Else
Trinity Ladies Aid
Schleswig, Iowa

JON BEN GETTY CASSEROLE

2 ½ lb. ground beef
1 lge. onion, chopped
1 12-oz. pkg. noodles
1 lb. Velveeta or American cheese
1 No. 2 can peas, drained
2 cans cream of mushroom soup
1 can cream of chicken soup
1 qt. milk
Crushed potato chips, buttered crumbs or crackers

Brown meat in skillet with onion. Add a small amount water. Simmer for 30 minutes to 1 hour. Cool noodles and drain. Mix all ingredients except potato chips in casserole; top with crushed potato chips. Bake at 350 degrees for 1 hour. Yield: 20 servings.

Mrs. Grethel Gardner
Peace Ladies Soc.
Des Moines, Iowa

HURRY-UP LASAGNA

1 lb. ground beef
½ tsp. salt
1 tsp. monosodium glutamate
⅛ tsp. pepper
1 sm. onion, diced
2 tbsp. corn oil
2 8-oz. cans tomato sauce
1 6-oz. can pizza sauce
1 c. water
8 oz. lasagna noodles
6 slices American cheese

Sprinkle beef with salt, monosodium glutamate and pepper. Toss gently with fork. Brown with onion in heated oil in skillet. Add sauces and water. Bring to a boil; reduce heat and simmer for 20 minutes. Cook noodles according to package directions. Alternate layers of beef mixture, cheese and noodles in 9 x 13-inch baking dish, ending with cheese. Bake at 375 degrees for 20 minutes. Yield: 6 servings.

Mrs. R. Goodridge, Pres.
Resurrection Ladies Guild
St. Louis, Missouri

LASAGNA

1 ½ lb. ground beef
2 tsp. seasoned salt
2 cloves of garlic
½ tsp. pepper
1 1-lb. 13-oz. can tomatoes
2 sm. cans tomato sauce
1 pkg. spaghetti sauce mix
½ lb. lasagna noodles
½ lb. Mozzarella cheese, sliced
½ lb. Ricotta cheese or cottage cheese, well rinsed
½ c. Parmesan cheese

Brown meat. Add seasonings; simmer for 10 minutes. Add tomatoes, tomato sauce and spaghetti mix; simmer for 30 minutes. Boil noodles until tender; drain and rinse. Pour one-third of

(Continued on next page)

meat mixture in 12 x 8 x 2-inch dish; cover with noodles. Arrange slices of Mozzarella and Ricotta over top. Repeat layers, ending with meat sauce. Sprinkle Parmesan cheese over top. Bake at 350 degrees for 30 minutes. Yield: 6-8 servings.

Mrs. Marvin Swanson, Sec.
Trinity LWML
Brawley, California

LASAGNA

1 lge. onion, chopped
2 lb. ground beef
1 tsp. salt
¼ tsp. pepper
½ stick margarine
1 qt. tomatoes
1 sm. can tomato paste
½ c. water
1 clove of garlic, minced
2 bay leaves

Brown onion, ground beef, salt and pepper in margarine; add tomatoes, tomato paste, water, garlic and bay leaves. Simmer for 45 minutes.

SAUCE:

½ c. margarine
3 tbsp. flour
2 c. milk
1 8-oz. pkg. American cheese, diced
1 egg, beaten
1 8-oz. pkg. lasagna noodles, cooked and
    drained

Melt margarine; blend in flour. Gradually stir in milk, cheese and egg; cook until thick. Alternate layers of noodles, meat sauce and cheese sauce in 13 x 9-inch pan, ending with noodles. Bake at 325 to 350 degrees for 40 minutes. Yield: 12-15 servings.

Millie Peters
St. John's Ladies Aid
Yuma, Colorado

LASAGNA

1 sm. onion, finely chopped
½ green pepper, diced
1 clove of garlic, minced (opt.)
Olive oil
1 lb. ground round steak
1 can tomatoes
1 can tomato puree
1 can tomato paste
½ c. red wine
Oregano
Parsley flakes
Salt and pepper to taste
½ stick margarine
2 tbsp. flour
1 c. milk
1 lb. grated Mozzarella cheese
½ c. cottage cheese
1 egg, beaten
6 lasagna noodles, cooked
1 c. Parmesan cheese

Brown onion, green pepper and garlic in olive oil; add ground meat and brown slightly. Add tomatoes, tomato puree, tomato paste, wine, herbs and seasonings. Simmer for 1 hour. Melt margarine; blend in flour. Gradually stir in milk; cook until thick. Add Mozzarella cheese; stir until blended. Combine cottage cheese and egg; add to sauce. Line a baking dish with one-half of noodles. Pour one-half of sauces over noodles; sprinkle 1/2 cup Parmesan cheese. Repeat. Bake at 350 degrees for 30 minutes. Yield: 6-8 servings.

Mrs. Hilda Bodendieck
Mt. Calvary LLL
Cahokia, Illinois

LASAGNA CASSEROLE

MEAT SAUCE:

1 lb. hamburger or Italian sausage
1 clove of garlic, minced
1 tbsp. whole basil
1 ½ tsp. salt
2 c. canned tomatoes
2 6-oz. cans tomato paste

Brown meat slowly; spoon off fat. Add remaining ingredients except noodles; simmer for 30 minutes, stirring occasionally.

CHEESE FILLING:

3 c. cottage cheese
2 tbsp. parsley flakes
½ c. grated Parmesan cheese
2 eggs, beaten
2 tsp. salt
½ tsp. pepper
1 lb. Mozzarella cheese, sliced
1 10-oz. pkg. wide noodles, cooked

Mix all ingredients except Mozzarella cheese and noodles; place one-half the noodles in a 13 x 9 x 2-inch baking dish. Spread with one-half of the cheese filling. Cover with one-half the Mozzarella cheese and one-half the Meat Sauce. Repeat layers. Bake at 375 degrees for 30 minutes. Let stand for 10 minutes; cut into squares. Yield: 12 servings.

Mrs. Karl Maier, Past Pres.
Bethany-Trinity Ladies Aid Soc.
Waynesboro, Virginia
Mrs. Ivan G. Althouse, Jr.
Christ Lutheran Mary Martha Soc.
Lynch, Nebraska

MAIN DISH CASSEROLE

1 lb. ground beef
2 stalks celery, minced
1 sm. onion, minced
1 8-oz. pkg. noodles
1 10-oz. can cream of chicken soup
1 10-oz. can cream of mushroom soup
Salt and pepper to taste
½ can Chinese noodles

(Continued on next page)

Combine meat with celery and onion in a heavy fry pan; cook until meat looses pink color. Cook noodles according to directions on package. Combine meat, noodles, soups, salt and pepper. Place in casserole. Garnish with Chinese noodles. Bake, uncovered, at 350 degrees for 30 minutes or until heated through. NOTE: Grated cheese may be substituted for Chinese noodles. Yield: 12 servings.

Mrs. W. J. Christians, Pres.
St. Peter's Ladies Aid
Woolstock, Iowa

SUNDAY SUPPER HAMBURGER

1 c. diced onions
2 tbsp. butter
1 ½ lb. hamburger
1 8-oz. pkg. noodles, cooked and drained
1 can chicken soup
1 can cream of mushroom soup
1 ¼ c. sour cream
1 12-oz. can whole kernel corn
1 ½ tsp. salt
¼ tsp. pepper
1 c. crushed wheat flakes

Brown onion lightly in butter; add hamburger and brown. Combine all remaining ingredients except wheat flakes. Blend well. Turn into buttered 7 1/2 x 11 3/4 x 1 3/4-inch baking dish. Top with crushed wheat flakes. Bake at 350 degrees for 45 minutes. Yield: 8-10 servings.

Mrs. M. Strand, Pres.
Zion Church Ladies Group
Nielsville, Minnesota

SUPER MEAT CASSEROLE

1 6-oz. pkg. wide noodles
6 c. water
1 tsp. salt
1 tbsp. chopped onion
1 lb. ground beef
½ c. diced celery
1 tbsp. butter
1 tsp. prepared mustard
3 to 4 c. tomato juice
½ tsp. celery salt

Cook noodles in water with salt until tender; drain. Saute onion, beef and celery in butter until celery is transparent. Add mustard, tomato juice and celery salt; heat to boiling. Add noodles; pour into 1 1/2-quart greased casserole. Bake at 350 degrees for 45 minutes. Sprinkle with paprika and garnish with pickled green pepper strips, if desired. Yield: 8 servings.

Mrs. L. F. Kraft, Rec. Sec.
St. Mathew's LCW
Honover, Ontario, Canada

TAGLIARINI

2 lb. ground beef
1 med. onion, chopped
1 green pepper, chopped

2 tbsp. drippings
1 can whole kernel corn, drained
1 lge. can mushrooms
2 cans tomato soup
1 can tomato sauce
1 tsp. chili powder
1 8-oz. pkg. fine noodles
Grated American cheese
1 can pitted ripe olives

Saute meat, onion and green pepper in drippings; add corn. Drain mushrooms, reserving liquid. Mix soup, sauce, chili powder and mushroom liquid. Place a layer of noodles in a large, shallow greased baking dish; add a layer of meat and sauce. Repeat layers. Sprinkle top generously with cheese. Press olives halfway down into cheese. Bake at 250 degrees for 2 hours. Yield: 12 servings.

Mrs. Harvey Shane, Pres.
Trinity LWML
Parsons, Kansas

TAGLIARINI

1 lb. hamburger
1 onion, chopped
2 tbsp. butter
1 can tomato soup
1 c. water
2 c. noodles, cooked and drained
1 can whole kernel corn
1 can pitted ripe olives
Salt and pepper to taste
1 c. grated cheese

Brown hamburger and onion in butter; add all remaining ingredients except cheese. Place in casserole; sprinkle with cheese. Bake at 350 degrees for 45 minutes. Yield: 6 servings.

Mrs. Katherine Dornow
St. Paul's Ladies Aid Soc.
Angelica, New York

TRUDY'S CASSEROLE

2 lb. ground beef
1 med. onion
1 sm. jar stuffed olives, chopped
1 c. cream of mushroom soup
1 ½ c. milk
Salt
1 8-oz. pkg. noodles, cooked
10 oz. sharp Cheddar cheese, grated
1 c. Chinese noodles
1 pkg. salted nuts

Cook meat and onion until meat is brown; add olives, soup and milk. Salt to taste. Place cooked noodles in bottom of casserole; add meat mixture. Spread cheese over meat. Top with Chinese noodles and chopped nuts. Bake at 350 degrees for 30 minutes or until hot and bubbly. Yield: 10-12 servings.

Mrs. C. Witte, Advisor
Trinity Ladies Aid
Vesper, Wisconsin

PERFECT COMPANY CASSEROLE

2 lb. ground beef
½ c. sour cream
3 tbsp. dried onion soup mix
1 egg, slightly beaten
1 ½ c. soft bread crumbs
¼ c. butter or margarine
1 8-oz. can mushrooms, undrained
1 10 ½-oz. can cream of chicken soup
1 ⅔ c. water

Combine beef, sour cream, onion soup mix, egg and crumbs; shape into 16 balls. Brown in butter. Add mushrooms, soup and water. Simmer for 20 minutes, adding additional water if needed. Place in 3-quart casserole.

BUTTER CRUMB DUMPLINGS:

2 c. sifted flour
4 tsp. baking powder
1 tbsp. poppy seed
1 tsp. celery salt
1 tsp. poultry seasoning
2 tsp. dried onion flakes
¼ c. oil
¾ c. plus 2 tbsp. milk
¼ c. melted butter or margarine
2 c. soft bread crumbs

Mix dry ingredients and seasonings; blend in oil and milk. Stir melted butter into crumbs. Drop dough by tablespoonfuls in 12 equal portions into buttered crumbs; roll to cover with crumbs. Place on top of casserole. Bake at 400 degrees for 20 to 25 minutes or until dumplings are golden. Yield: 8 servings.

Mrs. Dolores Lund, Pres.
Immanual Miss'y Guild
Loveland, Colorado

AMERICAN CHOW MEIN

1 lb. ground beef
1 lge. onion, chopped
2 tbsp. fat
1 c. chopped celery
½ c. rice
1 can chicken gumbo soup
1 can cream of mushroom soup
1 ½ tbsp. soy sauce
1 c. chow mein noodles

Brown ground beef and onion in fat. Add celery, rice, soups and soy sauce. Stir to blend; pour into 1 1/2-quart casserole. Bake at 350 degrees for 1 hour. Add chow mein noodles over top. Yield: 6 servings.

Mrs. Velma Novak
Bethlehem Ladies Aid Soc.
Crete, Nebraska

BAKED CHOP SUEY

1 lb. hamburger
1 c. diced onions or 2 onions, chopped
1 to 2 c. diced celery (opt.)
¼ c. butter or shortening (opt.)

1 can chicken noodle or cream of chicken
   soup
1 can cream of mushroom soup
Pepper to taste
1 tsp. salt
1 sm. can peas (opt.)
1 ½ to 2 c. water
2 to 4 tbsp. soy sauce
½ c. uncooked rice
1 3-oz. can chow mein noodles (opt.)
Pepper to taste

Saute hamburger, onions and celery in butter until hamburger is well broken up and light brown. Combine soups, pepper, salt, peas and water; add to hamburger mixture. Add soy sauce and rice. Place in a small roaster or cake pan. Bake at 325 to 350 degrees for 1 hour and 15 minutes to 1 hour and 30 minutes, stirring occasionally. Cover top with chow mein noodles; bake for 15 to 30 minutes longer. Watch closely so noodles will not burn. Yield: 6-8 servings.

Mrs. Mabel Schrankel
St. John's Evening Guild
Shell Lake, Wisconsin
Mrs. John Gaeke, Pres.
Salem LCW
Temple, Texas

BAKED CHOP SUEY

1 ½ lb. ground beef
½ c. chopped onion
½ c. chopped celery
1 can cream of chicken soup
1 can cream of mushroom soup
1 can chop suey vegetables
¼ c. soy sauce
1 c. cooked rice
Corn flake crumbs

Brown beef, onion and celery. Add remaining ingredients except corn flake crumbs; mix well. Place mixture in foil-lined roaster pan. Sprinkle with corn flake crumbs. Bake in 350 degree oven for 1 hour. Yield: 12 servings.

Agnes Troth, Treas.
Redeemer Ladies Aid
Joliet, Illinois

BAKED CHOP SUEY

1 lb. ground beef
1 can cream of mushroom soup
2 soup cans water
1 ½ c. chopped celery
Salt and pepper to taste
3 tbsp. soy sauce
1 c. rice
1 sm. onion, grated or chopped
1 green pepper, grated or chopped
1 can tomato paste (opt.)
Tabasco sauce (opt.)

Brown ground beef in a skillet. Add remaining ingredients. Place in greased casserole. Bake at 325 degrees for 1 hour and 30 minutes, stirring

(Continued on next page)

every 30 minutes. Add a little more water, if necessary. Yield: 6-8 servings.

Mrs. Charles Fiddes, Treas.
Faith Dorcas Soc.
Seaside, Oregon

BEEF CHOW MEIN

1 lb. ground beef
1 med. onion, chopped
2 stalks celery, diced
1 c. cooked rice
1 can cream of chicken soup
1 can cream of mushroom soup
½ c. water
3 tbsp. soy sauce
Chow mein noodles

Cook beef in large skillet until brown; pour off fat. Add remaining ingredients except noodles; mix well. Pour into a greased baking dish; top generously with chow mein noodles. Bake at 350 degrees for 30 minutes. Yield: 8 servings.

Mrs. J. R. Brinkhoff
Holy Cross LWML
Tuscaloosa, Alabama

BEEF-RICE CASSEROLE

1 ¼ lb. ground beef
1 sm. onion, diced
1 c. diced celery
½ c. uncooked rice
2 c. water
1 can cream of mushroom soup
1 can chicken with rice soup
2 tbsp. Worcestershire sauce
3 tbsp. soy sauce
1 sm. can peas
1 4-oz. can Chinese noodles

Brown beef and onion in a small amount of fat. Mix all ingredients except noodles in a large bowl. Pour into casserole dish or 8 x 8 x 2-inch baking dish. Bake at 350 degrees for 1 hour. Sprinkle with Chinese noodles. Bake for 30 minutes longer.

Mrs. Joseph P. Fabry
Faith Lutheran Church
Dunnville, Ontario, Canada

CHINESE HAMBURGER HASH

1 lb. hamburger
2 tbsp. oil (opt.)
2 med. onions, chopped
1 to 2 c. sliced celery
¼ c. soy sauce
¼ tsp. pepper
1 10 ½-oz. can cream of mushroom soup
1 10 ½-oz. can cream of chicken soup
1 ½ to 2 c. water
1 sm. can mushroom stems and pieces (opt.)
½ c. uncooked rice
1 can dry Chinese noodles

Brown meat in oil until crumbly; add more oil if necessary. Add onions, celery, soy sauce and pepper. Add soups; rinse cans with the water and add to meat mixture. Stir in mushrooms and rice. Pour into lightly greased casserole. Cover and bake at 350 degrees for 30 to 45 minutes. Uncover; bake for 30 to 45 minutes longer. Sprinkle with noodles; bake for 15 minutes longer. Yield: 8-12 servings.

Mrs. Kenneth Adams, Pres.
Trinity Ladies Guild
Walla Walla, Washington
Mrs. Richard Lammers
St. John's Ladies Aid
Alta, Iowa

CHOP SUEY CASSEROLE

2 lb. ground beef
2 c. sliced celery
1 c. chopped onions
⅔ c. rice
2 cans cream of mushroom soup
2 cans cream of chicken soup
Chow mein noodles

Brown beef; add all ingredients except noodles. Mix well. Bake in covered casserole at 350 degrees for 50 minutes. Cover with chow mein noodles; bake, uncovered, for 15 minutes longer. Yield: 10-12 servings.

Mrs. Glenn J. Deringer
Mt. Calvary Ladies Aid
Janesville, Wisconsin

CHOW MEIN CASSEROLE

1 lb. ground beef
1 sm. onion, diced
1 c. diced celery
2 tbsp. oil
1 can cream of mushroom soup
1 can mushrooms and liquid
1 can bean sprouts and liquid
½ c. water
½ c. uncooked rice
¼ c. soy sauce

Brown ground beef with onion and celery in oil. Combine all ingredients; pour into casserole. Bake at 350 degrees for 1 hour. Serve with chow mein noodles. Yield: 8 servings.

Mrs. Betty Hanson
Trinity Ladies Aid Soc.
Gillett, Wisconsin

CHOW MEIN HOT DISH

1 lb. hamburger
2 onions, chopped
1 c. uncooked rice
2 c. chopped celery
⅓ c. soy sauce
1 sm. can mushrooms
1 can cream of mushroom soup
3 soup cans water

(Continued on next page)

Brown meat slightly; add onions. Simmer slowly for 5 minutes. Add remaining ingredients. Place in baking dish. Bake at 350 degrees for 1 hour, stirring often. Yield: 6 servings.

Mrs. Lydia Wendling
Grace Ladies Guild
Longview, Washington

GROUND BEEF CASSEROLE

1 lb. ground beef
1 sm. onion, chopped
1 tsp. salt
½ tsp. coarsely ground pepper or
   seasoned pepper
⅓ c. uncooked rice
1 can cream of mushroom soup
1 can chicken noodle soup
1 ½ soup cans milk
Crushed potato chips (opt.)
Grated cheese (opt.)

Brown ground beef and onion; season. Add rice, soups and milk. Mix and place in casserole. Sprinkle crushed potato chips or grated cheese on top to cover. Bake at 375 degrees for 1 hour. Yield: 8 servings.

Ruth M. Knuth
Trinity LWML
Muskegon Heights, Michigan

HAMBURGER CHOW MEIN

1 to 1 ½ lb. hamburger
1 or 2 sm. onions, chopped
1 c. diced celery
2 to 2 ½ c. water
½ c. uncooked rice
1 can cream of mushroom soup
1 can cream of chicken soup
4 tbsp. soy sauce
2 tbsp. Worcestershire sauce (opt.)
1 can chow mein noodles

Brown hamburger and onion. Add remaining ingredients except noodles in 9 x 13-inch pan. Bake at 350 degrees for 1 hour to 1 hour and 30 minutes. Sprinkle with noodles; bake for 15 to 30 minutes longer. NOTE: May be baked in casserole or bean pot.

Mrs. Art Smith
Trinity Ladies Aid
Jansen, Nebraska
Mrs. Doris Foerster, Cor. Sec.
Our Savior Afternoon Division Women's Guild
Chicago, Illinois

MEAT CASSEROLE

½ c. chopped onion
½ c. diced celery
Butter
1 lb. hamburger
1 pkg. chicken-noodle soup mix
½ c. uncooked rice
⅓ c. soy sauce
1 can sliced mushrooms, undrained
2 c. boiling water
Chow mein noodles

Saute onion and celery in butter; add hamburger and brown. Add remaining ingredients except chow mein noodles. Pour into casserole; sprinkle with noodles. Bake at 350 degrees for 45 minutes. Yield: 6 servings.

Mrs. Jacob Rotheisler
Peace LWML
Gravelbourgh, Saskatchewan, Canada

MEAT IN CASSEROLE

1 lb. hamburger
½ c. uncooked rice
2 sm. onions, chopped
Salt and pepper
2 c. canned tomatoes

Mix meat, rice and onions; season to taste. Mix well. Shape into patties or place mixture in casserole. Pour tomatoes over mixture. Bake at 375 degrees for 45 minutes to 1 hour or until rice is done. Yield: 6 servings.

Mrs. Paul Stelter
Trinity LWML
Montello, Wisconsin

ONE-DISH MEAL SUPREME

4 med. potatoes, sliced
4 lge. carrots, sliced
1 lge. onion, chopped
⅓ c. uncooked rice
2 tsp. salt
Pepper
1 lb. hamburger
3 c. tomato juice

Place vegetables and rice in layers in greased casserole; add salt and pepper. Pat out hamburger to fit casserole; place on top. Cover with juice. Bake at 350 degrees for 1 hour and 30 minutes. Yield: 5-6 servings.

Mrs. Gene Richter
Peace Lutheran Church
Marcus, Iowa

PEPPY STUFFED PEPPERS

4 green peppers
1 lb. ground beef
2 c. cooked rice
¼ c. chopped onion (opt.)
1 ½ tsp. salt
⅛ tsp. pepper
1 15-oz. can tomato sauce

Cut peppers into halves lengthwise; remove seed and wash. Combine ground beef, rice, onion, salt, pepper and 1/4 can tomato sauce. Pile meat mixture lightly into pepper halves; place in large baking dish. Top each pepper with remaining tomato sauce. Cover dish tightly. Bake in 350 degree oven for 1 hour and 20 minutes, or until peppers are tender. Baste occasionally. Yield: 4-6 servings.

Mrs. C. W. Lizotte, Pres.
Immanuel LWML
Pensacola, Florida

ORIENTAL CASSEROLE

1 ½ lb. lean ground beef
2 c. chopped onions
1 c. sliced celery
2 tbsp. fat or salad oil
⅛ tsp. pepper
⅓ c. soy sauce
⅔ c. uncooked rice
1 4-oz. can water chestnuts
1 4-oz. can mushroom pieces, undrained

Cook beef, onions and celery in hot fat until meat is lightly browned; pour off drippings. Add pepper, soy sauce and rice. Add enough water to liquids drained from water chestnuts and mushrooms to make 2 cups. Heat to boiling; add with water chestnuts and mushrooms to meat mixture. Mix lightly; pour into greased 2-quart casserole. Cover tightly and bake at 350 degrees for 1 hour. Yield: 8-10 servings.

Mrs. Bonnie Egger, Sec.
Our Savior LWML
Muscatine, Iowa

POOR MAN'S DISH

1 lb. hamburger
1 med. onion, chopped
1 tbsp. salt
¼ tsp. pepper
4 c. sliced potatoes
1 c. sliced carrots
¼ c. uncooked rice
1 c. peas
1 can tomato soup
1 ½ c. water

Combine hamburger, onion and seasonings; brown. Place alternate layers of potatoes, carrots, rice, peas and hamburger mixture in casserole. Combine soup and water; pour over casserole. Bake at 350 degrees for 1 hour or until tender. Yield: 7 servings.

Dora Bristol
St. Matthew's Ladies Aid
White Lake, Wisconsin

QUICK CASSEROLE

1 lb. ground beef
1 med. onion, chopped
½ c. chopped celery (opt.)
1 pt. canned tomatoes
4 c. water
1 tbsp. chili powder
⅔ c. uncooked rice
1 envelope dry chicken noodle soup

Fry ground beef until brown; add onion and celery. Cook for about 5 minutes; add tomatoes, 1 cup water and chili powder. Simmer. Boil 3 cups water in saucepan; add rice and soup. Return to boil; add to meat mixture. Place in 3-quart casserole. Bake at 350 degrees for 30 minutes. Yield: 6-8 servings.

Mrs. Emmett Werchan, Sec.
Grace LWML
Coupland, Texas

QUICK HAMBURGER CASSEROLE

¾ lb. hamburger
2 tbsp. cooking oil
3 med. potatoes, sliced
Salt and pepper to taste
3 med. carrots, sliced
½ c. uncooked rice
1 onion, sliced
2 c. tomatoes
Buttered bread crumbs

Brown hamburger in oil. Place potatoes in bottom of greased casserole; season with salt and pepper. Layer carrots over potatoes; season with salt and pepper. Sprinkle rice over carrots. Spread hamburger over rice. Top with onion. Pour tomatoes over mixture; top with bread crumbs. Bake, uncovered, at 350 degrees for 1 hour. Yield: 6 servings.

Georgeanna Kleen, Sec.
Elk Mountain Ladies Aid
Elk Mountain, Wyoming

SEVEN-LAYER CASSEROLE

¾ c. uncooked rice
1 c. canned whole kernel corn
Salt and pepper to taste
2 cans tomato sauce
¾ sauce can water
½ c. finely chopped onion
½ c. finely chopped green pepper
1 lb. uncooked ground beef
4 strips bacon, cut into halves

Place rice in 2-quart baking dish; top with corn. Sprinkle with salt and pepper. Pour 1 can tomato sauce and one-half sauce can of water over top. Sprinkle onion and pepper over mixture. Sprinkle ground beef over top; season with additional salt and pepper. Pour remaining sauce and water over mixture. Top with bacon. Cover tightly. Bake at 350 degrees for 1 hour. Uncover; bake for 30 minutes longer.

Mrs. Charles Paar, Pres.
St. Mark's Ladies Aid
Waco, Texas

SPANISH RICE

1 lb. hamburger
1 tsp. onion flakes
Salt and pepper to taste
⅔ c. rice
1 28-oz. can tomatoes

Place a layer of hamburger in large casserole; sprinkle with onion flakes, salt and pepper. Add a layer of rice. Repeat layers. Pour tomatoes over all. Add a small amount of water. Bake at 350 degrees for 1 hour. Yield: 6 servings.

Mrs. Arnold Dyke
Trinity LWML
Rocanville, Saskatchewan, Canada

SUPPER CASSEROLE

⅔ c. uncooked rice
1 lb. hamburger
1 c. cut up celery
⅓ c. finely chopped onion
½ c. diced green pepper
1 No. 2 can tomatoes
2 c. water
2 tsp. salt
½ tsp. pepper

Mix all ingredients; pour into 3-quart casserole. Bake at 350 degrees for 1 hour and 30 minutes or until rice is tender. Yield: 6-8 servings.

Henrietta Link
St. Paul's Ladies Aid
Angelica, New York

TEXAS HASH

2 lb. ground beef
1 sm. onion, diced
3 tbsp. diced green pepper
1 tsp. salt
Pepper to taste
1 lge. can tomato juice
1 c. uncooked rice

Brown beef, onion and pepper; add seasonings. Place in large casserole. Add tomato juice and rice; mix well. Cover; bake at 375 degrees for 1 hour and 30 minutes. Yield: 6 servings.

Mrs. Norman Berning
Our Redeemer Ladies Aid
Knox, Indiana

TEXAS HASH

2 onions, diced
2 green peppers, finely chopped (opt.)
3 tbsp. fat
1 lb. ground beef
⅔ to 1 c. uncooked rice
1 qt. tomatoes
1 tsp. salt
¼ tsp. pepper (opt.)
½ to 1 tsp. chili powder

Brown onions and green peppers in fat; add ground beef. Brown. Add rice, tomatoes and seasonings. Place in baking dish. Bake at 350 degrees for 45 minutes to 1 hour. NOTE: One can tomato soup plus 1 soup can water may be substituted for tomatoes. Yield: 6-8 servings.

Mrs. Bill Hansen, Treas.
St. Paul's Ladies Aid
Wakefield, Nebraska
Anna Kopp, Key Lady
Concordia Ladies Aid
Cleveland, Ohio

CHOPPED BEEF CASSEROLE

1 lb. chopped beef
1 lge. onion, chopped
1 can mixed vegetables
1 can cream of mushroom soup
1 lge. can spaghetti
Crushed potato chips

Brown meat and onion. Drain vegetagles, reserving juice. Dilute soup with reserved juice. Layer spaghetti, meat, vegetables and potato chips alternately in casserole. Pour mushroom soup over casserole; top with potato chips. Bake at 325 degrees for 45 minutes. Yield: 6 servings.

Mrs. Arnold Kriplean
St. Paul's Ladies Aid
Sheboygan, Wisconsin

GOOD MEAT-SPAGHETTI CASSEROLE

2 c. spaghetti
3 c. boiling water
1 tsp. salt
1 onion, finely cut
2 tbsp. butter
1 lb. ground beef or hamburger
1 green pepper, minced
1 sm. bottle stuffed olives, sliced
1 can tomato soup
2 c. canned tomatoes

Cook spaghetti in boiling water with salt until tender; drain and blanch. Saute onion until light brown in butter. Add meat and cook until well seared. Add remaining ingredients except one-half of cheese. Mix well. Add spaghetti. Place in 2-quart covered casserole. Top with remaining cheese. Bake at 325 degrees for 1 hour. NOTE: This may be made and frozen until ready to use.

Mrs. George Nielsen, VP
Bethesda LCW
Creighton, Nebraska

SPAGHETTI AND MEAT

4 lb. ground beef
8 med. onions, chopped
3 tbsp. salt
2 tsp. pepper
2 lb. uncooked spaghetti, broken into 2-in. pieces
3 qt. tomato juice
6 c. catsup

Brown meat and onions in fat in oven or electric roaster at 500 degrees; cover roaster while meat is browning. Add remaining ingredients; mix well. Cover; cook at 375 degrees for 1 hour and 15 minutes or until spaghetti is done. Yield: 50 servings.

Mrs. Clifford Cross, Christen Serv.
Hope Evangelical LCW
Minneapolis, Minnesota

ONE-DISH MEAL

1 lb. ground beef
½ c. chopped onion
Salt and pepper to taste
2 stalks celery, cut up
1 c. peas
1 c. kidney beans
½ c. catsup
1 can spaghetti with cheese

Brown ground beef and onions in skillet; salt and pepper. Add remaining ingredients; mix well. Place in baking dish. Bake at 350 degrees for 30 minutes.

Mrs. Ed Leeds
St. John's Ladies Aid
Boyer, Iowa

TAMALE PIE

2 lb. ground beef
1 onion, chopped
2 8-oz. cans tomato sauce
4 4-oz. frozen tamales, thawed and cut up
1 can whole kernel corn
Salt and pepper to taste
1 can pitted black olives
Grated cheese

Brown ground beef with onion; add tomato sauce, tamales, corn and seasonings. Mix thoroughly. Stir in olives. Bake at 350 degrees for 20 minutes. Cover with grated cheese. Return to oven just long enough to melt cheese. Yield: 10-12 servings.

Mrs. Jane Doty, Pres.
Zion LWML
Terra Bella, California

TAMALE PIE

1 lb. ground beef
1 med. onion, chopped
1 No. 303 can cream-style corn
1 15-oz. can tomato sauce
1 tbsp. chili powder
1 tsp. salt
½ c. yellow corn meal
1 can pitted black ripe olives

Brown meat with onion. Cook corn with tomato sauce, chili powder and salt. Thicken with corn meal. Add meat mixture to corn mixture. Add olives. Bake at 350 degrees for 30 minutes. Yield: 4 servings.

Mrs. Donald Urlie, Pres.
Bethany LCW
Tuscon, Arizona

ENCHILADA PIE

1 lb. ground beef
1 onion, chopped
1 tsp. salt
¼ tsp. pepper
1 tsp. chili powder
1 8-oz. can tomato sauce
6 tortillas, buttered

1 4½-oz. can sliced ripe olives
1 ½ c. grated Cheddar cheese
1 c. water

Brown meat and onion; add seasonings and tomato sauce. Simmer for 20 minutes. Alternate layers of buttered tortillas, meat sauce, olives and cheese in casserole. Add water. Bake in preheated 400 degree oven for 25 minutes. Yield: 4-6 servings.

Mrs. J. M. Bowman, Sec.
Trinity Mary Martha Guild
San Diego, California

TANGY TORTILLA CASSEROLE

1 ½ lb. hamburger, crumbled
1 med. onion, chopped
1 No. 1 can tomatoes
1 10-oz. can enchilada sauce
1 2 ¼-oz. can sliced ripe olives, undrained
1 tsp. salt
⅛ tsp. pepper
¼ tsp. garlic powder
1 egg
1 c. small curd cottage cheese
½ lb. Jack cheese, grated
½ c. grated Cheddar cheese
8 tortillas, cut into halves
½ c. packaged tortilla chips, crushed

Brown hamburger and onion; blend in tomatoes, enchilada sauce, olives, salt, pepper and garlic powder. Beat egg into cottage cheese. Spread one-third meat sauce into greased 3-quart casserole or 9 x 12-inch glass cake pan; top with one-half of Jack cheese and one-half of cottage cheese. Top with one-half of tortilla halves. Repeat layers; cover with remaining meat sauce. Top with Cheddar cheese; border with crushed tortilla chips. Bake, uncovered, at 350 degrees for 20 minutes. Cut into s q u a r e s or wedges. Yield: 6-8 servings.

Mrs. Helen Landru, Pres.
Christ Lutheran Church LCW
Goleta, California

ALL-IN-ONE SKILLET

1 lb. hamburger
6 to 8 med. potatoes, sliced
1 can cream of mushroom soup
1 soup can milk
1 tsp. salt
⅛ tsp. pepper

Place a layer of hamburger in greased casserole. Add a layer of p o t a t o e s. Continue to alternate layers until all potatoes and hamburger are used. Pour mixture of soup, milk and seasonings over casserole. Bake at 350 degrees for 1 hour or until the potatoes are done. Yield: 8-10 servings.

Mrs. H. H. Hines, Pres.
United LCW
Hampton, Nebraska

BEWITCHED BEEF AND BEAN CASSEROLE

3 No. 303 cans baked beans
2 No. 2 cans kidney beans, drained
1 pkg. frozen green lima beans, partially thawed
¼ c. (packed) plus 1 tbsp. brown sugar
3 ½ tsp. dry mustard
5 tsp. salt
¾ tsp. pepper
2 lb. ground chuck
1 sm. onion, minced
¼ c. water
1 tbsp. fat or salad oil
1 c. catsup
2 tbsp. vinegar
1 tbsp. butter or margarine
1 16-oz. jar canned whole onions, drained

Mix all beans, 1/4 cup brown sugar, 3 tablespoonfuls mustard, 2 teaspoonfuls salt and 1/4 teaspoonful pepper in 3-quart casserole. Bake at 400 degrees for 45 minutes. Lightly mix meat, 3 teaspoonfuls salt, 1/2 teaspoonful pepper, minced onion and water; form into 16 balls. Brown in hot fat; remove from skillet. Wipe skillet. Combine catsup, vinegar, 1 tablespoonful brown sugar, 1/2 teaspoonful mustard, butter and meat balls in skillet. Simmer for 20 minutes. Arrange meat balls and whole onions on top of beans; spoon on sauce. Bake at 400 degrees for 15 minutes. Yield: 8 servings.

Mrs. Eugene C. Score
Holy Cross LCW
St. Paul, Minnesota

BURGER BEANS

1 lb. hamburger
1 med. onion, chopped
¼ tsp. salt
⅛ tsp. pepper
2 cans tomato soup
1 No. 2 can pork and beans
2 tbsp. (rounded) brown sugar
1 tbsp. mustard

Fry hamburger and onion with seasonings until done. Add remaining ingredients. Pour into greased 2 1/2 or 3-quart casserole. Bake at 400 degrees for 45 minutes. Yield: 6 servings.

Mrs. Helen Rader, Sec.-Treas.
Rader Immanuel Ladies Aid
Niangua, Missouri

CHINESE HOT DISH

1 lb. hamburger
1 to 2 c. chopped celery
1 box frozen peas
1 can cream of mushroom soup
2 tbsp. cream
1 to 1 ½ tsp. salt
Dash of pepper
1 sm. onion, chopped
1 c. crushed potato chips

Lightly brown hamburger; place in bottom of baking dish. Add layer of celery, then frozen peas. Combine remaining ingredients except potato chips; pour over casserole. Top with potato chips. Bake at 350 degrees for 45 minutes. NOTE: If started in a cold oven, the celery is still crunchy, but everything else is done. This may be varied by using water chestnuts, bamboo shoots and green peppers in addition to other ingredients. Yield: 6-8 servings.

Mrs. Irene C. Hoferer, Sec.-Treas.
Zion Priscilla Circle
Des Moines, Iowa
Mrs. Quentin Zell, Pres.
Holy Trinity Lutheran Body Bible Class
Bethlehem, Pennsylvania

DINNER IN A DISH

1 med. onion, chopped
2 green peppers, sliced
5 tbsp. fat
1 lb. hamburger
1 ½ tsp. salt
¼ tsp. pepper
2 eggs, well beaten
2 c. canned corn
4 med. tomatoes, sliced
½ c. dried bread crumbs

Saute onion and green peppers in 4 tablespoonfuls fat for 3 minutes. Add meat and seasonings. Remove from heat. Stir in eggs; mix well. Place 1 cup corn in a baking dish; add one-half the meat mixture. Add a layer of sliced tomatoes. Repeat layers. Cover with crumbs; dot with remaining fat. Bake at 350 degrees for 45 minutes. Yield: 4 servings.

Mrs. Curtis R. Wilkinson, Sec.
Emmanuel LWML
Littlefield, Texas

GOLDEN BEEF CASSEROLE

1 lb. lean ground beef
¼ c. diced onion
¼ c. diced green pepper
Shortening
1 10 ½-oz. can cream of mushroom soup
¾ tsp. salt
⅛ tsp. pepper
1 c. shredded Cheddar cheese
2 12-oz. cans whole kernel corn, drained

Brown beef, onion and green pepper in a small amount of melted shortening in large frying pan. Mix in undiluted soup and remaining ingredients. Spoon into greased 1 3/4-quart casserole. Bake in preheated 350 degree oven for 40 minutes. Yield: 4-6 servings.

Mrs. Barbara Prough, Sec.
Prince of Peace Dorcas Soc.
Southaven, Mississippi

GOLDEN CASSEROLE

½ lb. ground beef
2 c. cooked corn
⅔ c. cracker crumbs

(Continued on next page)

1 tsp. onion
⅓ tsp. salt
¼ tsp. pepper
1 egg
¾ c. milk
1 tsp. parsley (opt.)

Mix all ingredients. Place into buttered casserole. Bake at 375 degrees for 50 minutes.

Lola Thordsen
Trinity Ladies Aid
Persia, Iowa

GROUND BEEF HOT DISH

1 lge. onion, finely chopped
1 ½ lb. ground beef
2 tsp. salt
½ tsp. pepper
2 tbsp. shortening
7 c. sliced potatoes
1 10 ½-oz. can cream of chicken soup
1 10 ½-oz. can cream of mushroom soup
1 1-lb. can cream-style corn
1 ½ c. water

Fry onion, ground beef, salt and pepper in shortening. Chop ground beef into bite-sized pieces. Mix all ingredients in a roaster. Bake at 350 degrees for 1 hour, leaving cover on. Stir occasionally to keep from burning on bottom of roaster. Take cover off the last 15 minutes of baking. Yield: 12 servings.

Mrs. Kenneth Paulson
Immanuel Lutheran Church of Bejou
Winger, Minnesota

GROUND BEEF HOT DISH

1 ½ lb. ground beef
1 tsp. salt
1 sm. onion, diced
1 can cream of mushroom soup
1 can chicken with rice soup
1 c. chopped celery
1 pkg. frozen or 1 can mixed vegetable
½ pkg. or 1 sm. can chow mein noodles

Fry meat, salt and onion until lightly browned. Combine remaining ingredients except noodles. Add to meat mixture. Top with noodles. Bake at 350 degrees for 1 hour. Yield: 6 servings.

Mrs. Oliver K. Chose, Pres.
North Prairie LCW
Lake Mills, Iowa

HAMBURGER WITH BAKED BEANS

1 med. onion, chopped
2 strips bacon, cut into ½-in. pieces
1 lb. ground beef
2 1-lb. cans pork and beans
½ c. molasses
½ c. catsup
½ tsp. dry mustard
½ tsp. salt
½ tsp. Worcestershire sauce

Saute onion with b a c o n. Add ground beef and brown. Add remaining ingredients; mix well. Pour into 1 1/2-quart casserole. Bake at 375 degrees for 30 minutes. Garnish with sliced red tomatoes, if desired. Yield: 8-9 servings.

Mrs. Herbert C. Heinecke
St. Paul's Ladies Aid
Cumberland, Wisconsin

HAMBURGER-CORN CASSEROLE

1 lb. hamburger
1 med. onion, sliced
4 lge. potatoes, sliced
½ tsp. salt
¼ tsp. pepper
1 No. 2 can cream-style corn
½ c. milk

Brown meat. Place onion in greased casserole; add layer of potatoes, meat and seasoned corn. Pour milk over casserole. Bake, covered, in preheated 350 degree oven for 1 hour and 30 minutes to 2 hours. Yield: 4-6 servings.

Mrs. William Hartag
Our Redeemer Ladies Aid
Okabena, Minnesota

HAMBURGER DELUXE

1 ½ lb. ground beef
1 c. diced celery
1 med. onion, chopped
1 can cream of mushroom soup
1 can cream of chicken soup
1 sm. can peas and carrots, drained or 1
    pkg. frozen peas and carrots
1 can chow mein noodles

Brown beef, celery and onion in skillet; add all remaining ingredients except noodles. Place in greased casserole; top with chow mein noodles. Bake at 350 degrees for 35 to 45 minutes.

Mrs. Vernon D. Gundermann
Zion Ladies Aid Soc.
Arcadia, Iowa
Mrs. Hilda Thaete, Pres.
Trinity Dorcas Soc.
Rupert, Idaho

HAMBURGER HOT DISH

1 ½ lb. hamburger
1 med. onion
1 can cream of chicken soup
1 c. (scant) milk
4 c. cubed potatoes
1 ½ c. fresh or frozen peas
2 carrots, cubed
Salt to taste

Brown hamburger and onion. Add soup and milk; mix. Add vegetables and season; mix well. Place in medium casserole. Bake at 350 degrees for 1 hour. Yield: 8 servings.

Mrs. Irvin Harms, Pres.
Peace Ladies Aid
West Bend, Iowa

HAMBURGER HOT DISH

6 med. potatoes, sliced
1 lb. ground beef
1 med. onion, diced
1 tsp. salt
¼ tsp. pepper
1 can vegetable soup
1 can cream of mushroom soup
½ c. water

Place a layer of potatoes in large greased casserole. Add one-half the ground beef and onion. Repeat layers; add salt and pepper. Add soups mixed with water. Bake at 350 degrees for 1 hour and 30 minutes or until potatoes are done. Yield: 8 servings.

Mrs. Oscar Rodning, Pres.
Scandian Grove LCW
Gaylord, Minnesota

HAMBURGER PIE

2 lb. ground beef
4 c. diced potatoes
2 c. grated American cheese
2 tbsp. minced onion
1 No. 202 can whole-kernel corn
1 No. 202 can peas
1 can tomato soup
Salt and pepper to taste

Place one-half of ground beef in bottom of large casserole. Pat into sides of pan. Add alternate layers of potatoes, cheese, onion, corn and peas. Add soup diluted with water. Season with salt and pepper. Place remaining ground beef on top. Bake at 350 degrees for 1 hour or until potatoes are done. Yield: 8-10 servings.

Mrs. Eric Renner
St. Mark's Ladies Aid
Ruskin, Nebraska

HAMBURGER PIE CASSEROLE

1 med. onion, chopped
1 lb. ground beef
Salt and pepper to taste
2 ½ c. drained green beans

1 can tomato soup
5 med. potatoes, cooked
½ c. warm milk
1 egg, beaten

Brown onion; add meat and seasonings. Cook until brown. Add beans and soup; pour into buttered casserole. Mash potatoes; add milk, egg and seasonings. Spoon in mounds around edge of meat. Bake at 350 degrees for 30 minutes. Yield: 6 servings.

Mrs. Dean Senska, Pres.
Bethlehem Ladies Aid
Woonsocket, South Dakota

KRAUT WICKEL

10 or 12 outer cabbage leaves
1 lb. ground beef
2 c. boiled cabbage, chopped
1 stalk celery, chopped
1 onion, finely chopped
1 egg
Salt and pepper to taste

Scald outer cabbage leaves. Combine remaining ingredients, mixing well. Place 2 tablespoonfuls of mixture in each cabbage leaf. Fold around meat mixture. Place in a roasting pan with a little water. Bake at 350 degrees for 1 hour.

Mrs. J. N. McNott
Trinity Womens Miss'y Guild
Hanceville, Alabama

MEAL IN ONE

1 lb. hamburger
1 sm. onion, diced
Seasonings to taste
4 or 5 med. potatoes, sliced
1 can vegetable soup
1 soup can water

Brown hamburger and onion; season. Mix all ingredients; pour into baking dish. Bake at 350 degrees for 1 hour or until done. Yield: 6 servings.

Mrs. Herbert Schley, Pres.
Redeemer Tabea Miss'y Soc.
Owatonna, Minnesota

MINNESOTA SPECIAL

1 lb. ground beef
1 onion, chopped
1 green pepper, cut up
3 carrots, sliced
½ c. diced celery
3 potatoes, quartered
1 can peas
1 can water
Salt and pepper to taste

Brown meat and onion. Place in bottom of casserole. Place green pepper over meat, then carrots, celery, potatoes and peas. Add water

(Continued on next page)

and salt and pepper to taste. Bake at 350 degrees for 2 hours. Yield: 4-5 servings.

Mrs. Ruth Husemann
Rainbow Lakes Ladies Guild
Dunnellon, Florida

POTATO UPPER CRUST MEAT PIE

½ c. chopped onion
½ c. chopped celery
4 tbsp. butter or margarine
1 ½ lb. ground beef
1 c. cooked peas
1 10 ½-oz. can tomato soup
Salt
White pepper
3 c. hot mashed potatoes
1 egg, beaten
½ c. milk

Saute onion and celery in 2 tablespoonfuls butter until limp. Add ground beef and brown. Add peas, soup, 1 teaspoonful salt and 1/4 teaspoonful white pepper. Turn into 2-quart casserole. Combine remaining ingredients; mix well. Spread over casserole. Bake in preheated 350 degree oven for 50 minutes or until browned. Serve hot. Yield: 5-6 servings.

Mrs. Victor Fender, Pres.
St. John LCW
Erlanger, Kentucky

SHIPWRECK

2 med. onions, chopped
3 med. potatoes, sliced
½ to ¾ lb. ground beef, browned
1 c. cooked rice
½ c. chopped celery
1 15-oz. can kidney beans, drained
Salt and pepper
2 10 ¾-oz. cans tomato soup
1 soup can water

Layer onions, potatoes, meat, rice, celery and beans in 2-quart casserole, seasoning each layer. Pour soup diluted with water over each layer. Cover; bake at 350 degrees for 2 hours or until potatoes are done. Remove cover the last 15 minutes of baking. Yield: 4-6 servings.

Mrs. James T. Montgomery, Pres.
St. Mark's LCW
Grand Forks, North Dakota

SIDONIA'S OWN CASSEROLE

6 slices bacon, cut into 1-in. pieces
1 med. or lge. onion
Butter or margarine
2 lb. ground beef
Salt and pepper to taste
1 med. cabbage, cut up and cooked
4 lge. potatoes, mashed
Bacon drippings
Milk

Fry bacon until crisp. Saute onion in butter. Add ground beef; stir constantly over high heat. Add salt and pepper to taste. Grease large casserole; place cooked beef in bottom. Add bacon drippings and salt to taste. Place cabbage over beef. Add butter, milk and salt to potatoes. Spread evenly over cabbage. Cover; bake at 350 degrees for 45 minutes. Remove cover; brown potatoes under broiler. Yield: 5 servings.

Mrs. Karl Wulf
First Lutheran Church LCW
Toronto, Ontario, Canada

ST. LOUIS-ST. PAUL SPECIAL

1 med. onion, chopped
1 lb. ground beef
1 ½ tsp. salt
¼ tsp. pepper
1 can vegetable soup
4 med. potatoes
1 tbsp. butter
¼ to ⅓ c. milk

Saute onion and ground beef until meat loses redness; season with 1 teaspoonful salt and pepper. Place meat and onion mixture in a 2-quart casserole; cover with soup. Cook potatoes until soft; mash with butter and milk. Season with remaining salt. Spoon mashed potatoes over meat mixture. Bake at 425 to 450 degrees until bubbly. Yield: 4-6 servings.

Mrs. Erich Klipp, Sec.
St. Paul's Ladies Aid Soc.
St. Louis, Missouri

VEGETABLE-MEAT CASSEROLE

1 lb. hamburger
½ tsp. salt
Dash of pepper
1 sm. onion, chopped
1 can tomato soup
¼ to ½ soup can water
8 med. potatoes, sliced
1 15-oz. can peas, drained
Fine bread crumbs

Mix hamburger with salt, pepper and onion; brown. Add tomato soup mixed with water; heat. Add more water if too thick. Place layer of sliced potato in greased 2-quart casserole; add a layer of peas, then a layer of meat mixture. Repeat layers. Top with bread crumbs. Cover and bake at 350 degrees for 1 hour and 30 minutes. Yield: 8 servings.

Mrs. John Becker, Pres.
Trinity LCW
Neustadt, Ontario, Canada

AUTUMN MEAT LOAF

1 can onion soup
½ pkg. herb-seasoned stuffing mix
2 lb. ground beef
2 eggs, beaten
2 tbsp. catsup
Dash of cracked pepper

(Continued on next page)

Combine onion soup and stuffing mix. Add all remaining ingredients; mix thoroughly. Place in oiled loaf pan. Bake at 350 degrees for 1 hour and 30 minutes. Yield: 6-8 servings.

Mrs. A. F. Wedel
Mt. Olive Women's Guild
Minneapolis, Minnesota

BALLGAME MEAT LOAF

⅔ c. evaporated milk
1 egg, slightly beaten
1 c. cracker crumbs
1 ½ lb. ground beef
2 tbsp. chopped onion
1 ½ tsp. salt
1 tsp. prepared mustard

Combine all ingredients; pack into 8 x 5 x 3-inch pan. Bake at 350 degrees for 50 minutes to 1 hour. Yield: 12 servings.

Mrs. Norlin Nelson
First Lutheran Church
New Rockford, North Dakota

BARBECUED MEAT LOAF

1 ½ lb. ground chuck
2 med. onions, minced
4 tbsp. Worcestershire sauce
1 egg
1 c. milk
1 c. cracker crumbs
Salt and pepper
2 tbsp. butter
2 tbsp. vinegar
2 tbsp. brown sugar
4 tbsp. lemon juice
1 c. catsup
½ c. water
½ tbsp. dry mustard

Combine meat, 1 onion, 1 tablespoonful Worcestershire sauce, egg, milk, crumbs and seasonings. Shape into loaves; place in baking dish. Saute remaining onion in butter; add remaining ingredients. Simmer for a few minutes; pour over meat loaf. Bake at 325 to 350 degrees for 45 minutes. Yield: 6 servings.

Louise M. Flood
St. Johns Ladies Aid
Battle Creek, Nebraska

BEEF-RICE LOAF

1 lb. ground beef
1 c. cooked rice
1 sm. onion, diced
1 egg, beaten
1 tbsp. chopped parsley
½ tsp. Worcestershire sauce
½ tsp. salt
¼ tsp. pepper
¼ tsp. curry powder
1 can cream of celery soup

Combine all ingredients except 1/2 can soup; pack into loaf pan. Spread remaining soup on top.

Bake at 325 degrees for 1 hour. Yield: 4 servings.

Mrs. Virginia Reynolds, Pres.
St. Andrews Dorcas Soc.
Stateline, California

BEEF LOAF WITH ZESTY TOPPING

¾ c. milk
1 ½ c. soft bread crumbs
2 lb. ground beef
2 tsp. salt
⅛ tsp. pepper
1 med. carrot, grated
¼ c. diced onion
2 eggs, beaten
¼ c. catsup
3 tbsp. brown sugar
2 tbsp. prepared mustard

Pour milk over bread crumbs; add meat, salt, pepper, carrot, onion and eggs. Mix thoroughly. Pack into 5 x 9-inch loaf pan. Mix catsup, brown sugar and mustard; spread over loaf. Bake at 300 degrees for 1 hour and 30 minutes to 1 hour and 45 minutes. Yield: 8 servings.

Mrs. Levi Ersland
Our Savior's LCW
Richland, Montana

BLUE RIBBON MEAT LOAF

1 envelope dry onion soup mix
1 c. sour cream
2 eggs, slightly beaten
1 ½ lb. ground beef
1 c. soft bread crumbs
2 strips bacon

Combine onion soup mix with sour cream in a bowl; add eggs. Mix in ground beef. Add bread crumbs; mix well. Shape into a loaf. Place in loaf pan; lay bacon over top. Place in preheated 500 degree oven. Reduce heat. Bake at 375 degrees for 1 hour. Yield: 6-8 servings.

Mrs. Oscar Olson, Pres.
St. Joseph LCW
Rosholt, South Dakota

BUSH'S MEAT LOAF

1 c. toasted bread crumbs
2 tbsp. milk
1 med. onion, finely chopped
2 tbsp. finely diced green pepper
1 c. drained canned tomatoes
1 tsp. salt
¼ tsp. pepper
1 lb. ground beef
Tomato juice

Soften bread crumbs in milk; add onion, green pepper, tomatoes, salt and pepper. Mix well;

(Continued on next page)

add to meat. Shape into loaf. Place in slightly greased baking dish. Pour tomato juice around meat. Bake at 400 degrees for 1 hour. Yield: 4-6 servings.

Mrs. Richard M. Bush, Pres.
St. Stephen's LCW
Lenoir, North Carolina

CHEESE MEAT LOAF

1 8-oz. pkg. sliced American cheese
4 eggs, slightly beaten
4 lb. hamburger
2 ½ c. tomato sauce
2 sauce cans water
2 c. quick cooking oats
1 ½ c. chopped onions
2 tsp. salt
2 tbsp. mustard
2 tbsp. horseradish

Chop 1/2 package of cheese into small pieces. Combine all ingredients except unchopped cheese. Shape into two loaves; place in shallow pan. Bake at 375 degrees for 2 hours. Just before serving, place remainder of cheese over top. Return to oven to melt cheese. Yield: 20 servings.

Clara Trog, Pres.
Luther Memorial Women's Guild
St. Louis, Missouri

CHEESY MEAT LOAF

1 egg, beaten
1 lb. lean ground beef
¾ c. diced cheese
1 tbsp. chopped onion
1 tsp. salt
¼ c. chopped pepper
½ tsp. celery salt
1 c. milk
½ c. fine dry bread crumbs

Combine all ingredients; mix lightly. Pack lightly into buttered loaf pan. Bake at 350 degrees for 1 hour. Yield: 6 servings.

Mrs. Jake Den Herder
Peace Women League
Norwalk, Iowa

CHICKEN-FLAVORED MEAT LOAF

2 slices bread, moistened
1 ½ lb. ground beef
2 eggs
1 can chicken with rice soup
¾ tsp. salt

Tear bread into pieces. Mix ground beef, bread and eggs. Drain stock from soup; add with salt to bread mixture. Place in loaf pan or baking dish. Spread rice and chicken pieces from soup over meat loaf. Bake at 325 degrees for 1 hour. Yield: 6 servings.

Mrs. Elton E. Sump, Pres.
St. Mark Ladies Guild
Conroe, Texas

DELUXE MEAT LOAF

2 med. stalks, celery, chopped
1 med. onion, minced
1 med. carrot, minced
2 strips bacon, finely diced
1 3 to 4-oz. can mushrooms, sliced
1 med. green pepper, minced
½ tsp. monosodium glutamate
½ tsp. celery flakes
½ tsp. dry mustard
¼ tsp. garlic powder
½ tsp. sage
½ tsp. salt
¼ tsp. pepper
1 tbsp. soy sauce
1 tbsp. Worcestershire sauce
1 c. milk
2 eggs
1 c. dry bread crumbs
1 lb. ground lean beef
1 can tomato sauce (opt.)

Combine all ingredients except beef; mix well. Let stand for 30 minutes to 1 hour. Add beef; mix thoroughly. Spoon into greased 8 x 5 x 3-inch loaf pan. Bake at 350 degrees for 1 hour and 15 minutes. If desired, top with 1 can tomato sauce the last 15 minutes of baking time, or serve hot tomato sauce separately. Yield: 4-6 servings.

Mrs. Delores Benoit, Pres.
St. Luke Women's Guild
Mt. Clemens, Michigan

EASY MEAT LOAF

2 lb. ground beef
2 eggs
1 tsp. salt
¼ tsp. pepper
Onion to taste
4 slices bread, cut into small pieces
1 can tomato soup
¼ c. water

Combine all ingredients except 1/4 can soup and water; mold into a loaf. Dot with margarine or butter. Pour remaining tomato soup and water around meat loaf. Bake at 350 degrees for 1 hour and 15 minutes. Yield: 8 servings.

Mrs. Luella Schmeisser
Hope Evangelical Dorcas Soc.
Aurora, Illinois

FAMILY MEAT LOAF

1 ½ lb. minced beef
1 egg, beaten

(Continued on next page)

1 c. oats
1 c. milk
½ tsp. minced onion
½ tsp. dried parsley flakes
1 ½ tsp. salt
⅛ tsp. pepper
¼ tsp. monosodium glutamate
1 tsp. Worcestershire sauce
3 tbsp. catsup

Combine all ingredients except catsup; pack into 9 x 5-inch loaf pan. Make three diagonal indentions in top of meat loaf. Fill with catsup. Bake at 350 degrees for 1 hour and 15 minutes to 1 hour and 30 minutes. Yield: 6-8 servings.

Mrs. Louise Schmidt, Pres.
Bethel LCW
Marchwell, Saskatchewan, Canada

FAVORITE MEAT LOAF

2 lb. ground beef
6 tsp. horseradish
1 tbsp. salt
1 tsp. dry mustard
¼ c. milk
¼ c. catsup
¾ c. chopped onions
¼ c. finely chopped green pepper
2 eggs, beaten
2 c. bread crumbs

Combine all ingredients; mix well. Place in baking dish. Bake at 400 degrees for 40 minutes. Yield: 6-8 servings.

Mrs. Wilbert Hoermann
St. John Ladies Aid
Granville, Iowa

FLOSSIE'S MEAT LOAF

2 lb. ground beef
1 onion, chopped
¾ c. bread crumbs
1 egg, slightly beaten
1 8-oz. can tomato sauce
2 tsp. salt
¼ tsp. pepper
2 ½ tsp. dry mustard
1 tbsp. Worcestershire sauce
½ c. water
2 tbsp. brown sugar
2 tbsp. vinegar

Combine meat, onion, bread crumbs, egg, one-half of the tomato sauce, salt, pepper, 1/2 teaspoonful dry mustard and 2 teaspoonfuls Worcestershire sauce; place in loaf pan. Combine remaining tomato sauce, water, brown sugar, vinegar, remaining Worcestershire sauce and remaining dry mustard; stir. Pour over meat loaf. Bake at 325 degrees for 2 hours.

Mrs. Charles Smead, Treas.
Zion Naomi Circle
Bartlett, Illinois

FLUFFY MEAT LOAF

1 ½ lb. ground beef or veal
3 med. slices soft bread, torn into pieces
1 c. milk
1 egg, beaten
¼ c. minced onion
1 ¼ tsp. salt
¼ tsp. pepper
¼ tsp. dry mustard
¼ tsp. sage
¼ tsp. celery salt
¼ tsp. garlic salt
1 tbsp. Worcestershire sauce
3 tbsp. catsup (opt.)

Combine all ingredients except catsup; mix thoroughly. Shape into loaf on shallow baking pan. Spread catsup over top. Bake in preheated 350 degree oven for 1 hour and 30 minutes or until done. Serve hot or cold.

Inez Koechel, Pres.
First English LCW
Oshkosh, Wisconsin

GOOD MEAT LOAF

⅔ c. milk
1 egg, beaten
½ c. soft bread crumbs
1 ½ lb. ground beef
¼ c. catsup
¼ c. chopped green pepper
½ c. chopped onion
2 tsp. salt

Blend all ingredients until smooth; place in baking dish or loaf pan. Bake at 350 degrees for 1 hour. Yield: 4-6 servings.

Mrs. W. C. Farner, Pres.
St. John's LWML
Bismarck, Missouri

EVERYDAY MEAT LOAF

⅔ c. dry bread crumbs
1 c. milk
1 lb. ground beef
2 eggs, slightly beaten
¼ c. grated onion
1 tsp. salt
⅛ tsp. pepper
½ tsp. sage

Soak bread crumbs in milk; add meat, eggs, onion and seasonings. Mix well. Form individual loaves; place in greased pans.

PIQUANT SAUCE:

3 tbsp. brown sugar
¼ c. catsup
¼ tsp. nutmeg
1 tsp. dry mustard

(Continued on next page)

Combine brown sugar, catsup, nutmeg and mustard; pour over meat loaf. Bake at 350 degrees for 45 minutes to 1 hour. Yield: 4-5 servings.

Mrs. John E. Obed, Pres.
Our Redeemer LWML
Tampa, Florida

MEAT LOAF

1 ½ lb. ground beef
¾ c. oats
2 eggs, beaten
¼ c. chopped onion
2 tsp. salt or savory salt
¼ tsp. pepper
1 c. tomato juice
1 tbsp. Worcestershire sauce (opt.)
Dash of garlic salt (opt.)

Combine all ingredients thoroughly; pack firmly into a loaf pan. Bake at 350 degrees for 1 hour to 1 hour and 30 minutes. Yield: 8 servings.

Mrs. Frank Zednicek, Treas.
Bethany Guild
Charlevoix, Michigan
Mrs. Elmer Heller, Pres.
Holy Cross Ladies Aid
Fults, Illionis

MEAT LOAF

2 lb. hamburger
¾ c. quick cooking oats
2 eggs, well beaten
1 c. milk
1 lge. carrot, grated
1 lge. onion, diced
3 sm. pieces celery, diced
¼ green pepper, diced
2 tsp. salt
¼ tsp. pepper
¼ c. catsup

Combine all ingredients except catsup. Place in loaf pan. Top with catsup. Bake at 325 degrees for 1 hour and 30 minutes. Yield: 12 servings.

Mrs. Arthur Speckman
St. Peter Ladies Aid
Osceola, Indiana

MEAT LOAF

1 lean steak
Salt and pepper to taste
Dash of paprika
Dash of allspice
1 tbsp. chopped onion
1 tsp. butter
½ c. tomato juice

Put meat thorough food chopper twice. Mix meat, salt and pepper; shape into loaf. Sprinkle with paprika and allspice. Place loaf in baking pan; top

with onion and butter. Pour tomato juice over all. Bake at 350 degrees for 1 hour. Yield: 1 serving.

Mrs. Sam Musselman, Christian Service Chmn.
Zion LCW
Fairfield, Pennsylvania

MEAT LOAF

2 lb. ground beef
1 med. onion, sliced
2 eggs
1 ½ tsp. dry mustard
1 tsp. chili powder
1 ½ c. stewed tomatoes
2 slices bread, broken into pieces
2 tsp. salt
¼ tsp. pepper
4 strips bacon

Combine all ingredients except bacon. Pack into 9 x 5 x 3-inch loaf pan. Place bacon strips on top. Bake in preheated electric roaster or at 350 degrees for 1 hour and 30 minutes. Yield: 8-10 servings.

Mrs. Chris F. Holtzman, Sr., Pres.
St. Paul LWML
Ridgeway, North Carolina
Mrs. Ralph Blundon, Pres.
Calvary LCW
Grants Pass, Oregon

MEAT LOAF

1 lb. ground round steak
½ c. soft bread crumbs
⅛ c. milk
1 onion, minced
1 carrot
1 stalk celery
1 tsp. salt
¼ tsp. pepper

Place ground round steak in bowl; add bread crumbs and milk. Blend in onion, carrot, celery, salt and pepper. Shape into long roll; place in 8-inch buttered loaf pan. Bake at 450 degrees for 20 to 25 minutes. Yield: 6 servings.

Lucretia E. Riale, Pres.
Emanuel ULCW
Red Lion, Pennsylvania

MEAT LOAF

1 ½ to 2 lb. ground beef
1 c. bread crumbs
1 med. onion, chopped
1 tsp. salt
Pepper to taste
½ tsp. allspice or poultry seasoning
1 can tomatoes

Combine all ingredients except tomatoes; place in loaf pan. Bake at 350 degrees for 30 minutes.

(Continued on next page)

Pour tomatoes over loaf; bake until tomatoes boil and meat is done. Yield: 6 servings.

Mrs. M. Belsheim
Lea Park Bethel LCW
Marwayne, Alta, Canada

MEAT LOAF

2 lb. minced steak
1 ⅓ c. cracker crumbs
⅓ c. oats
1 med. onion, diced
2 eggs, beaten
1 10-oz. can tomato soup
1 tsp. prepared mustard
2 tsp. salt
¼ tsp. pepper

Place all ingredients in mixing bowl; mix well with hands. Shape into loaf in a 10 x 6 x 4-inch loaf pan. Bake at 325 degrees for 1 hour and 5 minutes to 1 hour and 10 minutes. Yield: 8 servings.

Mrs. Emma A. Weber, Pres.
North Soultrey Zion LWML
Gregherd, Saskatchewan, Canada

MEAT LOAF

1 lb. ground beef
1 sm. onion, grated
1 c. prepared bread stuffing
Seasonings to taste
1 egg, beaten
¼ c. catsup
¼ tsp. nutmeg
3 tbsp. brown sugar
1 tsp. mustard

Combine ground beef, onion, stuffing, seasonings and egg; place in loaf pan. Combine remaining ingredients; spread on top of loaf. Bake at 350 degrees for 1 hour. Yield: 6 servings.

Mrs. Alice Stewart
Grace Ladies Aid
Three Forks, Montana

MEAT LOAF IN A CRUST

MEAT LOAF:

3 lb. lean ground beef
2 eggs
1 c. chopped onions
1 can cream of mushroom soup
½ c. finely chopped parsley
1 tbsp. salt
½ tsp. (scant) pepper
2 tsp. Worcestershire sauce
1 ½ c. bread crumbs

Blend all ingredients; do not knead mixture. Mixture should be moist; add small amount of milk if needed. Shape into loaf pan; invert onto shallow baking pan. Bake at 450 degrees for 20 minutes. Reduce heat to 375 degrees. Continue to bake for about 1 hour longer.

CRUST:

2 c. flour
1 tsp. salt
1 c. shortening
Water

Combine all ingredients, using enough water to form ball. Roll pastry large enough to surround loaf. Wrap baked loaf in pastry; cut off excess. Seal pastry around loaf. Bake at 400 degrees until golden brown. NOTE: May be served plain or with meat sauce. Yield: 10 servings.

Mrs. Arloa Nelson
Salem Memorial LCW
Detroit, Michigan

MEAT LOAF FOR A PARTY

3 tbsp. light molasses
3 tbsp. prepared mustard
3 tbsp. vinegar
4 tbsp. catsup
1 c. milk
2 eggs
1 envelope onion soup mix
3 c. bread crumbs
½ tsp. hot pepper sauce
1 tsp. salt
½ tsp. leaf oregano
¼ c. chopped parsley
3 lb. ground beef

Blend molasses and mustard in large bowl; stir in vinegar, catsup, milk, eggs, onion soup mix and bread crumbs. Add remaining ingredients; mix well. Pack into greased loaf pan. Bake at 350 degrees for 1 hour and 30 minutes. Yield: 6 servings.

Mrs. Helen Hermanson
Good Shepherd LWML
Titusville, Florida

MEAT LOAF SPECIAL

2 lb. ground beef
¼ c. finely chopped onion or 2 tbsp. diced instant onion
2 tbsp. finely chopped celery (opt.)
2 tsp. salt
½ tsp. poultry seasoning
¼ tsp. pepper
¼ tsp. dry mustard
1 tbsp. Worcestershire sauce (opt.)
4 slices soft bread
½ c. milk
2 eggs
Corn flake crumbs
Catsup
½ c. boiling water

Place meat in large bowl; stir in onion, celery and seasonings. Remove crusts from bread;

101

(Continued on next page)

cube. Soak cubed bread in milk in a small bowl. Add eggs; beat with rotary beater. Combine meat mixture and egg mixture. Form into four or five small loaves. Roll loaves in corn flake crumbs; place in greased shallow pan. Press diagonal grooves into tops of loaves with a wooden spoon; fill grooves with catsup. Pour boiling water around loaves. Bake, uncovered, at 350 degrees for 1 hour. Serve hot or cold. Garnish with lettuce and tomato wedges. Yield: 8-10 servings.

Mrs. Norman Salte, Pres.
Bethlehem LCW
Outlook, Saskatchewan, Canada

MY BEST MEAT LOAF

1 lb. ground beef
1 med. onion, chopped
½ green pepper, chopped
1 ¼ c. bread crumbs
2 tsp. salt
½ tsp. pepper
2 eggs, beaten
1 c. canned tomatoes
1 tsp. prepared mustard
1 tsp. Worcestershire sauce

Combine all ingredients. Mix well. Place in loaf pan. Bake at 350 degrees for 45 to 50 minutes. NOTE: May use 3/4 cup tomatoes in loaf instead of 1 cup; spread remaining tomatoes over meat loaf. Yield: 6 servings.

Mrs. W. O. Kopp, Pres.
Grace Ladies Aux.
Freeport, Texas

PIQUANT MEAT LOAF

⅔ c. dry bread crumbs
1 c. milk
1 ½ lb. ground beef
2 eggs, slightly beaten
¼ c. grated onion
1 tsp. salt
⅛ tsp. pepper
½ tsp. sage

Soak bread crumbs in milk; add beef, eggs, onion and seasoning. Pack lightly into greased loaf pan.

PIQUANT SAUCE:

3 tsp. brown sugar
4 tsp. catsup
¼ tsp. nutmeg
1 tsp. mustard

Combine all ingredients; spread over meat loaf. Bake at 350 degrees for 1 hour and 15 minutes. Yield: 8 servings.

Mrs. Herbert Laroche, Pres.
Bethania Ladies Aid
Domremy, Saskatchewan, Canada

POT ROAST MEAT LOAF

1 lb. ground lean beef
⅔ c. evaporated milk
⅓ c. fine dry bread crumbs
¼ c. catsup or chili sauce
2 tsp. salt
2 tsp. Worcestershire sauce
Pepper to taste
2 tsp. dried parsley flakes
3 med. potatoes, sliced
3 med. onions, sliced
3 med. carrots, sliced

Combine ground beef, evaporated milk, bread crumbs, catsup or chili sauce, 1 teaspoonful salt, Worcestershire sauce and 1/4 teaspoonful pepper; shape into a loaf. Place in 13 x 9 x 2-inch pan. Mix dried parsley flakes with 1 teaspoonful salt and few grains of pepper. Place vegetables in layers around meat; sprinkle each layer with salt mixture. Cover with foil. Bake at 375 degrees for 1 hour or until vegetables are tender. Uncover; bake for 10 minutes longer. Yield: 4 servings.

Mrs. Luther Hovis
Trinity Lutheran Church
Fredericktown, Missouri

SAVORY MEAT LOAF

1 ½ lb. ground beef
1 pkg. dry onion soup mix
1 sm. can evaporated milk
½ c. bread crumbs

Mix ground beef, onion soup mix, milk and bread crumbs; shape into a loaf. Place in a 7 x 11-inch pan. Bake at 350 degrees for 45 minutes. Yield: 6-8 servings.

Mrs. Henry Brunner, VP
St. John Naomi Circle
Windsor, Colorado

SAVORY MEAT LOAF

1 c. ground dry bread crumbs
1 c. evaporated milk
3 eggs, slightly beaten
3 lb. ground beef
3 tsp. salt
Pinch of pepper
1 ½ tsp. monosodium glutamate
2 pkg. spaghetti sauce mix

Combine bread crumbs with evaporated milk; add eggs. Mix well. Add remaining ingredients; mix thoroughly. Shape into loaf; place in 7 x 10 x 2-inch foil-lined pan. Bake at 350 degrees for 1 hour. Yield: 8-12 servings.

Mrs. Dorothy Olds, Pres.
First Lutheran Church Ladies Guild
Grands Rapids, Minnesota

SKILLET MEAT LOAF

1 slice stale bread, crumbled
1 egg, beaten
¼ c. milk
1 tsp. Worcestershire sauce
2 tbsp. minced onion
½ tsp. salt
Pepper to taste
1 lb. ground beef
Flour
Meat drippings
¼ c. water

Combine bread, eggs, milk, Worcestershire sauce, onion, salt and pepper; add meat. Mix thoroughly. Shape into an oval loaf. Dust with flour; brown meat loaf in meat drippings in Dutch oven. Add water. Cover; cook over low heat for 50 minutes. Small potatoes, onions and carrots may be cooked around the loaf, if desired. Yield: 4-6 servings.

Mrs. Clarence Koth
St. Peter's LWML
Filion, Michigan

SPECIAL MEAT LOAF

¾ c. corn flake crumbs
1 c. milk
2 tbsp. onion
2 eggs, beaten
¼ c. diced green pepper
1 tbsp. Worcestershire sauce
1 tsp. salt
½ tsp. garlic salt
1 ½ lb. ground beef
1 c. Parmesan cheese
Catsup

Combine crumbs, milk, onion, eggs, green pepper, Worcestershire sauce, salt, garlic salt, ground beef and 1/2 cup Parmesan cheese. Roll into six loaves; place in 9 x 11-inch pan. Spread with catsup and sprinkle with remaining cheese. Bake at 350 degrees for 45 minutes. Yield: 6 servings.

Mrs. Elwin Ronk
St. John Lutheran Church
Dunlap, Iowa

SPECIAL MEAT LOAF

1 ½ lb. ground beef
¾ c. oats
2 eggs, beaten
¼ c. chopped onion
2 tsp. salt
¼ tsp. pepper
1 c. tomato juice

Combine all ingredients; mix thoroughly. Pack firmly into loaf pan. Bake at 350 degrees for 1 hour. Let stand for 5 minutes before slicing. Yield: 8 servings.

Mrs. Arnold Westfield, Pres.
Bethlehem LCW
Ellsworth, Wisconsin

SPICY MEAT LOAF

MEAT LOAF:

1 ½ c. bread crumbs
2 c. milk
3 lb. hamburger
4 eggs, beaten
½ c. chopped onion
2 tsp. salt
⅛ tsp. pepper
1 tsp. sage
½ tsp. dry mustard
½ tsp. poultry seasoning

Soak bread crumbs in milk; add meat, eggs, onion and seasonings. Mix well; form into two loaf pans. Top with sauce. Bake at 350 degrees for 1 hour.

SAUCE:

½ c. catsup
4 tbsp. brown saugr
1 tsp. dry mustard

Combine all ingredients; pour over Meat Loaf. Yield: 14 servings.

Mrs. Omer Maakestad, Pres.
Our Savior's LCW
Leland, Iowa

STUFFED MEAT LOAF

1 ½ lb. ground beef
1 egg
½ c. milk
Salt and pepper
1 tbsp. Worcestershire sauce
2 c. bread cubes
½ tsp. poultry seasoning
1 tbsp. minced onion
4 tbsp. melted butter

Mix ground beef with egg, milk, 1 teaspoonful salt, 1/8 teaspoonful pepper and Worcestershire sauce. Line a small loaf pan with part of mixture. Mix bread cubes, 1/2 teaspoonful salt and 1/2 teaspoonful pepper with remaining ingredients; spread over meat mixture. Cover with remaining meat mixture. Bake at 375 degrees for 45 minutes. Serve with mushroom sauce if desired. Yield: 6 servings.

Mrs. Nellie Croyle, Treas.
St. John Ladies Aid
Summerhill, Pennsylvania

SWEET LOAF DISH

⅔ c. dry bread crumbs
1 c. milk
1 ½ lb. ground beef
2 eggs, beaten
¼ c. grated onion
1 tsp. salt
¼ tsp. pepper
Sliced potatoes
1 can pork and beans
½ c. brown sugar
½ c. catsup

(Continued on next page)

Soak bread crumbs in the milk; add meat, eggs, onion and seasonings. Mix well. Form into loaf; place in a large casserole. Add potatoes around the outside of the loaf. Pour pork and beans over potatoes. Mix brown sugar and catsup; pour over meat loaf. Bake at 350 degrees for 1 hour and 30 minutes. Yield: 6 servings.

Mrs. Edna Schedler
St. John's Bethlehem Soc.
Pekin, Illinois

TOMATO MEAT LOAF

¼ c. chopped onion
½ tbsp. butter or margarine
1 lb. ground beef
½ tsp. salt
⅛ tsp. pepper
1 tbsp. chopped parsley
1 can tomato soup
1 egg
1 c. soft bread crumbs
2 slices white bread
⅛ c. water

Heat oven to 350 degrees. Cook onion in butter until tender; combine with meat. Add salt, pepper, parsley, 1/2 can tomato soup, egg and bread crumbs. Place one-half of mixture in 9 x 5 x 2 1/2-inch loaf pan. Place white bread over meat loosely. Add remaining meat mixture. Bake at 350 degrees for 1 hour. Combine remaining soup with water; pour over meat loaf during last 15 minutes of cooking. Yield: 4-6 servings.

Mrs. Alfred Leite
Urland Lutheran Church
Battleford, Saskatchewan, Canada

BAKED BEEF PATTIES

1 lb. ground beef
1 sm. onion, grated
1 tsp. chili powder
1 tsp. salt
⅛ tsp. pepper
½ c. chili sauce
4 strips bacon
4 apricot halves

Combine ground beef, onion, chili powder, salt, pepper and chili sauce; form into four patties. Wrap each with strip of bacon and fasten with wooden pick. Top each with an apricot half. Bake at 450 degrees for 20 to 25 minutes or until done. Yield: 4 servings.

Mrs. Carl Zaar, Sr., Pres.
Zion LCW
Hudson, Wisconsin

BAKED BEEF ROUNDS

2 lb. ground beef
1 c. soft bread crumbs
½ c. catsup
1 onion, chopped

1 egg, slightly beaten
1 tsp. Worcestershire sauce
1 ½ tsp. salt
¼ tsp. pepper
½ c. tomato juice
Onion rings

Mix all ingredients except tomato juice and onion rings. Shape into patties and place in a shallow baking pan. Spoon tomato juice around patties; cover with onion rings. Bake, uncovered, at 350 degrees for 1 hour. Yield: 4-6 servings.

Mrs. Clarence Vassberg, Pres.
Bethel LCW
Lyford, Texas

BARBECUED HAMBURGER

1 c. catsup
½ c. vinegar
½ c. chopped onion
1 tsp. chili powder
3 tsp. Worcestershire sauce
Hamburger patties

Mix all ingredients except patties; pour over patties. Bake at 350 degrees for 1 hour. Yield: 6 servings.

Mrs. Harold W. Schmolt, Pres.
St. Paul's LCW
Massillon, Ohio

BARBECUED MEAT PATTIES

1 c. soft bread crumbs
1 c. milk
1 lb. ground beef
1 sm. onion, chopped
1 tsp. salt
½ tsp. pepper
4 tbsp. powdered sugar
4 tbsp. fat

Soak bread crumbs in 1/2 cup milk. Add ground beef, onion, remaining milk, salt and pepper. Form into patties. Dip each pattie into powdered sugar; brown quickly in hot fat. Place in 8 x 8-inch baking pan. Top with Barbecue Sauce.

BARBECUE SAUCE:

1 tbsp. Worcestershire sauce
2 tbsp. vinegar
½ tsp. catsup
4 tbsp. chopped onion

Combine all ingredients in saucepan; bring to boil. Pour over meat balls. Bake in 350 degree oven for about 15 minutes. Yield: 10 servings.

Mrs. Earl C. Anderson, Treas.
Zion Ladies Aid
Hoskins, Nebraska

BEEF PATTIES

1 lb. ground beef
1 med. onion, chopped
3 eggs
½ c. quick cooking oats
1 tsp. salt
1 tsp. all purpose seasoning
Fat

Combine all ingredients except fat; mix thoroughly. Drop with tablespoon into skillet with fat. Fry until brown over medium heat. Yield: 8-10 servings.

Mrs. Albert Hohbein, Pres.
Zion LWML
Harbine, Nebraska

BROILED SALISBURY STEAK

1 lb. ground beef
1 tsp. salt
¼ tsp. pepper
Onion salt or chopped onion (opt.)
½ c. milk
Bread or cracker crumbs
2 tbsp. butter

Mix beef, salt, pepper, onion salt and milk. Form into one large steak. Cover on both sides with crumbs. Place on broiling rack and dot with butter; brown. Turn and dot with butter; brown. Place on hot platter; garnish with parsley and serve. Yield: 4 servings.

Mrs. Florence Gerfin
Hales Corners
Women's Serv. Guild
Hales Corner, Wisconsin

MEAL-IN-ONE COOKOUT

1 ½ lb. ground beef
1 ½ tsp. salt
1 tsp. pepper
4 lge. carrots, sliced
4 lge. potatoes, sliced
1 lge. onion, sliced

Mix ground beef, salt and pepper; shape into eight patties. Place a layer of carrots and potatoes on four squares of foil. Top with meat patties. Top with slices of onion and remaining meat patties, potatoes and carrots. Seal ends of foil together airtight. Cook for 15 minutes over hot coals; turn and cook on other side for 15 minutes. Yield: 4 servings.

Mrs. Clarence Wessel, Pres.
St. Paul Ladies Aid
Chaffee, Missouri

HAWAIIAN HAMBURGERS WITH SWEET 'N' SOUR SAUCE

⅔ c. evaporated milk
1 ½ lb. ground beef
½ c. chopped onion
⅔ c. cracker crumbs
1 tsp. salt
1 15-oz. can pineapple chunks
2 tbsp. cornstarch
¼ c. vinegar
¼ c. brown sugar
2 tbsp. soy sauce
1 c. coarsely chopped green peppers

Combine milk, ground beef, onion, crumbs and salt. Form into six 4-inch patties, pressing between sheets of waxed paper. Brown patties in a small amount of fat in skillet. Drain pineapple, reserving syrup. Add enough water to reserved syrup to equal 1 cup liquid. Combine syrup, cornstarch, vinegar, brown sugar and soy sauce; cook, stirring, until thick and clear. Pour off excess fat from burgers in skillet; cover with sauce mixture. Add pineapple chunks and green peppers. Cover; simmer over low heat for 15 minutes.

Mrs. Lorne Grife, Pres.
Grace Ladies Aid
Pembroke, Ontario, Canada

MOCK CHICKEN-FRIED STEAKS

1 lb. ground beef
1 tsp. onion salt
1 tsp. parsley flakes
1 egg
2 tbsp. milk
½ tsp. salt
1 tsp. chili powder
2 c. cracker crumbs or bread crumbs
Shortening

Mix all ingredients except 1 cup crumbs and shortening. Divide mixture into six balls. Sprinkle some cracker crumbs on board; roll and shape balls into steaks. Be sure both sides are well coated with crumbs. Place on waxed paper; chill for 30 minutes. Brown steaks on both sides in hot shortening. Serve hot. NOTE: Uncooked steaks may be frozen until needed. Yield: 6 servings.

Mrs. George Niehoff, Pres.
Zion Women's League
Quenemo, Kansas

MUSHROOM-GROUND BEEF PATTIES

1 lb. ground beef
2 med. onions, diced
½ tsp. salt
¼ tsp. pepper
1 can cream of mushroom soup

Form meat into flat patties; brown lightly on each side in heavy skillet. Drain off excess fat. Cover patties with onion; sprinkle with salt and pepper. Add soup. Cover; simmer for 30 minutes. Yield: 4-6 servings.

Mrs. Oscar Bredthauer, Sr., Chmn.
Trinity Ruth Soc. and Altar Guild
Grand Island, Nebraska

PEASANT'S FILLET

1 chicken or beef bouillon cube
1 ½ tbsp. water
1 lb. lean ground beef
⅛ tsp. onion salt
¼ to ½ tsp. salt
⅛ tsp. pepper
½ c. flour
3 tbsp. cooking oil
1 tbsp. butter
¼ c. red cooking wine

Dissolve bouillon cube in water. Mix beef, bouillon and seasonings. Separate into four parts; form into flat round patties about 3/4-inch thick and resembling a small filet. Flour patties on both sides; cook in oil with medium high heat to desired doneness. Turn only once and cook as a true fillet of the same size. Place on warm platter. Drain pan of all but 1 tablespoonful of drippings; reduce heat. Add butter and wine. Simmer a few minutes until sauce is a little thick. Pour over meat and serve immediately. Yield: 4 servings.

Mrs. W. A. Pearson, Pres.
Mighty Fortress LCW
Charlotte, North Carolina

PORK-U-PINES

1 med. onion, chopped
1 piece green pepper, chopped
4 tbsp. drippings
1 lb. ground beef
½ c. uncooked rice
1 c. mashed cooked potatoes
¾ tsp. chili powder (opt.)
1 ½ tsp. salt
½ tsp. pepper
1 egg
1 ½ c. water
1 ½ c. tomato soup or juice

Brown onion and green pepper in drippings; cook for 5 minutes. Remove from heat. Add meat, rice, potatoes and seasonings; mix well. Stir in egg. Shape into patties; place in roaster. Mix water and soup; pour over patties. Cover and bake at 375 degrees for 1 hour.

Mrs. Edward P. Jessen, Pres.
Zion LCW
Chicago, Illinois

RANCH BURGERS

1 lb. ground beef
1 ½ c. chopped onions
1 to 2 c. chopped celery
½ c. chopped green pepper
1 can tomato soup
½ to 1 tbsp. barbecue sauce
1 tsp. salt
Pepper to taste

Brown meat in small amount of hot fat; add onions, celery and green pepper. Cook in heavy skillet until soft. Add all remaining ingredients. Cover; simmer for 30 minutes. Yield: 6 servings.

Johanna Bauer
Grace Lutheran Church Miss'y Soc.
Sugar City, Colorado

SALISBURY STEAK

1 ⅔ c. cracker crumbs
2 tbsp. grated onion
1 tsp. Worcestershire sauce
½ tsp. pepper
½ tsp. nutmeg
2 lb. ground beef
½ c. catsup
2 eggs
2 tbsp. chopped parsley
2 tsp. salt
½ tsp. marjoram
1 can cream of mushroom soup
2 tbsp. butter
1 c. milk
1 tbsp. cooking Sherry
½ tsp. garlic salt
1 4-oz. can sliced mushrooms
1 tbsp. chopped pimento

Combine crumbs, onion, Worcestershire sauce, pepper, nutmeg, beef, catsup, eggs, parsley, salt and marjoram; mix well. Shape into eight oval patties. Place in shallow baking dish. Heat soup with butter, milk, cooking Sherry and garlic salt. Pour over meat patties in baking dish. Add mushrooms. Cover; bake at 350 degrees for 40 to 50 minutes. Garnish with pimento. Yield: 8 servings.

Mrs. Euna Jones, Pres.
Zion LWML
Old Glory, Texas

SALISBURY STEAK

1 lge. onion, chopped
1 lge. green pepper, chopped
Margarine
3 c. ground chuck
2 c. bread crumbs
2 eggs, well beaten
Salt and pepper to taste
2 tbsp. soy sauce
Flour

Saute onion and green pepper in margarine until tender. Mix all ingredients except flour. Sprinkle board with flour; place meat on floured board. Sprinkle top with flour and flatten down to about 1-inch in thickness. Cut into strips 1 x 3-inches; brown.

GRAVY:

2 c. water
2 beef bouillon cubes
½ tsp. thyme
Flour

(Continued on next page)

Combine ingredients to make a gravy. Pour over meat; simmer for 20 to 30 minutes. Yield: 12 servings.

> Mrs. Wilma Ferris
> Holy Trinity Mission and Aid Soc.
> Elizabeth, New Jersey

BEEF PASTRY

¼ c. shortening
1 c. flour
¼ tsp. salt
⅔ tsp. water
½ c. diced potatoes
¼ c. diced onion
3 oz. ground beef
Salt and pepper to taste

Cut shortening into flour; add salt. Sprinkle water onto flour mixture; mix until mixture forms a ball and cleans sides of bowl. Use 8-inch pie tin. Roll out dough into oblong shape; place in an 8-inch pie tin. Combine all remaining ingredients. Fill one-half of pie crust; dot with butter, salt and pepper. Fold remaining crust over filled portion. Bake at 425 degrees for 1 hour.

> Mrs. Roy S. Danner, Pres.
> St. John's Ladies Aid Soc.
> Tatamy, Pennsylvania

HAMBURGER- COTTAGE CHEESE PIE

1 c. chopped onions
¼ c. finely chopped green pepper
2 tbsp. butter
1 lb. minced beef
¾ tsp. salt
¼ tsp. pepper
1 tsp. Worcestershire sauce
2 tbsp. flour
1 9-inch pie shell, baked
1 c. cottage cheese
2 eggs, beaten
Dash of paprika

Saute onions and green pepper in melted butter for about 5 minutes or until limp. Add meat; brown for 4 to 5 minutes. Stir in seasonings and flour. Spread meat mixture into baked pie shell. Blend cottage cheese with beaten eggs; pour over meat. Sprinkle with paprika. Bake at 350 degrees for about 40 minutes or until nicely browned. Yield: 6 servings.

> Mrs. Miriam Loessin, Pres.
> St. Paul's LCW
> Radisson, Saskatchewan, Canada

HAMBURGER DELIGHT

1 ½ to 2 lb. hamburger
1 sm. onion, chopped
1 can onion soup
Salt and pepper to taste
Flour

4 med. potatoes, diced
4 med. carrots, diced
1 recipe pastry

Fry hamburger with onion; mix in onion soup, seasonings and thickening. Boil potatoes and carrots. Add vegetables and vegetable liquid to hamburger mixture. Cover with pastry. Bake at 400 degrees for 30 minutes. Yield: 6-8 servings.

> Mrs. Ray E. Varner
> Trinity Ladies Aid
> New Germany, Lunen, Nova Scotia, Canada

HAMBURGER PIE

1 ¼ lb. ground beef
1 tbsp. minced onion
¼ tsp. salt
Dash of pepper
1 ¼ c. instant rice
2 8-oz. cans tomato sauce
1 c. water
¼ lb. Cheddar cheese, cubed

Mix ground beef, onion, salt and pepper; pat like pie crust into a 9-inch pie pan. Mix rice, tomato sauce and water; pour into meat shell. Cover with aluminum foil. Bake at 325 degrees for 30 minutes. Remove foil; top with cheese. Continue baking for 10 minutes or until cheese melts. Cut into wedges. Yield: 6 servings.

> Mrs. Lloyd Clore
> St. Paul's Ladies Aid
> East St. Louis, Illinois

HAMBURGER PIE

1 lb. hamburger
2 tsp. salt
¼ tsp. pepper
1 tbsp. Worcestershire sauce
3 tbsp. catsup
1 tsp. prepared mustard
½ tsp. poultry seasoning
1 recipe pastry for two-crust 9-inch pie
2 med. potatoes, sliced
2 med. onions, coarsely chopped
¼ c. margarine or butter
1 can brown gravy with mushrooms

Mix hamburger with seasonings; pile into pastry-lined pie pan. Fry potatoes and onions in margarine until potatoes are just soft and onions lightly browned; mix in gravy. Pour mixture over the top of pie. Top with top crust. Bake at 375 degrees for 1 hour and 15 minutes. Yield: 4-5 servings.

> Mrs. Annette Phillips, Pres.
> Grace LWML
> Brandon, Manitoba, Canada

HAMBURGER PIE

1 lb. hamburger
Seasonings to taste
1 can vegetable soup
5 med. potatoes, cooked and mashed

(Continued on next page)

Mix hamburger with seasonings; put into bottom of 9-inch pie pan. Bake at 400 degrees for 20 minutes. Pour soup over hamburger; top with mashed potatoes. Heat in oven for 5 minutes. Yield: 4-5 servings.

Mrs. Audrey Lein, Pres.
Evergreen Ladies Guild
Evergreen, Colorado

HOT TAMALE PIE

5 c. yellow corn meal
5 qt. water
Salt
5 lb. hamburger
3 onions, finely diced
1 tsp. pepper
4 tbsp. chili powder
3 tbsp. sugar
2 qt. tomato sauce
2 No. 202 cans whole kernel yellow corn
2 cans sm. ripe pitted olives
3 tbsp. vinegar

Moisten corn meal with part of the water. Bring remaining water to a boil; add corn meal and 1 tablespoonful salt. Boil slowly for 10 minutes, stirring constantly. Pour 1 quart mush onto plate to cool; slice into 1 1/2-inch squares. Spread remaining mush into 2 x 10 x 16-inch baking pan. Brown hamburger in large skillet with onions. Cook until done, adding 5 teaspoonfuls salt and remaining ingredients. Bring to a boil; pour into mush-lined pan. Top with corn meal squares. Bake at 375 degrees for 40 minutes or until bubbly. Yield: 30 servings.

Mrs. Cleo M. Brinkman
First Lutheran Marys and Marthas
Fontana, California

MEAT-ZA PIE

1 lb. ground beef
¼ to 1 tsp. garlic salt
½ c. fine dry bread crumbs
⅔ c. evaporated milk
⅓ c. catsup or tomato paste
1 can mushrooms, drained and chopped
    or ¼ c. green pepper
2 to 3 slices American cheese, cut into strips
¼ tsp. oregano or poultry seasoning
2 tbsp. grated Parmesan cheese

Place beef, garlic salt and bread crumbs in 9-inch pan. Add evaporated milk; mix. Spread mixture, forming rim about 1/2-inch high around edge. Spread catsup or tomato paste over meat to rim. Arrange mushrooms or green pepper on catsup; place cheese strips in criss-cross pattern over top. Sprinkle with oregano or poultry seasoning; sprinkle generously with grated cheese. Bake in preheated 400 degree oven for 20 minutes, or until cheese is melted and lightly browned. Cut into wedges and serve. NOTE: one-half cup cracker crumbs may be substituted for dry bread crumbs. Yield: 4 servings.

Mrs. Roy Klingelhoefer, Pres.
Zion Ladies Aid
Mascoutah, Illinois

MEATZA PIE

1 lb. ground meat
⅔ c. evaporated milk
½ c. dry bread crumbs
1 tsp. garlic salt
1 sm. can tomato paste
1 2-oz. can mushrooms
1 c. shredded sharp cheese
¼ tsp. oregano
2 tbsp. grated Parmesan cheese

Mix meat with milk, crumbs and salt. Pat mixture into 9-inch pie plate, forming rims like pie shell. Spread tomato paste over meat mixture. Drain mushrooms; place on tomato paste. Top with shredded cheese. Sprinkle with oregano and Parmesan cheese. Bake at 375 degrees for 45 minutes. Yield: 4-5 servings.

Mrs. Gerald Johnson
St. John's LCW
Erie, Pennsylvania

MEATZA PIE

1 lb. ground beef
½ tsp. garlic salt
¾ c. fine bread crumbs
½ can cream of mushroom soup
⅓ c. catsup
2 or 3 slices process American cheese, cut
    into strips
¼ tsp. oregano
2 tbsp. grated Parmesan cheese

Place beef, garlic salt, crumbs and mushroom soup in 9-inch pie pan. Mix and spread evenly in pan. Spread catsup over top; place cheese strips in a criss-cross pattern over top. Sprinkle with oregano and Parmesan cheese. Bake at 400 degrees for 20 minutes. Yield: 6 servings.

Mrs. Lyall Moross, Chmn.
Bethesda LCW
Benson, Minnesota

INDIVIDUAL PIZZAS

1 can tomato sauce
½ tsp. salt
½ tsp. garlic salt
1 tsp. Worcestershire sauce
Oregano
1 can refrigerated biscuits
½ lb. ground chuck
½ lb. sharp cheese, grated

Combine all ingredients except biscuits, ground chuck and cheese. Roll biscuits between two pieces of waxed paper to a 4-inch circle. Place on ungreased cookie sheets. Shape meat into 4-inch patties. Place on biscuits; top with sauce and cheese. Bake at 450 degrees for 8 to 10 minutes or until brown. Yield: 10 servings.

Bernandette Fabin, Sec.
First Lutheran Guild
Phillipsburg, Kansas

TAMALE-PIZZA PIE

1 ½ c. yellow corn meal
6 c. boiling water
3 tsp. salt
1 c. chopped onions
1 tbsp. bacon drippings
1 ½ lb. lean ground beef
Pepper to taste
1 can pizza sauce
1 can tamales, cut into rounds
½ lb. sharp Cheddar cheese, grated

Stir corn meal with wire whip into boiling water with 2 teaspoonfuls salt. Cook slowly for 15 minutes or longer. Cook onions in bacon fat in skillet until limp. Add ground beef. Sprinkle with 1 teaspoonful salt and pepper; cook just until meat loses color. Add pizza sauce; cook for 10 minutes. Add tamales; gently stir into meat mixture. Simmer for 2 minutes. Spread corn meal into two 9 x 13-inch pans. Top with meat mixture. Sprinkle with cheese; garnish with olives, if desired. Bake at 375 degrees for 30 minutes or until bubbling hot and cheese is melted. Yield: 15 servings.

Mrs. Hazel W. Steinbeck
Zion LWML
Terra Bella, California

TINY PIZZAS

1 c. catsup
½ tsp. salt
½ tsp. Worcestershire sauce
½ tsp. garlic salt
2 drops Tabasco sauce
½ tsp. thyme (opt.)
1 can biscuits
½ lb. ground beef
¾ c. grated cheese

Combine catsup, salt, Worcestershire sauce, garlic salt, Tabasco sauce and thyme. Roll each biscuit to a thin 4-inch circle. Cover each with a layer of the uncooked ground beef; spread with catsup mixture. Sprinkle with cheese. Place on an ungreased cookie sheet. Bake at 425 degrees for 10 minutes. Yield: 5 servings.

Mrs. Louis Lundgren, Pres.
New Sweden LCW
Elgin, Texas

BARBECUED BEEF

1 ½ lb. ground beef
Fat
1 lge. onion, chopped
1 c. celery
1 green pepper, chopped
2 tbsp. vinegar
2 tbsp. sugar
1 c. catsup
1 c. water
1 tsp. mustard
1 tsp. Worcestershire sauce

Brown ground beef in fat; add onion, celery and green pepper. Add remaining ingredients. Simmer for 1 hour and 30 minutes. Yield: 12 servings.

Mrs. H. Pergande
Faith Ladies Guild
Dunedin, Florida

BARBECUE SAUCE FOR SPANISH RICE

1 green pepper, chopped
1 lge. onion, chopped
1 lb. round ground beef
½ tsp. salt
½ tsp. pepper
½ tsp. garlic salt
1 tsp. oregano
1 tsp. mint flakes
1 tsp. basil
1 tsp. celery flakes
3 cans tomato paste

Sear green pepper, onion and ground beef well; add all remaining ingredients. Simmer over very low heat for about 1 hour. Yield: 10-15 servings.

Marilyn Truitt
LWML
Charleston, South Carolina

GOULASH

2 tbsp. diced onion
2 tbsp. lard
2 lb. chopped beef
2 tsp. allspice
2 tbsp. vinegar
1 tbsp. sugar
2 tbsp. flour
10 gingersnaps, crumbled
2 tbsp. catsup
⅛ tsp. paprika
1 tsp. salt
3 qt. water

Brown onion in lard in 6-quart saucepan. Add beef, allspice, vinegar and sugar. Cook until meat is browned, stirring occasionally. Sprinkle with flour and gingersnaps. Cook, stirring until mixed. Stir in catsup, paprika and salt. Add water; simmer until meat is tender. Yield: 4 servings.

Mrs. Burnis Brahmer, Pres.
St. Matthews Ladies Aid
Wisner, Nebraska

BEEF AND MACARONI CASSEROLE

1 lb. ground beef, round or chuck
½ sm. onion, finely chopped
½ No. 303 can whole kernel corn
1 10 ½-oz. can tomato soup
¾ c. raw elbow macaroni, cooked and drained
Salt and pepper

Brown meat in large frying pan. Add onion, corn, soup and macaroni. Season to taste. Cook over medium heat for 20 to 25 minutes,

(Continued on next page)

adding water as needed; stir occasionally. Yield: 5 servings.

Mrs. Janet Ballard, Co-Chmn., Hospty. Com.
Mt. Olive LCW Guild
Palos Verdes Peninsula, California

CINNAMON CASSEROLE

1 c. uncooked macaroni
1 lb. ground round
1 sm. onion, chopped
Salt and pepper
1 tsp. cinnamon
1 10-oz. can tomato soup
¼ c. catsup

Cook macaroni; drain. Brown meat with onion in a skillet. Add salt pepper and cinnamon. Add remaining ingredients. Cover pan. Simmer for 15 minutes to blend flavors. Yield: 4 servings.

Mrs. S. James Krall, Pres.
St. Paul's LWML
Nanaimo, British Columbia, Canada

SKILLET MACARONI AND BEEF

1 ½ lb. ground beef
½ c. minced onion
½ lb. uncooked elbow macaroni
½ c. chopped green pepper
2 8-oz. cans tomato sauce or 1 qt. tomatoes
1 c. water
1 tsp. salt
¼ tsp. pepper
1 ½ tbsp. Worcestershire sauce

Cook beef in large skillet until redness disappears. Remove from skillet. Cook onion, macaroni and green pepper in meat fat until macaroni is yellow. Add additional fat if meat sticks. Return meat to skillet with tomato sauce, water, salt, pepper and Worcestershire sauce. Cover and simmer for 25 minutes or until macaroni is cooked. Yield: 6 servings.

Mrs. Jean Loveless, Pres.
Calvary Dorcas Soc.
Cromwell, Indiana

BEEF-NOODLE CASSEROLE

1 lb. ground beef
½ c. chopped onion
2 tbsp. fat
1 can tomato soup
1 ½ c. water
1 5-oz. pkg. noodles
½ pt. sour cream

Saute ground beef and onion in fat; Add soup, water and noodles; simmer until noodles are tender. Add sour cream; mix well. Garnish with green vegetables and parsley, if desired.

Mrs. Marvin Blada
St. John Lutheran Church
Newburg, North Dakota

GROUND BEEF AND NOODLES

¾ c. chopped onions
2 tbsp. margarine
1 lb. ground beef
3 c. uncooked noodles
3 c. tomato juice
1 tsp. salt
1 ½ tsp. celery salt
Dash of pepper
2 tsp. Worcestershire sauce
¼ c. chopped green pepper
1 c. sour cream
1 3-oz. can sliced mushrooms, drained

Cook onions in margarine until tender, but not brown. Add beef; brown lightly. Place noodles in layer over meat. Combine tomato juice and seasonings. Pour over noodles. Bring to a boil; cover and simmer over low heat for 20 minutes. Add green pepper; cover and simmer for 10 minutes or until noodles are tender. Stir in sour cream and mushrooms; heat just to boiling. Top with green pepper rings.

Mrs. Clayborne S. King, Pres.
Messiah LCW
Salisbury, North Carolina

HAMBURGER HEAVEN

1 lb. ground beef
1 tbsp. fat
1 med. onion, diced
1 tsp. salt
¼ tsp. pepper
½ lb. American cheese, sliced
1 c. chopped celery
2 c. fine dry noodles
1 No. 2 can tomatoes
¼ c. water

Brown meat slightly in fat in skillet. Add onion, salt and pepper; stir to blend well. Add all remaining ingredients except water in layers in order given; pour water over all. Cover. Cook over high heat until steaming; simmer for 30 minutes. Do not remove cover. Yield: 6 servings.

Mrs. Paul A. Dinterman, VP
St. Paul's LCW
Walkersville, Maryland

MacDONALD CASSEROLE

2 lb. hamburger
1 lge. onion, diced
1 clove of garlic, diced
1 red pepper, diced (opt.)
1 green pepper, diced (opt.)
2 stalks celery, diced
1 can cream of chicken soup
1 can Cheddar cheese soup
1 can cream of mushroom soup
1 pkg. noodles, cooked

Saute all ingredients except soups and noodles in frying pan. Add noodles and soups. Simmer, stirring, until heated. NOTE: May be cooked in

(Continued on next page)

casserole at low temperature for 1 hour. Yield: 10-12 servings.

Mrs. Florence Komnick, Pres.
St. John's Ladies Aid
New Berlin, Illinois

MOCK BEEF STROGANOFF

½ tsp. salt
1 lb. lean ground beef
½ c. chopped onion
1 clove of garlic, minced
1 sm. can mushrooms, chopped
¼ tsp. pepper
2 tbsp. flour
1 can cream of chicken soup
2 c. hot water
Cooked broad noodles or rice

Heat an iron skillet; sprinkle salt in skillet, using no fat. Make a large pattie of ground beef on a sheet of waxed paper. Place meat pattie in skillet; brown well on both sides. Remove pattie to large platter; cut into 1/2-inch cubes. Saute onion and garlic in meat drippings. Add more fat if needed. Add mushrooms, pepper, meat, flour, soup and hot water. Blend until smooth. Serve over noodles or rice; sprinkle with parsley and paprika, if desired. Yield: 6-8 servings.

Mrs. Joan Pitkin, Pres.
Trinity Ladies Guild
Exeter, California

SPANISH NOODLES

2 tbsp. fat
1 lb. ground beef
2 ½ tsp. salt
⅛ tsp. pepper
1 sm. onion
1 clove of garlic (opt.)
4 tbsp. green pepper
½ c. mushrooms
2 c. uncooked noodles
3 c. tomato juice
1 ½ tsp. sugar

Melt fat in skillet. Mix ground beef, salt and pepper; brown over high heat in hot fat. Add remaining ingredients. Cover; when steam comes from cover, reduce heat. Cook for 45 minutes without removing cover. Yield: 6 servings.

Mrs. John W. Nesgoda
Redeemer LCW
Erie, Pennsylvania

SPANISH NOODLES

1 lb. ground beef
1 green pepper, diced
1 onion, chopped
1 tsp. salt
2 c. uncooked noodles
3 ½ c. tomatoes
½ c. chili sauce
¼ tsp. pepper

Brown beef in large skillet. Add remaining ingredients in layers. Be sure all noodles are moistened. Cover; cook on high until steam escapes. Lower heat; simmer for 30 minutes. Yield: 4-6 servings.

Mrs. Frank Gajowski
Abiding Savior Miriam Circle
North Royalton, Ohio

ITALIAN SPAGHETTI

2 tbsp. olive oil
1 lge. onion, chopped
1 lge. green pepper, chopped
1 clove of garlic, minced
1 lb. ground beef
2 cans tomato paste
1 tsp. chili powder
¼ tsp. soda
2 tsp. sugar
2 c. water
Cooked spaghetti

Heat olive oil; add onion, green pepper, garlic and ground beef. Cook until brown. Add all ingredients except spaghetti; simmer for 1 hour and 30 minutes. Serve over cooked spaghetti. Yield: 4 servings.

Mrs. V. H. Waltemath
Maria Lutheran Church
Hershey, Nebraska

SPAGHETTI SAUCE

2 ½ onions, chopped
3 cloves of garlic
2 lb. hamburger
½ c. oil
Salt and pepper to taste
1 tsp. thyme
1 tsp. sweet basil
2 cans tomato paste
2 cans tomato sauce
Water
Dash of chili powder
¼ c. lemon juice
1 c. wine

Brown onions, garlic and hamburger in oil. Add remaining ingredients, adding as much water as tomato sauce and paste. Simmer for 2 hours. Serve over cooked spaghetti. NOTE: This sauce may be frozen.

Mrs. A. C. Larsen
Bethany Lutheran Church
Ord, Nebraska

SPANISH RICE WITH HOT CHILI SAUCE

2 c. rice
1 c. water
1 No. 2 can green peas
1 lb. hamburger
1 med. onion, chopped
¼ c. canned chopped green chilies
½ tsp. garlic salt
¼ tsp. salt
2 sm. cans tomato sauce

(Continued on next page)

Brown rice in large iron skillet; add water and simmer. Heat peas in saucepan. Brown hamburger, breaking up into small pea-sized pieces; add onion, green chilies, garlic salt and salt. When well done, add tomato sauce. Simmer for 15 to 25 minutes. Place rice in large bowl. Mix green peas in chili-hamburger mixture; pour on top of rice. Yield: 4-6 servings.

Mrs. Kathleen Burger, Librarian
Ladies of Trinity
Alamo Gordo, New Mexico

SPAGHETTI SAUCE

1 lge. onion, chopped
1 med. green pepper, chopped
2 tbsp. olive oil
1 lb. lean ground meat
1 can tomato paste
1 lge. can tomatoes
1 tsp. chili powder
Salt and pepper to taste
Dash of Texas Pete
Dash of cayenne
2 tsp. parsley flakes
1 tsp. Worcestershire sauce

Cook onion and pepper in olive oil for 5 minutes. Add meat and sear. Add remaining ingredients. Bring to a boil; simmer. NOTE: If desired, add a clove of garlic to onion and pepper; cook for 1 minute. Yield: 4 servings.

Sarah Lopp, Pres.
First Lutheran Church LCW
Lexington, North Carolina

BEEF STROGANOFF

2 lb. sirloin steak
Salt and pepper
5 tbsp. butter
1 tbsp. flour
2 c. beef stock
2 tbsp. sour cream
2 tbsp. tomato juice or paste
3 tbsp. grated onion

Cut beef into thin strips; sprinkle freely with salt and pepper. Let stand for 2 hours in cool place. Melt 2 tablespoonfuls butter over low heat; add flour. Stir until mixture bubbles and is smooth. Gradually stir in beef stock; cook until mixture begins to thicken. Boil for 2 minutes; strain into a saucepan. Add sour cream alternately with tomato juice or paste, stirring constantly. Simmer gently. Do not boil. Brown beef in 3 tablespoonfuls butter with onion. Stir beef and onion into sauce; season to taste. Simmer gently or cook in double boiler over hot water for 20 minutes. Yield: 6-8 servings.

Mrs. Lydia Schmanke, Pres.
St. John's LWML
Mt. Prospect, Illinois

GROUND BEEF STROGANOFF

1 tbsp. butter
1 lb. lean ground beef
2 tbsp. instant onion
1 1/2 tsp. paprika
1 can cream of mushroom soup
1 2 or 3-oz. can sliced mushrooms, undrained
1/2 c. sour cream
Salt and pepper to taste

Melt butter in pan; add beef and cook until lightly brown. Stir in onion and paprika. Add soup and mushrooms; simmer for 10 to 15 minutes. Blend in sour cream; season with salt and pepper. Sprinkle with parsley, if desired. Yield: 5 servings.

Mrs. Norma L. Matthews, Pres.
Living Word LCW
Memphis, Tennessee

HAMBURGER STROGANOFF

1 lb. ground beef
1/2 c. minced onion
1 clove of garlic, finely chopped
1/4 c. butter or margarine
2 tbsp. flour
2 tsp. salt
1/4 tsp. pepper
1 can cream of chicken soup
1 c. sour cream

Brown beef, onion and garlic in butter. Stir in flour, salt and pepper. Add soup; simmer, uncovered, for 10 minutes. Blend in sour cream just before serving. Serve over noodles. NOTE: One teaspoonful garlic salt may be substituted for 1 clove of garlic. Yield: 6-8 servings.

Mrs. Albert W. Moeller, Jr., Pres.
Cininnati Zone LWML
Cincinnati, Ohio

HAMBURGER STROGANOFF

1/2 c. minced onion
1/4 c. margarine
1 lb. ground beef
2 tbsp. flour
1 tsp. salt
1/4 tsp. pepper
1 10-oz. can mushrooms or 1 lb. fresh mushrooms
1 10-oz. can cream of mushroom or cream of chicken soup
1 c. sour cream
2 tbsp. parsley (opt.)

Saute onion in margarine. Add meat; brown. Add flour, seasonings and mushrooms; cook for 5 minutes. Add soup; simmer for 10 minutes. Stir in sour cream; heat through. Do not boil. Sprinkle with parsley. Serve with buttered egg noodles. Yield: 6 servings.

Mrs. Betty Olson
Faith LCW
Edmonton, Alberta, Canada

HAMBURGER STROGANOFF

½ c. diced onion
Butter
1 lb. ground beef
1 8-oz. can sliced mushrooms
1 can cream of chicken soup
1 c. sour cream
2 tbsp. minced parsley

Saute onion in small amount of butter; add meat. Cook until separated; add remaining ingredients. Cook for 5 to 10 minutes. Just before serving add sour cream. Serve over cooked noodles or rice, if desired. Yield: 4-5 servings.

Mrs. H. C. Stolldorf
Holy Trinity English Ladies Aid
Lafayette, Indiana

HAMBURGER STROGANOFF

¾ to 1 c. chopped onions
1 to 2 tbsp. fat or margarine
1 lb. ground beef
3 c. uncooked medium noodles
3 c. tomato juice
1 tsp. salt
1 ½ tsp. celery salt
Dash of pepper (opt.)
2 tsp. Worcestershire sauce
¼ c. chopped green pepper
1 c. sour cream
1 sm. can sliced mushrooms

Cook onions in hot fat until tender but not browned. Add beef; brown lightly. Place a layer of noodles over meat; top with tomato juice, seasonings and Worcestershire sauce. Bring to a boil. Cover; simmer over low heat for 20 to 30 minutes. Add green pepper, cook for 10 minutes longer. Stir in sour cream and mushrooms; heat just to boiling. Top with green pepper rings, if desired. Yield: 6-8 servings.

Mrs. David E. Deines
Trinity Women's Soc.
Mitchell, Nebraska
Mrs. George Germer
Berea Lutheran Church
Chappell, Nebraska
Mrs. Fred A. May, Pres.
Niobrara Evangelical LCW
Niobrara, Nebraska

HAMBURGER STROGANOFF

1 c. chopped onions
1 tbsp. fat
1 lb. ground beef
1 tsp. salt
1 ½ tsp. celery salt
2 tsp. Worcestershire sauce
Dash of pepper
3 c. uncooked medium noodles
3 c. tomato juice
¼ c. chopped green pepper
1 c. sour cream
1 can cream of mushroom soup

Cook onion in hot fat until tender but not brown. Add beef and brown lightly. Add with salt, celery salt, Worcestershire sauce, pepper and green pepper. Place noodles in a layer over meat; cover with tomato juice. Bring to a boil. Cover; simmer over low heat for 20 minutes. Add green pepper; cook for 10 minutes longer. Stir in sour cream and soup. Heat to boiling. Top with green pepper rings, if desired. Yield: 6 servings.

Mrs. James E. Williams, Supt.
Redeemer Lutheran Sunday School
Clearfield, South Dakota

INSTANT STROGANOFF

1 lb. hamburger
1 onion, chopped
1 clove of garlic, diced
1 10-oz. can cream of chicken soup
1 6 to 10-oz. can mushrooms
Salt to taste
½ to 1 c. sour cream

Fry hamburger, onion and garlic; add soup, mushrooms and salt. Simmer for 45 minutes. Just before serving, add sour cream and heat. Do not boil. Serve with noodles, macaroni or rice, if desired. Yield: 3 servings.

Mrs. E. E. Rosenquist, Sec.
St. Paul's Ladies Aid Soc.
South Edmonton, Alberta, Canada

CABBAGE AND HAMBURGER ROLLS

10 outside cabbage leaves
1 lb. ground beef
½ c. uncooked rice
2 tsp. salt
¼ tsp. pepper
¼ tsp. fine allspice
1 tbsp. chopped onion
3 stalks celery
3 lge. carrots
½ c. chopped onion
1 ½ c. cooked tomatoes
2 lge. potatoes
1 tbsp. sugar

Place cabbage leaves in 9 or 10-inch roaster. Cover with boiling water. Let stand, covered. Mix ground beef, rice, 1 teaspoonful salt, pepper, allspice and onion. Divide mixture equally onto cabbage leaves; roll up, folding up sides after first turn. Carefully place in roaster. Add 1 teaspoonful salt and remaining ingredients; cover with hot water. Boil gently for 1 hour. Yield: 6-8 servings.

Mrs. Arthur W. Ebel
Lutheran Ladies Aid
Hillsboro, Kansas

SPECIAL HAMBURGER STROGANOFF

½ c. minced onion
1 clove of garlic, minced
¼ c. butter
1 lb. ground beef
2 tsp. flour
2 tsp. salt
¼ tsp. pepper
1 lb. fresh mushrooms, sliced or 1 8-oz. can mushrooms
1 10 ½ oz. can cream of chicken soup
1 c. sour cream
2 tsp. minced parsley

Saute onion and garlic in butter over medium heat; add meat and brown. Add flour, salt, pepper and mushrooms. Cook for 5 minutes. Add soup. Simmer for 10 minutes. Stir in sour cream; heat thoroughly. Sprinkle with parsley. Serve with noodles, if desired. Yield: 4-6 servings.

Mrs. Lester Seibert, Pres.
Zion LCW
Silver Creek, New York

CABBAGE ROLLS

2 lb. hamburger
1 c. rice
1 med. onion, chopped
3 tsp. salt
1 tsp. pepper
1 8-oz. can tomato sauce
1 lge. cabbage
1 No. 2 can tomatoes
1 c. water

Mix meat, rice, onion, seasonings and tomato sauce. Cut core out of cabbage head. Put cabbage in kettle; pour boiling water over. Cover and let stand until cooled. Peal leaves off. Shape meat into small rolls; wrap cabbage leaf around each roll. Pack in kettle. Pour tomatoes and water over roll. Cook 15 minutes with 15 pound pressure in pressure cooker. NOTE: May be cooked in regular kettle with a extra cup of water; if so cook for 1 hour and 30 minutes. Yield: 20 cabbage rolls.

Mrs. R. M. Borth, Sec.
St. Paul LWML
Austin, Texas

CABBAGE ROLLS

Salt and pepper to taste
¼ c. chopped celery (opt.)
½ c. rice
1 lb. hamburger
1 med. cabbage
2 20-oz. cans tomatoes

Mix salt, pepper, celery, rice and hamburger. Remove core from cabbage; steam for 15 minutes or until tender and leaves come off easily. Roll meat mixture into 1 1/2-inch oblong rolls; roll in cabbage leaves, tucking in sides of leaves. Place additional cabbage over top. Place in greased pan; season with salt and pepper. Top

with tomatoes. Bring to a boil; simmer for 2 hours and 30 minutes. Yield: 10 servings.

Mrs. Else Siegle, Pres.
Immanuel Ladies Aid
Leslievelle, Alberta, Canada

FILLED CABBAGE

3 lb. meat loaf mix
1 egg
½ c. bread crumbs
1 tsp. onion salt
1 tsp. Worcestershire sauce
Salt and pepper to taste
1 lge. cabbage or 2 med. cabbages
Shortening

Mix meat loaf mix with egg, bread crumbs, onion salt, Worcestershire sauce, salt and pepper. Take each leaf off cabbage; parboil for 10 minutes. Drain and cool slightly. Criss-cross six pieces of cord string about 1 1/2 feet in length in a large pudding type pan. Place larger cabbage leaves on bottom of pan and around sides to form an outer shell of cabbage leaves, overlapping each leaf. Add a layer of meat, cabbage and salt. Repeat layers twice or until all ingredients are used. Place larger leaves for top. Pull strings up and tie securely. Brown filled cabbage in shortening on both sides in Dutch oven. Cover about half way and simmer for 3 to 4 hours. Serve with mustard sauce or gravy.

SAUCE:

2 eggs
1 tbsp. vinegar
2 tbsp. water
2 tbsp. sugar
¼ tsp. dry mustard

Combine all ingredients; cook until thickened. Yield: 8-10 servings.

Mary A. Hartt
St. Matthew LCW
Bloomsburg, Pennsylvania

STUFFED CABBAGE

1 lge. cabbage
2 lb. hamburger
1 ½ c. cooked rice
1 sm. onion, cubed
½ green pepper, cubed
Salt and pepper
2 eggs
Tomatoes

Core cabbage; heat in water until leaves separate. Combine remaining ingredients except tomatoes. Add tomatoes to moisten. Place part of meat mixture in each leaf. Roll; place in layers in pot. Cover with 1 quart tomatoes. Add salt to taste. Pressure cook for 10 minutes. If desired, thicken sauce and serve over cabbage.

Mrs. Fred Schoellig
St. Johns Lutheran Church
Garrattsville, New York

STUFFED CABBAGE CROWN

1 lb. ground beef
⅓ c. plus 2 tbsp. flour
1 ½ tsp. salt
¼ tsp. pepper
1 egg
1 c. milk
2 tbsp. grated onion
1 lge. cabbage
2 tbsp. butter or margarine

Combine ground beef, 1/3 cup flour, salt, pepper and egg in large bowl of electric mixer; beat until blended. Gradually beat in milk, a tablespoonful at a time, until smooth. Stir in onion. Trim off outside leaves of cabbage. Cut off slice about 1-inch thick from core end; set aside. Remove core from cabbage with sharp knife; hollow out cabbage to leave a shell 1/2-inch thick. Spoon meat mixture into shell; fit top slice back over top. Tie securely with string. Place stuffed cabbage, core-end down, in kettle; add boiling water to almost cover. Cover; simmer for 1 hour and 30 minutes or until cabbage is tender. Remove cabbage, reserving 1 1/2 cups liquid. Heat butter in small saucepan; blend in remaining flour. Cook, stirring constantly, just until bubbly. Stir in reserved liquid; cook, stirring, until gravy thickens. Boil for 1 minute. Season to taste. Place stuffed cabbage on heated platter; remove string. Cut cabbage into wedges; spoon gravy over wedges. Garnish with parsley, if desired. Yield: 4 servings.

Mrs. Lucy Mortland, Sec.
Immanuel First Ruth Soc.
West Covina, California

STUFFED CABBAGE ROLLS

1 sm. cabbage
1 lb. ground beef
2 tsp. chopped onion
1 egg, beaten
½ c. milk
1 tsp. salt
Butter
½ c. water

Trim off soiled leaves of cabbage and remove core. Cover with boiling water; let stand 5 minutes or until cabbage leaves are limp. Separate leaves carefully, reserving five of the largest leaves for the rolls. Combine meat thoroughly with onion, egg, milk and salt. Place one-fifth of the meat mixture on each of the five leaves; fold up envelope fashion. Fasten with toothpick. Brown delicately in butter in Dutch oven or saucepan. Add water; cover rolls with remaining cabbage leaves. Cover and simmer for 1 hour. Serve with tomato sauce. Yield: 5 servings.

Mrs. Doris E. Schwenke, Pres.
Our Savior Women's League
Muscatine, Iowa

STUFFED CABBAGE ROLLS

1 med. cabbage
2 tbsp. melted butter

2 c. ground beef
1 egg
1 c. minced onion
¾ c. uncooked rice
1 tsp. salt
½ tsp. pepper
½ c. cheese
1 can tomatoes

Simmer cabbage leaves, covered, in 1 inch boiling water for 5 minutes. Drain. Combine butter, beef, egg, onion, rice and seasoning. Fill leaves loosely with mixture. Fold each end of cabbage leaves toward center. Place in greased skillet. Sprinkle with cheese. Drain tomatoes, reserving liquid; place around edge of cabbage as border. Pour 1 cup tomato liquid over all. Cook until steam appears; reduce heat and cook for 1 hour.

Mrs. Earl W. Rose, Pres.
Grace LWML
Mitchell, Ontario, Canada

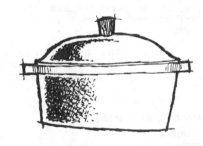

CHOPPED BEEF POT POURRI

1 lb. chopped meat
1 tbsp. butter
3 sm. onions, sliced
⅓ c. barley
2 c. tomatoes
1 ½ qt. water
1 tbsp. (scant) salt
½ tsp. pepper
3 carrots, diced
3 stalks celery, diced
1 tsp. Worcestershire sauce

Cook meat in butter, crumbling constantly; add onions. Cook for about 5 minutes. Add barley, tomatoes, water, salt and pepper. Cover; simmer over low heat for about 1 hour. Add vegetables and Worcestershire sauce; simmer for 1 hour longer. Yield: 4 servings.

Therese J. Lehr
Martin Luther Outreach and Fellowship
Milwaukee, Wisconsin

EGGPLANT RECIPE

1 eggplant, peeled and sliced
Salt to taste
1 lb. hamburger
Flour
Oil
1 can tomato juice or soup

Place eggplant into bowl; salt each slice and let stand. Fry meat until brown. Squeeze eggplant; roll in flour. Fry in oil in separate pan. Place meat into casserole. Add fried eggplant. Cover with tomato juice. Bake at 350 degrees until bubbly, about 30 minutes. Yield: 6 servings.

Mrs. A. Perry
Zion Evangelical Ladies Aid
Painesville, Ohio

GROUND BEEF STEW

1 onion, chopped
1 lb. ground beef
1 can tomatoes
1 pkg. frozen okra
1 tsp. salt

Brown onion and ground beef in pan; add tomatoes, frozen okra and salt. Cover and cook over low heat until okra is done. Yield: 4 servings.

Mrs. R. H. Treyler, Pres.
St. Marks LCW
Lenoir, North Carolina

HAMBURGER AND PEAS

1 ½ lb. hamburger
¼ c. chopped onion
1 tsp. monosodium glutamate
1 tsp. salt
1 pkg. frozen green peas
1 can beef broth
½ broth can water
1 tbsp. flour
3 tbsp. milk

Brown hamburger and onion in skillet; drain off excess fat. Add monosodium glutamate, salt, frozen peas, beef broth, and water. Bring to boil. Reduce heat; simmer for 30 minutes. Combine flour and milk; add to meat mixture. Simmer for 5 minutes longer. Serve with noodles or potatoes, if desired. Yield: 6 servings.

Mrs. Kay E. Parker, Pres.
Women of Shepherd King
Birmingham, Michigan

MORE

1 lb. ground beef
1 sm. onion, chopped
3 cloves of garlic, chopped
1 lge. can tomatoes
1 c. water
6 carrots, diced
4 med. potatoes, quartered
1 med. can corn
1 med. can string beans
1 med. can peas

Brown ground beef, onion and garlic; add tomatoes and water. Add carrots and potatoes; cook until tender. Add all remaining ingredients; salt and pepper to taste. Cook until done. Yield: 4-6 servings.

Mrs. Gerald Olney, Pres.
Grace Ladies Aid
Klickitat, Washington

SKILLET SAUERBRATEN

2 lb. ground beef
2 tsp. salt
¼ tsp. pepper
¼ tsp. ground cloves
¾ c. cider vinegar
1 med. onion, sliced
1 carrot, peeled and sliced
1 stalk celery, sliced
1 bay leaf
¾ c. water
2 tbsp. brown sugar
3 gingersnaps
½ c. hot water

Mix ground beef with salt, pepper and cloves. Add 1/4 cup of vinegar; shape into large pattie in skillet. Place onion, carrot, celery and bay leaf around meat. Mix water and remaining 1/2 cup vinegar with brown sugar; pour over meat. Cover and simmer for 1 hour, basting often. Place meat on heated platter; discard bay leaf. Soften gingersnaps in hot water; stir into drippings in pan. Heat, stirring constantly until gravy thickens. Pour over meat or serve separately. Yield: 8 servings.

Mrs. Arnel Hutton, Pres.
Prince of Peace LWML
Martinsville, Indiana

YUM YUMS

1 onion, finely chopped
Fat
1 ½ lb. ground beef
1 can undiluted chicken gumbo soup
1 tsp. chili powder
1 tbsp. prepared mustard
1 tsp. salt
½ c. catsup
Dash of pepper

Brown onion in a little fat; add ground beef and cook for 30 minutes. Add remaining ingredients; cook for 30 minutes longer. Add a little water if too thick; cook slowly and stir often. Yield: 10 servings.

Mrs. Frank Eckhart, Pres.
St. Paul's LWML
Holstein, Nebraska

BACON-WRAPPED BEEF LOGS

1 ½ lb. ground beef
¾ tsp. salt
⅛ tsp. pepper
½ tsp. celery salt
2 tbsp. minced onion
½ c. dry bread crumbs
½ c. grated carrots
½ c. grated Parmesan cheese
3 tbsp. melted butter
1 ½ tsp. Worcestershire sauce
6 slices bacon

Combine ground beef, seasonings and onion. Pat out to form 15 x 10-inch rectangle. Cut into six squares. Combine bread crumbs, carrots, cheese, butter and Worcestershire sauce. Spread 1/4 cup cheese mixture on each square. Roll as jelly roll. Wrap bacon slice around each roll; fasten with wooden pick. Place logs on rack in open roasting pan. Bake at 350 degrees for 40 minutes. Yield: 6 servings.

Mrs. Myra Tietz, Pres.
Zion LWML
Bancroft, Nebraska

BEEF ROLL ITALIANO

1 lb. lean ground beef
1 8-oz. can tomato sauce
½ tsp. salt
¼ tsp. pepper
1 c. dry cottage cheese
2 eggs, beaten
½ c. grated Parmesan cheese
2 tbsp. chopped parsley

Mix ground beef, 1/4 cup tomato sauce, salt and pepper. Shape into 9 x 12-inch rectangle on sheet of greased foil. Mix cottage cheese, eggs, Parmesan cheese and parsley. Spread on ground beef. Roll like jelly roll; shape foil around loaf, leaving top exposed. Pour remainder of tomato sauce over loaf. Bake at 325 degrees for 30 to 35 minutes. Yield: 6 servings.

Mrs. Robert Pariset, Pres.
St. Johns Ladies Aid
Vernon, Colorado

HAMBURGER GOURMET

2 lb. hamburger
1 sm. pkg. cream cheese
½ c. catsup
1 tsp. mustard
1 tsp. horseradish
1 tbsp. Bleu cheese
1 tbsp. minced onion
¼ tsp. salt
Pepper to taste

Shape hamburger into 12 patties. Cream the cheese; add catsup, mustard, horseradish, Bleu

cheese, onion and seasonings. Spoon cheese mixture on six patties. Cover with remaining patties. Seal edges. Broil for 5 minutes on each side. Yield: 6 servings.

Edna Grensing
Redeemer Ladies Merriam Soc.
North Las Vegas, Nevada

STEAK ROLLS

1 lb. hamburger
1 tsp. salt
⅛ tsp. pepper
1 sm. onion, finely chopped
1 beef bouillon cube
⅓ c. water
1 tsp. bisto
½ tsp. mustard
1 can cream of mushroom soup
⅔ c. flour
2 round steaks
4 tbsp. butter

Combine hamburger, salt, pepper and onion. Crush beef bouillon cube; dissolve in water. Bring to a boil. Add bisto and mustard. Cool. Add to hamburger mixture. Add soup; mix well. Add flour. Cut steak into squares. Place 1 tablespoonful of mixture on each square; roll. Preheat electric fry pan to 400 degrees. Fry steak rolls on all sides in butter. Place rolls into open baking dish. Bake at 325 degrees for 1 hour. Yield: 4-6 servings.

Mrs. David Erhardt, Pres.
Christ Lutheran Church LCW
Tisdale, Saskatchewan, Canada

STUFFED MEAT ROLL

2 lb. ground beef
1 ¼ tsp. salt
Pepper
1 can tomato soup
¼ c. chopped onion
3 tbsp. butter or margarine
1 egg, beaten
3 c. bread cubes
¼ tsp. thyme or sage

Combine meat, 1 teaspoonful salt, 1/4 teaspoonful pepper and soup; turn out onto waxed paper. Pat into 14 x 9-inch rectangle. Cook onion in butter; add to egg with 1/8 teaspoonful pepper, bread and thyme; mix well. Spread over meat; roll lengthwise. Place in shallow pan; bake at 350 degrees for 1 hour. Garnish with spiced crab apples. Yield: 6-8 servings.

Mrs. Frank E. Frie
Sattazahn's LCW
Jonestown, Pennsylvania

SURPRISE BURGERS

1 c. pkg. seasoned stuffing mix
⅓ c. evaporated milk
Salt and pepper
Monosodium glutamate
1 lb. round steak, ground
1 can cream of mushroom soup
2 tsp. Worcestershire sauce
1 tbsp. catsup

Prepare stuffing mix according to package directions. Combine milk and seasoned meat; divide into four patties. Pat each pattie to 6-inch circle on waxed paper. Place one-fourth the stuffing in center of each pattie. Bring meat over stuffing; seal. Place in 1 1/2-quart casserole. Combine remaining ingredients; pour over meat. Bake, uncovered, at 350 degrees for 45 minutes. Yield: 4 servings.

Mrs. Harry M. Welch, Pres.
St. Matthew's LCW
Harrisburg, Pennsylvania

WESTERN MEAT ROLL

1 ½ lb. ground beef
1 egg
¾ c. cracker crumbs
½ c. finely chopped onion
2 8-oz. cans tomato sauce with cheese
1 tsp. salt
½ tsp. oregano
⅛ tsp. pepper
2 c. shredded Mozzarella cheese

Combine ground beef, egg, cracker crumbs, onion, 1/3 cup tomato sauce, salt, oregano and pepper. Mix well; shape into 10 x 12-inch rectangle on waxed paper. Sprinkle Mozzarella cheese evenly over meat mixture. Roll up like jelly roll; press ends of roll to seal. Place in shallow baking dish. Bake at 350 degrees for 1 hour. Drain off excess fat; pour on remaining tomato sauce. Bake for 15 minutes longer. Slice before serving. Yield: 4-6 servings.

Mrs. Ervin Mintzloff, Treas.
Our Saviors Ladies Aux.
Hermosa, South Dakota

BAKED STUFFED PEPPERS

4 lge. green peppers
1 qt. boiling water
½ lb. ground beef
1 onion, chopped
1 tbsp. bacon fat
¼ c. tomato paste
Cooked rice
1 tsp. salt
½ tsp. chili powder
1 egg, separated
American cheese slices

Cut tops from green peppers; remove seeds and membrane. Cook in boiling water in large pot for 5 minutes; drain. Brown meat and onion in fat for 5 minutes. Stir in tomato paste, rice, salt and chili powder. Remove from heat. Beat egg yolk in bowl; add meat mixture. Fold in stiffly beaten egg white. Stuff into green peppers. Top with cheese slices. Place in casserole, adding just enough water to cover bottom of dish. Bake at 350 degrees for 35 minutes or until green peppers are tender and cheese is browned. Yield: 4 servings.

Alga Schafrick, Executive Bd. Member
Emmaus Mary Martha Guild
Brooklyn, New York

BEEF AND MUSHROOM ROLL

1 lb. ground beef
1 tsp. salt
¼ tsp. pepper
¼ c. chopped sweet pickles
¼ tsp. dry mustard
1 2-oz. can mushroom stems and pieces
1 sm. onion, minced
2 tbsp. flour
⅓ c. water
1 biscuit recipe
1 10-oz. can beef gravy

Cook beef, stirring, until no longer red. Add salt, pepper, pickles, mustard, mushrooms and onion. Pour off excess fat; blend in flour and water. Cook until thickened, stirring constantly. Cool. Roll biscuit dough in 12 x 9-inch rectangle. Spread meat mixture on dough; moisten edges. Roll as for jelly roll; pinch edges. Brush with milk. Place in greased shallow baking pan. Bake in 425 degree oven for 30 minutes. Slice; serve with heated gravy. Yield: 8 servings.

Mrs. Martin Wineberg, Pres.
St. Luke's LCW
Stow, Ohio

FLEISHKUCHLA

3 tbsp. cream
¾ c. milk
¾ c. water
Salt
6 c. flour
2 lb. ground beef
Pepper to taste
¼ c. finely chopped onion

Mix cream, milk, water and 1 tablespoonful salt; add flour. Knead for a few minutes. Roll out one-half of the dough thinly; cut into squares. Combine ground beef, salt to taste, pepper and onion; spread over one-half of dough square. Fold remaining half over meat mixture; seal edges. Repeat until all dough and meat are used. Fry in hot deep fat. Yield: 10-12 servings.

Mrs. Art Tornow, Pres.
St. Peter's Ladies Aid
Emery, South Dakota

CABBAGE BURGERS

1 pkg. dry or cake yeast
¼ c. warm water
2 c. milk, scalded
2 tsp. sugar
Salt
1 tbsp. shortening
6 to 7 c. flour or hot roll mix
1 lge. cabbage
1 c. chopped onions
1 ½ lb. ground beef
Pepper to taste

Soften yeast in warm water. Combine milk, sugar, 2 teaspoonfuls salt and shortening; cool to lukewarm. Add flour to make soft dough. Turn out onto floured board; knead for 8 minutes until smooth and satiny. Shape into ball; place in lightly greased bowl, turning once to grease surface. Cover; let rise for 45 minutes or until doubled in bulk. Cut dough 2 1/2 inches in diameter in form of ball; roll out to size of saucer. Combine salt to taste and remaining ingredients in kettle; steam over low heat until done. Cool. Place 3 tablespoonfuls cabbage mixture in center of each round. Bring up side and pinch together to seal. Turn upside down in greased pan. Let rise for 10 minutes. Bake at 375 degrees for 20 minutes. Yield: 8 servings.

Mrs. Ed Haun
Concordia Ladies Aid
Weiser, Idaho

HOBO DINNER

⅔ c. ground beef
Salt and pepper to taste
2 tbsp. chopped onion
1 carrot, cut into strips
4 sm. onion
1 sm. potato, quartered
½ ear corn
¼ c. chopped ripe olives

Season beef with salt, pepper and onion; pat to fit bottom of coffee can. Place vegetables on top of beef; sprinkle with salt, pepper and olives. Cover; cook over coals for 50 minutes or at 350 degrees for 1 hour. Yield: 1 serving.

Mrs. Fred Donner
St. Paul's Ladies Guild
Metamora, Michigan

MEAT ROLLS

2 eggs
Milk
1 lb. ground beef, pork or veal
2 c. soft bread crumbs
1 ¼ c. grated potatoes
1 tbsp. grated onion
Sage or garlic (opt.)

¼ tsp. pepper
Salt to taste

Beat eggs slightly; add to 1/2 cup milk. Mix remaining ingredients. Combine all ingredients; mix well. Shape into 1 1/2 x 3-inch rolls. Brown thoroughly in a large amount of fat. Place in baking pan or casserole; add about 1/2 inch milk. Bake, covered, at 350 degrees for 45 to 50 minutes. Yield: 8 servings.

Mrs. Jesse Filipi, VP
Holy Trinity LCW
Angus, Minnesota

PARTY PUPS

1 c. crushed cracker crumbs
2 tbsp. minced dried onion
1 c. milk
1 tsp. salt
¼ tsp. pepper
½ tsp. celery salt
2 lb. ground beef
Chopped green pepper (opt.)
12 slices bacon

Combine cracker crumbs, onion, milk, salt, pepper and celery salt. Add meat and green pepper; mix. Divide into 12 equal portions. Mold each portion into shape of frankfurter, 1-inch thick. Wrap with bacon; secure with wooden pick. Place on rack in broiler pan 5 inches from heat. Broil for 8 minutes on one side. Turn and broil for 6 minutes or until bacon is lightly browned. Remove picks and serve. Yield: 12 servings.

Mrs. William Eckstein, Pres.
Our Savior's LCW
Viborg, South Dakota

STUFFED BUNS WITH CABBAGE AND HAMBURGER

1 lb. hamburger
1 lge. onion, chopped
Salt and pepper to taste
1 sm. cabbage, chopped
Sweet roll yeast dough

Brown hamburger and onion; add salt and pepper. Add cabbage and small amount of water; simmer until cabbage is done. Cool. Let dough rise for 1 hour. Roll out and cut into 3-inch squares. Place a spoonful of hamburger mixture in center of each square; pinch edges of dough together. Place on a baking sheet; let rise for 30 minutes. Bake at 400 to 425 degrees until browned.

Mrs. Carl Matz
Zion Ladies Aid
Hillsboro, Kansas

VEGETABLE-MEAT ROLL

¾ c. plus 2 tbsp. vegetable soup
¾ c. evaporated milk
¾ tsp. salt
¾ lb. ground beef
1 ½ tsp. grated onion
⅛ tsp. pepper
2 c. biscuit mix
6 tbsp. water

Mix soup with 6 tablespoonfuls evaporated milk and remaining ingredients except biscuit mix and water. Let stand. Place biscuit mix in mixing bowl; stir in remaining milk and water. Turn out onto lightly floured board. Knead lightly until dough is smooth. Roll into 10 x 12-inch rectangle, 1/4-inch thick. Spread with meat mixture leaving a 2-inch margin. Roll like jelly roll; pinch overlapping edges together. Cut into 12 slices. Place in greased shallow pan, cut-side down. Bake in preheated 425 degree oven for 30 minutes or until brown.

VEGETABLE SAUCE:

3 tbsp. flour
1 ½ tbsp. butter or shortening, melted
¾ tsp. salt
⅛ tsp. pepper
¾ c. water
¾ c. evaporated milk
¼ c. vegetable soup

Blend flour into butter in saucepan. Add salt and pepper. Slowly stir in water. Boil for 2 minutes, stirring constantly. Stir in milk and soup. Heat thoroughly. Serve with meat roll. Yield: 12 servings.

Mrs. Leslie Sloan
St. Paul's Ladies Aid
Ridgedale, Missouri

TOMATO-MEAT SAUCE ON ONION BREAD

1 lb. ground beef
¼ c. chopped onion
½ c. chopped celery
½ c. chopped green pepper
2 tbsp. butter or margarine
1 tsp. salt
¼ tsp. pepper
1 ⅓ c. chili sauce
¾ c. water
¼ c. chopped parsley
¼ c. chopped stuffed olives

Saute ground beef, onion, celery and green pepper in butter until browned. Add salt, pepper, chili sauce and water; simmer for 1 hour. Stir in parsley and olives.

ONION BREAD:

2 c. sliced onions
5 tbsp. butter or margarine
1 ¾ tsp. salt
1 egg yolk
½ c. sour cream
1 c. sifted flour
1 ½ tsp. baking powder
1 egg, slightly beaten
½ c. milk

Saute onions in 2 tablespoonfuls butter until tender. Stir in 1 teaspoonful salt and egg yolk mixed with sour cream. Sift flour, baking powder and remaining 3/4 teaspoonful salt into bowl. Cut in 3 tablespoonfuls butter. Combine egg and milk; stir into flour mixture. Mix until moistened. Spread evenly in ungreased 9-inch pie pan. Top with onion mixture. Bake at 425 degrees for 25 minutes. Serve meat sauce over wedges of onion bread. Yield: 8 servings.

Mrs. John Wright, Pres.
Luther Memorial LCW
North Syracuse, New York

Pork Favorites

RECIPE FOR PORK-CORN SUEY ON PAGE 155

BAKED CANADIAN BACON

½ c. plus 2 tbsp. brown sugar
½ tsp. dry mustard
½ c. plus 1 tbsp. unsweetened pineapple juice
2 lb. unsliced Canadian bacon
Pineapple slices
1 tbsp. butter

Combine 1/2 cup brown sugar, mustard and 1/2 cup pineapple juice; spread over bacon. Bake, uncovered, at 325 degrees for 1 hour, basting at 15 minute intervals. Simmer pineapple slices in butter, remaining brown sugar and remaining pineapple juice; brown. Place along both sides of bacon on platter. Yield: 8 servings.

Ruth Olsen
St. Paul's LCW
Olds, Alberta, Canada

FRUIT-GLAZED BACON ROAST

4 to 5 lb. unsliced Canadian bacon
½ c. pineapple juice
½ c. pear juice
½ c. pickled peach juice
Canned pineapple slices
Brown sugar
Canned pear halves
Pickled peaches

Place Canadian bacon on rack in roasting pan. Combine juices; pour over meat. Roast at 350 degrees for 1 hour, basting frequently with juices in pan. Cut into 1/2-inch slices; arrange on a large platter. Sprinkle pineapple slices with brown sugar. Place under broiler until golden brown. Heat pears and peaches. Alternate pineapple and pear halves around meat. Top each pineapple slice with a peach. Garnish with parsley, if desired. Yield: 8-10 servings.

Mrs. Gladys A. Nelson
Our Redeemer Evangelical LWML
Augusta, Georgia

BAKED PORK CHOPS

Salt and pepper
6 pork chops
2 med. onions, sliced
1 can tomato soup
½ c. water

Salt and pepper pork chops. Place 3 chops in bottom of greased casserole; cover with one-half the onion slices. Repeat layers. Pour tomato soup over chops; add water. Bake at 350 degrees for 25 minutes. Yield: 6 servings.

Mrs. Albert Biebas
Ebenezer, LWML
Giddings, Texas

BAKED PORK CHOPS

6 pork chops
½ c. flour
Salt and pepper
1 can cream of celery soup

Dip chops into flour; brown in skillet. Season to taste. Place in casserole; pour on celery soup. Bake at 350 degrees until chops are done.

Mrs. Fred Groth
Redeemer Ladies Aid
Deer River, Minnesota

BAKED PORK CHOPS

4 pork chops, 1-in. thick
Flour
1 tbsp. oil or fat
1 med. onion, sliced (opt.)
1 c. sour cream
Salt and pepper

Dust chops generously with flour; brown in oil in skillet. Place chops in shallow baking pan; sprinkle with salt and pepper. Spread chops with sour cream; top with onion. Bake at 325 to 350 degrees for 1 hour, turning once. Yield: 4 servings.

Mrs. F. E. Brauer, Christian Growth Chmn.
St. Paul's LWML
Hardin, Illinois

BAKED PORK CHOPS

4 pork chops
Cooking oil
⅓ c. finely diced celery
2 tbsp. brown sugar
Juice of ½ lemon
½ tsp. salt
½ tsp. mustard
⅛ tsp. pepper
1 can tomato sauce
½ c. water

Brown chops in oil in frying pan. Place in shallow greased baking dish. Sprinkle with celery, brown sugar, lemon juice and seasonings. Pour tomato sauce and water over chops. Cover and bake at 350 degrees for 1 hour and 15 minutes or until chops are tender. Yield: 4 servings.

Mrs. Walter Brenner, Sec.
Our Savior LWML
West Palm Beach, Florida

BAKED PORK CHOPS WITH DRESSING

4 pork chops
Water
⅔ c. finely cut celery
1 tbsp. chopped onion
1 tsp. salt
1 No. 303 can applesauce
Pinch of sage
2 c. shredded bread

Brown chops; steam in 1/2 cup water over low heat for 15 minutes. Cook celery and onion in 2/3 cup water for 7 to 10 minutes; add salt, applesauce and sage. Add mixture to bread; mix until moistened. Divide dressing into four portions;

place over chops. Bake at 350 degrees for 40 to 45 minutes or until tender. Yield: 4 servings.

Mrs. Walter Klute, Pres.
Zion LWML
Hampton, Nebraska

BAKED STUFFED PORK CHOPS

6 double-rib pork chops
3 c. bread cubes
1 tsp. poultry seasoning
Pepper
1 tbsp. minced onion
½ c. finely diced celery
⅓ c. melted butter
¾ tsp. Season-all
¼ tsp. ginger
¼ tsp. dry mustard
2 tbsp. shortening
¼ c. water

Have pocket cut in each chop. Toss bread cubes with poultry seasoning, 1/4 teaspoonful pepper, onion, celery and butter. Fill each pocket with 1/2 cup stuffing; close opening with toothpicks. Combine 1/8 teaspoonful pepper and remaining seasonings; rub over chops, covering sides well. Brown in hot fat in skillet. Add water; cover tightly. Bake at 350 degrees for 1 hour or until tender. Yield: 6 servings.

Mrs. Nestor Kant, Pres.
St. Paul's LWML
Kirkland Lake Ontario, Canada

BARBECUE BAKED PORK CHOPS

4 pork chops
Fat
⅓ c. finely diced celery
Juice of ½ lemon
2 tbsp. brown sugar
½ tsp. salt
½ tsp. dry mustard
⅛ tsp. pepper
1 can tomato sauce
½ c. water

Brown chops in fat; place in shallow greased baking dish. Sprinkle with celery, lemon juice, brown sugar and seasonings. Pour tomato sauce and water over chops. Cover; bake at 350 degrees for 1 hour and 15 minutes or until chops are tender. Yield: 4 servings.

Mrs. Lois M. Miesner
Salem LWML
Brazeau, Missouri

BARBECUED PORK CHOPS

3 ⅓ lb. pork chops
2 lemons, sliced
2 med. onions, minced
2 c. water
1 c. catsup
2 tbsp. brown sugar
⅓ c. Worcestershire sauce

1 tsp. salt
1 tsp. mustard
2 dashes of Tabasco sauce

Place pork chops in shallow roasting pan. Place lemon slice on each chop. Bake at 450 degrees for 30 minutes. Boil onions for 10 minutes in water. Combine remaining ingredients; add to onions. Simmer for 30 minutes; pour over pork chops. Continue baking at 350 degrees for 30 to 45 minutes or until tender, basting with sauce every 15 minutes.

Mrs. Lester M. Bauer, Pres.
Concordia LWML
Beulah, North Dakota

OVEN-BARBECUED PORK CHOPS

Pork chops
Salt and pepper
Brown sugar
Catsup
Onion slices
Lemon slices

Place chops in shallow baking pan. Salt and pepper. On top of each chop, place 1 tablespoonful brown sugar, 1 tablespoonful catsup, 1 onion slice and 1 slice of lemon. Cover and bake at 325 degrees for 45 minutes to 1 hour. Remove cover during last 15 minutes of baking.

Mrs. Eldo Meyer
St. Marks Tabitha Soc.
Garrison, Iowa

CHOP 'N' STUFFING LOAF

4 pork chops, ½-in. thick
Salt and pepper
1 ½ c. packaged herb-seasoned stuffing
1 tsp. poultry seasoning
¾ c. chopped unpared apples
¼ c. seedless raisins
¼ c. chopped celery
¼ c. chopped onion

Trim excess fat from chops; salt and pepper. Prepare stuffing according to package directions; toss with remaining ingredients. Stand chops on edge, fat-side up, in center of 2-foot length of foil. Run skewer through center of chops, spacing them 1/2-inch apart. Spoon stuffing loosely between chops. Fold foil over and seal securely. Bake at 450 degrees for 1 hour and 15 minutes or until done. Yield: 4 servings.

Mrs. Rose Kautz
Emmanuel LWML
Nashville, Tennessee

CREOLE PORK CHOPS

4 loin or center cut pork chops, 1 ½-in. thick
1 tsp. salt
⅛ tsp. pepper
1 tbsp. fat or oil

(Continued on next page)

⅓ c. catsup
½ c. water
½ tsp. celery seed
3 tbsp. cider vinegar
¼ tsp. ginger
1 tsp. sugar
1 tsp. flour

Sprinkle chops lightly with 1/2 teaspoonful salt and pepper. Brown on both sides in fat in heavy skillet. Remove chops to casserole or baking dish. Combine remaining ingredients; pour over chops. Bake, uncovered, at 325 degrees for 1 hour and 30 minutes. Turn chops after first hour of baking. Yield: 4 servings.

Mrs. Darwin Heidbreder, Pres.
St. John's LWML
Lohman, Missouri

DIXIE PORK CHOPS

4 pork chops
½ tsp. salt
½ tsp. powdered sage
4 apples, cored and sliced
¼ c. brown sugar
2 tbsp. flour
1 tbsp. vinegar
½ c. raisins
1 c. hot water

Brown pork chops in skillet; drain and sprinkle with salt and sage. Place in baking dish; cover with apples and brown sugar. Make gravy with remaining ingredients; pour over apples and meat. Bake at 350 degrees for 1 hour. Yield: 4 servings.

Mrs. Vernet Soenksen
Faith Ladies Circle
Deloit, Iowa

FRENCH-STYLE PORK CHOPS

6 pork loin chops
Salt and pepper
3 apples, cored and pared
1 tbsp. brown sugar
1 tbsp. butter
¾ c. Sherry wine
¾ c. hot water

Trim chops; season with salt and pepper. Place close together in baking dish. Cover with thin apple rings; sprinkle with brown sugar and a small amount of salt. Dot with butter. Cover tightly; bake at 400 degrees until apples begin to soften and chops brown. Pour in wine and hot water. Reduce temperature to 300 degrees; bake until tender, basting occasionally. Yield: 6 servings.

Mrs. Willie Knoll, Project Chmn.
Trinity Ladies Aid
Shamrock, Texas

HEAVENLY PORK CHOPS

1 tbsp. salt
1 tsp. pepper

8 pork loin chops, 1 ¼-in. thick
8 tbsp. brown sugar
8 tbsp. catsup
8 slices lemon

Salt and pepper chops to taste. Place in roasting pan. Place 1 tablespoonful brown sugar, 1 tablespoonful catsup and 1 slice lemon on each chop. Cover; bake at 300 degrees for 2 hours. Remove cover; bake for 1 hour longer. Make gravy from drippings. Yield: 8 servings.

Mrs. Paul W. Hinz, Pres.
Grace Ladies Aid and LWML
Sheboygan, Wisconsin

ORANGE PORK CHOPS

6 pork chops
½ c. fresh orange juice
½ tsp. salt
⅛ tsp. pepper
¼ c. brown sugar

Place chops in shallow baking dish. Combine remaining ingredients; pour over chops. Bake at 350 degrees for 1 hour, basting as necessary. Yield: 6 servings.

Mrs. Kenneth C. Bowers, Pres.
Faith LWML
Sebring, Florida

OVEN-COOKED PORK CHOPS

6 pork chops
1 egg, beaten
1 c. crushed corn flakes
1 can tomato soup
½ c. brown sugar
Salt and pepper to taste
Dash of cloves
1 tbsp. vinegar

Dip chops into egg; dip into corn flakes. Brown in fat. Combine remaining ingredients; boil for 3 minutes. Pour over chops; bake at 350 degrees for 1 hour. Yield: 4-6 servings.

Mrs. Herb Arndt, Pres.
St. Peter LCW
Medicine Hat, Alberta, Canada

PORK CHOPS A LA DIXIE

Flour
4 to 6 lean pork chops
1 can chicken gumbo soup

Flour chops; brown quickly in hot fat in skillet. Remove from heat; place chops in casserole. Cover with soup. Cover; bake at 300 degrees for 45 minutes or until tender.

Mrs. Elaine Hahne, Sec.
St. Luke LWML
Itasca, Illinois

PORK CHOPS BAKED IN SOUR CREAM

4 pork chops, ½-in. thick
Flour
4 cloves
½ c. water
½ to 1 bay leaf
2 tbsp. vinegar
1 tbsp. sugar
½ c. sour cream

Dredge chops with flour. Insert 1 clove in each chop. Brown lightly; place in baking dish. Combine remaining ingredients; heat and pour over chops. Cover; bake at 350 degrees for 1 hour to 1 hour and 30 minutes.

Mrs. Rubin Erdman
Trinity LWML
Upham, North Dakota
Mrs. Otto Bartlet, Pres.
St. John's LWML
Gillett, Wisconsin

PORK CHOPS DELUXE

6 pork chops, 1-in. thick
1 tbsp. flour
1 pkg. dry onion soup mix
2 ½ c. hot water
1 c. sour cream

Brown chops in small amount of fat in preheated 325 degree electric skillet. Remove from skillet, reserving 1 tablespoonful fat. Stir in flour and soup mix. Blend well; stir in water. Add chops; Cook at 225 degrees for 1 hour. Remove chops; stir in sour cream. NOTE: May be baked at 350 degrees for 1 hour, if desired. Yield: 6 servings.

Mrs. Marvin Schoen, Pres.
Zion LWML
Downs, Kansas

PORK CHOP AND NOODLE CASSEROLE

6 pork chops
Salt
Prepared mustard
4 c. cooked noodles
2 cans cream of chicken soup
1 c. water
¼ c. chopped onion

Brown pork chops on one side. Turn and season with salt; spread lightly with mustard. Place noodles in rectangular 2-quart casserole. Top with chops, browned-side down. Pour soup, water and onion into skillet. Stir and heat until blended; pour over chops. Cover; bake at 350 degrees for 30 minutes. Uncover and bake for 30 minutes longer. Yield: 6 servings.

Mrs. George W. Rascoe
Zion LWML
Farmington, New Mexico

PORK CHOPS 'N' STUFFING

6 pork chops
4 c. soft bread crumbs
2 tbsp. chopped onion
½ c. melted butter
½ c. water
¼ tsp. poultry seasoning
1 can cream of mushroom soup
½ c. water

Brown pork chops on both sides in oven-proof skillet; pour off drippings. Lightly mix bread crumbs, onion, butter, water and poultry seasoning. Place a mound of stuffing on each pork chop. Blend soup and water; pour over stuffing. Bake at 350 degrees for 1 hour. Yield: 6 servings.

Mrs. A. William Bade, Pres.
St. Paul's Ladies Aid
Varna, Illinois

PORK CHOP CASSEROLE

6 lean chops
Salt and pepper to taste
5 tbsp. raw rice, cooked
6 tbsp. canned tomatoes
1 can cream of mushroom soup

Place pork chops in baking dish. Sprinkle with salt and pepper. Cover with rice. Add tomatoes; Cover with soup. Add enough water to cover chops. Bake at 350 degrees for 1 hour and 30 minutes. Yield: 6 servings.

Mrs. Alex Huls, Treas.
St. John's Ladies Aid
Shell Lake, Wisconsin

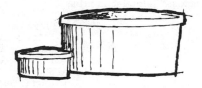

PORK CHOP AND RICE CASSEROLE

Salt and pepper to taste
4 thick chops
2 tbsp. fat
1 ½ onions, chopped
½ c. uncooked rice
1 ½ c. water or consomme
1 c. fresh or canned tomatoes
1 pkg. frozen lima beans
Pinch of monosodium glutamate

(Continued on next page)

Season chops; fry in fat. Remove from pan. Slightly fry onions. Add rice; fry slightly. Add liquid; return chops to rice mixture. Add tomtoes, lima beans, and monosodium glutamate. Cover; bake at 350 degrees until done. Yield: 5 servings.

Mrs. Selma Biedler, Pres.
Christ Lutheran Ladies Aid
Red Lake, Ontario, Canada

SPANISH PORK CHOPS

4 pork chops
½ c. uncooked rice
1 c. diced onions
¼ c. chopped green pepper
2 tsp. salt
¼ tsp. pepper
½ tsp. paprika
1 tsp. sugar
2 ½ c. tomatoes

Brown pork chops well in chicken fryer. Add remaining ingredients. Cover tightly; cook for 30 minutes or until rice is done. If too dry, add more water while cooking. Yield: 4 servings.

Mary Winkler, Pres.
Immanuel Ladies Aid Soc.
Alexander, Arkansas

RICE-PORK CHOP SUPREME

6 to 10 pork chops
1 can cream of chicken soup
1 c. milk (opt.)
1 c. instant rice

Brown chops in pan. Arrange in flat dish. Mix soup, milk and rice; pour over chops. Cover; bake at 350 degrees for 45 minutes to 1 hour and 15 minutes. Yield: 4-6 servings.

Mrs. J. Lloyd Davidson
St. Peter's LWML
Stratford, Ontario, Canada
Mrs. Arnold Brown, Pres.
Good Shepherd LCW
Atlanta, Georgia

GLORIFIED PORK CHOPS

6 pork chops
6 slices green pepper
6 slices onion
6 tbsp. partially cooked rice
Salt and pepper to taste
Tomato juice or 6 slices tomato

Brown chops; place in casserole. Top with green pepper, onion and rice. Add seasonings. Heat tomato juice in same pan; pour over chops. Cover; simmer for 1 hour and 30 minutes or

bake at 350 degrees for 1 hour. NOTE: One cup converted rice, cooked in 2 1/2 cups water may be substituted for 6 tablespoonfuls rice. Yield: 6 servings.

Mrs. Marcy King
Messiah Mary Magdelene Guild
Grand Rapids, Michigan
Mrs. Henry O. Thompson, Pres.
Salem Lutheran Church
Deerwood, Minnesota

PORK CHOPS AND RICE CREOLE

6 pork chops
Salt and pepper
2 onions, sliced
1 tbsp. fat
1 clove of garlic, minced
2 ½ c. hot water
1 can tomato soup
¼ c. chopped green onions
¼ c. diced celery
¼ green pepper, diced
2 tbsp. chopped parsley
¾ c. uncooked rice
½ bay leaf, crushed
Pinch of thyme (opt.)
Pinch of marjoram (opt.)

Season chops with salt and pepper; brown in hot skillet. Remove chops; drain off all fat but 1 tablespoonful. Brown onions in fat with garlic. Add hot water, soup, green onions, celery, green pepper, parsley and rice. Season with 1 teaspoonful salt, pepper, bay leaf, thyme and marjoram. Mix well; pour over chops in casserole. Cover and bake at 350 degrees for 1 hour and 30 minutes or until meat and rice are tender. If casserole becomes dry, add hot water. Yield: 6 servings.

Mrs. Russell Hughes
Messiah Women's Guild
Richardson, Texas

SAUERKRAUT AND PORK CHOPS

1 lge. onion, slices
1 can sauerkraut
4 pork chops
Salt and pepper to taste
Paprika
¼ c. rice
1 can tomato soup
2 c. water
1 tbsp. sugar

Line casserole with onion; place one-half of sauerkraut in casserole. Brown pork chops in casserole. Season with salt, pepper and paprika. Spread rice on top. Place remaining sauerkraut on rice. Mix soup with water and sugar. Pour over casserole. Bake at 350 degrees for 1 hour and 30 minutes. Yield: 4 servings.

Mrs. Sam Holt
St. Mathews LWML
Stony Plain, Alberta, Canada

SPANISH PORK CHOPS

6 pork chops
Seasoned flour
1 can tomato sauce
1 qt. water
1 med. onion, diced
1 tbsp. sugar

Roll pork chops in s e a s o n e d flour; brown in skillet. Place chops in baking dish; add all remaining ingredients. Bake at 350 degrees for 30 minutes or until done. Yield: 6 servings.

Mrs. Ed Kern, Treas.
St. John's Ladies Aid
Dent, Minnesota

SWEDISH PORK CHOPS

8 slices bread, broken into small pieces
2 c. peeled sliced apples
½ c. sliced onion
Salt and pepper to taste
6 pork chops

Place bread in well greased dish. Cover bread with layers of apples; add layer of onion. Place seasoned chops over bread and onion mixture. Bake, covered, at 325 to 350 degrees for 45 minutes. Uncover; continue baking until brown. Yield: 6 servings.

Mrs. Frank A. Rohde, VP
St. John's Dorcas Soc.
Woverly, Iowa

CORN CROWNED PORK CHOPS

6 pork chops, 1-in. thick
Salt and pepper to taste
1 No. 303 can cream-style corn
1 egg, beaten
1 med. onion, chopped
1 c. packaged seasoned bread dressing
1 tbsp. butter or margarine

Trim part of fat from chops; melt in skillet. Sprinkle chops with salt and pepper; brown on both sides in skillet. Place chops in baking dish. Mix corn, egg, onion, bread dressing and butter. Mound corn dressing over top of chops. Bake, covered, at 350 degrees for about 1 hour. Remove cover the last 15 minutes to brown. Yield: 6 servings.

Mrs. Douglas Richardson, Pres.
First English Mission Guild
Spring Valley, Minnesota

PORK CHOPS WITH CORN DRESSING

4 c. soft bread crumbs
1 c. bran
1 tbsp. chopped onion
¼ c. chopped celery
2 tbsp. fat
1 ½ tsp. salt
¼ tsp. poultry seasoning
¼ tsp. pepper
1 c. drained whole kernel corn
1 c. corn liquid or milk
4 pork chops

Combine bread crumbs and bran. Cook onion and celery in fat until lightly browned. Add to bread mixture 1 teaspoonful salt, remaining seasonings, corn and liquid. Mix thoroughly. Press dressing into baking dish, 8-inches in diameter. Arrange chops on dressing; sprinkle with remaining salt. Cover and bake at 375 degrees until done. Yield: 4 servings.

Mrs. Irene Florreish
Our Savior Dorcas Soc.
Columbus, Mississippi

FARMERS' PORK CHOPS

4 pork loin or shoulder chops
Flour
1 clove of garlic, chopped
Salt and pepper
4 potatoes, thinly sliced
2 lge. onions, sliced
1 ½ c. sour cream
½ tsp. dry mustard

Trim excess fat from chops; roll in flour. Brown chops and garlic in hot fat over medium heat. Season with salt and pepper. Place potatoes in 11 1/2 x 7 1/2 x 1 1/2-inch baking pan; top with browned chops. Separate onion slices into rings; lay over chops. Blend sour cream, 1 1/2 teaspoonfuls salt and mustard; pour over potatoes, chops and onions. Bake in preheated 350 degree oven for 1 hour and 30 minutes. Yield: 4 servings.

Mrs. Arnold L. Kienas, Pres.
Trinity LWML
Kalispell, Montana

PORK CHOPS AND LIMA BEANS

2 c. fresh or frozen lima beans, cooked
1 tbsp. margarine
Salt
1 tsp. sugar
1 tsp. prepared mustard
2 tbsp. minced onion
½ c. chili sauce
4 pork chops

Arrange lima beans in 1-quart casserole. Dot with margarine. Combine 1 teaspoonful salt, sugar, mustard, onion and chili sauce. Blend; pour over beans. Season chops to taste; arrange on beans. Bake at 350 degrees until chops are thoroughly cooked and brown. Yield: 4 servings.

Minette Ebers, Welfare Cir. Chmn.
Trinity LWML
Walnut Creek, California

HAWAIIAN PORK CHOPS

6 pork chops
Flour
1 ½ c. unsweetened pineapple juice
2 tbsp. vinegar
¼ tsp. salt
Dash of pepper
1 tsp. chili powder
1 tsp. dry mustard
1 tbsp. brown sugar
½ tsp. Worcestershire sauce
2 onions, chopped
5 carrots, quartered and partially cooked
Cooked sweet potatoes, peeled and halved

Season pork chops to taste; dredge in flour. Brown chops in a small amount of fat in skillet. Place chops in roaster. Add pineapple juice, vinegar, seasonings, brown sugar. Worcestershire sauce and onions to drippings in skillet; simmer for 5 minutes. Pour sauce mixture over chops; add carrots. Cover; bake at 325 degrees for 1 hour. Place sweet potatoes over top of casserole; bake for 30 minutes longer. Yield: 6 servings.

Mrs. Laura Tonniges
St. Peter's Miss'y League
Gresham, Nebraska

PORK CHOPS

Shortening
6 pork chops, 1-in. thick
2 onions, sliced
½ c. water
1 tbsp. flour
½ tsp. all purpose seasoning
½ tsp. onion seasoning
½ tsp. celery salt
Pepper to taste
½ c. milk
1 can cream of celery soup
1 pkg. frozen lima beans

Place shortening in skillet; brown chops on both sides. Place onion slices on chops; add water. Simmer for 1 hour or until tender. Remove chops to flat baking dish; place in single layer. Make a paste from flour; thicken pan drippings. Add seasonings, milk and soup. Cook limas until tender; add to soup mixture. Pour over chops. Bake at 325 degrees for 1 hour. More water may be added if necessary. Yield: 6 servings.

Mrs. C. Miller, Sec.
St. Peter Social Soc.
Sibbald, Alberta, Canada

PORK CHOPS AND POTATOES AU GRATIN

6 pork chops
6 potatoes, cooked and sliced
1 med. onion, sliced
3 tbsp. margarine
2 tbsp. flour
2 c. milk
Grated cheese

Brown pork chops in heavy frying pan. Place in deep baking dish. Add potatoes to cover. Saute onion in margarine until tender; add flour. Stir in milk; cook until thick. Pour over chops. Sprinkle generously with grated cheese. Bake at 350 degrees until chops are tender. Yield: 6 servings.

Mrs. Betty Barklage, Eunice Cir. Sec.-Treas.
St. Paul's LWML
Sedalia, Missouri

PORK CHOPS AND POTATOES

Salt and pepper to taste
6 pork chops
1 can cream of mushroom or cream of
    chicken soup
1 to 1 ¼ c. milk
6 to 8 potatoes, cut up

Season pork chops; brown on both sides in skillet. Warm soup with milk until well mixed; pour over chops. Add potatoes. Bake, covered, at 350 degrees for 1 hour to 1 hour and 30 minutes or until done. Yield: 6 servings.

Mrs. Hilda Rieker
St. Paul's Ladies Aid Soc.
Brimfield, Illinois
Mrs. Elmer Schmidt, Pres.
St. John's Ladies Aid
Beaufort, Missouri

PORK CHOPS WITH PEAS ESPAGNOL

4 pork loin
2 tbsp. vegetable oil
1 med. onion, sliced
½ c. diced celery
½ green pepper, diced
1 tsp. salt
½ tsp. basil or oregano
¼ tsp. seasoned pepper
2 tbsp. grated Parmesan cheese
1 1-lb. can tomatoes
1 1-lb. can green peas, drained

Brown chops in 1 tablespoonful hot oil in skillet; remove. Keep chops warm. Saute onion, celery and green pepper in remaining oil until soft; stir in salt, basil, pepper, cheese and tomatoes. Add peas; stir gently to blend. Place chops over top; cover. Bake at 350 degrees for 50 minutes or until chops are tender. Yield: 4 servings.

Mrs. Ralph Jaeger, Pres.
Trinity LWML
Cheyenne, Wyoming

PORK CHOPS, SOUTHERN-STYLE

5 pork chops
2 tbsp. flour
2 tbsp. cooking oil
¾ c. whole kernel corn
1 tbsp. chopped green pepper
1 tbsp. Worcestershire sauce
1 c. water

(Continued on next page)

Salt and pepper to taste
½ tsp. celery salt
Onion seasoning to taste
½ c. tomato sauce

Dredge chops in flour; brown on both sides in hot oil. Place in buttered baking dish. Drain off part of drippings; add remaining ingredients. Pour over chops. Bake at 325 to 350 degrees for 1 hour. Serve with applesauce. Yield: 5 servings.

Anna D. Bean
Good Shepherd Ruth Guild
Midwest City, Oklahoma

STUFFED PORK CHOPS WITH VEGETABLES

4 c. finely cubed dry bread
1 tbsp. finely chopped onion
2 tsp. salt
½ c. diced celery
2 tsp. powdered sage
1 tsp. chopped parsley
6 pork chops, 1-in. thick
Whole carrots
Whole potatoes

Combine all ingredients except chops and vegetables. Add just enough water so that mixture holds together. Cut pockets in chops; stuff with mixture. Secure with toothpicks. Brown chops in kettle in a small amount of fat; add 1/2 inch of water to bottom of kettle. Place carrots and potatoes around meat. Cook over high heat until steaming. Turn heat to low; cook for 1 hour. Yield: 6 servings.

Mrs. Ted Bernhardt, Walther League Counseler
St. John's Ladies Aid Soc.
Tampa, Kansas

CABBAGE ROLLS WITH SAUERKRAUT

½ c. uncooked rice
1 c. boiling water
1 lb. ground pork
⅛ tsp. pepper
¼ tsp. salt
6 leaves cabbage
Flour
Fat
1 lb. sauerkraut
4 tbsp. catsup

Cook rice in the boiling water for 10 minutes or until fluffy. Mix rice, meat, pepper and salt; divide mixture into six balls. Let cabbage leaves stand in boiling water for 1 minute. Place one meat ball in each leaf; roll up. Fasten with thread or skewer. Roll cabbage rolls in flour; brown on all sides in fat. Place in heavy pot. Rinse sauerkraut; place on rolls. Add catsup and small amount of water. Cover and cook for 1 hour. Yield: 4 servings.

Mrs. Leonida Mielke
Bethel Evangelical Ladies Aid
Kitchener, Ontario, Canada

PORKY PIE

1 ½ lb. shoulder pork
3 onions
4 tbsp. fat
1 ½ c. hot water
3 tbsp. flour
Milk
Sugar
1 tsp. salt
⅛ tsp. pepper
1 tsp. paprika
3 tart apples, peeled and sliced
1 recipe baking powder biscuits

Grind pork and onions. Fry for 5 minutes in fat. Add water; simmer for 10 minutes. Blend flour and a small amount of milk; add to meat. Add 1 tablespoonful sugar and seasonings; cook for 3 minutes longer. Sprinkle apples with sugar. Alternate layers of apples and meat in baking dish. Bake at 350 degrees for 30 minutes. Top with baking powder biscuits. Bake for 30 minutes longer. Yield: 6 servings.

Mrs. Edwin H. Schroeder
St. John's Dorcas Soc.
Waverly, Iowa

SWEET AND SOUR MEAT BALLS

1 ½ lb. ground lean pork
¼ c. minced green onions
½ tsp. ginger
⅓ c. plus 2 tbsp. soy sauce
½ c. fresh bread crumbs
3 tbsp. milk
1 egg, beaten
1 ½ tsp. salt
Pepper to taste
3 tbsp. cooking oil
1 20-oz. can pineapple chunks
2 tbsp. cornstarch
½ c. cider vinegar
1 tbsp. Worcestershire sauce
¼ c. brown sugar
1 green pepper, cut into strips
1 15-oz. can bean sprouts, drained and rinsed
½ lb. slivered almonds

Combine pork, onions, ginger, 2 tablespoonfuls soy sauce, bread crumbs, milk, egg, 1/2 teaspoonful salt and pepper, chill well. Shape mixture into balls. Heat oil in heavy pan or Dutch oven; brown meat balls well on all sides. Remove balls; drain all but 2 tablespoonfuls drippings from pan. Drain pineapple, reserving juice. Stir cornstarch into drippings in pan; remove from heat. Add reserved pineapple juice, vinegar, remaining soy sauce and Worcestershire sauce; stir well. Cook over medium heat until mixture comes to a boil; stir in brown sugar, remaining salt and pepper. Add meat balls. Cover; simmer for 30 minutes. Add pineapple chunks and green pepper; cook for 5 minutes. Add bean sprouts and nuts; heat for 5 minutes longer. Serve with rice. Yield: 6 servings.

Mrs. O. Nelson, VP
Hanley LCW
Hanley, Saskatchewan, Canada

SAUSAGE DELIGHT

1 lb. ground pork
1 tsp. finely chopped onion
½ c. bread crumbs
½ c. milk
1 egg
½ tsp. salt
¼ tsp. pepper
Hard-cooked eggs, quartered

Mix all ingredients thoroughly except hard-cooked eggs and crumbs; form into balls. Insert an egg quarter into each ball. Roll in crumbs. Fry until well done and browned evenly. Yield: 4 servings.

Mrs. Gus Temme
Immanuel Dorcas Sewing Cir.
Wentzville, Missouri

BARBECUED HAM

2 ½ tbsp. Worcestershire sauce
⅛ tsp. paprika
¼ c. butter or margarine
1 tbsp. sugar
1 tbsp. lemon juice
1 lb. chipped ham, broken into small pieces

Combine all ingredients except ham; simmer until well blended. Toss ham with sauce. Heat through. Serve on toasted buns. Yield: 6-8 servings.

Mrs. Mertin L. Sellinger, Pres.
Good Shepherd LCW
Greensburg, Pennsylvania

CHEESE-HAM STRATA

8 or 9 slices white bread
¾ lb. sharp cheese, sliced
1 pkg. chopped frozen broccoli, cooked
2 c. cubed ham
6 eggs, beaten
3 ½ c. milk

Cut bread with large round cutter. Place bread scraps on bottom of greased 11 x 13-inch pan; top with cheese, broccoli and ham. Place bread rounds on top. Pour on eggs and milk. Refrigerate overnight. Bake at 350 degrees for 55 minutes. Let stand for 15 minutes before serving. Yield: 8 servings.

Mrs. Mary Gerber, Cor. Sec.
St. Andrew-Redeemer Ladies Guild
Detroit, Michigan

DEVILED EGG AND HAM CASSEROLE

6 hard-cooked eggs
2 tbsp. mayonnaise
½ tsp. salt
½ tsp. dry mustard
Dash of pepper
¼ c. plus 2 tbsp. butter or margarine
¼ c. flour

2 c. milk
1 c. grated process cheese
1 ½ c. drained cooked peas
1 c. diced cooked or canned ham
½ c. dry bread crumbs

Halve eggs; remove yolks and mash with mayonnaise, salt, mustard and pepper. Fill whites. Arrange eggs in greased 10 x 6-inch baking dish. Blend 1/4 cup butter and flour. Gradually stir in milk; cook until thick, stirring constantly. Stir in cheese, peas and ham. Pour over eggs. Combine crumbs and remaining butter; sprinkle over mixture. Bake at 375 degrees for 15 minutes. Yield: 6 servings.

Mrs. Allie Keup, Pres.
Immanual Ladies Aid
Wild Rose, Wisconsin

EGGPLANT STUFFED WITH HAM

1 lge. eggplant
Salted water
1 onion, minced
1 green pepper, chopped
2 tomatoes, quartered
2 tbsp. butter
½ tsp. salt
⅛ tsp. pepper
1 c. diced ham
Bread crumbs

Wash and dry eggplant; cut off a slice from top. Scoop out inside to within 1/2-inch of skin. Cover shell with salted water. Chop eggplant pulp; combine with onion, green pepper and tomatoes. Cook in a small amount of boiling salted water until tender. Drain and mash. Add butter, salt, pepper and ham. Drain shell well; fill with mixture. Sprinkle top with bread crumbs. Bake at 350 degrees for 25 minutes. Sprinkle with Parmesan cheese, if desired. Yield: 4-6 servings.

Mrs. Paul Jump, Pres.
St. Paul's LWML
Marshfield, Missouri

HAM AND CHEESE PIE

4 eggs, slightly beaten
1 ½ c. milk
8 oz. Longhorn or Cheddar cheese
¼ tsp. salt
Dash of pepper
¾ c. diced cooked ham or other meat
1 9-in. pie shell, unbaked

Combine all ingredients except pie shell; mix well. Pour into pie shell. Bake at 350 degrees for 40 to 45 minutes. Garnish with parsley, pimento strips or ripe olives. Yield: 6 servings.

Lois A. Renneau, Pres.
St. Andrew's LCW
San Diego, California

HAM AND BROCCOLI CASSEROLE

1 ½ c. chopped onions
2 c. chopped fresh mushrooms
¼ c. butter
2 cans cream of mushroom soup
1 ½ c. milk
2 10-oz. pkg. frozen broccoli spears, cooked
½ tsp. salt
½ tsp. pepper
2 c. chopped baked ham
1 ½ c. dry stuffing mix
Dash of paprika

Saute onions and mushrooms in butter until very tender. Add soup; mix well. Stir in milk. Arrange one-third of broccoli in bottom of 2-quart casserole; add salt and pepper. Add layers of ham, sauce and stuffing mix. Repeat layers twice, ending with stuffing mix. Sprinkle with paprika. Bake at 350 degrees for 30 minutes. NOTE: Green beans or asparagus may be substituted for broccoli. Yield: 6 servings.

Mrs. Francis J. Heine
Nativity LCW
Chester, Pennsylvania

HAM-CHEESE SQUARES

1 c. cooked rice or noodles
2 c. ham, cut into ½-in. cubes
2 c. grated sharp cheese
½ tsp. salt
3 eggs, slightly beaten
1 c. milk

Mix rice and ham; add remaining ingredients, mixing well. Pour into greased 1 1/2-quart baking dish. Bake at 350 degrees for 45 minutes. Yield: 6 servings.

Mrs. J. H. Cornwell, Sec.
Plains Parish LCW
Smithville, Georgia

HAM AND LENTIL CASSEROLE

¾ lb. lentils
2 ⅓ lb. smoked ham, boned
1 or 2 cloves of garlic, minced
1 c. finely chopped onions
1 c. finely chopped carrots
1 c. finely chopped green peppers
1 c. finely chopped celery
1 No. 2 ½ can tomatoes
1 c. seedless white raisins
½ c. catsup
1 tbsp. sugar
1 tbsp. salt
Pepper to taste

Wash and soak lentils for 1 to 2 hours before cooking. Bring to a boil; simmer for 25 minutes. Drain. Trim fat from ham and reserve. Cut lean meat into bite-sized cubes. Place fat in skillet and cook slowly, stirring often, until most of fat has been rendered out, leaving crisp little crumbles. Drain off some of liquid fat. Saute garlic and vegetables in remaining fat, stirring often. Add remaining ingredients. Place a layer of lentils, layer of ham cubes and a layer of tomato-vegetable mixture in a 4-quart casserole. Repeat layers until casserole is filled, ending with tomato mixture. If casserole seems a bit dry, add a little tomato juice. Cover and bake at 350 degrees for 2 hours and 30 minutes or until lentils are tender. When almost finished, taste for salt. If more is needed, sprinkle it on top. Insert spoon here and there and work back and forth to distribute salt evenly. Do not stir. When done, the consistency should be moist, but not runny. If too moist, remove lid for final minute of cooking. NOTE: Casserole should be prepared for baking a day in advance; can be finished ahead of time and reheated before serving. Yield: 12 servings.

Mrs. Howard Westendorf, VP
First Lutheran LWML
Natchez, Mississippi

HAM AND MACARONI CASSEROLE

1 can cream of celery soup
½ c. milk
4 oz. raw macaroni, cooked
2 c. chopped baked ham
¼ c. chopped green pepper
2 tbsp. minced onion
1 tsp. dry mustard
1 c. grated Swiss cheese

Combine soup and milk; add macaroni, ham, green pepper, onion, mustard and 1/2 cup cheese. Heat thoroughly; pour into greased casserole. Sprinkle with remaining cheese. Bake at 350 degrees for 25 to 30 minutes. Yield: 6 servings.

Mamie Lewis, Pres.
Faith Church Ladies Aid
Council Bluffs, Iowa

HAM AND NOODLE CASSEROLE

½ lb. uncooked smoked ham
½ lb. American cheese
1 green pepper, chopped
6 oz. fine noodles
1 can mushrooms with juice or 1 can cream of mushroom soup
1 ½ c. water
1 tsp. salt

Put ham, cheese and green pepper through food chopper. Add remaining ingredients. Pour into a well greased casserole. Bake at 350 degrees for 1 hour. NOTE: If desired, 1 cup white sauce may be subsitutued for mushrooms. Yield: 8 servings.

Mrs. Arnold Dicke, Pres.
Grace Ladies Aid
Cottonwood Falls, Kansas

HAM-NOODLE CASSEROLE

1 ½ c. chopped cooked ham
1 c. grated cheese
1 8-oz. pkg. noodles, cooked and drained
1 can cream of chicken soup

(Continued on next page)

½ c. milk
½ tsp. curry powder
2 tbsp. butter

Combine ham and 3/4 cup cheese; alternate layers of noodles and ham in greased baking dish. Mix soup, milk and curry; pour over noodles. Sprinkle top with remaining cheese; dot with butter. Bake at 375 degrees for 20 to 30 minutes.

Mrs. Victor Erickson
Faith LCW
Oakville, Washington

HAM 'N' RICE

1 4-lb. cooked ham, cubed
1 1-lb. can diced carrots
1 pt. light cream
½ c. pickle relish
¼ c. chopped onion

Combine all ingredients; heat to boiling. Serve over rice or toast. Yield: 25 servings.

Mrs. Eugene Fisher, Pres.
St. John's LCW
London, Ohio

MACARONI AND HAM SCALLOP

1 ½ c. uncooked elbow macaroni
¼ c. chopped green pepper
¼ c. chopped onion
1 tbsp. butter
1 c. cooked ham
1 ¼ c. cream of mushroom soup
½ c. milk
1 tbsp. pimento
1 tbsp. parsley
Dash of pepper
½ c. grated cheese

Cook macaroni until tender; drain and rinse. Simmer green pepper and onion in butter for 5 minutes. Add ham; brown lightly. Combine ham mixture, soup, milk, pimento, parsley and pepper with macaroni. Pour into casserole. Sprinkle with cheese. Bake at 350 degrees for 45 minutes.

Mrs. Phyllis Mallory, Pres.
Morning Star LCW
Omaha, Nebraska

HAM STROGANOFF

1 c. diced cooked ham
¼ c. chopped onion
2 tbsp. margarine
2 tsp. flour
1 c. sour cream
1 4-oz. can mushrooms, drained

Cook ham and onion in margarine until onion is tender, but not brown. Sprinkle with flour; gradually stir in sour cream. Add mushrooms. Cook and stir over low heat just until mixture thickens.

Prolonged cooking will curdle the sour cream. Serve over fluffy rice. Yield: 2-3 servings.

Mrs. David E. Lange
Natchitoches, Louisiana

HAM TETRAZZINI

½ c. chopped onion
1 c. diced green peppers
1 ½ c. diced celery
½ c. butter
1 can cream of mushroom soup
1 ½ c. milk
2 c. grated Cheddar cheese
1 tsp. salt
¼ tsp. pepper
2 tbsp. Worcestershire sauce
3 c. diced ham
1 lb. raw thin spaghetti, cooked and drained
½ c. grated Parmesan cheese

Brown onion, green peppers and celery in butter until soft, but not browned. Stir in soup and milk; blend well. Mix cheese, seasonings, ham and spaghetti; pour into large casserole. Sprinkle Parmesan cheese over top. Bake at 350 degrees for 45 minutes to 1 hour. Yield: 12 servings.

Mrs. Marion Guffin, Sec.
Holy Cross Ladies Guild
Spokane, Washington

HOT HAM AND CHEESE ROLLS

½ lb. cubed baked ham
⅓ c. sliced green onions
½ c. sliced stuffed olives
½ c. chili sauce
½ lb. cubed Cheddar cheese
2 hard-cooked eggs, sliced
3 tbsp. mayonnaise
12 frankfurter rolls, split

Combine and mix all ingredients except rolls. Pile mixture onto rolls. Wrap each roll in a 6-inch square of foil. Twist ends securely. Place on grill over medium coals for 8 to 10 minutes. Turn frequently. NOTE: These may also be made in the oven. Wrap in foil. Bake at 400 degrees for 10 minutes. Yield: 12 servings.

Mrs. Dwight Kimmel, Pres.
St. James LCW
Jewett, Ohio

MACARONI AND HAM CASSEROLE

1 ½ c. uncooked macaroni
2 c. cubed ham
1 can cream of mushroom soup
¾ c. water
1 tbsp. minced onion
¾ c. grated Cheddar cheese

Cook macaroni in salted water until tender; drain. Mix ham, soup, water, onion and cheese.

(Continued on next page)

Add macaroni; place in 3-quart casserole. Bake at 400 degrees for 30 minutes. Yield: 6-8 servings.

Mrs. Herb Pohl, Treas.
Our Redeemer LWML
Emmett, Idaho

TWO-IN-ONE BAKE
1 med. cauliflower
1 can cream of chicken soup
¼ c. milk
2 c. diced cooked ham
⅛ tsp. dried savory
1 c. grated sharp Cheddar cheese

Cook cauliflower in 1 inch boiling salted water until tender-crisp; drain. Separate into flowerettes. Combine soup and milk in 10 x 6-inch baking dish. Add cauliflower, ham, savory and 1/2 cup cheese. Sprinkle remaining cheese on top. Bake at 350 degrees for 30 minutes. Yield: 6 servings.

Mrs. Otto Dehnbostel
St. John's Ladies Group
Napoleon, Ohio

HAM BALLS
1 lb. ground cured ham
1 lb. fresh ground pork
1 egg
⅔ c. cracker crumbs
1 can milk
½ tsp. salt
Pinch of thyme
Chopped onion

Mix all ingredients; form into balls. Place in 8 1/2 x 11-inch baking dish. Bake at 375 degrees for 20 minutes.

GLAZE:
½ c. brown sugar
1 ½ tbsp. vinegar
½ tsp. dry mustard

Combine all ingredients. Bring to full boil; boil for 1 minute. Spoon glaze over meat balls. Bake for 20 minutes longer. Yield: 6 servings.

Mrs. Harry S. Bowman
First Lutheran Church LCW
Watsontown, Pennsylvania

HAM BALLS
1 ½ lb. ground ham
1 lb. ground pork
1 c. milk
2 eggs
1 c. fine cracker crumbs
½ c. vinegar
1 c. water
1 ½ c. brown sugar
1 tsp. dry mustard

Combine meats, milk, eggs and cracker crumbs; mix well. Form into balls; brown on all sides. Place in casserole. Combine remaining ingredients; pour over ham balls. Cover and bake at 350 degrees for 2 hours, turning the balls after 1 hour. NOTE: Leftovers may be frozen for later use. Yield: 24 small or 16 large ham balls.

Mrs. Althea S. Farrand
St. John's LCW
Jordan, Montana

HAM BALLS
1 lb. fresh pork, ground
1 ½ lb. cured ham, ground
⅔ c. bread crumbs
1 egg
½ c. milk

Mix all ingredients; shape into 20 to 24 meat balls. Place in pan.

SAUCE:
1 c. brown sugar
1 c. water
½ c. vinegar

Combine all ingredients; heat to boiling. Cool; pour over ham balls. Bake at 325 degrees for 1 hour, turning ham balls once.

Mrs. Melbert Schnelle, Pres.
Immanuel LWML
Lockwood, Missouri

HAM BALLS
1 lb. ham
1 ½ lb. fresh pork
¼ tsp. pepper
¼ tsp. salt
2 eggs, well beaten
1 c. milk
1 c. bread crumbs
⅓ c. brown sugar
¼ c. vinegar
¼ c. water
1 tbsp. ground mustard

Grind meats together. Add pepper, salt, eggs, milk and crumbs. Roll into walnut-sized balls; place in pan. Combine remaining ingredients; pour over ham balls. Bake at 325 degrees for 2 hours to 2 hours and 30 minutes, basting frequently with sauce. Yield: 8 servings.

Mrs. Harold J. Bolm
Messiah LCW
Chicago, Illinois

HAM BALLS
2 lb. ground ham
1 lb. ground pork
2 eggs, beaten
1 c. milk
1 c. bread crumbs

(Continued on next page)

¾ c. brown sugar
1 c. water
½ c. vinegar

Combine meats, eggs, milk and crumbs; shape into balls. Combine remaining ingredients to make a sauce. Cook ham balls slowly in sauce for 2 hours, basting occasionally. Yield: 30 ham balls.

Mrs. Benny Nelson, Pres.
Immanuel LCW
Mediapolis, Iowa

HAM NUGGETS
½ lb. ground ham
½ lb. fresh pork or sausage
¼ c. chopped green onions
1 sm. can mushrooms, ground
1 egg, slightly beaten
1 tbsp. milk
Oil

Combine ham, pork, onions and ground mushrooms. Add egg and milk. Shape into balls; brown in small amount of oil until well done, about 30 minutes. Yield: 30 small meat balls.

Mrs. Maurice Nelson, Pres.
St. Paul's LCW
Frostburg, Maryland

SWEDISH HAM BALLS
1 lb. ground ham
1 ½ lb. ground fresh pork
2 eggs, beaten
1 c. milk
2 c. bread crumbs
¾ c. brown sugar
1 tsp. dry mustard
½ c. vinegar
½ c. water

Combine meats, eggs, milk and bread crumbs; mix thoroughly. Form into small balls; place in baking dish. Combine remaining ingredients; pour over ham balls. Bake at 325 degrees for 1 hour, basting often with sauce.

Jennie Nordin, Pres.
Augustana LCW
Clearbrook, Minnesota

BERNADINE'S HAM LOAF
1 lb. cured ham, ground
1 lb. fresh pork, ground
1 c. Krispies or corn flakes
⅛ tsp. pepper
1 egg, slightly beaten
1 c. pineapple juice
6 slices pineapple
24 whole cloves
¾ c. brown sugar
½ c. water
½ c. vinegar

Mix meats, cereal and pepper. Mix egg and pineapple juice; add to meat mixture. Pack into greased pan. Bake at 350 degrees for 2 hours. Before serving, surround with slices of pineapple stuck with cloves. Mix remaining ingredients; cook to make a syrup. Pour over ham loaf; return to oven and bake until glazed. Yield: 6 servings.

Mrs. Ed. J. Bredehoeft, Pres.
St. Paul's LCW
Emmetsburg, Iowa

DANISH SETTLEMENT FAVORITE HAM LOAF
1 ½ lb. pork shoulder
1 ½ lb. smoked ham
2 tbsp. brown sugar
1 tbsp. dry mustard
1 c. cracker crumbs
Salt and pepper to taste
2 eggs, beaten
3 c. milk
1 can tomato soup

Grind meats together. Combine meats, sugar, mustard, cracker crumbs, salt, pepper and eggs. Gradually add milk; mix well. Be sure that the mixture is moist; add additional milk if necessary. Place in well greased pan. Pour soup over top. Bake at 350 degrees for 1 hour and 30 minutes or until done. Yield: 12 servings.

Reeta Petersen, Sec.
Settlement LCW
Gowen, Michigan

FAMILY REUNION HAM LOAF
3 eggs, slightly beaten
1 can evaporated milk
1 can tomato soup
1 c. cracker crumbs
3 lb. ground smoked ham
3 lb. ground fresh pork

Combine eggs, milk, tomato soup and cracker crumbs. Add to meats; mix thoroughly. Pack into two 9 x 5-inch loaf pans. Bake at 325 degrees for 2 hours.

EPICUREAN SAUCE:
1 pt. heavy cream, whipped
¾ c. mayonnaise
½ c. prepared horseradish
2 tsp. salt
4 tsp. prepared mustard
¼ c. minced parsley

Fold all ingredients together until well blended; chill. Serve over ham loaf. Yield: 20 servings.

Mrs. Loren Pobanz, Pres.
Faith LWML
Green Bay, Wisconsin

HAM LOAF

1 egg, beaten
½ c. milk
½ c. cracker crumbs
½ lb. smoked ham, ground
1 ½ lb. lean pork shoulder, ground
¼ tsp. dry mustard
⅛ tsp. pepper

Mix egg, milk and cracker crumbs; add meats and seasonings. Shape into loaf. Bake at 325 degrees for 1 hour and 30 minutes. Yield: 6 servings.

Mrs. Fred Nittler
Trinity Ladies Aid
Greeley, Colorado

HAM LOAF

1 ½ lb. ham
1 lb. pork
Pepper to taste
2 eggs, slightly beaten
½ c. tomato juice
⅔ c. milk
Cloves
1 c. cracker crumbs
1 c. brown sugar
2 tsp. mustard
⅓ c. vinegar
½ c. water

Combine meats, pepper, eggs, tomato juice and milk; form into loaf. Stick with cloves. Combine remaining ingredients; boil for 2 minutes. Bake ham loaf at 350 degrees for 1 hour, basting with brown sugar mixture. Yield: 8 servings.

Ada B. Hansen
Christ Lutheran Church
Saylorsburg, Pennsylvania

HAM LOAF

1 ¼ lb. ground smoked ham
¾ lb. ground fresh pork
¾ c. cracker crumbs
2 eggs
½ c. milk
⅛ tsp. pepper
¾ c. pineapple juice
¾ c. brown sugar

Mix meats, cracker crumbs, eggs, milk and pepper; shape into loaf. Place in baking dish. Bake at 350 degrees for 1 hour. Baste loaf with mixture of pineapple juice and brown sugar. Bake for 30 minutes longer. Score with a spoon; garnish with a Maraschino cherry half anchored with a clove. Yield: 8-10 servings.

Mrs. Robert Thomas, Sr.
Trinity Ladies Aid Soc.
Flat River, Missouri

HAM LOAF

2 lb. ground ham
2 lb. ground pork

1 pt. milk
8 graham crackers, crushed
3 eggs
¼ c. vinegar
⅓ c. brown sugar
1 tbsp. dry mustard

Combine meats, milk, graham crackers and eggs. Pat flat in a greased baking pan or dish. Combine remaining ingredients; pour over meat mixture. Bake at 350 degrees for 45 minutes. Yield: 18 servings.

Mrs. Leda Mowrey
Cross Roads LCW
Daleville, Indiana

HAM LOAF

1 lb. ground cured ham
1 lb. lean ground beef
1 c. bread crumbs
¼ tsp. pepper
2 eggs, beaten
1 c. milk
⅓ c. brown sugar
1 tbsp. dry mustard
¼ c. vinegar

Combine meats, crumbs, pepper, eggs and milk; mix well. Shape into loaf. Combine remaining ingredients to make sauce. Bake ham loaf at 350 degrees for 1 hour, basting with sauce. Yield: 4 servings.

Mrs. R. C. Wiesehan, Pres.
Trinity LWML
Peoria, Illinois

HAM LOAF

⅔ lb. cured ham, ground
1 ⅓ lb. fresh pork, ground
1 c. dry bread crumbs
2 eggs, beaten
1 c. milk
½ tsp. pepper
⅓ c. brown sugar
1 tsp. dry mustard
¼ c. vinegar

Mix meats, bread crumbs, eggs, milk and pepper well. Shape into a loaf. Make a paste of brown sugar, mustard and vinegar; spread over top of loaf. Bake at 350 degrees for 1 hour. Yield: 6-8 servings.

Mrs. C. E. Roth
St. Jacobi Ladies Aid
St. Louis, Missouri

HAM LOAF WITH CHUTNEY SAUCE

1 ½ c. fine soft white bread crumbs
⅔ c. milk
1 lb. ground pork
1 lb. ground ham
⅓ c. chopped onion
6 drops of Tabasco sauce
1 egg

Soak bread crumbs in milk for 5 minutes. Add remaining ingredients; mix well. Bake at 350 degrees for 1 hour and 10 minutes or until done. Let stand in pan for 10 minutes.

CHUTNEY SAUCE:

½ c. light corn syrup
¼ c. brown sugar
⅔ c. drained sweet pickle relish
¼ c. seedless raisins
¼ c. chopped nuts
½ tsp. dry mustard

Mix all ingredients in pan. Bring to a boil; boil for 1 minute. Serve with ham loaf. Yield: 8 servings.

Mrs. Lois Wildman
St. Paul's Lutheran Church for the Deaf
Flint, Michigan

HAM LOAF WITH CRANBERRY SAUCE

3 c. left-over ground ham
1 egg
2 tbsp. minced onion
1 c. milk
Salt and pepper
1 c. bread crumbs
1 17-oz. can jellied cranberry sauce

Combine all ingredients except cranberry sauce. Crush cranberry sauce with fork; spread in a greased loaf pan. Arrange meat mixture over the cranberry sauce. Bake at 350 degrees for 30 to 40 minutes. If desired, cranberry sauce may be heated separately and poured over ham loaf after baking. Yield: 6 servings.

Mrs. Orvo Kausisto, Chmn.
St. Mark's LCW
Waukegan, Illinois

HAM AND PORK LOAF

1 ½ lb. pork steak
1 lb. smoked ham
1 c. cracker crumbs
1 c. milk
2 eggs, beaten
½ tsp. salt
⅛ tsp. pepper
½ c. water
½ c. brown sugar
1 tsp. mustard

Grind meats together. Combine all ingredients except water, sugar and mustard. Pack into loaf pan. Bake at 350 degrees for 1 hour and 30 minutes, basting with mixture of remaining ingredients. Yield: 8 servings.

Mrs. Lorraine Bauschke, Cor. Sec.
Prince of Peace Ladies Guild
Corinth, Mississippi

HAM-TOMATO LOAF

1 ½ lb. smoked ham, ground
¾ lb. ground pork
1 can tomato soup
1 c. cracker or bread crumbs
3 eggs, beaten
1 sm. onion, chopped
1 tsp. salt
½ tsp. pepper

Combine all ingredients; pack into pan. Bake at 350 degrees for 1 hour and 45 minutes.

SAUCE:

1 can cream of celery soup
½ soup can milk
1 tbsp. grated onion

Combine all ingredients; heat and serve over ham loaf. Yield: 8 servings.

Mrs. Norman P. Burau, Pres.
Holy Communion LCW
Grosse Pointe Farms, Michigan

MUSHROOM- HAM LOAF

1 ½ lb. smoked ham, ground
1 ½ lb. lean pork, ground
2 c. grated soft bread crumbs
1 can cream of mushroom soup
¼ c. water
2 eggs, slightly beaten
¼ c. chopped onion
¼ c. chopped green pepper
1 ½ tsp. monosodium glutamate
½ tsp. salt
¼ tsp. pepper

Mix all ingredients lightly, but thoroughly. Pack into loaf pan. Bake at 350 degrees for 1 hour and 30 minutes. Pour off juices from pan before unmolding. Serve hot or cold.

HORSERADISH-WHIPPED CREAM SAUCE:

3 tbsp. fine dry bread crumbs
2 tbsp. prepared horseradish
1 c. heavy cream, whipped
Salt and pepper to taste

Fold bread crumbs and horseradish into whipped cream. Add salt and pepper. Serve with ham loaf. Yield: 6-8 servings.

Dorathy Lewis, Pres.
St. Thomas LWML
Pittsburgh, Pennsylvania

PARSLEY-HAM LOAF

1 ½ lb. ground cured ham
1 lb. ground fresh pork
2 eggs
1 c. milk
1 c. bread crumbs
1 tsp. salt
¼ tsp. pepper
3 sprigs parsley, finely cut
1 ½ c. brown sugar

(Continued on next page)

1 tbsp. prepared mustard
½ c. vinegar
½ c. water

Combine meats, eggs, milk, bread crumbs, salt, pepper and parsley. Shape into a loaf. Combine remaining ingredients; cook for 5 minutes. Bake loaf at 350 degrees for 2 hours, basting every 20 minutes with sauce. Yield: 12 servings.

Betty J. Fisher
St. John's LCW
Milton, Pennsylvania

PARTY PINEAPPLE AND HAM LOAF

1 lb. ground smoked ham
1 lb. ground lean fresh pork
2 eggs
¾ c. soft bread crumbs
¾ c. milk
2 to 8 tbsp. catsup
8 slices pineapple, drained

Mix all ingredients except pineapple. Divide into 9 patties. Form a long roll in a shallow baking dish, alternating a pattie and pineapple slice, starting and ending with meat. Bake at 325 degrees for 30 minutes.

SPICY GLAZE:

1 c. light brown sugar
¼ c. pineapple syrup
2 tbsp. vinegar
1 tsp. prepared mustard

Combine all ingredients; baste ham loaf. Continue baking at 325 degrees for 1 hour longer, basting every 20 minutes. Yield: 8-9 servings.

Shirley Becker, Pres.
Good Shepherd Dorcas Soc.
Evansville, Indiana
Mrs. Don Friedrichs, Pres.
Denison Zone LWML
Charter Oak, Iowa

SMOKED HAM LOAF

1 lb. ground smoked ham
1 lb. ground lean pork
3 c. Wheaties
2 eggs, beaten
1 c. milk
1 tsp. salt
⅛ tsp. pepper

Mix all ingredients thoroughly; pack into greased 9 x 5-inch loaf pan. Bake at 350 degrees for 1 hour and 30 minutes. Unmold. Serve hot or cold. NOTE: For catsup topped loaf, spread 3 tablespoonfuls catsup over top before baking. Yield: 8 servings.

Mrs. Roy Redman
Zion Ladies Aid
Columbia City, Indiana

QUANTITY HAM LOAF

15 lb. fresh ham
15 lb. cured ham
20 eggs, beaten
4 ½ qt. milk
3 lb. crackers, ground
2 qt. tomato juice

Grind meats together. Mix in remaining ingredients. Shape into 10 loaves. Bake at 350 degrees for 1 hour and 30 minutes. Yield: 150 servings.

Mrs. Lawrence Rodland, Pres.
St. John's Ladies Aid Soc.
Waterside, Pennsylvania

SMOKED HAM LOAF

2 eggs, beaten
2 c. milk
1 tsp. (scant) salt
¼ to ½ tsp. pepper
2 tbsp. ground onion
½ c. instant tapioca
1 ½ lb. smoked ham, ground
1 lb. pork shoulder, ground
½ c. water
½ c. vinegar
¾ c. brown sugar
½ tsp. mustard

Combine eggs, milk, salt, pepper, onion and tapioca; mix well with meats. Pack into baking pan. Bake at 350 degrees for 40 minutes. Boil water, vinegar, brown sugar and mustard for 5 minutes. Score ham loaf with knife almost through into serving sized portions; pour sauce over loaf. Continue baking for 35 minutes longer. Yield: 8-10 servings.

Mrs. Esther Stecker
St. Martin Ladies Aid Soc.
Chilton, Wisconsin

CRUSTY HAM PATTIES

3 c. coarsely ground cooked ham
1 egg, lightly beaten
1 9-oz. can crushed pineapple, well drained
½ tsp. salt
¼ tsp. cinnamon
¼ tsp. nutmeg
2 c. mashed sweet potatoes
¾ c. crushed corn flakes
¼ c. lard or drippings

Combine ham with egg, pineapple, seasonings and sweet potatoes. Shape into 12 patties. Dip into corn flakes; fry in hot fat until well browned on both sides, 5 to 8 minutes. Yield: 4 servings.

Mrs. Kenneth Huth, Pres.
Clarks Fork Trinity Ladies Aid
Boonville, Missouri

HAM PATTIES

½ tsp. dry mustard
½ tsp. pepper
½ tsp. salt
½ c. tomato juice

137

(Continued on next page)

½ c. milk
¾ c. cracker crumbs
1 lb. ground ham
1 lb. ground pork

Combine all ingredients; mix well. Shape into patties. Place in cake pan. Bake at 300 degrees for 1 hour and 30 minutes or until done.

Mrs. Theo Remmers, Sec.
Heron Lake Evangelical Lutheran Church
Heron Lake, Minnesota

HAWAIIAN HAM RING

SAUCE:

3 tbsp. brown sugar
2 tbsp. vinegar
½ c. pineapple syrup
¼ tsp. mustard

Mix all ingredients; bring to a boil.

HAM RINGS:

1 lb. ground ham
1 lb. ground pork
2 eggs
1 c. corn flake crumbs
1 c. milk
1 can pineapple slices

Combine all ingredients except pineapple. Shape in form of doughnuts; place each on drained pineapple ring. Bake at 325 degrees for 1 hour and 15 minutes, basting frequently with sauce. If desired, grated cheese may be sprinkled on top just before removing from oven. Yield: 8-10 servings.

Mrs. Ann Maurhoff
Our Savior Ladies Guild
Pittsburgh, Pennsylvania

HAM RING WITH CHERRY SAUCE

1 lb. ground uncooked smoked ham
1 lb. fresh ground pork
2 eggs, beaten
1 ½ c. wheat flakes
½ c. milk
¼ c. brown sugar
1 tsp. prepared mustard
¼ tsp. cloves

Combine meats, eggs, wheat flakes and milk; mix well. Place in 1 1/2-quart ring mold. Combine remaining ingredients; spread over top. Bake at 350 degrees for 1 hour. Drain; invert onto platter.

CHERRY SAUCE:

1 No. 2 can sour pitted cherries
½ c. sugar
2 tbsp. cornstarch
¼ tsp. cloves
¼ tsp. red food coloring

Drain cherries, reserving liquid. Mix sugar, cornstarch and cloves. Gradually stir in cherry

liquid. Cook until mixture boils and thickens, stirring constantly. Add food coloring and drained cherries. Pour into bowl in center of ham ring. Garnish with sprigs of fresh parsley. Yield: 6 servings.

Hulda N. Langrehr, Del.
Christ Lutheran Dorcas Ladies Aid
Berwyn, Illinois

SOUTHERN HAM PUFF

1 ¼ c. evaporated milk
¾ c. water
1 tbsp. butter
¼ tsp. salt
¼ tsp. pepper
⅓ c. corn meal
1 c. grated cheese
3 eggs, separated
1 c. ground ham

Combine milk, water, butter, salt and pepper; heat to boiling. Stir in corn meal slowly; keep boiling for 5 minutes. Stir in cheese; cook until cheese melts. Remove from heat; cool. Slowly beat in egg yolks and ham. Fold in stiffly beaten egg whites. Bake at 325 degrees for 40 minutes.

Roberta N. Otten, Pres.
United LCW
Cole Camp, Missouri

TASTY HAM CASSEROLE

4 oz. uncooked noodles
3 c. ground cooked ham
2 c. sour cream
½ c. crushed corn flakes
1 tbsp. melted butter or margarine

Cook noodles in boiling salted water; drain. Combine noodles, ham and sour cream. Pour into 1 1/2-quart casserole. Combine corn flakes and butter; sprinkle over ham mixture. Place in a pan of hot water. Bake at 350 degrees for 40 minutes. Yield: 8-10 servings.

Mrs. Guy L. LaChine, Pres.
Grace LWML
Knoxville, Tennessee

BAKED SLICE OF HAM

1 slice ham, 1-in. thick
2 tbsp. light brown sugar
1 c. milk

Cut ham into serving pieces; place in heavy skillet. Sprinkle with brown sugar; add 1/2 cup milk. Bake, uncovered, at 375 degrees for 1 hour or until milk is abosorbed. Remove ham from skillet; add remaining milk and heat on top of stove for dressing. Yield: 3 servings.

Mrs. Walter H. Guigley, Pres.
LCW
Ringtown, Pennsylvania

CRANBERRY-GLAZED HAM ROLLS

2 c. instant rice
½ c. minced onion
½ c. diced celery
½ c. butter or margarine
½ tsp. salt
¼ tsp. pepper
2 cans whole cranberry sauce
½ c. (packed) brown sugar
¼ c. lemon juice
16 thin slices cooked ham

Prepare the rice and refrigerate. Saute onion and celery in butter until tender. Add salt and pepper; refrigerate. Combine cranberry sauce, brown sugar and lemon juice; refrigerate. At least 50 minutes before serving, combine rice and celery mixtures. On each slice of ham, place 1 teaspoonful rice mixture. Roll; place, seam-side down, in pan. Heat cranberry sauce mixture. Spoon 1 tablespoonful over each ham roll. Heat at 350 degrees for 20 minutes. Use remaining sauce to pass at the table. Yield: 8 servings.

Mrs. T. J. Rowens, Pres.
St. Paul's LCW
Charleston, West Virginia

DUTCH BAKED HAM SLICES

½ c. flour
1 tsp. dry mustard
½ c. brown sugar
1 sm. can evaporated milk
2 med. slices smoked ham
¼ c. water

Mix flour and mustard; sprinkle one-half of mixture over bottom of ungreased baking pan. Crumble one-half the brown sugar over flour mixture; pour one-half the milk over the dry ingredients. Arrange ham slices in a single layer; cover with remaining ingredients in same order used for bottom. Pour water around edges. Bake at 300 degrees for 1 hour. Yield: 4 servings.

Mrs. Harold I. Houtz, V P
Shiloh Ladies Guild
Lemont, Pennsylvania

HAM AND ASPARAGUS ROLL-UPS

CHEESE SAUCE:

2 tbsp. butter
2 tbsp. flour
1 c. milk
¼ tsp. salt
⅛ tsp. dry mustard
1 tbsp. catsup
1 c. Old English cheese

Melt butter; add flour gradually to make smooth paste. Gradually add milk. Add salt, mustard and catsup. Cook until mixture comes to full boil. Remove from heat; add cheese. Blend until cheese is completely dissolved. If necessary, heat for a few minutes to melt cheese.

ROLL-UPS:

18 stalks cooked asparagus
6 slices boiled ham, ⅛-in. thick
6 slices toast

Place 3 stalks asparagus in center of each slice of ham. Roll individually and secure with toothpicks. Place in shallow 10 x 6-inch pan. Cook at 325 degrees for 30 minutes. Serve on toasted bread; cover with Cheese Sauce. Serve immediately. Yield: 6 servings.

Mrs. Walter Huemrich
Concordia LCW
Pittsburgh, Pennsylvania

HAM WITH CARROT-PINEAPPLE SAUCE

1 ¾ qt. crushed pineapple
¾ qt. shredded carrots
1 c. brown sugar
½ tsp. cinnamon
1 tsp. cloves
¼ c. cornstarch
10 lb. canned ham, sliced

Combine pineapple, carrots, brown sugar, cinnamon, cloves and cornstarch; mix thoroughly. Cook until mixture boils and thickens. Arrange about 17 ham slices in each of three 9 x 13-inch baking pans. Pour sauce over ham. Bake at 350 degrees for 30 minutes. Serve each slice of ham with a spoonful of sauce. Yield: 50 servings.

Estella Schaefer, Pres.
St. Peter's LCW
Trenton, Ohio

HAM CASSEROLE

¾ loaf white bread
Butter
1 ½ lb. cooked ham
4 c. milk
3 eggs
¼ lb. Longhorn cheese, grated
1 sm. can cream of mushroom soup
¼ c. half and half or cream

Cut off crust of bread. Butter slices and place in a 10 x 18-inch baking dish, buttered-side down. Place ham slices over bread; add another layer of bread. Mix milk and eggs; pour over ham and bread. Refrigerate overnight. Top with cheese. Bake at 350 degrees for 45 minutes. Mix soup and cream; pour over top. Bake until bubbly, about 15 minutes longer. Yield: 18 servings.

Mrs. William Bergdall, Pres.
Marquardt LCW
Monroeville, Indiana

HAM SURPRISE

6 sweet potatoes
⅔ c. milk
¼ c. brown sugar

139

(Continued on next page)

1 tsp. salt
1 tsp. cinnamon
1 tsp. nutmeg
6 slices ham
1 can pineapple chunks

Boil and mash sweet potatoes; blend with milk, sugar, salt and spices. Lay ham slices in baking dish; cover each slice with the potato mixture. Garnish with pineapple chunks. Pour pineapple juice over each portion. Bake at 450 degrees for 10 minutes. Yield: 6 servings.

Mrs. Carl Everts, Pres.
Hope LWML
Austin, Texas

SMOTHERED HAM

1 slice center cut ham, 2-in. thick
1 c. boiling water
6 whole cloves
1 c. milk
1 c. bread crumbs
1 tbsp. chopped onion
½ tsp. salt
Pepper
Brown sugar

Place ham in baking dish. Add boiling water; stick cloves in top of ham. Scald milk; add bread crumbs and soak until soft. Add onion and seasonings; spread over ham. Cover with a layer of brown sugar. Bake at 350 degrees for 2 hours or until the top is crisp and brown and the ham is done. Yield: 4-6 servings.

Mrs. Charles K. Knisely, Pres.
Our Savior Ladies Guild
Boxford, Massachusetts

STUFFED HAM STEAK

2 c. soft bread crumbs
½ c. raisins
½ c. chopped peanuts
2 tbsp. dark corn syrup
½ tsp. dry mustard
¼ c. butter or margarine
2 slices ham, ½-in. thick
Cloves

Combine all ingredients except ham and cloves. Place one slice of ham in shallow baking pan; spread stuffing over ham. Top with second slice of ham. Stick whole cloves in fat. Bake at 300 degrees for 1 hour. Yield: 6 servings.

Mrs. Charles L. Griffin, Sec.
Trinity Dorcas League
Brownsville, Texas

APPLE-GLAZED ROAST PORK

1 tsp. salt
1 tsp. dry mustard
¼ tsp. pepper
1 tbsp. flour
1 4-lb. pork loin
1 1-lb. can applesauce

¼ c. (packed) brown sugar
¼ tsp. cinnamon
½ tsp. cloves
1 lb. sauerkraut

Rub salt, mustard, pepper and flour over pork. Place roast, fat-side up, in a shallow roasting pan. Roast at 350 degrees for 1 hour. Combine remaining ingredients except sauerkraut; spread one-half of applesauce mixture over top of roast. Bake for 30 minutes. Spread with remaining applesauce mixture. Bake for 15 minutes longer or until thermometer registers 185 degrees. Place sauerkraut around roast. Bake for 45 minutes longer. Yield: 8 servings.

Mrs. Estelle Meth, Unit Recorder
St. Paul's Evangelical LCW
Richmond Hill, New York

BARBECUED PORK

½ tsp. salt
¼ tsp. pepper
1 4-lb. pork roast
2 c. water
1 sm. onion, chopped
½ pt. tomato juice
2 tbsp. Worcestershire sauce
2 tbsp. flour

Salt and pepper roast; brown. Bake at 400 degrees until tender. Cool thoroughly. Slice roast. Place water in roaster; add onion, tomato juice and Worcestershire sauce. Thicken with flour. Place cold sliced meat in gravy; simmer for a few minutes. Yield: 6 servings.

Doris Voelker, Pres.
St. John's Women's League
Corydon, Indiana

CROWN ROAST OF PORK WITH CORN
STUFFING

1 16-rib crown roast of pork
2 tbsp. salt
Pepper
3 c. diced celery
2 c. boiling water
⅔ c. minced onions
½ c. butter
2 1-lb. cans whole kernel corn, drained
1 tsp. sage
2 qt. soft bread crumbs

Place meat, bone-side up, in open shallow pan. Sprinkle with 3 1/2 teaspoonfuls salt and 1/8 teaspoonful pepper. Place folded strip of foil over exposed ends of ribs. Roast, uncovered, in preheated 325 degree oven for 30 to 35 minutes per pound or until meat thermometer inserted in fleshiest part of roast reaches 185 degrees. Cook celery in water, covered, for about 15 minutes; drain. Cook onions in butter in small skillet until soft. Combine celery, onions, corn, sage, bread crumbs, remaining salt and 3/4 teaspoonful pepper; mix thoroughly. Place part of stuffing mixture in center of roast 45 minutes before roast is done. Place remaining stuffing on

(Continued on next page)

rack around roast. Remove foil; place paper frill on end of each rib to serve. Yield: 8 servings.

Mrs. Murray Bair
Trinity Women's Guild
Urbana, Illinois

FAVORITE PORK ROAST

1 4-lb. pork roast
Salt and pepper to taste
2 apples, peeled and quartered
1 sm. onion, sliced

Season roast with salt and pepper. Sear lightly; place in open roaster. Add 2 cups water, apples and onion, turning to brown. Add water as needed. Bake at 350 degrees for 2 hours. Add additional water; thicken for gravy.

Mrs. Erma Wallochlaeger
Zion Lutheran Church
Neshkoro, Wisconsin

HERBED ROAST PORK

1 6-lb. pork loin
3 tsp. salt
1 tsp. pepper
1 tsp. thyme
½ tsp. nutmeg or mace
2 carrots, sliced
2 onions, sliced
2 cloves of garlic
4 whole cloves
Few celery leaves
Parsley
3 bay leaves
1 10½-oz. can consomme
½ can water

Rub meat with mixture of salt, pepper, thyme and nutmeg. Bake at 450 degrees for 20 minutes. Reduce heat to 350 degrees. Add carrots, onions, garlic, cloves, celery leaves, parsley and bay leaves around roast. Pour in consomme and water. Roast for 2 hours or until tender, basting often. Place roast on hot platter. Skim fat from liquid in pan; work cooked vegetables and liquid through a sieve. Reheat if necessary. Serve as gravy with roast. Yield: 6 servings.

Mrs. William C. Lindholm
Grace LCW
East Tawas, Michigan

ISLAND PORK AMBROSIA

1 jar strained apricots
5 tbsp. honey
4 tbsp. lemon juice
4 tbsp. soya sauce
½ clove of garlic, minced
½ sm. onion, minced
⅓ c. ginger ale or 7-Up
⅛ tsp. ginger
⅛ tsp. pepper
1 5 lb. loin pork roast

Combine all ingredients; pour over roast. Let stand for 4 to 5 hours or overnight, turning meat frequently. Roast at 325 degrees for 3 hours and 30 minutes, basting frequently. Thicken remaining liquid for gravy. Yield: 6 servings.

Mrs. K. Guy Wasson
Trinity Ladies Aid
Greeley, Colorado

LOIN OF PORK WITH MUSHROOMS

1 5-lb. pork loin
Juice of ½ lemon
1 c. fresh mushrooms, cut into strips
Salt
1 ½ c. chicken broth
½ c. dry white wine

Rub pork loin with lemon juice; let stand for 15 minutes. Cut small slits in fat side of pork; place strip of mushroom in each slit. Place pork in Dutch oven or roaster; sprinkle with 1/2 teaspoonful salt, chicken broth and wine. cover; let set for 1 hour and 30 minutes. Roast, covered, at 325 degrees for about 3 hours. Remove cover the last 1 hour and 30 minutes. skim off fat; thicken gravy, if desired.

Mrs. Dorothy Alger
Good Shepherd LCW
Ft. Myers, Florida

PORK ROAST

1 4-lb. pork roast
1 tsp. salt
1 tsp. pepper
1 c. flour
20 whole cloves
1 qt. tomato juice
1 No. 2 can peas

Sprinkle roast with salt, pepper and flour. Brown until golden brown. Press cloves into each side of meat. Place in deep kettle. Cover with water; boil for 3 hours or until pork is tender. Add tomato juice and peas. Heat to a boil. Yield: 6 servings.

Mrs. Harold Koop, VP
Immanuel Ladies Aid
Seymour, Indiana

ROAST PORK TENDERLOIN

Juice of 1 lemon
Juice of 1 orange
1 tsp. salt
¼ tsp. pepper
1 lge. onion, thinly sliced
1 sm. clove of garlic, minced
2 1-lb. pork tenderloins
3 tbsp. flour
1 tsp. salt
1 c. milk

(Continued on next page)

Mix juices with seasonings, onion and garlic. Pour over meat; let stand for 2 hours, turning several times in marinade. Drain. Place in shallow pan. Bake, covered, at 350 degrees for 1 hour and 30 minutes; uncover last 30 minutes of cooking. Place on heated platter. Blend flour and salt in pan. Add milk; cook until thickened. Pour around meat. Garnish with onion rings if desired. Yield: 4 servings.

Mrs. Dorothy Henk, Ruth Cir. Pres.
Bethlehem Ladies Aid
Dundee, Illinois

AMERICAN CHOP SUEY

1 lb. breakfast sausage
1 c. chopped onions
1 c. chopped green peppers
1 c. chopped celery
1 c. brown rice
2 cans chicken with rice soup
2 soup cans water
½ can Cheddar cheese soup

Slightly fry sausage; add remaining ingredients. Cook until rice is tender. Pour into baking dish. Bake at 350 degrees for 1 hour. Yield: 8 servings.

Ruby Tensmeyer, Pres.
Immanuel First Ruth Soc. LWML
West Covina, California

DELICIOUS BARBECUED SAUSAGE

1 med. onion, chopped
½ c. chopped celery
Butter
1 lb. link sausages
½ c. catsup
¼ tsp. pepper
1 tsp. salt
4 tbsp. sugar
4 tbsp. vinegar
1 tbsp. prepared mustard
¾ c. water

Fry onion and celery in butter until transparent. Boil sausages for 2 minutes to remove excess fat; brown slightly in pan with celery and onion. Cut into bite-sized pieces. Combine remaining ingredients; add to sausage mixture. Cover and simmer for 30 minutes. Yield: 4 servings.

Mrs. T. C. Knutson
St. John's Evangelical LCW
Roseray, Saskatchewan, Canada

GERMAN OATMEAL SAUSAGE

1 pork shoulder
Salt to taste
1 tbsp. thyme
Quick cooking oats
Butter

Boil pork in water with 2 teaspoonfuls salt in covered kettle until well done. Remove from broth and cool. Grind pork; add to broth. Heat to boiling; add oats. Stir until oats drop from spoon. Add thyme and additional salt before mixture thickens. Pour into molds; let stand until firm. Remove and wrap in foil or freezer paper. Freeze; slice thin and fry crisp in butter to serve. Yield: 4-6 servings.

Mrs. John H. Kahrs
Immanuel Ladies Aid
Leland, Michigan

KITCHENER SPECIAL

¾ lb. lge. pork sausage
4 oz. wide noodles
½ c. chopped onion
½ c. sliced celery
½ tsp. salt
⅛ tsp. pepper
1 tsp. chili powder
½ tsp. dry mustard
½ tsp. white sugar
1 20-oz. can tomatoes
½ c. water
½ c. grated cheese

Cut sausage in 1-inch pieces; brown well. Drain off all fat. Add uncooked noodles, onion and celery. Sprinkle with seasonings and sugar. Combine tomatoes, water and cheese. Pour over mixture in pan. Cover tightly and simmer for 30 minutes, stirring occasionally. If necessary, add more boiling water during cooking. Serve hot with extra cheese. Yield: 4-5 servings.

Mrs. Robert Beilstein, Pres.
Ladies of Hope
Kitchener, Ontario, Canada

PIZZA PIE

CRUST:

1 c. water
1 tbsp. sugar
1 pkg. dry yeast
2 tbsp. corn oil
½ tsp. salt
3 to 4 c. bread flour

Combine water and sugar in large bowl; sprinkle yeast on top. Let stand for 10 minutes or until bubbly. Add remaining ingredients; mix well. Let rise until doubled in bulk. Punch down; let rise again until doubled. Knead; divide and fit dough into 2 pizza pans or 4 pie pans.

SAUCE:

1 onion, chopped
2 tbsp. corn oil
1 tsp. sugar
1 1-lb. 3-oz. can tomatoes
1 bay leaf
1 tsp. oregano
Dash of pepper
1 tsp. salt
3 pieces smoked sausage, cut into ¼-in. pieces
1 lb. cheese, thinly sliced

142

(Continued on next page)

Saute onion in oil until limp. Add sugar, tomatoes and seasonings; cover. Cook slowly for 30 minutes, stirring occasionally. Sauce will be thick. Cool; spread over dough. Lightly fry sausage; cool. Place over sauce; top with cheese. Bake at 400 degrees for 30 minutes. Yield: 6 servings.

Mrs. Rudolf A. Miller
Lemberg Trinity LCW
Lemberg, Saskatchewan, Canada

PORK-RICE CASSEROLE

¾ lb. pork sausage
1 med. onion, chopped
2 cans cream of chicken or mushroom soup
1 soup can water
1 c. uncooked rice
1 c. Cheddar cheese, cut into small cubes
1 4-oz. can mushrooms (opt.)

Brown sausage in skillet with onion; add remaining ingredients. Pour into shallow 1 1/2-quart baking dish. Bake at 350 degrees for 30 minutes. Yield: 4-6 servings.

Mrs. Verda M. Erdmann
Redeemer LWML
Huntington Beach, California

PORKY IN PEN

6 to 8 Idaho potatoes
1 lb. sm. pork sausages
1 can cream of mushroom soup

Peel potatoes; make holes through potatoes, crosswise, with corer. Insert sausages into holes. Place in pan. Place cored out part in corners of pan. Pour soup over all. Bake at 350 degrees for 1 hour and 30 minutes.

Mrs. Aug Hohl
Emmaus Evangelical Day Guild
Milwaukee, Wisconsin

RICE-SAUSAGE CASSEROLE

2 lb. mild sausage
1 c. chopped celery
1 onion, diced
1 green pepper, diced
1 pkg. chicken noodle soup mix
1 c. instant rice
5 c. water
¾ c. slivered almonds

Brown sausage; drain. Add celery, onion and green pepper; saute. Pour into casserole; add soup, rice and water. Mix well. Bake at 400 degrees for 40 minutes, adding almonds during last 15 minutes of baking time. Yield: 8 servings.

Mrs. Russell Thompson, Pres.
Campus Lutheran Dorcas Guild
Columbia, Missouri

SAUERKRAUT PIE

2 pkg. smoked link sausage
1 No. 2 can sauerkraut
1 or 2 cans refrigerated biscuits

Place layer of sausage in bottom of baking dish; place deep layer of sauerkraut over the sausage links. Place biscuits on top of sauerkraut. Bake at 375 to 400 degrees until biscuits are brown. NOTE: If desired, homemade biscuits may be used.

Mrs. Ruth Luedtke
Our Savior Ladies Guild
New London, Iowa

SAUSAGE PIE AND CHEESE PUFFS

1 lb. bulk pork sausage
1 c. coarsely chopped celery
⅓ c. chopped onion
¼ c. chopped green pepper
2 tbsp. minced parsley
½ tsp. salt
1 6-oz. can tomato paste
¾ c. water
1 c. cooked kidney beans

Brown meat; add celery, onion, green pepper, parsley and salt. Brown lightly. Combine tomato paste and water; add to meat mixture. Add beans; cover. Simmer for 10 minutes. Pour into large casserole.

CHEESE PUFFS:

1 c. biscuit mix
½ c. milk
½ c. grated sharp cheese

Combine all ingredients. Drop by spoonfuls over casserole. Bake at 425 degrees for 20 minutes.

Lydia Fliehler
Hope Lutheran Church
Hollywood, California

SAUSAGE AND RICE CASSEROLE

1 lb. sausage
1 envelope chicken noodle soup mix
1 qt. water
½ c. chopped onion
½ c. chopped celery
¾ c. uncooked rice

Break up and fry sausage until brown; remove half of grease. Cook soup in water; add to sausage and stir well. Add onion, celery and rice. Pour into greased casserole; Bake at 300 degrees for 1 hour and 30 minutes or until rice is well done. Yield: 5 servings.

Mrs. Hazel Hahner, Wlfr. Chmn.
Atonement Lydia Guild
Woodland Hills, California

SAUSAGE-RICE CASSEROLE

1 lb. bulk pork sausage
1 ½ c. chopped celery
½ c. chopped onion
½ c. chopped green pepper
1 pkg. chicken soup mix
1 can cream of mushroom soup
3 ½ c. boiling water
1 c. uncooked rice
Slivered almonds (opt.)

Brown sausage in skillet; remove sausage and pour off fat, reserving two tablespoonfuls. Cook celery, onion and green pepper in reserved fat until tender. Combine soup mix with mushroom soup; gradually stir in boiling water. Combine all ingredients in 2-quart casserole. Cover; bake at 350 degrees for 45 minutes. Top with slivered almonds, if desired. Yield: 8-10 servings.

Mrs. Robert Burer
Holy Cross LCW
Fairfield, Ohio

SAUSAGE PILAF

1 lb. bulk pork sausage
1 c. chopped celery
½ c. chopped onion
½ c. chopped green pepper
¼ c. chopped pimento
1 can cream of mushroom soup
1 ¼ c. milk
½ c. uncooked rice
½ tsp. poultry seasoning
¼ tsp. salt
1 c. soft bread crumbs
2 tbsp. butter, melted

Brown sausage; drain off excess fat. Add celery, onion and green pepper; cook until tender, but not brown. Stir in pimento, soup, milk, rice and seasonings. Pour into 1 1/2-quart casserole. Cover and bake at 350 degrees for 50 minutes, stirring occasionally. Mix crumbs and butter; sprinkle over casserole. Bake, uncovered, for 20 minutes longer. Garnish with pimento stars, if desired. Yield: 6 servings.

Mrs. Herbert A. Paar
Hope Ladies Aid Soc.
Dallas, Texas

SAUSAGE STUFFING

1 lb. sausage
1 c. diced onions
1 c. diced celery
1 can beef consomme
2 tbsp. minced parsley
5 tsp. poultry seasoning
1 tbsp. salt
1 tsp. pepper
4 qt. (lightly packed) day-old bread crumbs
2 eggs, well beaten

Cook sausage, onions and celery over medium heat until sausage breaks up in small pieces and is cooked, about 10 minutes. Add consomme; heat. Combine remaining ingredients; add sausage mixture. Mix well; stuff turkey. Yield: Stuffing for a 10-pound turkey.

Mrs. Alvin L. Olson, Pres.
First Lutheran Salol LCW
Roseau, Minnesota

SIX-LAYER DINNER

2 c. diced potatoes
½ c. rice
1 lb. pork sausage
1 c. diced carrots
1 c. diced onions
Dash of salt
1 can tomato soup
2 c. water

Spread layers of potatoes, rice, sausage, carrots and onions in baking dish, salting each layer. Mix soup and water; pour over all. Bake at 350 degrees for 1 hour and 30 minutes. Yield: 6 servings.

Mrs. Kenneth Weber, Chmn.
St. Paul's Women's Guild
Bertrand, Nebraska

STUFFED PORK SAUSAGE ROLL

2 lb. pork sausage
2 c. chopped tart apples
2 sm. onions, chopped
2 c. small bread cubes

Pat pork sausage on waxed paper into a flat rectangular shape about 1/2-inch thick. Mix apples, onions and bread cubes; spread over meat. Roll up like a jelly roll. Place on a trivet. Bake at 350 degrees for 1 hour. Yield: 4-6 servings.

Mrs. Scott Johnsen, Pres.
Our Savior LCW
Memphis, Tennessee

BAKED SPARERIBS

3 lb. spareribs
Salt and pepper
1 6-oz. can frozen pineapple-orange juice, thawed
¼ c. water
¼ c. brown sugar
1 tbsp. soy sauce
1 tbsp. butter
1 tsp. liquid smoke
⅛ tsp. garlic powder

Sprinkle spareribs with salt and pepper. Place on broiler rack; bake at 400 degrees for 30 minutes. Combine 1/4 teaspoonful salt and remaining ingredients in saucepan. Bring to a boil; simmer for 10 to 15 minutes. Reduce heat to 250 degrees; bake for 1 hour and 30 minutes, basting with sauce at intervals. Yield: 4 servings.

Mrs. Adda V. Herman
Zions Lutheran Church
Pillow, Pennsylvania

BARBECUED RIBS

1 c. vinegar
5 tbsp. brown sugar
3 tbsp. lemon juice
5 tbsp. Worcestershire sauce
3 to 4 lb. spareribs, cut into serving pieces
3 tbsp. oil
1 med. onion, minced
2 tbsp. prepared mustard
1 tsp. liquid smoke
¾ c. catsup
1 tsp. salt
⅓ c. barbecue sauce

Combine vinegar, 3 tablespoonfuls brown sugar, lemon juice and 3 tablespoonfuls Worcestershire sauce. Place ribs in roasting pan. Bake, uncovered, at 500 degrees for 10 to 15 minutes. Reduce heat to 325 degrees; bake for 2 hours, basting every 15 minutes with vinegar mixture. Combine remaining ingredients. Pour over ribs. Bake for 30 minutes longer. Yield: 6 servings.

Mrs. Lyle Hillmer, Pres.
Bethlehem LWML
Mason City, Iowa

BARBECUED RIBS

2 ½ to 3 lb. spareribs, cut into serving pieces
2 tsp. salt
¼ tsp. pepper
⅓ c. chopped onion
1 8-oz. can tomato sauce
2 tsp. vinegar
½ tsp. Worcestershire sauce
Dash of Tabasco sauce

Wipe spareribs with damp paper towel. Sprinkle with salt and pepper. Place in shallow baking pan; cover with foil. Bake, uncovered, at 400 degrees for 45 minutes. Drain off excess fat. Combine remaining ingredients; pour over spareribs. Continue baking, uncovered, for 45 minutes or until tender, turning meat once. Yield: 6 servings.

Mrs. Chris F. Holtzman, Sr. Pres.
St. Paul's LWML
Ridgeway, North Carolina

BARBECUED SPARERIBS

3 lb. spareribs, cut into serving pieces
1 med. onion, diced
½ c. catsup
1 ½ tsp. salt
¼ tsp. Worcestershire sauce
¼ tsp. chili powder
1 c. water
½ tsp. dry mustard
2 tbsp. brown sugar

Arrange spareribs in frying pan. Combine remaining ingredients; pour over ribs. Bake, covered, at 350 degrees for 2 hours. Skim off fat.

Bake, uncovered, for 30 minutes longer. Yield: 6 servings.

Mrs. Jake Balster, Pres.
Immanuel Ladies Aid
Silver Creek, Minnesota

BARBECUED SPARERIBS

4 lb. spareribs, cut into serving pieces
5 tsp. salt
¾ c. water
¾ c. catsup
½ tsp. red pepper
2 tbsp. vinegar
1 tsp. chili powder
1 tsp. pepper
1 tsp. paprika
2 tsp. Worcestershire sauce
2 onions, sliced

Sprinkle ribs on each side with 2 teaspoonfuls salt. Place side by side on 11 x 17 x 1-inch cookie sheet. Bake at 375 degrees for 45 minutes. Combine remaining ingredients. Pour over meat. Bake until done. Yield: 4 servings.

Mrs. Carl J. Haenfiling
Zion Ladies Aid
Accident, Maryland

BARBECUED SPARERIBS

5 lb. spareribs
1 tsp. salt
⅛ tsp. pepper
1 lemon, thinly sliced
½ c. minced onion
1 tsp. chili powder
1 tsp. celery seed
¼ c. vinegar
¼ c. Worcestershire sauce
1 c. catsup
2 c. boiling water
Dash of Tabasco sauce
¼ c. (firmly packed) brown sugar

Arrange spareribs, rounded-sides up in two shallow pans. Sprinkle with salt and pepper. Arrange lemon slices over spareribs; sprinkle with onion. Combine remaining ingredients; pour over spareribs. Bake at 450 degrees for 45 minutes. Bake at 350 degrees for 45 minutes longer. Yield: 6-8 servings.

Mrs. Robert M. Henrichs
St. Peter's Lutheran Church
Humboldt, Kansas

BARBECUED SPARERIBS

3 lb. spareribs
1 ¼ c. catsup
1 tbsp. prepared mustard
¾ c. water
⅓ c. vinegar
2 tbsp. Worcestershire sauce
2 tbsp. brown sugar
2 tsp. chili powder
Pinch of garlic salt

(Continued on next page)

Place ribs in 9 x 13-inch pan. Combine remaining ingredients. Pour over ribs. Bake at 350 degrees for 1 hour and 30 minutes, basting three times. Turn ribs only once. Yield: 4 servings.

Mrs. Roxana Duncan
Timothy Ladies Guild
Council Bluffs, Iowa

BARBECUED SPARERIBS

3 ½ to 4 lb. spareribs
1 ½ c. water
1 8-oz. can tomato sauce
2 med. onions, chopped
3 tbsp. vinegar
1 ½ tbsp. sugar
3 tbsp. Worcestershire sauce
1 tsp. salt
1 tsp. chili powder
1 tsp. dry mustard

Have butcher crack bones cross-wise. Cut between every 2 ribs to make serving-sized pieces. Place ribs meaty-side up, in single layer in a large baking pan. Combine remaining ingredients; bring to a boil. Pour over meat. Cover; chill for several hours or overnight. Bake, covered, at 450 degrees for 30 minutes, basting often with sauce. Remove cover; continue baking, basting frequently for 1 hour and 30 minutes to 2 hours or until meat is tender. Yield: 4 servings.

Mrs. Richard Delventhal, Church Sec.
Faith Ladies Guild
Dunedin, Florida

BARBECUED SPARERIBS OR PORK CHOPS

4 lb. spareribs or pork chops, cut into serving
   pieces
2 tbsp. fat
3 tbsp. flour
2 c. boiling water
½ c. catsup
1 bay leaf
4 tbsp. vinegar
1 tbsp. celery seed
1 tsp. ground cloves
1 tbsp. minced onion
½ tsp. paprika
1 tsp. salt

Brown meat in fat in electric frying pan. Remove meat. Add flour to fat in skillet; blend thoroughly. Slowly add water, stirring constantly until well mixed. Add remaining ingredients except meat. Cook until thickened. Add meat. Cover; simmer for 2 hours and 30 minutes to 3 hours. Yield: 12 servings.

Mrs. Andrew Claycamp
St. John Ladies Aid
Columbus, Indiana

BEST BARBECUED SPARERIBS

4 lb. spareribs, cut into serving pieces
1 tsp. salt
¼ tsp. pepper
3 tbsp. flour
¼ c. chopped onion
⅔ c. boiling water
½ c. catsup
¼ c. chili sauce
3 tbsp. vinegar
1 tsp. salt
1 tsp. Worcestershire sauce
¼ tsp. paprika
¼ tsp. celery seed
1 tbsp. brown sugar

Sprinkle ribs with salt, pepper and flour. Place in shallow baking pan. Top with onions. Combine remaining ingredients. Cover with one-half the sauce. Bake, covered, at 350 degrees for 1 hour and 30 minutes or until brown. Baste with remaining sauce. Uncover last few minutes of baking. Yield: 6-8 servings.

Mrs. Edna Paul, Pres.
First Lutheran Church LCW
Los Angeles, California

DARK BROWN BARBECUED RIBS

5 lb. lean spareribs
Salt and pepper to taste
½ c. mild molasses
⅓ c. vinegar
¼ c. mustard
¼ c. water
2 tbsp. Worcestershire sauce
½ tsp. Tabasco sauce
1 c. chili sauce

Place ribs seasoned with salt and pepper in shallow baking pan. Bake at 350 degrees for 1 hour. Combine remaining ingredients; pour over ribs. Bake for 1 hour longer, basting every 15 minutes with sauce. Yield: 6 servings.

Mrs. Emil H. Schmidt, Pres.
St. Paul Women's General Assembly
Pipestone, Minnesota

EASY BARBECUED SPARERIBS

½ c. vinegar
½ c. water
1 14-oz. bottle catsup
1 sm. onion, chopped
4 tbsp. Worcestershire sauce
2 tbsp. sugar
2 tbsp. lemon juice
3 lb. spareribs

Combine all ingredients except spareribs. Simmer until onion is clear. Pour over ribs; roast at 350 degrees for 2 hours or until tender, turning often. NOTE: Sauce may be used for chicken by adding 1/2 cup lard and 1/4 cup butter.

Mrs. Dennis L. Hartung
Zion Ladies Aid
Fairmont, Monnesota

GARLIC BARBECUED SPARERIBS

3 to 4 lb. spareribs, cut into 3-in. pieces
½ c. catsup
⅓ c. lemon juice
½ c. orange juice
¼ c. brown sugar
¼ tsp. salt
1 clove of garlic, finely chopped
1 sm. onion
½ tsp. dry mustard
¼ tsp. Worcestershire sauce
Pepper

Fry ribs until golden brown. Place in shallow pan. Combine remaining ingredients. Bring to a boil. Pour over ribs. Bake at 350 degrees for 35 minutes. Yield: 4-6 servings.

Mrs. Dennis Hanke, Pres.
Faith LWML
Middle Lake, Saskatchewan, Canada

OVEN BARBECUED SPARERIBS

2 lb. spareribs, cut into small pieces
Flour
Salt and pepper
1 c. brown sugar
½ c. vinegar
½ c. water
1 tbsp. soy sauce
½ c. catsup

Coat ribs with flour; sprinkle with salt and pepper. Brown in hot fat. Drain off all fat; coat ribs with flour again. Place in casserole. Combine remaining ingredients; pour over ribs. Bake at 325 to 350 degrees for 45 minutes. Serve with rice. Yield: 6 servings.

Mrs. Dorothy Holtby, Pres.
Mount Zion LWML
Cranbrook, British Columbia, Canada

SMOKE PORK BARBECUE

Liquid smoke
2 10½-oz. cans tomato soup
4 med. onions, chopped
1 tbsp. salt
2 tbsp. chili powder
2 lge. cloves of garlic
1½ tbsp. unsulphered molasses
4 lb. pork ribs or backbones

Combine all ingredients except meat; simmer for 20 minutes. Place meat in shallow pan; pour sauce over each piece of meat. Bake at 350 degrees for 10 minutes. Reduce heat to 250 degrees for 3 hours, basting every 30 minutes. Toward the end of the baking period, the accumulated fat may be removed.

Mrs. Robert J. Schell, Pres.
Emmanuel LWML
Asheville, North Carolina

TANGY BARBECUED SPARERIBS

2 lb. spareribs, cut into serving pieces
2 tsp. salt
2 tbsp. prepared mustard
2 tbsp. flour
¼ c. chopped onion
½ tsp. ground cloves
½ tsp. pepper
2 tbsp. Worcestershire sauce
1 c. pickle or peach juice
1 c. catsup

Brown spareribs; season with 1 teaspoonful salt. Mix mustard with flour. Add remaining ingredients; blend well. Pour over spareribs. Cover; bake at 300 degrees for 1 hour and 30 minutes, turning once during cooking. Serve sauce over mashed potatoes. NOTE: One cup water mixed with 3 tablespoonfuls vinegar and 3 tablespoonfuls sugar may be substituted for pickle juice. Yield: 4-6 servings.

Mrs. Pat Young, Pres.
St. Paul's LWML
Woodland, California

CHEF'S SPARERIBS

¼ c. brown sugar
1 tbsp. salt
1 tbsp. celery seed
1 tbsp. chili powder
1 tsp. paprika
2 to 3 lb. pork ribs
¼ c. vinegar
1 c. canned tomato sauce or puree

Mix dry ingredients; rub part of mixture into ribs. Let stand for 1 hour. Combine remaining mixture with vinegar and tomato sauce. Cook ribs on grill over slow fire until done, basting occasionally with sauce. Yield: 4 servings.

Mrs. Rex Moore, VP
Trinity Ladies Aid Soc.
Auburn, Indiana

FOUR R'S SPARERIBS

3 lb. ribs
2 onions, sliced
2 tbsp. vinegar
2 tbsp. Worcestershire sauce
1 tbsp. salt
1 tsp. paprika
¼ tsp. cayenne pepper
½ tsp. pepper
1 tsp. chili powder
¾ c. catsup
¾ c. water
2 tbsp. brown sugar

Place ribs in shallow pan. Combine remaining ingredients; pour over ribs. Bake, uncovered, at 350 degrees for 2 hours and 30 minutes, basting often. Yield: 4 servings.

Mrs. Hugo Alewel, Sec.
St. Paul's Ladies Aid
Concordia, Missouri

HAWAIIAN RIBS

4 lb. spareribs, cut into 1 ½-in. strips
¾ c. cornstarch
¼ c. molasses
¼ c. soy sauce
½ c. sugar
¾ c. vinegar
¾ c. water
¾ c. pineapple juice
1 can pineapple chunks
2 green peppers, cut into 1-in. strips

Brown ribs in heavy fry pan or Dutch oven. Mix cornstarch with molasses and soy sauce. Spread on each side of ribs. Brown in hot oven. Combine sugar, vinegar, water and pineapple juice; heat until sugar is dissolved. Pour over ribs. Cover; cook for 25 to 30 minutes or until tender. Add pineapple and green peppers. Cover; simmer for 5 minutes. Yield: 6 servings.

Mary L. Morse, Pres.
Redeemer Lutheran Guild
Napa, California

HAWAIIAN-STYLE SPARERIBS

3 lb. spareribs
2 tbsp. brown sugar
2 tbsp. cornstarch
½ tsp. salt
¼ c. vinegar
½ c. catsup
1 9-oz. can crushed pineapple
1 tbsp. soy sauce

Cut ribs into serving pieces. Combine remaining ingredients. Cook, stirring until slightly thickened. Arrange layer of ribs in roasting pan. Cover with one-half the sauce. Add another layer of ribs; top with remaining sauce. Cover tightly; bake at 350 degrees for 1 hour and 30 minutes to 2 hours. Yield: 4-6 servings.

Mary Winkler, Pres.
Immanuel Ladies Aid Soc.
Alexander, Arkansas

PEKING-STYLE SPARERIBS

2 to 2 ½ lb. small spareribs
1 c. white vinegar
6 c. boiling water
2 tbsp. cornstarch
3 tbsp. shoyu sauce
1 clove of garlic, grated
2 tbsp. salad oil
1 13 ½-oz. can pineapple chunks
¼ c. sugar
1 tsp. monosodium glutamate
1 green pepper, cut into 1-in. squares

Cut ribs into 3-inch lengths across bones. Bring 3/4 cup vinegar and water to a boil; add ribs and cook for 10 minutes. Drain; discard water. Place cornstarch in large bowl; add shoyu sauce and garlic. Mix well. Coat ribs in mixture. Let stand for 30 minutes. Heat oil in large heavy skillet; add ribs and brown slowly and thoroughly. Remove from skillet. Drain pineapple, reserving syrup. Pour reserved pineapple syrup, remaining vinegar, sugar and monosodium glutamate into skillet. Stir and cook for 1 minute. Add ribs; simmer for 30 to 40 minutes, stirring occasionally. Stir in cornstarch mixture left from marinating ribs, pineapple chunks and green pepper. Cook over high heat for 2 minutes, stirring frequently. Serve with white rice or Chinese fried rice, if desired. Yield: 3 servings.

Mrs. Dorothy Range, Pres.
St. Paul Ladies Guild
West Allis, Wisconsin

MOLOWA SPARERIBS

2 to 3 lb. spareribs, cut into 1 ½-in. squares
¾ c. shoyu sauce
¼ c. water
⅓ c. sugar

Brown spareribs lightly; pour off excess oil. Add shoyu, water and sugar. Bring to a boil. Simmer for 45 minutes to 1 hour or until tender, stirring every 5 to 10 minutes. Serve with rice. Yield: 4-6 servings.

Mrs. Edna Dacoscos, Pres.
Good Shepherd Lutheran Church
Honolulu, Hawaii

PORK AND KRAUT

2 to 3 lb. fresh pork ribs
Water
1 qt. sauerkraut
Salt and pepper

Place pork in large kettle; cover with cold water. Cook slowly for 1 hour. Add sauerkraut, making sure there is enough liquid in pan to cover. Cook slowly for 1 hour. Season to taste. Yield: 5-6 servings.

Lorena Nickel, Pres.
St. Paul's LCW
Gowanstown, Ontario, Canada

SPARERIB CASSEROLE

1 ½ lb. spareribs
¾ c. chopped celery
½ c. chopped green pepper
3 sm. onions, chopped
½ c. chopped cabbage
2 tbsp. chili sauce
3 c. tomatoes or tomato juice
2 c. diced potatoes

Brown spareribs. Combine celery, green pepper, onions, cabbage and chili sauce in sauce. Cook until browned. Pour over spareribs. Add remaining ingredients. Bake at 350 degrees until done. Yield: 6 servings.

Mrs. Veronica Packard, Pres.
Mount Calvary Ladies Aid
Maple Creek, Saskatchewan, Canada

SPARERIBS WITH CARAWAY KRAUT

3 lb. spareribs, cut into serving pieces
2 tsp. salt
¼ tsp. pepper
1 No. 2 ½ can sauerkraut, undrained
2 med. carrots, shredded
1 unpared tart apple, finely chopped
1 ½ c. tomato juice
2 tbsp. brown sugar
2 to 3 tsp. caraway seed

Season ribs with salt and pepper; place in Dutch oven. Combine sauerkraut with remaining ingredients; spoon over ribs. Bake, covered, at 350 degrees for 2 hours and 30 minutes to 3 hours and 30 minutes or until done. Baste several times with juices during last hour of cooking. Yield: 4-6 servings.

Mrs. Vera H. Palechek, Pres.
Zion Ladies Aid
Carlinville, Illinois

SWEET AND SOUR BAKED SPARERIBS

2 lb. spareribs
Salt and pepper
1 lemon, sliced
½ c. chopped onion
2 tbsp. dry mustard
⅓ c. chili sauce
1 c. brown sugar
¾ c. pineapple juice
1 tsp. lemon juice

Place ribs on rack in baking pan. Sprinkle with salt and pepper. Arrange lemon slices over ribs; top with onion. Combine remaining ingredients. Bake, uncovered, at 350 degrees for 2 hours. Spoon sauce over ribs two or three times during baking. NOTE: Spareribs may be threaded on rotisserie spit or cooked directly on grill over charcoal. Cook slowly, basting with barbecue sauce every 15 to 20 minutes. Yield: 3-4 servings.

Mrs. John E. Hoyer
Ebenezer LCW
Stickney, South Dakota

SWEET AND SOUR RIBS

2 lb. pork ribs
¼ c. sugar
¼ tsp. dry mustard
3 tbsp. vinegar
½ tsp. salt
2 tbsp. flour
3 tbsp. soy sauce
1 c. water

Brown ribs. Combine remaining ingredients; pour over ribs. Bake at 300 degrees for 2 hours, basting frequently. Yield: 6-8 servings.

Mrs. Ted Rub
Trinity Ruth Guild
Sterling, Colorado

SWEET AND SOUR BARBECUED SPARERIBS

3 to 4 lb. spareribs, cut into pieces
1 lemon, thinly sliced
1 lge. onion, thinly sliced
1 c. catsup
2 c. water
⅓ c. Worcestershire sauce
1 tsp. chili powder
1 tsp. salt
2 dashes of Tabasco sauce
1 c. brown sugar

Place ribs in shallow roasting pan, meaty-side up. Place 1 slice lemon and 1 slice onion on each piece of meat. Roast at 450 degrees for 30 minutes. Combine remaining ingredients except brown sugar. Bring to a boil; pour over ribs. Sprinkle with brown sugar. Bake at 350 degrees for 45 minutes to 1 hour or until tender. Baste with sauce every 15 minutes. Add water as needed. Yield: 4 servings.

Mrs. Raymond Thompson, Pres.
Barneneld Lutheran Church
Barneneld, Wisconsin

SWEET AND SOUR SPARERIBS

2 lb. spareribs, cut into 1-in. pieces
¾ c. soy sauce
½ c. plus 3 tbsp. sugar
5 tbsp. flour
½ c. vinegar
1 ½ c. water

Dip spareribs into soy sauce; roll in 3 tablespoonfuls sugar mixed with flour. Fry in deep fat until browned. Place spareribs in Dutch oven or saucepan. Add remaining ingredients. Cover; simmer for 30 minutes or until ribs are tender. Serve with rice. Yield: 4 servings.

Mrs. Irma Szol, Pres.
Fort Macleod LCW
Fort Macleod, Alberta, Canada

SWEET AND SOUR SPARERIBS

1 egg
½ c. milk
2 lb. lean spareribs, cut into 1-in. pieces
Bread crumbs
1 c. tomato juice
½ c. vinegar
1 c. catsup
1 c. brown sugar
2 tsp. Worcestershire sauce
1 tsp. salt
1 c. water

Beat egg with milk. Dip ribs into egg mixture. Roll in bread crumbs. Brown in pan. Combine remaining ingredients in large pan. Pour over spareribs. Bake at 350 degrees for 1 hour and 30 minutes. Serve with rice. Yield: 6 servings.

Mrs. K. Markman, Sec.
Zion Evangelical Esther Cir.
Port Arthur, Ontario, Canada

SWEET AND SOUR SPARERIBS

2 lb. spareribs, cut into 1-in. pieces
Flour
2 tbsp. cooking oil
2 tbsp. cornstarch
½ tsp. salt
2 tbsp. brown sugar
¼ c. vinegar
1 c. pineapple juice
2 tbsp. soy sauce

Roll spareribs in small amount of flour; brown in oil in pan. Cover; simmer for 20 minutes. Mix cornstarch with salt and brown sugar. Add vinegar, pineapple juice and soy sauce. Mix well; cook until thickened. Pour sauce over spareribs. Cook for 15 minutes. Serve on platter garnished with pineapple slices. Yield: 4 servings.

Mrs. Fred Gronvold, Pres.
Weldon Ladies Aid
Weldon, Saskatchewan, Canada

SWEET AND SOUR SPARERIBS

3 lb. spareribs, cut into 3-in. strips
2 tbsp. soy sauce
½ tsp. salt
¼ tsp. pepper
3 tbsp. butter, melted
1 ½ c. green pepper, cut into 1 x 1 ½-in. pieces
1 ¼ cans sliced pineapple, cut into ½-in. pieces
4 tbsp. cider vinegar
¾ c. chicken stock
¾ c. (packed) brown sugar
2 whole canned pimentos, cut into small pieces
1 lge. onion, cut into ½-in. pieces
½ c. water
2 tbsp. cornstarch

Cook spareribs in boiling water for 1 hour. Drain; wash thoroughly twice. Drain in sieve for 2 hours. Add spareribs, soy sauce, salt and pepper to butter in frying pan. Cook for 10 minutes, stirring constantly. Boil green pepper for 3 minutes; drain. Drain pineapple, reserving juice. Combine pineapple juice with vinegar and brown sugar. Add to spareribs with green pepper, pineapple, chicken stock and pimento. Cook over medium heat for 10 minutes, stirring constantly. Add onion. Cover; cook for 3 minutes. Mix water with cornstarch; pour over ribs. Cook for 3 minutes longer. Yield: 8 servings.

Evelyn E. Hagen
Trinity LWML
San Bernardino, California

SWEET-SOUR SPARERIBS

3 lb. spareribs, cut into serving pieces
⅔ c. (firmly packed) brown sugar
2 tbsp. cornstarch
2 tsp. dry mustard
⅔ c. vinegar
1 c. crushed pineapple, undrained
½ c. catsup
½ c. water
¼ c. finely chopped onion
2 tbsp. soy sauce
Salt and pepper to taste

Place ribs, meaty-side up, in single layers in large shallow pan. Brown at 425 degrees for 20 to 30 minutes. Drain off fat. Combine remaining ingredients except salt and pepper in saucepan. Stir until smooth. Cook over medium heat until thick and glossy, stirring constantly. Sprinkle ribs with salt and pepper. Spoon one-half the sauce over each piece. Reduce heat to 350 degrees; bake for 45 minutes. Turn ribs; cover with remaining sauce. Bake for 30 minutes or until done. Yield: 6-8 servings.

Mrs. Clarence Ohlde, Pres.
Zion LWML
Linn, Kansas

TERIYAKI SPARERIBS

Spareribs
1 c. soy sauce
1 c. sugar
2 cloves of garlic, sliced
2 tsp. fresh grated ginger

Place ribs in roaster. Cover; bake at 350 degrees until tender. Combine remaining ingredients; bring to a boil. Cool sauce. Cook ribs, basting with sauce until sauce has soaked into ribs.

Helen Riggs, Pres.
Trinity LCW
Manhattan Beach, California

CURED PORK SHOULDER AND VEGETABLES

5 slices pork shoulder or steak
1 lge. onion, sliced
3 med. potatoes, sliced
3 to 4 carrots, cut lengthwise
3 tbsp. uncooked rice
1 pt. canned tomatoes, diced
Salt and pepper to taste

Fry meat until partially brown on both sides Arrange in skillet. Place onion slice and potato slice on each piece of meat. Cut carrots crosswise; place on potatoes. Sprinkle with rice. Add tomatoes, salt and pepper. Cover; cook slowly for 30 to 40 minutes or until potatoes are done, adding water as needed.

Mrs. Lowry Anderson
St. Paul's Ladies Aid
Fruitland, Missouri

DANISH STUFFED PORK TENDERLOIN

2 pork tenderloins
1 c. pitted prunes
2 apples, peeled and sliced
3 tbsp. butter
Salt and pepper to taste

Remove sinews from meat; cut meat open lengthwise. Scald prunes; remove stones. Stuff meat with fruits and tie. Brown in butter; add salt and pepper. Add enough water to cover; simmer

(Continued on next page)

for 40 minutes or until meat is tender. Thicken gravy with flour blended with cold water. Yield: 4 servings.

Inge North
St. Thomas Ladies Cir.
St. Louis, Missouri

HAWAIIAN BAKED PORK

2 c. crushed pineapple
3 med. sweet potatoes, pared and sliced
2 tbsp. brown sugar
4 pork shoulder steaks
Salt and pepper
4 strips bacon

Place pineapple in a large baking dish; top with potatoes. Sprinkle with brown sugar. Season pork steaks with salt and pepper; place on top of potatoes. Arrange bacon strips over steaks. Cover; bake at 350 degrees for about 1 hour or until potatoes and chops are tender. Remove cover; increase temperature to 450 degrees. Cook for 10 minutes longer to brown steaks and bacon. NOTE: Individual baking dishes may be used. Yield: 4 servings.

Mrs. Paul F. Brandenburg, Pres.
St. John's LWML
Vincennes, Indiana
Mrs. Alma Valerius
Immanuel Ladies Aid
Bridgman, Michigan

ORIENTAL PORK STEAKS

1 beef bouillon cube
⅓ c. hot water
1 tsp. ginger
2 tsp. salt
1 tbsp. sugar
¼ c. honey
½ c. soy sauce
4 to 6 pork steaks

Dissolve bouillon cube in hot water; add ginger, salt, sugar, honey and soy sauce. Marinate steaks in honey mixture in refrigerator for at least 2 hours. Turn steaks occasionally. Remove steaks from marinade; place on rack in open roasting pan. Bake at 350 degrees for 1 hour. Yield: 4-6 servings.

Mrs. Ellen Fisher
St. Martin's LCW
Marine City, Michigan

PORK BARBECUE

STEAKS:

6 pork steaks, cut 1 ½-in. thick
1 c. vinegar
Pepper to taste

Trim excess fat from steaks; brush both sides with vinegar and pepper. Allow to set for about 30 minutes. Brown over hot coals; brush with Barbecue sauce. Turn often, brushing with additional sauce. Continue cooking until steaks are well done.

BARBECUE SAUCE:

¼ c. bacon drippings
¼ c. butter
2 sm. onions, finely chopped
½ clove of garlic
½ c. catsup
2 tsp. Worcestershire sauce
¼ tsp. mustard
10 drops Tabasco sauce
Salt to taste

Combine all ingredients in saucepan; simmer until onions are clear. NOTE: More seasoning may be added, if desired. Yield: 6 servings.

Mrs. Arthur Naumann, Pres.
Emanuel's LCW
Sequin, Texas

PORK STEAK CREOLE

4 pork steaks
Shortening
¾ c. diced green peppers
½ c. chopped onion
1 No. 2 ½ can tomatoes
⅔ c. uncooked rice
1 ½ tsp. salt
⅛ tsp. pepper
¼ c. water

Brown steaks on both sides in shortening in heavy skillet. Remove steaks from pan; pour off half fat. Saute green peppers and onion in remaining fat. Add tomatoes, rice, salt, pepper, water and browned pork steaks. Cover and simmer for 1 hour and 30 minutes, stirring occasionally. Yield: 4 servings.

Mrs. Russell Harms, Pres.
Faith LCW
Watseka, Illinois

PORK TENDERLOIN CASSEROLE

1 lb. pork tenderloin, cut into serving pieces
Evaporated milk
Seasoned flour
Fat
1 can cream of mushroom soup

Dip meat into evaporated milk; roll in seasoned flour. Brown lightly in hot skillet in a small amount of fat. Place meat in layers in greased casserole. Cover with soup; add 1/2 soup can of evaporated milk. Cover and bake at 300 degrees for 1 hour and 30 minutes or until tender. Yield: 4 servings.

Mrs. Oscar B. Martin, Pres.
St. James LCW
St. Jacobs, Ontario, Canada

SWEET AND SOUR PORK STEAK

1 lb. pork steak
1 egg, beaten
Fine bread crumbs
½ can tomatoes
½ tsp. allspice
¼ tsp. cloves
¼ c. vinegar
Salt and pepper to taste
½ c. brown sugar

Dip steak into egg; dip into crumbs. Brown steak in hot fat in skillet; place in casserole. Combine all remaining ingredients; pour over steak in casserole. Bake at 325 to 350 degrees for 1 hour. Serve with spaghetti.

Mrs. R. Pasker, Pres.
Martin Evangelical LCW
Vancouver, British Columbia, Canada

TENDERLOIN-NOODLE CASSEROLE

6 oz. noodles
6 slices pork tenderloin, ½-in. thick
Salt and pepper
3 tbsp. butter or margarine
3 tbsp. flour
1 c. milk
¾ c. grated cheese
2 tbsp. chopped green pepper
2 tbsp. chopped red pepper

Cook noodles in boiling salted water; rinse and drain. Brown meat on both sides in hot fat. Season with salt and pepper. Melt butter; blend in flour. Add 3/4 teaspoonful salt and dash of pepper. Stir in milk; cook and stir until thick. Add cheese; stir until cheese melts. Combine noodles, sauce and green and red peppers; place in 10 x 6 x 1 1/2-inch baking dish. Place meat on top. Bake at 350 degrees for 30 minutes or until done. Yield: 6 servings.

Catherine Hartman
Mt. Hope Miss'y Soc.
Upper Tract, West Virginia

CANTONESE SWEET AND SOUR PORK

Salt and pepper
1 3-lb. pork loin roast, cut into 1 ½-in. cubes
Flour
¼ c. vegetable shortening
¼ c. butter or margarine
1 c. coarsely sliced onions
6 slices canned pineapple
1 green pepper, sliced into strips
1 c. pineapple syrup
2 tbsp. cornstarch
2 tbsp. soy sauce
¼ c. vinegar
¼ c. brown sugar
¼ tsp. Worcestershire sauce
¼ tsp. ginger

Salt and pepper pork; coat with flour. Fry in shortening until done. Remove from skillet; set aside. Heat butter in large skillet; add onions.

Saute until golden. Cut pineapple into bite-sized chunks; add to onion with green pepper and 1/2 cup pineapple syrup. Cover and cook for 10 minutes. Mix remaining ingredients thoroughly. Add to pan; bring to a boil. Stir constantly until thickened; add pork. Simmer for 5 minutes. Serve with hot rice. Yield: 3-4 servings.

Mrs. Erwin Stein
St. Peter's Ladies Aid Soc.
New Baden, Illinois

CHICKEN MASQUERADE

1 lb. lean pork
1 10 ½-oz. can chicken with rice soup
2 soup cans water
2 c. broken noodles
1 No. 2 can cream-style corn
1 2-oz. can pimento, cut up
1 green pepper, cubed
3 c. grated Cheddar cheese

Mix pork, soup and water; simmer for 30 minutes to 1 hour. Remove meat, reserving broth; cut into 1-inch pieces. Cook noodles in reserved broth until tender; add pork, corn, pimento, green pepper and 2 cups cheese. Pour mixture into a greased 2-quart casserole or 13 x 9 1/2 x 2-inch baking dish. Sprinkle with remaining cheese. Bake, covered, in preheated 375 degree oven for 30 minutes. Remove cover; bake for 15 minutes longer. Yield: 10 servings.

Mrs. Horest Wilson, Sewing Chmn.
Bethlehem Lutheran
Columbus, Ohio

CHINESE PORK WITH PEPPERS

1 lb. pork shoulder, cut into 2-in. strips
2 tbsp. salad oil
¾ tsp. salt
1 bouillon cube
1 ¾ c. water
4 tsp. soy sauce
2 green peppers, cut into 1-in. pieces
1 c. celery, cut into ¼-in. pieces
2 tbsp. cornstarch
4 tsp. dark molasses

Brown pork in oil; add salt, bouillon, 1 1/2 cups water and soy sauce. Cook for 45 minutes. Add peppers and celery; cook for 15 minutes. Mix cornstarch and molasses into 1/4 cup cold water; stir into meat. Cook until thickened. Yield: 4 servings.

Mrs. Herbert Schmidt, Pres.
Good Shepherd Lutheran Church
Jacksonville, Florida

CHOP SUEY

2 c. boiling water
3 bouillon cubes
3 tbsp. soya sauce
3 lb. pork shoulder, diced
⅓ c. flour

(Continued on next page)

1 can sliced mushrooms
1 c. sliced onions
2 c. slivered celery

Pour water over bouillon sand soya sauce; stir until smooth. Brown pork in skillet; add flour and stir until blended. Add bouillon mixture; stir. Add mushrooms, onions and celery. Cook for 30 minutes or until done. Serve with boiled rice or noodles. NOTE: Beef or chicken may be substituted for pork. Yield: 8 servings.

Elizabeth Bildy, Pres.
Grace LWML
Rodney, Ontario, Canada

CHOW MEIN

½ lb. lean pork, finely cut
1 qt. diagonally sliced celery
3 ½ c. finely sliced cabbage
1 qt. finely sliced carrots
⅓ c. finely sliced green pepper
⅓ c. sliced white onion
½ tsp. salt
Garlic salt to taste
¼ tsp. pepper
¼ tsp. dry mustard
⅓ c. canned mushroom stems and pieces
3 tbsp. flour
⅓ c. water
Soy sauce
Monosodium glutamate

Brown pork; braise until tender. Combine all vegetables except mushrooms; add salts, pepper and mustard. Toss lightly; add to pork. Cook until vegetables are just done. Add mushrooms. Mix flour with water; stir into pork mixture. Add soy sauce; cook until thickened. Add monosodium glutamate. Serve over Chinese noodles, if desired. Yield: 8-10 servings.

Mrs. Alfred Winger
Trinity Lutheran Church
Pinewood, Minnesota

CHOW MEIN

2 c. finely chopped onions
½ c. shortening
4 c. finely chopped celery
1 tsp. salt
¼ tsp. pepper
3 c. hot water
1 can bean sprouts, drained
2 cans mixed Chinese vegetables, drained
4 c. cooked pork, cut into thin strips
1 tbsp. molasses
5 tbsp. cornstarch
3 tbsp. soy sauce
1 tsp. sugar
1 tbsp. brown gravy sauce

Fry onions in shortening for 3 minutes. Add celery, seasonings and water. Cover; cook for 5 minutes. Add bean sprouts, Chinese vegetables, meat and molasses. Cook 5 minutes longer. Add cornstarch, soy sauce, sugar and brown gravy sauce. Cook until thickened. Serve with rice or noodles. Yield: 8 servings.

Mrs. Ella Summers, Stewardship
Faith LCW
Yucaipa, California

FRENCH HUNTER'S DINNER

5 lge. stalks celery, chopped
3 lb. onions, chopped
½ lb. lard
3 lb. pork, cut into 1-in. pieces
½ lb. spaghetti
1 6-oz. can mushrooms
1 1-lb. can tomatoes
1 1-lb. can lima beans

Fry celery and onions in one-half the lard in large covered kettle until transparent. Fry pork in remaining lard in skillet until well done, turning constantly. Add to onion mixture. Pour 1 pint water into skillet; pour drippings and water into onion mixture. Cook spaghetti in 3 quarts boiling water for 20 minutes; add to onions with any remaining water in pan. Add mushrooms, tomatoes and beans. Add 4 teaspoonfuls salt. Serve on toast. Yield: 10 servings.

Mrs. H. T. Keister
Our Redeemer Willing Workers
Jackson, Mississippi

HUNGARIAN GOULASH

1 lb. lean pork shoulder
½ green pepper, chopped
1 lge. onion, chopped
Vegetable fat
1 tbsp. paprika
1 tsp. salt
½ lb. sauerkraut
1 8-oz. can stewed tomatoes
1 clove of garlic, minced
Sugar to taste
Pinch of caraway seed
½ c. sour cream (opt.)

Cut meat into 1-inch cubes. Braise green pepper and onion in fat until browned. Add pork, paprika and salt; mix well. Cover and simmer for 15 minutes, stirring occasionally. Wash sauerkraut in cold water; squeeze dry and chop. Add to meat mixture with tomatoes, garlic, sugar and caraway seed. Simmer for 2 hours. Add sour cream just before serving. Yield: 4-6 servings.

Hilda Thiessen, Sec.
Ascension LCW
Goose Lake, Iowa

MEAT TURNOVERS

1 sm. onion, minced
⅓ c. margarine or chicken fat
½ c. flour
1 ½ c. milk
1 tsp. beef extract or 1 pkg. instant beef broth
2 c. cooked diced pork or ham
1 recipe pastry

(Continued on next page)

Fry onion in a small amount of fat until lightly browned. Make a white sauce of margarine, flour and milk; dissolve beef extract in small amount of mixture. Add beef extract, meat and onion to white sauce; cool. Divide pastry into six equal portions; roll out thin. Cut each portion into a 6-inch circle. Place 1/2 cup meat mixture on one-half of circle; cut slit in remaining half. Moisten edges; fold slit side of pastry over meat mixture. Press edges together with fork. Brush top with additional milk. Bake at 425 degrees for about 25 minutes. NOTE: Pastry should be based on 3 cups flour and 1 teaspoonful baking powder.

Mrs. Minnie Allen, Pres.
St. Paul's Mission Soc.
Colon, Michigan

HUNGARIAN POT LUCK

Flour
2 lb. lean pork, cut into 1-in. cubes
1 lge. onion, chopped
Oil or shortening
1 tsp. paprika
2 tbsp. caraway seed
2 qt. sauerkraut, well rinsed
1 ½ lb. smoked summer sausage, Polish sausage or Keilbasa, cut into 1-in. pieces
Salt and pepper to taste
1 c. sour cream

Lightly flour pork cubes. Lightly saute onion in oil until soft, but not brown. Add pork; lightly brown. Add one-half the paprika and all the caraway seed. Add enough water to cover pork almost halfway. Cover and simmer for 30 minutes. Combine sauerkraut and sausage in roaster or casserole. Add pork mixture, salt and pepper to taste. Cover; bake at 350 degrees for 1 hour or longer. Before serving, stir in sour cream. Garnish with remaining paprika. Yield: 6-10 servings.

Mrs. H. E. McArthur, Pres.
LWML
North Madison, Ohio

PORK CASSEROLE

½ lb. pork steak, cubed
1 sm. onion, chopped
1 c. chopped celery
1 can cream of chicken soup
1 can cream of mushroom soup
1 soup can of water
½ c. uncooked rice
¼ tsp. salt

Brown meat. Add remaining ingredients; mix well. Pour into baking dish. Bake at 350 degrees for 1 hour and 15 minutes to 1 hour and 30 minutes. Yield: 4 servings.

Mrs. A. R. Baumgarten, Pres.
St. John's Women's Soc.
Evansville, Wisconsin

PORK CANTONESE

2 lb. boned pork shoulder, cut into 1-in. pieces
Oil
1 10-oz. can mushrooms
1 15-oz. can pineapple cubes
⅓ c. molasses
1 tbsp. soya sauce
¼ c. white vinegar
2 green peppers, chopped
2 med. onions, chopped
1 ½ tbsp. cornstarch

Saute meat in a small amount of oil. Drain liquid from mushrooms and pineapple; add water to make 2 cups. Add to meat; simmer for 1 hour. Add remaining ingredients except cornstarch; cook for 15 minutes. Thicken with mixture of cornstarch and water. Yield: 6 servings.

Mrs. Herman Arason
Glenboro Ladies Aid
Glenboro, Manitoba, Canada

PORK CHOP SUEY

3 lb. pork shoulder, cubed
4 ½ c. water
2 lge. onions, chopped
4 c. thinly sliced celery
4 envelopes chicken broth or 4 chicken bouillon cubes
6 tbsp. cornstarch
1 tbsp. brown sugar
2 tsp. ginger
½ tsp. salt
¼ tsp. pepper
1 6-oz. can sliced mushrooms
1 15-oz. can bean sprouts
4 tbsp. soy sauce (opt.)

Brown pork in pan; add water. Cook slowly until tender. Cook onions and celery until clear but still crisp. Add chicken broth to pork; thicken with cornstarch. Add onion mixture and all remaining ingredients; simmer for 10 minutes. Serve. Yield: 12 servings.

Dawn Graham, Pres.
Bethlehem LCW
Erickson, Manitoba, Canada

PORK CHOP SUEY

2 lb. pork shoulder, cut into ¼-in. cubes
1 tsp. salt
1 tsp. pepper
½ c. flour
2 c. water
3 chicken bouillon cubes
3 tbsp. soy sauce
1 c. chopped onions
2 c. chopped celery
1 sm. can mushrooms, chopped

Sprinkle meat with salt and pepper. Brown in 10-inch skillet. Sprinkle with flour; add water, bouillon and soy sauce. Simmer slowly about 30 minutes or until meat is tender. Add onions, celery and mushrooms. Simmer for 30 minutes longer or until vegetables are tender. Serve with

(Continued on next page)

chow mein noodles or rice. Yield: 6 large servings.

Mrs. Roy Neece, Pres.
St. Paul Ladies Aid Soc.
Ft. Worth, Texas

PORK-CORN STEW

2 to 3 lb. pork shoulder
3 c. water
2 tbsp. chili powder
1 sm. onion
Pinch of garlic salt
1 tsp. whole black pepper
Salt to taste
1 No. 2 can corn

Cut meat into pieces. Add remaining ingredients except corn. Cook in pressure cooker until meat is done; add corn. Simmer for a few minutes. Serve with catsup. Yield: 4 servings.

Mrs. B. Ellebrecht, Pres.
St. John's LWML
Truth or Consequences, New Mexico

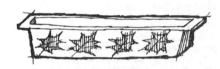

PORK-CORN SUEY

2 lb. boned pork shoulder, cut into 1-in. cubes
1 3 to 4-oz. can mushrooms
2 red or green peppers, cut into strips
2 med. onions, sliced
2 tbsp. unsulphured molasses
1 tbsp. soy sauce
2 tbsp. vinegar
1 12-oz. can whole kernel corn
½ tbsp. Accent
1 tbsp. cornstarch
½ c. water
Hot cooked rice

Brown meat in large heavy utensil. Drain mushrooms; measure liquid. Add enough water to make 2 1/2 cups. Add to meat; bring to a boil. Cover; reduce heat and simmer for 1 hour. Stir in mushrooms, red or green peppers and onions. Combine molasses, soy sauce and vinegar. Add to meat with corn; sprinkle with Accent. Cook, stirring occasionally, for 10 minutes longer. Blend cornstarch with water; stir into hot mixture. Cook, stirring, until thickened. Serve over hot cooked rice. Yield: 6-8 servings.

Photograph for this recipe on page 121 .

PORK-GREEN PEPPER CHOW MEIN

1 lb. pork, diced
2 tbsp. shortening
2 tsp. soya sauce
½ tsp. salt
1 c. beef bouillon
1 c. chopped onions
2 green peppers, chopped
2 tbsp. molasses
1 bay leaf
1 1-lb. can Chinese vegetables
2 tbsp. cornstarch
¼ c. water

Brown pork in shortening; add remaining ingredients except Chinese vegetables, cornstarch and water. Cover and cook until meat is tender. Add Chinese vegetables; cook 10 minutes longer. Blend cornstarch and water; stir into pork mixture. Cook and stir until thickened. Serve over rice or chow mein noodles, if desired. NOTE: May be cooked in pressure cooker. Yield: 4 servings.

Suzann Rumsby, Pres.
Christ Lutheran Church LCW
Las Vegas, Nevada

PORK AND PEPPER SUPREME

½ lb. lean pork, finely cut
2 tbsp. bacon drippings
½ green pepper, thinly sliced
1 onion, sliced
1 4-oz. can sliced mushrooms, drained
1 tbsp. cornstarch
2 ¼ c. tomato juice
1 tsp. salt
1 tsp. Worcestershire sauce
½ tsp. horseradish
1 ⅓ c. instant rice

Brown pork in bacon drippings; add green pepper, onion and mushrooms. Cook, stirring, until vegetables are tender. Mix cornstarch with 1/4 cup tomato juice; add remaining tomato juice, salt, Worcestershire sauce and horseradish. Add to meat mixture; cook, stirring, until thickened. Cover; cook for 10 minutes longer. Prepare rice according to package directions. Pour meat sauce over rice. Serve with soy sauce, if desired. Yield: 4 servings.

Mrs. Frank Berta
Trinity Mary and Martha Soc.
Streator, Illinois

PORK AND SAUERKRAUT WITH DUMPLINGS

1 lb. fresh or cooked pork, cut into 1-in. cubes
1 tsp. salt
¼ tsp. pepper
2 tbsp. fat
½ c. water
1 No. 2 ½ can sauerkraut
1 apple, pared and cored
1 onion, chopped
4 dumplings

(Continued on next page)

Season pork cubes with salt and pepper. Brown in fat in large heavy saucepan. Combine water, sauerkraut, apple and onion; add to pork. Simmer for 35 to 40 minutes. Place dumpling on sauerkraut; steam until done. Lift dumplings onto plate. Place sauerkraut in deep dish or large platter. C o v e r with pork cubes; top with dumplings. Yield: 4 servings.

Mrs. Carl Shumaker, Pres.
St. John Matrons Soc.
Akron, Ohio

SPANISH PORK

1 ½ lb. diced pork shoulder
1 med. onion, sliced
1 ½ c. cooked tomatoes
¼ c. diced green pepper
⅓ c. diced celery
1 tbsp. Worcestershire sauce (opt.)
1 tsp. salt

Brown pork in heavy skillet with onion. Combine remaining ingredients; add to pork in casserole. Cover and bake at 350 degrees for 1 hour or until pork is tender. Yield: 5-6 servings.

Marion Eckel, Pres.
Trinity LCW
Riga, Michigan

SWEET PORK

1 lb. lean pork
1 13 ½-oz. can pineapple chunks
2 tbsp. cornstarch
¼ c. vinegar
¼ c. brown sugar
¼ c. minced onion
2 tbsp. soy sauce
1 med. green pepper, coarsely chopped

Cut pork into 1-inch cubes. Brown pork in fat for 10 minutes. Drain pineapple, reserving juice. Add enough cold water to juice to make 1 cup. Pour into saucepan; stir in cornstarch, vinegar, brown sugar, onion and soy sauce. Cook until thickened and clear. Add pineapple chunks and green pepper. Pour over pork in skillet. Cover and simmer until meat and vegetables are done. Serve with hot fluffy rice. Yield: 4-6 servings.

Margaret Purdy
St. Luke's Priscilla Guild
Putnam Valley, New York

SWEET-SOUR PORK

2 lb. lean pork, cut into 1-in. cubes
4 tbsp. fat

1 tsp. salt
1 tsp. garlic salt
¼ tsp. pepper
6 tbsp. minced onion
2 med. green peppers, cut into strips
2 c. chopped celery
4 tbsp. cornstarch
½ c. water
2 c. prepared chicken bouillon cubes
4 tsp. soy sauce

Brown pork in fat; add salt, garlic salt, pepper and onion. Cook over medium heat until tender. Add green peppers and celery. Cover; simmer for 5 minutes. Combine cornstarch and water. Add cornstarch mixture and remaining ingredients. Cook for 3 to 4 minutes longer, stirring constantly until thickened. Serve over rice or mashed potatoes. Yield: 8 servings.

Joyce Schmidt
Immanuel LWML
Sebewaing, Michigan

SWEET AND SOUR PORK

1 ½ to 2 lb. lean pork, cut into 2-in. strips
2 tbsp. fat
¼ to ½ c. water
2 tbsp. cornstarch
½ tsp. salt
¼ c. brown sugar
¼ c. vinegar
1 c. pineapple juice
1 to 3 tbsp. soy sauce
¾ c. green peppers, cut into strips
¼ to ⅓ c. thinly sliced white onion
1 5-oz. can water chestnuts (opt.)
1 No. 2 can pineapple chunks
2 cans chow mein noodles (opt.)

Brown pork in hot fat; add water. Cover and simmer for 1 hour. Combine cornstarch, salt, brown sugar, vinegar, pineapple juice and soy sauce; mix well. Cook until slightly thick, stirring constantly. Pour sauce over hot pork; let stand for at least 10 minutes. Add green peppers, onion and c h e s t n u t s. Cook for 10 minutes. Add pineapple chunks; cook 2 to 3 minutes longer. Serve over noodles or hot rice, if desired. NOTE: Two tablespoonfuls water may be added to cornstarch mixture, if desired. Yield: 6 servings.

Mrs. H. A. Krahn, Sec.
Trinity Senior Aid
Cape Girardeau, Missouri
Mrs. Richard Albrecht, Pres.
Good Shepherd LCW
Kenosha, Wisconsin
Mrs. Robert G. Delker, Pres.
St. Paul's Lutheran Church
Riga, Michigan
Mrs. Walt Peterson, VP
St. John's Women's Deborah Guild
Idaho Falls, Idaho

Poultry Favorites

RECIPE FOR RAISIN CHICKEN CASABLANCA ON PAGE 208

BAKED CHICKEN

1 c. rice
1 3-lb. chicken,
1 can cream of mushroom soup
1 pkg. dry onion soup mix
1 c. milk

Place rice in large flat casserole. Arrange chicken over rice. Mix soup, soup mix and milk; pour over chciken. Bake, covered, at 350 degrees for 1 hour. Uncover; bake for 1 hour longer. Yield: 4-6 servings.

Mrs. H. Borchardt
Trinity LWML
Hudson, Wisconsin

BAKED CHICKEN DELUXE

1 2½ to 3-lb. frying chicken, cut up
1 10-oz. can cream of chicken soup

Place chicken pieces on a flat ungreased pan, large enough so pieces are not overlapped. Spoon undiluted soup over chicken. Bake at 325 to 350 degrees for 1 hour and 30 minutes to 2 hours. Do not turn chicken. Yield: 4 servings.

Mrs. John F. Gerken
St. John's Ladies Aid
Napoleon, Ohio

BAKED CHICKEN AND RICE

¾ c. uncooked rice
I chicken, cut up
¼ envelope onion soup mix
1 ½ c. water
1 10 ½-oz. can cream of chicken soup

Place rice in medium baking dish. Fry chicken; lay, skin-side up, on top of rice. Sprinkle onion soup mix over chicken. Mix water with soup; pour over all. Bake at 350 degrees for 2 hours. Yield: 4 servings.

Mrs. Wayne Jacobson, Pres.
Immanuel LWML
Stirum, North Dakota

BAKED CHICKEN AND RICE CASSEROLE

1 c. uncooked rice
1 can cream of chicken or mushroom soup
1 can cream of celery soup
½ to 1 soup can water or milk
1 to 2 broiler-fryer chickens, cut up
½ to 1 pkg. dry onion soup mix

Place rice in buttered baking pan. Combine chicken and celery soups and water; pour over rice. Place chicken on mixture, skin-side up. Sprinkle onion soup mix over chicken. Cover; bake at 325 degrees for 2 hours. NOTE:

One small box instant rice may be substituted for the regular rice. Yield: 6 servings.

Mrs. David Tuttle
Immanuel Lutheran Church
Ionia, Iowa
Mrs. Charles Farmer, Pres.
Emmanuel Ladies Aid
Laotto, Indiana
Mrs. Kay Isaacson, Pres.
Pike LCW
Embarraas, Minnesota
Mrs. Irvin Kriewaldt
St. Matthews Ladies Aid
White Lake, Wisconsin

BAKED FRYER

½ to 1 pkg. onion soup mix
1 c. instant or long grain rice
1 fryer, cut up
1 can cream of chicken or mushroom soup
1 ½ to 2 soup cans water

Sprinkle onion soup mix in greased glass 9 x 12-inch baking dish or small roaster. Spread with rice. Place chicken, skin-side up, on rice. Mix soup with water; pour mixture over chicken. Bake, uncovered, at 350 degrees for 1 hour and 30 minutes.

Mrs. Hans Johnson, Pres.
St. Mark's LWML
Toledo, Oregon
Mrs. Gerald Groth, Sec.
St. John's Mary and Martha Soc.
Wright, Minnesota

BAKED GARLIC CHICKEN

1 2½-lb. chicken
1 c. sour cream
1 tsp. Worcestershire sauce
1 tbsp. lemon juice
2 cloves of garlic, mashed
½ tsp. salt
¾ tsp. white pepper
¾ tsp. celery salt
½ tsp. paprika
Flour

Cut chicken into serving pieces; place in bowl. Mix all remaining ingredients except flour; pour over chicken. Refrigerate overnight. Drain; dredge in flour. Place chicken in single layer in shallow pan. Bake, covered, at 325 degrees for 1 hour or until tender. Uncover the last 20 minutes to crisp.

Mrs. Charles Farnsworth, Pres.
St. Paul's Evangelical LWML
South Bend, Indiana

BARBECUED CHICKEN

1 4 to 5-lb. chicken, cut into serving pieces
¼ c. vinegar
¼ c. shortening or cooking oil

(Continued on next page)

1 ½ c. tomato juice
¼ c. catsup
¼ tsp. dry mustard
Dash of red pepper
1 ½ tbsp. Worcestershire sauce
1 bay leaf
1 tbsp. brown sugar
¼ tsp. garlic powder
½ tsp. salt
½ tsp. liquid smoke

Place chicken in 13 x 6 x 3-inch baking pan. Combine remaining ingredients in saucepan; cook for 15 minutes. Pour over chicken. Bake, uncovered, at 325 degrees for 2 hours. Yield: 6 servings.

Mrs. Herman Fink
Bethany Ladies Aid
Kaukauna, Wisconsin

BARBECUED CHICKEN

1 chicken fryer, halved
1 c. catsup
1 tbsp. prepared mustard
2 tbsp. Worcestershire sauce
½ c. dark syrup
½ c. tomato juice
⅛ tsp. garlic
½ tsp. pepper
½ tsp. salt

Place chicken, skin-side down, on baking sheet. Combine remaining ingredients. Brush sauce on chicken. Bake at 350 degrees until tender, turning and basting sides. When tender pour remaining sauce over chicken. Bake for 5 minutes longer or until sauce bubbles. Yield: 4 servings.

Mrs. A. H. Janssen, Pres.
Emmanuel LWML
Hereford, Texas

BARBECUED CHICKEN

½ c. flour
2 tsp. salt
¼ tsp. pepper
1 frying chicken, cut into serving pieces
1 med. onion, chopped
2 tbsp. vinegar
¼ c. lemon juice
1 c. catsup
1 ½ tsp. prepared mustard
1 c. water

Place flour, salt and pepper in paper bag. Add chicken, several pieces at a time; shake. Brown chicken in 1/4-inch fat in skillet. Brown onion in fat in another skillet. Add remaining ingredients except chicken; simmer for 30 minutes. Place chicken in deep baking dish. Cover with sauce. Bake, uncovered, at 325 degrees for 1 hour. Yield: 4 servings.

Mrs. Lester Knop, Pres.
St. John's Ladies Aid
Hastings, Iowa

BARBECUED CHICKEN

1 2 ½ to 3-lb. broiler-fryer, quartered
Salt
½ tsp. pepper
¼ c. butter or margarine
¼ c. lemon juice
¼ c. Worcestershire sauce
¼ c. cider vinegar
¼ c. catsup

Wash chicken; sprinkle with salt and pepper. Arrange chicken, skin-side up, in single layer in shallow roasting pan. Broil 6 inches from heat for 5 minutes or until golden. Melt butter in small saucepan; add lemon juice, Worcestershire sauce, vinegar and catsup. Bring to a boil, stirring constantly. Boil for 1 minute. Pour sauce over chicken. Bake in preheated 325 degree oven for 1 hour, basting frequently with sauce. Yield: 4 servings.

Mrs. Ernest Lichtfuss
Bethany Ladies Aid
Kaukauna, Wisconsin

BARBECUED CHICKEN

⅓ c. vinegar
1 tsp. Worcestershire sauce
½ tsp. grated onion
1 clove of garlic (opt.)
¾ tsp. salt
¼ tsp. paprika
½ tsp. dry mustard
½ c. catsup
1 chicken, cut up
Few drops of Tabasco sauce

Combine all ingredients except chicken; mix well. Drown chicken in butter. Pour barbecue sauce over chicken. Bake at 375 degrees for 1 hour or until soft and will pull away from bone. Baste occasionally. NOTE: Chicken may be cooked in electric skillet.

Mrs. Leon Rudolph, Pres.
Salem Ladies Aid
Troutville, Pennsylvania

BARBECUED CHICKEN

¾ c. brown sugar
1 c. finely chopped onions
1 tbsp. Worcestershire sauce
1 tbsp. prepared mustard
½ c. catsup
1 c. boiling water
1 3 to 3 ½-lb. frying chicken
Flour
Salt and pepper
3 tbsp. butter or shortening

Combine sugar, onions, Worcestershire sauce, mustard, catsup and water; let stand for 1 hour to blend flavors. Cut chicken into serving pieces; dredge with flour, salt and pepper mixture. Fry until golden brown in butter or shortening. Remove chicken from fat and drain slightly. Place

(Continued on next page)

in shallow oblong cake pan; cover with barbecue sauce. Bake, uncovered, at 350 degrees for 1 hour. Baste occasionally. Yield: 6 servings.

Mrs. Gunnard Larson
Immanuel LCW
Jamestown, North Dakota

BARBECUED FRYERS IN FOIL

1 tsp. paprika
1 tsp. chili powder
1 tsp. salt
½ tsp. pepper
2 tsp. catsup
2 tsp. vinegar
2 tsp. Worcestershire sauce
4 tsp. water
1 tsp. prepared mustard
2 tsp. lemon juice
2 tsp. margarine
1 chicken

Mix all ingredients except chicken in a saucepan; bring slowly to a boil. Remove at once. Brush chicken with sauce. Place chicken in a large roaster with foil. Pour remaining sauce on chicken; wrap foil tightly around chicken. Cover roaster. Bake in preheated 550 degree oven for 15 minutes. Reduce temeperature to 350 degrees and bake for 1 hour and 15 minutes longer.

Mrs. George Wachsmann
Ebenezer LWML
Giddings, Texas

CHICKEN BARBECUE

2 tbsp. Worcestershire sauce
2 tbsp. vinegar
1 tbsp. lemon juice
4 tbsp. water
2 tbsp. melted butter
3 tbsp. brown sugar
3 tbsp. catsup
1 tsp. salt
1 tsp. dry mustard
¾ tsp. chili powder
1 tsp. paprika
1 3-lb. frying chicken, cut up

Mix all ingredients except chicken; beat thoroughly. Grease inside and outside of brown paper bag; place in roaster, open-side up. Salt and pepper chicken. Dip chicken into barbecue sauce ; place in bag. Pour remaining sauce into bag; seal. Cover roaster. Bake in preheated 500 degree oven for 15 minutes; reduce temperature to 350 degrees and bake for 1 hour and 15 minutes longer. Yield: 6 servings.

Mrs. Hugo Leimer
Bethlehem Lutheran Church
Perryton, Texas

CHICKEN BARBECUED IN FOIL

3 tbsp. butter
1 tbsp. brown sugar

¾ c. chopped onions
1 tsp. prepared mustard
¼ c. lemon juice
½ c. catsup
1 2 ½ to 3-lb. frying chicken, halved
Salt and pepper

Combine all ingredients except chicken. Bring to a boil. Reduce heat; simmer, uncovered, for 15 minutes. Rub chicken with salt and pepper. Place each half on heavy foil. Pour one-half of sauce on each chicken half; wrap. Bake at 350 degrees for 1 hour or at 200 degrees for 2 hours. Carefully open packets; turn back foil. Broil chicken until browned. Remove from foil; serve with remaining sauce. Yield: 2-4 servings.

Mrs. Harry Brolsma, Pres.
St. John's LWML
Sherburn, Minnesota

CHICKEN IN THE SACK

4 tbsp. water
6 tbsp. catsup
2 tbsp. vinegar
4 tbsp. brown sugar
1 tsp. salt
2 tsp. paprika
2 tsp. chili powder
2 tsp. mustard or dry mustard
Juice of 1 lemon
¼ lb. butter (opt.)
1 chicken, cut into serving pieces

Mix all ingredients except butter and chicken; bring to a rolling boil. Add butter. Place four No. 10 brown paper grocery bags inside each other. Grease inside of inner bag. Dip chicken into hot sauce, coating thoroughly; place in greased bags. Pour remaining sauce over chicken. Turn bag down at top and fasten well. Rotate bag so that sauce will run over chicken. Place bag in roaster; cover. Bake at 500 degrees for 15 minutes. Reduce heat to 325 to 350 degrees and bake for 1 hour and 15 minutes. NOTE: If desired, sauce may be made in advance and refrigerated until needed. Do not add butter to sauce until ready to use. Yield: 4-5 servings.

Mrs. Leo Johansen, Pres.
Mt. Olive Ladies Aid
Woonsocket, South Dakota
Mrs. Delfin Wilke, Pres.
Zion Ladies Aid
Lewisville, Minnesota

CHICKEN-TATER BARBECUTIE

½ c. chopped onion
¼ c. chopped green pepper
¼ c. chopped celery
⅓ c. salad oil
½ c. catsup
¼ c. water
2 tbsp. vinegar
2 tbsp. sugar
1 tbsp. Worcestershire sauce
1 tbsp. prepared mustard
2 tsp. salt

(Continued on next page)

¼ tsp. pepper
1 2 ½ to 3-lb. frying chicken, cut up
4 to 5 sm. Idaho potatoes, peeled

Saute onion, green pepper and celery in salad oil until tender, but not browned. Add catsup, water, vinegar, sugar and seasonings; simmer for 15 minutes. Arrange chicken and potatoes in shallow pan; pour barbecue sauce over chicken. Bake at 400 degrees for 40 minutes to 1 hour or until done. Baste frequently with sauce while baking. NOTE: Sauce may be doubled. Yield: 5 servings.

Mrs. Charles Kluball, Pres.
Messiah LWML
Valdosta, Georgia
Mrs. John H. Trimmer, Jr., Pres.
St. Matthew LCW
York, Pennsylvania

DELICIOUS BARBECUED CHICKEN

1 frying chicken, cut up
2 c. tomato juice
2 tsp. salt
4 ½ tsp. Worcestershire sauce
½ c. sugar
¼ tsp. dry mustard
1 bay leaf
¾ c. vinegar
3 tbsp. salad oil
¼ tsp. chili powder
¼ onion, chopped

Brown chicken as for frying. Place in roaster or casserole dish. Combine remaining ingredients; simmer for 10 minutes. Pour over chicken. Bake at 350 degrees for 1 hour or until tender. Baste frequently. Yield: 4-6 servings.

Mrs. Winton Wallin, Pres.
Concordia LCW
Concord, Nebraska

HOME-STYLE BARBECUED CHICKEN

1 egg
½ c. cooking oil
1 c. cider vinegar
2 tsp. salt
1 ½ tsp. poultry seasoning
¼ tsp. pepper
5 broiler halves

Beat egg; add oil and beat again. Add remaining ingredients except chicken. Dip chicken into sauce. Cook over medium coals for 45 minutes, turning and basting every 8 minutes. Yield: 6 servings.

Mrs. Marcy King
Messiah Mary Magdelene Guild
Grand Rapids, Michigan

OVEN-BARBECUED CHICKEN

1 2 ½ to 3-lb. fryer, halved
½ c. cooking oil

1 ½ tbsp. paprika
¼ c. vinegar
1 tbsp. salt

Wash and dry chicken. Dip into 1/4 cup oil; sprinkle with paprika. Place chicken in broiler pan, skin-side up. Bake at 350 degrees for 10 minutes. Mix vinegar and remaining oil; add salt. Baste chicken liberally with vinegar mixture. Return to broiler for 10 minutes more. Turn chicken and repeat procedure. Cook for 40 minutes or until done. Yield: 2 servings.

Mrs. Carl E. Key, Chmn.
Christ Lutheran Ladies Aid
Delavan, Illinois

OVEN-BARBECUED CHICKEN

1 med. onion, diced
Fat
2 tbsp. vinegar
2 tbsp. brown sugar
¼ c. lemon juice
1 c. catsup
3 tbsp. Worcestershire sauce
½ tbsp. prepared mustard
1 c. water
½ c. chopped celery
Salt and pepper to taste
2 chickens

Brown onion in a small amount fat. Add all remaining ingredients except chickens; simmer for 30 minutes. Cut chickens into quarters or serving pieces. Brown lightly. Place pieces in a single layer in a shallow pan. Bake, uncovered, at 325 degrees for 1 hour. Yield: 8 servings.

Mrs. Thomas Rue, Pres.
Taylors Falls First LCW
Shafer, Minnesota

OVEN-FRIED CHICKEN IN BARBECUE SAUCE

⅓ c. barbecue sauce
1 tbsp. Worcestershire sauce
⅓ c. catsup
1 ½ tsp. celery salt
½ tsp. onion salt
2 2 ½-lb. chickens, cut into serving pieces
2 c. fine cracker crumbs
½ c. melted butter

Combine barbecue sauce, Worcestershire sauce, catsup, celery salt and onion salt. Dip chickens into sauce. Place in mixing bowl. Pour remaining sauce over chickens; marinate for 2 hours. Roll chicken in cracker crumbs; place in large baking pan. Let stand for 30 minutes. Spoon butter over chicken. Bake at 350 degrees for 1 hour, turning once. Yield: 8 servings.

Mrs. Wilbur Lohse, Sec.
Clarks Fork Trinity Ladies Aid
Boonville, Missouri

OVEN BUTTER-BARBECUED CHICKEN

2 3-lb. frying chickens, cut into pieces or
   halved
Seasoned flour
Shortening
1 c. butter
¼ c. vinegar
2 c. water
1 tsp. salt
1 ½ tsp. dry mustard
1 ½ tsp. paprika
1 tbsp. chili powder
1 tbsp. chopped onion
½ c. tomato sauce or catsup
Dash of Tabasco sauce
1 tbsp. Worcestershire sauce

Coat chickens with seasoned flour. Brown in
hot fat in heavy skillet. Place chickens in shallow baking pan. Melt butter; add remaining ingredients. Bring to a boil. Reduce heat; simmer for 3 minutes. Brush chickens with sauce.
Bake at 325 degrees for 1 hour or until done,
brushing occasionally with additional sauce.
Yield: 8 servings.

Mrs. Darrell Teske, Pres.
Zion LWML
Kramer, North Dakota

PAPER BAG BARBECUED CHICKEN

Salt and pepper to taste
3 tbsp. catsup
2 tbsp. vinegar
1 tbsp. lemon juice
2 tbsp. Worcestershire sauce
4 tbsp. water
2 tbsp. melted butter
3 tbsp. brown sugar
1 tsp. dry mustard
1 tsp. chili powder
1 tsp. paprika
1 3-lb. fryer chicken, cut up

Heat 1 teaspoonful salt with remaining ingredients, except chicken, to make sauce. Salt and
pepper chicken. Grease inside of brown paper
bag; bag may be lined with aluminum foil. Dip
chicken into sauce; place inside bag. Pour remaining sauce over chicken. Tie ends of bag and
place in pan. Bake at 350 degrees for 1 hour and
30 minutes or until tender. Yield: 6 servings.

Mrs. Carl W. Schmidt, Aux. Pres.
Eventide Lutheran Home for Aged
Denison, Iowa

PAT'S SNAPPY BARBECUED CHICKEN WINGS

20 chicken wings
Salt and pepper
6 tbsp. molasses
4 tsp. prepared mustard
3 tbsp. vinegar
1 c. catsup
1 med. onion, thinly sliced
½ tsp. Tabasco sauce

Wash wings with salt and pepper. Arrange in shallow roasting pan. Combine remaining ingredients in saucepan. Bring mixture to a
boil. Boil for 1 minute, stirring constantly.
Pour sauce over chicken. Bake at 350 degrees
until tender. Brush with sauce at 15 minute
intervals. Serve with rice and sauce. Yield:
6 servings.

Mrs. Pat Noffke, VP
St. Luke's LWML
Ottawa, Ontario, Canada

BREAST OF CHICKEN WITH RICE

1 c. long grain rice
1 can cream of chicken soup
1 can cream of celery soup
1 soup can water
6 sm. whole chicken breasts
1 tsp. salt

Place rice in 9 x 12-inch baking pan. Mix soups
and water well; pour over rice. Place chicken
breasts over mixture. Season with salt. Cover
tightly with foil. Place in preheated 400 degree
oven; reduce temperature to 325 degrees and
bake for 2 hours and 30 minutes. Yield: 6 servings.

Mrs. Agnes Christiansen
All Saints Church
Brush, Colorado

SUPER DELUXE BARBECUED CHICKEN

1 chicken, cut up
⅓ c. flour
1 tsp. paprika
¾ tsp. salt
⅛ tsp. pepper
¼ c. fat
1 c. catsup
½ c. vinegar
1 med. onion, diced
⅓ c. water
2 tbsp. lemon juice
2 tbsp. butter
1 tbsp. brown sugar
1 tbsp. Worcestershire sauce

Coat chicken with flour, paprika, salt and pepper;
brown in fat. Place in 2-quart casserole. Combine remaining ingredients; bring to a boil. Pour
sauce over chicken. Cover; bake at 350 degrees
for 1 hour and 15 minutes. Yield: 4-6 servings.

Mrs. Darold Berhow, Pres.
Dolliver Ladies Aid
Dolliver, Iowa

CHICKEN BREASTS AND CREAM

2 whole chicken breasts, halved
3 tbsp. fat
⅓ c. chopped onion
1 sm. clove of garlic, minced

(Continued on next page)

¾ c. chicken broth
¾ c. light cream
1 ½ tsp. salt
⅛ tsp. pepper
2 tsp. Worcestershire sauce
3 tbsp. flour
1 c. water

Brown breasts in fat until golden brown. Heat onion, garlic, broth, cream and seasonings in saucepan. Place chicken in roaster; pour sauce over breasts. Bake, covered, in preheated 300 degree oven for 2 hours. Uncover and bake for 15 to 20 minutes longer. Remove chicken from pan and keep warm. Blend flour and water into drippings in pan; pour over chicken. Serve with wild rice. Yield: 4 servings.

Mrs. Stephen B. Fleming, Pres.
Concordia LWML
Miami, Florida

CHICKEN BREASTS IN CREAM

2 lb. chicken breasts
Salt and pepper
7 tbsp. butter, melted
¼ lb. fresh mushrooms, sliced or 1 c. canned
    mushrooms, drained
4 tbsp. flour
2 c. light cream
1 c. dry white wine or unsweetened pineapple
    juice
½ lb. seedless grapes or 1 c. canned grapes,
    drained

Season chicken breasts with salt and pepper. Brown in 4 tablespoonfuls butter. Place in deep 2 1/2-quart casserole. Top with mushrooms. Stir flour into remaining butter. Add cream and wine. Cook until smooth and thickened. Pour over chicken. Bake at 350 degrees for 1 hour or until chicken is tender. Add grapes. Bake for 10 minutes longer. NOTE: If canned grapes are used, bake for 5 minutes. Yield: 6 servings.

Mrs. Ronald Tiemann, Pres.
St. John's Ladies Aid
Buffalo, Minnesota

CHICKEN BREASTS WITH RICE

1 c. brown rice
1 can cream of celery soup
1 can cream of chicken soup
1 can cream of mushroom soup
8 chicken breasts
Mushrooms (opt.)
Slivered almonds (opt.)

Place brown rice in large baking dish. Add soups and chicken breasts. Cover; bake at 350 degrees for 1 hour and 30 minutes. Baste two or three times. Remove cover the last 30 minutes; add mushrooms and almonds. brown or broil until brown. Yield: 8 servings.

Mrs. Margie Asmann, Kitchen Chmn.
Immanuel LWML
Wichita, Kansas

CHICKEN BREAST SUPREME

1 stick butter
1 tsp. ground thyme leaves
Juice of 2 lemons
Salt
8 chicken breasts
Paprika
½ c. water

Melt butter; mix with thyme and lemon juice. Sprinkle salt over chicken; dash with paprika. Place chicken under broiler until light brown in color; turn and brown other side. Brush remaining butter mixture over chicken; add water. Cover with foil. Bake at 300 degrees for 1 hour and 30 minutes. NOTE: Chicken may be cooked over outside grill; watch constantly, turning often. Yield: 8 servings.

Mrs. Keith C. Carpenter, Church Sec.
Emmanuel LCW
Lincolnton, North Carolina

CHICKEN IN THE GARDEN

2 chicken breasts
5 chicken legs
2 chicken wings
¾ c. instant rice
6 med. potatoes
4 unpeeled tomatoes
4 tbsp. water
Salt to taste

Fold four 24-inch pieces of aluminum foil in half. Divide chicken pieces on foil. Place 3 tablespoonfuls rice, 1 1/2 potatoes and 1 tomato on each piece of foil. Sprinkle with 1 tablespoonful water each. Sprinkle generously with salt. Seal package tightly, using drugstore wrap on top; fold ends up over top. Bake at 350 degrees for 1 hour to 1 hour and 30 minutes. NOTE: Use fryer chicken pieces. Yield: 4 servings.

Mrs. Ruth Borcherding, Pres.
Trinity LWML
Iuka, Illinois

CHICKEN CASSEROLE

1 c. instant rice
1 pkg. dried onion soup mix
Chicken breasts and dark meat (opt.)
1 can cream of chicken soup
1 soup can milk
Paprika

Cover buttered glass 7 x 11-inch baking dish with rice. Sprinkle with soup mix. Place chicken over rice mixture. Dilute chicken soup with milk; pour over chicken. Sprinkle with paprika. Place foil over dish; bake at 350 degrees for 1 hour. Remove foil; reduce temperature to 300 degrees and bake for 1 hour longer. Yield: 4 servings.

Mrs. I. S. Perry, Pres.
St. Andrew's LCW
St. Petersburg, Florida

CHICKEN GOURMET

½ stick butter
1 ¼ c. brown rice
½ c. slivered almonds
8 chicken breasts, halved
1 can cream of chicken soup
1 can cream of mushroom soup
1 can cream of celery soup
1 can beef consomme
1 consomme can water
½ c. cooking Sherry
2 oz. grated Parmesan cheese
1 tbsp. minced onion

Spread butter around sides and bottom of large roaster. Spread rice over bottom of roaster; sprinkle with almonds. Lay chicken pieces over rice and almonds. Heat soups, consomme, water and cooking Sherry; stir until smooth. Pour over chicken; sprinkle with Parmesan cheese and onion. Bake, uncovered, at 275 degrees for 3 hours. Yield: 8 servings.

Mrs. Carl Helot, VP
Our Saviour Women's Guild
Evansville, Indiana

CHICKEN MORNAY

½ c. flour
1 tsp. salt
⅛ tsp. pepper
⅛ tsp. ginger
4 chicken breasts
½ c. butter
Water

Combine flour, salt, pepper and ginger; coat chicken with mixture. Brown in butter in heavy frying pan. Cover; cook over low heat 30 to 45 minutes or until tender, adding a small amount of water if necessary. Place chicken in shallow baking pan or casserole; add 1 cup water to drippings in pan; stir to loosen sediment.

SAUCE:

4 tbsp. butter
4 tbsp. flour
1 tsp. salt
½ c. cream
½ c. milk
1 c. grated American cheese
½ c. fresh or canned mushrooms

Melt butter in saucepan; blend in flour and salt. Stir in cream and milk. Blend in water from frying pan; cook, stirring constantly, until thickened. Add cheese and stir until melted; add mushrooms. Pour sauce over chicken. Sprinkle with additional cheese, if desired. Bake at 350 degrees for 25 to 30 minutes. Sprinkle with paprika and serve over rice, if desired.

Margaret Romberg
Lydia Serv. Guild
Woodland Hills, California

CHICKEN AND RICE

1 c. rice
1 ½ c. water
1 can cream of mushroom soup
1 can cream of chicken soup
1 can cream of celery soup
1 tbsp. poultry seasoning
1 tsp. salt
6 chicken breasts or whole chicken

Mix rice, water, soups and poultry seasonings in large casserole or small roaster. Salt chicken; place over rice mixture. Bake, covered, at 350 degrees for 2 hours. Yield: 4-6 servings.

Velma Brase
Grace LWML
Tulsa, Oklahoma

COMPANY CHICKEN

3 chicken breasts, cut into halves
6 to 8 drumsticks
6 to 8 thighs
⅓ c. soy sauce
⅓ c. white wine
Juice of 1 lime
1 clove of garlic
⅛ tsp. curry
1 tsp. ginger
Flour
1 ½ tsp. salt
¼ tsp. pepper
¼ c. butter
1 med. onion, chopped
1 tbsp. chopped pimento
½ c. sliced mushrooms

Arrange chicken parts in shallow dish. Combine soy sauce, wine, lime juice, garlic, curry and ginger; mix and pour over chicken. Refrigerate chicken for 3 to 4 hours, turning pieces several times. Remove chicken from sauce; drain. Mix flour with salt and pepper; toss chicken in mixture until well coated. Brown slowly in butter. Saute onion in separate pan; combine with 1/2 cup marinade, pimento and mushrooms. Pour

164

(Continued on next page)

over chicken; cover tightly. Bake at 350 degrees for 25 minutes; remove cover and continue baking for 15 to 20 minutes longer. Yield: 6 servings.

Mrs. Arlene Starkey, Pres.
King of Glory LCW
Indianapolis, Indiana

PINEAPPLE, CHICKEN AND RICE

4 chicken breasts
Butter
¾ c. uncooked rice
1 10-oz. can pineapple chuncks, undrained
1 c. diced celery
3 tsp. salt
¼ tsp. poultry seasoning
1 tbsp. soy sauce
1 ½ c. chicken stock or 2 chicken bouillon
    cubes dissolved in 1 ½ c. boiling water

Brown chicken in butter in fry pan. Combine remaining ingredients in 1 1/2-quart casserole. Place chicken over mixture; cover. Bake at 350 degrees for 1 hour and 30 minutes. Uncover; continue baking for 15 minutes longer. Yield: 4-6 servings.

Mrs. Barbara Peters
St. John's LCW
Laird, Saskatchewan, Canada

SMOTHERED CHICKEN

20 lb. fryer chicken breasts and thighs
Salt and pepper
Thyme
Mace (opt.)
Melted butter
1 minced white onion

Clean chicken thoroughly; dry with toweling. Season with pepper, salt, thyme and mace. Place on broiler; brush with melted butter. Broil quickly on both sides. Place chicken in roasting pan over onion. Bake, uncovered, at hot temperature for 10 to 15 minutes. Cover; bake at 300 degrees for 2 hours or until done. Baste chicken with juice. Yield: 30 servings.

Hulda Kivela, Cook Custodian
St. Francis Ladies Aid Soc.
San Francisco, California

YUMMY CHICKEN BAKE

Softened butter
2 lb. chicken breasts
Seasoning to taste
1 pkg. dry onion soup mix

Rub softened butter over chicken; season. Roll in onion soup mix. Place in a 13 x 9 x 2-inch

foil-lined pan. Cover with aluminum foil; seal foil edges. Bake at 375 degrees for 1 hour.

Mrs. Curtis Wilhoit, Pres.
Solomon LCW
Greenville, Tennessee

CANTONESE CHICKEN

10 chicken thighs and legs
2 tbsp. cornstarch
¼ c. honey
½ c. catsup
¼ c. soy sauce
¼ c. lemon juice

Place chicken in a 9 x 13-inch baking dish. Mix remaining ingredients; pour over chicken. Cover dish with foil. Refrigerate overnight. Bake at 325 degrees for 1 hour and 30 minutes. Remove foil; bake, uncovered, for 30 minutes longer. Serve on boiled rice. Yield: 10 servings.

Berniece Sward, Pres.
Our Redeemer LCW
Los Angeles, California

BAKED CHICKEN

1 chicken, cooked
3 eggs
6 c. chicken broth
1 onion, chopped
1 can cream of mushroom soup
1 tsp. pepper
1 tsp. salt
1 ½ c. chopped celery
1 c. grated cheese
4 c. crushed Ritz crackers

Chop chicken into chunks; mix with remaining ingredients in 9 x 13 x 2-inch baking pan. Bake at 350 degrees for 1 hour.

Mrs. William Bernhardt, Pres.
Mt. Calvary LWML
Watonga, Oklahoma

BAKED CHICKEN CASSEROLE

1 6-oz. can boned chicken, diced
1 10 ½-oz. can cream of chicken soup
1 c. diced celery
2 tsp. minced onion
½ c. almonds or pecans
½ tsp. salt
¼ tsp. pepper
1 tbsp. lemon juice
¾ c. mayonnaise
3 hard-cooked eggs, thinly sliced
2 c. crushed potato chips

Combine chicken and broth with soup. Mix remaining ingredients except potato chips; combine with chicken mixture. Place in casserole. Sprinkle with potato chips. Bake at 350 degrees for 30 minutes. NOTE: Left-over chicken or

(Continued on next page)

turkey may be substituted for canned chicken. Yield: 6-8 servings.

Mrs. Fred J. Frieling, Pres.
Trinity LWML
Austin, Texas

CHICKEN-ALMOND BAKE

2 cans cream of celery soup
2 cans cream of mushroom soup
1 c. chicken broth
4 oz. blanched slivered almonds
1 lge. onion, grated
1 chicken, cooked, boned and diced
1 ½ c. diced celery
1 can mushrooms
1 tsp. Worcestershire sauce
1 lge. pkg. Chinese noodles

Combine all ingredients except noodles. Place one-half the noodles on bottom of large casserole. Add chicken mixture; top with remaining noodles. Bake at 350 degrees for 1 hour. Yield: 8 servings.

Mrs. Randolph Bohlmann, V. Chmn.
St. John's Ladies Aid
Plato, Minnesota

CHICKEN CASSEROLE

2 c. cooked diced chicken
1 can cream of chicken soup
1 can cream of mushroom soup
1 can chow mein noodles
1 sm. can evaporated milk
½ c. chopped celery
¼ c. chopped onion
Salt and pepper to taste

Combine all ingredients. Bake at 325 degrees for 35 minutes. Yield: 8 servings.

Mrs. Nicholas Marrow, Martha Cir. Chmn.
St. Pauls Women's League
Boca Raton, Florida

CHICKEN CASSEROLE

2 c. cooked, chopped chicken
2 cans chow mein noodles
2 cans cream of mushroom soup
1 c. diced celery
1 c. milk or water

Mix all ingredients; reserving a small amount of noodles. Place in buttered baking dish. Top with remaining noodles. Bake at 325 degrees for 1 hour. NOTE: One can cream of chicken soup or 1 can cream of celery soup may be substituted for mushroom soup. Cashews may be placed on casserole instead of noodles. Yield: 8 servings.

Mrs. R. J. Fennell, Sec.
Good Shepherd Ladies Guild
Toledo, Ohio

CHICKEN CASSEROLE

2 cans cream of mushroom soup
1 c. water
½ c. chopped onion
2 c. chopped celery
½ lb. broken cashews
2 ½ c. cooked diced chicken
1 sm. can mushrooms
1 can Chinese noodles
Crushed corn flakes or potato chips
Butter

Mix soup with water; add onion, celery, nuts, chicken and mushrooms. Fold in noodles; pour into greased 4-quart casserole. Sprinkle with corn flakes; dot with butter. Bake, covered, at 325 degrees for 1 hour. Yield: 8 servings.

Mrs. Helen Wrana, Pres.
Bethesda LCW
Sherrodsville, Ohio

CHICKEN CASSEROLE

1 stewing hen
4 hard-cooked eggs, sliced
2 cans cream of mushroom soup
1 med. onion, diced
½ c. diced celery
2 pimentos
¼ tsp. salt
⅛ tsp. pepper
⅛ tsp. paprika
Cracker crumbs
Butter

Stew hen. Remove meat from bones in large pieces. Alternate layers of meat and eggs in casserole dish. Combine soup, onion, celery, pimentos, salt, pepper and paprika. Pour over chicken. Sprinkle with cracker crumbs; dot with butter. Bake at 350 degrees for 1 hour. Yield: 8 servings.

Mrs. Thomas L. Kleckley, Pres.
Zion LCW
Lexington, South Carolina

CHICKEN CASSEROLE

1 stewed chicken, boned and chopped
6 hard-cooked eggs, sliced
2 c. corn flakes
1 can cream of mushroom soup
2 soup cans chicken broth

Place a layer of chicken in casserole; spread one-half the sliced eggs over chicken. Cover with 1 cup corn flakes. Repeat layers until all the chicken is used. Dilute soup with broth; spread over mixture. Sprinkle top with corn flakes. Bake at 300 degrees for 2 hours.

Mrs. Carl Irmer
St. Peter's LWML
Gresham, Nebraska

CHICKEN CASSEROLE

1 6-oz. pkg. chow mein noodles
1 can cream of mushroom soup
1 5-oz. can mushrooms
3 c. cooked diced chicken
4 ½ oz. cashews
1 c. diced celery
2 tbsp. chopped onion
Salt and pepper to taste

Reserve 1/4 package noodles for top. Mix soup, mushrooms and liquid and 1 cup water in large casserole or baking dish. Add remaining ingredients. Top with reserved noodles. Bake at 350 degrees for 30 minutes.

Mrs. Nannie Giese, Pres.
Trinity Ladies Aid
St. Walburg, Saskatchewan, Canada

CHICKEN CASSEROLE DELIGHT

4 c. cooked boned chicken
1 c. chopped celery
1 sm. can evaporated milk
1 10 ½-oz. can cream of mushroom soup
1 10 ½-oz. can chicken with rice soup
1 3 ½-oz. can chow mein noodles

Mix all ingredients; place in a buttered casserole. Top with crushed potato chips, if desired. Bake at 350 degrees for 1 hour. Yield: 6-8 servings.

Mrs. Wilbert Reisenbichler, Pres.
Zion Ladies Aid
Pocahontas, Missouri

CHICKEN CHOP SUEY

1 lge. can chow mein noodles
2 c. chopped cooked chicken
1 can cream of mushroom soup
¼ c. water
1 c. cashews
1 tbsp. soy sauce
1 c. chopped celery
¼ c. green onions
1 4-oz. can sliced mushrooms

Line 9-inch baking dish with one-half noodles. Combine remaining ingredients. Pour over noodles; cover with remaining noodles. Bake at 375 degrees for 40 minutes. Yield: 6 servings.

Mrs. Gladys Clark
Zion LWML
Fallbrook, California

CHICKEN CHOW MEIN

1 chicken, boiled
2 cans cream of mushroom soup
½ to ¾ c. cashews
1 c. chopped onions
1 c. chopped celery
1 lge. can chow mein noodles

Cut up chicken; add soup, nuts, onions, celery and one-half noodles. Place mixture in buttered long flat baking pan; spread remaining noodles over the top. Bake at 350 degrees for 40 minutes.

Mrs. Adolph Yagow
Zion Ladies Aid
Lincoln, Illinois

CHICKEN-EGG CASSEROLE

1 sm. fryer
2 c. corn flakes
6 slices toast, cubed
1 sm. onion, chopped
2 c. chicken broth
Chopped giblets
3 hard-cooked eggs, chopped
1 can cream of chicken soup

Cook chicken until tender; reserve broth. Combine corn flakes, toast, onion, chicken broth and chopped giblets in casserole dish. Alternate layers of chicken and eggs. Cover with chicken soup. Bake at 300 degrees for 30 minutes. Yield: 6-8 servings.

Mrs. Ralph Ballington, VP
Nazareth LCW
Lexington, South Carolina

CHICKEN ENCHILADA CASSEROLE

2 cans boned chicken
1 lge. onion, chopped
2 cans cream of chicken soup
1 can milk
1 sm. can green chilies
1 pkg. tortillas
½ lb. Longhorn cheese, grated

Mix chicken, onion, soup, milk and chilies; set aside. Fry tortillas to soften. Line a greased 13 x 5 x 2-inch pan with tortillas; spread chicken mixture in pan alternately, ending with grated cheese. Bake at 350 degrees for 30 to 45 minutes. Yield: 8 servings.

Mrs. Dick Dunlap, Pres.
St. Peter's LCW
Carlsbad, New Mexico

CHICKEN SALAD CASSEROLE

1 c. chopped celery
2 tbsp. chopped onion
3 tbsp. margarine or butter
1 can cream of mushroom or cream of chicken soup
½ c. sliced thin almonds
1 tbsp. lemon juice
3 hard-cooked eggs, sliced
½ c. mayonnaise
1 ½ c. crushed corn flakes
1 ½ c. crushed potato chips
2 ½ c. cooked, cubed chicken

(Continued on next page)

Saute celery and onion in margarine in skillet for 10 minutes. Add all remaining ingredients except corn flakes and potato chips. Place one-half the corn flakes and potato chips on bottom of large casserole; place chicken mixture on top. Sprinkle remaining corn flakes and chips on top. Bake at 350 degrees for 30 minutes or until bubbly.

Mrs. Sharon Ewing, VP
Prince of Peace Ladies Guild
Corinth, Mississippi

CHICKEN SOPA

1 frying chicken
1 10 to 12-oz. pkg. tortillas
1 can cream of chicken soup
5 oz. Old English cheese
5 oz. Cheddar cheese
1 4-oz. can green chili peppers
6 to 8 fresh green onions, chopped

Boil chicken until tender; bone and cut into large pieces. Reserve broth. Lightly fry tortillas. Mix chicken soup, broth, cheeses, chilies and onions; heat until cheeses melt. Arrange layers of tortillas, chicken and sauce in a 2-quart casserole until all ingredients are used. Bake at 325 degrees for 20 minutes. Yield: 12 servings.

Mrs. J. L. Knoz, Sec.
Trinity Dorcas Soc.
Eden, Texas

CHICKEN SUPREME

½ c. flour
½ c. prepared biscuit mix
½ c. buttermilk pancake mix
1 ½ tsp. salt
¼ to ½ tsp. pepper
2 frying chickens, cut up
1 ½ c. lard
½ c. butter
2 med. onions, thinly sliced
2 or 3 fresh tomatoes, thinly sliced
1 4-oz. jar sliced mushrooms

Combine flour, biscuit mix, pancake mix, salt and pepper. Roll chicken in flour mixture; fry in lard and butter until golden brown. Alternate layers of chicken with layers of onions, tomatoes and mushrooms in roaster, ending with vegetable layer. Cover roaster. Bake at 325 degrees for 1 hour to 1 hour and 30 minutes. Yield: 8-10 servings.

Mrs. Irving E. Valvick, Pres.
Trinity LWML
Elmore, Minnesota

CHICKEN SUPREME DISH

1 can boned chicken or 3 breasts, cooked
1 can cream of mushroom soup
1 can cream of chicken soup
1 can evaporated milk
1 can Chinese noodles

Cut chicken into 1-inch pieces; add all remaining ingredients. Stir well. Place in casserole. Bake at 350 degrees for 1 hour. Yield: 8 servings.

Mrs. Frank Lepic
Our Savior Women's Guild
Chicago, Illinois

CHICKEN STRATA

8 slices bread, cubed
2 c. cooked chicken, cubed
½ c. chopped onion
½ c. chopped green pepper
½ c. chopped celery
½ c. mayonnaise
¾ tsp. salt
Dash of pepper
2 eggs, slightly beaten
1 ½ c. milk
1 can cream of mushroom soup
½ c. grated sharp cheese

Place one-half the bread cubes in baking dish. Combine chicken, vegetables, mayonnaise and seasonings; spread over bread. Add remaining bread. Combine eggs and milk; pour over bread cubes and cover. Chill for 1 hour or overnight. Add soup. Bake at 350 degrees for 50 minutes. Add cheese. Bake until cheese is melted. Yield: 8 servings.

Mrs. Frank Trimmer
Eberhard Church Ladies Aid
Columbia City, Indiana

CHINESE CHICKEN CASSEROLE

1 No. 2 ½ can Chinese noodles
1 c. diced celery
½ c. chopped onion
2 c. cubed cooked chicken
1 can cream of mushroom soup
½ c. water
½ c. cashews (opt.)

Cover the bottom of a baking dish with 1/2 can of Chinese noodles; top with celery, onions and chicken. Spoon soup over chicken; add water. Top with remaining noodles and nuts. Bake at 375 degrees for 30 minutes. Yield: 8-10 servings.

Mrs. Ralph Snyder, Pres.
Emmanuel LWML
York, Nebraska

BAKED CHICKEN

1 4-lb. chicken, cooked
2 c. soft bread crumbs
4 eggs, well beaten
1 tbsp. salt
1 c. cooked rice
¼ c. chicken fat or butter
3 c. broth

(Continued on next page)

Dice meat; force skin and giblets through food chopper. Add crumbs to eggs; let set. Mix crumb mixture with meat and ground giblets. Add remaining ingredients. Place mixture in baking pan. Bake in moderate oven for 1 hour.

Mrs. Norman R. Krebs
Immanuel Ester Soc.
Artesia, New Mexico

BAKED CHICKEN DISH

3 c. bread crumbs
3 c. diced cooked chicken
3 eggs, slightly beaten
4 tbsp. flour
Salt to taste
4 c. broth
Butter

Mix 1 cul bread crumbs with chicken and eggs. Moisten flour and salt with a small amount water; stir into broth. Cook until thickened. Place chicken mixture in buttered oblong baking dish. Mix remaining crumbs with a small amount butter; spread over chicken mixture. Bake at 300 degrees for 30 minutes. Yield: 12-15 servings.

Mrs. Carl Niemeier, Sec.
St. John's Ladies Aid
Galva, Iowa

BAKED CHICKEN SUPREME

2 chickens
3 eggs, separated
3 qt. dry bread crumbs
Salt and pepper to taste
5 stalks celery, chopped
½ c. finely chopped onion

Cook chicken, reserving broth. Remove skin and bones from chicken. Grind chicken skin. Cut meat into large pieces. Place meat in 9 x 13-inch loaf pan. Mix beaten egg yolks with bread crumbs and enough broth to moisten. Beat egg whites until stiff; add to dressing. Season with salt and pepper. Spread dressing over chicken. Cook celery in broth until tender. Add to ground chicken skin with onion. Sprinkle over dressing. Add small amount of milk if dressing seems too dry. Bake at 300 degrees for 1 hour and 30 minutes. Yield: 12 servings.

Mrs. Arnold Junck, Pres.
St. Paul's Ladies Aid
Carroll, Nebraska

BAKED CHICKEN SUPREME

6 to 8 c. soft bread crumbs
1 stalk celery, chopped
Salt and pepper
Sage
½ tsp. baking powder
1 med. onion, chopped
⅓ c. fat or butter

1 ½ to 2 c. milk
2 eggs, beaten
1 chicken, cooked and diced
Chicken broth
White sauce (opt.)
1 can cream of mushroom soup (opt.)

Combine crumbs, celery, salt, pepper, sage and baking powder. Fry onion in fat; mix with crumb mixture. Add milk and eggs. Place chicken in 9 x 13-inch pan. Place dressing over chicken. Pour broth over all to within 1 inch of covering. Bake at 350 degrees for 1 hour to 1 hour and 30 minutes. Combine white sauce with soup. Serve over chicken. Yield: 8 servings.

Mrs. Clifford Koch, Pres.
St. John's Ladies Aid
Pilger, Nebraska
Mrs. Harold Dreyer, Pres.
Immanuel LCW
Russville, Nebraska

BAKED CHICKEN SUPREME

1 baking chicken
Salt and pepper
1 onion, diced
⅓ c. fat or butter
6 to 8 c. broken bread
1 stalk celery, diced
½ tsp. baking powder
Sage to taste
1 ½ to 2 c. milk
2 eggs, well beaten

Boil chicken with salt and pepper until done; remove bones. Chop meat into small pieces; reserve broth. Run skin through food chopper. Fry onion in fat until brown; add bread, celery, baking powder and seasonings to taste. Add milk and eggs; beat well. Place chicken in baking dish; pour dressing over chicken. Spread ground skin on top of dressing; cover with broth. Bake at 375 degrees for 1 hour to 1 hour and 30 minutes.

Mrs. Mary Schutz
Salem Ladies Aid
Elwood, Nebraska
Mrs. Joe Olson, Pres.
Redeemer LCW
McLaughlin, South Dakota

CHICKEN A LA TOLONAISE

1 5-lb. hen
2 qt. boiling water
½ c. margarine
1 carrot, chopped
1 sliced onion
6 sprigs parsley
6 green onion tops, chopped
2 lge. stalks celery with tops, chopped
1 ½ loaves stale bread, cubed
1 tsp. poultry seasoning
Dash of pepper
Salt to taste
1 c. chicken fat
1 c. flour
1 c. milk, warmed
4 eggs, slightly beaten
Buttered crumbs

169

(Continued on next page)

Boil chicken in salted water slowly until meat begins to leave bones. Cool in both. Remove meat from bones in bite-sized pieces. Reserve broth. Grind skin and giblets. Cook vegetables in margarine slowly for 5 minutes; add skin, giblets and bread. Mix lightly with fork. Add 1/3 cup broth. Season with poultry seasoning, pepper and salt to taste. Melt fat in large heavy saucepan. Add flour; mix until bubbling. Add warmed milk and 3 2/3 cups broth; bring to a boil. Salt to taste. Add a small amount of sauce to eggs; gradually add to sauce in sauce pan. Cook slowly for 3 minutes. Alternate layers of chicken dressing and sauce in large greased casserole. Cover with buttered crumbs. Bake at 375 degrees for 25 minutes or until crumbs are brown and chicken is hot. Yield: 12 servings.

Mrs. C. W. Daniel, Pres.
St. Matthew's Mission Sewing Cir.
Sonora, California

CHICKEN CASSEROLE

1 4-lb. chicken
Butter
¾ c. flour
6 eggs, well beaten
2 tbsp. onion
6 c. soft bread crumbs
½ tsp. celery salt
½ tsp. poultry seasoning

Cook chicken and remove bones; reserve broth. Mix 1/2 cup butter with flour and 6 cups chicken broth; add eggs. Cook for 2 minutes. Saute onion in 6 tablespoonfuls butter; add bread crumbs, celery salt and poultry seasoning. In deep baking dish, place a layer of dressing; add chicken. Repeat layers until all chicken and dressing are used. Pour sauce over all. Bake at 350 degrees for 1 hour and 30 minutes. Yield: 8 servings.

Mrs. Ervin Fredrick
Christ Lutheran Church
Holyoke, Minnesota

CHICKEN CASSEROLE

14 slices dry bread
½ c. diced celery
⅓ c. diced onion
2 eggs, beaten
4 c. rich broth
1 tsp. salt
⅛ tsp. pepper
1 chicken, cooked and cubed
2 c. cooked noodles

Mix all ingredients except chicken and noodles. Alternate layers of dressing, chicken and noodles in greased 13 x 9-inch loaf pan. Cover with thin layer of dressing. Bake at 400 degrees for 15 minutes; reduce temperature to 350 degrees. Bake for 20 minutes longer.

Mrs. Louis Speckmann
Martin Luther LCW
Johnson, Nebraska

CHICKEN CASSEROLE

1 5 to 6-lb. hen
8 eggs
1 stick margarine
1 c. flour
2 c. milk
Salt and pepper
2 c. corn bread crumbs
2 c. light bread crumbs
1 c. chopped celery
⅓ c. chopped onion

Cook chicken until done. Remove chicken, reserving 4 cups broth. Remove meat from bones; cut into bite-sized pieces. Hard-cook 6 eggs; slice. Melt margarine; blend in flour. Slowly add broth and milk. Season with salt and pepper. Cook until thickened, stirring constantly. Combine bread crumbs, celery, onion and 2 well beaten eggs. Mix well. Place a layer of dressing, a layer of chicken and a layer of eggs in 2 casseroles. Repeat layers. Cover with sauce; bake at 350 degrees for 1 hour. Yield: 16 servings.

Mrs. Jimmy Torrence, Pres.
Mt. Tabor LCW
Little Mountain, South Carolina

CHICKEN WITH DRESSING

2 3 to 4-lb. whole frying chickens
1 tbsp. salt
1 tsp. pepper
½ tsp. ground sage
½ c. chopped onion
1 c. chopped celery
1 ½ c. water

Sprinkle outside of chickens with salt and pepper; sprinkle inside with salt, pepper and sage. Divide onion and celery; stuff each chicken cavity with mixture. Place chickens in roaster; add water. Steam in oven until chickens are tender enough to bone. Remove cover; brown chickens lightly on all sides. Cool; remove bones. Cut meat into pieces.

DRESSING:

2 1¼-lb. loaves two-day old white bread
1 tbsp. salt
1 tsp. pepper
2 tsp. ground sage
2 c. finely cubed celery
1 c. finely cubed onions
¾ lb. margarine
6 eggs
1 ½ qt. milk

Break bread slices into quarters in large bowl; sprinkle in salt, pepper and sage. Mix well. Saute celery and onions in margarine until tender; pour into bread mixture. Mix well. Beat eggs with milk; pour into bread mixture, blending well. Add broth from roaster and mix. Mixture should be soft. Spread one-half of dressing in a greased 12 x 15 x 2-inch pan; add chicken. Cover with remaining dressing. Bake at 350 degrees for 1 hour and 15 minutes to 1 hour and

(Continued on next page)

30 minutes or until center is solid to the touch. Yield: 12 servings.

Mrs. Irene Saager
Hope Ladies Aid Soc.
Cedar Lake, Indiana

CHICKEN AND DRESSING CASSEROLE

1 lge. stewing hen
¾ c. chopped celery
½ c. chopped onion
2 tbsp. chopped parsley
½ c. plus 2 tbsp. butter
1 1-lb. loaf bread, cubed
3 tsp. salt
Dash of pepper
½ to 1 tsp. poultry seasoning
1 c. chicken fat
1 c. sifted flour
1 c. milk
4 eggs, slightly beaten
1 c. dry bread crumbs

Cook hen until tender; bone and dice, Reserve broth. Grind skin. Saute celery, onion and parsley in 1/2 cup butter for 5 minutes. Combine cubed bread, chicken skin and onion mixture; toss lightly. Add 1 teaspoonful salt, pepper and poultry seasoning; sprinkle with 3 tablespoonfuls broth. Toss again. Place in 10 x 14-inch pan or 2 1/2-quart casserole. Melt fat in large pan; blend in flour. Gradually add 4 cups broth and milk. Cook until thick, stirring constantly. Add remaining salt. Blend a small amount of hot mixture into eggs; add eggs to remaining hot mixture. Cook over low heat for 3 to 4 minutes. Pour one-half of custard over dressing; cover with chicken. Pour remaining custard over chicken. Brown bread crumbs in remaining butter; sprinkle over casserole. Bake at 350 degrees for 20 to 25 minutes or until crumbs are golden brown. NOTE: Butter may be substituted for part of chicken fat.

Mrs. G. M. Ruck, Sec.
Zion Ladies Aid Soc.
Manchester, Missouri

CHICKEN AND DRESSING CASSEROLE

1 c. chicken fat
1 c. flour
8 c. plus 3 tbsp. chicken broth
1 c. milk
2 tsp. salt
4 eggs, slightly beaten
7 c. dry bread crumbs
½ c. plus 2 tbsp. butter
¾ c. chopped celery
½ c. chopped onion
2 tbsp. chopped parsley
1 tsp. pepper
1 tsp. poultry seasoning
4 c. diced cooked chicken

Melt chicken fat; blend in flour. Gradually add 8 cups chicken broth, milk and 1 teaspoonful salt; cook, stirring until thick. Blend a small amount of hot sauce into eggs, returning to remaining hot sauce. Set aside. Brown 1 cup bread crumbs in 2 tablespoonfuls butter. Set aside. Saute celery, onion and parsley in remaining butter for 5 minutes. Combine remaining bread crumbs, salt, pepper, poultry seasoning and sauted ingredients; toss lightly with remaining broth. Turn into greased 2 1/2-quart casserole. Cover with one-half of sauce. Top with chicken. Cover with remaining sauce. Sprinkle with browned bread crumbs. Bake at 350 degrees until heated through.

Mrs. Robert Callis
St. John's Ladies Aid
Howard, South Dakota

CHICKEN FLUFF

4 c. cooked diced chicken
2 c. cooked rice
2 c. fresh soft bread cubes
1 4-oz. can mushrooms, drained
2 ½ c. cooled chicken broth
4 eggs, beaten
2 tsp. salt
¼ c. milk
1 can cream of mushroom soup

Combine chicken, rice, bread and mushrooms. Mix chicken broth with eggs and salt. Add to chicken mixture. Pour into large flat greased pan. Bake at 350 degrees for 1 hour. Cut into squares. Heat milk and soup; stir until smooth. Serve over chicken squares. Yield: 12 servings.

Mrs. Fred Hoshek, Pres.
Redeemer Ladies Guild
Cleveland, Ohio

CHICKEN HOT DISH WITH MUSHROOM SAUCE

3 c. diced cooked chicken or turkey
1 c. cooked rice
2 c. soft bread crumbs
½ c. diced celery
¼ c. chopped pimento
4 eggs, beaten
2 tsp. salt
¼ tsp. poultry seasoning
2 c. chicken broth
½ c. milk
1 can cream of mushroom soup

Combine chicken, rice, bread crumbs, celery and pimento; add to beaten eggs. Add salt, poultry seasoning and broth. Mix thoroughly; stir in chicken mixture. Pour into 9 x 9 x 2-inch buttered baking dish. Bake at 350 degrees for 45 minutes to 1 hour. Cut into squares. Combine milk and soup; heat thoroughly. Serve with chicken dish. NOTE: Two chicken bouillon cubes dissolved in hot water may be substituted for broth. Yield: 9 servings.

Mrs. Waldemar Schwarz, Sec.
Trinity Lutheran Guild
Appleton, Minnesota

CHICKEN HOT DISH

1 onion, chopped
½ c. butter
6 c. bread crumbs
1 ½ to 2 c. milk
1 chicken, cooked and chopped
1 c. chopped celery
1 tsp. baking powder
Salt and pepper
Sage or poultry seasoning
Ground chicken skin
Chicken broth

Saute onion in butter. Combine with one-half the bread crumbs and milk in 9 x 13-inch cake pan. Add chicken, celery, baking powder and seasonings. Top with remaining crumbs; pat down. Add ground skin and enough broth to cover. Bake at 375 degrees for 1 hour and 30 minutes. Cut into squares; serve with cream sauce or thickened broth. Yield: 8-10 servings.

Mrs. Herman Krapf, Pres.
Trinity Ladies Aid
Jasper, Minnesota

CHICKEN SOUFFLE

Salt and pepper
1 5-lb. chicken
1 ½ c. diced celery
1 ½ c. diced cheese
1 onion, finely chopped
1 can cream of mushroom soup
2 eggs, well beaten
4 c. soft fine bread crumbs

Cook and season chicken; reserve 5 to 6 cups broth. Dice chicken. Mix 1/2 teaspoonful salt and 1/2 teaspoonful pepper with all ingredients except a few bread crumbs. Place in large casserole or roaster. Top with remaining crumbs. Cover. Bake at 350 degrees for 1 hour. Yield: 12-14 servings.

Mrs. Albert Rathert, Pres.
St. John's Pleasant Green Tabitha Ladies Aid
Agra, Kansas

CHICKEN 'N' STUFFING SCALLOP

1 8-oz. pkg. or 2 c. herb-seasoned stuffing
3 to 4 c. cubed cooked or canned chicken
½ c. butter or margarine
½ c. flour
¼ tsp. salt
Dash of pepper
4 c. chicken broth
6 eggs, slightly beaten
1 can cream of mushroom soup
¼ c. milk
½ to 1 c. sour cream
¼ c. chopped pimento

Prepare stuffing according to package directions. Spread in 13 x 9 x 2-inch baking dish; top with chicken. Melt butter in large saucepan; blend in flour, salt and pepper. Add cool broth; cook and stir until mixture thickens. Stir a small amount of hot mixture into eggs, return to remaining hot mixture. Pour over chicken.

Bake at 325 degrees for 40 minutes to 1 hour or until knife inserted halfway is clean. Let stand for 5 minutes; cut into squares. Mix soup, milk, sour cream and pimento. Stir until heated thoroughly. Serve sauce over chicken. NOTE: Sauce may be omitted. Yield: 8-12 servings.

Mrs. Edwin Krause, Pres.
Trinity Bethany Soc.
Faribault, Minnesota
Mrs. John H. Concoby, Pres.
First Evangelical Naomi Cir.
Painesville, Ohio
Flora Erickson, Pres.
Our Saviour Lutheran Church The Phebians
Paradise, California
Mrs. K. Schuster, Pres.
Concordia LCW
Pittsburg, Pennsylvania
Leona Kieffer
Our Redeemer Ladies Aid
Overland, Missouri
Mrs. Archie D. Barba
Wollaston Lutheran Guild
Quincy, Massachusetts

CHICKEN SUPREME

1 stewing chicken
½ tsp. poultry seasoning
1 chicken bouillon cube
Flour
1 c. chopped celery
½ c. chopped onion
2 eggs
1 ½ tsp. salt
1 sm. loaf bread, chopped
1 sm. can mushrooms
1 can cream of mushroom soup
½ c. dry bread crumbs

Boil chicken until meat falls from bones. Remove chicken; chop. Add poultry seasoning and bouillon cube to 1 quart broth; thicken with flour. Cook celery and onion until done; cool. Add eggs, salt, bread, chopped chicken and mushrooms; toss lightly. Place mixture in pans; pour gravy over mixture. Top with mushroom soup. Sprinkle crumbs over all. Bake at 325 degrees for 1 hour and 30 minutes. NOTE: Casseroles may be frozen, if desired. Yield: 10 servings.

Mrs. Harvey Einspahr
Concordia Ladies Aid
Weiser, Idaho

CHICKEN SUPREME

1 loaf stale bread
1 chicken, cut up
5 eggs, beaten
1 med. onion, chopped
1 tsp. sage
1 tsp. salt
¼ tsp. pepper

Tear bread into pieces. Boil chicken until done. Remove from bones; cut meat into bite-sized pieces. Reserve broth. Cut giblets. Combine bread, giblets, eggs, onion, seasonings and

172

(Continued on next page)

enough broth to make a thin dressing. Place one-half of dressing in 9 x 13-inch pan; cover with chicken. Add remaining dressing. Make gravy with remaining broth; pour over dressing. Prick dressing with fork. Bake at 375 degrees for 1 hour or longer. Yield: 12 servings.

Mrs. Ed Lobeda, Pres.
St. James LCW
Edgar, Nebraska

CHICKEN SUPREME

1 stewing hen
1 sm. onion, chopped
1 c. chopped celery
⅓ c. butter
5 c. toasted bread cubes
½ tsp. baking powder
Salt and pepper
½ tsp. sage
1 egg
1 ½ c. milk

Cook chicken until tender, reserving broth. Remove skin and bones. Cut skin fine or put through food chopper. Cut meat into large pieces. Place in baking pan. Thicken broth; pour over meat. Brown onion and celery slightly in butter in skillet. Mix bread cubes with chicken skin, baking powder, salt, pepper, sage, egg and milk. Add to onion and celery. Spread over chicken. Top with small amount of butter, if desired. Bake at 350 degrees for 45 minutes or until done.

Mrs. Phillip Weitzed, Treas.
St. Peter's English Lutheran Church
Newell, Iowa

CHURCH LUNCHEON CHICKEN

1 lge. stewing hen
2 cans cream of mushroom soup
¾ loaf dry bread, cubed
1 onion, diced
1 tsp. sage
Salt and pepper to taste
2 eggs, beaten

Stew chicken until tender. Remove meat from bones; cut into bite-sized pieces. Reserve broth. Combine meat with undiluted soup. Combine bread cubes, onion and seasonings. Add enough boiling broth to moisten. Toss lightly with a fork. Pat one-half the dressing in 9 x 13-inch baking pan. Spoon chicken mixture on top. Beat eggs into remaining dressing. Spoon over chicken layer. Bake at 350 degrees for 35 to 45 minutes. Make gravy of remaining broth. Cut casserole into squares to serve. Spoon gravy over each square.

Mrs. Bernice Schmitt, Sec.
Grace Ladies Aid
Muscatine, Iowa

OVEN-FRIED CHICKEN 'N' DRESSING

1 4-lb. chicken, cut into servings pieces
Salt and pepper
Flour
⅓ c. shortening
6 c. dry bread cubes
2 tbsp. chopped onion
1 ¼ tsp. sage
½ c. melted margarine
1 can cream of chicken soup
1 ¼ c. water

Sprinkle chicken with salt and pepper; coat with flour. Heat shortening in skillet; brown chicken. Place in 3-quart casserole or Dutch oven. Combine bread, onion, sage and margarine with 1/2 cup soup. Place dressing over chicken. Add 2 tablespoonfuls flour to drippings in skillet; heat until browned. Add remaining soup and water. Bring to a boil; cook, stirring constantly, until thickened. Pour over dressing. Cover; bake at 350 degrees for 1 hour or until tender. Yield: 6 servings.

Mrs. Ralph Mundt, Pres.
St. John's LCW
Golden Lake, Ontario, Canada

SCALLOPED CHICKEN

1 c. finely chopped celery
½ c. finely chopped onion
2 tbsp. butter
¾ c. water
4 c. cooked, boned chicken
3 c. broken stale bread or packaged dressing
2 tbsp. minced parsley
1 tsp. crushed sage
2 tsp. salt
½ tsp. pepper
4 eggs, slightly beaten
3 c. rich chicken stock

Cook celery, onion and butter in water until tender. Cut chicken into large pieces. Mix celery and onion with all remaining ingredients except eggs and chicken in large mixing bowl. Add eggs and chicken; mix lightly. Spread evenly in greased 10 x 10 x 2-inch pan. Bake at 350 degrees for 1 hour. Serve immediately with chicken gravy, if desired. Yield: 12-16 servings.

Mrs. Lawrence List, Pres.
St. Peter's LCW
Dayton, Ohio

SCALLOPED CHICKEN

4 tbsp. chicken fat
4 tbsp. flour
1 qt. broth
1 ½ qt. stale bread
¾ c. melted butter
1 ½ tsp. sage
¼ c. stock
¾ tsp. salt
⅛ tsp. pepper
2 tbsp. onion
1 qt. chopped stewed chicken

(Continued on next page)

Place chicken fat in skillet; add flour, stirring constantly. Pour broth in slowly, stirring. Combine all remaining ingredients except chicken; mix well. Place chicken in bottom of a 9 x 13 x 2-inch pan; cover with dressing mixture. Pour gravy over dressing. Bake at 350 degrees until dressing is done. Yield: 6-10 servings.

Ruth Manford, Pres.
Trinity Priscilla Guild
Manilla, Iowa
Hazel Eberhard
St. Paul's Women's League
Marion, Iowa

SCALLOPED CHICKEN

1 4 to 5-lb. chicken
2 qt. diced bread
3 eggs, slightly beaten
Salt and pepper to taste
1 tbsp. melted butter
1 can mushrooms
1 pimento

Cover chicken with salted water; boil until done. Reserve broth. Break chicken into small pieces. Add bread to broth. Mix remaining ingredients into broth. Pour into baking pan. Bake at 350 degrees for 45 minutes or until brown and moisture disappears. Yield: 15 servings.

Erna Ramsey
Trinity Ladies Aid
Persia, Iowa

STUFFED ROAST CHICKEN

1 4 ½-lb. chicken
Bread
2 eggs, beaten
1 tsp. salt
¼ tsp. pepper
1 tsp. poultry seasoning
1 sm. onion, chopped
Ground gizzard
Ground heart
Ground liver
¼ lb. pork sausage (opt.)

Wash chicken inside and out; wipe dry. Soak dry bread in warm water; squeeze out excess water, to make 2 1/2 cups of bread. Add eggs, salt, pepper, poultry seasoning, o n i o n, gizzard, heart, liver and sausage. Mix well. Fill chicken with stuffing; sew opening. Rub chicken with salt. Bake at 300 to 350 degrees for 25 minutes per pound. Do not baste or cover chicken.

Mrs. Wilbur F. Heuser, Pres.
St. Matthew's Ladies Aid
Germania, Pennsylvania

HOT CHICKEN SALAD

2 c. cooked cubed chicken
2 c. chopped celery
⅓ c. chopped green pepper
3 tbsp. pimento, cut into strips

2 tbsp minced onion
1 tsp. salt
2 tbsp. lemon juice
½ c. mayonnaise or salad dressing
⅓ c. shredded sharp or Swiss cheese
1 c. coarsely broken potato chips

Blend all ingredients except cheese and potato chips. Place in greased 1 1/2-quart baking dish. Sprinkle cheese and potato chips over top. Bake at 350 degrees for 25 to 30 minutes or until cheese is browned and bubbly. Yield: 6-8 servings.

Mrs. Bud C. Johnson, Christian Action Chmn.
Spencer, Nebraska

HOT CHICKEN SALAD

4 chicken breasts, cooked
1 tsp. salt or to taste
2 c. finely cut celery
1 sm. onion, grated
1 green pepper, cut finely
1 c. mayonnaise
½ c. grated cheese or 1 4-oz. can grated
   American cheese
2 c. crushed potato chips

Cover chicken breasts with water; season. Cook until tender. Cool; cut into bite-sized pieces. Add celery, onion, pepper and mayonnaise. Place in well buttered 9 x 13-inch flat baking dish or pan; sprinkle with cheese and crushed potato chips. Bake at 375 degrees for 20 minutes. Yield: 6-8 servings.

Doris Ritthaler, Pres.
Christ Lutheran Church LCW
Romulus, Michigan

MOCK CHICKEN SOUFFLE

10 to 12 slices bread
2 c. chopped cooked chicken
½ c. mayonnaise
¼ c. finely chopped green pepper (opt.)
1 sm. onion, minced
1 c. chopped celery
4 eggs
2 to 3 c. milk
1 can cream of mushroom soup
½ c. grated sharp cheese (opt.)
Paprika (opt.)

Dice one-half of bread, if desired; place in 9 x 13-inch buttered dish. Mix chicken with mayonnaise, green pepper, onion and celery; spread over bread. Trim crust from remaining bread; place whole slices over chicken mixture. Beat eggs until frothy; add milk. Pour over bread. Refrigerate overnight. Bake at 325 degrees for 15 minutes. Add soup and cheese; sprinkle with paprika. Bake for 1 hour longer. Yield: 8 servings.

Mrs. David W. Anton, Past Pres.
St. Thomas Women's Guild
Rocky River, Ohio
Mrs. William J. Yoder
Peace Lutheran Guild
Filer, Idaho

BAKED CHICKEN CASSEROLE

1 c. uncooked macaroni or noodles
¼ lge. green pepper, finely cut
1 6-oz. can boned chicken or 1 10 to
    12-oz. chicken breast
1 can cream of chicken soup
1 c. diced cooked celery
2 tsp. minced onion
⅓ red pimento, finely cut
¼ c. finely chopped almonds
½ tsp. salt
¼ tsp. pepper
1 tbsp. lemon juice
¾ c. mayonnaise
1 c. frozen peas
1 2-oz. can mushroom stems and pieces
2 hard-cooked eggs, thinly sliced
2 c. crushed potato chips

Boil macaroni until tender. Saute green pepper slightly. Mix all ingredients except potato chips, folding egg slices in last. Top with crushed potato chips. Bake at 450 degrees for 15 minutes. Yield: 8 servings.

Mrs. Eleonora Walton
Sts. Thomas and Peter Ladies Aid Soc.
Detroit, Michigan

CASSEROLE OF CHICKEN

2 c. cooked macaroni
4 c. cooked diced chicken
1 c. crumbled potato chips
1 c. chicken broth
1 c. cream
3 tbsp. melted butter
1 egg, beaten
Salt and pepper

Place macaroni, chicken and potato chips in layers in buttered baking dish. Mix remaining ingredients and pour over layers; season with salt and pepper. Bake at 350 degrees for 45 minutes. Yield: 12 servings.

Mrs. Irene Gasch, Pres.
St. Paul's Ladies Aid Soc.
Vesper, Wisconsin

CHICKEN CASSEROLE

2 c. chicken
2 cans cream of mushroom soup
2 c. milk
7 oz. uncooked macaroni
½ lb. Cheddar cheese, diced
4 hard-cooked eggs, diced

Combine all ingredients in casserole. Refrigerate overnight. Bake at 350 degrees for 1 hour. Yield: 10 servings.

Mrs. June Holmberg, Pres.
LCW
Orion, Illinois

CHICKEN CASSEROLE

1 stewing chicken, cooked and chopped
1 7-oz. pkg. macaroni
½ c. chopped onion
2 tbsp. chicken fat
¼ c. flour
2 c. milk
½ c. chopped green pepper
⅓ c. chopped pimento
2 3-oz. cans mushrooms
2 10 ½-oz. cans cream of chicken soup
1 stewing chicken, cooked and chopped

Cook macaroni according to package directions. Saute onion in chicken fat; blend in flour. Add milk; cook until thickened. Add green pepper, pimento, mushrooms, soup, chicken and macaroni. Mix well. Place in 9 x 12-inch greased baking dish. Bake at 350 degrees for 45 minutes. Yield: 8-10 servings.

Mrs. William C. Walde, Pres.
Concordia LWML
Fort Wayne, Indiana

CHICKEN CASSEROLE

½ c. butter or chicken fat
1 c. bread crumbs
1 4-oz. can mushrooms
1 ½ c. uncooked shell macaroni
3 c. cooked cubed chicken
1 c. grated Cheddar cheese
1 c. milk
1 c. chicken broth
¼ c. chopped green pepper
1 tsp. salt
3 eggs, slightly beaten
1 3-oz. can chow mein noodles

Melt butter or chicken fat in saucepan; stir in bread crumbs. Combine all remaining ingredients except noodles. Turn into a 13 x 9 1/2 x 2-inch baking pan. Sprinkle with noodles. Bake at 350 degrees for 45 minutes.

SAUCE:

½ c. butter or chicken fat, melted
½ c. flour
2 c. chicken broth
¼ c. cream
½ tsp. lemon juice
Parsley to taste
Salt to taste

Combine all ingredients; cook over low heat for 5 minutes. Serve with chicken. Yield: 12 servings.

Mrs. E. B. Biffle, Past Pres.
Faith Ladies Guild
Jefferson City, Missouri

CHICKEN CASSEROLE DELUXE

4 chicken legs and 2 chicken breasts
Butter
2 cans cream of mushroom soup
1 sm. pkg. Velveeta cheese
1 c. chopped celery

(Continued on next page)

1 green pepper, chopped
1 sm. onion, chopped
1 can mushrooms
1 sm. pkg. uncooked macaroni
1 pkg. frozen peas

Brown chicken in butter. Cool; cut into small pieces. Add soup and cheese to pan drippings; stir until cheese is melted. Mix chicken with celery, green pepper, onion, mushrooms, macaroni and peas. Add to soup m i x t u r e. Place in buttered casserole; bake at 350 degrees for 1 hour. Yield: 8 servings.

Mrs. Melvin Pratt
Corners Mary-Martha Altar Guild
East Troy, Wisconsin

CHICKEN-MACARONI CASSEROLE

1 3 to 4-lb. chicken
2 c. broth
Flour
1 c. grated American cheese
1 8-oz. pkg. shell macaroni, cooked and
     drained
½ c. melted butter
4 c. fine bread crumbs

Cook and season chicken; bone and dice. Place in large bowl. Thicken broth with flour; add to chicken. Add grated cheese and macaroni. Add 2 cups buttered bread crumbs; mix well. Pour into a 10 x 13-inch pan; spread remaining bread crumbs on top. Bake at 350 degrees for 30 minutes. Yield: 16-18 servings.

Mrs. Emanuel Mai
Concordia Dorcas Soc.
Hoisington, Kansas

CHICKEN CASSEROLE

1 3-lb. chicken
2 ½ c. noodles
1 box frozen peas
1 c. grated cheese
1 c. mushrooms
2 tbsp. chopped pimento
1 c. sweet cream
Flour

Cook chicken until tender; reserve 2 cups broth. Cook noodles in remaining broth. Arrange layers of noodles, chicken, peas, cheese and mushrooms in a large casserole until all mixture is used. Lay pimento over mixture. Pour sweet cream over the top. Thicken reserved broth with a small amount flour; pour over casserole. Bake at 350 degrees for 1 hour. Yield: 12 servings.

Mrs. Fern Rahe, Treas.
Zion Women's Soc.
Chappell, Nebraska

CHICKEN CASSEROLE

1 6-oz. can mushrooms
1 c. evaporated milk

½ c. butter, margarine or chicken fat
½ c. flour
½ tbsp. turmeric
¼ tsp. oregano
½ c. grated cheese
1 12 to 16-oz. pkg. med. noodles
1 4-lb. stewing chicken, cooked and boned

Drain liquid from mushrooms; add e n o u g h chicken broth to make 3 cups liquid. Add milk to liquid. Melt fat; blend in flour and spices. Add liquid; cook until thickened. Add 1/4 cup cheese; stir until melted. Spread noodles in greased casserole; add chicken and mushrooms. Pour sauce over mixture; add remaining cheese. Bake at 350 degrees for 45 minutes. Yield: 12 servings.

Mrs. Carl E. Carlson, Treas.
Silver Creek LCW
Monticello, Minnesota

CHICKEN CASSEROLE

1 qt. buttered bread crumbs
1 sm. pkg. noodles, cooked
3 hard-cooked eggs, chopped (opt.)
1 can cream of mushroom soup
1 c. milk
1 chicken, cooked and diced
Salt and pepper to taste

Line a buttered 8 x 12-inch casserole with 3/4 quart buttered crumbs. Mix noodles, eggs, mushroom soup, milk and chicken; pour over buttered crumbs. Dot with butter. Add salt and pepper to taste. Cover with remaining buttered crumbs. Bake at 300 degrees for 30 to 40 minutes or until heated through and browned on top. Yield: 6-8 servings.

Mrs. Charlie Schilb, Sec.
Immanuel Ladies Aid
Clarinda, Iowa

CHICKEN HOT DISH

4 lb. noodles
Salt
Chicken broth
3 chickens, cooked and diced
3 pkg. frozen peas
4 c. diced celery
4 c. diced carrots (opt.)
1 can pimento
4 cans cream of mushroom soup
4 cans chicken soup
1 c. milk
1 tbsp. pepper

Cook noodles with 2 tablespoonfuls salt in broth until partially done. Do not drain. Add salt to taste and remaining ingredients. Pour into large greased roaster or small greased casseroles. Bake at 350 degrees for 30 minutes or longer. Yield: 50 servings.

Mrs. Frank G. Koch, Pres.
St. Paul's Ladies Aid Soc.
Eden Valley, Minnesota

CHICKEN-NOODLE CASSEROLE

1 12-oz. pkg. egg noodles
4 tbsp. butter
¼ c. chopped green pepper
¼ c. minced onion
½ c. chopped celery
½ c. sliced mushrooms (opt.)
4 tbsp. flour
1 c. chicken stock
1 c. milk
Salt and pepper to taste
2 c. coarsely crushed potato chips
2 c. cooked cubed chicken

Cook noodles accroding to package directions. Melt butter in saucepan. Add green pepper, onion, celery and mushrooms; cook over low heat until celery is tender. Add flour; blend. Add chicken stock and milk. Cook; stir until smooth and thick. Season with salt and pepper. Arrange thin layer of crushed potato chips in casserole dish. Add layer of noodles and layer of cubed chicken. Pour a small amount of sauce mixture over layers. Repeat. Garnish with whole potato chips. Bake at 350 degrees for 30 minutes. Yield: 8 servings.

Mrs. Donald Hake, Pres.
Whitnall Park LCW
New Berlin, Wisconsin

CHICKEN-NOODLE CASSEROLE

1 lge. chicken, cut up
½ c. flour
2 c. milk
½ c. grated cheese
1 sm. can mushrooms, finely chopped
Salt to taste
1 pkg. noodles, cooked
12 soda crackers
½ c. crushed corn flakes

Stew chicken, reserving 3 cups broth. Make paste of 1 cup broth and flour; add to 2 cups broth and milk. Add cheese, mushrooms, salt and noodles. Mix with chicken. Place in buttered pan. Grind chicken skin with crackers; mix with corn flakes. Sprinkle topping on chicken. Bake at 325 degrees for 1 hour. Yield: 10 servings.

Mrs. Anna L. Esterly
Zion Dorcas Cir.
Ainsworth, Nebraska

CHICKEN-NOODLE CASSEROLE

2 tsp. salt
1 qt. boiling water
4 oz. noodles
3 tbsp. fat
3 tbsp. flour
¼ tsp. paprika
1 c. chicken broth
1 c. milk
1 tbsp. lemon juice
¼ c. chopped olives
2 c. cubed cooked chicken

Add 1 teaspoonful salt to boiling water. Gradually add noodles; boil for 7 minutes or until tender. Drain. Melt fat in top of double boiler. Add flour, 1/2 teaspoonful salt and paprika. Mix to a smooth paste; gradually add chicken broth and milk, stirring constantly. Cook until slightly thickened. Add lemon juice and olives. Combine noodles and chicken in a 1 1/2-quart casserole. Pour sauce over casserole. Bake, covered, at 350 degrees for 45 minutes. Serve hot. NOTE: Peas may be substituted for olives. Yield: 6-8 servings.

Mrs. Edgar Hecht
Immanuel Ladies Aid
New Wells, Missouri

CHICKEN-NOODLE CASSEROLE

1 10-oz. pkg. noodles
1 can cream of chicken soup
⅔ c. milk
1 tsp. salt
1 ½ c. shredded cheese
2 c. cooked chicken
1 c. chopped celery
¼ c. chopped green pepper
¼ c. chopped pimento

Cook noodles until done; drain. Add remaining ingredients. Mix well. Pour into greased casserole. Bake at 400 degrees for 40 minutes. Yield: 8 servings.

Mrs. Neal McKinney, Pres.
Good Shepherd Ladies Aid
Pasadena, Texas

CHICKEN AND NOODLE DISH

1 chicken, cooked and cubed
1 lb. wide noodles or macaroni, cooked and drained
1 4-oz. can pimento
2 cans cream of mushroom soup
½ c. bread crumbs
3 eggs, beaten
½ pt. heavy cream, whipped

Mix all ingredients well. Add cream last. Place in baking dish. Bake at 375 degrees for 45 minutes. Yield: 8-10 servings.

Mrs. Fred A. Wittler
Trinity LCW
Winside, Nebraska

CHICKEN-NOODLE HOT DISH

2 c. uncooked ripple noodles
4 c. boiling water
1 tsp. salt
1 can cream of chicken soup
½ c. evaporated milk
⅛ tsp. thyme
¼ c. chopped almonds
15 oz. chicken pieces
2 tbsp. melted butter
⅓ c. chopped green pepper
½ c. bread crumbs

(Continued on next page)

Cook noodles in boiling salted water. Place noodles in 6-cup baking dish. Mix soup with milk and thyme. Pour over noodles; mix well. Mix chicken with almonds. Add to noodles. Combine remaining ingredients; sprinkle over chicken. Bake at 350 degrees for 20 minutes or until sauce is bubbly. Yield: 6 servings.

Mrs. Lester Bargstadt, Pres.
Christ Lutheran Church LCW
Pierce, Nebraska

CHICKEN SUPREME

2 2 ¼-lb. fryers
1 c. chopped green peppers
1 c. chopped onions
1 c. chopped celery
1 stick butter
½ lb. Velveeta cheese
1 bottle stuffed olives, sliced
1 can whole mushrooms
2 cans cream of mushroom soup
1 pkg. spinach noodles

Boil chickens until done; reserve stock. Cool chicken; cut into pieces. Saute peppers, onions and celery in butter until tender. Add cheese, olives, mushrooms and mushroom soup; mix well. Cook noodles in chicken stock. Combine all ingredients with chicken pieces. Place in casserole. Heat in oven. Serve hot with sliced almonds on top.

Mrs. Charles Mitchell
First United LCW
Memphis, Tennessee

CHICKEN TETRAZZINI

1 ½ c. fine noodles
3 ½ c. chicken soup
⅓ c. butter
3 tbsp. flour
½ tsp. salt
Dash of pepper
1 egg yolk
3 tbsp. light cream
1 4-oz. can mushrooms
3 c. cooked diced chicken
2 to 3 tbsp. Parmesan cheese

Cook noodles in 2 cups chicken soup and water sufficient for cooking. Drain; spread in 6 x 11-inch baking dish. Melt butter in double boiler. Add flour; stir until smooth. Add remaining chicken soup slowly, keeping mixture smooth. Add salt and pepper. Cook until thickened. Beat egg yolk; add cream. Add egg yolk mixture to sauce very slowly, stirring constantly. Drain mushrooms; fry and add to sauce. Add cooked chicken. Pour chicken mixture over noodles. Sprinkle with Parmesan cheese. Bake at 350 degrees for 15 to 20 minutes; brown quickly in broiler. Yield: 6 servings.

Irma A. Klemer, Pres.
Cleveland Hill Women's Guild
Buffalo, New York

HEAVENLY HASH

1 med. stewing chicken, cooked and chopped
1 pkg. wide noodles, cooked
1 sm. can mushrooms
1 sm. can pimento
1 can corn
1 ½ tbsp. butter
1 ½ tbsp. flour
2 c. milk
¼ lb. American cheese, grated
Finely crushed cracker crumbs

Mix chicken, noodles, mushrooms, pimento and corn. Melt butter; blend in flour. Gradually add milk. Cook until thickened, stirring constantly. Add cheese; stir until melted. Add to chicken mixture. Pour into two casseroles or shallow pans. Pour chicken broth over casseroles; cover with crumbs. Bake at 350 degrees for 45 minutes.

Ruby Siefker
St. Paul's Evangelical Ladies Aid
Beecher, Illinois

STROGANOFF CASSEROLE

1 can cream of celery or chicken soup
½ c. sour cream
½ to ¾ c. milk
1 c. cubed cooked chicken or 1 7-oz. can tuna, drained and flaked
2 tbsp. chopped parsley
2 tbsp. chopped pimento (opt.)
¼ tsp. salt
Dash of pepper
2 c. cooked med. noodles
2 tbsp. buttered bread crumbs

Blend soup and sour cream; stir in milk. Add chicken or tuna, parsley, pimento, seasonings and noodles. Pour into 1 1/2-quart shallow baking dish. Top with crumbs. Bake at 350 degrees for 30 minutes. Yield: 4 servings.

Mrs. Arthur L. Peyer
Trinity LCW
Peoria, Illinois

YUMMY CHICKEN CASSEROLE

1 2 ½-lb. fryer
1 can cream of chicken soup
8 oz. noodles, cooked
1 soup can milk
Bread crumbs

Cook chicken until tender; cool. Remove chicken from bones; chop. Place in 2-quart casserole; add chicken soup, noodles and milk. Top with bread crumbs. Bake at 350 degrees for about 1 hour. Yield: 8 servings.

Mrs. Beatrice Swanson, Pres.
Our Savior's Dorcas Soc.
Marion, Kansas

CHICKEN-SPAGHETTI CASSEROLE

1   3 to 4-oz. can sliced mushrooms
Chicken broth
1 c. light cream
4 tbsp. butter or margarine
1 tbsp. flour
1 tsp. salt
⅛ tsp. pepper
2 c. diced cooked chicken
4 oz. spaghetti, cooked
¼ c. grated Parmesan cheese

Drain mushrooms; measure liquid. Add enough chicken broth to make 1/2 cup liquid; add cream. Melt 1 tablespoonful butter in saucepan. Add flour, salt and pepper; stir to a smooth paste. Gradually add broth mixture and cook, stirring constantly, until mixture thickens and comes to a boil. Add chicken and mushrooms; heat. Place spaghetti in a 2-quart casserole; spoon chicken mixture over top. Sprinkle with grated cheese and dot with remaining butter. Bake at 375 degrees for 15 minutes or until lightly browned. Yield: 4 servings.

Mrs. Harold E. Einem
Messiah LWML and Ladies Guild
Valdosta, Georgia

CHICKEN TETRAZZINI

1 tsp. minced onion
3 tbsp. butter
2 tbsp. flour
1 c. evaporated milk
1 c. chicken broth
3 c. diced chicken
1 hard-cooked egg, chopped
4 oz. spaghetti, cooked
1 c. diced celery
1 c. sliced mushrooms

Lightly brown onion in butter; add flour, milk and chicken broth. Blend thoroughly. Add remaining ingredients; pour into buttered casserole. Bake at 375 degrees for 30 minutes. Yield: 6 servings.

Mrs. A. C. Buetzow, Pres.
Mt. Calvary Ladies Guild
Pittsburgh, Pennsylvania

CHICKEN TETRAZZINI

1 med. onion, diced
1 stalk celery, diced
3 tbsp. butter
2 c. cooked cubed chicken
2 c. uncooked spaghetti
1 tsp. salt
¼ tsp. pepper
1 can cream of chicken soup
3 c. chicken broth
½ can sliced mushrooms

Saute onion and celery in butter; place in casserole. Top with chicken; sprinkle with spaghetti, salt and pepper. Combine soup with broth. Pour over spaghetti; cover with mushrooms. Bake in moderate oven for 30 minutes or until spaghetti is tender. Uncover; bake until brown. Yield: 6 servings.

Mrs. Ervin E. Basner, Pres.
St. Peter's Ladies Aid Soc.
Hemlock, Michigan

CHICKEN TETRAZZINI

4 lge. chicken breasts
1 med. onion, sliced
2 whole cloves
1 tsp. salt
¼ tsp. pepper
2 c. water
1 can cream of chicken soup
1 c. sour cream
¼ lb. sharp Cheddar cheese, grated
¼ c. Sherry wine
1 pt. fresh mushrooms
½ lb. spaghetti, cooked
½ c. grated Parmesan cheese
1 tbsp. butter

Place chicken, onion, cloves, salt, 1/8 teaspoonful pepper and water in large kettle. Cover and cook over low heat for 30 to 40 minutes. Remove chicken, reserving 1/2 cup broth. Bone chicken and cut meat into 1-inch pieces. Mix soup, sour cream, Cheddar cheese, Sherry and remaining pepper in saucepan; heat, but do not boil. Cook mushrooms in reserved chicken broth for 10 minutes. Combine all ingredients except Parmesan cheese and butter; place in 3-quart casserole. Sprinkle Parmesan cheese on top. Dot with butter. Bake at 350 degrees for 30 minutes. Yield: 8 servings.

Mrs. Albert Niemi
Trinity Ladies Aid Soc.
Fredericktown, Missouri

ARROZ CON POLLO

2 sm. fryers, cut up
Salt to taste
6 oz. olive oil
1 med. onion, diced
2 cloves of garlic, minced
1 sm. green pepper, diced
4 oz. canned tomatoes
1 qt. chicken broth
1 bay leaf
1 10-oz. pkg. yellow rice mix

Season chicken with salt; fry in olive oil. Remove chicken from olive oil; saute onion, garlic and green pepper in remaining olive oil; add tomatoes, salt, chicken broth and bay leaf. Bring to a boil. Place rice in casserole; pour mixture of chicken broth and seasonings over rice; stir well. Place fried chicken on top. Bake, uncovered, at 350 degrees for 1 hour. Garnish with green peas and pimento, if desired. Yield: 6-8 servings.

Mrs. Numa Bulot, Pres.
St. Matthew's LWML
New Orleans, Louisiana

BAKED CHICKEN

4 c. diced cooked chicken
1 c. cooked rice
1 tsp. salt
½ tsp. paprika
¼ c. chopped pimento
4 eggs, well beaten
¼ c. butter or chicken fat
3 c. chicken stock or half stock and cream of
    mushroom soup

Combine all ingredients. Pack into buttered pan. Bake at 350 degrees for 1 hour. Let stand for 10 minutes before removing from pan. Yield: 6 servings.

Mrs. Dorothy Hugo, Sec.
Beautiful Savior Ladies Guild
Milwaukee, Wisconsin

CHICKEN-ALMOND CASSEROLE

6 tbsp. butter
6 tbsp. flour
½ tsp. paprika
Dash of pepper
3 chicken bouillon cubes
2 c. hot water
1 ⅔ c. evaporated milk
Salt
½ c. slivered blanched almonds
1 4-oz. can mushrooms
3 c. cooked cubed chicken breast
3 c. cooked rice
1 pimento, chopped
⅔ c. buttered bread crumbs
Slivered almonds

Melt butter; blend in flour, paprika and pepper. Dissolve bouillon cubes in water; add to milk. Salt to taste. Add to flour mixture. Stir over low heat until smooth and thick. Add remaining ingredients except crumbs and almonds. Pour into buttered casserole. Cover with crumbs and almonds. Bake at 350 degrees for 30 minutes. Yield: 6-8 servings.

Mrs. Roscoe Mathews, Mission Chmn.
Trinity Ladies League
Hammond, Indiana

CHICKEN, ALMOND AND RICE CASSEROLE

1 lge. onion, chopped
½ bunch celery, chopped
½ green pepper, chopped
1 c. uncooked rice
2 pkg. chicken-noodle soup mix
4 c. boiling chicken broth or water
1 3 to 4-lb. stewing chicken, cooked and
    cubed
½ c. slivered almonds
½ tsp. curry powder

Saute onion, celery and green pepper in oil or chicken fat; add rice, soup mix and broth. Add chicken, almonds and curry powder. Place in 9 x 13-inch pan. Bake, covered, at 350 degrees

for 1 hour. Uncover last few minutes of baking time. Yield: 8-10 servings.

Mrs. Ray Schnitzmeyer, Pres.
Trinity LWML and Ladies Aid
Hoffman, Illinois

CHICKEN CASSEROLE

1 4-lb. chicken
2 c. cooked rice
3 c. chicken broth
1 10 ½-oz. can cream of mushroom soup
Salt to taste
Pepper (opt.)
4 eggs, slightly beaten
2 c. buttered bread crumbs
Butter

Boil chicken until tender; cool. Remove bones and dice meat. Mix rice, broth, mushroom soup, salt, pepper and eggs; add to meat. Place one-half of bread crumbs on bottom of a 2-quart casserole; add chicken mixture. Top with the remaining crumbs. Dot with butter. Bake at 350 degrees for 45 minutes to 1 hour or until browned on top. Yield: 8-10 servings.

Mrs. Irene Doctor
Emmanuel Soest, Ladies Aid
Fort Wayne, Indiana

CHICKEN CASSEROLE

3 c. diced cooked chicken
2 c. chopped celery
4 tbsp. diced onion
4 tbsp. diced pimento
4 tbsp. diced green pepper
6 hard-cooked eggs, diced
2 cans cream of chicken soup
1 ½ c. mayonnaise
2 tbsp. lemon juice
1 c. slivered almonds
3 c. cooked instant rice
1 c. water
Salt and pepper to taste

Combine chicken, celery, onion, pimento, green pepper and eggs. Add undiluted soup and remaining ingredients. Pour into baking dish. If desired, top with chow mein noodles. Bake at 400 degrees for 30 minutes. Yield: 20 servings.

Mrs. Edward M. Philips, Pres.
Plattville Women's Aux.
Minooka, Illinois

CHICKEN DELUXE

1 whole chicken
¼ c. chopped onion
1 c. cooked rice
¼ c. chopped green pepper
1 8-oz. can tomato sauce
1 10 ¾-oz. can cream of mushroom soup

Boil chicken until tender or meat falls off bones. Cool slightly and remove bones. Reserve

(Continued on next page)

2 1/4 cups broth. Mix chicken broth, onion, rice, pepper, tomato sauce and soup in large casserole. Bake at 350 degrees for 1 hour and 30 minutes to 2 hours. Yield: 8 servings.

Mrs. Marvin L. Nuss
Bethlehem Dorcas Soc.
Perryton, Texas

CHICKEN GERTRUDE

1 5-lb. stewing hen
1 qt. water
1 tbsp. salt
Few celery leaves
3 tbsp. butter
3 tbsp. flour
1 ½ c. chicken broth
1 c. light cream
2 c. New York State sharp cheese, grated
1 tsp. salt
½ tsp. monosodium glutamate
Dash of pepper
1 lb. or lge. can sliced mushrooms
1 c. cooked rice
1 c. slivered blanched almonds
1 tbsp. minced onion

Place hen in large kettle with water, salt and celery leaves. Simmer, covered, for several hours or until tender. Let cool in broth. Skim fat from broth. Remove chicken from bones; cut into bite-sized pieces. Melt butter; blend in flour. Gradually add broth and cream. Cook until thickened, stirring constantly. Add cheese; continue cooking until smooth. Season with salt, monosodium glutamate and pepper. Mix chicken with cream sauce in large bowl. Saute mushrooms in butter. Add rice, almonds and onion. Pour into 2-quart casserole. Sprinkle with a few chopped almonds. Bake at 350 degrees for 40 minutes or until golden and bubbly. Yield: 8 servings.

Mrs. John Anderson Wells
Christian Action Chmn.
St. Paul's LCW
Columbia, South Carolina

CHICKEN HOT DISH

1 lge. chicken
Celery
1 med. onion, chopped
1 c. cooked rice
1 ½ tsp. salt
2 tbsp. pimento
1 can cream of mushroom soup

Cook chicken, celery and onion in pressure cooker until tender, following cooker directions. Remove bones and dice chicken; combine remaining ingredients with chicken and broth. Place in casserole. Bake at 350 degrees for 1 hour. Yield: 12 servings.

Mrs. Conrad Rosvold
St. John Lutheran Church
Motley, Minnesota

CHICKEN SCALLOP

⅓ c. uncooked rice
2 c. chicken broth
2 ½ c. diced chicken
⅓ c. chopped celery
¼ c. pimento
2 eggs, beaten
¾ tsp. salt
⅛ tsp. poultry seasoning
¼ c. chopped onion
3 tbsp. butter
3 tbsp. flour
½ c. sour cream
1 c. mushrooms, drained

Cook rice in 2 cups broth for 10 minutes. Add chicken, celery, pimento, eggs, salt and poultry seasoning. Cook onion in butter until tender. Blend in flour. Stir in remaining broth, sour cream and mushrooms. Add rice, pour into large greased baking dish. Bake at 325 degrees for 40 minutes. Yield: 4-6 servings.

Mrs. Carolyn Weisheit
Epiphany LWML
Montgomery, Alabama

CHICKEN SUPREME

1 5-lb. stewing chicken
3 c. water
1 med. onion, sliced
1 carrot, scraped and halved
Celery tops
1 tbsp. salt
1 bay leaf
6 tbsp. chicken fat
Butter or margarine
6 tbsp. flour
1 c. whole milk
1 6-oz. can sliced mushrooms
1 4-oz. can pimento, diced
1 ¼ c. slivered almonds, toasted
6 c. cooked rice
1 c. buttered bread crumbs

Simmer chicken in water with onion, carrot, celery tops, salt and bay leaf in large covered kettle for 1 hour to 1 hour and 30 minutes or until tender. Cool chicken in stock; remove from bone and dice. Strain stock into a bowl; chill. Skim off and reserve fat. Pour 1 cup stock over cooked rice in bowl. Let stand. Melt chicken fat in saucepan, adding enough butter or margarine to make 2 tablespoonfuls; blend in flour. Remove from heat; stir in 2 cups chicken stock. Cook over low heat, stirring constantly, until thickened; boil for 1 minute. Remove from heat; gradually stir in milk, undrained mushrooms, pimento, almonds and chicken. Mix rice and chicken mixture in buttered 12-cup casserole. Sprinkle with buttered bread crumbs. Bake at 350 degrees for 50 minutes to 1 hour. Yield: 12-15 servings.

Mrs. Robert Wallin, Treas.
Trinity LCW
New Holland, Pennsylvania

CHICKEN WIGGLE

1 4 to 5-lb. hen
1 ½ qt. broth
1 c. rice
4 onions, diced
1 c. diced celery
1 green pepper, chopped
1 can peas
1 can mushrooms
1 can tomato sauce
1 can cream of celery soup
1 bottle stuffed olives
Salt and pepper to taste
1 c. buttered bread crumbs

Boil hen until tender. Cool in broth; cut into bite-sized pieces. Cook rice, not too done, in 1 quart broth; cool in broth. Saute onions, celery and green pepper in chicken fat. Mix all ingredients except bread crumbs; pour into buttered 10 x 14-inch casserole. Bake in moderate oven for 1 hour. Add buttered crumbs; brown for a few minutes before serving.

Mrs. Ruth Karner, Pres.
Immanuel LWML
Broken Arrow, Oklahoma

HOT CHICKEN SALAD

Diced cooked chicken
1 can cream of chicken soup
2 tbsp. chopped onion or 2 tsp. grated onion
2 tbsp. diced green pepper
1 to 1 ½ c. cooked rice
¼ c. water (opt.)
1 tsp. salt
½ tsp. pepper
¾ c. mayonnaise
½ c. sliced almonds
1 to 3 tsp. lemon juice (opt.)
3 hard-cooked eggs, chopped (opt.)
1 c. diced celery
Pimento
Buttered bread crumbs or shoestring potatoes

Combine all ingredients except crumbs; pour into a greased pan. Cover with buttered bread crumbs. Bake at 350 to 375 degrees for 45 minutes to 1 hour. NOTE: Buttered corn flakes or potato chips may be substituted for bread crumbs. Yield: 8 servings.

Mrs. Herman Merkel
Concordia Lutheran Church
Bourbon, Missouri
Mrs. Edward Hoffman
Faith LCW
Brookfield, Illinois
Mrs. Arnold Wendt, Cor. Sec.
Immanuel Women's Guild
Macomb, Illinois

RICE-CHICKEN CASSEROLE

1 c. instant rice
2 tbsp. diced onion
1 10-oz. pkg. frozen peas
2 c. cooked diced chicken or turkey

1 can cheese soup
1 c. milk
1 c. crushed round cheese crackers
3 tbsp. melted butter

Prepare rice according to package directions, adding onion to boiling water. Fluff rice with fork. Spread into 10 x 6 x 1 1/2-inch baking dish. Sprinkle with peas. Cover with meat. Blend soup and milk. Pour evenly over meat. Combine crumbs and butter; sprinkle over casserole. Bake at 350 degrees for 30 minutes. Yield: 4-6 servings.

Mrs. Elmer Roesener, Pres.
Emmanuel LCW
Goodland, Kansas

SCALLOPED CHICKEN WITH RICE

1 ½ c. diced cooked chicken
2 c. cooked rice
½ c. finely chopped celery
Salt and pepper to taste
2 c. chicken broth
3 eggs, beaten
1 can cream of mushroom soup
Buttered crumbs

Combine chicken, rice, celery, salt and pepper. Mix broth, eggs and soup; pour into chicken mixture. Mix well. Place in buttered baking dish; cover with crumbs. Bake at 350 degrees for 45 minutes. Yield: 8 servings.

Nancy Lu Holler, Treas.
Trinity LWML
Rutherfordton, North Carolina

SCALLOPED CHICKEN

2 c. crushed soda crackers
1 lge. hen, cooked and flaked
1 ½ c. American cheese, cut into chunks
1 ½ c. chopped celery
1 10 ½-oz. can cream of mushroom soup
1 lge. onion, chopped
2 eggs, beaten
4 c. chicken broth
4 crushed Ritz crackers

Place soda crackers in 12 x 15-inch buttered pan. Combine remaining ingredients except Ritz crackers; pour over soda crackers. Top with Ritz crackers. Bake at 350 degrees for 30 minutes. Yield: 20 servings.

Mrs. Cleo Theiler
LWML
Colby, Kansas

SCALLOPED CHICKEN DISH

2 c. chopped cooked or canned chicken
1 c. cream of mushroom soup
1 c. cream of chicken soup
1 can Chinese noodles
½ c. broth or water

(Continued on next page)

Mix chicken with remaining ingredients; place in baking dish. Bake at 350 degrees for 45 minutes. Yield: 6 servings.

Helen M. Carlson
Emmanuel LCW
Napa, California

CALYPSO CHICKEN CASSEROLE

1 pkg. frozen diced chicken
1 can cream of mushroom soup
1 can cream of celery or chicken soup
1 2-oz. can sliced mushrooms, drained
1 10-oz. pkg. frozen mixed vegetables
1 c. flour
1 ½ tsp. baking powder
½ tsp. salt
3 tbsp. shortening, melted
½ c. milk

Combine chicken, soups, mushrooms and mixed vegetables. Place in a 2-quart casserole. Combine flour, baking powder and salt; add shortening and milk. Drop dough by spoonfuls into casserole. Bake at 450 degrees for 45 minutes. Yield: 4-6 servings.

Dorothy H. Goff, VP
Grace Evening Guild
Aurora, Colorado

CHICK AND CHIPS

1 can cream of chicken soup
½ c. milk
1 c. cubed cooked chicken
1 ¼ c. crushed potato chips
1 c. cooked green peas, drained

Pour soup into 1-quart casserole. Add milk; mix thoroughly. Add chicken, 1 cup potato chips and peas; stir well. Sprinkle with remaining potato chips. Bake at 350 degrees for 25 minutes or until heated through. Yield: 4 servings.

Mrs. Donna Prelipp, Pres.
Zion Evangelical Ladies Aid
Oneida, Wisconsin

CHICKEN-BROCCOLI CASSEROLE

6 chicken breasts
2 pkg. frozen broccoli
2 cans cream of chicken soup
2 tbsp. cooking Sherry
2 egg yolks
Slivered almonds

Stew chicken in salted water until tender. Cool and remove bones. Cook broccoli according to directions on package. Place broccoli in shallow baking dish. Cover with chicken breasts. Combine soup, Sherry and egg yolks; pour over chicken. Sprinkle with slivered almonds. Bake

at 350 degrees for 30 minutes. Yield: 6-8 servings.

Phoebe Bylsma, Chmn. Cookbook Comm.
St. Paul Ladies Guild
Montgomery, Alabama

CHICKEN-BROCCOLI CASSEROLE

1 whole chicken or 4 chicken breasts
1 pkg. frozen broccoli
1 can cream of mushroom soup
¼ lb. American or sharp cheese, chopped
1 can French-fried onions

Cook chicken; reserve stock. Remove chicken from bones; cut into pieces. Cook broccoli according to package directions. Combine soup, 1 cup chicken stock and cheese. Heat mixture until cheese is melted. Alternate layers of chicken and broccoli in casserole. Pour cheese mixture over casserole. Bake at 350 degrees for 20 to 30 minutes. Spread onions over top the last 10 minutes of baking time. Yield: 8-10 servings.

Mildred Krager, Historian
St. Michael's LWML
Little Valley, New York

CHICKEN CASSEROLE

2 10-oz. pkg. frozen broccoli spears
2 to 3 c. cooked diced chicken
2 cans cream of chicken soup
1 c. mayonnaise
1 tsp. lemon juice
½ to 1 tsp. curry powder
½ c. shredded sharp American cheese
½ c. soft bread crumbs
1 tbsp. melted butter

Cook broccoli as directed on package; drain. Arrange broccoli in greased 11 1/2 x 7 1/2 x 1 1/2-inch baking dish, placing floweretts along edge of dish. Cover stalks with chicken. Combine soup, mayonnaise, lemon juice and curry powder; pour over chicken. Sprinkle floweretts with cheese. Combine bread crumbs with butter; sprinkle over top. Bake at 350 degrees for 25 to 30 minutes. Garnish as desired. Yield: 6-8 servings.

Mrs. Richard M. Nash, Jr., Pres.
Bethany Ladies Guild
Lompoc, California
Lila A. Scott
Holy Cross LCW
Concord, California

CHICKEN-CORN CASSEROLE

2 c. diced cooked chicken
½ c. diced celery
1 12-oz. can whole kernel corn
¼ c. chopped pimento
1 tbsp. chopped onion
¼ c. fat

183

(Continued on next page)

3 tbsp. flour
1 tsp. salt
1 c. stock
2 eggs, slightly beaten
Green pepper rings
⅔ c. buttered bread crumbs
¼ c. grated cheese

Arrange chicken, celery, corn and pimento in buttered baking dish. Cook onion slightly in hot fat; add flour and salt. Blend; gradually add stock. Cook until smooth and thick, stirring constantly. Quickly stir sauce into eggs. Pour over chicken mixture. Top with g r e e n pepper rings. Mix crumbs with cheese; sprinkle over top. Bake at 350 degrees for 30 minutes. Yield: 10 servings.

Mrs. Irv. Wallschlaeger, Pres.
Zion Ladies Aid
Neshkoro, Wisconsin

CHICKEN DIVAN

2 2½-lb. whole fryers
Seasoning salt
Pepper
3 pkg. frozen broccoli spears
2 cans cream of chicken soup
1 c. mayonnaise
3 tbsp. lemon juice
1 tsp. (heaping) curry powder
2 c. grated sharp Cheddar cheese
Paprika
¼ c. slivered almonds, toasted

Heavily season whole fryers inside and out with seasoning salt and pepper. Place in dry roaster. Bake at 325 degrees for 1 hour and 15 minutes. Cool chicken. Remove bones and skin; slice into long pieces. Place frozen b r o c c o l i spears in salted water; cook until thawed but not done. Combine u n d i l u t e d chicken soup with mayonnaise, lemon juice and curry powder. Drain broccoli; arrange on bottom of a 3-quart rectangular baking dish. Place chicken slices over broccoli; add soup mixture. Top with cheese. Sprinkle with paprika. Bake at 375 degrees for 25 to 30 minutes. Sprinkle almonds on top the last 10 minutes of baking. Let stand for 10 minutes before serving. Yield: 8 servings.

Mrs. Sam W. Sheddan, Pres.
Bethany LCW
Memphis, Tennessee

CHICKEN DIVAN

4 chicken breasts
1 chicken bouillon cube
¼ c. butter or margarine
¼ c. flour
½ tsp. salt
Dash of pepper
¼ c. chicken broth
½ c. heavy cream
3 tbsp. cooking Sherry (opt.)
2 10-oz. pkg. frozen broccoli or asparagus
½ c. grated Parmesan cheese

Boil chicken breasts until tender, adding bouillon cube to water. Cool and s l i c e chicken. Melt butter; add flour, salt and pepper. Mix well. Add broth, stirring until thick. Remove from heat; stir in cream, Sherry and additional salt and pepper. Cook broccoli or asparagus until tender; place crosswise in 13 x 9 x 2-inch baking dish. Pour one-half of sauce over mixture; top with chicken slices. Add cheese to remaining sauce; pour over chicken and sprinkle with additional cheese, if desired. Bake at 350 degrees for 20 minutes or until hot through. Broil until sauce is golden. NOTE: Fresh broccoli or asparagus may be substituted for frozen.

Marjory H. Kirk, Cor. Sec.
Redeemer Ladies Guild
Deming, New Mexico

CHICKEN PIE

3 c. cooked cubed chicken
6 sm. white onions, cooked
1 c. diced cooked carrots
1 tbsp. chopped parsley
1 c. chicken broth
1 c. evaporated milk or milk
2 tbsp. flour
1 tsp. salt
⅛ tsp. pepper

Arrange chicken, onions, carrots and parsley in layers in 1 1/2-quart casserole. Combine broth and milk; add flour. Blend well. Cook until thick, stirring constantly. Season with salt and pepper. Pour over layers in casserole.

SWEET POTATO CRUST:

1 c. flour
1 tsp. baking powder
½ tsp. salt
1 c. cool mashed sweet potatoes
⅓ c. melted butter
1 egg, beaten

Sift flour with baking powder and salt; stir in sweet potatoes, butter and egg. Chill. Roll out to 1/4-inch thick. Place on top of casserole. Bake at 350 degrees for 40 minutes or until crust is brown. Yield: 6-8 servings.

Mrs. Edwin Jacobs
Immanuel LWML
Daykin, Nebraska

CLASSIC CHICKEN DIVAN

2 bunches fresh broccoli or 2 10-oz. pkg.
  frozen broccoli
¼ c. butter or margarine
¼ c. flour
2 c. chicken broth
½ c. light cream
3 tbsp. Sherry wine
½ tsp. salt
Dash of pepper
3 chicken breasts, cooked and thinly sliced
¼ c. grated Parmesan cheese

(Continued on next page)

Cook broccoli in boiling salted water; drain. Melt butter; blend in flour. Add chicken broth until thick. Stir in c r e a m, Sherry, salt and pepper. Place broccoli crosswise in 13 x 9 x 2-inch baking dish. Pour one-half the sauce over broccoli; top with chicken slices. Add Parmesan cheese to remaining sauce; pour over chicken. Sprinkle with additional Parmesan cheese. Bake at 350 degrees for 20 minutes or until heated through. Broil until sauce is golden. Yield: 8 servings.

Mrs. Carl Freund, Sec.
Faith Women's Guild
Eustis, Florida

FRENCH HERBED CHICKEN

1 2 ½ to 3-lb. frying chicken
⅓ c. flour
1 ½ tsp. salt
½ tsp. pepper
Butter or fat
8 sm. whole peeled onions
½ c. coarsely chopped carrots
1 clove of garlic, crushed
3 or 4 sprigs parsley
1 med. bay leaf
¼ tsp. dried thyme or 1 tsp. fresh thyme
2 or 3 sprigs celery leaves
1 c. sliced fresh mushrooms or 1 3-oz. can
    sliced mushrooms
2 c. red Burgundy wine

Coat chicken in mixture of flour, salt and pepper. Brown c h i c k e n in small amount of butter in skillet. Remove chicken. Add onions, carrots and garlic to same skillet. Cover; cook for 5 minutes. Place parsley, bay leaf, thyme and celery leaves in muslin or cheesecloth bag. Place in 3-quart casserole. Add chicken, vegetables and mushrooms in l a y e r s. Add Burgundy wine to skillet in which chicken was browned; heat. Pour over chicken layers. Cover; bake at 350 degrees for 2 hours. Remove bag of herbs. Serve in casserole or remove to heated platter. Garnish with snipped parsley. Yield: 4-6 servings.

Mrs. Frank S. Bramby, Pres.
St. Paul's LCW
Roselle Park, New Jersey

HOT CHICKEN SALAD

2 c. chopped cooked chicken
1 ½ c. diced celery
½ c. chopped English walnuts
2 c. frozen peas, cooked and cooled
3 hard-cooked eggs, diced
¾ c. mayonnaise
1 can cream of chicken soup
1 can chow mein noodles

Combine all ingredients except noodles. Place in 9 x 13-inch baking dish. Cover with chow mein noodles. Bake at 450 degrees for 15 minutes. Yield: 6 servings.

Mrs. Arthur Beeker, Pres.
Zion LCW
Helena, Ohio

SCALLOPED CHICKEN

3 c. peas
2 c. chopped celery
2 tbsp. chopped pimento
2 tsp. salt
6 c. cooked chicken
4 c. broth
8 tbsp. flour
Buttered crackers, crumbled

Add peas, celery, pimento and salt to chicken. Thicken broth with flour. Add to chicken and vegetables. Top with cracker crumbs. Bake at 350 degrees for 1 hour. NOTE: Milk mixed with fat or butter may be substituted for broth.

Harriett Hyde, Chmn.
First Lutheran Church LCW
Sherrard, Illinois

CHICKEN CONTINENTAL

3 to 4 lb. frying chicken pieces
⅓ c. seasoned flour
¼ c. butter
1 can cream of chicken soup
2 ½ tbsp. grated onion
1 tbsp. chopped parsley
1 tsp. salt
⅛ tsp. thyme
½ tsp. celery flakes
1 ⅓ c. water
1 ⅓ c. instant rice

Roll chicken in flour; saute in butter until golden brown. Mix soup, onion and seasonings in saucepan; gradually stir in water. Bring to a boil stirring constantly. Pour rice into a shallow 2-quart casserole. Stir all except 1/3 cup soup mixture into rice; top with chicken. Pour remaining soup mixture over chicken. Cover; bake at 375 degrees for 30 minutes. Sprinkle with paprika. Yield: 4 servings.

Mrs. Margaret Knock
Good Shepherd LCW
Ashland, Pennsylvania

CHICKEN DELIGHT

2 med. frying chickens
1 c. flour
2 tbsp. shortening
4 green onions, chopped
1 green pepper, chopped
1 2-oz. can pimento, chopped
1 10-oz. can cream of mushroom soup
1 tbsp. salt
Monosodium glutamate

(Continued on next page)

Cut chickens into serving pieces; roll in flour. Brown in shortening. Place chicken in a 2-quart casserole; sprinkle onions, green pepper and pimento over chicken. Pour soup over all; sprinkle with salt and monosodium glutamate. Bake at 350 degrees for 1 hour. Yield: 8-10 servings.

Rosalind Shenk, Sec.
St. Paul's LCW
Detroit, Michigan

CHICKEN HAMBURGER

2 lb. uncooked chicken
1 lge. onion, ground
2 tsp. salt
¼ tsp. pepper
Flour
2 eggs
½ c. tomato juice or water

Grind chicken and onion; add salt, pepper, 1 cup flour and eggs. Mix. Form into 10 patties; roll in flour. Brown in hot fat. Place meat in casserole or roaster; add tomato juice. Cover; bake at 325 degrees for 1 hour and 30 minutes. Yield: 5 servings.

Mrs. Harold Micanek
Christ Lutheran Church Mary and Martha Soc.
Lynch, Nebraska

CHICKEN WITH PINEAPPLE

1 roasting chicken, cut into serving pieces
½ tsp. marjoram
½ tsp. salt
1 10-oz. can mushrooms, drained
½ c. chopped green pepper
½ c. diced celery
¼ c. chopped onion
½ c. pineapple chunks

Brown chicken in frying pan. Arrange in casserole. Sprinkle with marjoram, salt and mushrooms. Drain off excess fat. Cover tightly; bake at 325 degrees for 2 hours. Add green pepper, celery, onion and pineapple 30 minutes before serving. Yield: 4-5 servings.

Mrs. H. A. Olson, Pres.
Grace LCW
Medicine Hat, Alberta, Canada

CHICKEN AND RICE

1 c. rice
1 fryer chicken, cut into serving pieces
1 can cream of mushroom soup
1 soup can water
1 envelope onion soup mix
Paprika
Barbecue sauce (opt.)

Sprinkle rice on bottom of buttered casserole. Place chicken on rice. Mix mushroom soup, water and onion soup mix; pour over chicken and rice. Sprinkle with paprika and barbecue sauce.

Cover pan with foil. Bake at 350 degrees for 1 hour and 30 minutes. NOTE: This may be prepared in advance. Yield: 6 servings.

Mrs. Henry W. Klans, Pres.
Immanuel LWML
Salisburg, Missouri

CHICKEN AND RICE CASSEROLE

8 pieces chicken
Salt and pepper to taste
Margarine or shortening
½ c. uncooked rice
1 can cream of mushroom soup
1 ½ soup cans water
1 tsp. chopped pimento

Wash and dry chicken pieces; sprinkle with salt and pepper. Brown in a small amount of margarine or shortening. Place in a greased 8 x 12 x 2-inch pan. Sprinkle rice over chicken. Mix soup and water; pour over chicken and rice. Sprinkle with additional salt and pepper. Add pimento. Cover with foil. Bake at 325 degrees for 1 hour. Uncover and bake for 15 minutes longer. Increase heat to 350 degrees and bake for 15 minutes to brown. Add a small amount water or chicken broth to pan if mixture becomes dry. Yield: 4 servings.

Mrs. Menta Diebel
Grace Altar Guild
Victoria, Texas

CHICKEN 'N' RICE BAKE

1 chicken, cut into serving pieces
Salt and pepper to taste
1 stick margarine
1 med. onion, chopped
1 med. green pepper, chopped
4 chicken bouillon cubes
1 c. long grain rice
1 ½ c. water

Season chicken with salt and pepper; brown in margarine. Saute onion and green pepper in margarine after removing chicken. Crush bouillon cubes with fork; add to onion mixture. Stir in rice. Add 1/2 teaspoonful salt and the water. Place in baking pan. Place chicken on top of rice. Cover with foil. Bake at 250 degrees for 1 hour and 30 minutes.

Mrs. Ed Shingler
Holy Trinity Ladies Aid
Blackduck, Minnesota

CHICKEN RICE

1 ½ c. uncooked rice
1 pkg. dry onion soup mix
2 cans chicken with rice soup
1 ½ soup cans water
1 fryer, cut up
Margarine

(Continued on next page)

Combine rice, soups and water. Pour into greased 9 x 16-inch pan. Arrange chicken, skin-side up, over mixture. Brush with melted margarine. Bake at 350 degrees for 1 hour and 30 minutes. Yield: 4-6 servings.

Mrs. Richard Kelto, Pres.
Ruth Guild-Trinity National
Milwaukee, Wisconsin

CHICKEN-RICE-BAKE

1 c. uncooked rice
1 pkg. dry onion soup mix
1 can chicken with rice soup
1 soup can water
1 sm. can mushrooms, drained
1 2 ½-lb. frying chicken or 2 ½ to 3 lb.
   chicken pieces
¼ c. butter, melted
1 c. instant chicken bouillon

Spread rice over bottom of 7 x 11-inch glass baking dish. Add soups and water; mix well. Add mushrooms. Place chicken on top. Gently pour melted butter over chicken. Bake at 350 degrees for 1 hour. Pour bouillon over chicken; bake for 30 minutes longer. Serve in baking dish. Yield: 6 servings.

Mrs. Otto F. Stahlke
Immanuel Ladies Aid
Springfield, Illinois

CHICKEN WITH RICE

½ c. uncooked rice
2 c. chicken broth
2 c. chopped celery
¼ c. chopped onion
2 c. coarsely chopped cooked chicken
1 can cream of mushroom soup
1 tbsp. soy sauce
Bread cubes
Melted butter

Mix rice with chicken broth. Place in 2-quart dish. Bake at 350 degrees for 20 minutes. Add celery and onion. Bake for an additional 20 minutes. Add chicken, mushroom soup and soy sauce. Bake for 40 minutes longer. Roll bread cubes in butter; spread over chicken mixture the last 15 minutes of baking. Yield: 6-8 servings.

Mrs. Harold Bartz, Pres.
Zion Evangelical Ladies Aid
Oconto, Wisconsin

CHICKEN ON SUNDAY

1 can cream of celery soup
2 cans cream of mushroom soup
¾ c. milk
4 c. instant rice
1 frying chicken, cut-up
1 envelope dry onion soup mix

Combine soups and milk; add rice. Mix well. Place one-half the mixture in a greased 9 x 12-inch baking pan. Lay chicken on mixture; cover with remaining mixture. Sprinkle dry soup mix on top. Seal pan with foil. Bake at 325 degrees for 2 hours and 15 minutes. Yield: 6 servings.

Joyce Schroer, VP
Our Savior LWML
Red Oak, Iowa

CHICKEN TERIYAKI

2 sm. fryers
¾ c. soya sauce
½ c. sugar
1 tsp. grated ginger
1 clove of garlic, grated
½ tsp. monosodium glutamate

Cut chickens into serving pieces. Combine all remaining ingredients; marinate chickens overnight in refrigerator in mixture. Place chicken pieces on broiler rack. Bake at 350 degrees for 1 hour, basting with marinade once. Yield: 8 servings.

Louise Hullinger, Pres.
Mt. Greenwood Ladies Aid Soc.
Chicago, Illinois

CHICKEN WITH TINY BISCUITS

1 ½ qt. frozen cooked chicken with broth,
   thawed
3 tbsp. butter
2 ¼ c. flour
½ c. milk
Salt and pepper
2 ½ tsp. baking powder
¼ tsp. soda
6 tbsp. shortening
¾ c. sour milk

Drain chicken; reserve 2 cups broth. Melt butter in heavy saucepan. Add 1/4 cup flour; blend until smooth. Gradually add 2 cups broth and 1/2 cup milk. Cook until thickened, stirring constantly. Add salt and pepper to taste. Arrange chicken in 6 x 10-inch dish. Pour gravy over chicken. Mix 2 cups flour with baking powder and soda; cut in shortening. Add sour milk; roll out. Cut into small biscuits. Arrange biscuits on casserole. Bake at 400 degrees for 25 to 30 minutes. Yield: 6 servings.

Mrs. Dale Major, Pres.
LWML
Lyons, Kansas

CREAMED CHICKEN

1 5 to 6-lb. chicken
Diced onion
Diced celery
1 c. water
Salt and pepper
Cream sauce
1 sm. can mushrooms, cut into small pieces

(Continued on next page)

Place chicken in pressure cooker. Mix onion with celery to make 1/4 cup. Add with water to chicken. Add salt and pepper. Pressure cook for 25 minutes at 15 pounds pressure. Remove chicken, reserving broth. Let chicken cool. Remove bones; cut into small pieces. Make cream sauce using one-half broth and one-half milk. Add mushrooms; stir. Pour cream sauce over chicken; stir. Bake at 250 to 300 degrees for 30 minutes. Serve over pattie shells. Yield: 8 servings.

Mrs. Leona Nagel, Pres.
St. John's Ladies Aid
Red Bud, Illinois

CREAMED CHICKEN-BISCUIT RING

Butter
Flour
3 c. warm chicken stock
2 ½ c. milk
Salt
¼ tsp. pepper
¼ tsp. paprika
3 c. diced cooked chicken
2 tbsp. baking powder
½ c. sliced green stuffed olives
¼ c. pimento, cut into 1-in. squares

Melt 1/3 cup butter; add flour to form a smooth paste. Add chicken stock; blend well. Add 1/2 cup milk, salt to taste, pepper and paprika; cook until thick. Add chicken. Cook for 5 minutes or until thick. Sift 4 1/2 cups flour with baking powder and 1 1/2 teaspoonfuls salt; cut in 1/2 cup butter until mixture resembles meal. Add 2 cups milk; beat vigorously with spoon for 30 seconds. Pour into greased 9 1/2 x 2-inch ring mold; fill with chicken mixture. Garnish with olives and pimento. Bake at 350 degrees for 30 minutes. Increase temperature to 450 degrees and bake for 15 minutes longer or until brown. Let stand in mold for several minutes. Turn out onto large warm platter. Yield: 6 servings.

Ida G. Burgquist, Pres.
Bethany LCW Priscilla Cir.
Chicago, Illinois

DELICIOUS BAKED CHICKEN

¾ c. butter or margarine
¼ c. water
1 4-lb. frying chicken
1 3-oz. pkg. onion soup mix

Line a 9 x 12-inch glass cake pan with foil. Spread one-half the butter over foil; add water. Wash chicken, but do not dry. Cut into 12 pieces; lay on greased foil, skin-side up. Sprinkle onion soup over the chicken pieces. Dot with remaining butter. Seal with an additional piece of foil, making sure steam cannot escape. Bake in preheated 300 degree oven for 1 hour and 30 minutes. Yield: 4 servings.

Mrs. Emma Ullrich
Christ Lutheran Church Ladies Aid Soc.
Young, Saskatchewan, Canada

EASY CHICKEN

Salt
Flour
1 lge. fryer, cut up
Fat
½ c. water

Salt and flour chicken; brown quickly in hot fat. Place in casserole; add water. Bake at 350 degrees for 1 hour and 30 minutes or until tender. Yield: 6 servings.

Mt. T. F. Rampmaier
St. John's Ladies Aid
Iota, Louisiana

EASY CHICKEN CACCIATORE

1 frying chicken, cut up
1 1-lb. can meatless chicken-spaghetti sauce
1 onion, sliced
1 green pepper, thinly sliced
¼ c. brown sugar

Brown chicken in small amount of oil; place in baking dish or pan. Pour spaghetti sauce over chicken. Place onion and green pepper on top of chicken. Sprinkle with brown sugar. Bake at 350 degrees for 1 hour. Yield: 3-4 servings.

Mrs. Elsie Keckstein, Pres.
Prince of Peace LWML
Oregon, Ohio

FINGER LICKIN' CHICKEN DISH

1 2 ½-lb. fryer, cut up or chicken parts
½ c. flour
½ tsp. salt
¼ tsp. pepper
½ tsp. paprika
½ c. butter or margarine
2 cans cream of chicken soup
1 1-lb. can cooked onions, undrained
1 or 2 4-oz. cans mushroom stems and
    pieces, undrained
2 tbsp. chopped pimento
1 tbsp. chopped parsley
¼ c. dry Sherry wine

Dredge chicken in mixture of flour, salt, pepper and paprika. Melt butter in 9 x 13-inch baking dish. Place chicken in dish, skin-side up. Bake at 400 degrees for 30 minutes. Heat chicken soup, onions, mushrooms, pimento, parsley and Sherry to boiling. Turn chicken pieces; pour sauce over chicken. Bake for 35 to 45 minutes longer or until well browned. Yield: 4-6 servings.

Mrs. Richard J. Tuff, Pres.
Christ Lutheran Church LCW
Saldatna, Alaska

FORGOTTEN CHICKEN

½ c. uncooked wild or brown rice
½ c. uncooked white rice
1 pkg. onion soup mix

(Continued on next page)

1 2½ to 3-lb. fryer, cut up
1 can cream of chicken soup
3½ c. water

Place wild and white rice in large casserole; add onion soup mix and chicken. Dilute soup with water; pour over rice and chicken. Bake at 300 degrees for 2 hours and 30 minutes to 3 hours. Yield: 4 servings.

Mrs. Robert Fuller, Pres.
Our Savior LWML
Butler, Alabama

ONION-FLAVORED CHICKEN

2 c. instant rice
2 fryers, cut up
1 can cream of mushroom soup
1 can cream of celery soup
1 soup can milk
1 pkg. dry onion soup mix

Place rice in bottom of rectangular cake pan; lay chicken pieces on rice. Pour mushroom and celery soups evenly over chicken; add milk. Sprinkle onion soup mix over top. Bake at 350 degrees for 1 hour. Yield: 8 servings.

Jane Riedel, Treas.
Messiah LCW Assn.
Cocoa, Florida

CHEESE-FLAVORED CHICKEN

8 pieces chicken
2 c. Italian bread crumbs
⅓ c. grated Parmesan cheese
¼ c. grated Romano cheese
1 tsp. salt
½ to 1 tsp. garlic salt
¼ tsp. pepper
1 egg, slightly beaten
¼ c. water
2 to 3 c. oil

Wash chicken; dry with paper towel. Combine crumbs, cheeses, salt, garlic salt and pepper. Mix egg and water. Dip chicken pieces into egg mixture; roll in bread crumb mixture. Brown on both sides in hot oil. Drain off excess oil. Cover chicken. Bake at 375 degrees for 45 minutes. To crispen chicken, remove lid and increase temperature to 400 degrees and bake for 20 minutes. Yield: 4 servings.

Joyce Weston
Christ the King LCW
Youngstown, Ohio

CHICKEN A LA MODE

Chicken breasts
Melted butter
Salt and pepper
Crushed potato chips

Wash breasts and wipe dry. Dip into melted butter; salt and pepper. Roll until completely covered in crumbs. Lay chicken in rows in buttered baking dish. Bake at 350 degrees for 1 hour.

Mrs. Martin Nielsen, Pres.
First English Evangelical LCW
Grosse Pointe Park, Michigan

CHICKEN CRUNCH

1 can cream of mushroom soup
¾ c. milk
1 tbsp. finely chopped onion
1 tbsp. chopped parsley
1 c. fine dry bread crumbs
½ tsp. poultry dressing
½ tsp. salt
2 lb. chicken parts
2 tbsp. melted butter

Mix 1/2 cup soup, 1/4 cup milk, onion and parsley. Combine bread crumbs, poultry seasoning and salt. Dip chicken into soup mixture; roll in crumbs. Place in 12 x 8 x 2-inch baking dish. Drizzle butter on chicken. Bake at 400 degrees for 1 hour. Combine remaining soup and milk. Heat, stirring occasionally. Serve over chicken. NOTE: One package herb-seasoned stuffing, finely crushed, may be substituted for bread crumb mixture. Yield: 4-6 servings.

Mrs. Albert Welp
Wray Calvary Mission Guild
Wray, Colorado

CHICKEN DELIGHT

1 to 2 chickens, cut up
1 c. evaporated milk
2 c. crushed corn flake crumbs
2 tbsp. salt

Roll chicken pieces in evaporated milk; roll in corn flake crumbs with salt. Spread foil on cookie sheet; place chicken on foil. Bake at 350 degrees for 1 hour. Yield: 6 servings.

Mrs. Otto Boehme, Pres.
Mt. Calvary LWML
Eagle Grove, Iowa

CHICKEN DIABLE

1 3-lb. broiler-fryer, cut up
4 tbsp. butter or margarine
½ c. honey
¼ c. prepared mustard
1 tsp. salt
1 tsp. curry powder

Wash chicken pieces; pat dry and remove skin, if desired. Melt butter or margarine in a shallow baking pan; stir in remaining ingredients. Roll chicken pieces in butter mixture to coat both

(Continued on next page)

sides; arrange, meaty-side up, in a single layer in same pan. Bake at 375 degrees for 1 hour or until chicken is tender and richly glazed. Yield: 4 servings.

Rebie Reeves, Pres.
Summer Memorial LCW
Newberry, South Carolina
Mrs. Eve Kadrovach
Grace Mary Martha Soc.
Elk Rapids, Michigan

CORN-CRISPED CHICKEN

1 c. corn flake crumbs
1 tsp. salt
¼ tsp. pepper
1 2½ to 3-lb. fryer, cut up
½ c. evaporated milk
4 Cling peach halves, drained

Combine crumbs, salt and pepper. Dip chicken into milk; roll in crumbs. Place in foil-lined pan. Bake at 350 degrees for 50 minutes. Do not crowd chicken. Add peaches; bake for 10 minutes longer. Yield: 6 servings.

Mrs. Eva Kreft, Sec.
St. Peter's Ladies Aid
Sac City, Iowa

CORN-CRISPED CHICKEN

1 broiler-fryer chicken, cut into serving
    pieces
1 c. corn flake crumbs
1 ½ tsp. salt
¼ tsp. pepper
½ c. evaporated milk

Wash and dry chicken. Combine corn flake crumbs with salt and pepper. Dip chicken into milk, then roll in seasoned crumbs. Place chicken, skin-side up, on foil-lined pan. Do not crowd. Bake at 350 degrees for 1 to 2 hours or until tender. Cover lightly with foil the last 45 minutes of baking, if desired. Yield: 4-5 servings.

Mrs. Ervin F. Basner, Pres.
St. Peters Ladies Aid Soc.
Hemlock, Michigan
Mrs. Gerald C. Radtke
Grace Ladies Aid
Correll, Minnesota
Mrs. Susanna Weber
Paradise Ladies Aid Soc.
Reynoldsville, Pennsylvania
Mrs. Cora Adolph
St. Paul's Evangelical Lutheran Church
McCreary, Manitoba, Canada

CORNHUSKER FRIED CHICKEN

1 2½-lb. chicken, cut up
Salt
1 tsp. paprika
Flour
¼ lb. butter

Roll chicken in seasoned flour. Slice butter into 8 x 12-inch baking dish. Bake at 350 degrees for 45 minutes. Turn chicken; continue baking for 45 minutes. NOTE: Place under broiler for last 20 minutes for more golden brown chicken.

Mrs. Herman Katz, Pres.
Trinity Ladies Aid
Jansen, Nebraska

CRISPY CHICKEN

1 can cream of mushroom soup
¾ c. milk
1 tbsp. finely chopped onion
1 tbsp. chopped parsley
2 lb. chicken pieces
1 c. finely crushed packaged herb-seasoned
    stuffing or bread crumbs
2 tbsp. melted butter or margarine

Mix 1/3 cup soup with 1/4 cup milk, onion and parsley. Dip chicken into soup mixture; roll in stuffing. Place in shallow 12 x 8 x 2-inch baking dish; drizzle butter on chicken. Bake at 400 degrees for 1 hour. Combine remaining soup and milk; heat. Stir occasionally. Serve over chicken, if desired. Yield: 4-6 servings.

Mrs. Robert Breslin, VP
Eternal LWML
Milton, Florida

CRISP OVEN-FRIED CHICKEN

1 3½-lb. broiler-fryer
3 tbsp. flour
3 tbsp. flour
3 tbsp. yellow corn meal
1 ½ tsp. salt
¼ tsp. pepper
1 ½ tsp. dried crushed rosemary leaves
¼ tsp. paprika
¼ c. evaporated milk
Fat

Wash chicken; cut into serving pieces. Dry well on paper towels. Combine flour, corn meal, salt, pepper, rosemary and paprika in shallow pan; blend well. Pour milk into separate shallow pan. Dip chicken pieces into milk; roll in flour mixture, coating well. Heat fat in large skillet; fry chicken in hot fat, browning lightly. Remove to shallow roasting pan. Bake in preheated 350 degree oven for 40 to 45 minutes or until chicken is golden brown, tender and crisp. Yield: 4 servings.

Mrs. Emil Schad
St. John's Ladies Aid
Purdy, Missouri

CRUSTY BAKED CHICKEN

2 frying chickens, quartered
2 c. Rice Krispies
½ tsp. salt
½ tsp. pepper

190

(Continued on next page)

1 tbsp. monosodium glutamate
1 tsp. parsley flakes
1 can evaporated milk
¼ c. cooking oil

Wash chickens; pat dry with paper towels. Roll Rice Krispies until fine. Add salt, pepper, monosodium glutamate and parsley flakes; mix well. Combine milk and oil in large mixing bowl. Dip chicken into milk mixture; roll in Rice Krispie mixture. Place coated chicken parts, skin-side up, in shallow baking pan or cookie sheet with aluminum foil covering. Pour remaining milk and oil over chicken. Bake at 375 degrees for 1 hour or until golden brown and tender. Yield: 8 servings.

Mrs. Fred W. Badger
Concordia Lutheran Church
Manchester, Connecticut

CRUSTY FRIED CHICKEN

1 3-lb. frying chicken
2 pkg. dry garlic salad dressing mix
3 tbsp. flour
2 tsp. salt
¼ c. lemon juice
2 tbsp. soft butter
1 c. milk
1 ½ c. pancake mix
Fat or salad oil

Clean and wipe chicken with damp paper towel. Combine salad dressing mix, flour and salt in small mixing bowl. Mix lemon juice with butter to a smooth paste. Brush all sides of chicken pieces with lemon juice mixture. Place in bowl; cover. Refrigerate overnight. Dip chicken into milk, then into pancake mix. Coat well. Dust off excess pancake mix. Brown lightly in 1/4 to 1/2 inch fat in large skillet or Dutch oven. Place in baking dish. Spoon one-half the remaining milk over chicken. Bake, covered, at 375 degrees for 30 minutes. Baste with remaining milk. Cook, uncovered, for 30 minutes longer. Yield: 8 servings.

Mrs. Thomas Davis Taylor, Pres.
Ebenezer LCW
Columbia, South Carolina

EASY OVEN-FRIED CHICKEN

1 chicken, cut up
1 ½ sticks margarine
1 c. prepared biscuit mix
1 tsp. salt
Pepper to taste
1 tsp. paprika

Wash chicken; leave moist. Melt margarine in glass baking dish or broiler pan. Place prepared biscuit mix and seasonings in paper sack. Shake chicken in sack. Place coated chicken pieces in pan. Bake at 425 degrees for 20 to 25 minutes. Turn. Reduce heat to 350 degrees and continue

cooking for 45 minutes to 1 hour or until tender. Yield: 4-5 servings.

Mrs. Eugene Meyer, Pres.
Algona Zone LWML Iowa Dist. West
Burt, Iowa

DELICIOUS CHICKEN

1 frying chicken, cut into serving pieces
1 stick margarine or butter
1 pt. Rice Krispies, ground or finely rolled
Salt and pepper

Brush each piece of chicken with melted margarine or butter, using pastry brush. Roll in Rice Krispie crumbs. Season to taste. Place in shallow pan. Bake at 325 to 350 degrees for 1 hour to 1 hour and 20 minutes or until done. Turn chicken to brown both sides.

Mrs. Harry Demien
Immanuel Lutheran Church
Wentzville, Missouri
Mrs. Orville Goebel
St. Peter's Ladies Aid
Mishawaka, Indiana

OVEN-FRIED CHICKEN

1 2 ½ to 3-lb. broiler-fryer, cut up
¼ c. flour
1 ½ tsp. salt
¼ tsp. pepper
1 tsp. paprika
1 ½ tsp. curry powder
1 ½ tsp. poultry seasoning
½ c. butter

Wipe chicken with damp cloth. Combine flour, salt, pepper, paprika, curry powder and poultry seasoning in plastic bag. Shake two or three chicken pieces at a time in seasoned flour. Place butter in large shallow pan; melt in oven. Place chicken, skin-side down, in pan. Bake in preheated 450 degree oven for 30 minutes. Turn chicken; bake for 15 minutes longer. Yield: 4 servings.

Mrs. Ferne Gatenby, Pres.
Mary and Martha Soc.
Barrie, Ontario, Canada

OVEN-FRIED CHICKEN

1 fryer, cut into pieces
Salad oil
Crushed crackers or corn flakes
2 tbsp. corn meal
Salt and pepper to taste
Paprika to taste
Dash of basil

Dip chicken pieces into salad oil. Combine crushed crackers and corn meal. Roll chicken in crumb mixture. Place on foil-lined shallow baking pan; sprinkle with salt, pepper, paprika and basil. Bake at 325 degrees for 1 hour to 1

(Continued on next page)

hour and 30 minutes or until golden brown. Do not turn or baste. Yield: 4-6 servings.

Mrs. Jane Boren, Pres.
Our Savior Women's Guild
Carbondale, Illinois

OVEN-FRIED CHICKEN

1 2 ½ to 3-lb. fryer, cut up
Salt
¼ lb. butter, melted
Cracker crumbs

Sprinkle chicken with salt; dip into butter. Roll in crumbs. Place chicken in shallow baking dish; drizzle with remaining butter. Bake at 350 degrees for 1 hour. Yield: 4-5 servings.

Mrs. Wallace Kahler, Pres.
St. John's LWML
Brunswick, Missouri

OVEN-FRIED CHICKEN

½ lb. margarine or butter
½ tsp. pepper
2 c. crushed potato chips
6 chicken legs

Melt margarine; combine pepper with crushed potato chips. Dip chicken legs into melted butter; roll in potato chips. Place on a cookie sheet or shallow pan. Bake at 350 degrees for 1 hour. Yield: 6 servings.

Mrs. Earl Schmidt
St. John's Ladies Aid
Taylor, Michigan

OVEN-FRIED CHICKEN

1 c. plus 2 tbsp. flour
2 tsp. paprika (opt.)
2 tsp. salt
¼ tsp. pepper
1 fryer chicken, cut into serving pieces
½ c. margarine, melted
1 ½ c. hot water

Place 1 cup flour, paprika, salt and pepper in paper bag; add chicken. Shake until well coated. Place chicken pieces, skin-side down, in single layer in margarine in 13 x 9 1/2 x 2-inch pan. Bake in preheated 425 degree oven for 45 minutes. Turn; bake for 15 minutes longer. Blend remaining flour into pan drippings; add water. Boil for 1 minute. Serve with chicken.

Mrs. M. H. Ewing
Rehoboth Beach LWML
Bay Vista, Delaware

OVEN-FRIED CHICKEN WITH PECAN CRUST

1 2 ½ to 3-lb. broiler-fryer, cut up
1 c. biscuit mix
1 ½ tsp. salt
1 tsp. paprika
½ tsp. poultry seasoning
½ c. finely chopped pecans
½ c. evaporated milk
½ c. melted butter

Wash chicken and pat dry. Combine biscuit mix, seasonings and pecans. Dip chicken into evaporated milk, then into biscuit mixture. Place in 13 x 9-inch shallow baking dish; pour melted butter over pieces. Bake, uncovered, at 375 degrees for 1 hour. Yield: 4 servings.

Mrs. Ralph Aga
First LCW
Waco, Texas

PARMESAN ITALIAN-FRIED CHICKEN

1 fryer chicken, cut up
1 egg
2 tbsp. water
½ c. flour
½ c. grated Parmesan cheese
1 ½ tsp. salt
1 tsp. oregano
Dash of pepper
2 tbsp. butter or margarine, melted

Dip chicken into egg beaten with water. Combine flour, Parmesan cheese, salt, oregano and pepper. Roll chicken in mixture. Arrange chicken in baking dish with melted butter. Bake at 400 degrees for 45 minutes, brushing occasionally with melted butter. Sprinkle with additional Parmesan cheese before serving.

Mrs. Lois Wegner
Zion Ladies Aid
Scotia, Nebraska

OVEN-FRIED PARMESAN CHICKEN

1 c. crushed herb-seasoned stuffing mix
⅔ c. grated Parmesan cheese
¼ c. snipped parsley
1 2 ½ to 3-lb. broiler-fryer, cut up
½ c. butter or margarine, melted

Combine crushed stuffing, cheese and parsley. Dip chicken pieces into melted butter or margarine; roll in stuffing mixture. Arrange chicken pieces, skin-side up, on large shallow baking pan. Sprinkle with remaining butter and crumbs. Bake at 375 degrees for 45 minutes or until tender. Do not turn chicken while baking. Yield: 4 servings.

Mrs. Paul Weiss, Pres.
Faith Women's League
York, Nebraska

ROAST CHICKEN WITH GARLIC

1 chicken, cut into pieces
4 tbsp. melted margarine
2 c. crushed potato chips
Salt and pepper to taste
Garlic powder to taste

Dip pieces of chicken into melted margarine; roll in potato chip crumbs. Sprinkle with salt, pepper and garlic powder. Roast at 275 degrees for about 2 hours or until tender.

Eleanor Wangelin, Pres.
Redeemer LWML
Colden, New York

SOUTHERN OVEN-FRIED CHICKEN

1 4-oz. pkg. potato chips, crushed
¼ tsp. garlic salt
Dash of pepper
1 2 ½ to 3-lb. frying chicken, cut up
⅓ c. melted butter or margarine

Combine crushed chips and seasonings. Dip chicken into melted butter; roll in chip mixture. Place pieces, skin-side up, so pieces do not touch in greased shallow pan or jelly roll pan. Bake at 375 degrees for 1 hour or until tender. Do not turn chicken while baking. Yield: 8 servings.

Mrs. Ella Tallman
St. Timothy LCW
Columbus, Ohio

GEORGIA CHICKEN

2 broiling chickens, quartered or 4 breasts
   and 4 legs
1 2-lb. can Cling peach halves, undrained
2 tbsp. lemon juice
1 tbsp. Worcestershire sauce
1 ½ tsp. salt

Dry chicken pieces; arrange on rack in single layer in 12 x 8 x 2-inch baking pan. Drain 3/4 cup syrup from peaches; add lemon juice and Worcestershire sauce. Brush chicken with one-half the syrup mixture; sprinkle with salt. Bake in preheated 400 degree oven for 1 hour or until chicken is tender and rich golden brown. Baste every 15 minutes with remaining syrup mixture and pan juices. Place peach halves around chicken; brush with pan juices and remaining syrup mixture. Bake for 5 minutes or until peaches are heated. Yield: 8 servings.

Mrs. Robert Macdonald, Pres.
Good Shepherd LCW
Norwalk, Connecticut

HAWAIIAN CHICKEN

1 pkg. dry onion soup mix
1 can cream of chicken soup
2 soup cans water
¾ c. rice
1 ½ tsp. soy sauce
1 fryer, cut up

Combine soups, water, rice and soy sauce in 9 x 13-inch pan. Place chicken, bony-side up, in pan; turn when brown. Bake at 350 degrees for 2 hours. Yield: 5-6 servings.

Mrs. June Strand, Sec.
Good Shepherd LCW
Eugene, Oregon

HUNGARIAN STUFFED CHICKEN

1 4-lb. chicken
9 slices Vienna bread
1 med. onion, chopped
¾ stick butter
2 tbsp. chopped parsley
1 tsp. salt
½ tsp. pepper
½ tsp. paprika
4 eggs, separated
2 uncooked chicken livers, finely chopped

Wash and salt chicken. Soak bread in a small amount water; drain and squeeze. Place bread in a large bowl. Saute onion in butter until tender; add to bread. Add parsley and seasonings. Beat egg yolks; add to bread mixture with chopped livers. Mix well. Beat egg whites until stiff; fold into stuffing mixture. Loosen skin from breasts carefully, using a knife. Spoon stuffing between skin and meat; fill breast cavities with remaining stuffing. Sew up opening; rub well with butter. Bake at 350 degrees for 2 hours, basting occasionally. Yield: 4-6 servings.

Mrs. Mary Silk, VP
Holy Trinity Parma Faith Guild
Cleveland, Ohio

CHICKEN LOAF

1 qt. chopped cooked chicken
1 qt. chopped celery
2 c. soft bread crumbs
2 c. cooked rice
¼ c. diced pimento
5 eggs, beaten
1 can cream of mushroom soup
1 can cream of chicken soup
1 tsp. lemon juice
1 tsp. salt
Pepper
¼ c. butter or chicken fat
3 c. broth or milk

Combine chicken, celery, bread crumbs, rice, pimento and eggs. Pour into loaf pan. Bake at 325 degrees for 1 hour and 15 minutes. Cool; cover with sauce made of remaining ingredients. Serve hot or cold. Yield: 8-10 servings.

Mrs. John H. Dubbels
St. John's Ladies Aid
Stewartville, Minnesota

CHICKEN LOAF

1 c. hot chicken broth
2 eggs, slightly beaten
1 c. bread crumbs
2 tbsp. chicken fat
3 c. ground cooked chicken
¼ c. finely chopped celery
3 tbsp. finely chopped onion
¾ tsp. salt
¼ tsp. pepper

Gradually stir a small amount hot broth into eggs; return to broth. Add bread crumbs and chicken fat; mix well. Add remaining ingredients. Pour into an 8 x 4 x 2-inch loaf pan. Bake at 325 degrees for 1 hour or until firm. Yield: 6 servings.

Mrs. Elfred Detmer, Pres.
Mary and Martha Cir. LCW
Chapin, Illinois

CHICKEN LOAF

4 c. ground cooked chicken
1 c. milk
1 sm. onion, chopped
½ tsp. sage
2 c. soft bread crumbs
2 eggs, beaten
1 c. chicken broth
Salt to taste

Mix all ingredients. Place in 9 1/2 x 5-inch loaf pan. Bake at 350 degrees for 1 hour. Yield: 10 servings.

Mrs. Mildred Oberjohnn, Pres.
St. John's Ladies Aid Soc.
Kampsville, Illinois

CHICKEN LOAF

1 4 to 5-lb. chicken
2 c. soft bread crumbs
1 c. cooked rice
1 tsp. salt
½ tsp. paprika
½ c. chopped pimento (opt.)
4 eggs, well beaten
¼ c. butter or chicken fat

Cook chicken; reserve 2 1/2 cups broth. Cool and dice chicken. Mix remaining ingredients. Place in 9 x 13 x 2-inch pan. Bake at 325 degrees for 1 hour. Cut into squares or slices. Serve with chicken gravy or mushroom sauce. Yield: 10 servings.

Mrs. C. C. Kiziah
New Jerusalem LCW
Hickory, North Carolina

EASY CHICKEN LOAF

2 c. diced cooked chicken
1 c. soft bread cubes or ¾ c. rice plus ½ c.

soft bread cubes
1 c. milk or broth
1 tsp. chopped green pepper
2 tbsp. cooked chopped celery
½ tsp. salt
⅛ tsp. paprika
2 tbsp. melted butter
2 eggs, well beaten
1 can cream of mushroom soup

Mix all ingredients except soup; place in a well greased 8 x 8-inch pan. Set in a pan of water. Bake at 375 degrees for 45 minutes or until firm. Serve with mushroom sauce made with diluted mushroom soup. Yield: 4-6 servings.

Mrs. Frieda Magnor
Trinity Ladies Aid Soc.
Mt. Rainier, Maryland

ELEGANT CHICKEN LOAF

4 c. chicken broth
6 c. cooked rice
3 c. milk
6 c. chopped cooked chicken
2 cans cream of mushroom soup
4 tbsp. butter
¾ c. flour
1 tbsp. salt
⅛ tsp. pepper
Blanched almonds
1 sm. can pimento (opt.)

Make gravy of broth, flour, butter and milk; mix with remaining ingredients. Place in a large casserole. Bake in moderate oven for 45 minutes. minutes.

Mrs. John Wolff
Bethlehem LWML
Maple Lake, Minnesota

PATMOS LOAF

4 c. diced cooked chicken
3 tbsp. grated onion
4 tbsp. chopped pimento
1 ½ tsp. salt
1 ½ tsp. chili powder
1 ½ c. chicken stock
1 ½ c. milk
2 c. cracker crumbs
3 eggs, beaten

Combine all ingredients; mix thoroughly. Coat a greased loaf pan with a small amount of crumbs; fill with chicken mixture. Set pan in a pan filled with about 2 inches hot water. Bake at 350 degrees for 1 hour or until knife inserted comes out clean. Serve hot with chicken gravy, if desired. Yield: 6-8 servings.

Mrs. Sonja Stottler, Pres.
Concordia Women's Soc.
Hagerstown, Maryland

QUICKIE CHICKEN LOAF

3 c. finely chopped cooked chicken
2 c. chicken broth
1 c. fine bread crumbs
2 tbsp. chopped celery
1 tsp. salt
Dash of pepper (opt.)
4 eggs, beaten
½ c. chopped pimento (opt.)

Mix all ingredients. Place in buttered 9 x 13-inch pan. Bake at 350 degrees for 30 minutes. NOTE: Serve with mushroom soup which has been diluted with 1 soup can of milk, if desired. Yield: 12-15 servings.

Mrs. Joseph T. Gill, Pres.
St. Paul's Ladies Aid and LWML
Wood River, Illinois
Mrs. Dorina Ruff, Pres.
Immanuel Ladies Aid
Waterloo, Illinois

LONDON CHICKEN

24 pieces chicken
Butter
2 cans cream of chicken soup
1 can cream of mushroom soup
¾ lb. mushrooms, sliced
¼ c. Sherry wine

Wash and dry chicken. Brown lightly in butter. Place chicken pieces in shallow pan. Blend soups; pour over chicken. Saute mushrooms in chicken drippings for 5 minutes. Drain; sprinkle over soup. Add wine. Cover. Bake at 350 degrees for 1 hour and 30 minutes. NOTE: Use legs, thighs and breasts of chicken. Yield: 12 servings.

Mrs. Don Whitman
Immanuel Ladies Guild
DeKalb, Illinois

MARINATED CHICKEN

2 3-lb. fryers, cut up
1 bottle Italian dressing

Marinate chicken pieces in Italian dressing in bowl for 24 hours. Place chicken in a single layer in a large baking pan. Bake at 350 degrees for 2 hours, turning once. Garnish with cinnamon apples.

Mrs. Renate Weber, Pres.
Zion LWML
El Paso, Texas

NO PEEKIE CHICKEN

1 c. rice
3 c. boiling water
1 can cream of mushroom soup
1 envelope onion soup mix
6 pieces chicken
Kitchen Bouquet

Add rice to boiling water with mushroom and onion soups. Place mixture in 9 x 13 x 2-inch baking dish. Brush chicken pieces with Kitchen Bouquet; place over mixture in baking dish. Cover dish tightly with foil. Bake at 325 degrees for 2 hours. Do not open oven during cooking.

Jeanette Dice
House of Prayer LCW
Country Club Hills, Illinois

NORTH DAKOTA ROAST CHICKEN

1 chicken, cut into serving pieces
¾ c. flour
1 tsp. salt
¼ tsp. pepper
½ c. cooking oil or shortening
1 c. sweet or sour cream
White cooking wine (opt.)

Dredge chicken in flour seasoned with salt and pepper; brown in hot oil. Arrange chicken in roaster or casserole; add cream. Bake, covered, at 375 degrees for 1 to 2 hours or until tender. Add water as needed; baste occasionally with cream and drippings. Add a small amount of white wine the last 30 minutes of baking time. Yield: 4-5 servings.

Mrs. Ellen Aarfor
St. Paul's LWML
Sunset, Utah

OVEN CHICKEN

1 lge. chicken
Salt and pepper
1 can cream of mushroom soup
½ c. milk or 1 sm. can evaporated milk
Paprika

Cut chicken into serving pieces; salt and pepper to taste. Place in one layer on shallow pan. Mix soup with milk; spread over chicken. Sprinkle generously with paprika. Bake at 300 degrees for 2 hours or until done. Yield: 6 servings.

Mrs. Ernest Ramm, Chmn.
St. John's LWML
Muleshoe, Texas

PEACHY CHICKEN

1 No. 2 can peaches
¼ c. butter
1 tsp. soy sauce
1 tsp. onion salt
1 chicken
Salt to taste

Drain peaches, reserving juice. Place peach juice, butter, soy sauce and onion salt in saucepan. Bring to a boil. Place chicken in shallow baking pan; salt. Pour juice over chicken. Bake at 375 degrees for 1 hour or until chicken is done. Baste frequently. Place peach halves

195

(Continued on next page)

around chicken for last 5 minutes to warm. Garnish with parsley. Yield: 4 servings.

Mrs. Ray Hayden, Pres.
Luther Memorial LCW
Gays Mill, Wisconsin

CHICKEN PIE

1 7 to 8-lb. chicken
2 tbsp. butter
Flour
2 c. milk
2 tsp. baking powder
¼ tsp. salt
3 tbsp. shortening
1 egg

Cook chicken until tender; reserve 6 cups broth. Remove bones; line 2 1/2 x 18 x 10-inch pan with chicken. Heat reserved broth and butter; add mixture of 4 heaping table-spoonfuls flour and 1 cup milk. Cook until thickened. Thoroughly mix 2 cups flour with baking powder, salt and shortening. Add mixture of beaten egg and remaining milk. Pour gravy over chicken; top with crust. Bake at 450 to 475 degrees for 15 to 20 minutes or until brown. Yield: 15 servings.

Mrs. Floyd H. Whitten, Pres.
St. Matthew's LCW
Fillmore, Illinois

CHICKEN PIE

FILLING:

4 tbsp. butter or melted chicken fat
¼ c. flour
1 ½ tsp. salt
¼ tsp. pepper
2 c. chicken stock
⅔ c. cream or evaporated milk
2 c. cooked chopped chicken
1 ½ c. cooked peas
1 ½ c. cooked carrots

Melt butter; blend in flour and seasonings. Stir in chicken stock and cream; bring to a boil, stir-ring constantly. Boil for 1 minute. Divide chicken into six small casseroles; add peas and carrots. Pour on hot sauce.

CRUST:

⅓ c. shortening
1 c. sifted flour
½ tsp. salt
1 tsp. celery seed
½ tsp. paprika
2 tbsp. water

Cut shortening into flour and salt; add celery seed and paprika. Sprinkle mixture with water; mix well with fork until particles cling together and form ball. Roll to 1/4-inch thickness on floured board. Cut into circles; place on tops of

casseroles. Bake at 425 degrees for 35 minutes. Yield: 6 servings.

Ellen R. Rumsey
First Lutheran LWML
El Cajon, California

CHICKEN POT PIE

½ c. chopped onion
¼ c. chicken fat
2 ½ c. flour
¼ tsp. pepper
1 ½ tsp. salt
2 c. chicken stock
2 c. diced chicken
½ c. peas
½ c. carrots
Fried mushrooms (opt.)
¾ c. shortening
6 tbsp. water

Brown onion in chicken fat in saucepan. Blend in 1/4 cup flour, pepper and 1/2 teaspoonful salt; gradually add chicken stock, stirring constantly until thickened. Fold in diced chicken, peas and carrots. Add fried mushrooms, if desired. Place sauce in small bowls and cool. Sift 2 1/4 cups flour into bowl; add 1 tea-spoonful salt. Cut in shortening, blending with 2 knives. When mixture looks fine, add water. Form dough into a ball; roll into sections large enough to extend over tops of bowls. Bake at 450 degrees for 30 minutes or until crust is lightly browned. Yield: 4-6 servings.

Doris Hahn
Christ Lutheran Church Ladies Aid
Harrow, Ontario, Canada

CHICKEN PIE TO SET BEFORE A KING

Chicken fat or shortening
Flour
1 ½ c. chicken stock
1 c. milk
Salt and pepper
1 tbsp. chopped parsley
4 c. chopped, cooked and seasoned chicken
12 sm. onions
2 tbsp. baking powder
¾ tsp. curry powder

Melt 4 tablespoonfuls fat in saucepan; add 3 table-spoonfuls flour. Stir to a smooth paste; add chicken stock and 1/2 cup milk gradually. Cook until thickened, stirring constantly. Season with salt and pepper; add parsley and chicken. Cook onions in additional chicken stock. Add to chicken mixture. Turn into 13 x 9-inch baking dish. Sift 2 cups flour; add baking powder, salt and curry powder. Sift again. Cut in shortening; add 1/2 cup milk, stirring with fork until dough is formed. Turn out onto lightly floured board; roll 1/4-inch thick to fit baking dish. Cut slits in dough to allow escape of steam. Fit over meat pie, pressing dough against edge of dish to seal. Brush with cream, if desired, for browning. Bake at 450

(Continued on next page)

degrees for 15 to 20 minutes. Yield: 6-8 servings.

Mrs. Hertha Stuckwisch
St. John's Ladies Aid Soc.
Battle Creek, Nebraska

COLONIAL EASTERN SHORE CHICKEN POT PIE AND TOPPING

1 chicken
1 qt. water
2 tsp. salt
¼ tsp. pepper
½ tsp. celery seed
2 tbsp. flour
½ can peas
1 potato, cooked and cubed
½ onion, finely diced

Place chicken in kettle; cover with water. Add salt, pepper and celery seed. Cover; boil until chicken is tender enough to fall off bones. Remove chicken from liquid stock; cool. Remove meat from the bones. Place in a well buttered 2-quart baking dish. Add flour mixed with a small amount of water; stir into chicken stock; cook until thickened. Add salt and pepper; simmer for 5 minutes. Add peas, potato and onion. Stir until vegetables are mixed through gravy. Pour mixture over chicken in baking dish. Add small amount of milk, if necessary to fill dish.

TOPPING:

1 c. flour
2 tsp. baking powder
½ tsp. salt
3 tbsp. shortening
⅓ c. milk

Sift flour with baking powder; cut in shortening. Stir in milk to make a soft dough. Knead on slightly floured board; roll out. Place over top of pie. Bake at 375 degrees for 20 minutes or until crust is brown. Yield: 6 servings.

Mrs. Tillie A. Fraze
Immanuel Ladies Aid soc.
Preston, Maryland

RELISH CHICKEN DISH

1 fryer, cut up
Salt and pepper to taste
½ c. margarine
¼ c. India relish
1 tbsp. mustard
Paprika to taste

Arrange chicken in single layer in casserole; season. Melt margarine; add relish, mustard and paprika. Mix well. Pour over chicken. Cover with lid or aluminum foil. Bake at 325 degrees for 1 hour and 30 minutes to 2 hours. Yield: 6 servings.

Mrs. Clarence T. Rodgers, Pres.
Mt. Olive Ladies Aid Soc.
Columbia, South Carolina

SAVORY CHICKEN

2 tbsp. (heaping) flour
1 tsp. salt
¼ tsp. pepper
1 tsp. thyme
1 tsp. marjoram
1 chicken, cut up
½ c. water

Place flour, salt, pepper, thyme and marjoram in paper bag. Shake chicken in bag to coat only. Remove chicken to roaster; add water. Bake, covered, at 375 degrees for 1 hour and 30 minutes. Remove cover; bake for 30 minutes longer or until brown. Yield: 6-8 servings.

Mrs. Ada Berner, Pres.
Mt. Olive Ladies Aid
Milwaukee, Wisconsin

SAVORY OVEN LEMON CHICKEN

1 2½-lb. broiler-fryer, cut into 10 pieces
¼ lb. butter or margarine
2 tbsp. lemon juice
1 tsp. salt
1½ tsp. paprika
¼ tsp. garlic powder

Wash and dry chicken. Melt butter in 10 x 2-inch baking dish. Stir in remaining ingredients; blend. Coat chicken in mixture; turn skin-side up. Bake at 375 degrees for 45 minutes or until tender, basting occasionally. Serve with pan juices. Yield: 4 servings.

Mrs. George H. Emmitt
Atonement Lydia Serv. Guild
Woodland Hills, California

SMOTHERED CHICKEN

1 pkg. chicken noodle soup mix
1½ c. boiling water
½ c. plus 2 tbsp. flour
1 tsp. salt
⅛ tsp. pepper
1 chicken, cut into serving pieces
½ c. margarine
¼ c. minced onion
1 c. milk

Stir soup mix into boiling water; simmer for 7 minutes. Strain noodles; reserve broth. Place noodles in casserole. Combine 1/2 cup flour, salt and pepper; coat chicken with seasoned flour. Brown in 1/4 cup margarine. Arrange in casserole. Saute onion in remaining butter; blend in remaining flour, reserved broth and milk. Pour over chicken. Cover; bake at 325 degrees for 1 hour.

Gladys Engert, Pres.
Trinity LWML
Altenburg, Missouri

SMOTHERED CHICKEN

4 tbsp. flour
1 tsp. salt
½ tsp. paprika
⅛ tsp. garlic powder
1   4 to 5-lb. frying chicken or 2 sm. fryers,
    cut up
4 tbsp. cooking oil or fat
1 lge. onion, chopped
1 c. chopped carrots
3 stalks celery, chopped
1 10-oz. can cream of mushroom soup

Combine flour, salt, paprika and garlic powder
in paper bag; shake chicken until well coated.
Brown chicken in oil. Drain. Place chicken in
large casserole. Brown onions, carrots and
celery in same oil. Add vegetables to chicken;
pour soup over mixture. Bake, covered, at
325 degrees for 2 hours to 2 hours and 30 minutes. Yield: 6-8 servings.

Mrs. Doreen Kuntz, Sec.
Mount Calvary Lutheran Church
Maple Creek, Saskatchewan, Canada

SPANISH CHICKEN

¼ c. flour
1 lge. fryer
¼ c. salad oil
1 ½ c. uncooked rice
3 c. water
1 envelope Spanish rice seasoning mix
1 lge. pepper, cut into 8 rings
1 c. sliced stuffed green olives

Flour chicken; brown in salad oil. Place rice in
baking dish; place chicken on rice. Stir water into
drippings in fry pan. Blend in Spanish rice seasoning; heat to boiling. Pour over chicken. Cover.
Bake at 350 degrees for 30 minutes. Uncover;
place green pepper and olives on top. Cover; bake
for 30 minutes longer or until tender. Yield: 8
servings.

Mrs. W. Babcock
Beaver Creek LCW
Ratner, Saskatchewan, Canada

SWEET AND SOUR CHICKEN

1 chicken, cut up
1 c. vinegar
1 c. sugar
3 tbsp. cornstarch
1 lge. can pineapple chunks and juice
1 lge. green pepper, cut up
1 can pimento, cut into large pieces

Brown chicken; place in roaster. Combine vinegar, sugar and cornstarch, cooking until clear.
Add pineapple chunks, juice, green pepper and
pimento; cook for 5 minutes. Pour sauce over
chicken. Bake at 325 degrees for 1 hour. Yield:
6 servings.

Mrs. Joel Ramerth, Pres.
St. Paul's Ladies Aid
Fulda, Minnesota

TAVERN-STYLE BAKED CHICKEN

1 3 ½ to 5-lb. chicken, cut up
1 med. onion, sliced
Cold water
2 3-oz. cans broiled sliced mushrooms, or
   pieces
1 c. evaporated milk
½ c. butter
½ c. flour
1 tsp. salt
Dash of pepper
½ tsp. turmeric
¼ tsp. oregano
½ c. grated mild or sharp American cheese
3 c. cooked rice

Cover chicken and onion with cold water; add 1
teaspoonful salt. Bring slowly to a boil; simmer
for 1 hour or until chicken is tender. Remove
from bones. Measure liquid from mushrooms,
adding chicken broth to make 3 cups; add evaporated milk. Melt butter; blend in flour, salt,
pepper and turmeric. Add chicken broth mixture.
Cook over low heat, stirring constantly, until
thickened. Add oregano and 1/4 cup cheese, stirring until cheese melts. Spread rice in greased
shallow baking dish; top with chicken and mushrooms. Pour sauce over all; sprinkle with remaining cheese. Bake at 350 degrees for 30 minutes. Yield: 8 servings.

Mrs. Nellie B. King
First Lutheran Church LWML
Dunsmuir, California

BREADED CHICKEN

1 frying chicken, cut up
Salt and pepper to taste
Flour
2 eggs, beaten
Bread or cracker crumbs
½ c. shortening

Wash and dry chicken well. Season with salt and
pepper. Roll chicken in flour. Dip into egg, then
crumbs. Heat shortening in heavy skillet. Add
chicken; fry slowly at 325 degrees until golden
brown. Yield: 4-6 servings.

Mrs. Simon Schenn, Jr.
St. Peter's LWML
Vittoria, Ontario, Canada

CHICKEN KIEV

3 12 to 14-oz. chicken breasts, boned and split
Salt and pepper
¼ c. finely chopped onion
3 tbsp. finely chopped parsley
1 ¼ c. firm butter
2 eggs, slightly beaten
3 tbsp. milk
⅓ c. flour
1 c. fine dry bread crumbs

Place each chicken breast between two pieces of
waxed paper; pound with flat side of meat mallet
until very thin. Sprinkle each side with salt and

(Continued on next page)

pepper. Saute onion and parsley in 2 or 3 table-spoonfuls butter. Place 2 tablespoonfuls butter and onion mixture in center of each breast. Fold over the two short ends, then the long ends. Secure with wooden pick or skewer. Blend eggs and milk. Roll chicken in flour; dip into egg mixture. Roll again in crumbs; dip into egg mixture, then again into crumbs. Melt 1/2 cup butter in skillet. Add chicken, skewered-side down; fry for 5 to 7 minutes. Turn and fry for 5 to 7 minutes longer. Place skillet in oven; bake for 10 minutes. Remove picks and serve immediately.

Mrs. Edward N. Grosz, Pres.
Salem LCW
Parkston, South Dakota

CHICKEN KIEV

6 med. chicken breasts, boned
Salt and pepper
Garlic powder
Pinch of rosemary
6 tbsp. cold butter
Fat
2 eggs
1 tbsp. water
White dry bread crumbs

Pound and roll chicken with rolling pin until flat and tender. Sprinkle each piece lightly with salt, pepper, garlic powder and rosemary. Place butter, shaped into oval, in center of each piece. Roll meat around butter, shaping to simulate a drumstick. Press well with both hands. Beat eggs with water. Dip drumsticks into bread crumbs; dip into egg mixture and again into crumbs. Press crumbs well onto surface of meat. Place on waxed paper; let stand for 20 to 30 minutes, turning several times to permit surface to dry slightly. Deep fry in electric skillet at 300 degrees for 10 to 11 minutes. Place a frilled toothpick on one end before serving. Yield: 6 servings.

Mrs. Ester Strieter, Pres.
Trinty LWML
Lisle, Illinois

SOUTHERN-FRIED CHICKEN

1 2½ to 3-lb. broiler, cut up
Salt
¼ tsp. pepper
1 sm. onion, diced
1 egg, beaten
1 c. prepared biscuit mix
3 tbsp. shortening
3 tbsp. butter

Cook chicken until tender with 1 teaspoonful salt, pepper and onion in enough water to cover. Let cool in broth. Beat egg with a dash of salt. Roll chicken in egg; coat with biscuit mix. Fry in shortening and butter until brown over medium heat. If desired, make gravy from broth. Yield: 4 servings.

Mrs. Edna Priebe, Sec.
Zion Cir.
Princeton, Minnesota

BARBECUED BROILERS

2 broilers
1 c. honey
½ c. oil
½ c. tomato puree
4 tbsp. soy sauce
3 cloves of garlic, finely chopped
½ c. red wine

Split broilers into halves; remove backbones. Mix honey with remaining ingredients. Place broiler halves in dish; cover with mixture. Let stand for 2 hours. Remove broilers from sauce; place on barbecue grill with bone-side down. Place grill 5 to 6 inches from coals until sauce begins to bubble and cook. Move grill higher. Baste chicken often with sauce. Cook for 1 hour and 30 minutes to 2 hours or until done. Yield: 4 servings.

Mrs. John Killian, Pres.
Faith Women's Guild
Greenville, Mississippi

BARBECUED CHICKEN

1 c. cooking oil
2 c. vinegar
5 tbsp. salt
½ tsp. pepper
2 to 3 tsp. poultry seasoning
1 egg
6 to 10 2½ to 3-lb. broiler halves

Mix all ingredients except chicken, beating egg in last. Place broilers on grill 12 to 18 inches above bed of hot charcoal, breast-side up. Baste upper side with sauce, turning at 5 to 7 minute intervals. Basting liberally while turning. If charcoal gets too hot and chickens begin to char, sprinkle with water. Cook for 45 minutes to 1 hour and 15 minutes or until chickens test done. Yield: 10-12 servings.

Mrs. Norman Butts, Pres.
Trinity LCW
Castleton on Hudson, New York
Dorothy K. Geihsler, Christian Growth Chmn.
Immanuel Ladies Aid
Preston, Maryland
Mrs. Arnold Kunes
Trinity Vester Guild
Towanda, Pennsylvania

BARBECUED CHICKEN

Juice of 1 lemon
½ c. cooking oil
4 tbsp. vinegar
2 tbsp. Worcestershire sauce
¼ tsp. Tabasco sauce
2 tsp. salt
2 tsp. sugar
1 tsp. garlic salt
1 tsp. paprika
2 fryer chickens, cut into halves

Mix all ingredients except chickens. Brush sauce on both sides of chickens; marinate for 4 to 5

(Continued on next page)

hours or longer. Light charcoal in outdoor grill. Sear chickens outside. Baste occasionally with remaining sauce until chickens are well done. Yield: 4 servings.

Mrs. Margaret Woehlert, Pres.
Holy Cross LWML
Onaway, Michigan

BARBECUED CHICKEN

½ c. dry white wine
½ c. salad oil
1 tsp. tarragon
1 tsp. salt
1 frying chicken, cut up

Mix wine and all remaining ingredients except chicken. Place chicken on barbecue grill over coals; baste with sauce, continuing to baste as chicken is turned. Cook for 40 minutes or until done. Add additional salt, if desired. Yield: 4 servings.

Mrs. Roy W. Olson, Pres.
Our Savior LCW
Quincy, California

BARBECUED CHICKEN WITH LEMON SAUCE

¼ lb. butter or margarine
¼ c. lemon juice
¼ tsp. pepper
¼ tsp. basil
¼ tsp. garlic salt
1 tbsp. paprika
2 tsp. salt
2 1-lb. chickens, halved

Place butter or margarine, lemon juice and seasonings in pan; heat until all is well blended. Place chicken, skin-side down on barbecue rack; brush with lemon sauce. Turn after 15 minutes of cooking and brush other side. Continue turning and basting frequently until chickens are tender and browned. Yield: 4 servings.

Mrs. Roy E. Wood, Sec.
Trinity Ladies Aid Soc.
Lowell, Indiana

BARBECUED DRUMSTICKS

¼ c. catsup
2 to 3 tbsp. lemon juice
2 tbsp. soy sauce
¼ c. salad oil
½ tsp. monosodium glutamate
12 drumsticks

Combine all ingredients except chicken, mixing well. Add drumsticks to mixture; stir to coat. Refrigerate overnight or let stand at room temperature for 2 hours, spooning sauce over occasionally. Place drumsticks in wire broiling basket. Grill over slow coals for 25 minutes, basting with marinade occasionally. Turn and

cook other side for 20 minutes or until tender, basting with marinade. Yield: 6 servings.

Erlaine Plugge
Messiah LCW
Ralston, Nebraska

GARLIC BARBECUED CHICKEN

1 frying chicken, cut up
1 bottle garlic dressing

Marinate chicken in garlic dressing for 30 minutes; cook over charcoals for 45 minutes to 1 hour or until tender. Baste often with dressing, turning chicken. Yield: 5 servings.

Mrs. Merlin T. Latare, Pres.
St. Mark's LCW
Oxford Junction, Iowa

CHICKEN A LA KING

1 3-lb. stewing chicken
1 carrot, chopped
1 med. onion, chopped
1 stalk celery, chopped
Flour
1 can pimento, chopped
Salt and pepper to taste
Biscuits

Cook chicken in boiler, adding carrot, onion and several pieces celery; allow to cook in broth Remove chicken from bones, discarding skin. Cut meat into medium pieces. Strain broth. Cook remaining celery and add to chicken. Thicken broth with flour; add chicken, cooked celery, pimento, salt and pepper. Serve over biscuits.

Mrs. Bruce R. Shaffer, Pres.
St. John's LCW
Homestead, Pennsylvania

CHICKEN A LA KING SUPREME

¼ c. plus 2 tbsp. butter
½ green pepper, shredded
1 c. thinly sliced mushrooms
2 tbsp. flour
2 c. light cream
3 to 3 ½ c. chopped cooked chicken
3 egg yolks
1 tsp. onion juice
1 tbsp. lemon juice
½ tsp. paprika
Cooking Sherry to taste
Shredded pimento

Simmer 2 tablespoonfuls butter, green pepper and mushrooms for 5 minutes; add flour and seasonings to taste. Cook, stirring gently, until frothy. Mix in cream; stir until sauce is thickened. Pour into top of double boiler. Add chicken; heat thoroughly. Cream remaining butter; beat into egg yolks. Add onion juice, lemon juice and paprika; beat well. Add egg mixture to hot chicken

200

(Continued on next page)

mixture slowly, stirring until thickened. Add Sherry to taste. Add pimento; stir lightly. Serve at once in noodle nests, pattie cases or on hot buttered toast. Yield: 8 servings.

Mrs. Harold Friemark, Pres.
Immanuel Ladies Aid
Berlin, Wisconsin

CHICKEN ON BISCUIT

1 4-lb. chicken
4 c. water
2 ¾ tsp. salt
2 c. plus 2 tbsp. flour
1 egg
2 tsp. baking powder
⅓ c. fat
¾ c. milk

Cook chicken in water with 2 teaspoonfuls salt. Remove bones from chicken; return chicken to broth. Thicken broth by adding 2 tablespoonfuls flour and egg made into paste. Heat to boiling, stirring constantly. Add chicken. Combine dry ingredients and 3/4 teaspoonful salt; cut in fat. Add milk; make into small biscuits. Bake at 450 degrees for 15 minutes. Serve chicken mixture over biscuits. Yield: 12-15 servings.

Mrs. Jesse Shull
Trinity Dorcas Soc.
Sugar Grove, Ohio

CHICKEN CACCIATORE

1 2½ to 3 lb. chicken, cut into pieces
Salt and pepper
¼ c. oil
1 onion, chopped
1 clove of garlic, minced
½ c. mushrooms (opt.)
1 can tomato paste
2 c. hot water
1 bay leaf
¼ tsp. allspice

Sprinkle chicken with salt and pepper; brown in hot oil. Push chicken to side of skillet; add onion, garlic and mushrooms. Cook and stir for a few minutes. Mix tomato paste with water, bay leaf, allspice and 1/2 teaspoonful salt; pour over chicken. Stir well. Cover and simmer for 30 minutes or until chicken is tender. Uncover; simmer until sauce is thick.

Mrs. Helen Sheasley
Sts. Paul and John LCW
Loganton, Pennsylvania

CHICKEN CHOW MEIN

1 chicken, boiled and diced
2 c. chicken broth
1 c. bean sprouts
½ c. uncooked rice

1 c. cooked celery
1 tsp. salt
Chow mein noodles

Combine all ingredients except noodles in heavy saucepan; cook for 30 minutes. Pour over noodles to serve. Yield: 6-8 servings.

Mrs. Joyce Einspahr, Pres.
St. Paul's Ladies Aid
Wauneta, Nebraska

CHICKEN CURRY

4 or 5 onions, sliced
5 tbsp. butter
¾ c. flour
1 qt. hot chicken stock
Juice of ½ lemon
1 slice lemon
1 ½ c. heavy cream
2 to 4 tsp. curry powder
3 c. chopped chicken or turkey
Salt and pepper to taste

Saute onions in butter until soft; stir in flour. Cook slowly until golden. Slowly add hot chicken stock; simmer. Add lemon juice and lemon slice; simmer for 15 to 20 minutes. Add cream. Make a paste of curry and water; add to mixture with chicken and seasonings. Heat through. Serve with rice and condiments of chutney, peanuts, coconut, bacon, parsley, egg and raisins. Yield: 8 servings.

Elizabeth C. Post, Pres.
Zion LWML
Plymouth, Massachusetts

CHICKEN AND DUMPLINGS

1 stewing chicken, cut into serving pieces
Salt
8 med. potatoes, boiled and mashed
6 eggs, beaten
Flour

Boil chicken in enough water to cover until tender. Add salt. Remove chicken, reserving broth; keep warm. Mix mashed potatoes with eggs, salt and pepper. Add flour until stiff. Drop by spoonfuls into boiling reserved broth. Boil for 15 minutes. Serve with chicken. Yield: 8 servings.

Mrs. Anne Halfrich
Grace Guild
Killeen, Texas

CHICKEN WITH LEMON SAUCE

2 broiler-fryers, cut into serving pieces
3 c. water
1 onion, sliced
4 celery tops, chopped
2 bay leaves
2 tsp. monosodium glutamate
2 tsp. salt
½ tsp. peppercorns

(Continued on next page)

Place chicken in kettle; add remaining ingredients. Brint to a boil; cover tightly. Reduce heat and simmer for 45 minutes to 1 hour or until meat is tender. Remove from heat; strain broth. Place chicken on serving platter; keep warm.

SAUCE:

¼ c. butter or chicken fat
¼ c. flour
3 c. chicken stock
3 egg yolks
4 tbsp. lemon juice
½ c. finely chopped parsley

Melt butter in saucepan; blend in flour. Gradually add stock and cook, stirring constantly, until mixture thickens and comes to a boil. Beat egg yolks with lemon juice. Add to stock, stirring rapidly. Cook until mixture returns to a boil. Remove from heat; stir in parsley. Spoon part of sauce over chicken; serve remaining sauce in separate dish. Yield: 8 servings.

Mrs. W. H. Schlie, Cookbook Chmn.
St. John's Mission Cir.
Hubbard, Iowa

CHICKEN MARENGO

1 lge. frying chicken
1 ½ c. water
1 tbsp. olive oil
2 tbsp. butter
6 sm. white onions
1 ½ c. chicken broth
1 clove of garlic
2 tsp. chopped parsley
Salt and pepper to taste
½ c. dry white wine
2 egg yolks
1 tbsp. flour
8 pitted olives

Boil chicken neck, giblets and back in water. Cut remaining chicken into serving pieces; Fry in fat in a heavy iron skillet until golden brown. Parboil onions in salted water for 15 minutes; drain. Bring broth to a boil; pour over chicken. Add onions, garlic, parsley, salt, pepper and wine; simmer gently for 15 minutes. Beat egg yolks and flour; add a small amount cold broth. Add egg mixture to boiling sauce; stir until thickened. Add olives. Remove garlic. Arrange chicken on platter; pour sauce over chicken. Serve with rice or noodles. Yield: 6 servings.

Mrs. George Campbell
Mt. Calvary LWML
Brady, Texas

CHICKEN AND NOODLES

1 3 ½ lb. fryer, cut up
Flour
¼ c. fat or salad oil

1 onion, chopped
1 clove of garlic, minced
Salt and pepper
¼ tsp. ground ginger
1 c. water
8 oz. wide noodles
4 sprigs parsley, chopped

Wash chicken and dry on absorbent paper; roll in flour. Heat fat in large skillet; add chicken and brown on all sides. Add onion, garlic, 1 teaspoonful salt, 1/4 teaspoonful pepper, ginger and water. Cover; bring to boil. Simmer for 45 minutes or until chicken is tender. Cook noodles in boiling salted water until tender; drain. Remove chicken from broth; add noodles to broth in skillet. Add parsley; season with salt and pepper. Pile noodles in center of hot platter; arrange chicken around edge. Yield: 4 servings.

Mrs. C. H. Garberson, Pres.
Zion Ladies Aid LWML
Harper, Kansas

CHICKEN & PAPRIKAS

2 tsp. salt
½ tsp. pepper
2 chickens, cut up
1 ½ tsp. paprika
¾ c. water

Salt and pepper each piece of chicken separately; partially brown on both sides in deep iron skillet. Add paprika and water; let simmer for 1 hour and 30 minutes or until tender. NOTE: Chicken may be cooked in pressure cooker for 20 minutes. Yield: 8-10 servings.

Mrs. Helen Jurges
Mount Calvary Ladies Guild
Pittsburgh, Pennsylvania

CHICKEN WITH PEACHES AND GINGER

1 lge. chicken, cut into pieces
2 tsp. salt
¼ c. margarine or butter
1 1-lb. can Cling peaches
1 onion, sliced
1 tbsp. lemon juice
½ tsp. ginger
2 tsp. cornstarch
2 tbsp. water

Sprinkle chicken with part of salt; brown in margarine. Drain juice from peaches into skillet. Add onion, lemon juice, ginger and remaining salt. Cover and simmer for 40 minutes or until tender. Blend cornstarch and water; stir into chicken mixture when chicken is tender. Add peach halves. Simmer for 5 minutes longer. Yield: 6 servings.

Mrs. Howard C. Paul, Cir. Chmn.
St. John's LCW
Pittsburgh, Pennsylvania

CHICKEN POT PIE

4 c. flour
1 tsp. salt
½ tsp. baking powder
2 ½ tbsp. shortening
1 egg
¾ c. chicken broth
1 stewing chicken
1 stalk celery, diced
1 lge. onion, diced
1 med. potato, diced
Salt and pepper
Parsley flakes

Sift flour, salt and baking powder. Add shortening, egg and broth. Divide dough into four equal parts. Roll on lightly floured board until dough is thin. Cut into 2-inch squares; place on waxed paper. Cook chicken in 4 quarts water until tender. Remove chicken. Add celery, onion and potato to broth. Add dough squares, one at a time, to boiling broth. Season with salt, pepper and parsley flakes. Cook for 15 minutes, stirring occasionally to prevent sticking. Yield: 5 servings.

Mrs. Vincent Reed, Pres.
Trinity LCW
Coatesville, Pennsylvania

CHICKEN POT PIE

1 2 or 3-lb. stewing chicken
3 med. potatoes, diced
Parsley
2 tsp. salt
3 c. flour
3 tbsp. shortening
¾ c. cold water

Cook chicken until tender; remove from broth. Add potatoes, parsley and 1 teaspoonful salt to broth. Combine remaining ingredients to make dough. Roll thin; cut into small squares. Drop into boiling broth. Add diced chicken. Cook over low heat for 30 minutes, stirring often with wooden spoon. Yield: 6 servings.

Mrs. Beulah Wagner
St. Timothy's LCW
Dundalk, Maryland

CHICKEN SPAGHETTI

1 stewing hen
1 ½ c. chopped green peppers
1 c. chopped onions
Butter
1 can pimento, chopped
1 can mushrooms
Cayenne pepper
Garlic salt
Salt and black pepper
1 pkg. uncooked spaghetti
1 can cream of mushroom soup
1 can English peas

Cook chicken in large amount of liquid, reserving broth. Cool; remove chicken from bones. Saute green peppers and onions in butter in skillet. Add pimento, mushrooms, cayenne, garlic salt, salt and pepper. Cook spaghetti in reserved broth. Add soup, peas, chicken and vegetables. Serve. Yield: 3-4 servings.

Mrs. Glenn Haas, Pres.
Holy Cross LWML
Atwater, California

CHICKEN SPAGHETTI

1 hen
2 c. chopped onions
2 c. chopped green peppers
2 c. chopped celery
1 tsp. cumin
1 can tomatoes
2 tbsp. chili powder
1 can cream of mushroom soup
1 lb. Velveeta cheese
1 pkg. spaghetti

Simmer hen in water to cover for 3 hours or until done. Remove meat from bones and dice. Reserve broth. Cook onions, green peppers and celery in chicken fat. Add remaining ingredients except spaghetti. Cook spaghetti in chicken broth. Combine the two mixtures; simmer to heat. Yield: 10-12 servings.

Mrs. Walter Lentz
St. John's LCW
Auburn, Nebraska

CHICKEN STEW AND DUMPLINGS

1 stewing hen, cut up
2 tbsp. flour
3 tsp. salt
Pepper to taste
Paprika to taste
2 tbsp. margarine
2 c. flour
1 tsp. (heaping) baking powder
2 tbsp. butter
1 egg

Dredge chicken in mixture of flour, 1 1/2 teaspoonfuls salt, pepper and paprika. Brown chicken in margarine. Place in large kettle with water; cook until tender. Sift flour, baking powder and remaining salt. Add butter, egg and enough water to make soft biscuit dough. Spoon dough onto chicken; cover. Steam for 15 to 20 minutes. Remove dumplings and chicken to warm platter. Serve with gravy. NOTE: Dumplings should not be cooked in water but by steam from water under chicken.

Mrs. John Mahder, Pres.
St. John's of Robinson Ladies Aid
Grand Haven, Michigan

CHICKEN STEW WITH VEGETABLES

2 lb. chicken parts
2 tbsp. flour
¼ tsp. salt
Dash of pepper
3 tbsp. shortening
½ c. chopped onion
¼ tsp. crushed sweet basil
1 10-oz. can cream of mushroom soup
1 soup can water
2 c. carrots, cut into ½-in. pieces
1 9-oz. pkg. frozen, cut, green beans

Dust chicken with flour seasoned with salt and pepper. Brown chicken in shortening in heavy pan. Remove chicken; add onion and basil. Cook over low heat, stirring to loosen browned bits. Blend in soup and water. Add chicken and carrots. Cover; cook over low heat for 30 minutes, stirring occasionally. Add beans. Cover; cook for 30 minutes longer. Yield: 4-6 servings.

Mrs. R. Lissel
Emmanuel LCW
Dafor, Saskatchewan, Canada

CHICKEN TETRAZZINI

1 stewing hen
1 lb. raw spaghetti, cooked
2 c. diced cooked celery
1 c. coarsely chopped cooked onions
2 cans tomatoes
1 clove of garlic
1 tbsp. chili powder
1 tbsp. sugar
Dash of allspice
Dash of nutmeg
Salt and pepper to taste
1 can English peas, drained and cooked
1 can mushrooms (opt.)

Stew hen until well done, reserving broth. Cube. Add spaghetti to meat. Add remaining ingredients except peas and mushrooms. Just before serving, add peas and mushrooms; heat thoroughly. Yield: 15 servings.

Mrs. A. G. Guthals, Pres.
Immanuel LWML
Clovis, New Mexixo

CHICKEN IN WINE-CHERRY SAUCE

1 can sweet dark cherries
1 c. Port or Burgundy wine
3 tbsp. lemon juice
2 cloves of garlic
¼ tsp. ginger
½ tsp. oregano
1 2½ to 3½ lb. chicken, cut into serving pieces
½ c. flour
2 tsp. salt
Dash of pepper
¼ c. shortening
1 chicken bouillon cube

Drain cherries, reserving 1 cup juice. Combine cherry juice, wine, lemon juice, garlic, ginger and oregano. Pour over chicken; let stand for several hours or overnight. Remove chicken; wipe dry. Combine flour, salt and pepper. Dip chicken into flour mixture. Brown in shortening. Remove garlic from marinade; pour over chicken. Add bouillon cube; bring to a boil. Reduce heat and simmer. Add cherries; cook for 15 minutes. Yield: 4-6 servings.

Mrs. S. V. Susina
Vestavia Hills LWML
Birmingham, Alabama

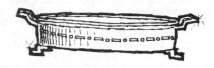

CREAMED CHICKEN

½ c. chopped celery
1 ½ tsp. chopped onion
1 tbsp. chopped green pepper
2 tbsp. fat
¼ c. flour
1 ½ c. chicken broth
½ c. milk or cream
1 ½ c. diced cooked chicken
Salt to taste

Cook celery, onion and green pepper in fat until tender. Blend flour into fat and vegetable mixture. Stir in chicken broth and milk; cook until smooth, stirring constantly. Add chicken; season with salt. Heat thoroughly; serve on rice, toast, or biscuits. Yield: 4 servings.

Bernice Bires, Pres.
Hope Evangelical Women of Hope
Beaver, Pennsylvania

CREAMED CHICKEN A LA KING

5 pkg. fresh frozen peas
Milk
5 lb. mushrooms
2 lge. green peppers, chopped
3 ¾ c. butter or margarine
3 ⅓ c. flour
5 tbsp. salt
2 ½ tsp. pepper
1 12½-lb. chicken or turkey, boned and
    chopped
40 oz. canned pimento, diced

Cook peas as package directs. Heat 4 quarts milk slowly. Saute mushrooms and green peppers in butter in large kettle until tender; stir in flour, salt and pepper until smooth. Stir in 10 cups cold milk; gradually stir in hot milk. Cook, stirring, until thickened. Add drained

(Continued on next page)

cooked peas, chicken and pimento. Carefully heat through. Yield: 125 servings.

Mrs. Theresia Mallon, Pres.
Our Redeemer Ladies Aux.
Buckingham, Quebec, Canada

CREAMED CHICKEN DELUXE

1 c. sliced carrots
1 c. diced celery
1 med. onion, chopped
2 tbsp. flour
2 tbsp. fat
1 c. milk or thin cream
¼ tsp. salt
⅛ tsp. pepper
2 c. cooked cubed chicken
1 tbsp. parsley
1 c. frozen peas

Cook carrots, celery and onion in a small amount of water to tender-crisp stage. Combine flour, fat, milk, salt and pepper. Add chicken and vegetables. Simmer gently for 15 minutes or bake at 300 degrees for 20 to 30 minutes or until vegetables are tender. Serve on rice, potatoes or toast. Garnish with parsley. NOTE: May be varied by adding mushrooms, chopped hard-cooked eggs, chopped pimento or olives. Yield: 6 servings.

Mrs. Alfred Caupert, Pres.
St. John Ladies Aid Soc.
Baldwin, Illinois

CREOLE CHICKEN AND SPAGHETTI

Salt and pepper
1 lge. fryer, cut up
2 8-oz. cans tomato sauce
1 6-oz. can tomato paste
1 c. water
2 tbsp. creole seasoning
1 pkg. thin spaghetti, cooked

Salt and pepper chicken; sear on both sides in heavy pot or pan without grease. Add tomato sauce, tomato paste, water, creole seasoning and additional salt and pepper. Cook until tender. Remove chicken to serving dish; add cooked spaghetti to sauce. Serve hot. Yield: 6 servings.

Inez Walker, Pres.
LWML
Pensacola, Florida

CURRIED CHICKEN

1 lb. cooked diced chicken
¼ c. water
1 tsp. curry powder
¼ tsp. salt
¼ tsp. ginger
¼ tsp. allspice
1 10-oz. can cream of mushroom or cream of celery soup

Combine all ingredients except soup; cook for 10 minutes. Add soup; heat through. Serve with rice. NOTE: Cooked raisins, sweet pickles, peanuts or

hard-cooked eggs may be served with chicken. Yield: 4 servings.

Mrs. Clarence J. Waybright, Ldr.
St. James LCW
Gettysburg, Pennsylvania

DANISH CHICKEN

1 4-lb. roasting chicken
Salt and pepper
1 lge. bunch parsley
3 to 4 tbsp. butter
¼ c. water
1 c. heavy cream
1 tbsp. flour

Wash chicken inside and out; pat dry. Season inside of chicken with salt and a liberal amount of pepper. Wash parsley; break off stems. Stuff whole bunch parsley inside chicken. Melt butter in a Dutch oven; slowly brown chicken on all sides. Add water. Simmer, covered, for 45 minutes or until drumsticks pull away from bird. Remove cover and add cream the last 15 minutes of cooking time. Keep heat on low to prevent curdling. Remove chicken; thicken broth with flour blended with cold water. Yield: 4 servings.

Mrs. George Uhl, VP
Our Saviour Ruth Guild
Mineola, New York

DEVILED CHICKEN

1 2 to 2 ½-lb. broiling or frying chicken, cut into serving pieces
Salt and pepper
½ c. fat, melted
2 tbsp. flour
1 c. hot water or soup stock
1 ½ tsp. dry mustard
2 tsp. Worcestershire sauce
2 tsp. tomato catsup
Paprika

Season chicken with salt and pepper. Brown in fat. Remove from pan. Stir in flour; add water. Cook until thick, stirring constantly. Add remaining ingredients. Add chicken. Cover; simmer for 1 hour or until chicken is tender. Yield: 3-4 servings.

Anne Antrim
Holy Trinity LWML
Macon, Georgia

FRIED CHICKEN WITH MUSHROOM SOUP

1 frying chicken, cut up
Butter
1 can cream of mushroom soup

Wash chicken; drain. Fry in butter until almost tender. Pour soup over chicken. Simmer until tender. Yield: 4 servings.

Mrs. Cora Harman
St. John Ladies Aid Soc.
Accident, Maryland

GOURMET CHICKEN BREASTS

6 chicken breasts
Flour
Salt and black pepper to taste
3 tbsp. shortening
1 onion, chopped
1 sweet red pepper, chopped
1 green pepper, chopped
1 ½ lb. mushrooms, thinly sliced
Cayenne pepper or Tabasco sauce
½ c. Port or Sherry wine
½ c. cream
1 egg yolk

Remove bones from chicken. Cut chicken into narrow 2-inch strips. Dredge in flour, salt and pepper. Fry slowly in large pan in shortening for 3 to 5 minutes. Add onion. Fry only until transparent; do not brown chicken and onion. Add more seasonings to taste; add red and green peppers, mushrooms, cayenne pepper and wine. Simmer for 8 to 10 minutes. Add cream blended with egg yolk. Heat, but do not boil. Serve over bed of rice; garnish with parsley. Yield: 6-8 servings.

Mrs. Audrey Drager, Treas.
Christ Lutheran Church Ladies Aid
Ontario, Canada

HOT CHICKEN SANDWICHES

1 chicken, cooked
1 pt. chicken broth
5 slices bread, broken into pieces
5 eggs, beaten

Remove chicken from bones. Combine chicken and broth in saucepan; bring to a boil. Drop in bread, stirring constantly. Bring to a boil again; gradually add eggs. Keep hot until ready to serve. Yield: 12-15 servings.

Mrs. Robert Weiss, Pres.
Trinity LCW
Ansonia, Ohio

HUNGARIAN CHICKEN

1 2 ½-lb. broiler, cut into serving pieces
¼ c. flour
¼ c. corn oil
½ c. finely chopped onion
½ tsp. salt
1 tbsp. paprika
3 tbsp. cornstarch
½ c. sour cream
1 tbsp. vinegar

Roll chicken lightly in flour. Heat corn oil in large skillet over medium heat for 2 minutes. Add chicken; brown lightly. Add onion, 3 table-spoonfuls water, salt and paprika. Cover tightly; simmer for 25 minutes or until chicken is tender. Remove chicken. Add cornstarch to 1/4 cup of water; mix with 3/4 cup water and sour cream. Pour slowly into pan drippings. Cook, stirring constantly, until thickened and smooth. Stir in

vinegar. Add chicken; reheat in gravy. Serve with rice. NOTE: May substitute 2 to 3 pounds cut-up chicken for one 2 1/2-pound broiler.

L. Mantey, Pres.
Trinity LWML
Winkler, Manitoba, Canada

HUNGARIAN CHICKEN PAPRIKAS

1 3 to 4-lb. chicken
1 lge. or 2 sm. onions, chopped
3 tbsp. fat
1 tsp. paprika
1 tbsp. salt
1 c. tomato juice
2 tbsp. flour
1 pt. sour cream
2 eggs, beaten
Pinch of baking powder
½ c. water

Cut chicken into sections. Brown onions in fat in large pot or Dutch oven; add paprika, chicken and salt. Brown chicken lightly. Add tomato juice; simmer until chicken is tender. Mix flour with sour cream until smooth in separate bowl. Add to chicken just before serving. Mix eggs with 2 cups flour, 1 tablespoonful salt, baking powder and water. Beat with spoon; drop by teaspoonfuls into boiling salted water. Cook until dumplings rise to top. Drain; rinse in cold water. Serve with chicken. Yield: 6 servings.

Helen Sathmary
St. John's LCW
Denver, Pennsylvania

HUNGARIAN CHICKEN PAPRIKAS

CHICKEN AND GRAVY SAUCE:

2 springer chickens, salted and cut up
4 tbsp. fat
1 lge. onion, diced
1 tsp. paprika
Salt and pepper to taste
½ pt. light cream
4 tbsp. (heaping) flour

Brown chickens in fat in deep frying pan. Add onion; continue browning for 4 minutes. Sprinkle paprika onto chicken. Add water to cover. Add salt and pepper to taste. Mix cream with flour; Stir until smooth. Add to chicken, stirring rapidly to prevent lumping. Continue cooking for 10 to 15 minutes.

HUNGARIAN DUMPLINGS:

4 c. flour
Pinch of salt
2 eggs

Mix flour, salt, eggs and enough water to make soft dough. Add a teaspoonful at a time dough to rapidly boiling water. Cook for 10 minutes or until done. Drain in colander; rinse with cold water. Dumpling noodles may be buttered or

(Continued on next page)

added to Chicken and Gravy Sauce. Yield: 6 servings.

Mrs. Bette Knudson
Holy Cross Lutheran Church
North Madison, Ohio

JAMAICA-STYLE CHICKEN

1 4-lb. roasting chicken
2 tbsp. butter or margarine
1 ½ c. chicken broth
¾ c. sliced celery
1 med. onion, chopped
½ tsp. garlic salt
2 dried red peppers, crushed
1 tbsp. vinegar
¼ tsp. allspice
¼ c. sliced green olives
1 med. green pepper, sliced
2 tbsp. cornstarch
Salt and pepper to taste

Brown chicken on all sides in butter in heavy kettle. Place chicken on rack in kettle; add broth, celery, onion, garlic salt, red peppers, vinegar and allspice. Cover; simmer for 1 hour and 30 minutes or until tender. Add olives and green pepper; cook for 10 minutes longer. Remove chicken; thicken mixture in kettle with cornstarch blended with a small amount of cold water. Season to taste; pour over chicken. Yield: 4 servings.

Mrs. Darrell Clocksene, Treas.
Emmanuel LCW
Groton, South Dakota

LEMON FRIED CHICKEN

1 c. flour
1 tsp. salt
¼ tsp. savory salt
¼ tsp. onion salt
¼ tsp. garlic salt
½ tsp. pepper
Pinch of oregano
1 or 2 fryers, cut up
Juice of 1 lemon
¼ c. sugar
¼ to ¾ c. water

Mix flour, salts, pepper and oregano in a plastic bag. Dust chicken pieces in flour mixture. Fry until brown on all sides in small amount of grease. Mix lemon juice, sugar and water; pour over chicken. Steam over low heat or in electric frying pan for 40 minutes to 1 hour. Serve hot or cold.

Mrs. John Trautman, Pres.
St. Paul's Ladies Aid
Driscoll, North Dakota

MARYLAND-STYLE CHICKEN WITH CREAM GRAVY

¾ c. flour
1 ½ tsp. salt
½ tsp. celery salt
½ tsp. paprika
½ tsp. garlic salt
¼ tsp. pepper
1 3-lb. chicken, cut up
2 eggs
¼ c. water
1 c. fine dry bread crumbs
½ c. cooking oil
3 tbsp. hot water

Combine flour, salt, celery salt, paprika, garlic salt and pepper in paper bag. Add chicken pieces, one or two at a time; shake bag to coat chicken. Beat eggs with water. Dip chicken into mixture; shake to remove excess. Roll in crumbs. Heat oil in large heavy skillet; add chicken. Cook gently until golden on all sides; transfer to baking dish. Add hot water to skillet; stir well, scraping all browned bits. Pour over chicken. Bake, uncovered, in preheated oven for 45 minutes or until chicken is tender.

CREAM GRAVY:

¼ c. butter
¼ c. seasoned flour
1 ½ c. chicken stock
1 c. light cream
Salt and pepper

Melt butter in heavy saucepan. Sprinkle in flour; cook until bubbly. Remove from heat; add chicken stock all at once. Stir in cream gradually. Place in moderate oven. Cook and stir until thick and smooth. Season to taste. Serve chicken with cream gravy. Yield: 4 servings.

Mrs. Carol Mukala, Mbrshp. Chmn. Com.
Immanuel Bethany Sisters
Nipigon, Ontario, Canada

MEXICAN FRIED CHICKEN

1 ½ c. flour
2 tsp. salt
1 tbsp. plus 2 tsp. chili powder
1 sm. frying chicken, cut into serving pieces
½ c. fat
1 sm. onion, chopped
1 clove of garlic, minced
1 green pepper, chopped
1 c. tomatoes
½ c. uncooked rice

Combine flour, salt and 1 tablespoonful chili powder. Roll chicken in flour mixture. Brown in fat on both sides. Add remaining ingredients. Cover; simmer for 1 hour. Yield: 4-6 servings.

Mrs. Louise Muller
Christ Lutheran Church LWML
Anderson, Illinois

RAISIN CHICKEN CASABLANCA

1 3-lb. frying chicken, cut up
¼ c. flour
1 ¾ tsp. salt
⅛ tsp. pepper
½ tsp. paprika
2 tbsp. cooking oil
2 tbsp. butter or margarine
2 tbsp. cornstarch
1 c. chicken broth
½ c. dark seedless raisins
1 c. orange juice
4 tsp. coarsely grated orange peel
½ tsp. white wine vinegar

Dredge chicken in flour mixed with 1 teaspoonful salt, pepper and paprika. Heat oil and butter in skillet; brown chicken lightly. Turn heat to low; cook chicken, uncovered, turning occasionally, for 40 minutes or until chicken is tender. Transfer to hot platter and keep warm while preparing sauce. Pour out fat in skillet, returning 1 tablespoonful. Mix cornstarch with chicken broth. Add to drippings; cook until mixture boils and thickens, stirring constantly. Stir in raisins, orange juice, orange peel, vinegar and remaining salt. Simmer for 5 minutes. Pour some of sauce over chicken; s e r v e remaining sauce in sauce boat. Serve with rice, if desired. Yield: 3-4 servings.

Photograph for this recipe on page 157.

SAUCE PIQUANT

1 tbsp. flour
2 tbsp. oil
1 lge. onion
1 med. green pepper
1 clove of garlic, minced
1 sm. can tomato sauce
1 can mushroom steak sauce
½ c. water
1 4-lb. hen, cooked and diced
½ lb. smoke sausage
1 tbsp. Worcestershire sauce
2 tsp. salt
¼ tsp. pepper
Parsley
Chopped onion tops
1 bay leaf
¼ c. dry wine

Brown flour in oil in 4 or 5-quart pot; add onion, green pepper and garlic; cook until tender. Add tomato sauce, steak sauce and water. Cook for 15 minutes. Add chicken, sausage, Worcestershire sauce, salt and pepper. Simmer for 45 minutes. Add a handful parsley, a handful onion tops, bay leaf and dry wine. Simmer for 20 minutes. Serve over rice, if desired. Yield: 6 servings.

Mrs. Bill Moore
Trinity Ladies Aux.
Baton Rouge, Louisiana

SKILLET BARBECUED CHICKEN

1 frying chicken, cut into serving pieces
Chopped giblets (opt.)

¼ c. salad oil
2 tbsp. vinegar
2 tbsp. brown sugar
⅓ c. catsup
1 tsp. Worcestershire sauce
¼ tsp. garlic salt
1 tsp. salt
½ tsp. pepper
½ tsp. celery seed
½ tsp. parsley flakes
¼ c. water

Wash chicken pieces; drain well. Simmer in water to cover. Combine remaining ingredients in electric frying pan or large heavy skillet. Place chicken in sauce. Cook, uncovered, over medium heat for 35 minutes, turning to brown evenly. Remove chicken to warm platter. Skim oil from sauce in skillet. Add 1 cup stock from cooking giblets or water. Stir to loosen all brown particles in pan. Add giblets. Serve sauce over chicken. Yield: 4 servings.

Mrs. Harvey Samuelson, Pres.
LCW
Harcourt, Iowa

SKILLET BARBECUED CHICKEN

2 lb. chicken parts
½ tsp. salt
Dash of pepper
¼ c. butter
1 can tomato soup
½ c. chopped onion
3 tbsp. vinegar
2 tbsp. brown sugar
1 tbsp. Worcestershire sauce
5 drops of Tabasco sauce (opt.)

Season chicken with salt and pepper. Brown well in butter. Stir in remaining ingredients. Cover; simmer for 45 minutes or until chicken is tender. Stir occasionally. Yield: 6 servings.

Mrs. Clarence Bentz, Pres.
St. John's LWML
Tampa, Kansas

SPICED CHICKEN

1 c. orange juice
1 ½ c. sliced peaches
2 tbsp. brown sugar
2 tbsp. vinegar
1 tsp. mace or nutmeg
1 tsp. sweet basil
1 clove of garlic, minced
6 fryer legs and thighs or 1 3-lb. chicken, disjointed
½ c. seasoned flour
Oil

Combine orange juice and peaches with brown sugar, vinegar and spices in saucepan; cook slowly for 10 minutes. Dredge chicken in seasoned flour; brown in 1/2 inch hot oil in fry pan. Remove chicken; pour off oil, retaining browned bits in fry pan. Replace chicken; pour

(Continued on next page)

fruit sauce over top. Cover. Simmer for 20 minutes. Yield: 4-6 servings.

Mrs. Robert Baker, VP
Gloria Dei LCW
New Milford, New Jersey

SWEET AND SOUR CHICKEN

1 No. 2 can pineapple chunks
2 tbsp. butter
2 tbsp. cornstarch
1 c. chicken broth
2 tbsp. soy sauce
2 tbsp. vinegar
1/3 c. sugar
2 c. cooked chopped chicken
1/2 tsp. salt
Pepper to taste
Chopped green pepper to taste

Drain pineapple, reserving 2/3 cup syrup. Cook pineapple in butter for 3 minutes; add 1/3 cup reserved syrup. Cover; simmer for 10 minutes. Mix cornstarch, broth and remaining reserved syrup. Add to pineapple mixture; cook until thick. Add all remaining ingredients. Serve over rice. Yield: 6 servings.

Mrs. Peer S. Hegg, Pres.
St. Mark's LCW
Hacienda Heights, California

ROAST ROCK CORNISH HEN

6 Rock cornish hens
Butter
Salt and pepper
6 slices bacon, minced
4 tbsp. chopped onion
4 c. cooked brown rice
1 c. chopped celery
1/4 tsp. sage
1/2 c. rich milk
1/2 c. white corn syrup
1/2 c. consomme

Wash and clean hens. Brush with melted butter; season with salt and pepper to taste. Saute bacon lightly with onions. Pour off all but 2 tablespoonfuls fat. Combine with rice, celery, 1 teaspoonful salt, 1/2 teaspoonful pepper, sage and milk. Stuff birds; place in roaster. Bake at 375 degrees for 1 hour or longer. Baste with sauce of corn syrup and consomme the last 15 minutes of baking. Yield: 6 servings.

Mrs. Harriet Brandau
Zion Guild
Blackburn, Missouri

ROCK CORNISH HENS WITH WILD RICE

6 1-lb. cornish hens
2 tbsp. butter
1 c. finely chopped onions
1/2 lb. bulk pork sausage or ground ham
1 4-oz. can mushrooms, drained
3 c. cooked wild rice
1/2 tsp. salt
1/2 tsp. marjoram
1/2 tsp. thyme

Wash hens; drain. Melt butter; add onions and simmer until tender. Do not brown. Add sausage; cook, stirring frequently, until done. Add remaining ingredients. Toss lightly until mixed. Stuff hens with mixture; close cavity with skewers. Tie legs and wings close to body. Sprinkle with additional salt and pepper. Cover each hen with three or four thicknesses of cheesecloth that has been dipped into melted butter or margarine. Bake at 325 degrees, on rack, in open shallow pan for 2 hours. Baste frequently with additional melted margarine or butter during baking. Yield: 6 servings.

Mrs. Herman Habitz, Pres.
Emmanuel Mary Martha Guild
Dearborn, Michigan

DUCKLING A L'ORANGE

1 5 to 5 1/2-lb. fresh or frozen duckling
Salt and pepper
Sugar
3/4 c. white wine
Giblets
3/4 c. chicken broth
4 tsp. flour
1 1/2 tbsp. lime juice
Juice and grated rind of 2 oranges
Juice and grated rind of 1 lemon
2 tbsp. currant jelly
1/4 c. brandy

Rub inside of cleaned duckling with salt, pepper and 1 teaspoonful sugar; tie legs. Roast in preheated 500 degree oven for 20 minutes. Reduce temperature to 325 degrees and roast for 1 hour and 40 minutes longer. Baste often with wine. Cook giblets, covered, in chicken broth and water. Remove and dice. Reserve giblets and broth. Place duck on heated platter. Remove fat from pan, reserving 2 tablespoonfuls fat; add flour. Blend, stirring, until well browned. Add 2 tablespoonfuls sugar; brown lightly. Add lime juice, reserved broth, orange and lemon juice, currant jelly and brandy. Cook until mixture is reduced by half, stirring constantly. Quarter duck. Serve with sauce, grated lime, lemon, orange, watercress and giblets. Yield: 4 servings.

Mrs. V. J. Hobratschk
Emmanuel LWML
Littlefield, Texas

ROAST MANDARIN DUCKLING

1/2 c. chopped celery
1/2 c. chopped onion
Soy sauce
1 tbsp. sugar

(Continued on next page)

1 tsp. salt
½ tsp. pepper
½ tsp. cinnamon
¾ tsp. ginger
1 4 to 5-lb. duckling
2 tbsp. honey
1 16-oz. can Mandarin oranges
1 14-oz. can pineapple chunks
3 tbsp. cornstarch

Combine celery, onion, 1/3 cup soy sauce, sugar, salt, pepper, cinnamon and 1/2 teaspoonful ginger. Place in cavity of duckling. Score skin over entire duckling at 1 inch intervals. Place on rack in shallow roasting pan. Roast at 325 degrees for 2 hours and 30 minutes or until drumsticks are tender. Remove from oven; pour off drippings. Combine honey with 1 teaspoonful soy sauce. Glaze duckling. Increase oven temperature to 400 degrees; bake for 15 to 20 minutes, basting frequently. Let cool. Drain oranges and pineapple, reserving liquid. Add enough water to make 3 cups liquid. Mix liquid with cornstarch, 3 tablespoonfuls soy sauce and remaining ginger. Cook, stirring constantly until thicken and clear. Remove duckling from bones; cut into 2-inch squares. Add oranges, pineapple and duckling to sauce; simmer for 5 minutes.

Mrs. Ila Thompson, Pres.
Trinity LCW
Dallas, Oregon

CHEDDAR-TURKEY CASSEROLE

1 c. rice
2 tbsp. instant minced onion
1 10-oz. pkg. green peas
4 to 6 slices cooked turkey, cubed
1 can Cheddar cheese soup or cream of mushroom soup
1 c. milk
1 c. finely crushed cheese crackers
3 tbsp. butter or margarine

Cook rice, adding onion to boiling water. Fluff rice with fork; place in baking dish. Sprinkle with peas; add turkey. Mix soup with milk; pour evenly over turkey. Combine crumbs and butter; sprinkle over turkey. Bake at 350 degrees for 35 minutes or until heated through. Yield: 4-6 servings.

Mrs. Thomas B. Georgi, Pres.
Our Hope Ladies Guild
Huntertown, Indiana

GRANDPA'S TURKEY 'N' DRESSING

1 19 to 22-lb. turkey
3 med. pig hearts, quartered
1 lb. pork sausage
4 med. onions, ground
1 ½ lb. celery, ground
1 sm. pkg. poultry seasoning
1 tsp. thyme
3 tbsp. salt
1 tbsp. sausage seasoning
4 1 ½-lb. loaves white bread, cubed

Salt turkey cavities. Soak hearts in cold water. Simmer hearts, neck and giblets for 1 to 2 hours or until tender. Reserve broth. Grind meat from neck. Brown sausage. Combine 3-quarts broth, vegetables, sausage and seasonings. Boil until vegetables are tender. Pour over bread; mix well. Stuff turkey. Bake at 325 degrees for 7 hours to 8 hours and 30 minutes. Yield: 15 servings.

Mrs. John E. Lignell, Pres.
Tabor LCW
Chicago, Illinois

ROASTED TURKEY

1 15-lb. turkey
Salt
Giblets, chopped
2 loaves old bread, finely cut
1 med. onion, chopped
1 c. chopped celery
2 eggs
1 c. milk
2 tbsp. sage
½ tsp. pepper

Place frozen turkey into pan with cold water to cover; add 1 cup salt. Cook giblets until tender. Pour hot giblets and juice over bread; cover and steam until soft. Add 1 teaspoonful salt and remaining ingredients; mix well. Stuff thawed turkey with dressing. Place into roaster, breast-side down; rub salt over turkey. Add 3 cups water. Cover tightly. Bake at 425 degrees for 1 hour. Reduce temperature to 350 degrees; continue roasting until tender. Length of cooking time depends on age and size turkey. NOTE: Place remaining dressing in greased casserole; bake for 1 hour.

Mrs. Murl Starr, Pres.
Lutheran Ladies Aid
Hillman, Minnesota

SMOKED TURKEY

1 6 ½ to 7-lb. turkey
½ tsp. garlic salt
Salt and pepper
⅓ c. liquid smoke
1 c. boiling water
Butter

Remove all pin feathers from turkey; rinse with cold water and pat dry with paper towels. Rub turkey cavity and skin with garlic salt, salt and pepper. Brush entire bird, inside out with 1/4 cup liquid meat smoke. Refrigerate overnight. Place turkey in a shallow roasting pan. Bake in preheated 500 degree oven for 15 to 20 minutes. Reduce heat to 400 degrees; pour a mixture of water, a small amount butter and remaining liquid smoke around turkey. Continue roasting for 2 hours or until bird is tender.

(Continued on next page)

Baste frequently. Cool and serve cold. NOTE: Fish may be prepared by the same method.

Mrs. Edwin Reinking
St. Paul's Ladies Aid Soc.
Decatur, Indiana

TEXAS TURKEY AND DRESSING

1 10 to 12-lb. turkey
4 c. corn bread crumbs
2 c. day-old bread crumbs
1 c. chopped celery
½ c. chopped onion
1 sm. tart apple, chopped
½ c. raisins
1 ½ tsp. salt
1 tsp. pepper
1 tsp. poultry seasoning
6 eggs, beaten
5 c. turkey broth

Place turkey in roaster; fill roaster one-half full of water. Bake, covered, at 350 degrees for 5 hours. Combine crumbs, celery, onion, apple, raisins and seasonings. Mix well. Combine eggs and broth; pour over mixture. Mix well. Let set for 15 to 20 minutes. Pour over turkey and stuffing. Return to oven and bake for 1 hour or until dressing and turkey are golden brown.

Mrs. August Bernhardt, Pres.
St. Lukes LWML
Olney, Texas

TURKEY-CHIP BAKE

2 c. diced cooked turkey or chicken
1 c. diced celery
3 green onions, chopped
1 10 ½-oz. can cream of mushroom soup
½ c. water
1 c. grated Cheddar cheese
2 c. crushed potato chips

Combine poultry or meat with celery and onions. Place one-half of mixture in casserole. Spoon 1/2 can soup and 1/4 cup water over meat mixture. Sprinkle with 1/2 cup cheese and 1 cup potato chips. Repeat layers. Bake at 350 degrees for 25 to 30 minutes. NOTE: Beef or pork may be substituted for turkey. Yield: 4 servings.

Mrs. Emil Johnson, Sec.
St. Paul's Ladies Guild
Grants Pass, Oregon

TURKEY CHOW MEIN ALOHA

3 c. chopped celery
1 lge. onion, chopped
3 carrots, chopped
1 c. turkey gravy

1 tsp. salt
Dash of pepper
4 c. chopped cooked turkey
1 can cream of mushroom soup
1 sm. can mushroom
1 tsp. soy sauce
1 7-oz. can crushed pineapple

Simmer vegetables in gravy until tender; add all remaining ingredients. Simmer for 30 minutes. Serve over chow mein noodles. Yield: 12 servings.

Mrs. Lloyd Johnson, Pres.
LCW
Harris, Minnesota

TURKEY LOAF

¼ c. shortening
1 c. hot milk
2 c. chopped cooked turkey
2 c. soft bread cubes
½ tsp. salt
¼ tsp. pepper
2 eggs, beaten
¼ c. chopped celery
¼ c. chopped onion

Melt shortening in milk. Combine all ingredients; pack lightly into greased loaf pan. If there is any left-over turkey skin, arrange it over top. Bake at 350 degrees for 45 minutes. Let stand for 5 minutes before slicing. Yield: 6 servings.

Mrs. Joel H. Timian, Pres.
Zion LWML
Corvallis, Oregon

TURKEY RECHAUFFE

1 c. sliced mushrooms
1 tsp. grated onion
4 tsp. butter
2 tbsp. flour
1 ½ c. broth
¼ c. cooking Sherry
1 c. light cream, scalded
1 tsp. salt
¼ tsp. pepper
3 egg yolks, beaten
3 c. cooked chopped turkey

(Continued on next page)

Brown mushrooms and onion lightly in butter; remove mushrooms. Add flour to remaining butter; stir until smooth and hot. Gradually add broth and Sherry; cook gently until thickened. Add scalded cream and seasonings. Blend a small amount of hot mixture into egg yolks and return to sauce, beating vigorously. Add turkey and mushrooms. Serve hot over toast points. Yield: 6-8 servings.

Mrs. Ralph Heine
Zion Ladies Aid
Columbia City, Indiana

TURKEY SUPREME

1 loaf day-old bread
1 onion, chopped
2 tsp. sage
1 tsp. salt
Pepper
¾ c. melted butter
2 eggs, beaten
Broth
1 6-lb. turkey, cooked and cubed
2 cans cream of mushroom soup
4 tbsp. pimento
¾ c. flour
2 c. milk

Mix bread, onion, sage, salt, pepper, 1/4 cup butter, eggs and enough broth to moisten dressing. Place in greased 10 x 14-inch baking dish. Arrange turkey over dressing. Combine 1/2 cup butter, soup, pimento, flour and milk. Pour sauce over turkey. Bake at 350 degrees for 1 hour. Yield: 8 servings.

Mrs. A. C. Thompson
Walhalla Ladies Aid Soc.
Walhalla, North Dakota

TURKEY SUPREME

2 c. herb-seasoned croutettes
2 c. diced turkey or tuna
1 can French cut green beans, drained
¼ c. slivered blanched almonds (opt.)
1 can cream of mushroom soup
½ c. milk
¼ c. hot water
2 tbsp. butter, melted

Distribute 2/3 cup croutettes in buttered shallow baking dish. Arrange a layer of turkey over croutettes, then a layer of beans. Scatter almonds over beans; top with a layer of turkey. Blend soup with milk; pour over casserole. Top with remaining croutettes blended with hot water and melted butter. Bake at 400 degrees for 25 to 30 minutes or until browned and bubbly. Yield: 4-6 servings.

Mrs. Rudolph Riedel, Pres.
Immanuel Ladies Aid
Parkers Prairie, Minnesota

TURKEY TETRAZZINI

2 c. shredded cooked turkey
1 can cream of mushroom soup
½ c. milk
2 c. cooked spaghetti
1 c. canned peas, drained
1 sm. can pimento
1 tsp. salt
1 c. shredded cheese

Mix all ingredients except cheese. Place in greased baking dish. Bake at 350 degrees for 30 minutes. Sprinkle cheese on top the last 15 minutes of baking. Yield: 6-8 servings.

Mrs. Robert L. Behlmer, Pres.
St. John's Ladies Aux.
Napoleon, Indiana

Fish and Shellfish Favorites

RECIPE FOR TABASCO OYSTER PIE ON PAGE 230

BAKED FILLETS

2 lb. haddock fillets
1 onion, chopped
2 tbsp. butter
1 tbsp. flour
1 tsp. salt
1 tsp. pepper
1 c. cream
Paprika

Cut fillets into serving sizes; place in greased baking dish. Saute onion in butter until tender; blend in flour, salt and pepper. Stir in cream. Pour over fish; sprinkle with paprika. Bake at 350 degrees for 30 minutes. Yield: 4 servings.

Mrs. James Penney
Mt. Calvary LCW
Bridgewater, Nova Scotia, Canada

BAKED HALIBUT

1 ½ lb. halibut fillets or 4 halibut steaks
1 can frozen cream of shrimp soup, thawed
½ c. dried bread crumbs
Paprika

Arrange fish fillets or steaks in a buttered dish. Spread soup over fish; sprinkle with bread crumbs. Sprinkle lightly with paprika. Bake at 350 degrees for 30 minutes or until fish flakes easily. Yield: 4 servings.

Mrs. Robert C. Schoen, 3rd VP
Christ Lutheran Church LWML
Brea, California

FISH CAKES

1 ½ lb. halibut
2 tbsp. flour
2 eggs
1 c. milk
½ tsp. nutmeg
Salt to taste
2 c. cream sauce
Chopped parsley
Paprika

Cut halibut into pieces; put through meat grinder. Add flour; mix well. Beat in an egg at a time. Add milk, nutmeg and salt; mix well. Shape with 2 soup spoons into rounded patties. Fry in small amount of shortening until brown on each side. Place in shallow casserole; pour cream sauce over top. Sprinkle with parsley and paprika. Bake at 325 degrees for 30 minutes. Yield: 6 servings.

Mrs. Doreen Merrell, Pres.
Faith Women's Guild
Juneau, Alaska

HALIBUT CREOLE

1 ½ lb. halibut, sliced
Sliced tomato
Chopped green pepper
Chopped onion
⅓ c. melted butter

Place halibut in a buttered glass baking dish; sprinkle with salt and pepper. Place tomato on each piece of halibut. Top each tomato slice with 1/2 teaspoonful green pepper and 1/2 teaspoonful onion. Baste with the butter. Bake at 350 degrees for 40 to 45 minutes.

Mrs. William Gehring, Treas.
St. John's Ladies Aid
Vegreville, Alberta, Canada

SOLOMON GUNDY

6 salt herring
Vinegar
1 c. sugar
½ tsp. pepper
1 tbsp. pickling spice
3 lge. onions, sliced

Soak herring in cold water overnight. Clean and remove skin. Fillet and cut into pieces. Bring enough vinegar to a boil to cover fish. Add sugar, pepper and pickling spice. Cool. Pour over herring and onions. Place in bottle; seal tightly. Keep in cool place. Yield: 20 servings.

Mrs. Allen M. Wentzell
Grace LCW
Luenburg County, Nova Scotia, Canada

BAKED FISH WITH CHEESE SAUCE

1 chopped onion, chopped
1 7-oz. pkg. spreading cheese, sliced
1 2 ½-lb. Walleye pike, halibut or perch
1 ½ tsp. Worcestershire
1 tsp. dry mustard
1 tsp. salt
½ tsp. pepper
1 c. milk

Place onion and one-half of cheese in cavity of fish. Place remaining cheese on top of fish. Combine remaining ingredients; pour over fish. Bake at 400 degrees for 25 to 30 minutes. Yield: 4 servings.

Mrs. Gene Hall, Pres.
Trinity Ladies Aid of Freistadt LWML
Mequon, Wisconsin

BAKED PICKEREL

Bacon
Cleaned dressed pickerel

Place a layer of bacon in bean pot; cover with a few layers of fish. Place a layer of bacon over fish. Cover with water, filling pot not quite full. Cover and bake at 250 to 300 degrees for 5 to 7 hours.

Mrs. Walter Neuberger, Chmn.
Zion Ladies Aid
Canistota, South Dakota

FISH CAKES

3 to 4 lb. Northern pike fillets
2 eggs
1 c. light cream
Salt and pepper to taste

Grind fillets in meat grinder; combine with eggs, cream, salt and pepper. Mix at high speed for 10 to 15 minutes. Drop by tablespoonfuls into hot fat. Fry for 3 to 5 minutes. Yield: 8 servings.

Mrs. Margaret Klees, Treas.
Mt. Zion Eventide Guild
Minneapolis, Minnesota

PICKLED WALLEYE FISH

1 lb. Walleye, filleted
1 tbsp. salt
1 c. water
1 c. vinegar
Pickling spice
1 tbsp. sugar
1 lge. onion, sliced

Cut fish into bite-sized pieces. Sprinkle with salt; pile fish into dish. Add water to make a brine to cover fish. Let set in a cool place over-night. Heat vinegar with pickling spice and add sugar; let cool slightly. Rinse fish and drain. Pack fish and onion in layers into jar. Cover with vinegar mixture. Seal.

Mrs. Verna Smith, Pres.
Our Savior Mary Martha Cir.
Dryden, Ontario, Canada

BAKED SALMON

1 can salmon
3 tbsp. shortening or butter
2 tbsp. onion
2 tbsp. flour
1 tsp. salt
¼ tsp. pepper
1 c. rich milk
1 8-oz. pkg. noodles, cooked

Drain salmon, reserving liquid. Melt butter; add onions, flour, salt, pepper, rich milk and salmon liquid. Line greased pan with one-half of noodles. Remove bones and black particles from salmon. Place salmon over noodles; top with remaining noodles. Pour sauce over noodles. Top with buttered bread crumbs or crushed potato chips, if desired. Bake at 375 degrees for 25 to 30 minutes. Yield: 6 servings.

Mrs. C. F. Juergensen
First Lutheran Church LWML
Sabetha, Kansas

BAKED SALMON

1 sm. onion, finely chopped
½ med. green pepper, chopped
1 tbsp. butter or margarine
1 can cream of mushroom soup
¼ c. milk
1 1-lb. can red salmon
½ c. coarse bread crumbs
1 tbsp. grated Parmesan cheese

Saute onion and green pepper in butter; add soup and milk. Blend well and heat almost to a boil. Drain salmon; remove skin and bones. Break into large chunks; place in a small greased casserole. Pour soup mixture over salmon; cover with crumbs. Sprinkle with cheese. Bake at 400 degrees for 20 minutes. Yield: 4 servings.

Mrs. Peter H. Schumaker, Jr., VP
Trinity Eventide Miss'y League
Davenport, Iowa

BAKED SALMON CASSEROLE

1 1-lb. can red salmon
2 c. bread cubes
1 c. milk
2 tbsp. melted butter
½ tsp. salt
¼ tsp. paprika
2 tbsp. chopped celery
1 tbsp. chopped onion
1 tbsp. chopped parsley
1 tbsp. chopped green pepper
2 eggs, beaten

Flake salmon and remove skin and bones. Soak bread in milk. Combine remaining ingredients. Turn into casserole. Bake at 350 degrees for 45 minutes or until lightly brown. Serve with white sauce, if desired. Yield: 4 servings.

Mrs. Elva Swanson
Bethany Ladies Aid
Hawthorne, Nevada

BAKED SALMON WITH GRAVY SAUCE

1 1-lb. can salmon
1 c. cracker crumbs
5 tbsp. melted butter
½ c. light cream
4 eggs
1 tsp. (rounded) flour
1 c. milk

Drain salmon, reserving liquid. Combine salmon, cracker crumbs, 4 tablespoonfuls butter, cream and beaten yolks of 3 eggs. Beat 3 egg whites until stiff. Fold into salmon mixture. Turn into casserole. Bake at 350 degrees for 25 minutes. Blend flour into remaining melted butter; gradually add milk and salmon liquid. Bring to a boil. Beat remaining egg; stir into hot mixture. Serve with baked salmon. Yield: 9 servings.

Frieda L. Hett
Zion Evangelical Ladies Aid
Hillsboro, Kansas

MUSHROOM-SALMON LOAF

2 c. flaked salmon
1 ½ c. dry bread crumbs
½ c. minced green pepper
2 eggs, slightly beaten
1 can cream of mushroom soup

Combine all ingredients; pack firmly into a greased small loaf pan. Bake at 350 degrees for 1 hour or until done. Turn out onto a warm platter.

MUSHROOM SAUCE:

1 can cream of mushroom soup
¼ c. milk

Combine all ingredients and heat; serve over loaf. Yield: 6 servings.

Mrs. Arthur Craig, Pres.
Trinity Women's League
Springfield, Missouri

OVEN BAKED SALMON CROQUETTES

1 1-lb. can salmon
Milk
¼ c. butter
2 tbsp. minced onion
⅓ c. flour
¼ tsp. salt
¾ tsp. Tabasco sauce
1 tbsp. lemon juice
1 c. corn flake crumbs

Drain salmon, reserving liquid. Add enough milk to liquid to make 1 cup. Melt butter in saucepan; add onion and cook until tender. Blend in flour, salt and Tabasco sauce; add milk mixture. Cook until thickened, stirring constantly. Flake salmon; add to sauce with lemon juice. Stir in one-half of corn flake crumbs; chill. Divide mixture into light or tea portions; shape into cones. Roll in remaining corn flake crumbs. Place on greased baking sheet. Bake at 400 degrees for 20 to 25 minutes or until golden brown. Yield: 8-10 servings.

Mrs. L. G. Fitzpatrick, Jr., Pres.
St. Paul Women's Guild
St. Joseph, Missouri

RICE AND SALMON PIE

⅓ c. raw rice, cooked
4 tbsp. butter
4 tbsp. grated cheese
1 9-in. pastry shell, baked
1 ½ c. canned salmon
2 tbsp. flour
1 c. milk
1 egg, lightly beaten

Mix hot rice with 2 tablespoonfuls butter and 2 tablespoonfuls cheese. Place in pie shell. Top with salmon. Melt remaining butter; blend in flour. Gradually add milk, stirring and cooking until thick. Remove from heat; stir in egg.

Pour over salmon. Sprinkle with the remaining cheese. Bake at 450 degrees for 10 minutes. Yield: 6 servings.

Mrs. Harold Kosmack
Our Redeemer Lutheran Church
Buckingham, Quebec, Canada

SALMON IN BARBECUE SAUCE

1 5-lb. salmon, whole or cut into large pieces
Salt
Pepper
Butter
1 lge. onion, chopped
1 bottle catsup
1 tsp. soy sauce
1 tsp. mustard
1 tsp. Worcestershire sauce
Few drops of Tabasco sauce

Place salmon in a foil-lined shallow baking dish. Sprinkle with salt, pepper and melted butter. Fold foil over fish. Bake at 350 degrees for 30 minutes or until fish is partially cooked. Saute onion in 1/4 pound butter; add remaining ingredients. Simmer until thick. Pour over salmon. Bake, uncovered, for 30 minutes or until fish is done, basting with sauce frequently. Yield: 8 servings.

Mrs. Glenn Parish, Pres.
Hope LCW
Lynden, Washington

SALMON CASSEROLE

½ c. carrots
½ c. onion
1 6-oz. can salmon, skin and bones removed
1 c. cooked macaroni
1 can cream of celery soup
1 tsp. salt
⅛ tsp. pepper
2 tbsp. butter
½ c. bread crumbs
¼ lb. cheese, cut into strips

Cook carrots and onion in small amount of water until tender; drain. Break salmon into chunks; place in greased 2-quart casserole. Spoon carrots, onions and macaroni over salmon. Combine soup, salt and pepper; add to casserole. Melt butter; toss with bread crumbs. Cover top of casserole with crumbs. Place strips of cheese over crumbs. Bake at 375 degrees for 20 minutes. Yield: 6 servings.

Mrs. Vincent Kampert, Pres.
Immanuel Ladies Aid
Fairmont, Minnesota

SALMON CROQUETTES

1 lge. can salmon
2 eggs
2 c. crushed cracker crumbs
½ c. milk
¼ tsp. pepper
1 tsp. salt

216

(Continued on next page)

Combine all ingredients; shape into patties. Fry in butter until brown. Yield: 4 servings.

Mrs. Arthur Bussmann, Pres.
Zion LWML
Cologne, Minnesota

SALMON DELUXE CASSEROLE

1 c. undrained salmon, mashed
1 c. cooked rice
1 sm. onion, chopped
2 tbsp. chopped green pepper
2 tbsp. butter
1 10-oz. can cream of mushroom soup
1 c. milk
1 ¼ c. crushed potato chips

Combine salmon and rice. Saute onion and green pepper in butter until tender. Add salmon, rice mixture and soup combined with milk. Add crushed potato chips, reserving 1/4 cup for topping. Turn into casserole. Sprinkle with remaining crushed potato chips. Bake at 375 degrees for 45 minutes. Yield: 4 servings.

Mrs. Evonne Bode
Faith Ladies Aid Soc.
Courtenay, British Columbia, Canada

SALMON FRITTERS

1 ¼ c. sifted flour
1 ½ tsp. baking powder
1 tsp. salt
¼ c. yellow corn meal
1 egg, slightly beaten
¾ c. milk
1 1-lb. can red salmon, drained

Sift flour with baking powder and salt; stir in corn meal. Combine egg and milk; stir into dry ingredients. Break salmon into bite-sized pieces; fold into batter. Drop by rounded tablespoonfuls into deep fat heated to 375 degrees. Fry until golden brown. Drain on paper towels.

Mrs. Albert Rommel, Treas.
St. John's LWML
Escalon, California

SALMON LOAF

1 egg, beaten
1 c. grated cheese
1 tbsp. grated onion
½ tsp. salt
2 c. undrained salmon chunks
1 c. soft bread crumbs
1 tbsp. melted butter
¼ tsp. pepper

Combine all ingredients; place in buttered casserole. Place casserole in pan of water. Cover; bake at 350 degrees until set. Yield: 6 servings.

Sylvia S. Richau
St. James Ladies Aid Soc.
Golden Valley, North Dakota

SALMON LOAF

1 1-lb. can salmon
1 tbsp. lemon juice
1 tsp. salt
2 eggs, beaten
⅔ c. chopped celery
1 ½ c. bread crumbs
½ c. milk

Drain salmon, reserving liquid; add enough water to make 1/2 cup. Combine all ingredients. Pack mixture firmly into a greased glass 1 1/2-quart loaf pan. Bake at 350 degrees for 30 to 40 minutes. Yield: 6-8 servings.

Mrs. Val Baumeister, Pres.
Immanuel Mary Martha Soc.
Butte, Nebraska

SALMON LOAF

1 16-oz. can salmon
Milk
1 ½ c. soft bread crumbs
2 tbsp. chopped sweet pickle
2 tsp. lemon juice
1 tsp. salt
¼ tsp. pepper
1 egg, slightly beaten

Drain salmon, reserving liquid. Add enough milk to liquid to make 1 cup. Flake salmon. Combine all ingredients. Pack into a greased small loaf pan. Bake at 375 degrees for 25 to 30 minutes or until browned. Serve with egg sauce or mock Hollandaise sauce, if desired. Yield: 4-6 servings.

Helene Enders, Pres.
Faith Women's League
North Surrey, British Columbia, Canada

SALMON LOAF

2 eggs, separated
2 c. cooked rice
1 c. undrained flaked salmon
Juice of ½ lemon
2 tbsp. melted butter
Dash of pepper
½ tsp. salt

Beat egg yolks; mix with rice, salmon and seasonings. Beat egg whites until stiff; fold into salmon mixture. Place in a greased baking pan; set pan in pan of hot water. Bake at 350 degrees for 45 minutes to 1 hour. Serve with tomato sauce, if desired.

Irma Hartman, Pres.
Our Redeemer LWML
Kokomo, Indiana

SCALLOPED SALMON

1 1-lb. can salmon
Milk
1 ½ c. cracker crumbs
¼ c. melted butter
2 tbsp. lemon juice
2 tbsp. diced onion
Dash of pepper

Drain salmon, reserving liquid; add enough milk to make 1 1/3 cups. Heat salmon liquid mixture. Combine all ingredients; place in buttered baking dish. Bake at 350 degrees for 30 minutes.

Mrs. Melvin Moore, Pres.
LWML
Creston, Iowa

TERIYAKI

¾ c. shoyu sauce
¼ c. sugar
¾ c. Sake
1 lb. salmon, tuna, rockfish or mackerel
    fillets

Combine shoyu sauce, sugar and Sake. Cut fillets into small steaks; marinate in sauce for 30 minutes. Remove from marinade. Broil on one side for 4 minutes. Turn and broil other side for 6 minutes. While broiling, baste three times in sauce. Yield: 4 servings.

Mildred E. Meissner, Chmn.
Peace LWML
Schererville, Indiana

BAKED RED SNAPPER WITH CREOLE SAUCE

6 slices bacon
1 6-lb. red snapper
Salt and pepper
3 or 4 stalks celery, finely chopped
4 med. onions, finely chopped
2 green peppers, finely chopped
4 cloves of garlic, finely chopped
6 tbsp. cooking oil
3 lge. cans tomatoes
½ tsp. Tabasco sauce
½ tsp. thyme
¼ tsp. oregano
Lemon slices
Parsley

Fry bacon slices until crisp. Grease snapper inside and out with part of bacon grease; rub in salt and pepper. Bake at 350 degrees for 30 minutes. Saute celery, onions, green peppers and garlic in remaining bacon grease and cooking oil. Add tomatoes, Tabasco sauce and seasonings. Pour over snapper. Garnish with lemon slices and sprigs of parsley. Yield: 8 servings.

Mrs. Mary H. Price
St. Paul's Ladies Guild
Montgomery, Alabama

STUFFED SOLE FILLETS

2 lb. sole fillets
½ c. drained, grated pared cucumber
1 ¼ c. seasoned bread crumbs
½ tsp. Worcestershire sauce
Dill pickle juice or milk
Salt and pepper to taste
2 lb. sole fillets
Seasoned flour
3 c. thinly sliced onions
Butter or margarine
½ tsp. dill seed
2 c. medium thick cream sauce or 1 can cream
    of celery soup
½ c. sweet or sour cream
3 tbsp. Parmesan cheese

Combine cucumber, bread crumbs and Worcestershire sauce; moisten with dill juice or milk. Season with salt and pepper. Spread the centers of each fillet with a heaping tablespoonful of mixture; roll up and secure with toothpicks. Sprinkle with seasoned flour. Saute onions in small amount of butter; sprinkle with salt, pepper and dill seed. Spread in a shallow 8 x 12-inch pan; place fish rolls on top of onions. Brush rolls with 1/4 cup melted butter. Bake at 400 degrees for 15 minutes. Remove toothpicks from fish rolls; drizzle with cream sauce. Sprinkle with cheese. Bake for 5 minutes longer. Sprinkle with paprika or chopped parsley. Yield: 6 servings.

Mrs. Ben Johnson, VP
St. Andrew's LCW
West Northfield, Nova Scotia, Canada

BAKED FISH

Salt
3 lb. thick trout or bass
½ c. flour
⅛ tsp. pepper
6 med. potatoes, chopped
4 to 6 sm. onions, halved
8 strips bacon
1 can tomato sauce
½ c. water

Salt fish lightly; set aside. Mix flour with 1 teaspoonful salt and pepper. Roll fish in flour mixture; place in 8 x 12 x 2-inch baking pan. place potatoes and onions around fish. Sprinkle with remaining flour. Top with bacon; add tomato paste mixed with water. Bake at 350 degrees for 15 minutes or until bacon is brown. Cover; bake for 1 hour and 15 minutes longer. Yield: 6 servings.

Mrs. H. F. Krusemark, Pres.
Zion Ladies Aid
Alamo, Texas

BAKED TUNA

½ green pepper, chopped
1 sm. onion, diced
2 tbsp. butter
4 tbsp. flour
1 qt. milk
1 tsp. salt

218

(Continued on next page)

13 oz. tuna
8 oz. mushrooms
1 25-cent bag potato chips, crushed

Brown green pepper and onion in butter. Add flour, milk and salt. Cook until thickened. Add tuna, mushrooms and three-fourths of potato chips. Pour into casserole; top with remaining potato chips. Bake at 350 degrees for 1 hour. Yield: 6 servings.

Mrs. M. V. Christensen, Treas.
St. Mark's Women's Aux.
Baton Rouge, Louisiana

CHEESE AND TUNA CASSEROLE

2 c. cooked rice
2 7-oz. cans tuna
¾ c. cooked vegetables
1 c. milk
1 can cream of celery soup
6 slices American cheese, cubed
Pimento cheese strips

Combine rice, tuna and mixed vegetables in greased 2-quart casserole. Gradually add milk to soup, blending well. Add with cubed cheese to rice mixture. Garnish with pimento cheese strips. Bake at 350 degrees for 35 to 40 minutes. Yield: 4 servings.

Mrs. Clarence Bruns
Trinity Evangelical Ladies Aid Soc.
Harvel, Illinois

CHOPSTICK TUNA

1 can cream of mushroom soup
¼ c. water or milk
1 can tuna, flaked
1 can chow mein noodles
1 c. finely sliced celery
¼ to ½ c. cashew nuts
Dash of pepper (opt.)
¼ c. finely chopped onion
1 sm. can Mandarin oranges, drained (opt.)

Combine soup and water. Add tuna, 1 cup noodles, celery, nuts, pepper and onion. Toss lightly. Place in ungreased 10 x 6-inch shallow baking dish or 1 1/2-quart casserole. Sprinkle remaining noodles on top. Bake at 375 degrees for 15 to 20 minutes or at 325 degrees for 40 minutes. Garnish with Mandarin oranges. NOTE: If desired, white Albacore tuna may be used. All noodles may be mixed in and dish topped with cashews. Yield: 4-8 servings.

Mrs. Earl F. Halverson, Sec.
St. Timothy's Lutheran Church
Skokie, Illinois
Helen Becker, Pres.
Faith Women's Guild
Westchester, Illinois

DEEP SEA DELIGHT

1 6-oz. pkg. noodles
1 can cream of mushroom soup
1 can button mushrooms
1 can tuna
1 1-lb. can asparagus tips
1 sm. green pepper, chopped
¾ c. cubed or grated American cheese
½ tsp. salt
⅛ tsp. pepper

Cook noodles in salted water. Drain, rinse and drain again. Add remaining ingredients, reserving some of the cheese. Pour into casserole; top with reserved cheese. Bake at 350 degrees for 45 minutes. Yield: 6 servings.

Edna Lemke
Faith LWML
Carpinteria, California

FISH AND NOODLE CASSEROLE

1 5-oz. pkg. noodles, cooked and drained
1 can tuna
1 pimento or green pepper
1 c. cubed cheese
3 hard-cooked eggs, diced (opt.)
Salt and pepper to taste

Combine all ingredients; pour into casserole.

WHITE SAUCE:

3 tbsp. butter, melted
3 tbsp. flour
1 sm. onion, finely cut
1 ½ c. milk

Blend butter and flour. Add onion. Slowly stir in milk; cook until thickened, stirring constantly. Pour over tuna mixture in casserole. Bake at 325 degrees for 1 hour. Yield: 6 servings.

Mrs. Mabel L. Lake
Gettysburg Emmanuel Lutheran Church
Gettysburg, South Dakota

ITALIAN-STYLE TUNA AND NOODLES

2 cans tuna
1 clove of garlic
1 bay leaf, crushed
¼ c. melted butter
½ c. water
1 tbsp. sugar
Dash of pepper
2 c. cubed cheese
½ c. chopped onion
⅓ c. chopped celery
1 No. 303 can tomatoes
1 can tomato paste
1 ½ tsp. salt
½ tsp. oregano
1 pkg. noodles, cooked

219

(Continued on next page)

Combine all ingredients in casserole. Bake at 375 degrees for 30 minutes. Yield: 10 servings.

Mrs. Ed J. Bredehoeft, Pres.
St. Paul's LCW
Emmetsburg, Iowa

PARTY TUNA DISH

2 c. cooked rice
1 c. water-packed tuna
⅛ tsp. pepper
½ tsp. salt
1 tbsp. chopped parsley
1 tbsp. grated onion
¾ c. grated cheese
⅔ c. thick white sauce
⅓ c. crushed corn flakes
2 tbsp. brown sugar
6 slices pineapple

Mix rice, tuna, seasonings, onion, 1/2 cup cheese and the white sauce; mold into six balls. Roll in mixture of corn flake crumbs, 1/4 cup cheese and brown sugar. Place balls on 6 pineapple slices. Bake at 325 degrees for 25 minutes. Yield: 6 servings.

Mrs. R. E. Clausen, VP
Immanuel Ladies Aid
Wisconsin Rapids, Wisconsin

PERFECT TUNA CASSEROLE

1 can cream of mushroom soup
½ c. milk
1 7-oz. can tuna, drained and coarsely
    flaked
1 ¼ c. crushed potato chips
1 c. cooked peas, drained

Empty soup into a small casserole; add milk and mix thoroughly. Add tuna, 1 cup potato chips and peas; stir well. Sprinkle top with remaining potato chips. Bake at 375 degrees for 20 minutes. Yield: 4 servings.

Mrs. R. W. Kimbrough
St. Mark's Ladies Aux.
Baton Rouge, Louisiana

TUNA CASSEROLE

1 c. chopped onions
1 c. tuna
1 ½ c. water
1 c. chopped celery
1 c. cream of mushroom soup
1 c. Chinese-fried noodles
Buttered crumbs

Mix all ingredients except crumbs; pour into casserole. Top with crumbs. Bake at 350 degrees for 1 hour.

Mrs. Gerhard Obermueller
Christ the King Lutheran Church
Cody, Wyoming

TUNA WITH BAKED RICE

1 c. rice
1 tbsp. butter
½ tsp. salt
1 c. shredded tuna
1 c. thin white sauce
1 egg, well beaten
Paprika

Cook rice in double boiler; add butter and salt. Mix lightly. Line well oiled baking dish with rice. Pour tuna into rice mold. Cover with white sauce combined with egg. Bake at 375 degrees for 30 minutes. Sprinkle with paprika. NOTE: if desired, minced beef, chicken or salmon may be substituted for tuna. Yield: 8 servings.

Mrs. Hugo Findeisen, Pres.
Trinity Ladies Aid
Sealy, Texas

TUNA CASSEROLE

1 5 ½-oz. can evaporated milk
1 6 ½-oz. can tuna
1 can chicken and rice soup
1 can cream of mushroom soup
1 3-oz. can chow mein noodles

Mix all ingredients in casserole. Bake at 375 degrees for 30 to 35 minutes. Yield: 6 servings.

Joyce Warner, Sec.
Hope Women's Guild
Plant City, Florida

TUNA CASSEROLE

2 c. diced celery
¼ c. diced onion
6 tbsp. butter
1 can tuna
1 lge. can Chinese noodles
1 can cream of chicken soup
1 can cream of mushroom soup

Saute celery and onion in butter; add remaining ingredients. Pour into casserole. Bake at 350 degrees for 1 hour. Yield: 8-10 servings.

Mrs. Herbert Quandt, Pres.
Zion Ladies Aid
Denison, Iowa

TUNA CASSEROLE

½ c. chopped onion
¼ c. chopped green pepper
3 tbsp. fat
2 tbsp. flour
1 ¼ c. milk
1 10 ½-oz. can cream of chicken soup
¼ c. pimento
1 6 ½-oz. can tuna
½ 6-oz. pkg. macaroni, cooked and drained

Cook onion and green pepper in fat until tender. Add flour and blend. Add milk; cook over low

220

(Continued on next page)

heat until thick, stirring. Stir in remaining ingredients. Pour into greased 1 1/2-quart casserole. Bake at 350 degrees for 30 minutes. Yield: 6 servings.

Mrs. Delbert Miller
Grace Ladies Aid
Waterloo, Iowa

TUNA MEDITERRANEAN

2 7-oz. cans tuna
1 c. sour cream
¼ tsp. oregano
2 c. cooked elbow macaroni
½ c. sliced olives
¾ c. mushrooms
¼ c. chopped green pepper
2 tbsp. chopped pimento
¼ c. chopped cashews or almonds
¾ tsp. salt
1 c. grated American cheese
¾ c. corn flakes, crushed

Mix all ingredients except cheese and crumbs; place in 1 1/2-quart casserole. Sprinkle with cheese, then with corn flake crumbs. Bake at 350 degrees for 30 minutes. Yield: 6 servings.

Mrs. Lorain Butler, Pres.
Our Savior's Lutheran Ladies
Chester, California

TUNA-NOODLE BAKE

2 c. wide noodles
1 7-oz. can tuna, flaked
1 10-oz. can mushroom soup
1 c. milk

Cook noodles until tender; drain well. Place in greased baking dish. Spread tuna over noodles. Mix soup and milk; pour over noodles and tuna. Bake at 375 degrees for 35 minutes. Yield: 6 servings.

Mrs. Claire Becker
Zion Ladies Aid
Nipawin, Saskatchewan, Canada

TUNA AND NOODLE CASSEROLE

3 tbsp. butter
2 tbsp. flour
1 ½ c. milk
1 tsp. salt
¼ tsp. pepper
½ tsp. paprika
½ lb. American cheese, grated or cubed
1 4-oz. can mushrooms
1 7 ½-oz. can tuna, flaked
1 4-oz. pkg. noodles, cooked

Make a white sauce of butter, flour, milk and seasonings; add cheese and stir until smooth. Place mushrooms, tuna and noodles in layers in greased baking dish, with part of cheese sauce over each layer. Garnish with a few button mushrooms, if desired. Bake at 400 degrees for 20 minutes or until golden brown.

Mrs. Paul Oertel, Pres.
Zion Dorcas Soc.
Markville, Minnesota
Mrs. W. T. Rosamond, Pres.
Salem LWML
Springdale, Arkansas

TUNA-NOODLE CASSEROLE

½ 8-oz. pkg. wide noodles
1 8-oz. can English peas
¼ tsp. salt
1 c. diced celery (opt.)
½ c. diced green pepper (opt.)
1 6 ½-oz. can white tuna, drained and flaked
1 can cream of mushroom soup
½ c. milk
¼ c. bread crumbs or corn flake crumbs
1 tsp. butter

Cook noodles until tender in salted water; drain. Drain peas, reserving liquid. Combine liquid from peas, salt and celery; cook until tender, adding green pepper during last 5 minutes. Mix noodles, peas, celery, green pepper, tuna, soup and milk. If mixture is too dry, a little more milk may be added. Place in large casserole; sprinkle with buttered crumbs. Refrigerate until about 1 hour before serving time. Bake at 350 degrees until browned, about 45 minutes. Yield: 6 servings.

Mrs. Lillian Haman
Faith Evangelical Ladies
Hialeah, Florida

TUNA POT PIE

1 ½ c. diced carrots
1 ½ c. diced potatoes
3 tbsp. chopped onion
1 c. canned peas
1 7-oz. can tuna
1 ½ to 2 c. milk
¼ c. butter or margarine, melted
¼ c. flour
Salt and pepper to taste
Biscuit dough

Cook carrots, potatoes and onion until just tender in liquid from can of peas. Drain, reserving liquid. Mix liquid with oil from tuna and enough milk to make 2 cups of liquid. Blend butter and flour; stir in liquid. Cook until thickened, stirring constantly. Pour over cooked vegetables; add tuna, peas, salt and pepper. Pour into 1 1/2-quart casserole; top with biscuit dough. Bake at 450 degrees until biscuits are done. Yield: 6 servings.

Mrs. John Martell, Pres.
Zion Ladies Aid Soc.
Wallingford, Connecticut

TUNA AND NOODLE CASSEROLE

½ lb. Velveeta cheese
1 can cream of mushroom soup
⅓ c. milk
1 sm. pkg. noodles, cooked
2 cans tuna
Bread crumbs
Melted butter

Melt cheese in soup and milk. Add noodles and tuna; pour into casserole. Top with bread crumbs soaked in melted butter. Bake at 350 degrees for 20 minutes. Yield: 6 servings.

Dollyanna Bauer, Treas.
Concordia LCW
Chula Vista, California

TUNA-NOODLE CASSEROLE

1 can cream of mushroom soup
¼ lb. cheese
½ c. milk
1 tsp. chopped onion
1 tbsp. chopped green pepper
¼ tsp. pepper
1 8-oz. pkg. noodles, cooked and drained
1 can chunk-style tuna

Mix soup, cheese, milk, onion, green pepper and pepper in pan; cook until smooth. Add noodles and tuna. Bake at 325 degrees for 15 minutes. Yield: 4 servings.

Mrs. Otto Baker, Treas.
Grace LWML
Clarksville, Arkansas

TWO-TONE LOAF

4 ½ c. cooked rice
½ c. thick white sauce
1 tsp. grated onion
1 tbsp. chopped parsley
1 egg, beaten
1 8-oz. can tomato juice
1 7-oz. can tuna
4 slices Velveeta cheese

Combine 3 cups rice with white sauce, onion and parsley. Pack in greased loaf pan. Combine remaining 1 1/2 cups rice with egg, tomato juice and tuna. Pack into loaf pan as the second layer. Bake at 350 degrees for 1 hour. Unmold onto a platter; top with the cheese slices. Heat under broiler until bubbly. Yield: 6 servings.

Mrs. John O. Wessel, Pres.
Zion LWML
Matteson, Illinois

BAKED FISH

STUFFINGS:

2 c. stale bread crumbs
1 tsp. chopped capers or pickle
1 tsp. onion juice
½ tsp. salt
¼ c. melted butter
⅛ tsp. pepper

Combine all ingredients, mixing well.

FISH:

Cleaned fish
Salt
Salt pork strips
Pork fat

Sprinkle fish with salt; fill with stuffing. Sew edges together. Cut gashes across fish on each side; put strips of salt pork in gashes. Fold a piece of well buttered paper around tail of fish. Place fish on greased baking sheet with pieces of pork fat. Bake at 400 to 425 degrees for 15 minutes per pound plus an extra 15 minutes. Baste every 10 minutes; add water if necessary.

Mrs. Mathilda Neumann
Concordia Women's League
Geneseo, Illinois

BAKED FISH FILLETS

2 lb. fish
¼ tsp. salt
Dash of pepper
¼ tsp. paprika
Juice of 1 lemon
2 tbsp. butter or margarine
2 tbsp. flour
Salt and pepper to taste
1 tbsp. dry mustard
1 c. top milk
½ c. buttered bread crumbs
1 tbsp. minced parsley

Cut fillets in serving pieces; place in greased shallow baking dish. Sprinkle with salt, pepper, paprika and lemon juice. Melt butter; blend in flour, seasonings and milk. Cook until thick. Pour over fillets. Sprinkle with crumbs and parsley. Bake at 350 degrees for 35 minutes. Yield: 6 servings.

Mrs. Martha Lostroh, Pres.
Grace Ladies Aid
Seguin, Texas

BARBECUED FISH FILLETS

1 white wine
¼ c. lemon juice
2 tbsp. butter
2 tbsp. margarine
Fish

Combine wine, lemon juice, butter and margarine in saucepan. Cook over low heat until butter and margarine are melted; cool. Marinate fish for 20 minutes in mixture. Place fish on grill; brush with wine sauce for basting. If using a covered

(Continued on next page)

grill, cook each side for 5 minutes or 7 minutes per pound for large fish. If using an open grill, allow slightly more cooking time and baste more frequently.

Marlys Kuehnert
Our Savior Dorcas Guild
Columbus, Mississippi

BATTER-FRIED FISH
Fish fillets
2 c. buttermilk pancake mix
Beer

Cut fish fillets into 1-inch pieces. Thin pancake mix to desired consistency with beer. Dip fish into batter. Fry in deep fat at 400 degrees until done.

Mrs. Violet Schacht, Pres.
Redeemer Ladies Guild
Rochester, Minnesota

CHEESE-FISH BAKE
1 lb. fish fillet
1 can cream of mushroom soup
Dash of pepper
¼ c. shredded Cheddar cheese
Dash of paprika

Arrange fish in single layer in greased 10 x 6 x 2-inch baking dish. Pour soup over fish. Season with pepper; sprinkle Cheddar cheese over soup. Sprinkle with paprika. Bake at 375 degrees for 45 minutes or until lightly browned. Yield: 4 servings.

Mrs. Doris J. Bingerheimer
Christ Lutheran Church LWML
Wathena, Kansas

DEEP-FRIED FISH FILLETS
2 to 3 lb. shortening
1 lb. fish fillets
Salt to taste
½ c. flour
1 egg, slightly beaten
1 tbsp. water
Fine bread crumbs

Melt shortening in deep fat fryer at 370 degrees. Rinse fish in water and dry. Season with salt; dip into flour. Beat egg with water. Dip fish into egg mixture and then in bread crumbs. Fry in hot oil until golden brown; drain well. Yield: 6-8 servings.

Mrs. Henry Hippen, VP
Emmanuel Ladies Aid
Brook Park, Minnesota

DELICIA FISH
1 lb. frozen fish, partially thawed
1 c. wine or beer
¼ c. lemon juice
1 tsp. salt
Flour
Oil

Cut fish into slices, 1/2-inch thick. Pour mixed wine and lemon juice over slices; let stand for several hours or overnight. Drain off liquid Sprinkle with salt. Dip fish into flour. Fry in oil until golden brown.

Mrs. Marie Welk, Pres.
St. Luke's LWML
Eganville, Ontario, Canada

FISH POACHED IN TOMATO SAUCE
2 c. tomatoes
½ tsp. salt
1 bay leaf
1 tbsp. minced onion
½ tsp. peppercorns
2 lb. fish fillets
1 tbsp. butter

Cook tomatoes, salt, bay leaf, onion and peppercorns in greased skillet until reduced by about one-half. Add fish. Simmer for 5 minutes; turn fish carefully and simmer 5 minutes longer. Remove fish to hot platter. Strain tomato sauce; add butter. Pour over fish. Yield: 6 servings.

Mrs. Eloise H. Wood, Pres.
St. Michael's LWML
Little Valley, New York

FLAKED FISH CASSEROLE
2 eggs, separated
2 c. milk
2 tbsp. instant tapioca
1 ½ tsp. salt
Dash of pepper
½ c. finely chopped celery
1 ½ tsp. grated onion
2 c. flaked cooked fish
2 tbsp. chopped parsley
½ c. crushed corn flakes

Mix egg yolks with a small amount of milk in saucepan; add remaining milk, tapioca, salt, pepper, celery and onion. Mix well. Cook and stir over medium heat until mixture comes to a boil; remove from heat. Add fish and parsley, mixing well. Beat egg whites until stiff peaks form; very gradually fold in milk mixture, blending well. Spoon into greased 1 1/2-quart casserole. Sprinkle with corn flake crumbs. Bake at 350 degrees for 50 minutes or until firm and crumbs are browned. Yield: 4 servings.

Mrs. Jarl Sonsteng
Bethleham Dorcas Guild
Hermiston, Oregon

FRIED FISH

Fish
½ c. milk
1 egg
Prepared biscuit mix
Fat or shortening

Cut fish into serving pieces. Mix milk and egg. Dip fish into egg mixture, then into biscuit mix. Fry in deep fat until browned.

Martha Harms
Mt. Olive English Evangelical Women's League
Duluth, Minnesota

FRENCH-FRIED FISH FILLETS

Fish
Flour
Beaten egg
Cracker crumbs
Fat or rendered suet
Seasonings to taste

Dip fish in flour, egg and cracker crumbs. Fry in deep fat until done. Season to taste. Drain on paper towels.

Mrs. Bertha A. Rausch, Counselor
St. Peter's Ladies Guild
Napoleon, Ohio

FRENCH-FRIED FISH

1 lb. fish fillets
½ tsp. monosodium glutamate
Salt and pepper to taste
4 to 5 lb. beef suet, cut into small pieces

Dry fillets as much as possible. Rub monosodium glutamate into fillets; sprinkle with salt and pepper. Cook suet slowly until all fat is rendered; strain fat into French-frying pot, filling pot to desired depth.

MILK BATTER:

2 c. milk
¼ tsp. salt
Flour

Combine milk and salt; stir well. Soak fish in milk for 20 minutes. Remove from milk; roll lightly in flour. Fry in the beef fat at 380 to 390 degrees until done. Yield: 2 servings.

Mrs. Richard E. Hecht
Our Redeemer Ladies Aid
St. Louis, Missouri

OVEN BAKED FILLETS

4 fish fillets
1 tsp. salt
⅛ tsp. pepper
1 egg, beaten
1 tbsp. milk or water

Cracker meal, bread crumbs or corn meal
Melted butter

Roll fillets in mixture of salt, pepper, egg and milk; dredge in cracker meal. Place in greased pan. Brush with melted butter. Bake in preheated 350 degree oven for 20 to 25 minutes. Yield: 4 servings.

Mrs. Marlow McGowan, Pres.
Redeemer Bethany Soc.
Owatonna, Minnesota

PICKLED FISH

2 fish, 12-in. long
Salt
2 c. vinegar
2 bay leaves
10 whole allspice
¼ c. sugar
1 med. onion, sliced

Cut fish into 1-inch pieces; salt generously. Let stand for 6 hours. Rinse with cold water. Combine remaining ingredients; add 1 cup water. Bring to a boil. Add fish; boil for a few minutes longer. Place in hot sterilized jars and seal. Yield: 14 servings.

Mrs. Alfred Biberdorf
St. Paul's Ladies Aid Soc.
Willow City, North Dakota

PICKLED FISH

½ c. brown sugar
½ c. white wine
1 tbsp. pickling spice in cheesecloth
½ c. water
1 tbsp. salt
1 tbsp. concentrated lemon juice
1 ½ c. white vinegar
3 lb. fish, cut into bite-sized pieces
2 sm. or 1 lge. onion, thinly sliced

Combine all ingredients except vinegar, onion and fish; boil for 5 minutes. Cool. Add vinegar. Alternate layers of fish and onion in jars; pour strained vinegar mixture over all. Cover tightly and let set for at least 48 hours, turning jar upside down occasionally.

Mrs. Ray Kasma, Pres.
St. Paul's LWML
Wyoming, Minnesota

SWEET-SOUR FISH

1 1 ½ to 2-lb. fleshy fish
2 cloves of garlic, mashed
1 lge. onion, sliced
1 lge. sweet pepper, cut into strips
½ in. ginger, thinly sliced
2 c. water
¼ c. vinegar
3 tbsp. soy sauce
2 tbsp. flour
4 tbsp. sugar

(Continued on next page)

Fry fish and set aside. Saute garlic, onion, green pepper and ginger. Make a thick sauce of water, vinegar, soy sauce, flour and sugar. Add fried onion mixture. Boil until thick. Pour over fried fish on platter. Yield: 4-6 servings.

Mrs. Edward Pick, Sec.-Treas.
Trinity Evening Guild
Riesel, Texas

SEAFOOD STUFFED CREPES

FILLING AND SAUCE:

1 8-oz. can salmon, drained, boned, and flaked
1 7-oz. can tuna, drained and flaked
1 5-oz. can water chestnuts, drained and chopped or ½ c. finely chopped celery
1 tbsp. minced onion
5 tbsp. butter or margarine
⅓ c. flour
1 tsp. salt
⅛ tsp. pepper
2 c. milk
2 tbsp. grated Parmesan cheese
1 tbsp. lemon juice

Mix salmon, tuna and water chestnuts. Saute onion in butter just until soft. Blend in flour, salt and pepper; cook, stirring constantly, just until mixture bubbles. Stir in milk; continue cooking and stirring until sauce thickens and boils for 1 minute. Remove from heat; blend in cheese and lemon juice. Stir 1 cup sauce into tuna-salmon mixture; set remaining aside for later.

CREPES:

¾ c. flour
1 tbsp. sugar
½ tsp. salt
3 eggs
1 c. milk
1 tbsp. melted butter or margarine
¼ c. heavy cream, whipped
2 tbsp. Parmesan cheese

Measure flour, sugar and salt into sifter. Beat eggs until thick in a medium bowl; sift dry ingredients over. Beat just until smooth. Stir in milk and butter. Heat an 8-inch heavy frying pan slowly; test temperature by sprinkling in a few drops of water. When drops bounce about, temperature is right. Grease pan with butter or margarine. Pour scant 1/3 cup batter into pan, tilting pan to cover bottom completely. Bake 1 to 2 minutes or until top of pancake is set. Turn and brown other side. Repeat 7 times, lightly greasing pan before each pancake. Spoon about 1/3 cup filling into center of each crepe as it is baked. Roll up and place seam-side down in a shallow baking dish. Fold remaining sauce into whipped cream. Spoon over crepes. Sprinkle with Parmesan cheese. Bake at 350 degrees for 30 minutes or until filling is hot and cheese is golden. Yield: 8 servings.

Mrs. John Carlson, Pres.
Our Savior LWML and Guild
Satellite Beach, Florida

CLAM FRITTERS

2 c. ground clams
2 eggs
2 c. bread or cracker crumbs
1 tsp. salt

Clean clams under running water; put clams through food chopper. Beat eggs; add bread or cracker crumbs, ground clams and salt. Form into patties; fry quickly in a little hot oil. Serve immediately. Yield: 6 servings.

Mrs. Werner Holstein, Pres.
Faith Dorcas Soc.
Hammond, Oregon

DEEP-FRIED CLAMS

1 c. flour
2 tbsp. baking powder
½ tsp. salt
1 egg
1 c. evaporated milk
1 pt. clams, ground
Oil

Sift dry ingredients. Beat egg well; add milk. Combine dry ingredients and egg-milk mixture. Add clams; spoon into hot oil heated to 325 degrees. Cook for 10 seconds on each side. Drain on paper towel. Keep warm in moderate oven. Yield: 4-6 servings.

Mrs. Floyd Thompson, Pres.
St. Mark's Priscilla Cir.
Rochester, Washington

MEEK SCALLOPED OYSTERS

1 eggplant, pared and cut into 1-in. cubes
16 crackers, crushed
1 tsp. salt
1 can minced clams, undrained
1 ½ c. milk
3 tbsp. butter

Cook eggplant in small amount of water for 10 minutes. Add remaining ingredients except butter. Turn into casserole. Dot with butter. Bake at 350 degrees for 30 minutes. Yield: 10-12 servings.

Mrs. Matilda Zink, Past Pres.
St. John's Ladies Aid
Alpena, South Dakota

NEW CLAM CASSEROLE

2 eggs
1 can cream of mushroom soup
1 c. milk
30 saltine crackers, crushed
1 7½-oz. can minced clams
¼ c. melted margarine

(Continued on next page)

Beat eggs slightly; add soup, milk, cracker crumbs, clams and melted margarine. Turn into a greased 1 1/2-quart casserole. Bake at 350 degrees for 1 hour. Yield: 4 servings.

Mrs. Fred L. Endicott, Pres.
Emmaus LCW
Falmouth, Maine

COMPANY CRAB CASSEROLE

1 green pepper, diced
½ c. chopped green onion
½ c. butter
½ c. flour
1 tsp. dry mustard
1 ½ tsp. salt
½ tsp. white pepper
1 qt. milk
¼ tsp. Tabasco sauce
1 tsp. Worcestershire sauce
1 4-oz. can mushrooms, drained
1 4-oz. can pimento, diced
1 lb. crab meat
1 14-oz. pkg. midget sea shells, cooked
2 c. grated Cheddar cheese

Saute green pepper and onion in butter. Stir in flour, mustard, salt and pepper. Add milk gradually; stir and cook until thickened. Add Tabasco sauce, Worcestershire sauce, mushrooms, pimento, crab and drained sea shells. Pour into a greased casserole; top with cheese. Garnish with crab legs and ripe olives. Bake at 350 degrees for 30 minutes. Yield: 6-8 servings.

Mrs. Julia Wickman, Charter Member
Grace Ladies Aid
Klickitat, Washington

CRAB MEAT AU DIABLE

2 tbsp. flour
2 tbsp. butter, melted
¾ c. half and half cream
1 egg yolk, slightly beaten
½ tsp. salt
⅛ tsp. curry powder
2 tbsp. finely chopped green onion and tops
½ c. sliced mushrooms
1 6 ½-oz. can crab meat
Bread crumbs

Blend flour into butter. Add cream; cook until thickened. Cool slightly; add egg yolk, blending well. Add seasonings, onion and mushrooms which have been sauteed in a small amount of butter. Fold in crab meat chunks. Serve in pattie shells or in individual baking shells; sprinkle with bread crumbs and brown lightly under broiler. Yield: 6 servings.

Marie B. Cizmar
Trinity Mary Martha Cir.
Streator, Illinois

CRAB MEAT-BISCUIT CASSEROLE

½ c. chopped green pepper
⅓ c. chopped onion
½ c. shortening
½ c. sifted flour
¾ c. milk
1 c. shredded sharp cheese
1 tsp. dry mustard
½ tsp. monosodium glutamate
1 ½ c. drained tomatoes
1 c. crab meat
2 tsp. Worcestershire sauce
½ tsp. salt

Cook green pepper and onion in shortening for 15 minutes or until tender. Blend in flour, milk, cheese, dry mustard and monosodium glutamate. Cook, stirring constantly, until cheese is melted and mixture is thick. Add remaining ingredients; mix well. Pour into 2-quart casserole.

BISCUITS:

1 c. flour
2 tsp. baking powder
½ tsp. salt
¼ c. shredded sharp cheese
2 tbsp. shortening
½ c. milk
½ tsp. chopped pimento

Sift flour with baking powder and salt. Add cheese. Cut in shortening until it resembles coarse meal. Add milk and pimento; stir only until dry ingredients are dampened. Drop by rounded teaspoonfuls on top of casserole. Bake at 450 degrees for 20 minutes. Yield: 6-8 servings.

Mrs. Lucile Einess, Pres.
St. Michael's Guild
Minneapolis, Minnesota

CRAB MEAT CASSEROLE

½ c. butter
⅔ c. flour
2 ⅔ c. milk
2 6 ½-oz. cans crab meat, flaked
4 c. chopped celery
½ c. chopped green pepper
2 pimentoes, chopped
⅓ c. slivered blanched almonds
4 hard-cooked eggs, chopped
2 tsp. salt
1 c. shredded sharp Cheddar cheese
Buttered bread crumbs

Melt butter in saucepan; add flour and mix well. Remove from heat; slowly stir in milk. Return to heat; cook, stirring constantly, until thickened. Add crab, celery, green pepper, pimento, almonds, eggs and salt. Pour mixture into greased casserole. Top with cheese and bread crumbs. Bake at 350 degrees for 45 minutes. Yield: 6 servings.

Mrs. Emil Sunderland
Faith Ladies Guild
Sequim, Washington

CRAB MEAT SANDWICHES

1 7-oz. can King crab meat, drained
2 tbsp. finely chopped onion
¼ c. finely chopped parsley
½ tsp. vinegar
Salt and pepper to taste
2 lge. hard-cooked eggs
½ c. mayonnaise

Crumble crab meat into bowl; add remaining ingredients. Mix well; cover and refrigerate for 1 hour. Yield: 6 servings.

Dorothy Perry, Pres.
First Lutheran Church LWML
Ventura, California

HOT CRAB SPREAD

1 8-oz. pkg. cream cheese, softened
1 tbsp. milk
1 6½-oz. can crab meat, flaked
2 tbsp. chopped onion
½ tbsp. horseradish
¼ tsp. salt
Dash of pepper
1 tsp. capers (opt.)
3 tbsp. slivered almonds

Beat cream cheese and milk until smooth. Fold in crab meat, onion, horseradish salt, pepper and capers. Spoon into casserole. Sprinkle slivered almonds over top. Bake at 375 degrees for 15 minutes. Yield: 10 servings.

Mrs. Alice Bruns, Sec.
Zion Women's Soc.
Chappell, Nebraska

MARYLAND CRAB IMPERIAL

1 lb. lump crab meat
1 tsp. minced green pepper
1 tsp. minced onion
1 tbsp. butter
2½ tsp. cracker crumbs
¾ c. milk or cream
2 eggs, lightly beaten
½ tsp. salt
1½ tsp. mustard
Dash of red pepper
Mayonnaise
Paprika

Flake crab meat into bowl. Cook green pepper and onion in butter until soft. Add cracker crumbs and milk; cook slowly until thickened. Remove from heat. Add eggs, salt, mustard and red pepper; mix with crab meat. Pack into shells or ramekins. Top each with 1 teaspoonful mayonnaise and a dash of paprika. Bake at 400 degrees for 30 minutes or until brown. Yield: 5-6 servings.

Mrs. Louis C. Weller
Emmanuel Ladies Aid
Baltimore, Maryland

KING CRAB CASSEROLE

8 slices white bread
2 lb. King crab meat
½ to ¾ c. mayonnaise
1 sm. onion, finely chopped
1 green pepper, finely chopped
1 c. chopped celery (opt.)
3 c. milk
4 eggs, beaten
Salt and pepper
1 can cream of mushroom soup
1 c. grated American cheese
Paprika to taste (opt.)

Dice 4 slices of bread; place in greased 16-inch pan. Mix crab meat, mayonnaise, onion, green pepper and celery; place on diced bread. Trim crust from remaining bread; place on top of crab mixture. Mix eggs, milk, 1 teaspoonful salt and pepper; pour over all. Let set in refrigerator overnight. Pour soup over top; sprinkle with cheese, paprika and salt and pepper to taste. Let stand at room temperature for 1 hour. Bake at 325 degrees for 1 hour. Yield: 8-10 servings.

Mrs. Margaret Lehmann, Pres.
Our Savior Ladies Guild
Louisville, Kentucky
Sandra Lindroth
Messiah Ladies Cir.
Santa Cruz, California

MARYLAND-STYLE CRAB IMPERIAL

1 1-lb. can fresh crab meat
¼ tsp. salt
Dash of pepper
1 egg, beaten
1 c. heavy mayonnaise
Dash of paprika

Remove all shell from each lump of crab meat, working gently so as not to break the lumps. Place crab meat in bowl; add salt and pepper. Combine egg and mayonnaise; stir well. Place enough of dressing mixture in crab meat to allow it to stick together. Place the crab meat mixture lightly in a crab shell; do not pack down. A shell can be fashioned by shaping aluminum foil into a shallow shell. Try to have a high oval mound of crab mixture; cover with a thick coating of dressing mixture. Place in a shallow pan. Bake at 350 to 375 degrees for 30 minutes. Remove from oven and sprinkle top with paprika. Serve while hot. Yield: 4-5 servings.

E. LaVerne Cook
St. Andrew's Gloria Dei Cir. LWML
Silver Spring, Maryland

SEAFOOD SOUFFLE

½ c. evaporated milk
1 c. shredded Cracker Barrel sharp Cheddar cheese
½ tsp. salt
Dash of pepper
6 eggs, separated
1 c. crab meat, flaked

(Continued on next page)

Heat milk in double boiler. Add cheese, salt and pepper. Remove from heat; cool. Gradually add to slightly beaten egg yolks. Fold in stiffly beaten egg whites. Place crab meat in 1 1/2-quart casserole; top with mixture. Bake at 325 degrees for 45 minutes. Yield: 10 servings.

Bernice Leslein
St. Paul's LWML
Dubuque, Iowa

CASSEROLE OF LOBSTER THERMIDOR

⅓ c. butter, melted
½ c. sifted flour
3 c. warm light cream or 2 c. cream plus
   1 c. milk
Pinch of cayenne pepper
¼ tsp. dry mustard
1 can mushrooms
3 c. cooked lobster meat, cut into 1-in. pieces
¾ tsp. salt
¼ c. grated Parmesan cheese

Blend butter and flour to make paste; gradually add cream, stirring constantly. Cook until thick. Simmer several minutes longer. Add remaining ingredients; mix well. If the mixture is too thick, add more cream. Pour into casserole; sprinkle top thickly with additional cheese and drizzle melted butter over the cheese. Place the casserole on a cookie sheet. Bake at 400 degrees for 15 minutes; broil until top is brown. Yield: 6 servings.

Mrs. Ezra Miller, Pres.
St. John's LCW
Mt. Wolf, Pennsylvania

LOBSTER WITH DRESSING

5 hard-cooked eggs
1 can lobster, drained
2 eggs, beaten
1 tsp. mustard
½ tsp. pepper
½ tsp. olive oil
1 c. vinegar
2 tbsp. butter
⅛ tsp. salt

Finely mash egg yolks; mix with lobster. Chop egg whites; add to lobster. Place remaining ingredients in saucepan. Cook until thickened; cool. Pour over lobster mixture. Yield: 4-5 servings.

Mrs. B. S. Brown
Redeemer LCW
Kannapolis, North Carolina

LOBSTER MORNAY IN TOAST CUPS

¼ c. butter
¼ c. flour
2 ½ c. milk
⅛ tsp. cayenne
¼ tsp. nutmeg
¾ c. grated process Swiss cheese

¼ c. grated Parmesan cheese
2 5-oz. cans lobster, broken in chunks
8 to 10 toast cups

Melt butter over low heat; blend in flour. Cook over low heat, stirring until mixture is smooth and bubbly; remove from heat. Gradually stir in milk. Bring to boil, stirring constantly. Boil for 1 minute. Blend in seasonings and cheeses. Fold in lobster. Serve in toast cups garnished with parsley. Yield: 8-10 servings.

Catherine Butler, Pres.
Our Savior Ladies Soc.
Thistletown, Ontario, Canada

LOBSTER THERMIDOR

1 broiled lobster
3 mushrooms, sliced
¼ c. butter
Dash of paprika
⅛ tsp. mustard
1 tbsp. minced parsley
½ c. Sherry
1 ½ c. cream sauce
2 tbsp. grated Parmesan cheese

Cut lobster lengthwise into halves; remove meat and break into small pieces. Cook mushrooms for 5 minutes in butter; add paprika, mustard, parsley, Sherry and 1 cup cream sauce. Mix well; fill lobster shell with mixture. Cover with remaining sauce; sprinkle with cheese. Bake at 450 degrees for 10 minutes. NOTE: The cream sauce may be seasoned more highly, if desired. Increase mustard to 1 teaspoonful; add 1 teaspoonful grated onion and a dash of celery salt instead of parsley. Increase mushrooms to 3/4 cut. Proceed as above. Yield: 2 servings.

Mrs. Elmer Dietz
Mt. Calvary Ladies Guild
Excelsior Springs, Missouri

FRIED OYSTERS

1 pt. oysters
Salt and pepper to taste
Fine dry bread or cracker crumbs
1 egg, beaten
Fat

Drain oysters thoroughly; dry lightly between two sheets of paper toweling to remove moisture. Sprinkle with salt and pepper. Roll in dry crumbs, then in egg. Roll in dry crumbs again; place one layer deep in a wire frying basket. Lower into deep fat which has been heated to 375 degrees. Fry about 4 minutes or until browned and tender. Drain and serve hot. Yield: 3 servings.

Mrs. Lee W. Barrier, Pres.
Mt. Gilead LCW
Mt. Pleasant, North Carolina

OYSTER PANCAKES

2 eggs, beaten
2 c. milk
2 tbsp. shortening
2 c. flour
1 tsp. salt
4 tsp. baking powder
2 tbsp. sugar
1 pt. oysters, drained

Combine eggs, milk and shortening. Add flour sifted with salt, baking powder and sugar. Beat until smooth. Add oysters. Bake on ungreased griddle. Yield: 12-15 pancakes.

Mrs. Ray Wilkening
Grace Ladies Aid
Appleton, Minnesota

OYSTER PARTY PIE

2 c. water
1 tsp. salt
1 c. uncooked rice
¼ c. finely chopped canned pimento
3 tbsp. butter
⅛ tsp. pepper
1 pt. oysters, drained
1 tsp. cream-style horseradish
1 can condensed cream of mushroom soup
½ c. water
Paprika

Combine water, salt and rice in 2-quart saucepan; bring to a vigorous boil. Reduce heat as low as possible. Cover; simmer for 14 minutes. Remove from heat, leaving lid on 10 minutes longer. Stir pimento, butter and pepper into rice. Press rice over bottom and sides of greased 8 x 12-inch baking dish. Put oysters over rice; spread horseradish over oysters. Mix mushroom soup and water; pour over oysters and rice, carefully covering all exposed rice. Sprinkle with paprika. Bake at 400 degrees for 30 minutes. Serve hot. Yield: 4 servings.

Mrs. Charles Birx
Trinity Memorial LCW
Sharpsburg, Maryland

SCALLOPED OYSTERS

½ lb. mushrooms, sliced or 2 4-oz. cans
    mushrooms, drained
1 c. butter
¼ c. chopped green pepper
1 tsp. salt
1 pt. oysters or 1 12-oz. can frozen oysters,
    thawed
3 c. crushed soda crackers
½ c. light cream or half-and-half

Saute mushrooms in 1/4 cup butter for 5 to 10 minutes. Add green pepper and salt; cook gently for an additional 5 minutes. Drain oysters, reserving liquid. Sprinkle one-third of crackers over bottom of baking dish. Top with one-half of mushrooms and one-half of oysters. Dot with 1/4 cup butter. Repeat. Sprinkle remaining third of crackers on top; dot with remaining 1/4

cup butter. Add cream to reserved oyster liquid; pour over all. Bake at 350 degrees for 30 to 35 minutes. Yield: 6-8 servings.

Mrs. William H. Holtcamp, Jr., Pres.
Bethlehem LCW
Sedro Woolley, Washington

SCALLOPED OYSTERS

2 c. saltine crackers
½ pt. oysters, halved
¼ tsp. salt
4 tbsp. butter
Milk

Place alternate layers of cracker crumbs with oysters in greased casserole, beginning and ending with cracker crumbs. Sprinkle with salt and dot each layer with butter. Pour enough milk over all to completely soak crackers thoroughly. Let stand a few minutes. Add more milk until crackers will absorb no more. Bake at 350 degrees for 30 to 35 minutes or until top is browned. Yield: 4 servings.

Mrs. Edward F. Schinnerer, Pres.
First Lutheran Church Women's League
Long Beach, California

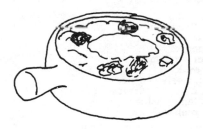

SCALLOPED OYSTERS

1 pt. oysters
½ lb. butter, melted
1 c. crushed plain or Ritz crackers
½ c. dry bread crumbs
Milk

Drain oysters, reserving liquid. Mix butter, crackers and bread crumbs. Place alternate layers of crumbs and oysters in buttered casserole, beginning and ending with crumbs. Mix liquid from oysters with enough milk to make 1 cup liquid. Pour into casserole. Bake at 450 degrees for 20 minutes. Reduce heat

(Continued on next page)

to 250 degrees and bake for 40 minutes longer. Yield: 4 servings.

Mrs. A. W. Trinklein, Publ. Com.
St. Matthew Parent-Teacher League
New York, New York

TABASCO OYSTER PIE

1 pkg. pastry mix or pastry for 9-in. two-crust pie
1 ½ qt. med. oysters
Salt
2 tbsp. flour
¼ c. butter
½ tsp. Tabasco sauce

Prepare pastry according to package directions. Line bottom and sides of 9-inch pie plate with half the pastry. Drain oysters; reserve 1/4 cup liquor. Turn oysters into pie plate; sprinkle with salt and flour. Dot with butter. Combine reserved oyster liquor and Tabasco sauce; pour over oysters. Top with remaining pastry; flute edges to seal. Cut slits in top crust to allow steam to escape. Bake at 450 degrees for 30 minutes. Yield: 6-8 servings.

Photograph for this recipe on page 213.

CREAMED SCALLOPS

4 tbsp. butter
4 tbsp. flour
1 tsp. salt
¼ tsp. pepper
½ tsp. dry mustard
1 ½ pt. milk
1 onion, finely chopped
1 tbsp. chopped parsley
1 tbsp. lemon juice
1 ½ pt. scallops

Melt butter in top of double boiler; add flour, salt, pepper and mustard. Stir until well blended. Remove from heat. Gradually stir in milk; return to heat. Add onion, parsley and lemon juice. Cook, stirring constantly until thick and smooth. Add scallops; heat thoroughly. Serve on toast. Yield: 4-6 servings.

Mrs. H. E. Rhodenizer, Pres.
Mt. Zion Ladies Aid
Lunen County, Nova Scotia, Canada

SCALLOPED SCALLOPS

1 lb. scallops
⅔ c. cream
½ c. butter
1 to 1 ¼ c. cracker crumbs

Place ingredients in casserole in layers. Bake at 350 degrees for 1 hour. Yield: 4 large or 6 small servings.

Mrs. Alfred E. Christiansen, Sr., Pres.
Trinity Women's Group
Westbrook, Maine

SCALLOPED SCALLOPS

1 ½ lb. scallops
¼ tsp. salt
½ c. crushed soda crackers
½ c. melted butter
3 tbsp. light cream
Dash of pepper
Dash of paprika

Season scallops with salt. Toss crackers with melted butter. Alternate layers of crumbs and scallops in baking dish, beginning and ending with crumbs. Pour cream over top; sprinkle with pepper and paprika. Bake at 425 degrees for 30 minutes. Yield: 4-5 servings.

Mrs. Joan M. Bailey, Pres.
Clifton Ladies Guild
Salem, Massachusetts

SKEWERED SCALLOPS

4 tbsp. dry white wine
4 tbsp. prepared mustard
4 tbsp. heavy cream
1 lb. fresh Chesapeak scallops
2 c. bread crumbs
1 tsp. salt
½ tsp. pepper
1 c. olive oil

Combine wine, mustard and cream. Skewer scallops; roll in wine mixture, then in bread crumbs. Sprinkle with salt, pepper and olive oil. Broil on outdoor grill 5 inches from fire for about 8 minutes or until golden brown. Yield: 4 servings.

Mrs. Hilmar L. Fricke, Pres.
Our Redeemer LCW
Wilmington, Delaware

ALFALPHA COCKTAIL

1 c. finely chopped green onions
1 c. finely chopped celery
2 c. catsup
1 48-oz. can V-8 juice
Juice of 1 lemon
¾ tsp. Worcestershire sauce
⅛ tsp. Tabasco sauce
1 4 ½-oz. can shrimp

Mix all ingredients; chill well. Stir again before serving. NOTE: Smoked oysters, or mushrooms

(Continued on next page)

may be substituted for shrimp. Yield: 10 servings.

Mrs. O. W. Kendel, Past Pres.
Christ Lutheran Church LWML
Mellowdale, Alberta, Canada

BOILED SHRIMP IN SAUCE

2 qt. water
1 lge. onion, chopped
2 tbsp. thick cooking sauce
6 tbsp. Worcestershire sauce
1 tsp. Tabasco sauce
½ c. catsup
2 tbsp. lemon juice
½ tsp. garlic salt
6 whole cloves
2 bay leaves
1 tsp. whole allspice
1 tbsp. chili powder
¼ tsp. oregano
½ stick margarine
Salt and pepper to taste
2 lb. sm. shrimp in shells

Put water into 5-quart Dutch oven; bring to a rapid boil. Add all ingredients except shrimp. Bring to a boil. Add shrimp. Simmer for 20 to 25 minutes. Turn off heat. Let stand for 30 minutes before serving. Yield: 4 servings.

Mrs. John Prigge
Grace Ladies Aux.
Freeport, Texas

CREOLE SHRIMP

½ c. minced onion
2 tbsp. butter
2 tbsp. flour
1 bay leaf
¼ to ½ c. diced celery
1 tsp. minced parsley
½ c. minced green pepper
Dash of cayenne
¼ tsp. pepper sauce
½ tsp. salt
1 6 ¼-oz. can tomato paste
3 c. water
2 c. cooked shrimp

Cook onion in butter until yellow. Blend in flour, bay leaf, celery, parsley, green pepper, cayenne, pepper sauce and salt. Add tomato paste and water. Cook slowly, stirring occasionally, until thickened, about 30 minutes. Stir in shrimp. Remove bay leaf before serving over rice. NOTE: This recipe may be made in advance and frozen until used. It may be warmed over once. Yield: 6-8 servings.

Mrs. D. E. Vickstrom, Pres.
Christ Lutheran Church LCW
Richmond, Virginia
Mrs. Vernon Lorenz
Holy Trinity LWML
Macon, Georgia

QUICK SHRIMP CURRY

½ c. chopped onion
1 to 2 tbsp. butter
1 can frozen condensed cream of shrimp soup
1 c. sour cream
½ to 1 tsp. curry powder
1 or 2 c. cleaned cooked shrimp

Cook onion in butter until tender, but not brown. Add soup; heat and stir until smooth. Stir in sour cream and curry powder. Add shrimp and heat. Garnish with paprika and add a sprig of parsley. Serve over rice, wild rice or noodles. Yield: 4-8 servings.

Mrs. Rhoda Gersmehl
Bethlehem LWML
Fort Wayne, Indiana
Mrs. Benjamin Irwin, Sec.
Emmanuel LCW
Lancaster, Pennsylvania

SCALLOPED SHRIMP

¾ c. dry bread crumbs
¾ c. cracker crumbs
1 5 to 7-oz. can shrimp
Chopped celery (opt.)
Butter
⅔ c. top milk or light cream

Place a layer of one-half bread crumbs and one-half cracker crumbs in a well buttered 10 x 6-inch baking dish. Cover with a layer of shrimp. Add parsley and celery. Repeat layers. Pour milk over top. Dot generously with butter. Bake at 450 degrees for 30 minutes. NOTE: Oysters may be substituted for the shrimp and oyster liquid for one-half the milk or cream. Yield: 4-6 servings.

Mrs. Howard Frerichs, Pres.
Trinity LWML
Ogallala, Nebraska

SHRIMP CACCIATORE

2 lb. fresh or frozen shrimp
⅓ c. olive oil or fat
½ c. minced onion
½ c. minced green pepper
2 cloves of garlic, minced
1 No. 2 can tomatoes
1 8-oz. can tomato sauce
½ c. red wine
2 tbsp. salt
¼ tsp. black pepper
½ tsp. allspice
1 bay leaf, crumbled
¼ tsp. thyme
Dash of cayenne pepper

Shell and devein shrimp. Cook 3 to 5 minutes in simmering water. Heat olive oil in large skillet. Add onion, green pepper and garlic; cook gently,

(Continued on next page)

stirring occasionally, until onion is tender. Add remaining ingredients. Simmer rapidly, uncovered, for 20 minutes. Add shrimp and heat thoroughly. Serve with rice, spaghetti or toasted croutons. Yield: 6 servings.

Martha Neugebauer
Immanuel Ladies Guild
Schenectady, New York

SHRIMP AND CHEESE CASSEROLE

6 slices white bread
½ lb. Old English cheese
1 lb. cooked shrimp
¼ c. butter or margarine, melted
3 whole eggs, beaten
½ tsp. dry mustard
Salt to taste
1 pt. milk

Break bread in pieces about size of a quarter. Break cheese into bite-sized pieces. Arrange shrimp, bread and cheese in several layers in greased casserole. Pour margarine over mixture. Combine eggs, mustard and salt. Add milk. Mix and pour over ingredients in casserole. Cover and let stand at least 3 hours or overnight. Bake, covered, at 350 degrees for 1 hour. NOTE: If you slightly increase the amount of shrimp, you improve the dish. When doubling recipe, use 3 pounds shrimp. Yield: 4 servings.

Mrs. Edwin Zielske
Emmanuel Altar and Organ Guild
Baltimore, Maryland

SHRIMP CHOW MEIN

1 c. celery, cut into ½-in. pieces
½ c. onion, chopped
1 can beef consomme
½ can water
1 can bean sprouts, drained
1 sm. can mushrooms, drained
1 sm. can water chestnuts, drained and sliced
1 lb. cooked and cleaned shrimp
3 tbsp. cornstarch
2 tbsp. sugar
¼ c. water

Combine celery, onion, soup and water; cook until tender. Add bean sprouts, mushrooms, water chestnuts and shrimp; cook for 10 minutes. Combine cornstarch, sugar and 1/4 cup water; add to chow mein and cook for 5 minutes. Serve over fluffy rice and chow mein noodles. NOTE: Left-over chicken or pork roast can be substituted for shrimp. Yield: 4 servings.

Mrs. Viola Striegl, Pres.
St. Paul's Esther Guild Soc.
East Northport, New York

SHRIMP NEWBURG

2 c. steamed and diced shrimp
2 tbsp. Sherry
4 tbsp. butter or margarine, melted
2 tbsp. flour
½ tsp. salt
⅛ tsp. cayenne pepper
¼ tsp. nutmeg (opt.)
1 c. top milk
2 egg yolks, slightly beaten

Heat shrimp thoroughly in Sherry and 3 tablespoonfuls butter. Melt remaining butter in a saucepan; remove from heat and blend in flour and seasonings. Add milk and return to heat. Cook, stirring constantly, until thickened. Stir a small amount of hot sauce into egg yolks; gradually return to remaining sauce. Cook over very low heat, stirring constantly for 2 to 3 minutes. Add shrimp and mix well. Serve immediately on toast points, crackers or in pattie shells, if desired. NOTE: If desired, 1 tablespoonful brandy may be substituted for 1 tablespoonful Sherry. Yield: 5 servings.

Viola M. Oebel
Redeemer Lutheran
Baltimore, Maryland

SHRIMP DELIGHT

1 ⅓ c. instant rice
1 c. finely chopped onions
⅓ c. finely chopped green pepper
4 tbsp. butter or margarine
2 tbsp. flour
1 ½ c. canned tomato juice
1 c. grated process cheese
2 4½-oz. cans shrimp or 1 pkg. frozen
    shrimp
1 tsp. salt
½ tsp. Worcestershire sauce
Dash of Tabasco sauce (opt.)
1 c. dry bread crumbs

Prepare rice as directed on package. Cook onions and green pepper in 2 tablespoonfuls butter until tender, but not brown. Blend in flour. Gradually stir in tomato juice; cook until thick. Add cheese; stir until melted. Add shrimp, rice and seasonings; stir well. Pour into greased 1 1/2-quart casserole. Top with bread crumbs; dot with 2 tablespoonfuls butter. Bake at 350 degrees for 30 to 45 minutes or until browned. NOTE: Tuna, salmon or diced cooked chicken may be substituted for shrimp. Yield: 6-8 servings.

Mrs. Fred Robertson, VP
St. John's Ladies Guild
Toronto, Ontario, Canada
Mrs. D. B. Semple, VP
Redeemer Women's Guild
Wayzata, Minnesota

SHRIMP STROGANOFF

6 tbsp. butter or margarine
1 ½ to 2 lb. cleaned shrimp
1 ½ c. sliced mushrooms
2 tbsp. minced onion
1 clove of garlic, minced
3 tbsp. flour
1 c. chicken stock or consomme
1 tsp. catsup
½ tsp. Worcestershire sauce
1 c. sour cream
1 tbsp. minced parsley or dill salt to taste
Salt to taste

Melt half the butter in a big skillet; add shrimp and stir while heating for 3 or 4 minutes. Remove from pan and keep warm. Melt remaining butter in same pan; Add mushrooms; saute for 2 minutes. Add onion and garlic; simmer until onion is tender and golden, but not browned. Sprinkle flour over and stir in. Add the chicken stock; stir while it cooks to blend. Stir in catsup and Worcestershire sauce. Remove from heat; quickly stir in sour cream and parsley. Add salt and shrimp. Return pan to heat for only a moment to get shrimp heated; high heat or too long cooking may curdle the cream. Serve at once over hot rice or noodles. NOTE: If desired, 1/4 cup white wine may be substituted for 1/4 cup stock.

Mrs. Fred Willms
St. John's LCW
Philadelphia, Pennsylvania

BAKED STUFFED SHRIMP

12 jumbo shrimp
½ lb. scallops
4 tbsp. butter
¼ tsp. paprika
2 tbsp. crushed potato chips
¼ c. cracker meal
3 tbsp. grated Parmesan cheese
1 to 2 tbsp. cooking Sherry
Lemon wedges

Clean shrimp and devein. Chop scallops; fill shrimp with scallops. Melt butter; add paprika. Cook over low heat for 10 minutes to take out raw taste of paprika. Add potato chips, cracker meal and cheese. Cover shrimp with mixture; place shrimp in a shallow baking dish with a small amount of water. Bake at 350 degrees for 20 to 25 minutes. Sprinkle with Sherry just before removing from oven. Garnish with lemon wedges. Yield: 6 servings.

Mrs. Howard Lidtke
Our Savior Ladies Guild
Pittsburgh, Pennsylvania

CRAB CIOPPINO

8 lge. onions, finely diced
10 stalks celery, diced
8 lge. cloves of garlic
1 c. olive oil or salad oil
4 No 2 ½ cans solid pack tomatoes, crushed
4 No 2 ½ cans tomato puree
2 bunches parsley, chopped
12 46-oz. cans cooked, buttered whole clams
Salt and pepper to taste
Monosodium glutamate
10 lb. raw medium prawns in shells
25 crabs, cleaned, cooked and cracked

Fry onions, celery and garlic in oil until tender. Add tomatoes and puree; bring to a boil. Add parsley. Add juice from clams; simmer for 30 minutes. Add seasonings and prawns; bring to a boil. Add whole clams and cooked crabs. Bring to a quick boil and serve. NOTE: If desired, 20 fresh live clams may be used. Wash fresh clams and steam in 1 pint water until done. Yield: 50 servings.

Lucile Perkins, Treas.
Mt. Olive Lutheran
Sebastopol, California

DELUXE SHRIMP AND CRAB CASSEROLE

1 lb. backfin crab meat
1 c. diced celery
¼ c. chopped parsley
¾ c. salad dressing
1 tsp. salt
1 tsp. dry mustard
½ tsp. pepper
1 lb. cooked shrimp
½ c. buttered bread crumbs

Combine all ingredients except shrimp and crumbs; place in greased baking dish. Add shrimp; stir slightly. Sprinkle buttered bread crumbs over top. Bake at 350 degrees for 1 hour. Yield: 6 servings.

Mrs. Charles D. Amrein
First Lutheran Church LWML
Towson, Maryland

SEAFOOD CASSEROLE

1 can cream of mushroom soup
1 c. milk
1 tbsp. chopped onion
½ green pepper, chopped
¼ tsp. pepper
½ c. Cheez Whiz
1 can sliced mushrooms
1 pkg. shell macaroni, cooked
1 can crab meat
1 c. deveined shrimp

Combine soup, milk, onion, green pepper and pepper; place over low heat. Add Cheese Whiz; stir occasionally until cheese is melted. Add mushrooms. Combine macaroni with crab meat, shrimp and cheese sauce. Refrigerate overnight. Bake at 350 degrees for 30 to 35 minutes. Yield: 10 servings.

Mrs. John Shingler, Jr.
Holy Trinity Lutheran Church
Blackduck, Minnesota

SEAFOOD WITH RICE

1 1½-lb. pkg. frozen shrimp, thawed
1 onion, sliced
Juice of 1 lemon
2 tbsp. butter
1 pkg. lobster tails
2 6-oz. pkg. frozen crab meat, thawed
2 cans frozen shrimp soup, thawed
1 c. mushrooms (opt.)
2 c. cooked rice

Cook shrimp, onion, lemon juice and butter for 2 to 3 minutes. Add remaining ingredients except rice; simmer until hot. Pour over rice. Yield: 8 servings.

Mrs. Ralph A. Emling, Rec. Sec.
Village Women's Guild
Bronxville, New York

SEAFOOD AND NOODLE CASSEROLE

¾ c. margarine
¼ c. flour
1 tsp. salt
¼ tsp. pepper
2½ c. milk
1 8-oz. pkg. crinkly noodles, cooked
½ lb. shrimp, cleaned
1 c. flaked crab meat
¾ c. grated sharp cheese
⅓ c. bread crumbs

Melt 1/2 cup margarine; blend in flour, salt and pepper. Gradually add milk; cook stirring until thick. Layer noodles, shrimp and crab meat in buttered 2-quart casserole. Pour sauce over layers; sprinkle with cheese. Cover with bread crumbs; dot with remaining butter. Bake at 350 degrees for 40 minutes. Yield: 6-8 servings.

Martha Van Gorden
Memorial Ladies Aid
Bremerton, Washinton

Variety
Meat Favorites

RECIPE FOR LEG OF LAMB WITH APRICOT STUFFING ON PAGE 237

BRAISED LAMB SHANK

4 lamb shanks
Flour
Fat
Salt and pepper to taste
¼ tsp. thyme
½ tsp. rosemary
2 c. hot water
1 c. chopped carrots
1 c. chopped potatoes
¼ c. chopped celery
1 med. onion, chopped

Crack bones in shanks. Roll shanks in flour; brown well in hot fat. Add seasonings and hot water. Cover; simmer for 1 hour and 30 minutes. Add vegetables. Cook for 30 minutes longer or until vegetables are tender. Yield: 4 servings.

Mrs. Clara Bodell
Zion Ladies Aid
Warren, Minnesota

CUMBERLAND LAMB ROAST

1 6 to 7-lb. leg of lamb
1 tsp. salt
1 tsp. dry mustard
½ tsp. ground ginger
5 thin slices lemon, cut into halves
⅔ c. currant jelly
1 tbsp. lemon juice

Trim excess fat from lamb; rub well with mixture of salt, mustard and ginger. Place, uncovered, on a rack in roasting pan, rounded-side up. Roast at 325 degrees for 2 hours. Remove from oven. Arrange lemon slices petal-fashion on side of roast, holding in place with dampened wooden picks. Combine jelly with lemon juice; spread over lamb. Return to oven. Continue roasting for 30 minutes to 1 hour longer. NOTE: Gravy may be made from pan drippings. Yield: 12 servings.

Emma A. Wiegand
Grace Ladies Aid Soc.
Mastic Beach, New York

DINNER CHOPS

6 lamb chops, thickly cut
Salt and pepper
1 green pepper, cut into rings
1 lge. onion, sliced
1 lemon, sliced
2 c. tomato juice

Brown chops in hot fat; season. Place in baking dish or pan; top each chop with pepper ring, onion slice and lemon slice. Pour tomato juice over chops. Cover; cook slowly or bake in 325 to 350 degree oven for 1 hour and 30 minutes. Yield: 6 servings.

Mrs. Kenneth Gunderson, Chmn.
Baltic Ladies Aid
Renner, South Dakota

LAMB AND CABBAGE

3 to 4 lb. stewing lamb, cut into pieces
1 lge. cabbage, cut into pieces
Flour
Salt and pepper to taste
1 tbsp. whole spices
Water

Place layer of meat in skillet; cover with layer of cabbage. Sprinkle flour between layers. Season with salt, pepper and spices. Cover with water; simmer for 2 to 3 hours or until done.

Laura Bradley, Sec.
Senior LWML
Mullan, Idaho

LAMB CHOPS WITH FRUIT DRESSING

4 double rib lamb chops
2 canned peaches, finely chopped
1 c. crushed pineapple
½ c. soft diced bread crumbs
4 tbsp. brown sugar
4 tbsp. melted butter

Brown pork chops; place in baking pan. Combine remaining ingredients; pour over chops. Bake at 350 degrees for 20 minutes. Yield: 4 servings.

Lolita Hamm
First Lutheran Church LCW
Nashville, Tennessee

LAMB CURRY

3 c. lean stewing lamb, cut into 1-in. cubes
1 qt. hot water
1 cinnamon stick
2 bay leaves
4 tbsp. butter or margarine, melted
2 onions, sliced
1 lge. green apple, peeled and sliced
4 tbsp. flour
½ tsp. curry powder
½ tsp. salt
⅛ tsp. pepper
Juice and grated rind of ½ lemon
½ c. seedless raisins
2 whole cloves

Cover meat with water; add cinnamon stick and bay leaves. Simmer until meat is tender. Discard cinnamon stick and bay leaves; remove meat. Strain; reserve liquid. Add butter, onions and apple; saute until golden yellow. Add flour mixed with curry powder, salt and pepper. Blend well; slowly add reserved liquid. Bring to a boil; add lemon juice, lemon rind, raisins and cloves. Serve with rice. Yield: 6 servings.

Mrs. Andrew A. Dashner, Pres.
Redeemer Evangelical LCW
Fisherville, Ontario, Canada

LAMB PATTIES

2 lb. ground lamb
3 tsp. salt
½ tsp. pepper
½ c. grated onion
1 c. corn flakes
1 ½ c. milk

Combine lamb, salt, pepper and onion; add corn flakes and milk. Form into patties. Broil for 10 to 15 minutes on each side or until golden brown. Yield: 12 patties.

Mrs. Elinor Ramsey, Cor. Sec.
St. John's Ladies Guild
Upper Montclair, New Jersey

LEG OF LAMB

1 clove of garlic
⅔ c. olive or salad oil
½ c. wine vinegar
2 tsp. salt
1 tsp. white pepper
1 tsp. rosemary
1 tsp. garlic powder

Place garlic pieces throughout leg of lamb. Mix all remaining ingredients; pour over lamb. Bake at 300 degrees for 5 hours. Reduce temperature to 250 to 275 degrees if lamb cooks too fast. Cover with foil the last hour of baking. Baste occasionally. NOTE: Lamb cooks faster in electric roaster. Yield: 12 servings.

Mrs. Carl A. B. Swanson
Walsburg LCW
Leonardville, Kansas

LEG OF LAMB WITH APRICOT STUFFING

1 ⅓ c. packaged instant rice
1 ⅓ c. sliced dried apricots
⅔ c. chopped celery
¼ c. chopped parsley
2 tsp. salt
¼ tsp. pepper
½ tsp. instant minced onion
½ tsp. crushed rosemary leaves
1 c. chicken bouillon
1 5-lb. boned leg of lamb

Mix rice, apricots, celery, parsley, seasonings and bouillon; let stand for 10 minutes for liquid to absorb. Stuff lamw with one-half the mixture; wrap remaining in aluminum foil. Secure lamb with string and skewers. Place on rack in shallow roasting pan. Bake at 325 degrees for 3 hours or until meat thermometer registers 175 degrees. Bake foil-wrapped stuffing for 1 hour. Serve lamb on platter with extra stuffing. Prepare gravy, if desired. Yield: 8-10 servings.

Photograph for this recipe on page 235 .

MUSHROOM CURRIED MEAT

1 tbsp. butter
1 med. onion, diced
½ c. diced green pepper
½ c. sliced mushrooms
½ c. sliced celery or 1 tsp. celery salt
Curry powder to taste
1 10-oz. can cream of mushroom soup
2 c. diced cooked lamb, chicken or veal
Hot milk or water
Hot cooked noodles or rice

Melt butter in medium-sized skillet; add onion, green pepper, mushrooms and celery. Saute slowly until partially cooked. Blend in curry powder, soup and meat; add enough milk to thin to desired consistency. Stir and heat thoroughly. Serve on a bed of hot rice or noodles. Yield: 5-6 servings.

Laura Van Deventer, Pres.
Messiah Ladies Guild
Stoney Creek, Ontario, Canada

NUTTED LAMB STEAKS

4 lean lamb steaks, ½-in. thick
2 tbsp. butter or margarine
Salt and pepper to taste
6 tbsp. dry Sherry
1 c. sour cream
⅓ c. finely chopped salted peanuts
2 tbsp. chopped fresh parsley

Trim steaks well; brown on both sides in heavy skillet in butter over medium heat. Season with salt and pepper. Reduce heat; add 4 tablespoonfuls Sherry. Cover; simmer for 15 minutes or until tender. Remove steaks from pan; keep warm. Add sour cream and remaining Sherry to drippings; heat slowly, stirring to blend. Return steaks to pan with nuts and parsley; cover with sauce from pan. Heat through. Yield: 4 servings.

Mrs. Harold W. Anderson, Pres.
First Lutheran Church ALCW
Mahnomen, Minnesota

PARTY PERFECT LAMB LOAF

2 3-oz. cans chopped mushrooms
2 tbsp. chopped onion
2 tbsp. butter or margarine
⅓ c. finely chopped cooked ham (opt.)
¼ c. fine dry bread crumbs
½ tsp. salt
¼ tsp. pepper
2 tbsp. dry Sherry
2 lb. lean ground lamb

Drain mushrooms, reserving liquid. Saute onion in butter until tender; add reserved mushroom liquid. Add mushrooms. Simmer until liquid is reduced to about 1 tablespoonful. Remove from heat; add ham, crumbs, salt, pepper and Sherry. Divide lamb into three parts. Alternate layers of lamb and mushroom mixture in 9 x 5 x 3-inch loaf pan, ending with lamb. Bake at 350

(Continued on next page)

degrees for 1 hour and 15 minutes. Drain off drippings. Yield: 6 servings.

Mrs. Gladys Deans, Chmn. Christian Serv.
St. John's LCW
Northumberland, Pennsylvania

ROAST LEG OF LAMB

1 5 to 6-lb. leg of lamb
2 tsp. salt
1 tsp monosodium glutamate
¼ tsp. pepper
Garlic

Wipe lamb with a clean damp cloth; do not remove the fell. Combine salt, monosodium glutamate and pepper; rub meat with mixture. Cut several small slits in surface of meat; insert a sliver of garlic into each. Place lamb, skin-side down, on rack in roasting pan. Insert meat thermometer in center of thickest part of meat, being sure that bulb does not rest on bone or in fat. Roast lamb, uncovered, at 300 degrees for about 3 hours or until thermometer reads 175 to 180 degrees. Place paper frill around end of leg bone. Serve on warm platter; garnish with cooked carrots, clusters of grapes on pineapple slices and parsley. Yield: 12-14 servings.

Mrs. Isabelle Crotcher, Pres.
St. John ALCW
Bellevue, Ohio

SHISH KABOB

Leg of lamb
½ lb. onions, chopped
1 tbsp. salt
1 tsp. pepper
Juice of 1 lemon
2 tbsp. olive or vegetable oil
1 tsp. sweet basil
1 lge. green pepper, chopped
½ c. chopped parsley

Bone meat; remove most of fat and gristle. Cut meat into 1 1/2-inch squares. Combine remaining ingredients. Mix with meat; let stand for several hours. Place meat on skewers; grill over charcoal, turning until meat is evenly browned. Serve with broiled tomatoes, green pepper and eggplant, if desired. NOTE: Salt may be added just before cooking instead of adding to marinade. Meat may be broiled in stove instead of grilled over charcoal.

Mrs. Sooren H. Darbinian
Trinity LCW
Fresno, California

TEXAS LEG OF LAMB

1 clove of garlic, crushed
¾ c. salad oil
¼ c. wine or cider vinegar
1 ½ tsp. salt
½ tsp. pepper
⅔ c. chopped onions

2 tsp. barbecue spice
¼ tsp. oregano
1 bay leaf, crushed
1 7 to 8-lb. leg of lamb, boned

Combine all ingredients except lamb to form marinade. Pour over lamb in large bowl; refrigerate overnight or longer. Turn meat occasionally while marinating. Broil meat, fat-side up, 4 inches from heat for 10 minutes; turn. Baste; brown for 10 minutes longer. Reduce heat to 450 degrees; bake lamb for 30 to 35 minutes. Reverse meat; bake for 5 minutes longer. Lamb should be pinkish in color. NOTE: To cook lamb outdoors, place on wire rack; broil for 45 minutes to 1 hour, turning and basting frequently. Yield: 12 servings.

Mrs. Vernon Jeschke, Pres.
Trinity LCW
Miles, Texas

THRIFTY LAMB PIE

2 c. diced cooked lamb
1 c. diced potatoes
1 onion, finely chopped
⅓ c. diced green pepper
⅔ c. diced celery
⅔ c. canned tomatoes, drained
½ tsp. sugar
1 ½ tsp. salt
2 c. meat stock and gravy
1 recipe biscuit dough

Combine all ingredients except dough; boil gently for 10 to 15 minutes or until vegetables are almost done. Place in 1 1/2-quart baking dish. Prepare biscuit dough; roll 1/2-inch thick. Place 1-inch strip around top of baking dish; cut remaining dough into biscuits; place over pie. Bake at 400 degrees for about 20 minutes. Yield: 4 servings.

Mrs. Doris M. Smith
Pilgrim LCW
Warwick, Rhode Island

ZIPPY LAMB SHANKS

8 lamb shanks
1 lge. onion, coarsely cut
1 c. coarsely cut celery
2 cloves of garlic, pressed
1 bottle catsup
1 can tomato soup
1 tsp. Worcestershire sauce
1 tbsp. soy sauce

Rinse lamb shanks in cold water; dry. Remove excess fat; brown well in heavy skillet or Dutch oven. Combine remaining ingredients in saucepan; cook for 5 minutes. Pour cooked sauce over browned lamb shanks; continue cooking, covered, for 2 hours longer. Yield: 8 servings.

Mrs. John Lee, Pres.
Peace Ladies Guild
Arroyo Grande, California

CHIPPED BEEF CASSEROLE

1 8-oz. pkg. egg noodles, cooked
6 tbsp. butter or margarine
1 4-oz. pkg. chipped beef, diced
1 can cream of mushroom soup
3 soup cans milk
6 oz. soft cheese, diced
1 5-oz. pkg. potato chips

Boil egg noodles in unsalted water. Drain and rinse with hot water. Melt butter. Add beef, soup, milk and cheese. Bring to a boil, stirring until cheese is melted. Stir in noodles. Pour in a greased casserole dish or loaf pan. Top with crushed potato chips. Bake at 325 degrees for 45 minutes. Yield: 12 servings.

Mrs. Adrian Honsbruch, Pres.
Immanuel Ladies Aid
Aurelia, Iowa

DAIRY CASSEROLE

¼ lb. chipped beef, cut into bite-sized pieces
½ lb. sharp Cheddar cheese, cut into bite-sized
   pieces
1 7-oz. pkg. macaroni, uncooked
2 cans cream of mushroom soup
1 pt. milk
4 hard-cooked eggs, chopped

Mix all ingredients except eggs; refrigerate overnight. Combine mixture with eggs just before baking. Pour into 9 x 12-inch pan. Bake at 350 degrees for 1 hour. Yield: 8 servings.

Mrs. Robert Peterson, Pres.
St. Paul's LCW
Rock City, Illinois

CORNED BEEF HOT DISH

2 8-oz. pkg. noodles
1 10 ½-oz. can cream of mushroom soup
1 10 ½-oz. can cream of celery soup
2 ½ c. milk
2 12-oz. cans corned beef, cubed
1 tbsp. minced onion
1 sm. jar or can pimento, minced
Crumbled potato chips

Cook noodles in salted water; drain. Blend soups with milk. Add remaining ingredients except potato chips, to noodles. Pour into a 3-quart buttered casserole. Top with potato chips. Bake at 350 degrees for 1 hour. Yield: 10 servings.

Mrs. Robert Godfrey, Publ. Chmn.
Ascension Women's Guild
Huntsville, Alabama

CORNED BEEF CASSEROLE

1 12-oz. can corned beef, broken into chunks
¼ lb. cheese, grated
1 can cream of chicken soup
1 to 1 ¼ c. milk
¼ to ½ c. chopped onion
1 6 to 8-oz. pkg. noodles, cooked and drained
¾ c. buttered crumbs (opt.)

Alternate layers of corned beef, cheese, soup, onion and noodles in greased 2-quart baking dish. Top with buttered crumbs. Bake at 350 to 375 degrees for 30 to 45 minutes. NOTE: Casserole may be combined instead of layered, if desired.

Mildred A. Jerr
Christ Lutheran Church
Southwick, Massachusetts
Mrs. Evelyn Ahlstrom
Zion Ladies Aid
Painesville, Ohio
Mrs. Mabel Jackson, Education Chmn.
St. Paul Womens Guild
Lynwood, California
Mrs. Erik Welsand, Past Pres.
Immanuel Ladies Aid
Brookston, Minnesota
Mrs. Virgil Sunsdahl, Pres.
St. Paul's LCW
Soudan, Minnesota

CORNED BEEF, ONION AND POTATO CASSEROLE

6 med. potatoes, thinly sliced
2 c. fresh or canned corned beef
Salt and pepper to taste
1 ½ to 2 c. milk
1 or 2 onions, sliced into rings
Parsley
1 tbsp. butter

Arrange alternate layers of sliced potatoes and corned beef in a large greased casserole, ending with potatoes. Salt and pepper each layer. Pour milk over all. Bake at 350 degrees for 45 minutes. Remove from oven. Add onion rings and parsley; dot with butter. Continue baking at 350 degrees for 20 minutes longer or until potatoes are tender and onion rings are lightly browned. Yield: 4-5 servings.

Mrs. C. I. Mayer, Pres.
St. Paul's Ladies Guild
Sacramento, Pennsylvania

CORNED BEEF ROLL WITH FLUFFY MUSTARD SAUCE

1 12-oz. can corned beef, broken
1 8-oz. can potatoes, drained and diced
1 egg, slightly beaten
2 tbsp. chopped onion
2 c. prepared biscuit mix
Milk
½ c. sour cream
½ c. mayonnaise or salad dressing
1 tbsp. prepared mustard

Combine corned beef, potatoes, egg and onion. Combine biscuit mix and 2/3 cup milk; knead 5 to 10 strokes on lightly floured board or surface. Roll to 12-inch square. Spread corned beef mixture on dough, to within 1/2-inch of edges. Roll like jelly roll, sealing edges. Place, seam-side down, on greased baking sheet. Cut slits on top roll. Bake at 425 degrees for 25 minutes. Cover lightly with foil for last 10 minutes, if browns too quickly. Cool for 5 minutes before removing to

(Continued on next page)

serving platter. Combine sour cream, mayonnaise and mustard; heat through. Serve sauce over corned beef roll. Yield: 6 servings.

Mrs. A. Ellsworth Grove
Salem Lutheran Church
Miffinburg, Pennsylvania

CHIPPED BEEF POT PIE

1 c. chopped onions
1 4-oz. pkg. dried beef, diced
¼ c. fat
2 tbsp. flour
¼ to ½ tsp. salt
¼ tsp. pepper
2 c. thinly sliced carrots
2 c. thinly sliced potatoes
2 c. water
1 beef bouillon cube

Saute onions and beef in hot fat; stir in flour and seasonings. Add remaining ingredients; bring to a boil. Cover; simmer for 5 minutes. Pour into 2-quart casserole.

TOPPING:

1 c. flour
½ tsp. salt
⅓ c. shortening
2 tbsp. water

Combine flour and salt; cut in shortening. Sprinkle water over mixture, mixing with fork until dough clings together. Roll out dough; fit over casserole. Slash top to allow steam to escape. Bake at 425 degrees for 25 to 30 minutes. Yield: 6-8 servings.

Mrs. Reta Cramer
Trinity Ladies Aid
Parsons, Kansas

COW IN THE GARDEN

1 No. 2 can peas
3 tbsp. butter
3 tbsp. flour
1 6-oz. can evaporated milk
1 c. shredded dried beef
4 baked potatoes, split or 4 servings
    mashed potatoes

Drain peas; reserve 2/3 cup liquid. Melt butter; blend in flour. Add reserved liquid and milk; cook, stirring constantly, until thick. Add peas and dried beef. Pour beef mixture over potatoes. Yield: 4 servings.

Mrs. Everett Jacobs, Pres.
Trinity Ladies Soc.
Edinburg, Illinois

DRIED BEEF CASSEROLE

¼ lb. dried beef
4 tbsp. butter
4 tbsp. flour

2 c. milk
¼ lb. cheese
1 can cream of mushroom soup
1 sm. pimento or green pepper, chopped
1 8-oz. pkg. noodles, cooked

Brown beef in butter; blend in flour. Add milk; cook until thick. Add cheese, soup and pimento; stir until cheese is melted. Add noodles; place in baking dish. Top with potato chips. Bake in moderate oven for 30 minutes to 1 hour. Yield: 6 servings.

Mrs. Clyde Pruett, Pres.
Trinity Ladies Aid
Cherokee, Iowa

DRIED BEEF CASSEROLE

2 c. uncooked macaroni
¼ lb. dried beef
½ lb. cheese, grated
4 hard-cooked eggs, chopped
2 cans cream of mushroom soup
1 pt. milk
Chopped onion to taste

Combine all ingredients; place in casserole. Let stand overnight. Bake at 350 degrees for 1 hour. Yield: 8 servings.

Mrs. Herbert Schlickelman, Pres.
St. Paul's Naomi Cir.
Emmetsburg, Iowa

DRIED BEEF CASSEROLE

¼ c. chopped onions
¼ c. chopped celery
¼ lb. dried beef, chopped
¼ c. fat
4 tbsp. flour
2 c. milk
2 c. cooked macaroni
½ tsp. salt
1 tbsp. minced parsley
⅓ c. grated cheese

Cook onion, celery and dried beef in hot fat until onion is golden. Stir in flour. Add milk gradually; stir until slightly thickened. Add macaroni, salt and parsley. Pour into greased 1 1/2-quart casserole. Sprinkle with grated cheese. Bake in 350 degree oven for 15 minutes. Yield: 6 servings.

Mrs. LaVine Kumm, Pres.
Faith LWML
Stanton, Nebraska

DRIED BEEF CASSEROLE

1 can cream of celery soup
1 soup can milk
1 c. uncooked macaroni
1 tbsp. grated onion
1 c. grated cheese
2 oz. dried beef

(Continued on next page)

Mix all ingredients; let stand for at least 4 hours or overnight. Bake at 350 degrees for 1 hour. Yield: 6 servings.

Mrs. Robert Bown
Emmanuel Ladies Aid
Gettysburg, South Dakota

DRIED BEEF DELIGHT

⅓ c. butter
½ c. flour
1 qt. milk
1 jar smoky cheese
4 c. raw noodles, cooked
1 pkg. dried beef
1 can cream of mushroom soup
Chopped pimento (opt.)
Crushed potato chips

Melt butter; blend in flour. Stir in milk. Cook until slightly thickened. Add cheese, noodles, dried beef, soup and pimento. Place in baking dish; sprinkle with potato chips. Bake at 375 degrees for 30 minutes. Yield: 6 servings.

Mrs. Lloyd Roeber, Pres.
Immanuel Ladies Aid
Wakefield, Nebraska

DICED BEEF HOT DISH

1 lge. onion, sliced
½ green pepper, diced
4 tbsp. butter
1 c. mushrooms
3 tbsp. flour
1 tbsp. sugar
Salt and pepper to taste
2 c. milk
½ c. cubed cheese
2 pkg. dried beef, chopped
6 stuffed olives, sliced
2 c. cooked macaroni or noodles
Grated cheese
Bread crumbs

Brown onion and green pepper in butter; add mushrooms. Stir in flour, sugar, salt and pepper. Add milk, cubed cheese, dried beef and olives, stirring constantly, until cheese is melted. Pour over noodles; mix well. Place in a greased baking dish or pan. Cover with grated cheese and bread crumbs. Bake at 350 degrees for 1 hour. Yield: 6 servings.

Mrs. Lawrence M. Larson, Pres.
Our Savior's LCW
Menomonie, Wisconsin

DRIED BEEF SUPREME

¼ lb. dried beef, shredded
¼ lb. mushrooms
1 lge. onion, diced
1 red mango, cut into ⅛-in. strips
1 green mango, cut into ⅛-in. strips
4 tbsp. butter

2 tbsp. flour
1 ½ c. milk
¼ lb. sharp cheese

Saute beef, mushrooms, onion and mangoes in 2 tablespoonfuls butter. Melt remaining butter; blend in flour. Gradually stir in milk, cooking until thick. Add sauted ingredients and cheese. Let stand for 4 hours; heat to serve. Serve over toast, if desired. Yield: 6 servings.

Augusta Eckman, Pres.
St. Michael's LCW
Berlin, Pennsylvania

SHOPPER'S CASSEROLE

¼ lb. dried beef, shredded
1 c. uncooked macaroni
2 hard-cooked eggs, diced
¼ tsp. salt
¼ tsp. rosemary
1 can cream of mushroom soup
1 c. milk
½ lb. grated Cheddar cheese
2 tbsp. grated onion

Combine all ingredients. Pour into greased 2-quart casserole. Cover; refrigerate overnight. Bake, uncovered, at 350 degrees for 35 minutes or until macaroni is tender. Yield: 4-6 servings.

Mrs. Kenneth Dockter, Chmn. Christian Action
Faith LCW
Prairie Village, Kansas

BRAIN CANAPES

1 set calf brains
Water
Vinegar
2 eggs
1 tsp. salt
1 tsp. pepper
1 tbsp. Worcestershire sauce
2 tbsp. catsup
4 hard-cooked eggs, diced
6 tbsp. mayonnaise
15 stuffed green olives or ¼ c. salad olives

Soak brains in water for 20 minutes; drain. Cover with mixture of vinegar and water, using 1 tablespoonful vinegar to each quart of water. Simmer for 15 minutes. Drain. Cover with cold water; let stand for 10 minutes and drain. Remove membrane and excess tissue; separate into segments. Combine beaten eggs, brains and seasonings; stir into small amount hot shortening; cool. Add hard-cooked eggs, mayonnaise and olives.

Mrs. S. T. Schreeder
North Side Lutheran Church
Houston, Texas

BAKED HEART

1 3½-lb. beef heart or 2 veal hearts
2 c. bread crumbs
¾ c. chopped onions
4 tbsp. butter
1 tsp. salt
1 tsp. thyme
1 tsp. sage
2 tsp. savory
Bacon fat
1 10-oz. can beef broth or consomme
1 10-oz. can tomato soup
6 slices bacon

Cut away hard muscular part at top of heart. Soak heart in cold water for 1 hour. Dry. Place bread crumbs in bowl. Fry onions in butter. Pour onions and butter over crumbs. Add salt, thyme, sage and savory; toss. Fill heart with stuffing. Secure with skewers; wind string around heart. Add bacon fat. Pour beef broth and soup around and over heart. Bake at 350 degrees for 3 hours and 30 minutes, basting frequently. Place bacon slices across heart after it has been baking several hours. Serve after removing strings. Garnish with parsley. Yield: 6 servings.

Mrs. Helen House, Pres.
Trinity LCW
Edmonton, Alberta, Canada

CHICKEN-FRIED HEART

1 1 to 1½-lb. beef or calf heart
Salted flour
3 to 4 tbsp. fat

Wash heart; remove any tough membranes. Cut crosswise into 3/4-inch slices. Dredge heart slices in salted flour. Brown in fat over low heat for 5 minutes. Make gravy from pan drippings, if desired.

Nancy B. Zastrow, Pres.
St. Andrew's LWML
Silver Springs, Maryland

ROAST BEEF HEART AND GRAVY

3 1-lb. beef hearts
1 pkg. dry onion soup mix
1 can cream of mushroom soup
¼ soup can water

Place beef hearts on large square of aluminum foil; sprinkle with dry onion soup mix. Mix soup with water; pour over beef hearts. Tightly close foil around beef hearts. Place in shallow pan. Bake at 350 degrees for 2 hours. Yield: 4-5 servings.

Mrs. Edwin Bjork, Pres.
First Lutheran Church LCW
Crystal Falls, Michigan

BAKED BEEF LIVER AND BACON

Shortening
1 egg, slightly beaten
¼ c. milk
4 slices liver
Flour
Bread crumbs
Salt and pepper
8 slices bacon

Grease shallow pan generously with cold shortening. Mix egg and milk. Dip liver into flour and then into egg mixture; roll in bread crumbs. Place liver in greased pan. Sprinkle with salt and pepper. Cover liver with bacon. Bake at 350 degrees for 20 minutes. Yield: 4 servings.

Mrs. George Heinen, Jr., Pres.
Zion LCW
Warroad, Minnesota

BAKED LIVER

½ lb. bacon
2 lb. sliced liver
Flour
Salt and pepper to taste
1 lge. Spanish onion, sliced

Place a layer of bacon and liver in baking dish; sprinkle with flour, salt and pepper. Top with a layer of onion. Repeat, ending with a layer of bacon. Bake at 375 degrees for 1 hour and 30 minutes to 2 hours. Yield: 4 servings.

Mrs. Hilda Wiesenger, Pres.
Peace LCW
Leduc, Alberta, Canada

BAKED LIVER

Sliced liver
Vinegar
Flour
Salt and pepper
Lard or butter
Diced onions
Milk

Cover liver with boiling water; add 1 teaspoonful vinegar to each cup of water. Let stand for 5 to 10 minutes. Pour off liquid; roll liver in flour mixed with salt and pepper. Brown in lard. Place in baking dish; cover with onions and milk. Bake at 350 degrees for 30 to 40 minutes. Serve with creamed potatoes.

Mrs. Edwin Lerum
Kickapoo United Church
Soldiers Grove, Wisconsin

BAKED LIVER AND ONIONS

2 Bermuda onions, sliced
3 tbsp. butter, melted
⅓ c. water
1 lb. sliced calves or beef liver

(Continued on next page)

242

Seasoned flour
2 tbsp. minced parsley
¼ tsp. thyme
1 bay leaf

Place onions in a shallow baking dish. Drizzle butter and water on top. Cover dish. Bake at 350 degrees for 25 minutes. Dredge liver in seasoned flour; place on top of onions. Add parsley, thyme and bay leaf. Cover casserole; bake for 30 minutes longer. Remove bay leaf and serve immediately. Yield: 4 servings.

Mrs. John Schaleger, Bd. Member
Our Savior LWML
North Aurora, Illinois

BARBECUED LIVER

1 lb. baby beef liver, sliced
2 tbsp. butter or margarine
⅓ c. bottled barbecue sauce
⅓ c. water

Brown liver in butter over medium heat. Combine remaining ingredients. Pour over liver. Heat for 10 minutes on low heat. Yield: 4 servings.

Mrs. Phyllis Heil, Pres.
Good Hope LCW
Lind, Washington

BEEF LIVER

2 lb. beef liver, sliced
1 c. milk
1 c. flour
Salt and pepper to taste

Soak liver in milk for 30 minutes. Drain; dip into flour, coating each piece. Season with salt and pepper. Fry in small amount of shortening until brown on both sides. Yield: 6 servings.

Mrs. Loraine Offhaus, Co. Chmn.
Faith Hospty. Cir.
Elma, New York

BRAISED LIVER WITH VEGETABLES

1 lb. liver
3 tbsp. flour
¾ tsp. salt
⅛ tsp. pepper
4 tbsp. fat
2 carrots, diced
6 potatoes, sliced 1-in. thick
1 sm. onion, chopped
1 c. tomato juice
1 c. boiling water

Cut liver into 2-inch squares; roll in flour seasoned with salt and pepper. Brown in hot fat.

Remove from grease. Place carrots, potatoes and onion in pan; brown lightly. Add liver, tomato juice, boiling water and 1/2 teaspoonful additional salt to vegetables. Cover and simmer for 1 hour. Thicken gravy, if desired. NOTE: A small amount lemon juice, vinegar or catsup may be added to mixture. Yield: 6 servings.

Mrs. William Cook, Sr., Teacher
St. Peter's LCW
Gadshill, Ontario, Canada

BRAZILIAN LIVER

1 lb. liver, cubed
2 tbsp. vinegar
½ tsp. salt
Dash of pepper
2 cloves of garlic, crushed
1 bay leaf, crushed
3 onions, sliced
1 lge. green pepper, chopped
½ c. butter or margarine
1 tbsp. flour

Place liver in bowl; mix vinegar, salt, pepper, garlic and bay leaf; pour over liver. Marinate for 30 minutes. Saute onions and green pepper in butter until soft; stir in flour. Remove liver from marinade. Combine all ingredients; cook for 2 minutes. Cover; steam for 2 minutes longer. Yield: 4-6 servings.

Mrs. Martha Koehler, Pres.
Faith Dorcas Soc.
Crook, Colorado

CHUCKWAGON-STYLE LIVER

1 ½ lb. liver, sliced ½-in. thick
¼ c. flour
Salt and pepper
3 tbsp. lard or drippings
2 c. thinly sliced carrots
1 c. diced onions
1 med. green pepper, diced
¼ c. water

Cut liver into serving-sized pieces. Combine flour, 1 1/2 teaspoonfuls salt and 1/8 teaspoonful pepper; dredge liver in seasoned flour. Brown in lard or drippings. Pour off drippings. Arrange vegetables on browned liver. Season vegetables with salt and pepper; add water. Cover tightly and simmer for 35 to 40 minutes or until done. Yield: 6 servings.

Mrs. Paul Hagge, Pres.
Trinity Ladies Guild
Lehigh, Iowa

CREOLE LIVER WITH A DISH OF RICE

4 slices bacon
1 lb. beef liver, sliced
Flour
½ green pepper, chopped

(Continued on next page)

1 pt. tomatoes
⅛ tsp. red pepper
1 ½ tsp. chili powder

Cut bacon into small pieces; fry until crisp. Remove cooked bacon from pan. Dip sliced liver into flour; brown in bacon fat. Add remaining ingredients and cooked bacon. Cover and simmer tently for 45 minutes. Serve with fluffy white rice, if desired. Yield: 5 servings.

Mrs. George V. Keyser, Pres.
Redeemer Ladies Guild
Mountain Home, Arkansas

EASY LIVER AND ONIONS
4 slices bacon
1 lb. liver, sliced
2 tbsp. flour
1 can onion soup
¼ c. chili sauce

Cook bacon until crisp; remove from pan. Drain and crumble. Dust liver with flour; brown in bacon drippings. Add bacon and remaining ingredients. Cover; simmer for 30 minutes or until liver is tender. Uncover; cook for a few minutes to thicken sauce. Yield: 4 servings.

Mrs. Charles R. Jones, Pres.
St. John's LCW
Anderson, Indiana

ENERGY LOAF
1 ½ lb. beef liver
1 ½ c. dry bread crumbs
¼ c. melted shortening
1 egg
1 ¼ tsp. salt
⅛ tsp. pepper
¼ tsp. paprika
3 tbsp. minced onion
3 tbsp. parsley
1 c. tomato juice (opt.)

Pour boiling water over liver; let stand for 5 minutes. Drain liver and chop. Add remaining ingredients, except tomato juice; mix thoroughly. Shape into loaf. Brush top with additional melted shortening. Place loaf in baking dish; add 1 1/2 cups water. Bake at 350 degrees for 1 hour, basting occasionally. Add tomato juice 15 minutes before removing loaf from oven. Yield: 6 servings.

Mrs. Jerrold Elling
Resurrection LCW
St. Paul Park, Minnesota

FOILED LIVER
1 lb. calves liver, sliced ⅓ to ½-in. thick
2 med. onions, sliced

Butter
Salt and pepper

Remove skin and veins from liver. Cut into serving pieces. Place 4 onion slices on 9 x 12-inch piece of greased foil. Place one piece liver over each onion slice. Place 1 pat of butter over each piece of liver. Sprinkle with salt and pepper. Cover each with remaining onion slices. Bring up corners of foil; fold. Bake at 350 degrees for 40 minutes. Open foil; bake for 10 minutes longer. Yield: 4 servings.

Mrs. Geroge Reule
Trinity Mary-Martha Soc.
Hillsboro, Oregon

LIVER AND BACON LOAF
1 lb. beef liver
6 slices bacon
1 med. onion
¼ c. finely chopped celery
1 c. coarsely crushed corn flakes
1 ½ tsp. salt
⅛ tsp. pepper
¼ tsp. marjoram
¼ c. chili sauce
¼ c. cold water
1 tbsp. flour
1 egg, lightly beaten

Place liver in saucepan; cover with boiling water. Simmer for 10 minutes; drain, reserving 1 cup liquid. Cut liver into pieces; put liver, bacon and onion through food chopper. Combine liver mixture with celery, corn flakes, salt, pepper, marjoram and chili sauce. Combine cold water and flour, blending until smooth. Heat reserved liver liquid; gradually stir into flour mixture. Cook until smooth and thickened, stirring constantly. Gradually beat hot mixture into egg. Add to liver mixture, blending well. Pack into buttered 9 x 5 x 3-inch pan. Bake at 350 degrees for 1 hour.

Mrs. Norman Baetz
St. John's LCW
Eden Grove, Ontario, Canada

LIVER BAKE
1 ½ lb. beef liver
Paprika
Flour
Bacon drippings
1 ½ c. water
2 bouillon cubes
2 tsp. Worcestershire sauce
½ c. catsup
1 lge. onion, sliced

Wipe liver with damp cloth; trim carefully. Cut into pieces. Combine paprika with flour. Dredge liver pieces into flour mixture. Brown in bacon drippings; arrange in greased casserole. Add water to pan drippings; stir in bouillon cubes, Worcestershire sauce and catsup. Pour gravy over liver; top with onion rings. Bake, covered,

(Continued on next page)

at 350 degrees for 1 hour. Garnish with bacon strips. Yield: 4-6 servings.

Mrs. Norma Gabert, Sec.-Treas.
Bethany LWML
Fort Saskatchewan, Alberta, Canada

LIVERBURGERS

1 lb. liver
2 c. diced uncooked potatoes
1 c. chopped onions
2 ½ tsp. salt
⅛ tsp. pepper
2 tbsp. fat
3 tbsp. tomato paste
1 tbsp. flour
1 ½ c. milk
½ c. cream

Put liver, potatoes and onion through meat grinder; add 1 1/2 teaspoonfuls salt and pepper. Drop liver mixture by spoonfuls into hot fat in skillet. Fry quickly; remove from pan. Blend tomato paste and flour into drippings in pan; add milk, cream and remaining salt. Bring to a boil, stirring constantly. Add liver burgers. Cover; simmer for 15 minutes. Yield: 8 servings.

Mrs. Herb Bureman
Trinity Ladies Aid
Gillett, Wisconsin

LIVER DUMPLINGS

1 ½ lb. liver
1 lge. onion, diced
2 qt. bread crumbs
1 tbsp. butter
2 eggs, beaten
½ c. flour
Salt and pepper to taste
Beef or chicken broth

Cook liver for 5 minutes; put liver through meat chopper. Fry onions and bread crumbs in butter. Mix liver with eggs; add onions and bread crumbs; season to taste. Stir in flour. Drop by spoonfuls into kettle of hot broth. Cook, covered, for 30 minutes, shaking frequently, to prevent sticking. NOTE: Soup may be substituted for beef or chicken broth. Yield: 6-8 servings.

Mrs. Ethel Williams
Hope Mary and Martha Guild
McMurray, Pennsylvania

LIVER DUMPLINGS

1 lb. beef liver
Grated onion to taste (opt.)
Salt to taste
2 eggs
Flour
Parsley (opt.)
Chopped bacon
Chopped onion

Remove skin from liver; put liver through food chopper. Add grated onion, salt and eggs. Mix well. Add enough flour to make a stiff dough. Drop by tablespoonfuls into a pot of boiling water. Cover; boil for 3 minutes. Remove from water with spoon; place in colander to drain. Saute bacon and chopped onion in small amount of butter; pour over dumplings. Yield: 4-5 servings.

Eva Braatz, Pres.
Redeemer LCW
Irvington, New Jersey

LIVER EN CASSEROLE

1 lb. calves liver, cubed
2 lge. onions, diced
Butter or bacon grease
½ green pepper, diced
1 stalk celery, diced
Mushrooms (opt.)
1 can tomato soup
1 soup can water
Salt and pepper

Sear liver and onions in butter; place in casserole. Add green pepper, celery and mushrooms. Pour soup and water over top. Season to taste. Bake at 350 degrees for 30 minutes. Yield: 4 servings.

Mrs. John Tugend, Pres.
Peace Ladies Guild
Scranton, Pennsylvania

LIVER LOAF

1 ½ lb. liver
2 tbsp. minced onion
1 tbsp. pepper
2 tbsp. minced green pepper
1 c. cracker or bread crumbs
1 tbsp. salt
1 egg, well beaten
½ c. chili sauce or catsup
1 c. hot water

Boil liver; put through food chopped. Mix with onion, pepper, green pepper, cracker or bread crumbs, salt, egg and chili sauce or catsup. Shape into loaf; place in greased pan. Bake at 350 degrees for 30 minutes or until done. Remove meat from pan; add water to remaining juice. Thicken with flour; serve gravy with meat. NOTE: Ten minutes before removing loaf from oven, chili sauce or catsup may be poured over top of loaf. Yield: 8 servings.

Mrs. E. A. Session, Pres.
Hope LWML
Muskogee, Oklahoma

LIVER NIPS

½ lb. liver
½ lb. suet
Few green leaves of sweet marjoram
1 sm. onion
3 c. flour
1 ½ tsp. salt
¼ tsp. baking powder
Dash of pepper
2 eggs
Beef broth

Grind liver, suet, marjoram and onion in meat grinder; add flour, salt, baking powder, pepper and eggs. Mix well to make a stiff batter, adding water if necessary. Drop by small spoonfuls into beef broth; let boil until liver mixture is thoroughly done.

Mrs. Ruby Derrick
St. John's LCW
Irmo, South Carolinia

LIVER AND ONIONS

1 lb. liver, sliced
4 tbsp. fat
½ c. flour
Salt and pepper
½ c. chopped onion

Wash liver in cold water; drain. Heat fat in skillet. Dip liver into flour; place in hot fat. Season with salt and pepper. Cover liver with the onion; fry over low heat. Sprinkle in remaining flour occasionally, turning liver often. Fry until brown; cover with water. Simmer for 30 minutes. Yield: 4 servings.

Mrs. Jennie Hiller
First Lutheran Church Ladies Aid
Missouri Valley, Iowa

LIVER AND ONIONS

1 lb. liver
1 tsp. salt
¼ tsp. pepper
1 c. flour
1 onion, chopped
3 tbsp. fat
½ c. water

Cut liver into serving pieces; sprinkle with salt and pepper. Roll in flour. Brown in fat on both sides over moderate heat. Add onion and brown. Add water. Cover; bake at 350 degrees for 30 minutes or until tender. Yield: 4-6 servings.

Mrs. Sam Mowry, Pres.
Mt. Zion LCW
Acme, Pennsylvania

LIVER PATE

1 med. onion, chopped
3 tbsp. butter or margarine
1 lb. liver, ground
3 hard rolls, cubed
3 eggs, beaten
1 tsp. salt
½ tsp. pepper

Saute onion in butter. Mix liver with onion and remaining ingredients. Place in greased 1-quart glass dish. Bake at 300 degrees for 1 hour. Yield: 4 servings.

Sophie Miess
St. Peter's German and Saxon LCW
Detroit, Michigan

LIVER IN SOUR CREAM

1 ½ lb. liver
⅓ c. butter
2 tbsp. flour
1 ¼ tsp. salt
Dash of pepper
1 ½ c. sour cream

Brown liver on both sides in butter. Remove liver from pan; add flour, salt and pepper. Blend until smooth. Add sour cream; cook for 1 minute, stirring constantly. Place liver in casserole; pour gravy over liver. Cover; bake at 300 degrees for 1 hour or until liver is tender. Yield: 4-6 servings.

Mrs. Elna Sims, Sec.
St. John's Ladies Aid Soc.
Taylor, Michigan

SPECIAL LIVER

3 slices bacon
1 lb. sliced beef liver
2 tbsp. flour
¼ c. chopped green pepper
3 tbsp. chopped onion
1 tsp. salt
⅛ tsp. pepper
¼ tsp. curry powder
2 c. canned tomatoes

Fry bacon; drain on absorbent paper. Dredge liver in flour; brown in bacon fat. Remove liver from pan. Cut liver into 2 x 3 x 1/2-inch pieces. Return liver to pan; add remaining ingredients. Cover and simmer for 45 minutes. Add crumbled bacon. Yield: 4 servings.

Mrs. Olger B. Lenning, Pres.
Bethel LCW
Story City, Iowa

CHICKEN LIVERS

1 lge. onion, sliced
1 sm. apple, peeled and sliced
2 stalks celery, sliced
Butter
1 lb. chicken livers
Flour
1 can cream of mushroom soup
½ c. water
Salt and pepper to taste

Saute onion, apple and celery in butter. Dust livers with flour; saute until done. Heat soup diluted with water. Combine all ingredients. Serve with buttered egg noodles or rice. Yield: 6-7 servings.

Mrs. Elaine Gobel
Redeemer Cir.
Hinsdale, Illinois

CHICKEN LIVERS IN BACON

Mustard
Pickle relish
Chicken livers
Fine bread crumbs
Bacon slices

Prepare a mixture of mustard and pickle relish. Cut chicken livers into fourths. Dip each piece into pickle relish and then into fine bread crumbs. Cut bacon slices into halves; place small amount of liver on bacon halves. Roll up; secure with toothpicks. Bake at 400 degrees for 10 to 12 minutes.

Mrs. Armin Lichtfuss, Pres.
Grace Ladies Guild
Boulder, Colorado

CHICKEN LIVERS AND GIZZARDS SAUTE

1 to 1 ½ lb. chicken livers and gizzards
¼ c. butter
¼ c. flour
1 tsp. salt
2 tsp. bottled meat sauce

Clean chicken gizzards and livers; cut into halves. Cook gizzards for 30 to 45 minutes or until tender; reserve 2 cups broth. Saute livers in butter in frying pan, over low heat, until lightly browned. Remove meat. Stir in flour; add chicken gizzards and reserved broth, stirring constantly. Add salt, meat sauce, chicken livers and gizzards. Serve on toast or over cooked rice. Yield: 6-8 servings.

Madelyn Gruenhagen, Chmn.
St. John's LWML
Napa, California

CHICKEN LIVERS GOURMET

1 4-oz. can sliced mushrooms
¼ c. flour
1 ½ tsp. salt
¼ tsp. pepper
1 lb. chicken livers
2 tbsp. instant minced onion
3 tbsp. butter
¼ tsp. Worcestershire sauce
1 ⅔ c. evaporated milk
½ c. sliced celery
2 tbsp. lemon juice
2 tbsp. chopped dried parsley
2 c. instant rice, cooked

Drain mushrooms, reserving liquid. Combine flour, salt and pepper; roll chicken livers in seasoned flour. Saute livers, mushrooms and onion in hot butter for 10 minutes. Add reserved mushroom liquid and Worcestershire. Cover; simmer for 5 to 8 minutes. Remove from heat; gradually stir in milk and celery. Cover; cook over heat for 5 minutes or until thick. Stir in lemon juice and parsley just before serving. Serve over rice.

Photograph for this recipe on inside front cover.

CHICKEN LIVERS WITH RICE

½ c. butter
½ c. minced onion
½ c. uncooked rice
½ tsp. saffron
2 c. chicken stock
½ c. grated Parmesan cheese
Salt and pepper to taste

Cook livers in boiling salted water until tender; chop and measure 1 cup. Melt butter in bottom of heavy kettle; saute onion lightly. Wash and drain rice; add to skillet. Stir as rice browns. Dissolve saffron in a small amount broth; stir into rice. Add remaining broth. Simmer for 30 minutes. Add one-half the cheese and livers. Season. Simmer, stirring, for 15 minutes. Turn into buttered casserole; sprinkle with remaining cheese. Brown quickly in oven. Yield: 4-6 servings.

Edna Koehler
St. John's LCW
Fredericksburg, Pennsylvania

CHICKEN LIVERS SUPREME

1 lb. chicken livers
¼ c. sifted flour
½ tsp. salt
⅛ tsp. pepper

247

(Continued on next page)

2 tbsp. butter or margarine
1 3 or 4-oz. can sliced mushrooms
1 ½ tsp. Worcestershire sauce

Shake chicken livers, a few at a time, in mixture of flour, salt and pepper in paper bag to coat evenly. Brown in butter in large heavy frying pan over low heat; stir in undrained mushrooms and Worcestershire sauce. Cover loosely; cook slowly for 10 minutes or just until liquid is absorbed. Yield: 4 servings.

Mrs. Elmer Johnson
Pella Ladies Aid
Waupun, Wisconsin

NENDEL'S SAUTED CHICKEN LIVERS

1 lb. chicken livers
Salt and pepper
Oil
¼ c. butter or rendered chicken fat
1 lge. onion, coarsely chopped
½ c. sliced mushrooms
1 tbsp. Sherry

Toss livers in flour seasoned with salt and pepper. Sauve livers, a few at a time, in small amount of heated oil for a few minutes or until browned. Melt butter or rendered chicken fat in another pan; add onion and cook until translucent. Add mushrooms; cook, stirring frequently, for several minutes longer. Add livers and Sherry; simmer mixture for 5 minutes. Yield: 4 servings.

Mrs. Louis Schmitz, Sec.
Mt. Olive Ladies Aid Soc.
Omaha, Nebraska

SMOTHERED CHICKEN LIVERS

½ lb. chicken livers
2 tsp. salt
½ tsp. pepper
⅔ c. milk
½ c. flour
3 tbsp. shortening
1 10 ½-oz. can cream of mushroom soup

Pierce chicken livers with meat fork to reduce popping; season with salt and pepper. Pour 1/3 cup milk over livers. Let stand for a few minutes; coat livers with flour. Fry livers in shortening until done; pour off remaining shortening. Add soup and remaining milk. Simmer over low heat for 10 minutes. Serve with potatoes or toast, if desired. Yield: 6 servings.

Patricia Hamlin, Pres.
Holy Trinity LWML
Macon, Georgia

SWEET AND PUGENT CHICKEN LIVERS

1 lb. chicken livers
2 tbsp. vegetable oil
Salt and pepper
1 8 ½-oz. can sliced pineapple
3 green peppers, cut into 1-in. pieces
1 c. chicken stock
½ c. vinegar
½ c. sugar
3 tbsp. cornstarch
1 tbsp. soy sauce

Cut each chicken liver into two or three pieces. Saute in oil until lightly browned. Season; place liver on hot platter. Cut each pineapple slice into six pieces. Simmer green peppers and pineapple pieces in chicken stock for 3 minutes. Mix vinegar with sugar, cornstarch and soy sauce. Add to green peppers and pineapple. Cook, stirring, until thickened. Pour chicken livers. Serve with rice. Yield: 6 servings.

Mrs. Adam Mark, Pres.
Our Savior's LCW
Beaconsfield, Quebec, Canada

LIVER PASTE

1 lb. pork liver
¾ lb. pork fat
1 lge. onion
2 tbsp. butter
2 tbsp. flour
2 c. milk
2 eggs, beaten
¾ tsp. pepper
1 tbsp. salt
½ tsp. allspice
¼ tsp. cloves

Put liver, fat and onion through meat grinder three times. Melt butter; blend in flour. Gradually add milk; cook, stirring until thick. Add liver mixture. Add eggs and spices; beat well. Turn into loaf pan; set loaf pan in pan of water. Bake at 350 degrees for 1 hour and 15 minutes.

Dorothy M. Larsen, Pres.
Faith LCW
Calgary, Alberta, Canada

MEAT BUNS

2 lge. onions, chopped
Butter or margarine
6 c. liver, sausage or cooked ground meat
¼ c. plus 2 tsp. sugar
½ c. lukewarm water
2 pkg. powdered yeast
2 c. scalded milk, cooled
2 tsp. salt
2 eggs, beaten
7 c. flour

(Continued on next page)

Cook onions in 1 tablespoonful butter for 5 minutes; add meat. Mix well. Set aside to cool. Add 2 teaspoonfuls sugar to water; sprinkle in yeast. Let stand for 10 minutes. Add lukewarm milk, 1/4 cup sugar, salt, eggs and 1/3 cup melted margarine; add 4 cups flour. Beat for a few minutes with a spoon. Add 3 cups flour and knead. Dough will be soft and sticky. Grease bowl and dough well; cover with waxed paper and a cloth. Let rise until doubled in bulk. Roll small pieces of dough the side of an egg on table top without flour to 3 x 5 inches. Place cold meat mixture in lengthwise roll; bring up sides of dough overlapping. Pinch edges together; roll lightly in flour. Place in greased pans. Let rise for 1 hour. Bake at 350 degrees for 20 minutes. Yield: 75 buns.

Mrs. Ella Beck, Treas.
Good Hope Schuler Ladies Aid
Schuler, Alberta, Canada

MEAT AND TURNIP CASSEROLE

4 c. diced turnips
1 c. fine dry bread crumbs
¾ c. shredded Cheddar cheese
½ c. white sauce mix
1 tsp. salt
Dash of pepper
1 12-oz. can luncheon meat, diced

Cook turnips for 20 minutes or until tender. Drain, reserving 2 cups liquid. Blend crumbs and cheese together. Mix white sauce mix with reserved turnip liquid. Mix three-fourths of crumb mixture with white sauce. Season with salt and pepper; stir in turnips and meat. Pour into buttered 2-quart casserole. Sprinkle with remaining crumb-cheese mixture. Bake at 350 degrees for 25 to 30 minutes. Yield: 6-8 servings.

Mrs. Jule Dalby, Sec.-Treas.
Metiskow LCW
Czar, Alberta, Canada

SHORT CUT SPAGHETTI

1 12-oz. can luncheon meat
1 green pepper, cut into rings
1 onion, sliced
1 8-oz. pkg. spaghetti, cooked
½ lb. Cheddar cheese, cubed
2 8-oz. cans tomato sauce

Saute meat, green pepper and onion in oil; add spaghetti and cheese. Pour in tomato sauce. Cover; simmer for 5 minutes or until cheese melts. Yield: 4 servings.

Mrs. Jeanette Bryant, Pres.
St. Andrew's Evangelical LCW
Millwood, Maryland

OXTAIL RAGOUT

2 oxtails, disjointed
¼ c. flour
1 tsp. salt
2 tbsp. fat
1 lge. onion, chopped
1 clove of garlic, chopped
1 tsp. paprika
2 ripe tomatoes or 1 c. canned tomatoes
12 scallions, diced or 12 sm. white onions
12 lge. mushrooms
1 c. diced potatoes

Coat oxtails with flour; sprinkle with salt. Brown in large skillet in hot fat. Stir in chopped onion, garlic, paprika and tomatoes. Cover; simmer for 2 hours or until meat is tender. Add a small amount of water as needed, to prevent sticking. Arrange scallions, mushrooms and potatoes around meat; add enough water to make 1/4 cup liquid. Cover; cook for 30 minutes or until vegetables are tender. Yield: 6 servings.

Mrs. Fred Flohr, Pres.
Grace Ladies Aid
Toronto, Ontario, Canada

OXTAILS IN SAVORY SAUCE

3 lb. oxtails, cut into 1½-in. pieces
2 tbsp. butter
¼ c. instant minced onion
¼ c. water
1 tbsp. dry mustard
1 tbsp. arrowroot
1 tbsp. dried mushrooms
1 10½-oz. can beef bouillon
1 c. red wine
2 tbsp. tomato paste
1 tsp. seasoned salt
1 tsp. salt
1 tsp. monosodium glutamate
Dash of cayenne
½ c. sour cream
Chopped parsley

(Continued on next page)

Brown oxtails in butter; remove from skillet. Soak onion in water for 5 minutes; stir into pan drippings. Add dry mustard, arrowroot, mushrooms, bouillon and wine. Cook over low heat, stirring constantly, until thickened and smooth. Stir in tomato paste, seasoned salt, salt, monosodium glutamate and cayenne. Return oxtails to sauce. Cover; simmer or bake at 250 degrees for 3 hours or until oxtails are tender. Stir in sour cream; sprinkle with parsley. Heat through and serve with noodles or steamed rice. if desired. Yield: 6 servings.

Harriett Johnson, Pres.
Our Savior's LWML
Fresno, California

PIG TAILS

10 pig tails
1 30-oz. bottle ginger ale
2 tbsp. brown sugar
2 tbsp. Worcestershire sauce
1 tsp. dry mustard
4 tsp. chili powder
½ c. water
¼ c. vinegar
1 tsp. salt
1 tbsp. paprika
1 c. tomato juice
Dash of cayenne
Flour

Place pig tails in roasting pan with enough ginger ale for tails to set in, but not be covered. Bake at 300 to 325 degrees for 2 hours or until tails are nearly cooked. Combine remaining ingredients, adding enough flour to thicken; cook until thickened. Pour over pig tails. Roast until meat is tender, about 2 hours. Yield: 3-4 servings.

Mrs. William Heinbuch, Pres.
St. Matthew's Charisma Guild
Stratford, Ontario, Canada

ROAST PIG TAILS

2 tbsp. Bovril cordial
1 c. hot water
5 lb. lean pig tails
2 qt. liquid from boiled ham
5 med. onions, diced
Salt and pepper to taste

Dissolve cordial in hot water. Place all ingredients in deep roasting pan. Cover and bake at 325 degrees for 4 hours or until most of liquid has evaporated. Remove cover and brown before serving, if necessary. Yield: 4 servings.

Mrs. George Strack
St. John's LCW
Petawawa, Ontario, Canada

WATERLOO COUNTY ROAST PIG TAILS

2 to 3 lb. pig tails
Salt
2 med. onions, chopped
½ c. brown sugar
2 tbsp. dry mustard
2 tbsp. molasses
½ tsp. pepper
Barbecue sauce to taste

Boil pigtails slowly for 1 hour in water and 2 tablespoonfuls salt; drain. Line roasting pan with onions. Add 1 cup water. Arrange pig tails on onions. Combine remaining ingredients except barbecue sauce with a small amount of water. Drizzle mixture over pig tails; cover. Bake at 300 degrees for 1 hour. Add a small amount of barbecue sauce. Bake, uncovered, for 30 minutes longer. Yield: 6-8 servings.

Mrs. Albert Kropf, Sec.
St. Matthew's Evangelical LCW
Kitchener, Ontario, Canada

BRAISED BEEF TONGUE

1 lge. beef tongue
Salt and black pepper to taste
Dash of red pepper
1 1-pt. bottle catsup
1 lge. onion, finely chopped
2 bunches parsley
2 stalks celery, finely chopped
3 lge. carrots, diced
1 tbsp. sugar
2 tbsp. vinegar
2 tbsp. flour
2 tbsp. butter
3 whole cloves
½ green pepper, finely chopped

Place tongue in boiling water. Add salt and black pepper to taste and red pepper; boil for 2 hours. Let stand overnight in stock. Clean and skin tongue; strain stock. Combine remaining ingredients; cook for 2 hours. Place tongue in roaster; pour sauce over tongue. Bake at 325 degrees for 2 hours or until tender. Yield: 6 servings.

Mrs. Mabel Decker
Memorial LCW
Harrisburg, Pennsylvania

COLD SLICED BEEF TONGUE

1 med. beef tongue
1 sm. onion, diced
1 stalk celery, diced
Salt
Water

(Continued on next page)

Cover tongue, onion and celery with boiling water; simmer until tender. Cool tongue in liquid; peel off skin. Place tongue in jar. Make a brine, using 1 tablespoonful salt to 1 quart water. Cover tongue with brine; let stand for one week in refrigerator. Cut into slices.

Mrs. R. Seastrand
Hoquiam Lutheran Church
Hoquiam, Washington

SOUR POTTED PORK TONGUES

2 ¼ c. water
2 c. white vinegar
2 tsp. pickling spices
1 med. and 1 lge. onion, sliced
6 fresh pork tongues
1 tbsp. lard
½ tsp. salt
½ tsp. pepper
½ tsp. paprika
1 tbsp. tomato sauce
1 tbsp. flour

Boil 2 cups water and vinegar; add spices. Remove from heat; add medium onion. Wash tongues; place in large bowl. Cover with vinegar mixture; cover bowl and let stand overnight in cool place. Brown tongues in lard in 5-quart Dutch oven. Season with salt, pepper and paprika; add remaining onion and brown. Add 1 1/2 cups of vinegar mixture and spices. Add tomato sauce. Cover; cook slowly for 1 hour and 15 minutes to 1 hour and 30 minutes. Remove tongues; remove skins with sharp knife. Cut off back ends. Thicken gravy with combination of flour and remaining water. Strain gravy; pour over tongues. Yield: 6 servings.

Mrs. William Jaissle, Statistician
Advent LCW
Palisade, New Jersey

SPICED TONGUE

1 tongue, cleaned
3 bay leaves
12 peppercorns
2 tbsp. salt
1 tsp. mustard
½ c. brown sugar
½ c. vinegar

Place all ingredients in pressure cooker; cover with water. Cook at 10 pounds pressure for 20 minutes. Release steam slowly until indicator turns to zero. Remove skin from tongue; return

meat to liquid. Let stand in liquid overnight. Slice for serving.

Mrs. Harold Zimmerschied, Pres.
Immanuel Guild
Higginsville, Missouri

TONGUE WITH CHERRY SAUCE

4 lb. fresh beef tongue
1 tsp. peppercorns
1 tbsp. salt
1 med. onion
6 whole cloves
1 bay leaf

Place tongue and spices in large saucepan. Cover with water; bring to boil. Simmer until tender. Peel tongue; cut into 1/2-inch slices. Arrange in glass baking dish.

CHERRY SAUCE:

½ c. brown sugar
1 c. tongue broth
1 tbsp. cornstarch
½ tsp. powdered cloves
1 c. pitted sour cherries, drained
1 tbsp. lemon juice
2 tbsp. butter

Combine sugar, broth, cornstarch and cloves; cook until thick and clear. Add cherries, lemon and butter. Pour over tongue. Bake at 350 degrees for 30 minutes. Yield: 6 servings.

Mrs. Alma Denstedt, Pres.
St. Paul's Ladies Aid
Tavistock, Ontario, Canada

TORRID TRIPE

1 ½ lb. honeycomb tripe
4 marrow bones, cut into 1 ½-in. pieces
2 qt. water
½ c. beef bouillon
1 c. vegetable stock
1 ⅓ c. chopped fresh or canned tomatoes
1 tbsp. vinegar
1 med. onion stick with clove
Pinch of savory
Pinch of thyme
4 sprigs parsley
½ sm. bay leaf
2 ½ tsp. salt
½ tsp. freshly ground pepper
½ c. unpeeled diced potatoes
½ c. peeled diced yellow turnip
½ c. unpeeled carrots

Wash and shred tripe; place in a large saucepan with bones, water, bouillon, stock, tomatoes, vinegar, onion stick, savory, thyme, parsley, bay leaf, salt and pepper. Cover; simmer for 2 hours.

(Continued on next page)

Add diced vegetables; cover and simmer for 1 hour or until vegetables are tender. Yield: 4-6 servings.

Mrs. Florence Morton
Bethel Evangelical Lutheran Church
Cheltenham, Pennsylvania

SAUSAGE ROLL

1 can refrigerated crescent rolls
1 can Vienna sausages or 1 pkg. small brown and serve sausages

Place rolls flat; place sausage at the wide end of each piece of dough. Roll dough around sausage; seal firmly. Bake according to instructions on roll package. Serve hot.

Mrs. Elfrieda Boese
St. Peter's LWML
Compton, California

BATTER DIPPED WIENERS

⅔ c. pancake mix
¼ c. corn meal
½ tsp. onion salt
1 tsp. dry mustard
½ tsp. garlic powder
12 wieners

Combine pancake mix, corn meal, onion salt, dry mustard and garlic powder; add enough water to make batter. Beat with rotary beater for 2 minutes. Dip wieners into batter, holding with kitchen fork or tongs. Drain off excess batter; fry in 375 degree hot fat in electric skillet for 2 to 3 minutes. Drain on absorbent paper. Serve at once with mustard or catsup. NOTE:For appetizers, slice wieners into small circles; coat each piece with batter. Fry in same manner. Serve bite-sized pieces on toothpick with spicy hot sauce. Yield: 4-5 servings.

Mrs. Alvin Kothe
Immanuel LCW
Salisbury, Missouri

CHINESE-STYLE SWEET AND SOUR FRANKS

1 lb. franks or wieners
1 1-lb. 4½-oz. can pineapple chunks
¼ c. water
¼ c. vinegar
3 tbsp. brown sugar
2 tbsp. cornstarch
1 tbsp. soy sauce
1 c. thinly sliced onions
1 c. thinly sliced celery
2 tbsp. shortening
1 med. green pepper, cut into strips
Cooked rice

Cut franks or wieners into 1-inch diagonal pieces. Drain pineapple chunks; reserve syrup. Combine syrup, water, vinegar, brown sugar, cornstarch and soy sauce; mix. Saute onions and celery in hot shortening until heated but crisp. Add franks, pineapple chunks and sauce mixture. Cook, stirring carefully, until sauce thickens and clears. Add green pepper and heat. Serve over hot buttered rice. Yield: 4-5 servings.

Mrs. Doughlas H. Brehm
St. Mark Mele-Mileke Guild
Kaneohe, Oahu, Hawaii

FRANKFURTERS AND SAUERKRAUT

3 slices bacon
Salad oil
¼ c. vinegar
1 ½ tsp. onion salt
¼ tsp. sugar
½ tsp. pepper
3 c. diced cooked potatoes
7 frankfurters
2 c. undrained sauerkraut
1 med. green pepper, sliced
Paprika

Cook bacon over low heat until crisp; reserve fat. Drain bacon and crumble. Add enough oil to reserved bacon drippings to make 1/2 cup. Combine oil mixture, vinegar, onion salt, pepper, sugar and bacon. Stir well; pour oil mixture over potatoes. Let stand for 10 minutes. Cut franks into 1-inch pieces. Combine sauerkraut and franks. Cover and cook for 5 minutes. Add potato mixture. Cook for 5 minutes longer. Stir in green pepper. Turn into serving dish; sprinkle with paprika. Yield: 6 servings.

Mrs. Elizabeth Omasta, Treas.
Holy Trinity Ladies Aid
North Hatfield, Massachusetts

FRENCH-FRIED HOT DOGS

1 c. pancake mix
2 tbsp. corn meal
1 tbsp. sugar
⅔ c. water
8 wieners

Combine pancake mix, corn meal and sugar; add water and beat with rotary beater for 2 minutes. Dip wieners into batter. Fry in hot fat for 2 to 3 minutes. Drain on paper towel. Yield: 8 servings.

Mrs. Pete Pedersen
St. Paul's Ladies Aid
Ellsworth, Kansas

PARTY FRANKS

1 ½ c. instant rice
½ tsp. salt
1 ½ c. water
12 frankfurters
2 tbsp. prepared mustard
1 10 ½-oz. can cream of mushroom soup
¼ c. chopped parsley
2 tbsp. grated onion
2 tbsp. chopped pimento
⅓ c. grated sharp Cheddar cheese

Combine rice and salt in boiling water; mix just enough to moisten all rice. Cover and remove from heat. Let stand for 13 minutes. Slit frankfurters lengthwise; spread out surface with mustard. Place franks in long shallow baking dish. Combine rice, undiluted mushroom soup, parsley, onion and pimento. Pile lightly into franks. Sprinkle with grated cheese. Bake at 350 degrees for 20 minutes. Yield: 12 servings.

Mrs. Viola Ketelhut
St. Mark's Evangelist Ladies Aid
East Detroit, Michigan

Cook onions and green pepper in small amount of fat until tender, but not brown. Add brown sugar, vinegar, mustard, Worcestershire sauce, tomato sauce and catsup. Bring to a boil. Cut frankfurters into 2-inch pieces; add to sauce. Simmer for 10 minutes. Serve with buttered noodles, if desired. Yield: 5-6 servings.

Ann Prott
Dorcas Ladies Aid
East Gary, Indiana

KIDS' CORN DOGS

1 c. prepared biscuit mix
2 tbsp. yellow corn meal
¼ tsp. paprika
½ tsp. dry mustard
1 egg, beaten
½ c. milk
1 1-lb. pkg. frankfurters

Preheat shortening or oil. Combine biscuit mix, corn meal and seasonings; add egg and milk. Stir until blended. Dip frankfurters into batter, allowing to drip slightly. Fry in preheated 400 degree electric skillet until golden brown, turning. Drain. Push a wooden skewer into one end. Yield: 8-10 servings.

Mrs. Dorothy Backman, Pres.
Faith and Charity Cir.
Coquille, Oregon

SKILLET FRANKS

1 c. chopped onions
½ c. chopped green pepper
¼ c. brown sugar
3 tsp. vinegar
1 tsp. mustard
2 tsp. Worcestershire sauce
1 8-oz. can seasoned tomato sauce
½ c. catsup
1 lb. frankfurters

SPAGHETTI LOAF WITH SWOONER SAUCE

LOAF:

1 8-oz. pkg. spaghetti
1 ½ c. milk
3 eggs, slightly beaten
1 tbsp. chopped parsley
⅓ c. chopped green pepper
1 tsp. salt
⅛ tsp. pepper

Cook spaghetti according to package directions. Combine milk, eggs, parsley, green pepper, salt and pepper; mix well. Add spaghetti. Pour into greased 9 x 5 x 2 3/4-inch loaf pan. Place in pan containing warm water up to level of loaf. Bake at 375 degrees for 45 minutes.

SAUCE:

3 tbsp. finely chopped onion
3 tbsp. melted fat or salad oil
2 tbsp. flour
3 c. canned tomatoes
1 tsp. sugar
1 tsp. salt
⅛ tsp. pepper
½ lb. frankfurters, sliced

Cook onion slowly in fat until soft; blend in flour. Remove from heat; add tomatoes. Stir until blended; add seasonings. Add frankfurters to sauce; cook until slightly thickened. Unmold loaf; serve with sauce. Yield: 6 servings.

Mrs. Mescal Gooden, Pres.
Lime Creek ALCW
Emmons, Minnesota

SPICY HOT DOGS

½ c. chopped onion
2 tbsp. chopped green pepper
2 tbsp. salad oil
1 lb. frankfurters or left-over roast
¾ c. catsup
2 tbsp. brown sugar
2 tbsp. prepared mustard
1 tbsp. Worcestershire sauce
1 tsp. salt

Cook onion and green pepper in oil until tender. Score frankfurters diagonally. Add remaining ingredients. Cover; simmer for 5 to 8 minutes.

Mrs. Edward Blum
Calvary Lutheran Church
Indianapolis, Indiana

WIENER CASSEROLE

4 tbsp. margarine
4 tbsp. flour
2 c. milk
6 c. cooked diced potatoes
8 to 10 wieners, sliced

Melt margarine; blend in flour, stirring until smooth. Gradually add milk, stirring constantly, until thickened. Combine potatoes and wieners in casserole dish. Pour sauce over mixture. Bake at 300 degrees for 1 hour.

Mrs. Robert W. Poirier, Pres.
Christ Lutheran Church Ladies Guild
Virginia Beach, Virginia

WIENERS CREOLE

3 wieners, sliced
1 tbsp. fat
¾ c. chili sauce
⅓ c. chopped onion
⅓ c. chopped green pepper
1 10-oz. can whole kernel corn

Brown wieners in fat; add chili sauce, onion and green pepper. Simmer until tender. Add corn; simmer for 15 minutes longer. Garnish with green pepper rings, if desired. Yield: 4 servings.

Mrs. Fred Donner
St. Paul's Ladies Guild
Metamora, Michigan

WIENER-NOODLE CASSEROLE

½ pkg. noodles
7 or 8 wieners, cut up
1 can cream of celery soup
2 tbsp. dry onion soup mix
½ c. milk
Bread crumbs

Boil noodles in salted water until done. Brown wieners in butter. Combine wieners and noodles with soup, soup mix and milk. Place in buttered 1-quart casserole; top with bread crumbs. Bake at 350 degrees for 20 to 25 minutes.

Angeline Kadous
Peace Ladies Aid
Shell Rock, Iowa

Wild Game Favorites

RECIPE FOR ROAST WATER FOWL ON PAGE 256

NORTHWOODS ROAST BEAR

1 4 to 5 lb. bear roast
½ c. vinegar
1 ½ tsp. salt
Pepper
2 onions, sliced
Ham skin or strips of soft pork or bacon

Remove all fat from roast. Place in large kettle; cover with water. Add vinegar; bring to boil. Simmer for 20 minutes. Remove roast from water; discard water. Place in roaster. Add salt and pepper. Secure onion rings on roast with toothpicks. Cover with ham skin. Cover; roast at 350 degrees for 3 hours, adding water as needed. Thicken gravy, if desired. Yield: 8 servings.

Mrs. Ira Lee, Pres.
St. Stephen's LCW
Denver, Colorado

DOVE AND DRESSING

12 dove breasts
½ c. light oil
Salt
4 c. poultry stuffing mix
2 tsp. dried parsley leaves
1 tsp. pepper
1 tsp. minced garlic
½ tsp. ground thyme
½ c. melted butter
1 tsp. paprika

Wash dove breasts in cold water; dry thoroughly with paper towels. Rub each dove with oil and salt lightly. Mix stuffing mix with 1 teaspoonful salt and remaining ingredients. Place dove breasts in greased shallow casserole on layer of stuffing. Sprinkle remaining stuffing over doves. Bake at 350 degrees for 45 minutes. Cover with foil if casserole browns too fast. Yield: 6 servings.

Mrs. Arnold Witzke, Pres.
Resurrection Ladies Guild
Brunswick, Georgia

PINEAPPLE DUCKLING

1 4 to 5 lb. Long Island duckling
2 tsp. Kitchen Bouquet
2 tbsp. fat, melted
1 tsp. salt
½ tsp. onion salt
½ tsp. celery salt
½ tsp. ginger
1 c. canned pineapple juice
2 c. diagonally sliced carrots
1 9-oz. can sliced pineapple, cut into 8 pieces
2 med. green peppers, cut into 8 pieces
2 tbsp. cornstarch
2 tbsp. cold water

Skin duckling; cut into serving pieces. Brush lightly with Kitchen Bouquet. Brown duckling on both sides in fat in large frying pan or Dutch oven. Combine seasonings; add to duckling. Add pineapple juice and carrots. Cover; simmer for 45 minutes or until duckling is tender. Add pineapple and green pepper. Cook for 5 minutes or until green peppers are tender. Mix cornstarch with water; stir into sauce. Cook, stirring constantly, until sauce thickens and boils. Yield: 4 servings.

Mrs. J. A. Stadler, Pres.
Our Savior Lutheran Church Aux.
Port Washington, New York

ROAST WATER FOWL

2 1 ¼-lb. wild ducks, oven ready
1 onion, chopped
1 clove of garlic, minced
2 tbsp. unsalted butter
1 tsp. paprika
½ tsp. salt
¼ tsp. Tabasco sauce
1 lb. sliced bacon
4 c. cooked wild rice

Rub cavities of birds with onion and garlic. Combine butter, paprika, salt and Tabasco sauce; rub into duck skin. Wrap duck in cheese cloth; place bird, breast-down, on rack in greased shallow pan. Roast, uncovered, at 325 degrees for 1 hour and 30 minutes to 2 hours, basting occasionally. Turn when half done. Remove cheese cloth; cover each bird with strips of bacon. Continue roasting until done. Serve with wild rice.

Photograph for this recipe on page 255 .

ROASTED WILD DUCK

1 wild duck
2 tsp. soda
2 qt. water
1 stalk celery with leaves, chopped
1 onion, cut up
1 unpeeled apple, cut up
1 tbsp. salt
¼ tsp. pepper
2 strips bacon or salt pork

Clean duck; place in kettle. Cover with water and soda; parboil for 10 minutes. Remove from water; drain. Stuff with celery, onion and apple. Salt and pepper the duck; tie down legs, tuck wings behind back. Lay strips bacon over breast of duck. Place in roasting; cover. Roast at 350 degrees, allowing 30 minutes per pound. Water may be added to pan if needed; baste often. Discard stuffing when done. Yield: 2-4 servings.

Mrs. C. W. Miller, Pres.
Zion LWML
Eland, Wisconsin

ROAST WILD DUCK DELUXE

Salt
2 tbsp. vinegar
2 ½ lb. wild duck, drawn and washed
Pepper to taste
1 ½ c. fine bread crumbs
¼ c. chopped apple
½ c. pork sausage
1 sm. onion, chopped
½ tsp. sage or poultry seasoning
Milk
2 slices bacon

Add 2 tablespoonfuls salt and vinegar to water; cover duck with water. Soak for 1 to 2 hours. Combine remaining ingredients except bacon with a small amount of milk. Stuff duck with dressing. Place in roaster. Sprinkle with salt and pepper; place bacon on duck breast. Add 1/4 cup water. Bake at 400 degrees for 2 hours or until done. Baste occasionally with liquid in pan. NOTE: For extra flavor baste with 1/2 cup red wine. Yield: 3-4 servings.

Mrs. Verna A. Dressler
Concordia LCW
Churchbridge, Saskatchewan, Canada

STUFFED ROASTED WILD DUCK IN WINE

2 c. chopped celery
1 onion, chopped
3 sprigs parsley or parsley flakes
12 lge. stuffed olives
Sliver of garlic
½ c. butter
1 c. fresh bread crumbs
Salt and pepper to taste
1 c. plus 1 tbsp. dry red wine
¼ c. water
2 ducks, dressed

Simmer celery, onion, parsley, olives and garlic in butter; add bread crumbs. Fry for few minutes; add salt and pepper to taste. Add 1 tablespoonful wine. Salt ducks lightly inside and out; stuff with above dressing. Rub duck's breast with butter. Place in roasting pan; pour red wine and water over ducks. Roast at 375 degrees for 30 minutes, basting once or twice. Reduce temperature to 325 degrees, cover, and bake for 1 hour to 1 hour and 30 minutes or until tender. Add a small amount of wine to gravy; do not thicken. Yield: 2-4 servings.

Mrs. H. E. Henriksen, Pres.
Zion LWML
Abilene, Texas

WILD DUCK

1 wild duck, cut into serving pieces
1 onion, sliced
Salt and pepper
2 c. water
1 c. fresh or canned mushrooms, sliced
¼ c. butter

2 tsp. flour
¼ tsp. thyme

Brown duck with onion in butter. Add salt, pepper and water. Cover; cook for 1 hour and 30 minutes. Saute mushrooms in small amount of additional butter. Add flour and thyme. Add to duck; cook for 30 minutes. Serve with wild rice. NOTE: Pheasant may be substituted for wild duck. Yield: 4 servings.

Mrs. Knute Monson, Pres.
American LCW
Newark, Illinois

WILD DUCK CASSEROLE

Breasts of 3 wild ducks
1 tsp. salt
Dash of pepper
Dash of cayenne
1 onion, finely chopped
1 c. soft bread crumbs
1 carrot, finely grated
3 tbsp. melted butter
Hot water
6 slices bacon

Arrange duck breasts in casserole leaving hole in center for dressing. Mix remaining ingredients except bacon. Fill center with dressing; arrange bacon strips across top. Bake at 375 degrees for 2 hours or until done. Serve hot. NOTE: Ducks should be skinned, not plucked.

Mrs. Vivian Broberg, Pres.
Donre Evangelical LCW
Spalding, Saskatchewan, Canada

WILD DUCK AND GRAVY

1 wild duck
Salt and pepper to taste
1 lge. onion
1 bay leaf
Pinch of garlic salt or monosodium glutamate
2 carrots, finely diced (opt.)
Cornstarch
Flour

Place duck in large cooker; cover with water. Add salt and pepper. Cook until almost done. Add onion, bay leaf, garlic and carrots. Additional onions and carrots may be added. Mix cornstarch with flour. Gradually add to broth. Cook until desired consistency. Yield: 8-10 servings.

Mrs. Carl G. Lippelt
St. John's Evangelical Church
LaCrosse, Indiana

WILD DUCK AND DRESSING

6 sm. wild ducks
½ c. chopped celery
½ c. chopped onion
¼ c. melted butter or margarine
4 c. diced tart apples
1 c. raisins or chopped prunes
¼ c. water
Salt
¼ tsp. pepper
½ tsp. thyme
4 c. cubed dry bread

Cook celery and onion in butter until transparent. Add apples, raisins and water; simmer until apples are tender. Add 1 teaspoonful salt and remaining ingredients except ducks; toss lightly until well mixed. Salt cavity of ducks; Place in greased baking pan with cover. Place remaining stuffing in pan around birds. Bake at 350 degrees for 1 hour for small ducks or 45 minutes per pound for larger ducks. Baste with additional butter. NOTE: Small wild duck is more easily cleaned and stuffed if split down breast bone. Yield: 5-6 servings.

Mrs. James R. Holste
St. Paul's LWML
Hardin, Illinois

WILD DUCKLING WITH ORANGE DRESSING

1 wild duckling
1 tsp. salt
¼ tsp. pepper
1 orange, peeled
2 tbsp. minced onion
¼ c. chopped celery
Fat
4 c. soft bread crumbs
¼ c. melted shortening
Grated rind of 1 orange
1 c. dry Sherry

Clean duck; rub body cavity with salt and pepper. Place orange in body cavity. Place in a small roasting pan or casserole. Saute onion and celery in fat; add remaining ingredients except Sherry. Toss lightly. Surround duckling with dressing, leaving only point of breast showing. Pour Sherry over duckling and dressing. Cover; bake at 350 degrees for 3 hours or until tender. Baste with additional Sherry if necessary. Uncover the last 30 minutes of cooking. Yield: 4 servings.

Mrs. Helen Chandler
St. John's Dorcas Guild
Lawton, Oklahoma

WILD DUCK, TEXAS-STYLE

1 c. diced celery
1 c. minced onions
1 c. seeded raisins
1 c. coarsely chopped pecans
2 eggs
4 c. soft bread crumbs
½ c. scalded milk
2 2 ½-lb. wild ducks
6 slices bacon

Combine celery, onions, raisins, pecans, eggs and bread crumbs; mix well. Add milk and mix. Stuff ducks with mixture; sew or skewer openings. Place three slices bacon on breast of each duck. Place ducks on rack of roasting pan. Bake, uncovered, at 500 degrees for 15 minutes. Reduce heat to 350 degrees and bake for 1 hour and 45 minutes longer. Serve hot. Yield: 4 servings.

Mrs. Robert Handrick
Trintiy LWML
Albany, Texas

BAKED PHEASANT

1 pheasant, cut up
Flour
Fat
¼ c. chopped onion
1 tbsp. salt
1 ½ tsp. Worcestershire sauce
1 c. sweet cream, evaporated milk or half and half
½ clove of garlic (opt.)
Dash of pepper

Roll pheasant in flour; brown in hot fat in skillet. Place pheasant pieces in baking dish; pour remaining ingredients over pheasant. Cover with foil. Bake at 300 degrees until tender. Add additional cream, if needed. Yield: 6-8 servings.

Mrs. George H. Nelson, Jr., Pres.
Zion LCW
Newman Grove, Nebraska

PHEASANT BARBECUE

1 can tomato soup
1 ½ c. catsup
3 tbsp. brown sugar
3 tbsp. vinegar
3 tsp. Worcestershire sauce (opt.)
1 med. onion, chopped
3 tsp. chili powder
½ c. water
1 pheasant
Fat

Combine soup, catsup, brown sugar, vinegar, Worcestershire sauce, onion, chili powder and water. Cut pheasant into serving pieces; brown in small amount of fat. Pour sauce over all. Bake at 300 degrees for 2 hours and 30 minutes. Additional water may be added, if needed.

Mrs. Clyde Dunn
St. John's Ladies Guild
Tyndall, South Dakota
Mrs. Arthur Vilhauer, Pres.
St. John's LWML
Tyndall, South Dakota

PHEASANT WITH CRANBERRY JUICE

1 pheasant, cut into serving pieces
2 tbsp. butter, melted
Salt and pepper to taste
Celery salt
Mixed dry herbs
1 c. chopped onions
1 tbsp. grated lemon rind
½ c. cranberry juice

Brown pheasant in butter for 45 minutes. Add seasonings, turning frequently. Add onions, lemon rind and cranberry juice. Cover; simmer for 15 to 20 minutes.

Mrs. Norman Johnson, Pres.
Trinity LCW
Stevens Point, Wisconsin

PHEASANT IN CREAM

¾ tsp. salt
⅛ tsp. pepper
¼ c. flour
1 tsp. paprika
1 pheasant, cut into pieces
¼ c. cooking fat
1 3½-oz. can mushrooms (opt.)
2 tbsp. chopped onion
¼ to ½ c. sour cream

Mix seasonings with flour. Dredge pheasant pieces in seasoned flour; brown evenly and slowly in preheated 1/4-inch deep fat. Cook for 15 to 20 minutes or until brown. Remove pheasant from skillet; place in a shallow casserole. Brown mushrooms and onion in remaining fat in skillet; add to pheasant; drizzle 1 to 2 tablespoonfuls sour cream over each pheasant piece in casserole. Bake at 325 degrees for 45 minutes to 1 hour or until fork tender. Do not cover young bird. Add additional cream if the meat becomes dry. Yield: 6 servings.

Mrs. Arnold Pfeiffer
First English Ladies Aid
Parker, South Dakota

PHEASANT DELIGHT

1 egg
½ c. milk
1 pheasant, cut into serving pieces
½ c. flour
½ c. corn meal
Fat
½ c. chopped onion
1 c. water

Mix egg with milk; dip pheasant pieces into egg mixture. Place flour and cornmeal in paper bag. Add pheasant; shake. Brown pheasant in fat. Place in baking dish; add onion and water. Bake at 325 degrees for 1 hour. Yield: 2 servings.

Norma Johnson, Pres.
Zion LWML
Presho, South Dakota

PHEASANT IN SOUR CREAM

1 pheasant
Lard or drippings
Salt and pepper
1 c. sour cream
1 med. onion

Brown pheasant in lard; season. Place in baking dish or pan. Cover with sour cream; bake in moderate oven for 1 hour or until tender. Place whole onion in pan with bird. Yield: 6 servings.

Mrs. Eugene H. Wiest, Pres.
Peace LCW
Herreid, South Dakota

PHEASANT WITH WILD RICE

3 pheasant
1 ¼ c. wild rice
1 c. flour
2 ½ tsp. salt
1 tsp. pepper
¼ c. melted butter
¼ c. melted lard
2 cans cream of mushroom soup
2 onions, chopped
1 c. milk
1 c. chopped celery
1 sm. can mushrooms

Skin, clean and cut up pheasant. Wash thoroughly; chill. Soak rice overnight. Dip pheasant pieces into flour, salt and pepper. Brown in hot butter and lard. Place in hot roaster. Add 1 can soup; sprinkle with 1 small onion. Cover; bake at 300 degrees for 1 hour. Boil rice for 10 minutes; rinse in clear water. Drain. Combine 1 can soup and milk; add to rice. Add celery, 1 large onion and mushrooms. Season with 1/2 teaspoonful salt and 1/2 teaspoonful pepper. Mix well. Pour into buttered casserole. Bake at 300 degrees for 1 hour. Serve with pheasant. Yield: 8-10 servings.

Mrs. Martin J. Olson
Calvary LCW
Mora, Minnesota

SMOTHERED PHEASANT

1 3-lb. pheasant, cut into serving pieces
Salt and pepper
Flour
Butter
1 c. sour cream
1 c. bread crumbs
½ c. finely chopped celery

Season pheasant with salt and pepper. Roll in flour. Brown meat in butter in skillet. Add sour cream. Mix bread crumbs with celery. Sprinkle over meat. Cover; bake at 350 degrees for 1 hour or until tender. Bake, uncovered, the last 10 minutes of cooking. Yield: 4-6 servings.

Mrs. Ronald Janneke, Pres.
Redeemer Ladies Aid Soc.
Willmar, Minnesota

SKILLET- FRIED PHEASANT

1 pheasant
1 tsp. salt
⅛ tsp. pepper
Flour
Shortening
1 can cream of mushroom soup
½ c. cream

Wash pheasant; cut into serving pieces and pat dry. Rub in salt and pepper; roll pieces in flour. Melt shortening in heavy skillet; brown pheasant thoroughly. Reduce heat. Mix mushroom soup with cream; stir into skillet. Cook slowly for 45 minutes or until pheasant is tender. NOTE: Mushroom soup may be omitted and the amount of cream increased to 1 cup. Yield: 4 servings.

Mrs. Leo Rystrom, Pres.
St. Paul's LCW
Frederick, South Dakota

QUAIL IN CASSEROLE

8 quail breasts
1 can cream of mushroom soup
1 3-oz. can mushrooms, undrained
1 c. sour cream
½ c. Sherry wine
Seasoning salt

Place quail in small shallow glass pan. Mix soup with mushrooms, sour cream and Sherry. Pour over quail; sprinkle with seasoning salt. Bake, uncovered, at 350 degrees for 1 hour and 30 minutes to 2 hours or until tender. Yield: 4 servings.

Mrs. Arnie Carlson, Chmn.
St. Mark's Flwp. Cir.
Wilmington, Delaware

ROAST QUAIL

10 wild quail
4 or 5 tbsp. bacon grease
⅔ c. water
Salt and pepper to taste
Butter

Brown quail in bacon grease. Place in roaster. Add water, salt and pepper to taste. Add one-half stick of butter for each 2 quails. Baste quail with melted butter at 15 minute intervals. Bake, covered, at 300 degrees for 1 hour. Yield: 4-5 servings.

Mrs. George J. McMunn
Messiah LWML
Vicksburg, Mississippi

BAKED RABBIT

2 2-lb. rabbits, cut up
Flour

2 tsp. salt
⅛ tsp. pepper
¼ c. fat or salad oil
¼ c. sliced onion
2 bouillon cubes
2 c. boiling water
¼ c. water

Coat rabbit pieces in 1/4 cup flour combined with salt and pepper. Cook onion until tender in fat in Dutch oven. Remove onion, brown rabbit in same fat. Arrange onion over rabbit. Add bouillon cubes and boiling water, stirring until cubes dissolve. Bake, covered, at 350 degrees for 1 hour and 30 minutes or until tender. Thicken gravy with 2 tablespoonfuls flour and water. Season to taste. Yield: 5-6 servings.

Mrs. Bill Koss, Pres.
Faith Ladies Aid Soc.
Dodge Center, Minnesota

PENNSYLVANIA DUTCH RABBIT PIE

1 rabbit
8 potatoes
1 lge. onion, chopped
Butter
2 eggs, beaten
Milk
1 tbsp. chopped parsley
1 slice bread, cubed
¼ tsp. pepper

Stew rabbit; reserve broth. Remove meat from bones in small pieces. Cook potatoes in salt water. Fry onions in butter until tender. Mash potatoes; add eggs and beat. Add milk to make thin consistency. Fold in onion, parsley, bread and pepper. Spread layer potato mixture in casserole; cover with layer of rabbit. Sprinkle with 1 tablespoonful rabbit broth. Continue to layer casserole, ending with potatoes. Bake at 325 degrees for 25 minutes. Serve with gravy make from remaining broth. NOTE: Chicken or pheasant may be substituted for rabbit. Yield: 6 servings.

Mrs. Mary Mengel, Pres.
Salem LCW
Leesport, Pennsylvania

RABBIT PIE

1 rabbit, cut into serving pieces
1 c. Port wine
1 onion, chopped
1 can cream of mushroom soup
1 recipe biscuit dough

Brown rabbit in frying pan. Remove meat; cool. Cut into small pieces. Add wine to pan drippings. Place rabbit and juices in deep baking dish. Add onion. Bake at 350 degrees until tender. Add soup. Cover with biscuit

(Continued on next page)

dough; bake until topping is done. Yield: 6-8 servings.

Mrs. Miriam Salmon, Pres.
St. Paul's LCW
Morrisburg, Ontario, Canada

RABBIT STEW

1 rabbit, cut into serving pieces
3 tbsp. shortening
1 med. onion, finely chopped
¼ c. chopped celery
2 tbsp. tomato paste
½ c. wine
1 tsp. mixed spices
1 clove of garlic, minced
Salt and pepper to taste
2 tsp. vinegar

Brown rabbit in shortening. Add remaining ingredients. Simmer until meat is done. Add vinegar 5 minutes before serving. Add water as needed. Yield: 4 servings.

Mrs. Ralph Fisher, Pres.
St. Matthew's LCW
Benwood, West Virginia

SOUTHERN BAKED RABBIT

2 tender young rabbits
4 tbsp. vinegar
4 tbsp. flour
Butter or margarine
2 onions, finely minced
¼ tsp. salt
⅛ tsp. pepper
1 10 ½-oz. can cream of mushroom soup
1 soup can water

Clean rabbits; cover with cold water and vinegar. Let stand overnight or until ready to cook. Drain thoroughly; sprinkle with flour. Brown in butter with onion, salt and pepper. Place in baking dish; add soup mixed with water. Bake at 350 degrees for 1 hour or until tender.

Mrs. Pearl Gregory
Trinity LWML
West Chicago, Illinois

RABBIT SMOTHERED WITH ONIONS

3 lge. onions, sliced
1 3-lb. rabbit, cut into serving pieces
Flour
3 tbsp. shortening
1 c. sour cream
Salt and pepper to taste

Fry onions slightly in skillet; remove from skillet. Dredge rabbit in flour. Saute rabbit in skillet until brown on both sides. Cover with onions. Pour sour cream over onions. Cover skillet; cook slowly for 1 hour or bake, covered, at 350 degrees for 35 to 45 minutes. Remove cover; bake for 15 minutes longer or until tender.

Mrs. Jerry Mennenga
Peace Ladies Aid
Shell Rock, Iowa

ANTELOPE LEG ROAST

1 lb. antelope leg
Olive oil
1 clove of garlic, mashed
Salt and pepper to taste
2 c. water
1 tbsp. Worcestershire sauce
1 onion, diced

Rub meat with olive oil, garlic, salt and pepper. Bake, uncovered, at 350 degrees for 2 hours or until brown, turning occasionally. Pour off excess fat; add water, Worcestershire sauce, salt, pepper and onion. Cover; cook for 2 hours more. Strain pan liquid for gravy; thicken with flour and water to taste. Yield: 4 servings.

Mrs. Mathilda M. Palmer, Pres.
Trinity Ladies Aid
Mena, Arkansas

BARBECUED VENISON CHOPS

6 venison chops
¼ c. flour
2 tsp. salt
½ tsp. pepper
2 tbsp. bacon fat
1 lge. onion, sliced
¾ c. catsup
1 tsp. prepared mustard
½ c. water
1 tbsp. Worcestershire sauce
2 tsp. vinegar
1 tbsp. brown sugar
½ tsp. oregano

Cut excess fat off venison; wipe with clean damp cloth. Combine flour, salt and pepper. Roll chops in flour; brown in hot fat. Arrange in large casserole with onion slices. Combine remaining ingredients. Pour over onions and chops. Cover; bake at 325 degrees for 1 hour. Remove cover; Yield: 4 servings.

Mrs. Harry Christensen, Pres.
Trinity LCW
Revillo, South Dakota

BARBECUED VENISON CHOPS

2 tsp. dry mustard
1 tbsp. minced onion
1 tbsp. minced parsley
½ c. soft butter
½ c. chili sauce
⅓ c. lemon juice
1 tsp. salt
6 venison chops

Blend mustard, onion, parsley and butter; shape into roll. Chill hard. Combine chilli sauce, lemon juice and salt; dip chops into mixture. Broil chops for 45 minutes over charcoal heat, about 12 to 14 inches from coals. Turn chops once, 20 minutes before done. Slice butter roll; place slice on each hot chop. Yield: 6 servings.

Marie Powell
Faith LWML
Mountain Home, Idaho

BARBECUED VENISON RIBS

3 lb. venison ribs
3 tbsp. flour
2 tsp. salt
Dash of pepper
Dash of paprika
2 tbsp. fat
1 onion, chopped
¼ c. cider vinegar
2 tbsp. brown sugar
1 c. chili sauce
½ c. water
½ tsp. dry mustard
½ c. diced celery

Cut ribs into small pieces. Combine flour, 1 teaspoonful salt, pepper and paprika; dip rib pieces into mixture. Sear floured ribs in hot fat; lift into casserole. Add onion to fat; cook and stir until golden brown. Add remaining ingredients; heat to almost boiling. Pour over ribs. Cover closely. Bake at 325 degrees for 3 hours or until tender. Serve with baked potatoes. Yield: 6 servings.

Mrs. Doris Wallace
Bethany Ladies Aid
Campbell River, British Columbia, Canada

BRAISED VENISON CHOPS

6 thick venison chops
3 slices bacon, diced
¼ c. salad oil
1 Spanish onion, sliced
½ tsp. salt
Dash of pepper
⅛ tsp. savory
1 c. consomme
2 tbsp. lemon juice

Remove fat from chops; wipe with damp cloth. Cut slits in sides of chops; insert bacon in slits.

Heat oil in skillet; brown chops on both sides. Drain. Place onion on chops; season with salt, pepper and savory. Add consomme and lemon juice. Cover skillet; simmer for 1 hour or until fork tender. Yield: 6 servings.

Mrs. Lillian Schreyer, Pres.
Grace Ladies Aid
Beausejour, Manitoba, Canada

DEER STEAK

3 lb. deer steak
Sliced onions
1 c. tomato soup
1 tbsp. vinegar
1 tbsp. Worcestershire sauce
Salt
¼ c. brown sugar
½ c. water

Fry steak until well done. Cover steak with onion. Simmer for 1 hour. Mix soup with vinegar, Worcestershire sauce, salt, brown sugar and water. Pour over steak and onions. Bake at 350 degrees for 1 hour. Add additional water if needed. Yield: 8 servings.

Mrs. Robert Shafter, VP
Melankton Good Will Cir.
Upham, North Dakota

ELK LOAVES

2 slices dry bread
Milk
1 ½ lb. ground elk
1 ½ tsp. salt
½ tsp. pepper
1 egg, beaten
½ c. minced onion
½ c. diced celery
½ c. barbecue sauce
2 tbsp. butter

Soak bread in small amount milk; add meat, salt, pepper, egg, onion, celery and barbecue sauce.

(Continued on next page)

Blend well; shape into two small loaves. Wrap in waxed paper; refrigerate for 30 minutes. Melt butter in pressure cooker; brown loaves in butter, using 10 pounds pressure for 15 minutes. Yield: 5 servings.

Mrs. James D. Wallace, Pres.
Good Shepherd Ladies Guild
Leadville, Colorado

ELK ROAST

1 2½-lb. frozen elk roast
2 tsp. salt
2 tsp. baking soda
½ pkg. dry onion soup mix

Place frozen elk roast in water. After roast is thoroughly thawed, pour off water and place roast in fresh water, adding salt and baking soda. Soak for 2 hours. Rinse roast with fresh water. Place in a large piece of aluminum foil; sprinkle onion soup mix over meat. Close foil tightly around the meat. Bake at 350 degrees for 2 hours. Yield: 6 servings.

Mrs. H. J. Brunkhorst
Augustana LCW
Denver, Colorado

HUNTERS' STEAK

⅓ c. cooking oil
1 ½ to 2 lb. moose or deer steak
1 ½ tsp. salt
¼ tsp. pepper
1 lge. onion, thinly sliced
1 clove of garlic
½ tsp. oregano
½ c. dry red cooking wine
2 tbsp. tomato paste

Heat oil in skillet; brown steak slowly on both sides, turning often. Season with salt and pepper. Add onion slices and garlic. Cook gently for 2 minutes; add oregano. Cover tightly; cook in 325 degree oven for 1 hour. Mix wine with tomato paste; add to meat. Cook for 30 minutes longer, turning once. Yield: 4 servings.

Mrs. Lillian Hildelrant
St. Timothy's Lutheran Church
Cliff, Ontario, Canada

MOOSE OR CARIBOU STROGANOFF

1 lb. moose or caribou
Flour
1 onion, sliced
1 c. water
1 tsp. salt

¾ tsp. dry mustard
½ tsp. pepper
¼ tsp. marjoram or ½ tsp. oregano
⅓ c. catsup or red wine
1 sm. can mushrooms
½ to 1 c. sour cream

Cut meat into finger-sized pieces. Dip into flour; brown well. Add onions, water, spices and catsup. Cook over low heat for 1 hour. Add mushrooms; simmer for 1 hour longer. Add sour cream; heat 2 to 3 minutes. Serve over rice or noodles. NOTE: Recipe may be used for venison or beef. Yield: 4-6 servings.

Mrs. Michael McBain, Pres.
Anchorage Women's Guild
Anchorage, Alaska

SPANISH MOOSE STEAK

2 lb. moose steak
½ tsp. salt
Pepper to taste
Flour
2 tbsp. hot fat
1 green pepper, chopped
1 clove of garlic, chopped
6 sm. onions, sliced
1 c. tomatoes
1 c. peas
Potato puffs

Dredge meat with seasoned flour; brown on both sides in hot fat. Remove from pan. Saute pepper and garlic in same fat until tender. Place pepper and garlic on meat; return meat to pan. Add onions and tomatoes; simmer for 2 hours or until tender. Shortly before meat is cooked, add peas and additional seasoning if necessary. Arrange meat on a platter with vegetables on top; surround with a border of potato puffs. Yield: 6 servings.

Mrs. Carole Mann, Pres.
Trinity LWML
Wilkie, Saskatchewan, Canada

OKANAGAN VENISON

¾ c. vinegar
1 ½ c. water
¾ c. brown sugar
Pinch of salt
¼ tsp. allspice
1 sm. bay leaf
¼ tsp. ground cloves
2 tbsp. soya sauce
3 tbsp. Casino dressing
1 3 to 4-lb. standing rib or loin venison roast
Several slices bacon
1 onion, sliced
1 tsp. salt
Pepper to taste
Garlic powder to taste
2 or 3 tbsp. lard

(Continued on next page)

Boil vinegar, water, sugar, spices, soy sauce and dressing for 5 minutes. Cut several deep slices into roast 1 1/2-inches apart or between each bone on rib roast. Marinate for 3 hours or overnight. Drain slightly. Place bacon slice and onion slice in each cut. Sprinkle roast with seasonings. Place in roaster. Brown lightly in lard. Add 3 cups warm water; cover. Bake at 350 degrees for 3 hours or until tneder, basting generously with marinade sauce 2 or 3 times. Yield: 4-6 servings.

Mrs. Alma Vogel, Pres.
St. John's Ladies Aid
Summerland, Brithish Columbia, Canada

SCALLOPINI OF VENISON

2 ½ lb. venison
1 ½ c. flour
1 tbsp. salt
1 tbsp. pepper
½ tsp. paprika
Fat
2 med. onions, sliced
1 tbsp. sugar
1 4-oz. can mushrooms (opt.)
1 ¼ c. tomato puree
1 ¼ c. tomato juice

Wipe meat with vinegar-soaked cloth. Flatten slightly with meat pounder. Combine flour, salt, pepper and paprika. Cut meat into serving pieces; roll in seasoned flour. Fry in hot fat until golden brown. Add onions after first turning. Place in greased casserole; add remaining ingredients. Bake at 325 degrees for 2 hours or until tender. Yield: 8-10 servings.

Mrs. Olga Van DeBruggen
St. Pauls Mary Martha Guild
Marengo, Wisconsin

SUCCULENT VENISON ROAST

1 6 to 8-lb. venison roast
4 slices bacon
1 tbsp. freshly ground pepper
½ tsp. thyme
½ tsp. savory
½ tsp. marjoram
2 tbsp. salt
1 clove of garlic, thinly sliced
1 bay leaf
2 onions, cut into ½-in. slices
1 c. chopped celery, leaves and stalk
3 carrots, thickly sliced
4 bouillon cubes
4 c. hot water

Place meat in deep roaster. Lay bacon over top. Sprinkle spices, salt and garlic over meat. Add bay leaf and vegetables. Place bouillon cubes in pan; add hot water. Cover; bake at 325 degrees for 2 hours and 30 minutes to 3 hours. Yield: 8-10 servings.

Mrs. David L. Brown, Pres.
Bethany LCW
Des Moines, Iowa

SWEET AND SOUR VENISON

2 lb. venison, cut into 2-in. cubes
2 c. water
2 tsp. salt
8 whole cloves
8 whole allspice
1 cinnamon stick, broken up
1 tbsp. sugar
4 tbsp. flour
1 tbsp. shortening
½ c. vinegar
1 med. onion, chopped

Simmer meat cubes in water seasoned with salt, spices and sugar for 1 hour and 30 minutes or until tender. Spread flour in shallow pan; brown in 350 degree oven for 10 minutes. Melt shortening in 1 1/2-quart pan; blend in flour until smooth. Drain stock from meat; stir into flour mixture with vinegar. Stir and cook until smooth and thick. Add meat cubes and onion; continue simmering for 30 minutes.

Mrs. Luther Berntson
LCW
Edinburg, North Dakota

VENISON BARBECUE

3 lb. venison chops or steaks
3 slices bacon
1 c. catsup
1 tbsp. salt
3 slices lemon
1 onion, thinly sliced
⅓ c. steak sauce
2 tbsp. vinegar (opt.)
1 tbsp. chili powder

Sear venison in frying pan with bacon. Mix remaining ingredients in saucepan; bring mixture to a boil. Stir to prevent burning. Cover venison with sauce. Bake at 350 for 1 hour and 30 minutes to 2 hours. Yield: 6 servings.

Mrs. Emil J. Sitz
Immaunel LWML
Drake, North Dakota

VENISON CHOPS GLORIFIED

1 ½ lb. venison chops
1 med. onion, chopped
½ tsp. paprika
½ c. tomatoes or tomato juice
2 oz. dry Sherry wine
Minced garlic to taste
1 tbsp. chopped parsley
¼ tsp. oregano
¼ tsp. thyme
½ piece bay leaf

Brown chops; remove from pan. Brown onion in pan drippings. Add remaining ingredients; bring to a boil. Pour over chops. Cover; bake at 350 degrees for 45 minutes.

Mrs. Alvin F. Hartmann
St. Paul's Evangelical Ladies Aid
Sheboygan, Wisconsin

VENISON PARMIGIANA

1 ½ lb. venison or round steak, 1 ½-in. thick
1 egg, beaten
⅓ c. fine dry bread crumbs
⅓ c. grated Parmesan cheese
⅓ c. cooking oil
1 med. onion, minced
1 tsp. salt
¼ tsp. pepper
½ tsp. sugar
½ tsp. marjoram
1 6-oz. can tomato paste
2 c. hot water
½ lb. Mozzarella or process cheese, sliced

Pound meat thin; cut into serving pieces. Dip meat into egg; roll in crumbs and Parmesan cheese. Brown in oil in skillet. Place meat in shallow, wide baking dish. Cook onion in remaining oil in skillet until soft; add salt, pepper, sugar, marjoram and tomato paste. Gradually add hot water. Boil for 5 minutes. Pour most of sauce over meat; top with cheese slices. Add remaining sauce. Bake at 350 degrees for 1 hour. Yield: 4-6 servings.

Mrs. Carl H. Panzer, Pres.
Peace Ladies Aid
Sweetwater, Texas

VENISON ROAST

2 tbsp. horseradish
½ c. red wine
½ c. tomato juice
4 lb. venison roast

Mix horseradish, red wine and tomato juice. Baste roast occasionally with mixture. Bake at 325 degrees for 2 hours and 15 minutes. Yield: 8 servings.

Mrs. Marilyn Staake
Immanuael Ladies Aid Soc.
Arenzville, Illinois

VENISON ROAST

1 6-lb. venison roast
1 4x6-in. piece bacon rind

Place roast in roasting pan, fastening bacon rind on top of roast with skewers. Bake in preheated 325 degree oven until roast is tender. Allow 15 minutes per pound. Yield: 8-10 servings.

Mrs. K. C. Stewart, Pres.
Gloria Dei LCW
Winnipeg, Manatoba, Canada

VENISON ROAST

1 3 to 5-lb. venison roast
1 pkg. dry onion soup mix
1 10 ½-oz. can cream of mushroom soup

Place meat on double thickness of foil large enough to wrap securely. Pour soup mix and mushroom soup over meat. Wrap securely; place in 8 x 8-inch baking pan. Bake at 275 degrees for 4 to 5 hours. Unwrap; place meat on hot platter. Serve at once with gravy. Yield: 6-8 servings.

Mrs. B. C. Olson, Pres.
First Lutheran Church LCW
Bemidji, Minnesota
Mrs. Carl Figge, Sec.
Mt. Calvary Ladies Aid
Wamego, Kansas

VENISON SKILLET DINNER

4 venison or veal chops, ½-in. thick
2 tbsp. flour
3 tbsp. fat
⅓ c. grated Parmesan cheese
1 tsp. salt
¼ tsp. pepper
4 c. thinly sliced potatoes
2 c. thinly sliced onions
3 beef bouillon cubes
¾ c. hot water
1 tbsp. lemon juice

Coat chops with flour; brown slowly on both sides in fat in skillet. Combine Parmesan cheese with salt and pepper. Sprinkle meat with 2 tablespoonfuls cheese mixture. Cover with potato slices. Sprinkle with 2 tablespoonfuls cheese mixture. Add onion slices. Sprinkle with remaining cheese mixture. Dissolve bouillon cubes in hot water. Add lemon juice. Pour over meat mixture. Cover; simmer for 45 minutes or until meat is done. Yield: 4 servings.

Arlene Stolp, Pres.
Grace Ladies Aid
Hudson, Colorado

VENISON STEAK ROLLS

2 lb. venison round steak, ½-in. thick
1 dill pickle
3 slices bacon, halved
½ c. flour
½ tsp. salt
¼ tsp. pepper
3 tbsp. shortening
1 c. tomato sauce
1 tsp. Worcestershire sauce

Cut steak into six 3 x 6-inch strips. Cut pickle lengthwise into six strips. Place bacon and pickle on venison strips. Roll lengthwise; fasten with toothpicks. Roll in flour, seasoned with salt and pepper. Melt shortening in skillet; brown rolls on all sides. Mix tomato sauce and Worcestershire sauce; pour over meat. Cover. Simmer slowly for 1 hour and 30 minutes or bake at 350 degrees for 2 hours. Yield: 6 servings.

Mrs. Albert Plo, Pres.
Good Shepherd LWML
Goleta, California

VENISON STROGANOFF

1 ½ lb. venison steak
Salt
Flour
Butter
1 c. chopped onions
1 6-oz. can mushrooms
1 c. beef broth
1 tsp. Worcestershire sauce
1 tsp. soy sauce
1 c. sour cream

Soak venison in salted water overnight. Remove all fat and tendons; cut into 3/4-inch strips. Roll in flour; brown in butter. Remove meat; saute onion and mushrooms in pan drippings. Add meat, broth, Worcestershire sauce, soy sauce and salt to taste. Cover; simmer for 45 minutes to 1 hour. Add cream just before serving; heat through. Yield: 4 servings.

Mrs. Jeanette Willey, Pres.
Warba Bethel LCW
Warba, Minnesota

Combination
Meat Favorites

RECIPE FOR PAELLA ON PAGE 273

COMPANY MEAT BALLS

2 lb. ground round steak
1 lb. lean pork
2 eggs, slightly beaten
4 or 5 club crackers, crumbled
3 tsp. salt
1 tsp. pepper
½ tsp. nutmeg
1 tbsp. dry parsley leaves
1 tsp. oregano
Milk or water
1 sm. onion, finely minced
4 tsp. flour
1 can beef consomme
1 can water

Have butcher grind meats three times. Combine all ingredients except flour, consomme and water. Form into medium or small balls; brown on all sides in small amount of fat. Remove meat balls. Pour off all but 4 tablespoonfuls fat. Blend flour into remaining fat; add consomme and water. Stir until thickened; add meat balls. Bake, covered, at 325 degrees for 1 hour. Remove cover the last 15 minutes of baking time. Yield: 12-15 servings.

Arlene E. Weikle, Pres.
St. Luke's LCW
Minneapolis, Minnesota

HAM BALLS

1 lb. ground ham
⅔ lb. ground beef
⅓ lb. ground pork
2 c. bread crumbs
1 c. milk
2 eggs
½ tsp. salt
¼ tsp. pepper

Combine all ingredients thoroughly; shape into 24 balls. Place in a 10 x 13-inch pan.

SAUCE:

¾ c. water
¼ c. vinegar
1 c. brown sugar
1 tsp. dry mustard

Combine all ingredients; pour over ham balls. Bake at 275 degrees for 1 hour and 15 minutes. Yield: 10-12 servings.

Mrs. Jeanette Hengelfelt, Pres.
Salem LCW
Stromsburg, Nebraska

HAMETTES

1 lb. ground ham
1 lb. ground pork
½ lb. ground veal
2 c. bread crumbs
1 to 1⅛ c. milk
2 eggs
Salt and pepper to taste

1 c. brown sugar
½ c. vinegar
½ c. water
1 tsp. mustard

Combine meats, bread crumbs, milk and eggs. Shape into balls the size of an egg or loaves. Place in baking dish. Bake at 350 degrees for 1 hour to 1 hour and 30 minutes. Combine remaining ingredients; baste meat balls with mixture during baking time. Yield: 14 servings.

Georgia Jane Holt, Pres.
Trinity LCW
Rockford, Illinois
Mrs. W. A. Bielefeld
Peace LCW
San Antonio, Texas

NORWEGIAN MEAT BALLS

1 lb. ground steak
¼ lb. ground pork
1 egg, slightly beaten
⅓ to ½ c. milk, scalded
1 tbsp. cornstarch
1 med. onion, minced
Salt and pepper to taste
⅛ tsp. nutmeg
⅛ tsp. allspice
⅛ tsp. ginger
Butter
Flour

Grind beef with pork. Add egg with milk and cornstarch to meat. Mix well. Add remaining ingredients except butter and flour. Beat thoroughly until light. Shape into small balls. Brown in butter; simmer until done, adding a small amount of water, if necessary. Remove meat balls; add more butter to drippings. Add flour; brown. Add enough water to make a medium-thick gravy. Season with salt and pepper; add meat balls. Meat balls may be prepared several hours before serving. Yield: 6-8 servings.

Mrs. Samuel B. Austin, Pres.
Ascension LCW
Ogden, Utah

PARTY HAM BALLS

2 lb. ground ham
1 lb. lean ground pork
1 lb. ground veal
½ c. milk
2 eggs, beaten
2 c. graham cracker crumbs
Pineapple slices
¾ c. brown sugar
¼ c. vinegar
½ c. pineapple juice
1½ tsp. dry mustard

Combine ham, pork and veal; add milk, eggs and cracker crumbs; shape into balls, using 1/3 cup for each ball. Place on pineapple slices. Place on cookie sheet. Bake at 350 degrees for 1 hour.

(Continued on next page)

Combine remaining ingredients; baste ham balls with mixture every 15 minutes during baking time. Yield: 24 servings.

Mrs. Carl Peters, Pres.
St. James LCW
Mason City, Iowa

Soak rusk in milk for a few minutes. Add egg, meats, salt, sugar and pepper. Mix well. Shape into small balls. Drop in boiling water in saucepan. Boil for 5 to 7 minutes. Drain; roll in crumbs. Brown in small amount of melted butter in frying pan. Yield: 4-6 servings.

Mrs. Dorothy N. Knudsen, Pres.
Christ the King Women's Guild
Grosse Pointe Woods, Michigan

SPAGHETTI AND MEAT BALLS

1 lb. Italian sweet sausage
2 No. 2 ½ cans tomato puree
2 No. 2 ½ puree cans water
1 ½ tsp. garlic salt
1 tbsp. dried sweet basil leaves
2 tbsp. dried parsley flakes
1 ½ tsp. salt

Brown sausage in large saucepan; do not drain off fat. Add tomato puree, water, garlic salt, basil leaves, parsley flakes and salt. Bring to a boil. Simmer for 1 hour and 30 minutes to 2 hours, stirring every 20 minutes.

MEATBALLS:

1 lb. ground chuck
½ c. bread crumbs
1 egg
1 tbsp. parsley flakes
1 ½ tbsp. grated Romano cheese
¾ tsp. garlic salt
½ tsp. salt
Dash of pepper
⅛ c. water

Combine all ingredients; shape into balls. Chill for a few minutes. Add to sauce; simmer for 1 hour.

SPAGHETTI:

1 lb. spaghetti
¼ lb. Romano cheese, grated

Cook spaghetti according to package directions; drain. Serve with meat balls and sauce; sprinkle with cheese. Yield: 6 servings.

Mrs. Vivian Reiglehoff
Whitestone Immanuel Dorcas Soc.
Whitestone, New York

SWEDISH MEAT BALLS

1 lb. ground beef
½ lb. ground pork
½ c. minced onion
¾ c. fine dry bread crumbs
1 tbsp. minced parsley
2 tsp. salt
¼ tsp. pepper
1 tsp. Worcestershire sauce
1 egg
½ c. milk
¼ c. fat or salad oil
¼ c. flour
1 tsp. paprika
2 c. boiling water
¾ c. sweet or sour cream

Combine meats, onion, bread crumbs, parsley, 1 1/2 teaspoonfuls salt, 1/8 teaspoonfuls pepper, Worcestershire sauce, egg and milk. Shape into balls. Brown in fat or oil. Remove meat balls; stir into pan drippings, flour, paprika, remaining salt and pepper. Gradually add water and cream, stirring until thick. Return meat balls in gravy; cook for 15 to 20 minutes. Yield: 6-8 servings.

Leona Wildgrube
Christ the King Workers
Edmonton, Alberta, Canada

SWEDISH MEAT BALLS

2 rusk, crushed
½ to ¾ c. milk
1 egg, beaten
1 lb. ground beef
¼ lb. ground pork
1 tsp. salt
½ tsp. sugar
Dash of pepper
Bread crumbs (opt.)

ALL-IN-ONE SUPPER CASSEROLE

1 can cream of chicken soup
½ c. milk
1 c. diced cooked or canned chicken
1 c. julienne strips cooked or canned ham or
    luncheon meat
¼ tsp. crushed marjoram
¼ tsp. crushed rosemary
1 c. canned peas, drained or ½ pkg. frozen peas,
    partially thawed
1 pkg. fried potato puffs

Combine all ingredients e x c e p t potato puffs;
place in 1/2-quart casserole. Top with potato
puffs. Bake at 425 degrees for 40 to 45 minutes.
Yield: 4-5 servings.

Mrs. Vernon Muehl
St. Stephen's Friendship Club
Detroit, Michigan

BAKED CHOP SUEY

1 lb. veal, chopped
½ lb. pork, chopped
Pepper to taste
1 c. diced onions
½ c. diced green pepper
2 c. water
2 c. diced celery
½ c. uncooked rice
1 can chicken noodle soup
1 can cream of mushroom soup
4 tbsp. soy sauce

Brown veal and pork. Season with pepper. Add
onions, green pepper, water, celery and rice.
Simmer for 10 minutes. Add soups and soy sauce.
Mix well. Bake at 350 degrees for 1 hour. Serve
over chow mein noodles, if desired. Yield: 8
servings.

Doris Fosgard, Pres.
Faith LCW
St. Clair Shores, Michigan

BAKED CHOP SUEY

1 lb. veal and pork, cubed
1 c. diced celery
2 med. onions, diced
1 tbsp. butter
½ c. uncooked rice
1 can chicken with rice soup
1 can cream of mushroom soup
1 c. water
Salt and pepper to taste
Soy sauce to taste

Brown meat, celery and onions in butter; add
rice, soups, water and seasoning to taste. Bake at
350 degrees for 1 hour or until rice is done.
Yield: 6 servings.

Mrs. Clarence Koenig
St. John's LCW
Milwaukee, Wisconsin

BAKED SANDWICH FILLING

1 ½ lb. beef
1 lb. pork
3 stalks celery, finely chopped
2 eggs
2 c. cracker crumbs
1 pt. tomato juice
1 pt. milk
2 onions, finely chopped
Salt and pepper to taste

Combine all ingredients. Cover; bake at 350
degrees for 2 hours, stirring occasionally.
Yield: 12 servings.

Mrs. Harmon Schumacher
Grace LCW
Luckey, Ohio

BASIC ONE-DISH MEAL

1 lb. ground beef
½ lb. pork sausage
1 onion, chopped
1 8-oz. pkg. noodles, cooked
1 can tomatoes, undrained
4 c. grated cheese
1 lge. bunch celery, chopped

Brown meats and onion; add noodles. Combine all
ingredients in baking dish. Bake at 350 degrees
for 1 hour and 30 minutes. Yield: 8-10 servings.

Edith L. Stamp
Trinity Ladies Aid
Persia, Iowa

CHICKEN PACIFIC

2 c. sour cream
1 tsp. tarragon
1 tsp. thyme
½ tsp. garlic powder
1 tsp. paprika
2 ½ tsp. salt
6 chicken breasts or 1 2-lb. broiler-fryer
    chicken
1 ½ c. corn flake crumbs
¼ c. butter
1 c. small canned shrimp
¼ c. diced ripe olives

Combine sour cream with tarragon, thyme, garlic powder, paprika and salt. Dip chicken into
sour cream mixture and then into corn flake
crumbs, coating well. Melt butter in baking dish;
place chicken, skin-side down, in dish. Bake at
350 degrees for 45 minutes. Turn and bake for
25 minutes longer. Add shrimp and olives to remaining sour cream mixture; pour over chicken
during last 10 minutes of baking time. NOTE:
sauce may be heated and served s e p a r a t e l y.
Yield: 6 servings.

Mrs. Emil Meinke, Sec.
St. John's Ladies Aid
Webster, Minnesota

CHICKEN CASSEROLE SUPREME

1 4-oz. pkg. dried beef, shredded
3 slices bacon, halved
3 chicken breasts, halved and boned
Pepper
1 can cream of mushroom soup
1 c. sour cream

Place dried beef in shallow casserole. Wrap bacon around each piece of chicken; place on top of beef. Sprinkle with pepper. Blend soup with sour cream; pour over chicken. Cover; bake at 275 degrees for 3 hours. Yield: 6 servings.

Mrs. Albert C. Stafford, Pres.
St. John's LCW
Asheboro, North Carolina

CHURCHILL'S HOT DISH

1 lb. veal
1 lb. pork
Seasoned flour
½ lb. sharp cheese, grated
½ pkg. fine noodles, cooked
1 can mushrooms, undrained
1 can pimento, cut into strips
1 No. 2 can cream-style corn
1 can cream of mushroom soup
1 can chicken with rice soup
Buttered bread crumbs

Cut veal and pork into small cubes; dredge in seasoned flour. Saute in small amount of fat for 25 minutes or until well browned. Place one-half of cheese, meat and noodles in layers in casserole. Cover with mushrooms, pimento and corn. Top with layers of remaining meat and noodles; cover with soups and remaining cheese. Top with buttered crumbs. Bake at 350 degrees for 1 hour.

Mrs. Gerald Clemens
Klamath LCW
Klamath Falls, Oregon

FAMILY HOT DISH

1 ½ lb. ground beef
½ lb. pork sausage
1 onion, chopped
1 ½ c. cooked undrained celery
1 can cream of chicken soup
1 can cream of mushroom soup
2 pkg. frozen mixed vegetables, thawed
1 8-oz. pkg. chow mein noodles

Brown meats and onion in small amount of fat. Combine all ingredients; place in casserole. Bake at 375 degrees for 1 hour. Yield: 15 servings.

Mrs. Herman Carstons, Pres.
St. Paul's LWML
Melrose, Minnesota

LASAGNA

½ lb. Italian sweet sausage
½ lb. ground beef
1 envelope spaghetti sauce mix
2 8-oz. cans tomato sauce
1 can tomato paste
1 ½ c. water
2 tbsp. grated Parmesan cheese
½ lb. lasagna noodles
1 lb. cottage cheese
2 tbsp. chopped parsley
1 8-oz. pkg. Mozzarella or Muenster cheese

Remove casing from sausage; cut sausage into small pieces. Cook in skillet over medium heat until brown. Add beef; cook until beef loses its pink color, tossing lightly with fork. Drain off fat. Stir in spaghetti sauce mix, tomato sauce, tomato paste, water and Parmesan cheese. Simmer for 10 minutes. Cook noodles; drain. Spoon enough sauce into a 7 x 11 x 2-inch pan to cover bottom. Place one-half of noodles on top; cover with one-half of cottage cheese and one-half of parsley. Cover with sauce. Repeat layers. Cut Mozzarella or Muenster cheese into wide strips. Arrange in a cross-bar design on top. Bake at 350 degrees for 30 minutes or until cheese melts and sauce is bubbly. Yield: 4 servings.

Augusta Timm, Pres.
St. Paul's Ladies Aid
Colon, Michigan

LASAGNA

1 ½ pkg. long flat noodles
3 lb. ground beef
1 lb. ground pork
1 tsp. garlic salt
2 tsp. salt
1 tsp. pepper
1 tsp. oregano
1 pkg. Mozzarella cheese
1 ½ lb. cottage cheese
1 sm. can grated Parmesan cheese
1 pkg. Swiss cheese
2 bottles pizza-flavored catsup

Cook noodles in salted water; drain. Fry meats with garlic salt, salt, pepper and oregano. Alternate layers of noodles, meat, cheeses and catsup in greased baking dish. Top with additional Parmesan cheese, if desired. Bake at 350 degrees for 1 hour. Yield: 25 servings.

Mrs. Ervin Pottschmidt
Redeemer Ladies Aid
Seymour, Indiana

LASAGNA BAKE

1 ½ lb. ground beef
½ lb. ground pork or Italian sausage
1 onion, diced
1 sm. can tomato sauce
1 can tomato paste
1 No. 3 can whole tomatoes
1 ½ tbsp. oregano

(Continued on next page)

1 clove of garlic, minced
Salt and pepper to taste
12 wide lasagna noodles, cooked
¾ lb. Ricotta cheese
1 can Parmesan cheese
1 lb. Mozzarella cheese
Tomato juice

Brown meats with onion; pour off grease. Add tomato sauce, tomato paste, tomatoes, oregano, garlic, salt and pepper. Simmer for 1 hour. Place 3 noodles in shallow baking dish. Cover with layers of sauce, Ricotta cheese, Parmesan cheese and Mozzarella cheese. Repeat until all ingredients are used. Add enough juice to moisten. Bake at 350 degrees for 45 minutes. Yield: 10 servings.

Mrs. Frieda Hirsch, 1st VP
Trinity LWML
San Bernardino, California

LASAGNA CASSEROLE

12 oz. lasagna noodles
½ lb. ground beef
½ lb. pork sausage
1 clove of garlic, mashed
1 onion, chopped
2 6-oz. cans tomato paste
3 c. water
2 tsp. salt
½ tsp. pepper
1 2-oz. can sliced mushrooms
1 lb. creamed cottage or Ricotta cheese
1 lb. Mozzarella cheese, sliced
½ c. grated Parmesan cheese

Cook noodles according to directions on package. Fry meats in a skillet until all pink color has disappeared. Stir to separate. Drain off excess fat. Add garlic, onion, tomato paste, water, salt, pepper and mushrooms. Cook slowly for 30 minutes, stirring frequently. Pour a thin layer of sauce into a 10 x 13-inch baking pan. Arrange a layer of noodles, side by side, over sauce. Spoon one-half of cottage cheese over noodles; top with layer of Mozzarella cheese. Cover with remaining noodles, cottage cheese, Mozzarella cheese. Top with remaining sauce; sprinkle with Parmesan cheese. Bake at 350 degrees for 45 minutes. Yield: 8-10 servings.

Mrs. Nancy Stine, Pres.
Trinity LWML
Simi, California

MEAT STEW

1 ½ lb. cubed beef
1 ½ lb. pork
1 green pepper or onion, chopped
1 10-oz. pkg. uncooked noodles
1 lb. American cheese, grated
2 pkg. dry chicken soup mix
1 can cream-style corn
Bread crumbs or crumbled potato chips

Cook meats with green pepper until done. Remove meats and green pepper, reserving broth. Cook noodles until done in reserved broth. Add cheese, meats, green pepper and soup. Pour into a 9 x 12-inch loaf pan. Add corn; sprinkle with bread crumbs. Bake at 375 degrees for 1 hour. Yield: 18-20 servings.

Mrs. Dan Hyatt, Pres.
First Lutheran Church Dorcas Ladies Aid
Onawa, Iowa

MOCK CHICKEN

1 lb. boiling beef
1 lb. lean pork
3 slices fresh bread, crumbled
1 can cream of chicken soup
1 c. broth
1 egg

Boil beef in small amount of water until tender. Remove meat from broth, reserving broth. Dice meat. Combine all ingredients; place in baking dish. Bake at 350 degrees for 45 minutes. Yield: 6 servings.

Mrs. Adolph W. Maas, Pres.
Immanuel Ladies Aid Soc.
Charter Oak, Iowa

MOM'S HOT DISH

1 lb. pork, diced
1 lb. veal, diced
½ lb. ham, diced
½ c. minced onion
2 tsp. salt
¼ tsp. pepper
½ c. water
2 c. uncooked diced potatoes
2 c. uncooked diced carrots
2 c. frozen green peas
1 can cream of chicken soup
1 can cream of celery soup

Brown pork, veal, ham and onion in 11 or 12-inch electric skillet; season with salt and pepper. Add water. Cover; simmer for 30 minutes or until meat is nearly done. Add potatoes, carrots, peas and soups. Bring to a boil; stir well. Cover; cook at 325 degrees for 30 to 40 minutes or until vegetables are tender, stirring occasionally. NOTE: Beef or lamb may be substituted for pork or veal. Yield: 8-10 servings.

Mrs. Fred Polak
Luther Memorial Ladies Aid
Gleason, Wisconsin

NOODLE CASSEROLE

1 pkg. noodles
Broth
1 lb. veal, chopped
1 lb. pork, chopped
1 can corn

(Continued on next page)

1 can mushrooms
Cream sauce
2 tbsp. flour
1 tbsp. butter
2 c. milk
½ lb. cheese, grated
1 c. pimento
Buttered bread crumbs

Cook noodles in broth until tender; drain. Add remaining ingredients except crumbs. Place in casserole. Cover with bread crumbs. Bake at 350 degrees for 1 hour. Yield: 6 servings.

Mrs. J. S. McGrath
St. John's Lutheran Church
Greenville, Pennsylvania

PAELLA

1 3-lb. broiler-fryer chicken, cut into serving
    pieces
1 ¼ tsp. salt
½ tsp. paprika
4 tbsp. cooking oil or butter
½ lb. ham, diced
1 med. onion, chopped
½ c. diced green pepper
1 1-lb. can peas
1 12-oz. bottle or can
    beer
½ tsp. Tabasco sauce
2 bouillon cubes
¼ tsp. saffron
1 ½ c. uncooked rice
6 mussels
6 clams
½ lb. shrimp, cooked and
    cleaned
2 pimentos, cut into pieces

Sprinkle chicken with 1 teaspoonful salt and paprika. Heat oil in skillet; brown chicken in oil. Remove to baking dish with tight-fitting lid. Cook ham in skillet; add to chicken. Cook onion and green pepper until onion is tender, but not brown. Drain liquid from peas; add to beer. Measure; add enough water to make 3 cups. Add Tabasco sauce. Stir liquid into skillet, scraping brown particles from bottom of pan; add bouillon cubes, saffron and remaining salt. Bring to a boil; pour over chicken and ham. Sprinkle rice over chicken; stir so that all of rice is moistened. Cover tightly and bake at 350 degrees for 25 minutes. Uncover; toss rice. Arrange mussels and clams on top of rice with shrimp, pimentos and peas. Cover; return to oven for 10 minutes longer. NOTE: Dish may be simmered on top of range in heavy skillet with tight-fitting lid. Yield: 6 servings.

Photograph for this recipe on page 267.

PTA CASSEROLE

½ lb. ground beef
½ lb. pork
2 cans cream of mushroom soup
1 green pepper, chopped
1 sm. can pimento

1 sm. can whole kernel corn
1 sm. can peas, drained
Salt to taste
Cooked noodles or macaroni
½ lb. Longhorn cheese, grated

Fry meats until brown; add soup, green pepper, pimento, corn and peas. Season with salt. Add noodles or macaroni; mix well. Add cheese. Place in casserole. Cover with crushed potato chips or bread crumbs, if desired. Bake at 350 degrees for 40 minutes. Yield: 15 servings.

Mrs. Eldon Eckhart
St. Mark's Lutheran Church
Norcatur, Kansas

SAUSAGE-RICE CASSEROLE

1 lb. hamburger
1 lb. pork sausage
1 c. chopped onions
1 c. chopped celery
1 c. chopped green peppers
3 pkg. chicken-noodle soup mix
2 c. uncooked rice
2 ½ qt. boiling water
8 oz. shaved almonds
1 can cream of mushroom soup
1 soup can water
Buttered Wheaties

Place hamburger, sausage, onions, celery and green peppers in a 3-quart casserole. Add soup mix and rice; pour boiling water over top. Sprinkle with almonds. Cover; bake at 350 degrees for 1 hour. Refrigerate for 24 hours. Dilute mushroom soup with water; pour over casserole. Sprinkle top with buttered Wheaties. Bake, uncovered, at 350 degrees for 1 hour. Yield: 20 servings.

Mrs. Ralph Erickson
Sharon LCW
Irma, Alberta, Canada

SCALLOPED VEAL AND PORK

2 lb. veal
1 lb. pork
3 c. water
6 slices toast, cubed
1 tsp. salt
¼ tsp. pepper
¼ c. chopped onion
¼ c. chopped celery

Boil veal and pork in water until tender; dice meat and reserve broth. Place meat and toast cubes in 2-quart casserole. Add salt, pepper and reserved broth. Stir until well mixed. Top with onion and celery. Bake at 350 degrees for 30 minutes. Yield: 8-10 servings.

Mrs. W. Walter Wilson
Israel's LCW
Paris, Ohio

SUPPER DISH

1 ½ lb. veal, cut into ½-in. cubes
1 ½ lb. pork, cut into ½-in. cubes
1 ½ lb. beef, cut into ½-in. cubes
1 14-oz. pkg. fine noodles
Chopped green pepper
1 can cream-style corn
½ lb. Velveeta cheese, diced
1 can cream of chicken soup
Cracker crumbs
Grated cheese
Paprika

Season meats with salt; boil in small amount of water until tender. Drain off liquid. Cook noodles in salted water for 20 minutes; rinse and drain. Cook green pepper for 20 minutes. Combine all ingredients except cracker crumbs, grated cheese and paprika. Turn into casserole; sprinkle with crumbs, grated cheese and paprika. Bake at 350 degrees for 40 minutes. NOTE: Casserole may be frozen before baking. Yield: 12-15 servings.

Neola Mericle, Pres.
Trinity LCW
Greenleaf, Kansas

TURKEY CASSEROLE

4 c. water
1 ½ c. wild rice
1 tsp. salt
1 lb. bulk pork sausage
1 3-oz. can mushrooms
2 cans cream of mushroom soup
1 tsp. Worcestershire sauce
Sliced left-over turkey
1 ½ c. buttered bread crumbs

Bring water to a boil; add rice and salt. Cook until rice is tender. Fry sausage; drain off fat. Add mushrooms, soup and Worcestershire sauce. Grease an 8 x 12 x 2-inch casserole or pan. Mix rice with sausage. Place one-half of rice mixture in casserole; cover with turkey. Place remaining rice over turkey. Top with buttered bread crumbs. Bake at 375 degrees for 45 minutes. Yield: 12 servings.

Alice Horpedahl, Pres.
Bethlehem LCW
Los Alamos, New Mexico

YUM YUM CASSEROLE

¾ lb. veal or beef
¾ lb. pork
2 tbsp. shortening
1 c. chopped celery
1 med. onion, chopped
1 can cream of mushroom soup
1 can cream of chicken soup
1 4-oz. pkg. macaroni or noodles,
  cooked
1 pkg. frozen peas, cooked
Crushed potato chips

Brown meats and onion in shortening. Add enough water to barely cover meat. Add celery; simmer for 20 minutes or until tender. Add remaining ingredients except potato chips; place in casserole. Top with potato chips. Bake at 350 degrees for 45 minutes. Yield: 8 servings.

Clara Tanner, Treas.
LWML
Shelby, Michigan

BARBECUED MEAT LOAVES

1 ½ lb. ground beef
½ lb. ground pork
½ c. bread crumbs
½ c. milk
½ c. chopped onion
1 ½ tsp. salt
⅛ tsp. pepper
½ c. catsup
⅓ c. vinegar
2 tbsp. Worcestershire sauce
1 tsp. chili powder

Combine meats, bread crumbs, milk, 1/4 cup chopped onion, salt and pepper. Shape into four to eight loaves. Place in shallow baking dish. Combine remaining ingredients. Pour over loaves. Bake at 350 degrees for 1 hour, basting every 15 minutes with sauce. Yield: 8 servings.

Mrs. Melvin M. Buss, Pres.
Faith LCW
Plymouth, Illinois

BEEF-SAUSAGE LOAF

2 lb. ground beef
½ lb. bulk sausage
2 tsp. salt
¼ tsp. pepper
Pinch of savory
Pinch poultry seasoning
1 egg
1 c. soft bread crumbs
1 c. tomato juice

Mix beef and sausage; season with salt, pepper, savory and poultry seasoning. Add egg, bread crumbs and tomato juice. Mix well; pack into 9 x 5 x 2 3/4-inch loaf pan. Bake at 350 degrees for 1 hour and 30 minutes. Yield: 6-8 servings.

Mrs. Clarence Seyferth
Trinity Ladies Aid
Racine, Wisconsin

BROWN AND GOLD MEAT LOAF

1 ½ lb. ground beef
½ lb. ground fresh pork
4 eggs, separated
1 ½ c. bread crumbs
½ c. tomato juice
1 ½ tsp. salt
½ tsp. pepper

(Continued on next page)

6 tsp. mustard
1 ½ tsp. horseradish
3 tsp. diced green pepper
2 tbsp. diced onion
¼ tsp. cream of tartar

Combine all ingredients except egg whites, 4 tea-spoonfuls mustard and cream of tartar; press into a loaf pan. Bake at 350 degrees for 50 minutes. Beat egg whites and cream of tartar until stiff. Fold in mustard. Spread over loaf. Bake for 10 minutes longer. Yield: 6 servings.

Mrs. John Knarr, Pres.
St. Paul's LWML
Tavistock, Ontario, Canada

DELICIOUS MEAT LOAF

2 lb. ground beef and pork
2 eggs, beaten
10 crackers, crushed
1 med. onion, diced
1 ½ tsp. salt
½ tsp. pepper
1 c. light cream
1 can tomato soup

Combine meat, eggs, cracker crumbs, onion, salt, pepper and cream. Form into a loaf; place in loaf pan. Pour soup over loaf. Bake at 350 degrees for 1 hour and 30 minutes. NOTE: Use two parts ground beef and one part ground pork to make the 2 pounds of meat required. Yield: 8 servings.

Mrs. Nels Forkrud
Opdal Lutheran Church
Sacred Heart, Minnesota

FLUFFY MEAT LOAF

1 lb. ground beef
½ lb. ground pork
3 slices soft bread, torn into
   pieces
1 ¼ c. milk
1 egg, beaten
¼ tsp. salt
¼ tsp. pepper
¼ tsp. dry mustard
¼ tsp. sage
¼ tsp. salt
¼ tsp. celery seed or powder
1 tbsp. Worcestershire sauce
¼ tsp. garlic salt
3 tbsp. catsup (opt.)

Combine all ingredients except catsup; shape into loaf. Place in shallow pan. Spread with catsup. Bake at 350 degrees for 1 hour and 30 minutes. Yield: 8 servings.

Mrs. Gustave Schaller
Christ Lutheran Church Mission Soc.
Ellendale, North Dakota

HAM LOAF

8 eggs, beaten
5 lb. ground veal
5 lb. ground pork
5 lb. ground ham
2 cans tomato soup
2 c. bread crumbs
2 c. milk
2 tbsp. salt
Onion juice

Combine all ingredients; place in loaf pans. Bake at 350 degrees for 1 hour to 1 hour and 30 minutes. Yield: 30-35 servings.

Mrs. Melvin Geske, Pres.
LWML
Fall Creek, Wisconsin

HAM LOAF

1 lb. ground ham
½ lb. ground lean pork
½ lb. ground lean beef
1 c. fine cracker crumbs
2 tbsp. chopped onion
2 tbsp. chopped celery
2 tbsp. chopped green pepper
½ tsp. salt
¼ tsp. pepper
2 eggs, beaten
1 c. milk

Combine all ingredients; shape into 10 to 12 individual loaves. Arrange in shallow baking pan.

TANGY SAUCE:

1 8-oz. can tomato sauce
3 tbsp. vinegar
1 tsp. dry mustard
1 c. (firmly packed) brown sugar

Combine all ingredients; pour over loaves. Bake at 350 degrees for 50 minutes to 1 hour, basting twice. Yield: 10-12 servings.

Oneta Dahl, Pres.
Trinity Ladies Aid
Akron, Colorado

HAM LOAF

1 lb. ground smoked ham
1 lb. ground veal
2 eggs, beaten
1 c. fresh orange juice
1 c. dry bread crumbs
½ tsp. salt
¼ tsp. pepper

Combine all ingredients; form into loaf. Bake at 350 degrees for 1 hour and 30 minutes.

SAUCE:

1 ½ c. orange juice
3 tbsp. sugar
1 tbsp. cornstarch

(Continued on next page)

Combine ingredients; cook until thickened. Baste ham loaf frequently with sauce during baking time. Yield: 8 servings.

Mrs. Al Schlensker
Christ Lutheran Church LWML
Noblesville, Indiana

INDIVIDUAL MEAT LOAVES

2 ½ lb. hamburger
½ lb. sausage
3 eggs
1 c. mashed potatoes
1 sm. onion
Pepper and salt to taste
Cracker crumbs
1 c. milk

Combine hamburger, sausage, 2 beaten eggs, potatoes, onion, pepper and salt. Shape into small loaves. Dip into remaining beaten eggs; roll in cracker crumbs. Fry in small amount of fat until brown. Place in roaster; pour milk over loaves. Bake at 300 degrees for 2 hours. Yield: 12 servings.

Doris Rehn, Pres.
Grace LCW
Lynn Center, Illinois

MEAT LOAF

1 lb. lean beef
½ lb. pork sausage
1 ½ c. bread crumbs
2 eggs, well beaten
¾ c. milk
½ c. catsup
¼ c. chopped pimento
1 sm. onion, chopped
Salt to taste
3 or 4 strips bacon

Combine all ingredients except bacon; place in a loaf pan. Top with bacon. Bake at 300 degrees until brown and meat begins to turn loose from sides of pan. Yield: 8-10 servings.

Mrs. Evan Lail, Pres.
Sardis Miss'y Soc.
Vale, North Carolina

MEAT LOAF

1 lb. ground beef
½ lb. ground pork
1 egg, beaten
1 c. corn bread crumbs
1 onion, finely chopped
1 tbsp. horseradish
1 ½ tsp. salt
¼ tsp. pepper
½ can tomato sauce

Combine all ingredients; shape into one large or two small loaves; place in shallow pan.

SAUCE:

½ can tomato sauce
2 tbsp. prepared mustard
2 tbsp. brown sugar
1 c. water

Combine all ingredients; pour over loaf. Bake at 350 degrees for 1 hour, basting every 15 minutes with sauce. Yield: 12 servings.

Mrs. E. A. Crowell
Crowell's LCW
Shelbyville, Tennessee

MEAT LOAF SUPREME

1 ¼ lb. ground beef
¼ lb. ground pork
⅔ c. bread crumbs
1 c. milk
2 eggs, beaten
¼ c. grated onion
1 tsp. salt
⅛ tsp. pepper
½ tsp. rubbed sage
3 tbsp. brown sugar
¼ c. catsup
¼ tsp. nutmeg

Combine all ingredients except brown sugar, catsup and nutmeg; pack into loaf pan. Combine remaining ingredients; spread over top. Bake at 350 degrees for 45 minutes to 1 hour.

Mrs. Grant Heuer, Pres.
Faith LCW
Moline, Illinois

MINCED BEEF AND SAUSAGE LOAF

1 lb. minced beef
2 c. soft bread crumbs
1 egg
1 tsp. salt
¼ tsp. pepper
½ tsp. savory
1 med. onion, chopped
2 stalks celery, diced
1 c. tomato juice
1 tsp. dry mustard
1 c. milk
2 tbsp. chopped parsley
½ lb. pork sausage

Combine all ingredients except sausage. Grease loaf pan with small amount of pan drippings; arrange sausage, side by side, in pan. Press beef mixture over sausage; brush top with additional tomato juice. Bake in preheated 350 degree oven for 1 hour. Pour gravy off loaf into a saucepan;

276

(Continued on next page)

thicken with flour or cornstarch mixed smooth in small amount of cold water, if desired. Turn loaf onto a preheated platter; garnish as desired. Yield: 6 servings.

Mrs. Viola Krause, Pres.
St. John's LWML
Parkbeg, Saskatchewan, Canada

MUSHROOM MEAT LOAF

1 lb. ground veal or lean pork
1 lb. ground smoked ham
2 eggs, beaten
1 c. bread crumbs
1 can cream of mushroom soup
1 sm. onion, finely chopped
½ tsp. salt
⅛ tsp. pepper
Chopped green pepper (opt.)
Catsup to taste (opt.)

Combine all ingredients; pack into buttered loaf pan. Bake at 375 degrees for 1 hour. Yield: 6 servings.

Kari G. Gulbrandson
Trinity Ladies Aid
Rock Springs, Wyoming

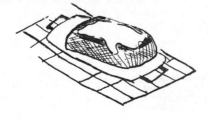

UPSIDE-DOWN HAM LOAF

4 slices pineapple
4 red cherries
1 orange, peeled and sectioned
½ c. brown sugar
¼ c. melted butter
½ lb. ground ham

1 ½ lb. ground veal
1 c. milk
2 eggs, beaten
2 c. corn flakes

Arrange pineapple in baking dish; place a cherry in the center of each slice. Arrange orange sections around the pineapple. Sprinkle with brown sugar and butter. Combine remaining ingredients; pack firmly into pan. Bake at 350 to 375 degrees for 1 hour. Yield: 8-10 servings.

Mrs. Myrtle Arnold, Sec.
Redeemer Ladies Soc.
Perris, California

BUSY DAY SPAGHETTI

1 lb. ground beef
¼ lb. bulk sausage
1 onion, chopped
1 green pepper, chopped
1 c. sliced mushrooms (opt.)
1 8-oz. can tomato sauce
1 No. 2 can tomatoes
1 tsp. salt
¼ tsp. Worcestershire sauce
6 drops of Tabasco sauce
7 oz. spaghetti

Brown beef and sausage; add onion and green pepper. Cook for 5 minutes. Add remaining ingredients; bring to a boil. Reduce heat to low. Cover; simmer for 30 to 35 minutes, stirring occasionally.

Mrs. John Skroback
Nazareth Ladies Soc.
Hopewell, Virginia

CABBAGE ROLLS

3 lb. ground beef
1 lb. ground pork
1 c. uncooked rice
3 tbsp. salt
Pepper to taste
6 med. onions, diced
3 tbsp. shortening
2 cabbages
2 qt. tomato juice

Combine ground beef, ground pork, rice, salt and pepper in large mixing bowl. Fry onions in shortening; add to meat mixture. Mix well. Remove leaves from cabbages; place in large pan. Pour boiling water over leaves; cover. Let stand for 3 minutes until wilted but not soggy. Pour off boiling water. Place small amount of meat mixture on each leaf; fold right side of cabbage over meat; roll up and tuck left side of cabbage leaf

277

(Continued on next page)

inside left side of cabbage roll. Cover with tomato juice; bring to a boil. Reduce heat to low or simmer; cook for 2 hours. Yield: 36 servings.

Mrs. Eleanor L. Bauer, VP
Holy Cross LWML
Madison, Ohio

LEBANESE MEAT AND CABBAGE

½ lb. ground beef
½ lb. ground fresh pork
1 egg
1 onion, finely chopped
¼ tsp. salt
12 leaves cabbage
¼ c. lemon juice
½ c. brown sugar
3 whole cloves
¾ c. tomato catsup
½ c. white raisins
1 c. water

Combine meats, egg, onion and salt. Place cabbage leaves in a pot of hot water for 10 minutes. Drain on paper towel. Place a ball of meat mixture on each leaf; roll up, tucking leaves under. Place in a heavy pan. Combine lemon juice, brown sugar, cloves, catsup, raisins and water. Pour over cabbage rolls. Cover; cook over medium heat for 30 minutes. Reduce heat; simmer for 20 minutes longer, adding additional water, if necessary. Yield: 6 servings.

Mrs. Clyde Seaks, Pres.
LCW
Stewartstown, Pennsylvania

CABBAGE ROLLS

1 cabbage
¾ lb. ground meat
¼ lb. ground pork
¾ c. uncooked rice
1 lge. onion, chopped
2 cloves of garlic, minced
1 tbsp. chopped parsley
1 tsp. chili powder
2 tsp. salt
¼ tsp. red pepper
2 tbsp. evaporated milk
½ can tomato paste

Strip off coarse outer leaves; use two or three of the leaves to line large skillet. Remove core; drop cabbage into large pot of boiling water. Steam until leaves become pliable and limp. Separate 12 leaves for rolls. Combine remaining ingredients; place spoonfuls of mixture on wilted cabbage leaves. Roll up and secure with toothpicks. Pack cabbage rolls into skillet lined with leaves.

SAUCE:

1 ½ cans tomato paste
2 c. boiling water
2 beef bouillon cubes
1 bay leaf
Salt and red pepper to taste

Combine all ingredients; pour sauce over cabbage rolls, adding hot water if necessary to more than one-half cover the rolls. Cover; simmer for 45 minutes to 1 hour. Yield: 6 servings.

Mrs. H. V. Fortune
Redeemer Martha Cir.
Houston, Texas

CHICKEN CHOW MEIN

½ lb. lean pork
3 tbsp. butter
2 tbsp. chopped onion
2 ½ tbsp. flour
2 ½ c. chicken stock
3 c. diced cooked chicken
¾ c. diced celery
¾ c. mushrooms
2 tbsp. soy sauce
¾ c. blanched slivered almonds
Salt and pepper to taste

Cut pork into cubes. Melt butter in heavy pan. Add onion and cook for 2 minutes; blend in flour. Gradually stir in chicken stock. Add chicken, pork, celery and mushrooms. Simmer for 15 minutes. Add soy sauce, almonds and seasonings. Serve with fried noodles, if desired. Yield: 6 servings.

Mrs. Harald Mastad
McCord-Mankota Mission
McCord, Saskatchewan, Canada

CHOP SUEY

½ lb. ground pork
½ lb. ground beef
Salt and pepper to taste
1 c. diced onions
2 c. celery
1 tbsp. cornstarch
1 tbsp. gravy coloring (opt.)
1 sm. can mushrooms

Brown meats; season with salt and pepper. Remove meats; from pan. Boil onions and celery in small amount of water until tender. Thicken liquid with cornstarch. Add to pan drippings, stirring until thick. Add gravy coloring and mushrooms. Combine all ingredients. Serve with rice and chow mein noodles, if desired. Yield: 4 servings.

Mrs. David Redman
Trinity LCW
Cedarburg, Wisconsin

CHOP SUEY

1 ½ lb. pork steak, cubed
1 ½ lb. round steak, cubed
1 lb. veal steak, cubed
Salt and pepper to taste
1 c. diced onions
2 c. diced celery
1 can bean sprouts
1 4-oz. can mushrooms
2 tbsp. chop suey molasses

Brown meats in small amount of shortening; season with salt and pepper. Remove meat from pan; fry onions until yellow in pan drippings; add celery and meats. Simmer for 1 hour or until meat is tender. Add bean sprouts, mushrooms and molasses; thicken with cornstarch, if desired. May be served over steamed rice and topped with Chinese noodles and soy sauce. Yield: 10 servings.

Mrs. Waldo R. Krug, Pres.
Bethlehem LWML
Kennewick, Washington

CHOP SUEY

2 cans Chinese vegetables
2 lb. chop suey meat
1 tsp. salt
1 tsp. monosodium glutamate
1 lge. onion, sliced and separated
  into rings
1 clove of garlic, crushed
3 c. sliced celery
1 green pepper, cut into 1-in. long
  strips
⅓ c. flour
1 tbsp. bead molasses
1 tsp. soy sauce

Drain Chinese vegetables, reserving 1 1/3 cups liquid. Brown meat; add salt, monosodium glutamate, onion, garlic, celery, green pepper and 1 cup vegetable liquid. Simmer for 40 minutes or until meat is tender. Combine flour with remaining vegetable liquid. Add to meat mixture with molasses and soy sauce; cook until thick, stirring constantly. Add Chinese vegetables. Serve on rice and top with chow mein noodles, if desired. Yield: 6-8 servings.

Mrs. Theodore Anderson
Hope Dorcas Soc.
Aurora, Illinois

CITY CHICKEN

1 lb. veal, cut into 1-in. cubes
1 lb. pork cut into 1-in. cubes
½ c. fine bread crumbs
1 tsp. salt
1 egg
2 tbsp. water

Alternate veal and pork on 4-inch skewers. Mix crumbs with salt; dip meat into crumbs, then into a mixture of egg and water and again into crumbs. Brown in small amount of fat. Cover and reduce heat; cook for 45 minutes or until meat is tender. Yield: 5-6 servings.

Beatrice A. Daily
Redeemer Miriam Soc.
North Las Vegas, Nevada

MEAT PATTIES WITH SAUERKRAUT

1 lb. pork
1 lb. beef
1 lge. onion, diced
1 clove of garlic, diced
¾ c. rice, parboiled
2 eggs, slightly beaten
Salt and pepper to taste
1 lge. can sauerkraut
Bay leaf
Caraway seed

Grind pork with beef. Brown onion and garlic in small amount of fat. Remove from heat; add rice, meat, eggs, salt and pepper. Shape into 2 1/2-inch patties; brown in small amount of fat. Place a layer of sauerkraut in large pot; add 1 bay leaf and a few caraway seed. Cover with a layer of meat patties. Repeat until all sauerkraut and patties are used. Add enough water to cover. Simmer over low heat for 2 hours and 30 minutes to 3 hours. Yield: 7 servings.

Mrs. John Fillo, Pres.
Holy Trinity Dorcas Mission Guild
Bridgeport, Connecticut

PRITTLES

1 fresh picnic ham
5 lb. lean beef
1 lge. beef tongue
1 lge. beef heart
1 lb. quick cooking oats
Salt and pepper to taste

Cover meats with water; cook until tender. Pour off broth. Add oats to broth; simmer for 1 hour, stirring often. Grind meats; add to oat mixture. Season with salt and pepper. Freeze or cold pack mixture. Yield: 2 gallons.

Mrs. Orville Thieroff
St. John's Ladies Aid
Defiance, Ohio

SAUERKRAUT WITH BEEF AND PORK

1 ½ lb. lean boneless fresh pork
1 ½ lb. ground beef
1 sm. onion, chopped

279

(Continued on next page)

Salt to taste
1 tsp. pepper
1 28-oz. can sauerkraut
1 28-oz. can tomatoes
1 lge. green pepper, sliced
2 c. sour cream

Dice pork into 1/2-inch squares; place in large frying pan. Add beef, onion, salt and pepper; fry over moderate heat, stirring, until meat is browned. Drain sauerkraut, reserving liquid. Place sauerkraut in large heavy kettle; arrange meat over sauerkraut. Drain tomatoes, reserving liquid; break up tomatoes and arrange on top of meat. Cover with green pepper; combine tomato juice and one-half of sauerkraut liquid. Pour over meat. Cover; simmer for 50 minutes. Spoon sour cream over top; cook for 10 minutes longer. Yield: 8 servings.

Mrs. H. G. Busch, Pres.
Hope LWML
Victoria, British Columbia, Canada

SPAGHETTI MEAT SAUCE

1 lb. pork links, cases removed
2 to 2 ½ lb. hamburger
2 lb. ground round steak
1 tbsp. salt
2 or 3 green peppers, cut into thin
  strips
2 carrots, sliced
6 med. onions, chopped
3 stalks celery, thinly sliced
4 No. 303 cans whole tomatoes
1 pkg. mushroom soup mix
1 lge. bottle button mushrooms, drained
1 can tomato soup
2 12-oz. cans tomato paste
½ tsp. oregano
½ tsp. black pepper
½ tsp. red pepper
½ tsp. celery salt
½ tsp. onion salt
½ tsp. rosemary
½ tsp. crushed bay leaf
2 cloves of garlic

Fry pork; drain off fat. Place pork in large kettle. Brown remaining meats; place in kettle with pork. Add remaining ingredients; simmer for 2 hours and 30 minutes to 3 hours. Remove

garlic. Serve over spaghetti. NOTE: Sauce may be frozen. Yield: 6 quarts.

Mrs. Carroll Vipond, Altar Chmn.
First Lutheran Church Evangelical Ladies Guild
Grand Rapids, Minnesota

CORNISH PASTIES

3 c. flour
1 tbsp. salt
1 c. lard
1 c. cold water
1 sm. rutabaga, grated
5 potatoes, cut into ½ x ⅛-in. pieces
1 lb. flank steak, cut into 1-in. cubes
6 oz. fresh pork, cut into 1-in. cubes
Salt and pepper to taste
Chopped suet
Minced onion
Finely diced potatoes

Sift flour and salt twice. Cut lard into flour mixture until pieces are size of small peas. Add water, a little at a time. Toss until mixture holds together. Handle as little as possible. Cut into five portions. Roll each portion of dough on floured board to a 9-inch circle. Place 2 tablespoonfuls rutabaga, 3/4 cup potatoes, 3 ounces steak and 1 ounce fresh pork on one-half of each circle; season with salt and pepper. Sprinkle with 1 teaspoonful suet, 1 tablespoonful onion and 2 tablespoonfuls diced potatoes. Fold crust over and seal edges. Cut slit in top of each pastry to allow steam to escape. Bake at 400 degrees for 1 hour. Yield: 5 servings.

Eloise D. Berg, Pres.
Messiah LCW
Marquette, Michigan

EGG ROLLS

FILLING:

½ c. finely chopped celery
¾ c. shredded cabbage
½ c. water
½ c. diced cooked shrimp
½ c. diced cooked pork
3 tbsp. oil
4 scallions, finely chopped
½ c. finely chopped water chestnuts, drained
1 clove of garlic, minced
¼ c. soy sauce

Place celery and cabbage in water in saucepan. Bring to a boil; drain. Add shrimp and pork to oil in skillet. Fry for 3 minutes, stirring constantly. Add celery, cabbage, scallions, water chestnuts, garlic and soy sauce. Fry for 5 minutes.

BATTER:

¾ c. plus 1 tbsp. sifted flour
1 tbsp. cornstarch
1 tsp. salt
2 eggs, beaten
Sugar

(Continued on next page)

Sift 3/4 cup flour with cornstarch and salt into a bowl. Beat in eggs; add a pinch of sugar. Add 1 1/2 cups water gradually, beating constantly, until batter is smooth. Grease a hot 6-inch skillet with 1 teaspoonful oil. Pour 3 tablespoonfuls batter into skillet, tipping skillet to spread batter. Fry over medium heat until batter shrinks from sides of skillet. Turn; fry for 1 minute. Repeat, adding oil each time, until all batter is used. Cool. Place 4 tablespoonfuls filling in center of each pancake. Fold edges over filling; roll up. Combine remaining flour with 2 tablespoonfuls water. Seal pancakes with flour mixture. Fry in 1/2 cup oil until golden. Yield: 6 servings.

June Ulm, Christian Growth Chmn.
Hope Ruth Guild
Overland Park, Kansas

FLEISCH KUECHLE

3 c. flour
1 tsp. salt
½ c. water
½ c. cream
1 c. ground beef
1 c. ground pork or beef
1 sm. onion, finely chopped
Salt and pepper to taste

Mix flour and salt with enough of combined water and cream to make a stiff dough. Roll out into circles the size of a pie plate. Combine remaining ingredients. Spread one-half of each circle with a thin layer of meat mixture; fold over. Pat down and seal by rolling a smooth edged saucer around edges. Fry in deep hot fat. Serve hot.

Mrs. Otto Bonnet
St. John's LWML
McClusky, North Dakota

GOURMET ROAST CHICKEN

6 tbsp. butter or margarine
1 2 to 2 ½-lb. chicken, cut up
2 doz. mushrooms
10 to 15 tiny onions
½ lb. uncooked ham
2 tsp. salt
¼ tsp. pepper
¾ c. dry wine

Melt 6 tablespoonfuls butter in large skillet. Brown chicken on all sides in butter. Place in roaster or Dutch oven. Saute mushrooms in 2 tablespoonfuls butter until brown; arrange around chicken. Make holes in onions. Cut up ham and chicken liver; place with onions around chicken. Sprinkle with salt and pepper. Add wine.

Cover tightly. Bake in moderate oven until tender. Yield: 4 servings.

Mrs. Harry Miley
Zion Ladies Guild
Wabash, Indiana

SHISH KABOBS

½ lb. beef, cubed
½ lb. veal, cubed
½ lb. pork, cubed
Seasoned flour
3 tbsp. shortening
1 ½ c. water or 1 can onion soup

Alternate beef, veal and pork on skewers; roll in seasoned flour. Brown in shortening. Place in roasting pan. Pour in water. Bake at 325 degrees for 2 hours and 30 minutes. Yield: 6 servings.

Mrs. Julius A. Peitsch, Pres.
Bethlehem Ladies Aid Soc.
Saginaw, Michigan

STUFFED HAM ROLLS WITH CREAMED CHICKEN

¾ c. cooked rice
2 tbsp. chopped parsley
¾ c. chopped almonds or walnuts
Salt and pepper to taste
3 tbsp. melted butter
Pinch of poultry seasoning
16 slices boiled ham
2 c. creamed chicken

Combine all ingredients except ham and creamed chicken; mix thoroughly. Spread over ham slices. Roll up ham slices; place, seam-side down, in a shallow baking pan. Cover with creamed chicken. Bake at 350 degrees until heated through. Do not overheat. Yield: 8 servings.

Mrs. Ben J. F. Romer, Pres.
Resurrection LCW
Detroit, Michigan

STUFFED MEAT PATTIES

1 c. soft bread crumbs
2 tbsp. chopped onion
1 tbsp. chopped parsley
½ tsp. poultry seasoning
½ lb. ground beef
½ lb. ground pork
2 c. slightly crushed corn flakes
1 tsp. salt
¼ tsp. pepper

281

(Continued on next page)

¼ c. rich milk
1 tbsp. drippings
1 c. cream of mushroom soup
⅔ c. water

Combine crumbs, onion, parsley and poultry seasoning. Combine meats, corn flakes, salt, pepper and milk. Shape meat mixture into 12 patties. Place a spoonful of stuffing on six patties; cover with remaining patties. Press edges together. Brown in drippings. Place in baking pan. Cover; bake at 350 degrees for 20 minutes. Drain off fat from pan; pour soup and water over patties. Bake for 15 minutes longer. Yield: 4 servings.

Mrs. O. H. Marten, Sec.
St. Luke's LWML
New Richmond, Wisconsin

STUFFED BEEF TENDERLOIN

1 3 to 4-lb. beef tenderloin
1 clove of garlic, split
1 8 to 10-oz. box mushrooms
¼ c. butter
1 lb. ground veal
2 ½ c. white wine
½ lb. ground cooked ham
¾ c. plus 2 tbsp. sour cream
4 tbsp. fine dry bread crumbs
Salt and pepper to taste
⅓ c. Maderia wine
1 can beef consomme

Split tenderloin lengthwise through the middle to about three-fourths of its depth; place between waxed paper; pound until flat. Rub with garlic. Saute mushrooms in 3 tablespoonfuls butter; add veal and 1 cup white wine. Cover; steam for 10 minutes. Add ground ham, 3/4 cup sour cream, bread crumbs, salt and pepper; mix thoroughly. Spread over tenderloin. Roll up; tie securely. Place in baking pan. Bake at 375 degrees for 30 minutes, basting with remaining white wine. Blend remaining sour cream, Maderia wine and beef consomme; add to pan juices. Strain and serve with meat. Yield: 12 servings.

Mrs. Glenn Stewart
Trinity LWML
Fredricktown, Missouri

WIENER-CHEESE BAKE

8 wieners
2 slices American or Cheddar cheese
8 slices bacon

Split wieners about three-fourths way through. Cut each slice of cheese into four strips; insert 1 strip of cheese into each wiener. Spiral bacon around wieners; secure with toothpicks. Place in pan. Bake at 325 degrees for 15 minutes or until bacon is crisp. Yield: 4 servings.

Mrs. Walter Gragert, Pres.
Zion LWML
Fairmont, Oklahoma

Dressing, Stuffing & Sauce Favorites

RECIPES FOR CURRY SAUCE, MUSTARD SAUCE, ONION-HORSERADISH SAUCE ON PAGE 291
RECIPES FOR SEAFOOD COCKTAIL SAUCE, TOMATO-MUSHROOM SAUCE ON PAGE 292

BASIC POULTRY DRESSING

1 lb. stale bread
½ c. chopped onion
3 c. diced celery
3 tsp. salt
3 tsp. salt
3 tsp. poultry seasoning
Dash of pepper
4 eggs, slightly beaten

Soak bread in cold water; squeeze dry. Melt butter in pan; add onion and celery. Fry until tender but not brown. Add to bread. Season with seasonings. Add eggs. Yield: 6 servings.

Mrs. Swen Carlson
Salem LCW
Strandquist, Minnesota

BREAD DRESSING

2 16-oz. loaves bread
Chicken or turkey heart, liver and neck
1 c. chopped onions
2 c. chopped celery
Salt and pepper to taste
2 to 3 tbsp. sage or poultry seasoning
2 eggs, beaten

Dry bread in oven until lightly browned. Put bread through food chopper or roll until crumbly. Cook heart, liver and neck; reserve broth. Put meat through food chopper. Mix onion and celery with bread mixture. Add salt, pepper and sage. Add eggs and broth; mix well. Stuff turkey. Yield: Stuffing for 20 pound turkey.

Mrs. Miriam Symbol, Pres.
Ostenfeld Lutheran Church
Ostenfeld, Manitoba, Canada

CHEF'S TURKEY DRESSING

4 c. finely chopped onion
4 c. finely chopped celery
1 tsp. crushed sage leaf
4 tbsp. salt
1 tsp. white pepper
2 c. margarine or butter
4 c. turkey stock
Ground cooked giblets
4 qt. dry bread, cut into ¼-in. squares

Saute onion, celery and seasonings in margarine until translucent. Add all ingredients to bread. Add a small amount of stock or water to moisten. Yield: Stuffing for 16 pound turkey.

Mrs. Carl F. Selle, Pres.
St. Stephen LWML
Horicon, Wisconsin

DRESSING FOR TURKEY

1 ½ lge. loaves white bread, toasted
4 stalks celery, finely chopped
1 stick melted margarine or butter
3 eggs
2 tsp. salt
½ tsp. pepper

Mix all ingredients. Add enough hot water to soften mixture. Yield: Stuffing for large turkey.

Mrs. William Stettes
St. Paul Ladies Aid
Pacific, Missouri

FOWL DRESSING

8 c. bread, broken into small pieces
Liquid from giblets
¼ lb. butter
1 c. ground cooked giblets
¾ c. chopped onions
¼ c. diced celery
4 eggs, well beaten
¼ tsp. pepper
¼ tsp. sage
1 tbsp. salt
1 tsp. poultry seasoning

Soak bread in water and giblet liquid. Mix to consistency of corn meal. Melt butter in frying pan; add ground giblets, onions and celery. Cook slowly until onions and celery are tender. Combine onion mixture with eggs and seasonings. Mix well. Use as stuffing for fowl.

Mrs. L. E. Swanson, Sec.
Pilgrim Ladies Aid
Lake City, Iowa

LORRAINE'S TURKEY DRESSING

2 loaves dry bread
2 lge. onions, chopped
Turkey liver
Turkey heart
Turkey gizzard
3 tbsp. lard
2 tsp. ginger
1 tsp. poultry spice (opt.)
3 tbsp. salt
2 tbsp. sugar

Soak dry bread in cold water until moist and crumbly. Grind onions and turkey liver, heart and gizzard together. Add lard. Sprinkle with salt, pepper and sugar. Combine with bread; mix well. NOTE: Sufficient stuffing for 22 pound turkey. Yield: 30 servings.

Mrs. Adolph Sanne, Pres.
Corcordia LWML
Clearwater, Nebraska

MOIST DRESSING FOR TURKEY

½ lb. butter
Heart and gizzard (opt.)
2 c. thinly sliced onions
2 c. chopped celery
1 1-lb. loaf white bread, toasted
1 tbsp. sage or poultry seasoning
1 tbsp. salt
¼ tsp. pepper
3 eggs

Melt butter slowly; add liver and gizzard. Cook for 5 minutes. Add onions and celery; cover pan and steam for 15 minutes. Cover bread with cold water until it swirls; press until very fluffy. Pour butter mixture over bread. Season with salt, pepper, add eggs. Mix lightly with two forks. Add more melted butter if mixture appears dry. Yield: Stuffing for 15 to 18 pound turkey.

Lucille Bruegmann, Pres.
St. Paul's LWML
Thornton, Illinois

ORANGE DRESSING

½ c. hot water
3 c. bread crumbs, toasted
2 tsp. grated orange rind
⅔ c. diced orange pulp
2 c. diced celery
¼ c. melted butter
1 egg, beaten
½ tsp. salt
⅛ tsp. pepper
¼ tsp. savory
½ c. raisins

Pour hot water over bread crumbs in large bowl; let stand for 10 minutes. Add remaining ingredients, stir lightly to combine. Stuff duckling. NOTE: If dry stuffing is desired, omit hot water. Yield: 6 servings.

Mrs. Sophie Fenske, Pres.
St. Luke LWML
North Surrey, British Columbia, Canada

POTATO-GIBLET DRESSING

4 lge. red potatoes
Giblets
4½ c. soft bread crumbs
2 c. chopped celery
½ c. chopped onion
5 tbsp. cooking oil
2½ tsp. salt
¼ tsp. pepper
3 eggs
1½ c. undiluted evaporated milk
2¼ tsp. poultry seasoning
2 tbsp. dry parsley

Cook potatoes. Cool; shred fine. Cook giblets until tender; cut into small pieces. Saute crumbs, celery and onions in oil. Combine potatoes with crumb mixture; season with salt and

pepper. Beat milk into eggs; add to potato mixture. Combine poultry seasoning and parsley with giblets; fold into dressing. Form dressing into balls; place in greased baking dish. Bake at 375 degrees for 30 minutes. Yield: 10-15 servings.

Mrs. Anne Boecler
Lutheran Village Church Women's Group
St. Louis, Missouri

SWEET POTATO-NUT DRESSING

8 lge. sweet potatoes
½ c. melted butter
¼ c. cream
1 egg
½ tsp. poultry seasoning
1 tsp. salt
¼ tsp. pepper
1 c. chopped nuts

Cook sweet potatoes until done. Peel and mash. Add remaining ingredients; mix well. Stuff chicken or turkey before roasting. Yield: Stuffing for 12 pound fowl.

Mrs. Elmer J. Lindholm
First Lutheran Church LCW
Pecatonica, Illinois

RICE DRESSING

1 c. uncooked rice
2 tsp. butter
½ c. chopped celery
1 tsp. chopped parsley
1 med. onion, chopped
½ lb. seasoned sausage
½ lb. ground round
2 eggs, well beaten
½ tsp. salt
½ tsp. pepper
½ tsp. thyme
2 tsp. cornstarch

Cook rice until tender. Rinse. Heat butter in saucepan. Add celery, parsley and onion; simmer until onion is tender. Add mixture to rice. Add remaining ingredients; Mix well with fork. Stuff into fowl. Yield: 10-12 servings.

Mrs. Kurt Wolf, Sec.
Zion Ladies Aid
Fisher, Arkansas

DRESSING FOR TURKEY

1 loaf dry bread
½ lb. gizzards
½ c. chopped celery
2 apples, chopped
1 onion, chopped
Liver
Heart

285

(Continued on next page)

Salt and pepper
½ tsp. (scant) sage
2 to 4 eggs, beaten
1 lb. pork sausage

Soak bread; squeeze out water. Grind gizzards, celery, apples, onion, liver and heart. Fry pork sausage. Mix all ingredients. Yield: stuffing for 1 turkey.

Mrs. John Knutson
Immanuel Ladies Aid
Hewitt, Wisconsin

PORK SAUSAGE DRESSING

2 med. onions, chopped
1 lb. pork sausage, diced
½ to 1 loaf bread, cubed
1 can cream of celery soup
1 can cream of chicken soup
2 eggs
2 tsp. poultry seasoning
Salt and pepper to taste
Milk

Brown onions in frying pan; add sausage. Fry until meat loses red color. Combine remaining ingredients, adding sufficient milk to soften. Add sausage mixture; mix well. Yield: 8 servings.

Mrs. William Koenig
St. Paul's LWML
Woodworth, North Dakota

SAUSAGE DRESSING

1 lb. bulk sausage
6 c. bread crumbs
½ c. chopped onion
½ c. chopped celery
¼ lb. butter
1 egg
Milk

Combine sausage and bread crumbs. Brown onion and celery in butter; add to sausage. Beat egg in cup; fill remainder of cup with milk. Add to sausage mixture. Place in baking dish. Bake at 350 degrees for 1 hour. Yield: 5-6 servings.

Mrs. J. V. Hess, Pres.
St. John's Women of the Church
Piqua, Ohio

TURKEY DRESSING

1 lge. loaf white bread
1 lb. link pork sausages
1 lge. or 2 med. parsnips, finely cut
1 bunch celery, finely cut
1 tbsp. butter
1 c. water

Toast bread and cut into cubes. Fry sausages and cut into bite-sized pieces. Pour off all but 2 tablespoonfuls grease. Place parsnips and celery in same pan; add butter and water. Simmer until done. Mix with toast and sausages. NOTE: May be made in advance and refrigerated until next day. Yield: Stuffing for one 15 pound turkey.

Florence Wilbrandt
St. John's Ladies Aid
Algonquin, Illinois

TURKEY DRESSING

Turkey neck and giblets
1 1½-lb. dry loaf bread
½ lb. pork sausage
2 c. finely diced celery
2 eggs, beaten
½ c. melted butter
1 tbsp. minced onion
⅛ tsp. poultry seasoning
Salt and pepper to taste

Cook neck and giblets except liver in water until tender. Reserve broth. Pick meat from neck. Grind giblets and raw liver in food chopper. Soak bread in water and drain. Mix all ingredients. Place in turkey. Yield: Stuffing for one 12 to 15 pound turkey.

Mrs. Leola Matzke, Pres.
St. John's Ladies Aid
Good Thunder, Minnesota

VEGETABLE DRESSING

3 c. grated cabbage
2 c. grated carrots
2 onions, diced
2 tsp. salt
2 tbsp. melted butter
1 egg, beaten
4 tbsp. whole wheat flour
1 tsp. poultry seasoning

Mix all ingredients well. Stuff chicken or salmon. NOTE: Stuffing may be used for veal roll or other meat. Yield: 8 servings.

Stella Schultz
St. Paul's LCW
Langenburg, Saskatchewan, Canada

MEAT FILLING FOR TURKEY

1 lge. onion, finely chopped
3 stalks celery, finely chopped
2 tbsp. oil or margarine
1 to 1½-lb. pork and veal, ground
6 to 8 slices dry Vienna bread

(Continued on next page)

2 or 3 eggs
¼ tsp. marjoram
½ tsp. salt
¼ tsp. pepper

Braise onion and celery in oil. Add meat; toss until redness of meat disappears. Soak bread in small amount of water; squeeze and crumble. Add to meat mixture; mix well. Add remaining ingredients; mix well. Cool; fill turkey. Add more bread, if needed. Yield: 10 servings.

Mrs. Carl Baumgart
Holy Trinity LCW
Chicago, Illinois

OYSTER STUFFING

1 c. chopped stewing oysters
4 c. stale bread cubes
2 tsp. salt
⅛ tsp. pepper
⅛ tsp. sage
3 tbsp. butter
1 onion, minced
2 tbsp. minced parsley
¾ c. minced celery

Place oysters in fry pan; cover. Saute for 5 minutes; drain. Combine bread cubes, salt, pepper and sage; add oysters. Melt butter in fry pan; add remaining ingredients. Saute until tender. Add to bread mixture; blend. Yield: Stuffing for 4-pound fowl.

Marie Bernblow
Emmanuel Ladies Aid
Rifle, Colorado

RICE STUFFING

¼ c. minced onion
½ c. diced celery
¼ c. shortening
½ c. sliced mushrooms (opt.)
1 tsp. salt
⅛ tsp. pepper
¼ to ½ tsp. poultry seasoning
3 c. cooked brown rice
1 ½ c. diced apples
½ c. stock and finely cut giblets
1 c. diced chestnuts (opt.)

Cook onion and celery in shortening until tender. Add mushrooms and seasonings. Simmer for 5 minutes. Combine with remaining ingredients. Mix well. Cool before stuffing bird. NOTE: Sufficient stuffing for 5 to 7 pound bird. Yield: 8 servings.

Mrs. Everrett Hank, Sec.
Immanuel Ladies Aid
Carroll, Nebraska

POULTRY STUFFING

1 onion, chopped
½ c. butter
4 c. cubed bread
½ tsp. salt
½ tsp. sage
½ tsp. thyme
¼ tsp. celery seed
Celery (opt.)
Celery leaves (opt.)
Raisins (opt.)
1 egg

Saute onion in butter. Mix remaining dry ingredients. Add egg; mix well. Yield: 4 servings.

Mrs. Rachel Hilderman
Christ Lutheran Church LCW
Rhein, Saskatchewan, Canada

SAUSAGE AND BREAD STUFFING FOR TURKEY

1 lb. pork sausage
¾ c. chopped onions
4 stalks celery
3 to 4 qt. stale bread cubes
1 tbsp. salt
¼ tsp. pepper
1 ½ tsp. poultry seasoning
1 c. water

Break sausage into small chunks; brown lightly. Add remaining ingredients. Mix thoroughly. Stuff cavity of turkey. Yield: Stuffing for 12 to 16-pound turkey.

Mrs. Gerald McDaniel
First Lutheran Church Women's Org.
East Orange, New Jersey

SAVORY RICE-APPLE STUFFING

¼ c. butter
½ c. chopped onion
1 ½ c. water
1 sm. box instant rice
2 ½ tsp. salt
Dash of pepper
½ tsp. poultry seasoning
2 c. diced, peeled fresh tart apples
1 c. diced celery
¼ c. chopped celery leaves
¼ c. chopped parsley
½ c. raisins (opt.)

Melt butter in saucpan. Add onions; saute until tender, stirring constantly. Add remaining ingredients, except raisins. Mix to moisten all rice. Bring to a boil over high heat, fluffing rice gently with fork. Cover; remove from heat. Let stand until rice is steamed. Add raisins; mix lightly with fork. Yield: 5 1/2 cups.

Mrs. Leonard H. Wortman
St. Mark's Ladies Aid Soc.
Ruskin, Nebraska

SWEET STUFFING

8 to 10 hamburger buns, cubed
¾ c. sugar
½ tsp. salt
1 med. apple, diced
2 eggs
1 tsp. allspice
¾ c. raisins
Cream or evaporated milk

Place all ingredients in bowl, using enough cream to moisten thoroughly. Yield: 8 servings.

Mrs. Clarence Boxberger
Immanuel Ladies Aid
Russell, Kansas

WILD RICE-ORANGE STUFFING

1 c. uncooked wild rice
2 tbsp. butter or margarine
¼ c. chopped onion
½ c. chopped celery
¼ tsp. Tabasco sauce
3 ½ c. toasted bread cubes
1 tsp. poultry seasoning
½ tsp. rosemary
2 tsp. salt
2 tsp. grated orange rind
4 oranges, cut into chunks
2 eggs, lightly beaten (opt.)

Wash rice thoroughly. Cover with boiling water; let stand for 15 minutes. Drain. Cover again with boiling water; let stand for 15 minutes longer. Drain; combine with remaining ingredients. Yield: Stuffing for 12 pound bird.

Mrs. William E. Macbeth, Pres.
Gloria Dei Evangelical LCW
Tecumseh, Michigan

BARBECUE SAUCE

1 med. onion, minced
2 tbsp. butter
2 tbsp. Worcestershire sauce
1 tsp. salt
1 sm. green pepper, minced
¾ c. catsup
2 tbsp. brown sugar

Combine all ingredients; simmer in heavy pan for 15 minutes. Serve with barbecued meat.

Mrs. Betty Mohney, Pres.
Oklahoma Ladies Aid
DuBois, Pennsylvania

BARBECUE SAUCE

2 onions, ground
½ c. brown sugar
4 tbsp. vinegar
1 bottle catsup

Combine all ingredients; heat thoroughly. Serve hot or cold on any kind of meat.

Alta Mahoney, Sec.-Treas.
Nevdorfer Ruth Circle
Jordan, Montana

BARBECUE SAUCE

¼ c. vinegar
½ c. water
2 tbsp. sugar
1 tbsp. mustard
½ tsp. pepper
1 ½ tsp. salt
1 ½ tsp. liquid or powdered smoke (opt.)
¼ tsp. cayenne pepper
1 thick slice lemon
1 slice onion
¼ c. butter or margarine
½ c. catsup
2 tbsp. Worcestershire sauce

Combine all ingredients except catsup, butter and Worcestershire sauce in saucepan. Simmer, uncovered, for 20 minutes. Add catsup, butter and Worcestershire sauce; bring to a boil. Yield: 1 3/4 cups.

Twila Robb, Sec.
United LCW
New Middletown, Ohio

BARBECUE SAUCE

1 tbsp. butter
1 med. onion, chopped
1 8-oz. can tomato sauce
1 tbsp. vinegar
1 tbsp. lemon juice
2 tbsp. brown sugar
1 tsp. salt
1 tsp. dry mustard
1 tsp. Tabasco sauce
1 bay leaf
1 clove of garlic
¼ c. water

Combine all ingredients in saucepan. Bring to a boil. Use as basting sauce for spareribs, frankfurters, chicken or beef. Yield: 1 2/3 cups.

Mrs. Elmer Seelow, Pres.
Trinity LWML
Ft. Lauderdale, Florida

BARBECUE SAUCE

½ c. catsup
1 tsp. salt
1 tsp. celery seed
½ c. vinegar
1 c. water
¼ c. brown sugar

Combine all ingredients; pour over pork chops or spareribs. Yield: 2 cups.

Mrs. Max Brager, Pres.
Kountze Memorial LCW
Omaha, Nebraska

BARBECUED RIB SAUCE

4 tbsp. liquid smoke
1 c. tomato catsup
1 lge. onion, minced
2 c. water
1 tbsp. salt
1 tbsp. chili powder
1 tbsp. celery seed
¼ c. brown sugar
¼ c. vinegar
¼ c. Worcestershire sauce
Few drops of Tabasco sauce
1 lemon, thinly sliced

Mix all ingredients except lemon; bring to a boil. Place lemon slices on browned meat; baste with sauce until meat is done. Yield: Sauce for 4 to 5 pounds ribs.

Marlys J. Tuller, Pres.
Ruskin Heights Lutheran WOC
Kansas City, Montana

BARBECUE SAUCE FOR CHICKEN

1 tsp. salt
½ tsp. pepper
1 tbsp. paprika
1 tbsp. sugar
½ tsp. garlic salt
1 c. catsup
1 med. onion, finely chopped
½ c. water
½ c. lemon juice or vinegar
1 tbsp. Worcestershire sauce
¼ c. butter

Blend all ingredients except lemon juice, Worcestershire sauce and butter. Heat to boiling. Remove from heat. Add remaining ingredients. Yield: 2 1/2 cups.

Grace N. Anderson, Treas.
LCW
Thomaston, Connecticut

JIFFY BARBECUE SAUCE

¾ c. chopped onions
½ c. cooking oil
¾ c. tomato catsup
¾ c. water
⅓ c. lemon juice
3 tbsp. sugar
3 tbsp. Worcestershire sauce
2 tbsp. prepared mustard
2 tsp. salt
½ tsp. pepper

Cook onions in hot oil until soft. Add remaining ingredients. Simmer for 15 minutes. NOTE: Chopped beef may be added to sauce for barbecued beefburgers.

Mrs. Fred Sauder, Treas.
St. Paul's Ladies Aid
Frazee, Minnesota

PANHANDLE BARBECUE SAUCE

½ c. butter
½ c. light brown sugar
¼ tsp. cayenne pepper
1 c. salad oil
1 tsp. dry mustard
½ c. Worcestershire sauce
1 14-oz. bottle catsup
2 tbsp. chili sauce
2 cloves of garlic, crushed
1 onion, finely chopped
¼ c. lemon juice
3 drops of Tabasco sauce

Melt butter in saucepan; add remaining ingredients, stirring constantly. Simmer for 15 minutes, stirring frequently. Sauce may be stored in tightly closed jar in refrigerator for 1 week or in freezer indefinitely. Use as marinade, basting or serving sauce for poultry, veal, lamb or beef. Yield: 6 cups.

Mrs. Esther Schroeder
Christ Lutheran Church Guild
Lincoln, Nebraska

RIB SAUCE

1 tbsp. melted butter
1 sm. onion, chopped
½ tsp. pepper
2 tsp. sugar
½ tsp. dry mustard
½ tsp. celery salt
½ tsp. paprika
4 tbsp. catsup
2 tsp. Worcestershire sauce
½ tsp. Tabasco sauce (opt.)
2 tbsp. vinegar
4 drops of garlic juice
6 tbsp. water

Melt butter; brown onion until tender. Add remaining ingredients. Bring to a boil. May be used to baste any kind of meat.

Mrs. Elmer A. Lehman, Ohio Synod Board
First Lutheran Church LCW
Leipsic, Ohio

THIN BARBECUE SAUCE

½ lb. butter or margarine
1 pt. vinegar
½ c. water
1 tsp. dry mustard
2 tbsp. chopped onion
1 ½ tsp. sugar
½ c. Worcestershire sauce
½ c. catsup
½ c. chili sauce
Juice of ½ lemon
Cayenne pepper (opt.)

Combine all ingredients; simmer for 1 hour to blend seasonings. Add cayenne pepper for hot sauce. Sauce may be made in advance and refrigerated.

Mrs. Olai Egeland
Ibbestad LCW
Vauxhall, Alberta, Canada

THREE-MINUTE BARBECUE SAUCE

2 cans tomato sauce
1 envelope old-fashioned French salad
    dressing mix
1 tsp. mustard
2 tbsp. vinegar
2 tbsp. salad oil
1 tbsp. sugar

Combine all ingredients in small saucepan. Simmer gently for 3 minutes, stirring occasionally. Serve with barbecue steaks, chicken or meat balls. Yield: 2 cups.

Mrs. Sue White, Pres.
St. Paul's LCW
Aberdeen, Maryland

UNCLE BEN'S BARBECUE SAUCE

1 ½ bottles catsup
½ to ¾ lb. margarine
Juice of 4 lemons
½ sm. can tomato juice
½ onion, grated
2 tsp. chili powder
2 tsp. paprika
2 tbsp. prepared mustard
3 lge. cloves of garlic, crushed
1 tsp. pepper

Combine all ingredients; heat only until margarine is melted. Yield: 4-5 cups.

Mrs. August Gruetzner, VP
Grace LWML
Elgin, Texas

CHERRY-MUSTARD SAUCE FOR HAM

1 13 ½-oz. can pineapple chunks
2 tbsp. sugar
3 tbsp. cornstarch
¼ tsp. salt
3 tbsp. mustard
12 Maraschino cherries, sliced

Drain and reserve juice from pineapple; add enough water to juice to make 1 cup. Combine sugar, cornstarch and salt in pan. Stir in liquid. Cook until thick and clear. Add mustard, pineapple and cherries. Serve hot.

Mrs. Robert Cordes
St. Johns Ladies Aid
Elk River, Minnesota

CHERRY SAUCE FOR HAM

2 c. cherries
¾ c. sugar
Pinch of salt
1 tbsp. cornstarch
1 tsp. almond flavoring
½ tsp. vanilla flavoring (opt.)

Drain cherries; reserve juice. Combine cherry juice, sugar and salt; bring to a slow boil. Mix cornstarch with water; add slowly to juice, stirring until thickened. Add cherries and flavorings. Serve over ham.

Mrs. Wilma Hellmuth
Hope Mary and Martha Guild
Bethel Park, Pennsylvania

CROQUETTE SAUCE

3 tbsp. butter
5 tbsp. sifted flour
1 c. milk
¼ tsp. onion juice
¼ tsp. celery salt
¼ tsp. salt
⅛ tsp. pepper
¼ tsp. lemon juice
½ tsp. Worcestershire sauce

Melt butter; add flour and thoroughly mix. Add remaining ingredients; cook until very thick, stirring slowly. Makes sufficent sauce to thicken 2 1/2 cups any meat or fish for croquettes.

Mrs. K. H. B. Carman, Pres.
St. Peter Evangelical LCW
Baldwin, Long Island, New York

HORSERADISH SAUCE FOR BAKED HAM

3 tbsp. mayonnaise
2 tbsp. horseradish
¾ tsp. dry mustard
1 tbsp. vinegar
½ c. heavy cream, whipped

Fold mayonnaise, horseradish, dry mustard and vinegar into cream. Serve with ham.

Mrs. Tony Conrad, Sec.
St. John's Mission Guild
Racine, Wisconsin

CURRY SAUCE

½ c. mayonnaise
2 tbsp. milk
1 tbsp. curry powder
¼ tsp. Tabasco sauce

Combine all ingredeints; refrigerate until ready to serve. Yield: 1/2 cup.

Photograph for this recipe on page 283.

MARINADE FOR ROLLED BEEF ROAST

¾ c. finely chopped onion
½ c. salad oil
¾ c. catsup
¾ c. water
⅓ c. lemon juice
3 tbsp. sugar
3 tbsp. Worcestershire sauce
2 tbsp. mustard
2 tsp. salt
½ tsp. pepper
2 bay leaves (opt.)

Cook onion in salad oil until tender. Add remaining ingredients; simmer for 15 minutes. Use as marinade and basting sauce for rolled, boned roast.

Mrs. Harrison Kaar, Pres.
Prince of Peace Lutheran Church
Geneva, Nebraska

MUSHROOM SAUCE FOR STEAK

1 pt. mushrooms
3 tbsp. butter
1 tbsp. flour
1 tsp. soy sauce
¾ c. light cream
Salt and pepper to taste

Slice mushrooms through cap and stem. Melt butter in skillet; add mushrooms. Sprinkle flour over mushrooms; toss to coat. Cook over medium heat for 8 to 10 minutes or until tender and lightly brown, stirring occasionally. Add soy sauce; slowly stir in cream. Cook and stir until mixture bubbles and thickens. Season with salt and pepper. Serve with broiled steak or spoon over toast points. Yield: 4 servings.

Arlene Krueger
Holy Cross Evening Guild
St. Cloud, Minnesota

MUSTARD SAUCE

¼ c. prepared mustard
¼ c. mayonnaise
1 clove of garlic, crushed
¼ tsp. Tabasco sauce

Combine all ingredients. Refrigerate until ready to serve. Yield: 1/2 cup.

Photograph for this recipe on page 283.

MUSTARD SAUCE

½ c. tomato soup
½ c. mustard
½ c. vinegar
½ c. sugar
½ c. butter
3 eggs, beaten

Combine all ingredients; cook in double boiler. Serve hot with ham.

Mrs. Clyde Bohn, Pres.
Trinity LWML
Hankinson, North Dakota

ONION-HORSERADISH SAUCE

¼ c. chopped onion
1 tbsp. horseradish
1 tbsp. water
¼ tsp. Tabasco sauce

Combine all ingredients. Yield: 1/2 cup.

Photograph for this recipe on page 283.

SAUCE FOR ROAST DUCK

½ c. red currant jelly
¼ c. California Port wine
¼ c. catsup
½ tsp. Worcestershire sauce
2 tbsp. butter or margarine

Combine all ingredients in small saucepan. Melt over low heat. Serve warm with duck. Yield: 1 cup.

Mrs. Nick Lovdjieff, Pres.
Grace LCW
Prospect Heights, Illinois

SEAFOOD COCKTAIL SAUCE

2 tbsp. prepared horseradish
¾ c. catsup
3 tbsp. chili sauce
2 tbsp. lemon juice
Salt to taste
Dash of Tabasco sauce

Combine all ingredients; serve in separate bowl or pour over individual cocktails. Yield: 1 cup.

Photograph for this recipe on page 283.

SHRIMP SAUCE

½ c. salad oil
½ c. white vinegar
4 tbsp. horseradish mustard
6 drops of anise flavoring
1 tbsp. paprika
¼ tsp. cayenne pepper
1 tsp. salt
¼ c. finely chopped parsley
¼ c. finely grated pimento
½ c. pureed celery
½ c. pureed onion
1 clove of garlic or ½ tsp. powdered garlic
5 tbsp. tomato puree

Mix all ingredients except, celery, onion, garlic and puree. Add remaining ingredients. Store sauce in glass jar in refrigerator. Serve with any kind of fish.

Mrs. H. A. Daniel
Christ Lutheran Church LCW
Waterford, Michigan

TOMATO-MUSHROOM SAUCE

⅔ c. catsup
2 tbsp. chopped cooked or canned mushrooms
¼ tsp. Tabasco sauce

Combine all ingredients. Refrigerate until ready to serve. Yield: 1/2 cup.

Photograph for this recipe on page 283.

TOMATO SOUP SAUCE

1 15-oz. can tomato soup
½ soup can water
2 tbsp. (heaping) brown sugar
⅛ tsp. turmeric
Pinch of cayenne pepper
2 tbsp. hot pepper sauce

Combine ingredients in saucepan. Cook over medium heat, stirring constantly, until mixture is well blended and smooth. Yield: 4-6 servings.

Mrs. A. Kundert, Pres.
Bethlehem LCW
Hilda, Alberta, Canada

TOPPING FOR BAKED HAM

1 c. apple jelly
¾ tsp. dry mustard
¼ tsp. cloves
¼ tsp. cinnamon
2 tbsp. vinegar

Combine all ingredients; heat until jelly is melted. Pour over baked ham last 30 minutes of baking time; continue baking. Serve with hot or cold ham.

Mrs. Mildred Clausen, Pres.
Zion LCW
Waterbury, Connecticut

Salad Favorites

RECIPE FOR ONE-TWO-THREE LENTEN SALAD ON PAGE 299

CAPRI BEEF SALAD

2 lb. round steak, cut in strips
1 8-oz. bottle Italian dressing
2 c. sliced carrots, cooked
2 c. lima beans, drained
1 c. chopped green peppers
½ c. pimento strips
1 c. red onion rings
1 head lettuce, cut in 2-in. chunks

Brown meat in small amount of Italian dressing.
Combine meat with carrots, lima beans, green
peppers, pimento strips, onion rings and remaining dressing. Chill. Add lettuce; toss lightly.
Yield: 6 servings.

Mrs. Duane Jacobson, Pres.
Elim LCW
Alvarado, Minnesota

HERRING SALAD

2 fillets of herring, cubed
1 ½ c. cubed boiled carrots
2 pickled cucumbers, cubed
2 hard-cooked eggs
2 c. boiled, cubed beet root
1 c. boiled, cubed potatoes
2 apples, cubed

Mix all ingredients except 1 egg; toss lightly.
Mash the reserved egg yolk and white separately
with a fork; arrange in strips across the top of
the salad. Prepare a sharp sauce with fresh or
sour whipped cream; season with mustard,
vinegar and sugar. Color the sauce red or pink
with boiled beet root juice.

Mrs. Nick M. Jarvi, Treas.
Zion Ladies Aid
Amasa, Michigan

"RASSOLJE"

DRESSING:

1 ½ c. sour cream
Mustard
Vinegar
Sugar
Salt and pepper to taste

Combine all ingredients.

SALAD:

2 or 3 pickled beets, diced
1 herring, diced
5 or 6 cooked potatoes, diced
2 pickled cucumbers, diced
1 med. apple, diced
1 or 2 hard-cooked eggs, diced
¾ lb. cold roast, diced
½ raw carrot, diced
½ onion, diced

Mix all ingredients; add dressing, mixing lightly.
Garnish with finely diced egg yolks, egg whites
and cooked beets. Yield: 6 servings.

Mrs. Elli Kalvik, Pres.
St. Peters Ladies Group
Toronto, Ontario, Canada

SILLISALAATI--HERRING SALAD

1 med. salt herring
1 c. diced cooked beets
1 c. diced cooked carrots
1 c. diced cooked potatoes
1 sm. onion, diced

Freshen the herring in cold water. Remove skin
and large bones; dice. Toss all ingredients lightly; chill for several hours. NOTE: No dressing
is used, but freshly ground pepper and vinegar
may be added to taste. Yield: 4 servings.

Mrs. Jenny Salonen
St. John's LCW
Clayridge, Saskatchewan, Canada

FISH SALAD

1 3-oz. pkg. lemon gelatin
½ c. boiling water
½ tsp. salt
2 tsp. vinegar
1 1-lb. can salmon or 2 7-oz. cans
   tuna
¾ c. chopped celery
½ tsp. grated onion
3 hard-cooked eggs
½ c. mayonnaise
1 sm. can pimento or 1 tbsp.
   chopped red pepper

Mix gelatin, water, salt and vinegar; cool until
slightly thickened. Add remaining ingredients;
pour into fish mold or other 1 1/2-quart mold.
Chill, preferably overnight. NOTE: Two cups
chopped cooked chicken may be substituted for
fish. Yield: 10-12 servings.

Mrs. Herman A. Wietbrock, Pres.
Trinity Ladies Aid Soc.
Lowell, Indiana

JELLIED SALMON LOAF

1 envelope unflavored gelatin
¼ c. cold water
¾ c. boiling water
¼ c. lemon juice
1 tbsp. vinegar
2 tbsp. sugar
½ tsp. salt
1 c. salad dressing
1 1-lb. can salmon or tuna
1 c. chopped celery
1 hard-cooked egg, sliced
10 stuffed olives

(Continued on next page)

Soak gelatin in cold water for 3 minutes. Add boiling water; stir until dissolved. Add lemon juice, vinegar, sugar and salt. Cool; stir in salad dressing. Mix thoroughly. Remove bones from salmon; flake. Add salmon to gelatin mixture. Add celery. Place slices of egg and olives in bottom of loaf pan or mold. Pour salmon mixture into mold. Chill overnight. Unmold; garnish with lettuce. Yield: 6 servings.

Mrs. Hans Egede
St. Johns LCW
Hampton, Iowa

RED SALMON SALAD

1 1-lb. lean red salmon, flaked
  and boned
5 hard-cooked eggs, finely chopped
1 ½ c. crushed soda crackers
1 c. mayonnaise or salad dressing
¼ to ½ c. Henri's Tastee dressing

Combine all ingredients; stir lightly. Serve immediately or refrigerate. Yield: 6-8 servings.

Mrs. O. F. Huster
Salem Ladies Guild
Affton, Missouri

SALMON MOUSSE

2 pkg. unflavored gelatin
½ c. cold water
2 c. red salmon
Dash of paprika
Dash of pepper
2 tbsp. vinegar
2 tbsp. catsup
1 c. mayonnaise
2 hard-cooked eggs, chopped
20 slices stuffed olives
2 tbsp. sweet pickle relish
1 c. heavy cream, whipped

Soften gelatin in cold water; place pan over hot water, stirring until gelatin is dissolved. Remove skin and bones from salmon; flake into small pieces. Combine salmon, seasonings, vinegar, catsup and mayonnaise. Blend in eggs, olives, relish and dissolved gelatin. Chill until partially set; fold in whipped cream. Pour into a 1-quart fish milk which has been well oiled. Chill overnight. Unmold onto lettuce greens; garnish with tomato slices and green pepper. Yield: 8 servings.

Mabel M. Schibonski, Pres.
Mt. Olive Ladies Guild
Denver, Colorado

SALMON-BANANA SALAD

3 ripe bananas
½ c. diced canned pineapple
1 ½ c. canned salmon, flaked
¼ c. diced celery
½ tsp. salt
1 tbsp. chopped sweet pickle
Mayonnaise

Mix bananas and pineapple; add salmon. Fold in remaining ingredients, adding enough mayonnaise to moisten. Serve on lettuce leaves. Yield: 4-6 servings.

Mrs. Philip List, Pres.
Immanuel Ladies Aid of Frankentrost
Saginaw, Michigan

SALMON AND RICE LOAF

½ envelope unflavored gelatin
¼ c. cold water
¾ c. milk, heated
1 tsp. salt
½ tsp. pepper
1 can salmon
1 c. cooked rice
1 tbsp. melted butter

Soak gelatin in cold water for 10 minutes; dissolve by adding hot milk. Add remaining ingredients. Pour into a wet mold; chill until set. Serve cold on lettuce as a salad, or with a hot tomato sauce in place of meat at dinner.

Mrs. Minnie Allen, Pres.
St. Paul's Mission Soc.
Colon, Michigan

SALMON SALAD

2 c. salmon, flaked
½ c. diced celery
2 tbsp. diced sweet pickle
2 c. corn flakes
¾ c. mayonnaise
2 tbsp. lemon juice

Combine salmon, celery, pickle and corn flakes. Blend mayonnaise and lemon juice; mix with salmon mixture. Serve immediately. Yield: 6 servings.

Mrs. Paul Kruse, Pres.
St. John LCW
Sunman, Indiana

SALMON SALAD LOAF

1 pkg. lemon gelatin
3 tbsp. vinegar
½ c. mayonnaise or salad dressing
¼ tsp. salt
1 1-lb. can salmon, drained and
  coarsely flaked
1 c. chopped celery
¼ c. chopped parsley
¼ c. chopped onion

Dissolve gelatin in 1 cup hot water. Add 1/2 cup cold water, vinegar, mayonnaise and salt. Beat well. Chill until partially set; beat until fluffy; fold in remaining ingredients. Pour into 8 1/2 x 4 1/2 x 2 1/2-inch loaf pan. Chill until set. Unmold onto crisp greens. Yield: 6 servings.

Mrs. Annette Lons, VP
Hope Ladies Guild
Arcade, New York

SEASHORE SALAD

1 tbsp. salt
3 qt. boiling water
4 oz. shell macaroni
¾ c. flaked salmon
½ c. diced celery
½ c. diced sweet pickles
½ c. salad dressing

Add salt to boiling water. Gradually add macaroni and cook until tender, about 10 minutes. Drain and rinse in cold water. Toss macaroni with salmon, celery, pickles and salad dressing. Chill before serving. Yield: 4 servings.

Mrs. Raymond Bowser
Zion Ladies Aid Soc.
Accident, Maryland

SUMMER SALMON SALAD

1 8-oz. can red salmon, drained
2 ½ c. cooked macaroni, chilled
1 c. diced celery
1 c. frozen peas, cooked
1 c. diced cooked carrots (opt.)
½ c. mayonnaise
½ tsp. cream
½ tsp. vinegar
¼ tsp. sugar

Divide salmon into small chunks; mix with macaroni, celery, chilled peas and chilled carrots. Combine mayonnaise with cream, vinegar and sugar. Add to salad; chill thoroughly. When ready to serve, lightly pile into 5 or 6 lettuce cups and arrange garnishes around it. Yield: 5-6 servings.

Mrs. Richard G. Peterson
Peace LCW
Wainwright, Alberta, Canada

CRUNCHY TUNA SALAD

1 6 ½ to 7-oz. can tuna, flaked
½ c. finely chopped onion
3 tbsp. finely chopped green pepper
3 tbsp. chopped ripe olives
2 tbsp. chopped pimento
½ c. mayonnaise
1 tsp. garlic vinegar
1 tbsp. light cream
1 3-oz. can crisp Chinese noodles

Combine tuna, onion, green pepper, olives and pimento. Blend mayonnaise, vinegar and cream until smooth; pour over tuna mixture and mix well. Chill. When ready to serve, add noodles and mix lightly. Serve on salad greens. Yield: 6 servings.

Mrs. Donald Lindner, Pres.
St. Stephen's Lutheran Church
Seattle, Washington
Mrs. Phil Wood
Faith LWML
Kinston, North Carolina

FIFTY STATE SALAD

¼ c. milk
½ c. mayonnaise or salad dressing
1 c. diced celery
1 c. grated carrots
¼ c. finely cut onion
1 6 ½-oz. can tuna, drained
1 c. or ½ box frozen peas, thawed (opt.)
1 c. or sm. can shoestring potatoes

Mix the milk with the dressing; add all ingredients except potatoes. Chill; add potatoes just before serving. Serve on lettuce leaves. Yield: 6 servings.

Mrs. Eva Hoerber
Redeemer Ladies Aux.
West Palm Beach, Florida

FRUITEO TUNA SALAD

1 6 ½ or 7-oz. can tuna, flaked
1 c. halved seedless grapes
½ c. chopped celery
⅓ to ½ c. mayonnaise
2 tbsp. undrained sweet pickle
  relish
Salt to taste

Combine tuna, grapes and celery. Blend mayonnaise with pickle relish; add to tuna mixture. Add salt and blend. Chill; serve in crisp lettuce cups or on a bed of salad greens. Yield: 4 servings.

Mrs. Alfred Scheiwe, Past Pres.
Trinity Ladies Aid
Goodland, Indiana

MACARONI SALAD

2 c. uncooked shell macaroni
1 c. Tokay grapes, halved and seeded
1 c. diced celery
1 sm. onion, finely chopped
1 6 ½-oz. can chunk tuna
½ c. mayonnaise
3 tbsp. sugar

Cook macaroni in salted water until tender; rinse and cool. Add grapes, celery, onion and tuna to macaroni. Mix mayonnaise and sugar; pour over macaroni. Mix well. NOTE: Drained fruit cocktail may be substituted for grapes. Yield: 10-12 servings.

Mrs. James Varvel, Pres.
Zion Ladies Aid
Hay Springs, Nebraska

MOLDED TUNA SALAD

1 pkg. lime gelatin
2 c. hot water
1 can tuna, flaked
1 tsp. lemon juice
½ tsp. salt
¼ tsp. paprika
1 c. chopped celery
2 hard-cooked eggs, chopped
1 green pepper, diced
1 sm. onion, diced
1 cucumber, chopped
1 sprig parsley

Dissolve gelatin in hot water. Chill until slightly thickened. Combine tuna, lemon juice, salt and paprika. Add tuna mixture, celery, eggs, green pepper, onion and cucumber to gelatin. Pour into a mold; chill until firm. Garnish with parsley. Yield: 8 servings.

Mrs. Walter King, Sec.
Bethlehem LWML
Upham, North Dakota

TOASTED TUNA-CURRY-MACARONI SALAD

1 8-oz. pkg. elbow macaroni
3 qt. boiling water
Salt and pepper to taste
2 6 ½-oz. cans tuna, flaked
1 c. cooked peas
½ c. sliced ripe olives
½ c. toasted almonds
½ c. chopped celery
½ c. coconut, toasted
1 c. mayonnaise
1 ½ tsp. curry powder

Cook macaroni in boiling water with 1 tablespoonful salt until tender. Drain; rinse with cold water. Drain and chill. Combine tuna, macaroni and remaining ingredients. Mix lightly, but thoroughly. Chill well. Yield: 6-8 servings.

Mrs. Francis Plapp
Good Shepherd LCW
Sanford, Florida

TUNA-ASPIC MOLD

1 envelope unflavored gelatin
2 ¼ c. cold water
1 tsp. prepared mustard
1 7-oz. can tuna
1 c. chopped celery
2 tbsp. lemon juice
¼ tsp. salt
¼ tsp. Paprika
½ c. salad dressing

Soften gelatin in 1/4 cup cold water. Add remaining water and all ingredients. Chill until set.

TOMATO ASPIC:

1 pkg. lemon gelatin
2 c. tomato juice, heated
Cloves
Onion
Salt to taste
Celery salt

Dissolve gelatin in tomato juice; add remaining ingredients. Cool; pour over tuna salad. Chill until firm.

Mrs. Helen E. Buss
Good Shepherd LWML
Winnepeg, Alberta, Canada

TUNA-MACARONI-PEA SALAD

1 7-oz. can tuna
3 to 4 c. cooked shell macaroni
1 No. 2 can peas, drained
5 hard-cooked eggs
½ c. celery
1 med. onion, chopped
Salt to taste
Mayonnaise

Combine all ingredients; add enough mayonnaise to bind. May be served hot or cold. Yield: 6 servings.

Mrs. Donald Peck, Pres.
St. John Flatrock Ladies Aid
Monroeville, Indiana

TUNA MOLD

2 envelopes unflavored gelatin
½ c. cold water
1 can tomato soup
2 3-oz. pkg. cream cheese
1 c. mayonnaise
2 tbsp. A-1 sauce
1 c. finely chopped celery
2 tbsp. finely chopped onion
¼ tsp. salt
Dash of pepper
2 6 ½-oz. cans chunk-style tuna, drained

(Continued on next page)

Dissolve gelatin in cold water. Heat soup in double boiler. Add cheese; stir until smooth, using rotary egg beater. Add mayonnaise, gelatin and A-1 Sauce. Blend mixture thoroughly; cool. Add remaining ingredients. Mix well. Pour into mold; chill until very firm. Serve with dressing made by mixing 3 tablespoonfuls A-1 sauce with 1 cup mayonnaise. Yield: 6-8 servings.

Mrs. Frances Loser
St. Luke Ladies Guild
Mt. Clemens, Michigan

TUNA-POTATO SALAD

½ lb. carrots, grated
2 cans tuna
1 sm. onion, chopped
3 stalks celery, chopped
2 hard-cooked eggs, chopped
Salad dressing
½ pkg. shoestring potatoes

Combine carrots, tuna, onion, celery and eggs with enough salad dressing to moisten. Stir in potatoes just before serving. Yield: 6 servings.

Mrs. Alfred Studahski, Pres.
St. John's Popple Creek Ladies Group
Sauk Rapids, Minnesota

TUNA SALAD

1 7-oz. can tuna, drained and flaked
3 tbsp. sweet pickle relish
1 tbsp. minced onion
½ c. mayonnaise
1 tbsp. lemon juice
1 ½ c. shredded cabbage
½ c. coarsely chopped salted peanuts

Combine tuna, pickle relish, onion, mayonnaise and lemon juice. Cover and chill well. Add cabbage and peanuts; toss lightly. Spoon into lettuce cups; garnish with tomato wedges and deviled eggs. Yield: 4-6 servings.

Mrs. Cameron Varey, Pres.
Mount Olive LWML
London, Ontario, Canada

TUNA SALAD

7-oz. shell creamettes
2 tsp. salt
1 can tuna
4 hard-cooked eggs
1 pt. cooked green peas
4 green onions, chopped
1 sm. head of lettuce, cut into small chunks
1 c. chopped celery
1 c. salad dressing

Cook creamettes in boiling salted water. Mix with remaining ingredients. Yield: 10-12 servings.

Mrs. William Petz, Pres.
St. John's Ladies Aid
Shell Lake, Wisconsin

TUNA SALAD MOLD

1 3-oz. pkg. lemon gelatin
½ c. boiling water
1 6½-oz. can chunk tuna
1 can chicken gumbo soup
2 tbsp. chopped green pepper and celery
1 tbsp. chopped onion

Dissolve gelatin in boiling water. Fold in remaining ingredients. Pour into greased mold; chill until firm. Yield: 6-8 servings.

Mrs. Elmer Zurcher
Bethlehem LWML
Upham, North Dakota

CRAB-GELATIN SALAD

1 pkg. lemon gelatin
¾ c. boiling water
1 can tomato soup
2 tbsp. lemon juice
2 pkg. cream cheese
⅔ c. mayonnaise
1 c. finely cut celery
¼ c. grated onion
¼ c. chopped green pepper
½ c. crab meat

Dissolve gelatin in boiling water; add tomato soup, lemon juice, cream cheese and mayonnaise. Blend well. Add remaining ingredients. Chill until firm. Yield: 9 servings.

Mrs. Edgar Marburger
St. John's Dorcas Guild
Lawton, Oklahoma

CRAB LOUIE

1 c. shredded lettuce
¼ c. shredded crab meat
1 tomato, cut into eighths
¼ c. chopped celery
¼ tsp. salt
2 tbsp. salad dressing
2 tbsp. thin cream
1 tsp. sugar
1 hard-cooked egg, quartered

Arrange shredded lettuce on dinner plate or small platter. Distribute crab meat, tomatoes and celery over lettuce. Sprinkle with salt. Mix salad dressing, cream and sugar; drizzle over crab. Garnish with egg. Yield: 1 serving.

Mrs. Howard Peters
Trinity Ladies Soc.
Lancaster, Ohio

CRAB MEAT SALAD

1 3-oz. pkg. lemon gelatin
1 ½ c. boiling water
3 tbsp. white vinegar
½ tsp. salt
½ tsp. onion juice
2 c. crab meat
¾ c. finely cut celery
1 tbsp. pimento

Dissolve gelatin in boiling water. Add vinegar, salt and onion juice; cool until thickened. Add crab meat, celery and pimento. Pour into 6 individual salad molds; chill until firm. Unmold onto lettuce. Yield: 6 servings.

Mrs. Irvin C. Eckert, Sr.
Trinity Laymen's League
Racine, Wisconsin

CRAB-POTATO SALAD

1 7 ½-oz. can crab meat, cleaned and
    flaked
6 potatoes, boiled and diced
3 med. dill pickles, diced
4 stalks celery, finely chopped
4 hard-cooked eggs, diced
2 tbsp. mayonnaise
1 tbsp. milk
1 tsp. vinegar

Combine crab meat, potatoes, pickles, celery and eggs. Add mayonnaise, milk and vinegar; toss. Refrigerate until ready to serve. NOTE: Frozen crab meat may be substituted for canned crab meat. Yield: 6 servings.

Ruth E. Korn, Pres.
St. John's Ladies Aid Soc.
North Merrick, New York

CRAB SALAD MOLD

1 pkg. unflavored gelatin
½ c. cold water
½ c. boiling water
1 c. mayonnaise
1 c. chili sauce
1 c. crab
4 hard-cooked eggs
2 tbsp. Worcestershire sauce
¼ c. chopped olives
1 can pimento

Soak gelatin in cold water; add boiling water. Add remaining ingredients; pour into mold. Chill. Yield: 6 servings.

Mrs. Kathryn Smette, Pres.
Bloomfield LCW
Upham, North Dakota

CRAB SALAD CASSEROLE

4 egg whites
1 c. mayonnaise
Salt and pepper to taste
2 cans crab meat
Bread crumbs
Paprika

Beat egg whites until stiff; fold in mayonnaise, salt and pepper. Fold in crab meat. Pour into casserole. Put bread crumbs and paprika on top. Bake at 350 degrees for 15 minutes. Yield: 5-6 servings.

Mrs. Robert Martin, Pres.
Epiphany LCW
Pleasantville, New Jersey

CRAB, TUNA OR SHRIMP SALAD

2 c. flaked crab meat, tuna or cleaned
    shrimp
½ c. diced cucumber
1 c. chopped celery
3 hard-cooked eggs, quartered
¼ tsp. salt
⅛ tsp. pepper
Juice of 1 lemon
2 tbsp. mayonnaise

Combine all ingredients; toss lightly. Chill; serve on crisp lettuce. NOTE: For tuna salad, add 4 sweet pickles, chopped. Yield: 6 servings.

Mrs. Herbert Buettner
St. Matthew Church
White Lake, Wisconsin

ONE-TWO-THREE LENTEN SALAD

1 7 ½-oz. can crab, flaked
1 c. diced celery
1 ½ c. diced Florida grapefruit
¼ c. French dressing
Salad greens

Combine crab, celery and grapefruit with French dressing; toss gently. Refrigerate for 2 to 3 hours. Drain and arrange on salad greens, topping with additional grapefruit sections, if desired. Serve with mayonnaise. Yield: 3 servings.

Photograph for this recipe on page 293.

LOBSTER SALAD

1 sm. can lobster
1 tomato, cut into small pieces
1 hard-cooked egg, chopped
Chopped lettuce
Salad dressing

(Continued on next page)

Mix lobster with tomato, egg, lettuce and enough salad dressing to moisten. Serve on buttered toast.

Mrs. Theodore Saar
Grace LWML
Pembroke, Ontario, Canada

LOBSTER-ORANGE SALAD PUFFS

2 c. cubed cooked lobster
2 c. diced orange sections
¼ c. minced green onions
2 tbsp. minced parsley
1 c. sour cream
¼ c. mayonnaise
1 ½ tsp. salt
1 tsp. hot pepper sauce

Combine lobster, orange sections, onion and parsley. Combine sour cream, mayonnaise, salt and pepper sauce, blending well. Add to lobster mixture; blend well. Chill until r e a d y to fill shells.

PUFF SHELLS:

1 c. water
½ c. butter or margarine
1 c. sifted flour
Dash of salt
4 eggs
1 envelope unflavored gelatin
¾ c. cold milk
1 can condensed tomato soup
3 3-oz. pkg. cream cheese
½ c. minced celery
1 ½ c. diced boiled
½ c. mayonnaise

Bring water and butter to a boil in a heavy saucepan, stirring until butter melts. Add flour and salt all at once. Reduce heat. Cook and stir until mixture is smooth and forms a soft ball, 1 to 2 minutes. Remove from heat and cool mixture slightly. Add an egg at a time, beating well after each addition. Drop batter by rounded tablespoonfuls in 8 mounds onto lightly greased baking sheet. Bake at 400 degrees for 40 to 45 minutes or until firm to the touch. Cool; cut off tops of shells and scoop out insides. Fill with chilled lobster mixture. Refrigerate until ready to serve. Yield: 8 servings.

Mrs. Lloyd Sorenson, Pres.
Mt. Olive Women's Guild
Torrance, California

TOMATO-ROCK LOBSTER MOLD

1 envelope unflavored gelatin
¾ c. cold milk
1 can condensed tomato soup
3 3-oz. pkg. cream cheese
½ c. minced celery
1 ½ c. diced boiled South African Rock
   Lobster Tail meat
½ c. mayonnaise

Soften gelatin in cold milk. Combine undiluted tomato soup and cream cheese in top of double boiler. Stir over boiling water until smooth and hot. Add softened gelatin; stir until thoroughly dissolved. Chill until thickened. Fold in celery, lobster and mayonnaise. Pour into 1-quart ring mold. Chill until firm. Unmold onto plate. Garnish with salad greens. Stuffed ripe olives may also be used for decoration, if desired. Yield: 8-10 servings.

Mrs. Lillian Pavlichek, Past Pres.
St. Paul's Ladies Guild
West Allis, Wisconsin

CELERY ROOT-SHRIMP SALAD

2 lge. celery roots
Bleu cheese dressing
1 green onion, chopped
1 tsp. Tabasco sauce
1 lb. cleaned shrimp
2 tbsp. mayonnaise
Parsley

Boil celery root in the skin until soft; peel and mash. Mix with Bleu cheese dressing. Add onion, Tabasco sauce and a few broken shrimp. Fill sherbet glasses half full with mixture. Put remaining shrimp on top. Garnish with mayonnaise and parsley. Yield: 8 servings.

Elouise Schmidt, Treas.
Shepherd of the Daughters of the Hills
Tiburon, California

MOLDED SHRIMP SALAD

SALAD:

2 pkg. lemon gelatin
2 c. boiling water
1 pt. heavy cream, whipped
1 3-oz. pkg. cream cheese
1 c. chopped celery
1 c. green or stuffed olives, chopped

Dissolve gelatin in boiling water. Cool until mixture starts to jell. Fold in whipped cream; mix well. Soften cheese; fold into gelatin with celery and olives. Pour into 8 x 10-inch pan; refrigerate until ready to serve. Unmold onto lettuce leaf.

TOPPING:

⅔ c. mayonnaise
2 tbsp. heavy cream
1 can shrimp, cleaned and drained
½ c. chopped pimento
1 tsp. lemon juice
1 tsp. minced onion

(Continued on next page)

Combine all ingredients. Spoon over salad. Yield: 10 servings.

Mrs. William Kundy, Jr.
Grace Church
Three Forks, Montana

PINEAPPLE-SHRIMP SALAD

1 lge. can pineapple
2 lb. cleaned shrimp
1 onion, diced
2 lemons, quartered and squeezed
1 tsp. liquid garlic
1 bag Crab Boil or other seafood
  seasoning
1 c. mayonnaise
1 c. diced celery
½ c. chopped walnuts
½ c. sliced ripe olives

Drain pineapple, reserving liquid. Boil shrimp in large pan with onion, lemons, liquid garlic and Crab boil for 20 to 25 minutes. Drain. Thin mayonnaise with pineapple juice. Combine shrimp, pineapple, celery, walnuts and olives with mayonnaise; chill for 1 hour. Serve on crisp lettuce. Yield: 5-6 servings.

Lois Jamsen
St. Michaels LWML
Fort Myers, Florida

SHRIMP MOLD

1 can tomato soup
1 or 2 envelope unflavored gelatin
½ c. cold water
3 3-oz. or 1 8-oz. pkg. cream cheese
½ to 1 c. finely chopped celery
½ c. chopped or ground green pepper
¼ or ½ c. minced onion
1 c. mayonnaise
1 or 2 cans shrimp, halved

Heat soup. Soak gelatin in cold water for 5 minutes. Mix with hot soup. Blend in cream cheese. Cool until thickened; stir in remaining ingredients. Pour into mold. Chill for 4 hours or overnight. Serve with a dressing made with mayonnaise and whipped cream. Yield: 10 servings.

Mrs. Berta Klatte
St. Thomas LCW
Bronx, New York
Mrs. Georgia Perrine, Pres.
Messiah LCW
Bremerton, Washington

QUICK SHRIMP SALAD

1 sm. head lettuce, shredded
2 sm. tomatoes, chopped
1 green pepper, chopped (opt.)
2 sticks celery, chopped
1 sm. onion
1 sm. can shrimp

Combine all ingredients; toss lightly. Serve with favorite salad dressing. Yield: 8 servings.

Mrs. Robert Kern, Pres.
St. John's LWML
St. Xavier, Montana

SHRIMP SALAD

1 pkg. lemon gelatin
1 c. boiling water
1 can tomato soup
3 3-oz. pkg. cream cheese
1 c. mayonnaise
1 c. diced celery
1 green pepper, chopped
1 can shrimp, cut up
1 No. 2 can peas, drained
1 onion, minced

Dissolve gelatin in boiling water; cool slightly. Heat soup until it simmers. Beat cream cheese into soup; cool and add mayonnaise. Add to gelatin mixture. Stir in remaining ingredients. Chill until firm.

Vi Schultz
St. Peter's Mary-Martha Guild
San Leandro, California

SHRIMP SALAD

DRESSING:

½ c. mayonnaise
⅛ tsp. prepared mustard
1 tbsp. vinegar
1 tbsp. Worcestershire sauce
Dash of Tabasco
Dash of Paprika
Salt and pepper

Combine all ingredients; mix well.

SALAD:

1 ½ c. shrimp
1 c. pineapple chunks
¼ c. chopped stuffed olives
1 tbsp. lemon juice
½ c. walnuts
1 c. chopped celery
2 tsp. chopped onion

(Continued on next page)

Combine all ingredients. Mix with dressing; chill. Serve on salad plates with shredded lettuce. Garnish with banana halves rolled in chopped nuts, ripe olives and parsley. Yield: 8 servings.

Mrs. Dorothy Henkelman
Redeemer Ladies Aid Soc.
Didsbury, Alberta, Canada

SHRIMP SALAD

2 lb. deveined and cleaned shrimp, chopped
6 hard-cooked eggs, chopped
1 c. finely chopped celery
1 sm. onion, finely chopped
Dash of garlic powder
½ c. salad dressing

Combine all ingredients; mix lightly. Serve on lettuce leaf.

Mrs. E. C. Kuhlman, Recipe Chmn.
St. John's Lutheran Church
Lake Charles, Louisiana

SHRIMP SALAD

4 c. uncooked shell macaroni
½ c. French dressing
½ c. chili sauce
1 c. chopped onions
1 tsp. salt
¼ tsp. pepper
2 pkg. frozen shrimp, deveined
1 c. sliced olives
1 c. mayonnaise
Hard-cooked eggs, diced (opt.)
Celery, diced (opt.)
Green pepper, diced (opt.)

Cook and drain macaroni; mix in French dressing and chili sauce. Let set for 1 hour. Add remaining ingredients; chill until ready to serve. Yield: 12 servings.

Mrs. Luella M. Weiss
Messiah Ladies Guild
Saginaw, Michigan

SHRIMP SALAD

2 c. noodle rings
1 c. chopped celery
1 tbsp. grated onion
⅓ c. chopped green pepper
1 pimento, chopped
3 hard-cooked eggs, chopped
1 c. salad dressing
¾ tsp. salt
1 ½ c. chopped shrimp or crab meat

Cook noodle rings in boiling water for 7 minutes. Drain; rinse with cold water. Place in large bowl; add remaining ingredients. Chill for 1 hour before serving. Yield: 12 servings.

Mrs. James Rath
St. Luke's LWML
Rapid City, South Dakota

SHRIMP-MACARONI SALAD

1 ½ lb. elbow macaroni, cooked and drained
Olive oil or butter
2 lb. tiny shrimp
⅓ stalk celery, finely diced
Salt to taste
1 med. onion, finely diced
1 green pepper, finely diced
Juice of 2 lemons
⅛ bottle Tabasco sauce
1 med. bottle catsup
1 pt. salad dressing

Mix macaroni with olive oil. Combine all ingredients; mix well.

Mrs. H. L. Voelkert
Grace Dorcas Soc.
High Point, North Carolina

SHRIMP-MACARONI SALAD

1 pkg. ring macaroni
1 c. cooked and broken shrimp
1 tomato, finely cut
½ c. diced celery
⅓ cucumber, chopped
¼ c. finely sliced green onion
1 sm. green pepper, finely cut
¼ c. sliced radishes
½ c. mayonnaise
½ tsp. salt
⅛ tsp. pepper

Cook macaroni; rinse with cold water and drain. Add shrimp and vegetables. Fold in mayonnaise. Season with salt and pepper; chill. Serve on lettuce. Yield: 4-6 servings.

Mrs. Peter Johnson, Sec.
Our Savior Ladies Aid
Brownsdale, Minnesota

SHRIMP-VERMICELLI SALAD

4 oz. small vermicelli
½ green pepper, chopped
1 lge. onion, chopped
4 stalks celery, chopped
3 tbsp. sweet pickle relish
1 sm. can pimento, chopped

(Continued on next page)

2 cans medium deveined shrimp or crab
Salt and pepper
Monosodium glutamate
Mayonnaise

Boil vermicelli in salted water until tender. Drain and rinse. Add remaining ingredients, adding enough mayonnaise to hold together. Chill at least 1 hour before servings. Yield: 10-12 servings.

Mrs. Marcella H. Kennedy, Pres.
Faith Lutheran LWML
Ukiah, California

BAKED SEAFOOD SALAD

1 green pepper, chopped
1 sm. onion, chopped
1 c. finely chopped celery
1 lb. crab meat, flaked
1 c. cooked or canned shrimp
1 c. mayonnaise
½ to 1 tsp. salt
¼ to ½ tsp. pepper
¼ tsp. Worcestershire sauce (opt.)
1 c. buttered bread crumbs

Mix all ingredients except bread crumbs. Pour into casserole or individual shells. Top with buttered bread crumbs. Bake at 350 degrees for 30 to 35 minutes or until browned. Yield: 4-6 servings.

Mrs. Ellis Hanson
Our Redeemer ALCW
Watertown, South Dakota
Donna Crouse, Sec.
Zion LWML
Anchorage, Alaska

HOT SEAFOOD SALAD

3 or 4 avocados
1 can shrimp, chopped
1 can crab meat or tuna
1 cup mayonnaise
1 sm. onion or 3 green onions, chopped
¾ c. chopped celery
⅛ tsp. salt
⅛ tsp. pepper
Juice of 1 lemon
½ c. crushed potato chips

Cut unpeeled avocados into halves and remove seeds. Combine shrimp, tuna, mayonnaise, onion, celery and seasonings; mix thoroughly. Squeeze lemon juice into each avocado half; fill with seafood mixture. Top with potato chips. Bake at 375 degrees for 30 minutes. Yield: 6-8 servings.

Mrs. Elsie Sharkus
Immanuel Ruth Soc. LWML
West Covina, California

SEAFOOD SALAD

1 5-oz. can lobster
1 5-oz. can shrimp
1 6 ½-oz. can crab meat
1 c. diced celery
1 tbsp. minced onion
1 tbsp. lemon juice
1 tsp. salt
¼ tsp. pepper
¾ c. mayonnaise or salad dressing

Combine all ingredients; mix well. Chill; serve on lettuce and garnish with paprika. Yield: 4-6 servings.

Mrs. Will Harms, Pres.
Christ Lutheran Church LWML
Highland, Wisconsin

SEAFOOD SALAD

2 6 ½-oz. cans tuna, flaked
2 4 ½-oz. cans jumbo shrimp, cut up
1 c. diced celery
1 lge. onion, diced
½ c. salad dressing
1 tsp. prepared mustard
2 tbsp. vinegar
2 hard-cooked eggs, diced
Salt and pepper to taste

Mix all ingredients; chill. Yield: 6-8 servings.

Mrs. Malitta Rahn
Our Redeemer Ladies Guild
Sheboygan, Wisconsin

SEAFOOD SALAD

1 can tuna, flaked
1 can shrimp, chopped
1 can lobster, diced
1 can crab meat, flaked
½ c. diced green pepper
½ onion, chopped
1 stalk celery, diced
2 tsp. sweet pickles
1 c. mayonnaise

Combine all ingredients; mix well. Chill before serving. Yield: 4 servings.

Mrs. Loraine Wendt
Our Savior Afternoon Guild
Chicago, Illinois

SHRIMP AND CRAB SALAD

1 lge. pkg. macaroni
1 med. jar pickle relish
2 cans shrimp, deveined
2 cans crab meat

(Continued on next page)

1 jar pimento
1 c. chopped celery
Salt to taste
Paprika to taste
½ c. chopped parsley
Mayonnaise
Pickle juice

Cook macaroni; drain. Drain pickle relish, reserving juice. Mix all ingredients except mayonnaise and pickle juice. Mix mayonnaise with pickle juice; add to macaroni mixture. Yield: 6 servings.

Mrs. Gail Goodan, Sec.
Faith LCW
Lynwood, California

HAM AND MACARONI SALAD

½ lb. boiled or baked ham, cubed
½ c. diced yellow cheese
2 c. cooked elbow macaroni
1 c. chopped celery
1 sm. onion, chopped
½ c. diced dill pickles
½ c. mayonnaise
2 tsp. mustard
6 hard-cooked eggs, sliced
3 tomatoes, cut into quarters

Combine ham, cheese, macaroni, celery, onion and pickles. Mix mayonnaise and mustard, stir into macaroni mixture, mixing well. Chill until ready to serve. Heap salad on lettuce leaves. Garnish with eggs and tomatoes. Yield: 6 servings.

Mrs. Jim Kuhlman, Pres.
Redeemer LWML
Osakis, Minnesota

HOT BAKED HAM SALAD

3 c. diced cooked ham
1 c. diced celery
½ c. chopped stuffed olives
2 hard-cooked eggs, diced
2 tsp. diced onion
1 tbsp. lemon juice
2 tbsp. prepared mustard
⅛ tsp. pepper
¾ c. margarine
1 c. crushed potato chips

Combine all ingredients except potato chips; place in greased 8 x 8-inch square pan. Sprinkle with potato chips. Bake at 400 degrees for 20 minutes. Yield: 6 servings.

Mrs. Pershing Kettelson, Pres.
Immanuel ALCW
Albion, Nebraska

HAM SALAD MOUNDS

3 lb. cubed ham
¼ lb. Longhorn cheese, cubed
⅓ pkg. circle noodles, cooked
2 hard-cooked eggs, cubed
2 sticks celery, finely cut
Finely chopped onion to taste
⅓ can pimento, finely cut
1 qt. salad dressing
1 16-oz. can evaporated milk, chilled and whipped
4 tbsp. mustard
1 c. honey
Juice of 1 lemon
1 can peas, drained

Combine ham, cheese, noodles, eggs, celery, onion and pimento. Whip remaining ingredients except peas to make a dressing. Add as much dressing as needed to ham mixture. Add peas. Serve in mounds on lettuce; garnish top with a slice of olive. Yield: 30 servings.

Mrs. James Bousfield, Chmn.
First English Ladies Aid
Parker, South, Dakota

POPEYE SALAD

1 lb. spinach
1 tsp. grated onion
½ tsp. salt
2 hard-cooked eggs, chopped
4 slices bacon, diced
4 tbsp. malt vinegar
2 tsp. sugar

Wash and dry spinach; trim and finely chop. Add onion and salt. Toss lightly with eggs. Fry bacon slowly until crisp; add vinegar and sugar. Mix well; our over spinach. Toss and serve. Yield: 4 servings.

Mrs. Orville Rose
Holy Cross Ladies Evening Guild
Lincoln, Nebraska

CHICKEN-ALMOND SALAD

1 tbsp. unflavored gelatin
¼ c. cold water
1 c. mayonnaise
1 c. heavy cream, whipped
½ tsp. salt
1 ½ c. diced chicken
¾ c. blanched, toasted chopped almonds
¾ c. seedless green grapes, halved

Soften gelatin in cold water; dissolve over hot water. Cool slightly; mix with mayonnaise, whipped cream and salt. Fold in remaining ingredients. Chill in mold until firm; unmold on lettuce. Yield: 6 servings.

Mrs. John I. Leslie, Jr., Treas.
Holy Cross Lydia Guild
Greenbelt, Maryland

CHICKEN-FRUIT SALAD

2 or 3 tbsp. cream
1 c. mayonnaise
1 c. diced chicken
1 c. diced celery
1 apple, diced
1 handful seedless grapes
½ banana

Add cream to mayonnaise; mix with remaining ingredients. Yield: 4 servings.

Anna Grothmann, Pres.
Grace LWML
Grandin, North Dakota

CHICKEN-FRUIT SALAD

3 c. diced cooked chicken
1 orange, chopped
1 sm. can pineapple chunks
1 apple, diced
15 grapes, halved and seeded
1 c. diced celery
15 slivered almonds or pecans
½ c. mayonnaise

Mix all ingredient; toss lightly. Serve on lettuce leaf. Yield: 10 servings.

Mrs. Albert Schnakenberg
Immanuel Ladies Aid
Lincoln, Missouri

CHICKEN-MACARONI SALAD

1 chicken, cooked and chopped
1 pkg. frozen peas and carrots, cooked
¼ c. chopped green pepper
1 c. chopped celery
1 tbsp. chopped dill pickle
6 hard-cooked eggs, diced
6 oz. macaroni, cooked
¾ c. heavy cream, whipped
1 ½ c. salad dressing
2 tsp. parsley
Salt and pepper to taste
Garlic salt

Combine chicken, vegetables, pickle, eggs and macaroni. Combine whipped cream and salad dressing; fold into chicken mixture. Add parsley; season to taste. Garnish with tomato slices, olives and parsley, if desired. Yield: 12-15 servings.

Mrs. Russell M. Collins, Pres.
Resurrection Women's Serv. League
St. Paul, Minnesota

CHICKEN-MACARONI SALAD

3 qt. cooked shell macaroni
3 qt. chopped cooked chicken
1 ½ qt. chopped celery
2 10-oz. pkg. frozen peas, cooked
6 hard-cooked eggs, chopped
½ c. chopped pimentos
1 qt. mayonnaise
Milk
Seasonings to taste

Combine macaroni, chicken, celery, peas, eggs and pimentos in large bowl. Thin mayonnaise with milk; add to chicken mixture. Season with salt and pepper to taste. Yield: 50 servings.

Mrs. Robert C. Greening, Sec.
Peace Ladies Guild
Alma, Michigan

CHICKEN SALAD

1 4 to 5-lb. boiling chicken
1 onion
1 bay lef
5 hard-cooked eggs
1 c. chopped celery
½ c. chopped onion
1 sm. jar pimento
3 c. cooked macaroni
1 ½ c. salad dressing
½ c. chopped green pepper
Salt and pepper to taste

Cook chicken with onion and bay leaf until done. Cool; remove bones and cut meat into small pieces. Mix with remaining ingredients. Yield: 10 servings.

Mrs. Jake Schlager
St. John's Ladies Aid
Culbertson, Nebraska

CHICKEN SALAD

2 c. coarsely diced chicken
2 tbsp. lemon juice
½ tsp. salt
1 c. diced celery
1 c. seedless white grapes
2 hard-cooked eggs, chilled and chopped
½ c. salad dressing
¼ c. slivered, blanched toasted almonds
Salt and pepper to taste

Sprinkle chicken with lemon juice and salt. Chill for several hours. Add celery, grapes, eggs, salad dressing and almonds. Toss lightly. Season. Serve on lettuce cups. Yield: 4-5 servings. Yield: 4-5 servings.

Mrs. Dora M. Luke, Pres.
Good Shepherd Guild
Glencoe, Minnesota

CHICKEN SALAD

1 3-oz. pkg. lemon gelatin
2 c. hot chicken broth
2 tbsp. vinegar
½ tsp. salt
1 c. diced cooked chicken
1 c. cooked peas, drained
½ c. celery
½ c. seedless or Tokay grapes
2 pimentos, cut up

Dissolve gelatin in chicken broth. Add vinegar and salt. Chill until thickened. Add remaining ingredients. Chill in individual serving molds or a large mold. Unmold on lettuce leaf; garnish with mayonnaise, if desired. Yield: 12 servings.

Mrs. J. W. Dyer, Pres.
Trinity LWML
Atchinson, Kansas

CHICKEN SALAD

1 stewing hen
Salt
½ c. cubed celery
2 hard-cooked eggs
½ c. diced sweet pickles
¼ c. diced stuffed olives
1 carrot, grated
½ c. salad dressing

Partially cover hen with water. Add 1 table-spoonful salt; boil slowly until tender. Remove meat from bones and dice. Add remaining ingredients; season to taste. Mix lightly, but well. serve on lettuce leaves. Yield: 6 servings.

Mrs. Olga Bammes, Pres.
Mt. Calvary Ladies Aid
Wamego, Kansas

CHICKEN SALAD SUPREME

4 c. (packed) diced cooked chicken
4 c. finely diced celery
2 c. sliced ripe olives
½ c. minced onion
2 c. finely chopped green peppers
½ c. finely chopped pimento
½ c. lemon juice
1 ¾ c. mayonnaise
1 ½ c. heavy cream, whipped

Combine chicken, celery, olives, onion, green peppers, pimento and lemon juice; toss to mix. Fold mayonnaise into whipped cream; add to chicken mixture, folding in carefully. Chill for several hours. Yield: 15-20 servings.

Mrs. Velma Moe
Beautiful Savior Ladies Guild
Milwaukee, Wisconsin

CHICKEN SALAD

3 c. diced cooked chicken
4 hard-cooked eggs, chopped
1 stalk celery, chopped
½ tsp. salt
Dash of pepper
Mayonnaise

Combine all ingredients, adding enough mayonnaise to moisten. Yield: 6 servings.

Mrs. Docilla Oehl
Trinity Ladies Aid
Friedheim, Missouri

CHICKEN SUPREME SALAD

3 c. finely diced cooked chicken
1 tsp. salt
1 c. crushed pineapple, drained
1 c. red grapes, halved and seeded
1 c. mayonnaise

Combine all ingredients; toss lightly. serve on lettuce. Yield: 12 servings.

Mrs. Joe Bange, Pres.
Immanuel Evening Guild LWML
Salisbury, Missouri

COMPANY CHICKEN SALAD

SALAD DRESSING:

½ c. vinegar
½ c. sugar
2 eggs, beaten
2 tbsp. flour
1 tsp. dry mustard
1 tsp. salt
1 tbsp. butter
Pepper to taste

Mix vinegar and sugar in saucepan; boil. Add remaining ingredients; chill.

SALAD:

1 chicken
3 stalks celery
Parsley
1 tsp. onion
Salt
½ c. heavy cream, whipped
1 c. seedless grapes

Cook chicken in water to cover with celery, parsley and onion until well done. Remove meat from bones; dice. Season to taste; chill. Mix 1 cup dressing with whipped cream; add chicken and grapes. Serve on lettuce. NOTE:

(Continued on next page)

If desired, 1 package prepared dessert topping mix may be substituted for whipped cream. Yield: 6 servings.

Mrs. Willard A. Meyer, Pres.
St. Paul's LCW
Postville, Iowa

CRANBERRY- CHICKEN SALAD

1 envelope unflavored gelatin
¼ c. cold water
1 1-lb. can cranberry sauce
1 c. crushed pineapple
½ c. nuts
1 tbsp. lemon juice

Soften gelatin in cold water; dissolve over hot water. Add remaining ingredients. Pour into 10 x 6-inch pan. Chill until firm.

SECOND LAYER:

1 pkg. unflavored gelatin
¾ c. water
1 c. mayonnaise
3 tbsp. lemon juice
¾ tsp. salt
2 c. diced chicken
½ c. celery
2 tbsp. chopped parsley

Soak gelatin in 1/4 cup cold water; dissolve over hot water. Add remaining 1/2 cup water and all ingredients. Pour over cranberry layer; chill until firm. Cut into s q u a r e s; serve on salad greens. Top with mayonnaise and walnut halves. Yield: 6-8 servings.

Mrs. Elton Shedd, Pres.
Brule Creek LCW
Elk Point, South Dakota

HOT CHICKEN SALAD

2 c. diced cooked chicken
¼ c. chopped almonds
1 ½ c. diced celery
½ tsp. grated onion
1 tbsp. lemon juice
¼ tsp. salt
Pepper to taste
⅔ c. mayonnaise
1 c. grated mild Cheddar cheese
1 c. crushed potato chips

Combine chicken, almonds, celery, onion, lemon juice, salt and pepper. Add mayonnaise; toss gently. Place into buttered casserole. Sprinkle with cheese; top with potato chips. Bake at 375 degrees for 25 minutes or until cheese is bubbly. Yield: 4 servings.

Mrs. Raymond Truwe, Pres.
Zion Ladies Aid
Mayer, Minnesota

HOLIDAY CHICKEN SALAD

2 c. chopped cooked chicken
½ c. chopped walnuts
2 c. diced celery
¾ tsp. salt
2 tsp. minced onion
½ c. diced ripe olives
½ c. diced green olives
¼ c. chopped pimento
½ tsp. paprika
½ c. mayonnaise
1 c. whipped cream

Mix all ingredients except whipped cream. Chill for at least 2 hours. When ready to serve, fold in whipped cream. Serve on lettuce leaf. Yield: 10-12 servings.

Mrs. Dorothy Morong, Nursing Home Chmn.
First Lutheran Church LWML
El Cajon, California

HOT CHICKEN SALAD

3 c. cooked chicken, salted
2 c. diced celery
1 med. can water chestnuts
1 ½ c. diced Cheddar cheese
1 c. salad dressing
1 ¼ c. white grapes (opt.)
1 c. potato chips

Combine chicken, celery, water chestnuts, 1 cup cheese, salad dressing and grapes; toss gently to mix. Pour into a buttered 12 x 8-inch pan. Mix potato chips and remaining 1/2 cup cheese; sprinkle over chicken mixture. Bake at 350 degrees for 45 minutes. Serve hot. Yield: 8 servings.

Mrs. Howard Detloff, Mite Box Chmn.
LWML
Bloomington, Illinois

HOT CHICKEN SALAD

2 c. cubed cooked chicken
2 c. diced celery
½ c. chopped almonds
½ tsp. salt
½ tsp. monosodium glutamate (opt.)
¼ tsp. tarragon (opt.)
2 tsp. grated onion
2 tsp. or 2 tbsp. lemon juice
1 c. mayonnaise
½ c. cubed or grated Cheddar cheese
1 c. crushed potato chips

Combine chicken, celery, almonds, seasonings, onion, lemon juice and mayonnaise; toss lightly. Pour into casserole. Top with cheese and potato chips. Bake at 450 degrees for 10 to 15 minutes or until hot. Yield: 6 servings.

Mrs. Wilfred Burginger, Pres.
Dorcas Soc. Stately
Sanborn, Minnesota
Mrs. Donald W. Glaser
Village LCW Guild
Bronxville, New York

LUNCHEON CHICKEN SALAD

3 c. diced cooked chicken
1 c. diced celery
1 c. diced pineapple, drained
1 c. orange sections
1 c. chopped walnuts or slivered almonds
2 tbsp. salad oil (opt.)
2 tbsp. vinegar (opt.)
2 tbsp. orange juice
½ tsp. salt (opt.)
Dash of marjoram (opt.)
½ c. mayonnaise or to taste

Combine chicken, celery, fruits and nuts. Blend oil, vinegar, orange juice and salt. Add to chicken mixture; chill for 1 hour. Drain off juice. Add mayonnaise and toss lightly. NOTE: If desired, mayonnaise may be added before chilling. Yield: 8-10 servings.

Mrs. C. W. Harner, Pres.
Reformation LCW
New Market, Virginia
Mrs. Milton R. Sheehan, Pres.
St. John's LCW
Rochester, New York
Mrs. Emil E. Adolphson, Pres.
Good Shepherd LCW
North Aurora, Illinois

MACARONI-CHICKEN SALAD

1 14-oz. pkg. shell macaroni, cooked and
    cooled
1 chicken, stewed
Onion
Salt and pepper
1 can peas
1 c. diced celery

Remove chicken from bones; break into small pieces. Combine remaining ingredients. Add chicken.

DRESSING:

½ c. sugar
1 tsp. salt
1 tbsp. flour
½ tsp. dry mustard
¼ c. vinegar
¼ c. water
1 egg, beaten
Salad dressing
Cream

Combine all ingredients except egg, dressing and cream. Mix well; add egg. Boil until thickened. Add a small amount of salad dressing and cream just before serving. Chill. Mix with chicken salad. Yield: 4 servings.

Mrs. Dwayne Wallace
Trinity LWML
Port Edward, Wisconsin

MOLDED CHICKEN SALAD

1 pkg. lemon gelatin
1 c. hot water
1 can cream of chicken soup
½ c. chopped celery
¼ c. diced green pepper
2 tbsp. diced pimento
1 tsp. diced onion
1 c. finely chopped cooked chicken
Hard-cooked egg slices

Dissolve gelatin in hot water; cool. Add remaining ingredients except egg; chill. Garnish with egg slices. Serve on bed of lettuce. Yield: 8-10 servings.

Mrs. Sam Hess, Pres.
St. Mark's Ladies Guild
Wausau, Wisconsin

SUNSHINE SALAD

1 pkg. lemon gelatin
1 tsp. salt
1 c. boiling water
½ c. salad dressing
3 c. cooked macaroni
1 c. diced cooked chicken
1 c. cooked peas
2 tbsp. sweet pickle
2 tbsp. chopped onion
½ c. diced cheese

Mix gelatin, salt and boiling water; cool. Blend in salad dressing; chill until slightly thickened. Whip gelatin mixture. Combine remaining ingredients; fold in gelatin mixture. Chill well. Yield: 12 servings.

Mrs. William Block
St. Paul's LWML
Willow City, North Dakota

ORIENTAL CHICKEN SALAD

3 c. cubed cooked chicken
1 c. canned Mandarin oranges, drained
1 c. chopped celery
⅛ tsp. ginger
1 tbsp. soy sauce
Mayonnaise
Salt and pepper to taste
2 c. chow mein noodles

Combine chicken, orange slices, celery, ginger and soy sauce. Add enough mayonnaise to moisten well; season to taste. Chill thoroughly. Serve on a bed of crisp noodles. Yield: 4 servings.

Mrs. B. J. Ulrich, Pres.
Immanuel Mary and Martha Soc.
Callaway, Minnesota

HOT TURKEY SALAD

2 c. cooked turkey, cut in ½-in. cubes
1 ½ c. celery, cut in ¼-inch cubes
¼ c. coarsely chopped toasted almonds
2 tsp. finely chopped onion
Rind of ½ lemon, grated
1 tbsp. lemon juice
½ to ⅔ c. salad dressing

 (Continued on next page)

⅛ tsp. pepper
Salt to taste
1 c. grated Cheddar cheese
1 c. crushed potato chips

Combine turkey, celery, almonds, onion, lemon rind and lemon juice. Add salad dressing; toss lightly to blend. Add pepper and salt. Put into oblong casserole. Sprinkle with cheese; top with potato chips. Put casserole on a baking sheet. Bake at 375 degrees for 25 minutes or until cheese begins to bubble. Yield: 4-6 servings.

Mrs. R. C. Pendleton, Pres.
Christ Lutheran Church Ladies Aid
Tulia, Texas

TURKEY SALAD

25 c. coarsely chopped cooked turkey
20 c. diced celery
20 c. rice, cooked and well strained
48 hard-cooked eggs
2 qt. salad dressing
½ c. vinegar
1 tbsp. paprika
1 tbsp. salt

Combine turkey, celery, rice and eggs. Combine remaining ingredients; add to turkey mixture. Serve on lettuce cups. Yield: 80 servings.

Mrs. Impi Mayry, Christian Action Chmn.
St. John's LCW
Detroit, Michigan

TURKEY SALAD

2 c. diced turkey
1 ½ c. celery
¼ c. French dressing
Salt and pepper to taste
½ c. mayonnaise
⅓ c. sour cream
¼ c. slivered almonds
2 c. crushed potato chips
1 c. grated cheese

Combine turkey, celery and French dressing; marinate for 1 hour. Add remaining ingredients. Pour into individual shells or casserole. Bake at 375 degrees for 20 minutes.

Helen E. Alusic, Sec.
Pentecost Evangelical Ruth Cir.
Racine, Wisconsin

TURKEY-FRUIT SALAD

4 c. chopped cooked turkey
1 c. pineapple chunks
1 c. seedless grapes
1 c. chopped apples
1 c. chopped walnuts
1 ½ c. mayonnaise

Combine all ingredients; toss lightly. Chill and serve. Yield: 6 servings.

Mrs. Arnold Davis, Pres.
Grace LCW
North Tonawanda, New York

WILD RICE AND TURKEY SALAD

½ lb. wild rice
4 c. cooked chopped turkey or chicken
1 c. mayonnaise
½ c. French dressing
Salt to taste
1 5-oz. can sliced almonds
1 c. diced celery
2 cans Mandarin oranges
1 No. 2 can pineapple chunks

Cook rice according to package directions; cool. Add turkey, mayonnaise, French dressing, salt, almonds and celery; chill. Just before serving, add oranges and pineapple. Serve on lettuce.

Annette Long Brooks
Mt. Pilgrim LCW
Prosperity, South Carolina

MOCK HAM SALAD

½ c. sugar
1 tbsp. (heaping) flour
Salt to taste
1 egg
½ c. vinegar
⅔ c. water
1 lb. bologna, ground
6 sweet pickles, ground
1 sm. onion, ground

Combine sugar, flour and salt in saucepan; mix well. Mix in egg. Add vinegar and water, mixing well. Cook over low heat, stirring constantly until mixture is consistency of salad dressing. Cool. Add remaining ingredients.

Mrs. Martin Huebner
Immanuel Evangelical Dorcas Soc.
Hanover, Wisconsin

CORNED BEEF SALAD

1 ½ c. V-8 juice
½ c. water
1 pkg. lemon gelatin
1 can corned beef, shredded
2 hard-cooked eggs, chopped
1 ½ c. chopped celery
2 tbsp. chopped green pepper
½ sm. onion, finely minced
1 c. salad dressing

Heat V-8 juice and water; dissolve gelatin in mixture. Cool. Add remaining ingredients. Pour into 8 x 8-inch pan; refrigerate overnight. Cut into squares for serving. Yield: 6-8 servings.

Mrs. Donald Hawks, Pres.
Hope LCW
Sioux Falls, South Dakota

CORNED BEEF SALAD

1 pkg. unflavored gelatin
¼ c. cold water
1 ½ c. hot tomato juice
1 tsp. lemon juice
½ tsp. salt
1 12-oz. can corned beef, shredded
3 hard-cooked eggs, chopped
2 c. diced celery
½ c. chopped cucumber
1 tbsp. onion juice
1 c. mayonnaise

Soften gelatin in water; dissolve in tomato juice. Add lemon juice and salt. Chill until partially set. Fold in remaining ingredients; chill until firm. Yield: 8 servings.

Mrs. Alfred P. Gebhardt, Pres.
Trinity Evangelical Mary-Martha Guild
Swissvale, Pennsylvania
Esther Erickson, Pres.
Friendship LCW
Pittsburgh, Pennsylvania

CORNED BEEF SALAD

1 3-oz. box lemon gelatin
1 to 1 ½ c. hot water
1 can corned beef, chopped
1 to 2 c. chopped celery
1 or 2 red or green peppers, chopped (opt.)
2 green onions, chopped (opt.)
3 or 4 hard-cooked eggs, chopped
Dash of salt (opt.)
1 c. salad dressing

Dissolve gelatin in hot water; cool until slightly thickened. Add remaining ingredients. Mix and pour into shallow dish. Chill. Yield: 8 servings.

Mrs. Forest Smith, Pres.
Stone LCW
Ashland, Ohio
Mrs. Vernon Anderson, Pres.
Mamrelund LCW
Pennock, Minnesota
Mrs. C. S. Weimer
Immanuel Ladies Aid
Avilla, Indiana

JELLIED CORNED BEEF SALAD

1 ½ c. tomato juice
1 envelope unflavored gelatin
¼ c. cold water
1 tbsp. lemon juice
Dash of salt
1 c. mayonnaise
1 tbsp. prepared mustard
1 tbsp. finely minced onion
2 c. finely chopped celery
½ c. chopped dill pickles or dill weed
1 12-oz. can corned beef, shredded
3 hard-cooked eggs, chopped

Heat tomato juice to boiling; add gelatin which has been softened in cold water. Heat until gelatin is dissolved. Stir in lemon juice and salt; refrigerate until slightly thickened. Blend mayonnaise with mustard, onion, celery and pickle. Stir in corned beef. Stir into partially set gelatin mixture with eggs. Carefully pour mixture into a 10-inch ring mold or 5 x 9-inch loaf pan. Chill until set. Turn out onto serving plate; garnish with crisp greens, if desired. NOTE: If desired, 2 envelopes gelatin may be used. If so, increase water to 1/2 cup. Yield: 8-10 servings.

Mrs. George W. Tripp, Chmn.
Honolulu Ruth Cir. LCW
Honolulu, Hawaii

JELLIED VEAL OR CHICKEN

2 tbsp. unflavored gelatin
2 c. beef consomme or meat juice
3 c. diced veal or chicken
1 ½ tsp. salt
½ c. finely diced carrots
1 c. diced celery
Tomato slices
Peas

Dissolve gelatin in heated consomme. Add remaining ingredients except tomatoes and peas. Arrange tomatoes and peas in bottom of individual dishes. Add gelatin mixture. Chill until firm. Serve on lettuce leaf and garnish.

Mrs. Nannie Giese, Pres.
Trinity Ladies Aid
Walburg, Saskatchewan, Canada

JELLIED VEAL WITH SAUCE

4 lb. veal and knuckle, cut into pieces
1 lge. onion
1 bunch celery tops
1 tbsp. salt
1 tbsp. gelatin
¼ c. water
3 tsp. Worcestershire sauce

Combine veal, onion, celery tops and salt. Cover with water; cook until tender. Remove veal; strain broth. Grind meat. Dissolve gelatin in cold water; add to hot broth. Add meat and Worcestershire sauce; chill until set.

SAUCE:

1 c. mayonnaise
2 hard-cooked eggs, chopped
½ c. English walnuts
12 stuffed olives, sliced
1 tsp. grated onion
½ pt. heavy cream, whipped
2 c. diced celery

Combine all ingredients; serve with jellied veal. Yield: 12 servings.

Mrs. David L. Schneider
Calvary LCW
Chillicothe, Ohio

Sandwich Favorites

RECIPE FOR CORNED BEEF DIPWICHES ON PAGE 325

BARBECUE

1 lb. onions, chopped
3 tbsp. fat
10 lb. ground beef
2 c. tomato puree
4 tbsp. brown sugar
3 tbsp. salt

Saute onions in fat. Add ground beef; boil. Add remaining ingredients, stirring frequently. Simmer for 1 hour or longer, stirring occasionally. Serve on warm buns. Yield: 100 servings.

Mrs. Darlene Brunner, Pres.
Christ Lutheran Church LCW
Sharon, Wisconsin

BARBEBURGERS

1 lb. hamburher
1 med. onion, diced
1 tsp. liquid smoke
1 c. water
½ bottle catsup or barbecue sauce
1 tbsp. sugar
1 tbsp. prepared mustard
1 tbsp. vinegar
Hamburger buns

Place hamburger, onion, liquid smoke and water into a frying pan. Cook over medium heat, stirring constantly, until the water has evaporated. Add catsup or barbecue sauce, sugar, mustard and vinegar; cook, stirring, until thick. Serve on hamburger buns. Yield: 8 servings.

Mrs. Doris Wiese
Christ the King Mary-Martha Soc.
Enterprise, Alabama

BARBECUED BURGERS

1 lb. ground beef
⅔ c. chopped onions
2 tbsp. fat
½ tsp. salt
⅛ tsp. pepper
1 10 ½ to 11-oz. can chicken gumbo soup
¼ c. water
1 tbsp. catsup
1 tbsp. prepared mustard

Cook meat and onions in hot fat until onions are golden. Stir in remaining ingredients; simmer over low heat for 30 minutes. Spoon over buns. Yield: 8 servings.

Mrs. Cecil Goodnough, Pres.
Good Shepherd Ladies Aid
Babbitt, Minnesota

BARBECUED BEEF

1 lb. beef, cubed
1 tbsp. fat
1 med. onion, chopped
½ c. diced celery
⅓ c. diced green pepper
1 c. catsup
¼ c. brown sugar
2 tbsp. vinegar
2 tbsp. Worcestershire sauce
1 tsp. salt
1 tsp. chili powder
12 toasted buns

Brown beef in hot fat. Add 1 1/2 cups water; simmer in covered skillet for 1 hour and 30 minutes. Reserve broth; add water to make 2/3 cup. Break beef into small pieces. Cook onion, celery and green pepper in fat until tender; add beef broth and remaining ingredients except buns. Simmer, uncovered, for 20 to 30 minutes. Serve on toasted buns. Yield: 12 servings.

Mrs. Henry Hagenlock
St. Paul's Ladies Aid
Seneca, South Dakota

BARBECUE BEEF

3 med. or 2 lge. chuck roasts
3 onions, chopped
3 mango peppers, chopped
2 c. catsup
½ tsp. powdered barbecue seasoning
1 c. chopped celery
3 tbsp. mayonnaise
3 tbsp. vinegar
1 can tomato soup
3 tbsp. sugar
3 tbsp. dry mustard
4 drops hot pepper sauce
1 tbsp. chili powder
1 6-oz. can tomato puree
5 tbsp. Worcestershire sauce

Roast meat; cut into small pieces. Let cool. Combine remaining ingredients. Simmer for 1 hour. Add to meat. Serve on buns. Yield: 20 servings.

Mrs. Jody Stelk, Sec.
Our Savior Women's Guild
Bradley, Illinois

BARBECUED BEEF

5 lb. beef
1 tsp. mustard
1 14-oz. can tomato puree
1 onion
1 green pepper, chopped
1 tsp. chili powder
1 tbsp. brown sugar
1 tbsp. vinegar
1 tbsp. Worcestershire sauce
Salt to taste
Warmed hamburger buns

Boil beef until well done. Shread into small pieces. Add remaining ingredients except buns. Boil slowly for 2 hours. Serve on buns. Yield: 20 servings.

Mrs. L. Keller
St. John's Bethlehem Soc.
Perkin, Illinois

BARBECUED BEEF

1 to 1 ½ lb. chopped beef
1 c. catsup
½ c. water
3 tbsp. vinegar
3 tbp. Worcestershire sauce
3 tbsp. sugar
6 tbsp. minced onion
Hamburger buns

Brown meat; add remaining ingredients. Cover; cook over medium heat for 45 minutes. Serve on buns. Yield: 12-15 servings.

Mrs. Marvin Feiner, Pres.
Holy Ghost Lutheran Church Ladies Aid
Milwaukee, Wisconsin

BARBECUED BEEF SANDWICH

1 lb. lean ground beef
1 med. onion, chopped
1 bottle catsup
1 tbsp. vinegar
1 egg
1 tbsp. prepared mustard
1 c. corn flakes

Brown ground beef and onion well. Mix remaining ingredients; add to beef. Simmer for 1 hour. Serve on buns. Yield: 6 servings.

Mrs. Helen L. Myers, Pres.
Holy Communion LCW
Portsmouth, Virginia

BARBECUED HAMBURGERS

1 lge. onion, chopped
5 lb. hamburger
2 c. tomato soup
1 tbsp. chili powder
Salt to taste
½ c. flour
Hamburger buns

Fry onion with hamburger until browned. Add soup, chili powder, salt and pepper. Cook for 1 hour. Thicken with flour. Serve on hamburger buns. Yield: 8-12 servings.

Marjorie Schendel, Parkland Zone Pres.
St. Peter's LWML
Oxbow, Saskatchewan, Canada

BARBECUED HAMBURGER

1 c. chopped onions
2 tbsp. butter
4 lb. ground beef
1 14-oz. bottle catsup
1 c. water
½ c. chopped celery
¼ c. lemon juice
2 tbsp. brown sugar
1 tbsp. Worcestershire sauce
1 tbsp. salt
2 tsp. vinegar
1 tsp. monosodium glutamate
½ tsp. dry mustard

Saute onions in butter. Add ground beef; brown lightly. Drain off excess fat. Add remaining ingredients; cover and simmer for 30 minutes. Use to fill warm hamburger buns or cool and freeze in five 1-pint freezing containers. Yield: 30-40 servings.

Mrs. Shirley A. Baumann
St. Matthew's LWML
Corning, Arkansas

BARBECUED HAMBURGERS

2 lb. ground beef
1 med. onion, finely chopped
2 tbsp. butter, melted
¼ c. chopped green pepper (opt.)
2 tbsp. catsup
1 c. tomato juice
½ can tomato soup
1 tsp. dry mustard
1 tsp. steak sauce
2 tsp. Worcestershire sauce
1 tsp. sugar
Salt and pepper to taste
18 hamburger buns

313

(Continued on next page)

Brown meat and onion in butter. Add remaining ingredients except buns. Simmer for 1 hour. Thin with additional tomato juice if needed. Serve on hamburger buns. Yield: 18 servings.

Mrs. Patricia McNamara, Sec.
St. James' Women's Guild
Imperial Beach, California

BARBECUED HAMBURGERS

1 tbsp. flour
1 tbsp. bacon grease, melted
1 c. cold water
1 lb. beef
½ med. onion, chopped
½ green pepper, chopped
½ bottle catsup
1 tbsp. mustard
3 tbsp. Worcestershire sauce
1 tbsp. sugar
Salt and pepper

Blend flour into grease. Add water; cook until thickened. Add remaining ingredients; cook for 1 hour. Dip off grease. Serve on hamburger buns. Yield: 0 servings.

Mrs. Janet Lennan
St. Paul's Dorcas Guild
Naugatuck, Connecticut

BARBECUED HAMBURGER

1 lb. ground beef
2 tbsp. fat
½ c. finely chopped onion
½ c. chopped celery
3 tbsp. chili sauce
3 tbsp. catsup
1 tbsp. Worcestershire sauce
1 can tomato soup
6 hamburger buns, split and toasted

Shape ground beef into six patties. Brown in fat; place in a buttered 1-quart casserole. Brown onion in remaining fat. Add remaining ingredients except hamburger buns. Simmer for 5 minutes. Pour over patties. Cover; bake at 350 degrees for 30 minutes. Spread on buns. Yield: 6 servings.

Mrs. Martin Christian, Pres.
St. John's Evangelical Ladies Aid
Algonquin, Illinois

BARBECUED HAMBURGERS

1 lb. ground beef
4 tbsp. chopped onion
1 c. chili sauce or catsup
¾ c. water
1 tsp. salt
3 tbsp. vinegar
2 tsp. Worcestershire sauce
1 tsp. paprika
1 tsp. chili powder

Brown ground beef and onion. Combine remaining ingredients in heavy saucepan. Cook over medium heat for 10 minutes. Serve on hamburger buns. Yield: 6 servings.

Josephine Sigfridson, Chmn.
St. James' Ladies Aid
Cokato, Minnesota

BARBECUE SAUCE

1 bunch celery
Chopped onion
4 tbsp. fat
1 bottle catsup
3 tbsp. plus 1 tsp. prepared mustard
¾ c. vinegar
1 c. brown sugar
1 c. water
Salt and pepper
2 ¼ lb. ground beef

Cut up celery; measure and use same amount chopped onion. Fry celery and onion in fat until tender, turning frequently. Place in heavy saucepan; add catsup, mustard, vinegar, sugar, water, salt and pepper to taste. Simmer for 1 hour or until thick. Place 1 teaspoonful salt in heavy fry pan; add beef and fry slowly until done, turning and breaking beef apart. Add beef to sauce. Serve over hot buns if desired. Yield: 20 servings.

Mrs. Otto Martz, Sec.
Tabitha Ladies Aid Soc.
Big Rapids, Michigan

BEEF BARBECUE

1 tsp. sugar
1 sm. onion, chopped
1 tbsp. butter
2 tbsp. vinegar
2 tbsp. Worcestershire sauce
1 c. catsup
1 lb. beef stew meat, cooked and shredded

Cook sugar, onion and butter; add vinegar, Worcestershire sauce and catsup. Add meat; simmer for 30 minutes. Serve on warm buns.

Mrs. Earl Spaulding, Pres.
St. John's LCW
Dundee, Michigan

BEEF BARBECUE

4 to 5 lb. lean stew meat
1 lge. can tomatoes
2 med. onions, chopped
½ c. catsup
½ c. vinegar
½ c. Worcestershire sauce
1 qt. water
8 cloves of garlic
½ tsp. chili powder
Dash of Tabasco sauce
Salt and pepper to taste

Combine all ingredients in large saucepan; cook for 5 to 6 hours or until beef falls into shreds. Serve on buns. Yield: 20 servings.

Mrs. James Williams, Pres.
Grace Ladies Guild
Woodbridge, Virginia

BEEF BARBECUE

2 lb. ground round steak
2 med. onions, chopped
2 tbsp. shortening
1 sm. green pepper, chopped
1 sm. stalk celery, chopped
1 10 ½-oz. can tomato soup
1 c. tomato juice
Catsup (opt.)
Salt and pepper to taste

Brown meat and onions in shortening. Add remaining ingredients; simmer for 1 hour to 1 hour and 30 minutes. Serve on hamburger buns. Yield: 15-20 servings.

Olga Rinko, Sec.
Lord Jesus Ladies Aid
Chicago, Illinois

BEEF SANDWICHES

2 ½ c. ground roast beef, pork or turkey
½ c. ground celery
½ lge. green pepper, ground
1 sm. onion, ground
12 stuffed olives, ground
3 tbsp. sweet pickle relish
⅓ c. salad dressing or mayonnaise

Mix all ingredients. Use for sandwich filling. Yield: 10-12 servings.

Mrs. Paul J. Lister, Pres.
St. John's Evangelical Sunset Cir.
Akron, Ohio

BEEF SANDWICH FILLING

Cooked beef
Ground or finely chopped sweet pickles
1 c. mayonnaise
6 tbsp. sugar
6 tbsp. vinegar

Grind cooked beef in a food chopper. Mix mayonnaise, sugar and vinegar; add to meat and pickles. Yield: 6 servings.

Mrs. Leo Hunsley, Pres.
St. John's Ladies Aid
LaCrosse, Indiana

BEEF SANDWICH SPREAD

Ground left-over roast beef
1 sm. onion
¼ tsp. salt
⅛ tsp. pepper
2 to 3 tbsp. mayonnaise

Mix all ingredients; refrigerate for at least 1 hour. Spread on buns or bread; serve. Yield: 6 servings.

Mrs. Nettie Wiese, Pres.
Our Redeemer's ALCW
Hancock, Minnesota

BURGER BUNS

1 c. catsup
½ c. water
2 tbsp. sugar
2 tbsp. cider vinegar
2 tsp. prepared mustard
2 tbsp. butter
1 c. chopped onions
2 lb. hamburger
Salt and pepper to taste
1 can chicken gumbo soup
Buns

Combine catsup, water, sugar, vinegar and prepared mustard. Mix well; place in a pint jar. Keep in refrigerator. Melt butter in pan; add onions. Cook until done. Add hamburger and seasonings to taste. Fry until meat is browned. Add soup and sauce. Simmer for 15 minutes. Serve hot on buns. Yield:12-15 servings.

Mrs. Marvin E. Meyer, Sec.
St. John's Ladies Aid Soc.
Loganville, Wisconsin

DYNAMITE

1 lb. ground beef
1 lb. hamburger
2 c. finely cut celery
1 c. finely cut onions
1 c. finely cut green peppers
Salt and pepper to taste
1 or 2 peppercorns (opt.)
½ c. water

Combine all ingredients. Heat slowly; stir frequently. Simmer for 1 hour. Serve on split rolls or buns. NOTE: Mixture can be frozen. Yield: 24 servings.

Emma M. Gregory
St. Peter's Tabitha Ladies Aid
Rodney, Michigan

GROUND MEAT SANDWICHES

1 to 1 ½ lb. ground meat
¼ c. water
1 sm. can tomato sauce
Salt and black pepper to taste
Chili pepper to taste
Catsup to taste
1 loaf bread

Brown meat in frying pan; add water. Add tomato sauce, salt, black pepper, chili pepper and catsup. Cook until done. Drain off excess gravy. Spread mixture between bread slices. Serve warm or cool. Yield: 24 servings.

Mrs. John Haun, Treas.
St. John's Evangelical LCW
Meyersville, Texas

HAMBURGERS FOR A CROWD

2 lb. hamburger
1 med. onion, chopped
Salt and pepper to taste
1 pkg. buns

Brown hamburger and onion in skillet; add salt and pepper. Place on buns; wrap in aluminum foil. Bake at 350 degrees for 15 minutes.

Mrs. Orville Wiechert, Pres.
Redeemer Ladies Aid
Marshall, Missouri

HAMBURGER SALAD SANDWICH

1 lb. ground beef
2 tbsp. salad oil
Salt and pepper to taste
4 c. finely chopped lettuce
½ c. finely chopped onion
¼ c. finely chopped green pepper
½ c. finely chopped celery
2 med. tomatoes, finely chopped
2 tsp. prepared mustard
½ pt. sandwich spread
Butter
1 lge. loaf bread

Brown meat in oil. Add salt and pepper. Mix lettuce, onion, green pepper, celery and tomatoes; add to meat. Combine mustard and sandwich spread; add to meat and vegetables. Spread slices of bread with butter, then meat mixture. Top with another slice of bread. Yield: 12 sandwiches. Yield: 12 servings.

Mrs. Paul Ftak, Pres.
Our Savior LWML
Dallas, Texas

HAMBURGER SANDWICH SPREAD

1 lb. hamburger
Fat or butter
2 tbsp. flour
¼ c. catsup
½ c. water
Salt and pepper to taste
1 tbsp. chopped green pepper
1 tbsp. chopped onion

Fry hamburger in fat until done. Add flour, catsup, water, salt, pepper, green pepper and onion. Cook until done. Serve on hot hamburger buns if desired. Yield: 6 servings.

Mrs. Martha M. Stockburger
Grace Ladies Aid
Three Forks, Montana

HAMBURGERS SUPREME

1 lb. ground beef
½ pkg. dry onion soup mix
½ c. sour cream

Combine all ingredients; shape into four patties. Cook on outdoor grill for 30 minutes. Serve on buns, if desired. Yield: 4 servings.

Glenda Dretke, Pres.
Trinity LWML
New Orleans, Louisiana

JACKBURGERS

1 loaf bread
1 lb. hamburger
1 egg
1 sm. onion, chopped
3 tsp. horseradish mustard
Salt and pepper to taste

Place nine slices of bread on broiler pan 3 inches from heat. Broil for 5 minutes or until toasted on one side. Combine hamburger and egg in a mixing bowl. Add remaining ingredients; mix thoroughly. Spread meat mixture thinly over untoasted side of bread. Broil until edge of bread is slightly brown. Yield: 4-5 servings.

Mrs. Albert Moe, Pres.
Christ Lutheran Church LCW
DeForest, Wisconsin

JUICY BURGERS

1 can chicken gumbo soup
1 tbsp. catsup
1 tbsp. mustard (opt.)
1 lb. ground beef, browned
Hamburger buns

Add soup, catsup and mustard to browned meat in saucepan. Simmer for 30 minutes. Stir after 15 minutes. Serve in hamburger buns. Yield: 4-6 servings.

Mrs. Ernest H. Lundgren, Pres.
Alpine LCW
Rockford, Illinois

JUICY BURGER

1 ½ lb. ground beef
1 onion, chopped
1 ½ tsp. salt
1 can tomato soup
1 can cream of mushroom soup
1 tbsp. dry mustard
2 tsp. chili powder
Buns

Brown ground beef and onion. Add remaining ingredients except buns. Simmer for 30 minutes, stirring several times. Spoon onto hamburger buns. Yield: 12 servings.

Mrs. Robert E. Mersey, VP
Clarks Fork Lutheran Church
Bunceton, Missouri

MAID RITES

1 lb. hamburger or ground chuck
½ to 1 tsp. pepper
1 tsp. sugar
2 tsp. mustard
Salt to taste

Combine all ingredients. Cook in top of double boiler for 20 to 25 minutes over medium heat, stirring occasionally. Serve on buns. Yield: 10-12 servings.

Mrs. Bobby McKibben, Pres.
Pitsburg Trinity Miss'y Soc.
Arcanum, Ohio
Doris Sander, Sec.
St. John's LCW
Greenville, Ohio

PIZZA BURGER

1 lb. ground beef
⅛ c. grated Parmesan cheese
¼ c. chopped onion
¼ c. chopped ripe olives
1 6-oz. can tomato paste
1 tsp. salt
½ tsp. oregano
⅛ tsp. pepper
Rolls, buns or English muffins
3 tomatoes, sliced
Cheddar cheese slices

Combine all ingredients except bread, tomatoes and cheese slices. Spread meat mixture on both halves of bread. Broil 5 inches from heat for 10 to 12 minutes. Top with tomatoes and cheese slices. Broil for 1 to 2 minutes or until cheese begins to melt. NOTE: French, Italian or Vienna bread, cut into halves lengthwise, may be used. Yield: 6 servings.

Mrs. Vernon H. Schwartz
Mt. Calvary LWML
Galesburg, Illinois

QUICK BARBECUE

2 lb. hamburger
1 can vegetable soup
¾ c. catsup

Brown hamburger in a small amount of fat; add soup and catsup. Simmer for 10 minutes. Serve in buns or on slices of bread. Garnish with sliced garlic dill pickles. Yield: 6 servings.

Mrs. Lyle Barth, Pres.
St. Paul's Ladies Aid
Rushville, Nebraska

PIZZA BURGERS

½ lb. ground beef
1 6-oz. can tomato juice
2 tbsp. chopped green pepper
½ tsp. oregano
2 tbsp. chopped onion
1 tsp. salt
½ tsp. dried parsley
½ c. grated Cheddar cheese
Buns

Combine all ingredients except cheese and buns. Spread thinly on bun halves. Sprinkle with cheese. Broil on lowest broiler rack for 5 to 8 minutes or until cheese is bubbly and meat is done. Yield: 10 servings.

Mrs. Tom Stinar
Holy Trinity Ladies Aid Soc.
Lakefield, Minnesota

QUICK BEEF AND ONION SANDWICH

1 lb. ground beef
1 10 ¾-oz. can onion soup
4 to 6 slices toast

Brown beef in skillet; add soup and heat. Spoon over toast. NOTE: Toast may be spread with mustard if desired. Yield: 4 servings.

Mrs. Roger Sell, Pres.
Emmanuel LWML
Littlefield, Texas

SLOPPY JOES

1 sm. bunch celery, diced
1 med. onion, diced
2 lb. ground beef
1 1-lb. 2-oz. bottle barbecue sauce
1 tsp. salt
¼ tsp. pepper
Hamburger buns

Cook celery in small amount of water until tender. Saute onion slightly in small amount of fat; remove from pan. Brown ground beef; drain off two-thirds of fat. Add celery, onion, barbecue sauce, salt and pepper. Bring to a boil. Serve on buns. NOTE: Sloppy Joes may be frozen. Yield: 14-18 servings.

Mrs. Marilyn Grasz, Pres.
Zion Ladies Aid
Garland, Nebraska

ROAST BEEF FILLING

2 c. ground roast beef
1 c. grated cheese
¼ c. sandwich spread
2 tbsp. ground pickle or relish
1 tsp. minced onion
Salt and pepper
Buttered buns or slices bread

Combine all ingredients; spread on buns or bread. Place on cookie sheet. Bake at 350 degrees until slightly toasted. Yield: 5-6 servings.

Mrs. W. A. Guinn
Our Savior Ladies Guild
Fort Madison, Iowa

SLOPPY JOES

10 med. onions, chopped
10 lb. hamburger
2 qt. catsup
4 tbsp. Worcestershire sauce
6 tsp. curry powder
2 qt. water
50 hamburger buns

Fry onions until brown; remove. Brown meat; add all ingredients. Simmer for 2 hours. Serve over hamburger buns. Yield: 50 servings.

Mrs. Galen Schaffert, Food Com. Chmn.
Redeemer Mary-Martha Cir.
Chico, California

SLOPPY JOES

1 ½ lb. ground beef
1 onion, chopped
1 ½ tsp. salt
⅛ tsp. pepper
3 tbsp. flour
½ tsp. Worcestershire sauce
1 c. catsup
1 ¼ c. water
Green pepper (opt.)
8 buns

Cook beef, onion, salt and pepper until meat loses its red color. Blend in flour, Worcestershire sauce, catsup, water and green pepper. Simmer for 20 minutes or until thick, stirring frequently. Serve between buns. Yield: 8 servings.

Mrs. Earl R. Beal, Pres.
St. Luke's LCW
Hickory, North Carolina

SLOPPY JOES

1 1 ½-lb. ground beef
1 sm. onion, diced
Salt and pepper
¼ c. prepared chili sauce mix
1 can chicken gumbo soup
½ c. catsup
Toasted buns

Combine ground beef, onion, salt and pepper. Cook over medium heat until done. Add chili sauce, soup and catsup. Cook to spreading consistency. Spread on buns. Yield: 5-6 servings.

Mrs. Ray Freeman
Redeemer Couples Club
Seymour, Indiana

SLOPPY JOES

2 tbsp. finely chopped onion
¼ c. finely chopped green pepper
½ c. finely chopped celery
1 lb. ground beef
½ c. catsup
1 tsp. salt
1 tsp. pepper
1 c. Cheese Whiz
Buns

Brown onion, pepper and celery in small amount of fat. Add ground beef; fry slowly until done. Add catsup, salt, pepper and Cheese Whiz. Fill buns with mixture. Wrap in aluminum foil. Heat in oven until cheese melts. Yield: 8 servings.

Mrs. Robert Fosnacht, Pres.
St. John's LWML
Center Point, Iowa

SLOPPY JOES

1 lb. ground beef
Butter or shortening
Salt to taste
½ c. finely chopped celery
½ c. finely chopped onion
1 10-oz. can prepared gravy or tomato sauce
¼ c. catsup

Brown beef in butter; add salt. Add remaining ingredients; simmer until done. Serve on heated buns. Yield: 4-5 servings.

Mrs. Harry C. Berndt, Pres.
St. Matthew's Evangelical Ladies Aid
Buckingham, Quebec, Canada

SLOPPY JOE HAMBURGERS

1 lb. hamburger
1 sm. onion, diced
1 can tomato soup
Salt and pepper to taste
1 tsp. chili powder
Hamburger buns

Brown hamburger and onion; add soup, salt, pepper and chili powder. Cook for 20 to 30 minutes or until meat is done. Serve on buns. Yield: 12 servings.

Mrs. Fred Klepper, Pres.
Peace Ladies Guild
Omaha, Nebraska

SLOPPY JOE HAMBURGERS

1 lb. ground beef
2 med. onions, cut up
1 can tomato soup
1 tsp. cornstarch
1 tbsp. salt
Hamburger buns

Brown meat and onions; add remaining ingredients. Simmer for 15 minutes. Serve on hamburger buns. Yield: 8 servings.

Mrs. Wilbert Preuss
St. Peter's Ladies Aid
Hemlock, Michigan

SPREAD-A-BURGERS

10 to 12 hamburger buns
1 ½ lb. hamburger
1 tbsp. prepared mustard
1 tsp. salt
1 can tomato soup
½ c. finely chopped onion
1 tbsp. Worcestershire sauce
Dash of pepper

Toast buns. Combine all ingredients except buns. Spread mixture on buns; broil 5 inches from heat until hot and meat is done. Yield: 10-12 servings.

Mrs. George F. Johnson, Chmn.
Mt. Hermon LCW
Annondale, Minnesota

SUPPER ON A BREAD SLICE

⅔ c. evaporated milk
1 ½ lb. ground beef
½ c. cracker crumbs
½ c. chopped onion
1 egg (opt.)
1 tbsp. prepared mustard
1 ½ tsp. salt
¾ tsp. monosodium glutamate
⅛ tsp. pepper
2 c. grated cheese
1 loaf French bread

Combine all ingredients except bread. Cut French bread in half lengthwise. Spread meat mixture over each half. Wrap foil around crust side of each half, leaving top uncovered. Bake at 350 degrees for 25 minutes. Garnish with strips of cheese if desired. Bake for 5 minutes or until cheese melts.

Mrs. Gerge Dandy
Salem LWML
Springdale, Arkansas
Mrs. Howard Junck, Pres.
Zion Ladies Aid
Ogden, Iowa

YUM YUM SANDWICHES

1 c. water
1 tsp. chili powder
¾ c. catsup
½ lge. onion, chopped
1 tsp. dry mustard
2 lb. hamburger
Salt to taste

Boil water, chili powder, catsup, onion and mustard for 5 minutes. Add hamburger and salt. Simmer for 30 minutes or longer. Serve on buns. Yield: 12 servings.

Mrs. Cora Hansen
Resurrection LCW
Ames, Nebraska

YUM YUM SANDWICH FILLING

5 lb. hamburger
5 tbsp. chili powder
5 tbsp. Worcestershire sauce
5 tbsp. sugar
10 tbsp. vinegar
10 tbsp. catsup
2 ½ c. grated potatoes
5 tsp. salt
2 ½ tsp. pepper
Onion (opt.)

Brown hamburger; add remaining ingredients. Simmer for 1 hour or longer. Serve on warm buns. Yield: 50 sandwiches.

Mrs. Melvin Meyer
Lakeside Ladies Aid
Venice, Florida

HOT CHICKEN SALAD SANDWICH

2 c. diced cooked chicken
½ c. diced celery
¼ c. chopped green pepper
3 green onions, chopped
Salt and pepper to taste
¼ c. mayonnaise
Butter
Hamburger buns
Grated Cheddar cheese (opt.)
Butter

Combine all ingredients except hamburger buns, cheese and butter. Spread on hamburger buns. Top each sandwich with 1/4 cup cheese. Dot each sandwich with butter. Wrap each sandwich in a square of foil. Refrigerate until ready to serve. Bake in preheated 450 degree oven for 15 minutes or until heated through.

Mrs. Arline Marquardt
Pilgrims Women's Guild
Lakewood, Ohio

BROILED ALASKA CRAB BURGERS

6 hamburger buns
Butter
1 6 ½-oz. can Alaskan crab, flaked
¼ c. mayonnaise
1 tsp. Worcestershire sauce
¼ c. diced celery
1 dill pickle, diced
6 thin slices cheese

Split and butter buns; toast on split side. Mix remaining ingredients except cheese; spoon onto lower half of buns. Top with cheese slices. Broil 5 inches from heat until cheese melts. Place top on each bun. Yield: 6 servings.

Mrs. Fredrick Stelling, Sec.-Treas.
Our Redeemer Ladies Aid
Chugiak, Alaska

OYSTER SANDWICH FILLING
¼ lb. butter
1 pt. oysters, finely cut
¼ tsp. salt
⅛ tsp. pepper
8 eggs, beaten
¼ c. cracker crumbs

Melt butter in fry pan. Add o y s t e r s, salt and pepper. Simmer for 5 minutes. Add beaten eggs and cracker crumbs. Cook until eggs are done. Serve on white or brown bread, if desired. Yield: 6 servings.

Awanda Feeney, Christian Growth Chmn.
St. Paul's Mary-Martha Cir.
Marengo, Wisconsin

SALMON BURGER
1 1-lb. can salmon, drained and flaked
½ lb. cheese, grated
¼ c. minced onion
1 c. minced celery
½ c. catsup
2 tbsp. sweet relish or chopped sweet pickle
¼ c. mayonnaise
½ tsp. salt
12 hamburger buns

Combine all ingredients in bowl except buns; mix well. Spread on hamburger buns. Wrap each bun in foil. Place on cookie sheet. Bake at 350 degrees for 20 minutes. Yield: 12 servings.

Mrs. William Schnell, Pres.
St. Paul's LWML
Sidney, Nebraska

SALMON-COTTAGE CHEESE SANDWICH
Toasted whole wheat bread
Butter
Salmon
Cottage cheese
Sliced tomato
Seasoning

Spread one slice of bread with butter; add a layer of flaked salmon and a layer of cottage cheese. Add tomato slices and seasoning. Top with remaining slice of bread.

Mrs. Arthur Rude, Pres.
Rendahl ALCW
Dunseith, North Dakota

SALMON SANDWICHES
1 7 ½-oz. can salmon, flaked
¼ c. salad dressing
¼ c. minced celery
1 dill pickle, chopped
Dash of salt
16 slices brown or rye bread, buttered

Mix salmon with salad dressing, celery, pickle and salt. Spread between slices of buttered bread. NOTE: Sweet pickles or pickle relish may be substituted for dill. Yield: 8 servings.

Mrs. Myrna Eyjolfsson, Pres.
Bethel Christian Life Guilds
Port Arthur, Ontario, Canada

SALMON SANDWICH FILLING
1 sm. can red salmon
1 c. cottage cheese, sieved
1 tbsp. minced onion
1 tbsp. minced celery
1 tbsp. minced sweet pickle
2 tbsp. salad dressing
1 tsp. paprika
1 tsp. salt

Drain salmon; remove skin and bones. Flake. Add remaining ingredients; blend. Spread on slices of bread. Yield: 12 sandwiches.

Mrs. Lawrence Wolf, Pres.
Swede Valley LCW
Ogden, Iowa

SHRIMP SANDWICHES
2 tbsp. mayonnaise
1 3-oz. pkg. cream cheese
1 tbsp. catsup
1 tsp. prepared mustard
Dash of garlic salt
1 c. canned or cooked chopped shrimp
¼ c. finely chopped celery
1 tsp. minced onion
10 slices bread

Cream mayonnaise, cream cheese, catsup, mustard and garlic salt. Add shrimp, celery and onion; blend well. Spread 5 slices bread with filling; top with remaining bread. Cut each sandwich into fourths, forming triangles. Yield: 20 servings.

Mrs. Alfred Horrmann, Christian Growth Chmn.
Peace Dorcas Club
Hutchinson, Minnesota

BUN-STEADS

¼ lb. American cheese, cubed
3 hard-cooked eggs, chopped
1 7-oz. can tuna
2 tbsp. chopped celery (opt.)
2 tbsp. chopped onion
2 tbsp. chopped stuffed olives (opt.)
2 tbsp. chopped sweet or dill pickle
2 tbsp. chopped green pepper (opt.)
½ c. mayonnaise
Buns

Combine all ingredients except buns. Spread filling on buns. Wrap in foil. Bake at 250 to 275 degrees for 30 minutes of until filling is heated and cheese melts. Serve hot. Yield: 18 servings.

Mrs. Clyde Kolsrud, Pres.
First Lutheran Church LCW
Mesa, Arizona
Mrs. Frida Christopherson
Zion LCW
Lancaster, Minnesota
Mrs. Edward F. Stegman
St. Paul's Altar Guild
South Bend, Indiana
Mrs. Myrna Bell, Sec.
Grace LCW
Worland, Wyoming
Mrs. Ronald Wagner, Treas.
Zion LWML
Detroit Lakes, Minnesota
Mrs. James Johnson, Pres.
Faith Ladies Soc.
Churubusco, Indiana

DAGWOOD SANDWICHES

5 hard-cooked eggs
1 6-oz. can tuna, flaked
2 c. cubed American cheese
2 tbsp. chopped onion
2 tbsp. chopped stuffed olives
2 tbsp. chopped green pepper
2 tbsp. sweet pickle relish
½ c. salad dressing or mayonnaise

Combine all ingredients. Spread on hamburger buns. Wrap in foil. Bake at 250 degrees for 30 minutes. Yield: 12 servings.

Mrs. M. C. Sandvig, Sales Promoter
Redeemer LCW
Plymouth, Wisconsin

HOT FILLED SANDWICH

1 can tuna, drained and flaked
1 c. chopped cheese
½ c. mayonnaise
2 tbsp. chopped onion
2 tbsp. chopped pickle
3 hard-cooked eggs, chopped
24 buns

Combine all ingredients except buns; mix well. Spread on buns. Wrap each bun in a piece of foil. Bake at 350 degrees for 1 hour. Yield: 24 servings.

Mrs. Walter Hickman
Zion Ladies Aid
Warren, Minnesota

SUBMARINES

1 6½-oz. can tuna
2 hard-cooked eggs
1 tbsp. chopped onion
½ c. chopped celery
½ tsp. prepared mustard
½ c. salad dressing or mayonnaise
8 hot dog buns

Combine tuna, eggs, onion and celery; mix well. Add mustard and salad dressing; stir to mix well. Cut buns into halves lengthwise. With a fork, remove part of the inside of the roll. Heap with tuna mixture. Place top slice back on roll. Yield: 8 servings.

Mrs. Lester Debrick, Sec.
Trinity Ladies Aid
Paola, Kansas

TUNA BURGERS

1 7-oz. can tuna, drained and flaked
1 c. chopped celery
1 sm. onion, minced
½ c. diced Cheddar cheese
½ c. chopped ripe olives
¼ c. mayonnaise
Salt and pepper to taste
6 hamburger buns, buttered

Combine all ingredients except buns. Fill buns with tuna mixture. Wrap each bun in foil. Refrigerate. Bake at 350 degrees for 15 to 20 minutes. NOTE: One cup cut-up chicken may be substituted for 1 can tuna. Yield: 6 servings.

Mrs. Willard Brown, Pres.
St. Paul's Ruth Cir.
Emmetsburg, Iowa

OPEN-FACED TUNA BURGERS

1 6 ½-oz. can tuna
¼ c. finely diced celery
2 tbsp. finely chopped onion
½ c. Cheddar cheese
1 tsp. prepared horseradish mustard
½ c. mayonnaise
Buns

Mix all ingredients except buns; spread on each half of bun. Place under broiler; cook until bubbly.

Mrs. Kenneth Greiman, Pres.
St. Paul's Ladies Aid Soc.
Garner, Iowa

TUNA SANDWICHES

2 cans tuna
3 hard-cooked eggs, chopped
2 stalks celery, finely chopped
1 sm. onion, grated
Salad dressing
8 to 10 buns, buttered
8 to 10 slices cheese

Mix tuna, eggs, celery and onion; add enough salad dressing to moisten. Spread filling on buns. Add slice of cheese; cover with top of bun. Wrap in foil. Bake at 350 degrees until cheese begins to melt. NOTE: Chopped ham or luncheon meat may be substituted for tuna. Yield: 8-10 servings.

Mrs. Thomas W. Pagel, Pres.
Good Shepherd ALCW
Bismarck, North Dakota

TUNA BURGERS

3 slices bread
⅔ c. evaporated milk
1 tbsp. catsup
1 tbsp. prepared mustard
1 tbsp. pickle relish
2 6 ½ or 7-oz. cans tuna
6 buns

Remove crusts from bread; place bread in bowl. Pour evaporated milk over bread. Add catsup, mustard and relish; mix with fork until blended. Add tuna; mix well. Spoon mixture onto bun halves. Broil for 8 minutes or until browned. Top with remaining bun halves. Yield: 6 servings.

Mrs. Richard Haag, Sec.
St. Paul's Ladies Aid
Three Rivers, Texas

TUNA SANDWICHES

12 hard-cooked eggs, chopped
1 sm. bunch celery, diced
6 sweet or sour pickles or olives, diced
4 tbsp. salad dressing
¼ c. half and half
½ tsp. salt
2 6 ½-oz. cans tuna

Combine eggs, celery and pickles. Mix salad dressing, half and half and salt; add to eggs, celery and pickles. Add to tuna. Chill until ready to use. Spread on slices of bread or buns with lettuce leaves, if desired. Yield: 10 servings.

Mrs. Bertha H. Kemp, Pres.
Immanuel Ladies Aid
Arriba, Colorado

TUNA BUNWICHES

1 can tuna
4 hard-cooked eggs, chopped
2 tbsp. minced onion
½ c. diced Velveeta cheese
Salad dressing
Buns

Combine tuna, eggs, onion and cheese, adding enough salad dressing to moisten. Spread on buns. Place in 350 degree oven; cook until cheese melts.

Mrs. Roy Biberdorf
Immanual Lutheran Church
Greenville, Tennessee

HAM AND CHEESE ROLL-UPS

½ lb. boiled ham, cubed
½ lb. sharp Cheddar cheese, ground
2 hard-cooked eggs, finely chopped
⅓ c. finely chopped onion
½ c. chili sauce
½ c. pitted green or salad olives
3 tbsp. mayonnaise
Hot dog buns

Combine all ingredients except buns; fill buns. Wrap in foil. Bake at 450 degrees for 10 minutes. Yield: 12 servings.

Mrs. Elizabeth Lentz, Pres.
St. John's Ladies Aid
Withee, Wisconsin

LOUISE'S FAVORITE SANDWICH

½ lb. bacon, cut into small pieces
¼ lb. American or Cheddar cheese, grated
Finely chopped onion
Buns

Fry bacon until partially cooked. Mix bacon, cheese and onion; spread on bun halves. Broil until cheese is bubbly and bacon is cooked. Serve hot. NOTE: May be prepared in advance and broiled just before serving.

Mrs. Henry S. Hanson, Pres.
Faith LCW
Balsam Lake, Wisconsin

HAM-PINEAPPLE FILLING

2 lb. cooked ham
4 8-oz. pkg. cream cheese
2 No. 2 cans crushed pineapple, drained

Grind ham coarsely. Mix with cream cheese and pineapple. Yield: 50 servings.

Allonia M. Morris, Treas.
St. Paul's Miss'y Cir.
Hancock, Maryland

HOT HAM SALAD SANDWICHES

1 c. ground cooked ham
1 c. sharp Cheddar cheese
1 sm. onion
1 hard-cooked egg
¼ c. relish
¼ to ½ c. salad dressing
1 tbsp. salad mustard
5 brown and serve French rolls or hamburger
  buns

Grind ham, cheese, onion and egg. Add relish, salad dressing and mustard; mix thoroughly. Place ham mixture on rolls or buns. Bake at 325 degrees for 10 minutes or until cheese melts and bread browns. Yield: 5 servings.

Mrs. Robert W. Schulz, Pres.
Good Shepherd LCW
Monroeville, Pennsylvania

HOT HAM BUNS

¼ c. soft butter
2 tbsp. horseradish mustard
2 tsp. poppy seed
2 tbsp. finely chopped onion
4 hamburger buns, split
4 thin slices boiled ham
4 slices process cheese

Mix butter, mustard, poppy seed and onion. Spread on buns. Add slice of ham and cheese to each bun. Place on baking sheet. Bake at 350 degrees for 20 minutes. Yield: 4 servings.

Mrs. Jacob Tjepkema, Pres.
St. John's LWML
Norwood, Minnesota

HOT HAM SANDWICH

1 can chopped ham
½ lb. Cheddar cheese
1 med. onion
16 slices bread, buttered
4 eggs, beaten
3 c. milk
1 can cream of mushroom soup
Sliced mushrooms

Grind ham, cheese and onion. Place 8 slices of bread, buttered-side down, in 10 x 14-inch baking dish or pan. Spread with ham, cheese and onion mixture. Cover with remaining bread, buttered-side up. Combine eggs and milk; pour over mixture in baking dish. Refrigerate for 24 hours. Bake at 250 degrees for 2 hours. Cut into eight pieces; serve with sauce of soup and mushrooms. Yield: 8 servings.

Mrs. Lester L. Hawkes, Pres.
St. John's ALCW
Madison, Wisconsin

SATURDAY SUPPER SANDWICHES

2 eggs, beaten
1 c. evaporated milk
½ tsp. salt
Dash of pepper
8 slices bread
Butter
8 slices boiled ham
Prepared mustard
4 slices Swiss cheese
Shortening

Blend eggs, milk, salt and pepper; set aside. Spread 4 slices of bread lightly with butter; add a slice of ham to each slice of bread. Spread lightly with mustard; add slice of cheese and second slice of ham. Top with unbuttered slice of bread. Dip each sandwich into egg and milk mixture; fry in shortening until golden, turning once. Yield: 4 servings.

Mrs. Herbert F. Chapman, Sec.
Redeemer Women's Guild
Colden, New York

BARBECUED PORK SANDWICHES

4 lb. lean pork shoulder,
1 bunch pascal celery, cut up
2 sm. onions, sliced
1 qt. tomatoes
Salt and pepper to taste
2 doz. buns

Place all ingredients except buns in kettle; simmer all day. Serve on buns. Yield: 24 servings.

Mrs. H. O. Porter, Pres.
St. Paul's LWML
Decatur, Alabama

BARBECUE SAUCE

1 bottle catsup
1 tbsp. prepared mustard
2 tbsp. Worcestershire sauce
½ tsp. salt
¼ tsp. pepper
1 tbsp. chopped green pepper
1 tsp. chopped pimento
1 tbsp. vinegar
1 c. water
Left-over thinly sliced pork or beef

Combine all ingredients except meat. Boil for 3 minutes. Add meat.

Mrs. Walter Mueller
St. John's Ladies Aid
Litchfield, Illinois

BARBECUED CORNED BEEF SANDWICHES

½ tsp. chili powder
2 tbsp. vinegar
Dash of pepper
1 c. tomato sauce
1 12-oz. can corned beef
6 slices bread or toast
1 onion, sliced (opt.)

Combine chili powder, vinegar, pepper, tomato sauce and corned beef in heavy skillet. Simmer for 20 minutes or until thick. Spoon onto slice of bread. Add slice of onion to top of barbecue. NOTE: Sandwich may be topped with a second slice of bread. Yield: 6 servings.

Mrs. Ross J. Stern, Cor. Sec.
Samuel's Bertha Walker LCW
Somerset, Pennsylvania

CORNED BEEF BURGER

1 12-oz. can corned beef, chopped
3 tbsp. finely chopped onion
1 tbsp. prepared mustard
3 tbsp. mayonnaise
1 ½ tsp. horseradish
3 tbsp. butter or margarine
9 hamburger buns, split
Butter
9 slices process cheese

Combine all ingredients except buns, butter and cheese. Spread buns with butter. Spread mixture on bottom halves of buns; top with slice of cheese. Toast under broiler until cheese melts; cover with toasted tops. Yield: 9 servings.

Mrs. H. G. Busch, Pres.
Hope LCW
Victoria, British Columbia, Canada

CORNED BEEF DIPWICHES

16 slices white bread
1 5-oz. jar cheese and olive spread
2 12-oz. cans corned beef, chilled
3 eggs
⅔ c. milk
1 tbsp. prepared mustard
2 tsp. caraway seed
Butter

Spread bread with cheese spread. Slice each can of corned beef into four slices. Place corned beef on one-half the bread slices, top with remaining bread, cheese-side down. Beat eggs, milk, mustard and caraway seed. Dip each sandwich into mixture, covering both sides. Brown on both sides in butter in skillet. Serve hot. Yield: 8 servings.

Photograph for this recipe on page 311.

SCHOOL DAY SANDWICH

1 12-oz. can corned beef, shredded
½ c. catsup
½ c. mayonnaise
2 tbsp. chopped sweet pickle
1 tbsp. grated onion

Combine all ingredients; stir until blended. Spread between slices of rye bread. Yield: 2 1/2 cups.

Dorothy Tuttle, Pres.
Immanuel Ladies Aid
Tacoma, Washington

HOT CORNED BEEF BARBS

½ tsp. chili powder
1 tbsp. cider vinegar
1 tbsp. Worcestershire sauce
Pinch of cayenne (opt.)
¼ c. plus 2 tbsp. catsup
¼ c. plus 2 tbsp. water
1 12-oz. can corned beef, broken up
Whole sweet pickles
Buns

Combine all ingredients except pickles and buns in skillet. Cook, uncovered, over medium heat, stirring occasionally, for 20 minutes or until most of liquid has evaporated and mixture is thickened. Broil buns 4 inches from broiler until toasted. Garnish with pickle. Yield: 10 servings.

Mrs. Albert Sample, Parish Sec.
Leganger ALCW
Toronto, South Dakota

DRIED BEEF AND TAPIOCA SANDWICH FILLING

1 ¾ c. tomato soup
⅛ tsp. pepper
2 tbsp. instant tapioca
¼ tsp. dry mustard
2 ½ c. grated brick or American cheese
1 ¼ c. ground dried beef
¼ tsp. Worcestershire sauce

Combine all ingredients in a double boiler except cheese, beef and Worcestershire sauce; cook for 5 minutes. Add cheese; stir until blended. Add dried beef and Worcestershire sauce. Yield: 2 1/2 cups.

Mrs. Lillie Gilster
St. John's LWML
Pender, Nebraska

LUNCHEON MEAT ON BROILED BUNS

1 can luncheon meat
¼ lb. Velveeta or American cheese
Grated onion
2 tbsp. milk
4 tbsp. mayonnaise
2 tbsp. catsup
12 hamburger buns

Grind luncheon meat with cheese. Add a small amount of onion. Add milk, mayonnaise and catsup. Mix until moist. Spread luncheon meat mixture on each bun half. Broil for a few minutes until cheese melts and is slightly browned. Yield: 12 servings.

Mrs. Edwin Schroder
St. John's Ladies Aid
Plato, Minnesota

FUN ON A BUN

1 can luncheon meat
1 sm. onion
½ lb. Cheddar cheese
1 can cream of mushroom soup
12 buns

Grind luncheon meat with onion and cheese. Stir in soup. Scoop out centers of buns. Fill with luncheon meat mixture. Wrap in foil; heat in oven or on grill. Yield: 12 servings.

Mrs. Harold Vinson, VP
St. Paul's Ladies Aid
Fort Dodge, Iowa

GOOEY BUNS

1 lb. minced ham or bologna
¾ lb. sharp cheese
8 sweet pickles
1 sm. onion
¼ c. mustard
⅓ c. salad dressing
Buttered buns

Grind ham, cheese, pickles and onion. Add mustard and dressing. Fill buns with spread. Wrap in foil. Bake at 300 degrees for 30 minutes. Yield: 12 servings.

Mrs. Doris Mauer, Pres.
Our Redeemer Evening Guild
Dubuque, Iowa

HOT MEAT SANDWICH

½ can luncheon meat
1 tbsp. diced onion
½ c. diced cheese
1 tbsp. catsup
2 tbsp. diced sweet pickle
2 hard-cooked eggs, chopped
3 tbsp. cream or melted butter
6 buns

Combine ingredients except buns; spread on buns. Wrap in foil; heat in oven until hot. Yield: 6 servings.

Mrs. Wallace Schwarz, Pres.
St. Peter's Evangelical Lutheran Church
Vernon Center, Minnesota

LUNCHEON MEAT SANDWICH

1 can luncheon meat
½ c. chopped onion
½ c. chopped green pepper
1 c. grated American cheese
Butter
16 hamburger buns

Chop meat; add onion, green pepper and grated cheese. Mix well. Butter buns; fill and wrap in foil. Heat at 350 degrees for 20 minutes. Serve warm. Yield: 16 servings.

Mrs. W. J. Stedtfeld, Pres.
St. Michael's LCW
St. Paul, Minnesota

LUNCHEON MEAT SANDWICH

1 can luncheon meat
1 med. onion
½ lb. Velveeta cheese
½ can tomato soup
12 hamburger buns, halved

Grind luncheon meat with onion and cheese; mix in soup. Spread luncheon meat mixture on each bun half. Broil for a few minutes until cheese is melted and slightly browned. Serve hot.

Mrs. Sally J. Caboth
St. John's Ladies Aid
Galva, Iowa

SANDWICH FILLING

1 lb. minced ham, ground
½ c. shredded Cheddar cheese
¼ c. chopped stuffed olives
2 ½ tbsp. chopped onion
2 hard-cooked eggs, chopped
4 tbsp. mayonnaise
2 tbsp. catsup
Dash of Worcestershire sauce

Mix all ingredients. Spread on buns; wrap in foil. Bake at 350 degrees for 15 to 20 minutes. Yield: 12 servings.

Mrs. Alvin E. Brandt, Chmn.
Zion Ladies Aid
Avon, South Dakota

SURPRISE SANDWICH SPREAD

1 can luncheon meat
6 hard-cooked eggs
6 sweet or dill pickles
½ sm. box Velveeta cheese
1 sm. onion
5 tbsp. salad dressing
Buttered hamburger buns

Grind all ingredients except dressing and buns. Add salad dressing to moisten; mix well. Spread on buns. Wrap in foil. Bake at 350 degrees for 20 minutes. NOTE: If made into open-faced sandwiches, broil until cheese melts. Yield: 10 servings.

Mrs. Robert Freeman, Pres.
Cottage Grove Ladies Aid and LWML
Cottage Grove, Oregon

BARBECUE SAUCE FOR WIENERS

¼ c. chopped onion
½ c. catsup
½ c. water
1 tbsp. sugar
1 tbsp. Worcestershire sauce
2 tbsp. vinegar
1 tsp. dry mustard
1 lb. frankfurters

Cook onion in hot fat; add remaining ingredients except frankfurters. Simmer, covered, for 10 minutes. Add frankfurters; simmer for 15 minutes longer. Serve on split buns or on rice. Yield: 5 servings.

Mrs. Danny Luedke, Pres.
Grace Persis Soc.
Marlin, Texas

QUICK TASTY HOT DOGS

Catsup
Mustard
Minced onion
Relish
8 wiener rolls
8 wieners
Cheese strips

Spread catsup, mustard, 1 teaspoonful onion and relish on each roll. Insert wiener into roll; top with strip of cheese. Wrap each roll in foil. Bake at 400 degrees for 20 minutes. Yield: 8 servings.

Mrs. Aden W. Cole
Martin Luther Lutheran Church
Savannah, Georgia

HAWAIIAN-STYLE SANDWICHES

4 slices white bread, buttered
4 slices cooked chicken
4 sliced ham
4 slices American cheese
1 egg
1 tbsp. milk
Pinch of sugar
Pinch of salt
Butter

Remove crusts from bread. Add a slice of chicken, ham and cheese to each slice of bread. Roll like jelly roll. Slice rolls into three portions. Mix egg, milk, sugar and salt. Dip each sandwich into egg mixture. Fry in butter on all sides until lightly browned and cheese is melted. Yield: 4 servings.

Mrs. Ralph Gunsenhouser, Sec.-Treas.
Redeemer Esther Guild
Ft. Wayne, Indiana

MOCK CHICKEN SANDWICHES

¾ lb. beef
¾ lb. pork
3 or 4 hard-cooked eggs
1 med. onion
3 med. pickles
Celery
Mayonnaise
Salt and pepper to taste

Boil meats until well done; reserve broth. Put meats, eggs, onion, pickles and celery through food chopper. Mix with mayonnaise and broth. Add salt and pepper. Spread on thin slices of bread.

Mrs. Don Struebing, Sec.
Salem LWML
Springdale, Arkansas

PIZZA BURGERS

¾ lb. ground beef
¾ lb. ground pork
Salt and pepper
2 tbsp. minced onion
¾ c. catsup
¼ c. barbecue sauce
6 hamburger buns
1 c. grated cheese

Season meats with salt, pepper and onion; fry in small amount of butter. Add catsup and barbecue sauce; spread on split buns. Sprinkle cheese on top. Broil until cheese melts. Yield: 12 servings.

Mrs. George Emich
St. Paul's LWML
Lester Prairie, Minnesota

SCRUMPTIOUS SANDWICH SPREAD

1 can luncheon meat, ground
1 can tuna
1 can cream of chicken soup

Combine all ingredients; serve on bread or buns.

Mrs. Hartwin Flitter, Pres.
Salem Ladies Aid
Madelia, Minnesota

SASKATCHEWAN CHICKEN AND HAM

¼ c. chopped fresh mushrooms
1 tbsp. butter
1 tbsp. flour
2 c. minced cooked or canned chicken
½ c. cream
½ to ¾ lb. precooked ham, ¼-in. thick
Paprika
4 slices hot toast

Cook mushrooms in butter for 5 minutes. Blend in flour. Add chicken and cream; set aside. Cut ham into four pieces; sprinkle both sides with paprika. Brown for 5 to 7 minutes on both sides in hot skillet. Place ham on toast; keep hot. Heat chicken mixture. Heap on top of ham. Yield: 4 servings.

Irene Childs
Immanuel LCW
Naicam, Saskatchewan, Canada

SKEWER DOGS

1 lb. ground beef
¾ c. soft bread crumbs
¼ c. milk
2 tbsp. chopped onion
1 egg, slightly beaten
½ tsp. salt
Dash of pepper
6 frankfurters
1 c. catsup
¼ c. butter, melted
¼ c. molasses
2 tbsp. vinegar
6 slices bacon
Toasted wiener buns

Combine ground beef, bread crumbs, milk, onion, egg, salt and pepper. Divide meat mixture into six portions. Shape meat around frankfurters, covering completely. Roll between waxed paper to make uniform. Chill; insert skewers lengthwise into frankfurters. Combine remaining ingredients except bacon and buns. Simmer for about 15 minutes. Wrap each frankfurter spirial-fashioned with bacon slice. Secure with toothpick. Broil frankfurters 3-inches from heat for 15 minutes. Brush with hot sauce just before removing from heat. Serve on toasted wiener buns.

Mrs. Carol Sorensen, Pres.
Mt. Olive Ladies Soc.
Des Moines, Iowa

Soup and
Stew Favorites

RECIPE FOR VENISON STEW WITH DUMPLINGS ON PAGE 343

ARABIAN STEW

Oil
5 med. potatoes, sliced
1 c. rice
1 med. onion, sliced
4 stalks celery, diced
¼ tsp. salt
Pepper to taste
1 lb. hamburger or 4 to 6 pork chops
1 can tomato soup
½ soup can water

Place a small amount of oil in casserole. Add potatoes, rice, onion, celery, salt and pepper. Place meat on top of mixture. Add soup and water. Bake at 350 degrees for 1 hour and 30 minutes. Reduce heat to 250 degrees and bake for 30 minutes longer. Yield: 6 servings.

Mrs. Gordon Raaflaub
St. Paul's Ladies Aid
Magnetarvan, Ontario, Canada

BEEF CHUCK STEW

2 lb. chuck stew meat
1 can cream of mushroom soup
1 soup can water
1 can tomato sauce
1 pkg. dry onion soup mix
Diced potatoes
Diced carrots
Diced turnips
Chopped celery

Combine meat, mushroom soup, water, tomato sauce and onion soup mix in heavy kettle or casserole. Cook, uncovered, at 325 degrees for 2 hours. Add vegetables. Cook, covered, 1 hour longer. Yield: 6 servings.

Mrs. Frances E. Neumann
Trinity Ladies Aid
Stockton, California

Brown meat slowly in fat until well browned. Add onion and celery; cook for a few minutes longer. Sprinkle with flour and stir quickly to blend; add tomatoes and enough hot water to cover. Add salt and pepper; cover tightly and simmer for 2 hours. Add diced carrots and potatoes; continue cooking until vegetables are tender. Add peas and cook for 5 to 10 minutes longer. Yield: 6-8 servings.

Mrs. Arnold Ammeter, Pres.
Starbuck LCW
Headingley, Manitoba, Canada

BEEF STEW

3 lb. beef cubes
¼ c. flour
3 tsp. salt
¼ tsp. pepper
4 tbsp. fat
4 c. boiling water
1 c. tomato sauce
1 onion, sliced
1 bay leaf
4 whole cloves
12 sm. whole onions
6 potatoes
6 carrots
1 pkg. frozen lima beans

Shake beef cubes in paper bag with flour, 1 teaspoonful salt and pepper. Brown in hot fat. Add hot water, tomato sauce, sliced onion, bay leaf, remaining salt and cloves. Simmer for 1 hour and 30 minutes to 2 hours. Add remaining ingredients except beans. Cook for 30 minutes. Add beans and cook for 15 minutes longer. Yield: 6-8 servings.

Mrs. Arthur M. Bicker
St. John's Evangelical Ladies Aid
Accident, Maryland

BEEF STEW

2 ½ to 3 lb. stew beef, cut into bite-sized
    pieces
2 to 3 tbsp. fat or drippings
1 med. onion, chopped
1 stalk celery, chopped
2 to 3 tbsp. flour
2 c. canned tomatoes
Hot water
Salt and pepper to taste
3 or 4 carrots, quartered
3 or 4 potatoes, quartered
2 c. fresh or frozen peas

BEEF STEW

2 lb. lean beef
¼ c. flour
2 tsp. salt
2 tbsp. pure vegetable oil
1 c. hot water
2 8-oz. cans tomato sauce
⅛ tsp. pepper
½ bay leaf
⅛ tsp. thyme
6 carrots
6 potatoes
6 onions
1 c. chopped celery

(Continued on next page)

Roll meat in flour mixed with salt. Brown slowly in hot oil; add water, tomato sauce and seasonings. Cover tightly; simmer for 1 hour and 30 minutes. Cut vegetables to desired size; add to meat mixture. Sprinkle with additional salt and pepper. Cover and simmer for 45 minutes or longer. Yield: 6 servings.

Mrs. Otto Morlock, Pres.
Zion Dorcas Cir.
Valley City, Ohio

BEEF STEW

2 lb. beef, cut into 1 ½-in. cubes
Fat
2 c. water
2 tbsp. lemon juice
1 tbsp. Worcestershire sauce
1 clove of garlic
4 tsp. salt
⅛ tsp. pepper
½ tsp. allspice
2 bay leaves
1 tsp. sugar
1 onion, sliced
1 lb. whole onions
12 potatoes
6 carrots

Brown meat well in fat. Simmer with remaining ingredients except whole onions, potatoes and carrots for 2 hours or until meat is tender. Add vegetables; cook until tender. Yield: 6 servings.

Mrs. Steve Karlik
Skaneateles Women's Cir.
Skaneateles, New York

BEEF STEW

2 lb. beef
Flour
Fat
1 onion, diced
½ c. diced carrots
½ c. diced celery
1 qt. stock or water
Salt
¼ tsp. pepper
6 potatoes, diced
4 tsp. baking powder
½ c. tomatoes

Cut meat into small pieces; dredge in flour. Brown meat in a small amount fat in a heavy skillet. Saute onion, carrot and celery; add to meat. Add stock or water. Add 1 teaspoonful salt, pepper and potatoes. Cook until potatoes are soft. Sift 2 cups flour with baking powder and 1/2 teaspoonful salt into mixing bowl. Mix mix enough water to make drop batter consistency. Drop batter from spoon into baking stew,

adding tomatoes and additional water if needed. Cover with tight fitting lid. Cook rapidly for 10 to 20 minutes, depending on size of dumplings.

Mrs. Lellian Quandt
Trinity LWML
Tuka, Illinois

BEEF STEW BOURBONNAISE

1 ½ lb. beef chuck, cut into 1-in. cubes
1 tbsp. shortening
1 clove of garlic, minced
1 med. onion, chopped
½ tsp. salt
⅛ tsp. pepper
1 can tomato soup
¾ c. red wine
¼ c. water
¼ tsp. powdered basil
¼ tsp. thyme
½ c. catsup
3 med. carrots, coarsely chopped
1 ½ c. celery, cut into 1-in. pieces
4 med. potatoes, cut up

Lightly brown beef in shortening; add garlic and onion. Saute until transparent. Sprinkle with salt and pepper; stir in undiluted soup, wine and water. Cover and simmer for 30 minutes. Add herbs and catsup. Arrange vegetables on top of meat and gravy. Cover. Simmer for 1 hour and 30 minutes or until meat and vegetables are tender. Add additional water if necessary. NOTE: One-half cup lemon juice may be substituted for red wine. Increase water for 1/4 to 3/4 cup. Yield: 6 servings.

Ethel Waterbury
Zion Ladies Aid Soc.
East Haven, Connecticut

BROWN BEEF STEW

2 lb. lean chuck or round steak
1 tbsp. salt
½ tsp. pepper
Flour
2 tbsp. vegetable oil
2 c. boiling water
½ tsp. paprika
1 tsp. brown sugar
1 tsp. Worcestershire sauce
1 sm. onion, chopped
Dash of garlic powder
Dash of ground cloves or allspice
1 bay leaf
4 sm. carrots, cubed
8 sm. white onions
1 pkg. frozen peas
Several stalks of celery, cut into 1-in. pieces
¼ c. chopped parsley

(Continued on next page)

Cut meat into thick cubes. Rub meat with salt and pepper. Pound all flour possible into beef pieces. Sear slowly until brown on all sides in hot oil. Add water, p a p r i k a, brown sugar, Worcestershire sauce, chopped onion, garlic powder, ground c l o v e s and bay leaf. Simmer slowly for 2 hours, stirring occasionally. Cook carrots, whole white onions, peas and celery separately until tender. Add to meat and stir well. Simmer until ready to serve. Add parsley. NOTE: Small potatoes may be added if desired. Yield: 8 servings.

Mrs. Rosemarie West
Bethlehem LWML
Richmond, Virginia

CHILI

1 ½ lb. hamburger
1 lge. onion, chopped
2 tbsp. butter
1 qt. tomatoes
1 qt. water
1 tbsp. sugar
1 tsp. salt
¼ tsp. pepper
1 green pepper, chopped
1 tsp. chili powder
2 tbsp. rice
2 cans kidney beans

Saute hamburger and onion in butter. Season to taste. Combine tomatoes, w a t e r, sugar, salt, pepper, green pepper, chili powder and rice in 3-quart kettle. Add browned hamburger mixture and simmer for 2 hours. Add kidney beans 20 minutes before serving. Yield: 8 servings.

Mrs. Marvin Gesell, Pres.
Christ Lutheran Church Ladies Cir.
Norfolk, Nebraska

CHILI

2 lb. ground beef
2 cans Chili-ets
2 1-qt. tomato juice
2 tbsp. chili powder
1 c. diced onions
Salt to taste

Fry meat until medium done. Add to Chili-ets, tomato juice and chili powder. Cook onions in water; drain. Add onions to mixture. Cook for at least 1 hour, adding water if necessary. Yield: 6 servings.

Mrs. Alma Wiese
LWML
Schleswig, Iowa

CHILI

2 lb. ground chuck
2 tbsp. salt
1 lge. onion, chopped
½ lb. ground suet
1 46-oz. can tomato juice
3 cans red beans
1 ½ tbsp. chili powder
1 tsp. ground red pepper
1 tsp. vinegar

Cook beef, salt and onion in suet in skillet until done. Do not brown. Combine all ingredients in large pot or electric cooker. Simmer for several hours. Yield: 8 servings.

Mrs. Gilbert C. Nieburg, Pres.
Ebenezer Ladies Aid Soc.
St. Louis, Missouri

CHILI

1 lb. ground beef
1 tbsp. salad oil
1 med. can tomatoes
1 tbsp. chili powder
1 tbsp. cold water
1 tsp. salt
1 tsp. sugar
1 tsp. Worcestershire sauce
2 c. cooked or canned red kidney beans

Brown beef in oil over medium heat, stirring constantly. Mix tomatoes and chili powder in cold water. Add to meat with salt, sugar and Worcestershire sauce. Bring to a boil. Cover; simmer for 1 hour. Add beans; cook, uncovered, until well heated. Yield: 4 servings.

Mrs. Jim R. Wesson
Redeemer Lutheran Church
Elizabethton, Tennessee

CHILI CON CARNE

½ to ¾ lb. ground beef
1 med. onion, chopped
1 tbsp. flour
1 pt. tomatoes
2 c. kidney or pinto beans, cooked
4 tbsp. chili sauce
2 to 3 tsp. chili powder
⅛ tsp. garlic powder
1 ½ to 2 c. water
1 beef bouillon cube
Salt and pepper
Pinch of oregano

Brown meat and onion in 3-quart saucepan. Add remaining ingredients except beans. Simmer for 2 hours, adding beans 1 hour before serving. Yield: 4-6 servings.

Carol K. Ernsthausen, Pres.
Trinity Guild
Spencerport, New York

CHILI CON CARNE

1 tbsp. shortening
2 med. onion, cut up
1 ½ lb. ground beef
1 ½ tsp. salt
¼ tsp. pepper
1 tsp. chili powder
½ tsp. monosodium glutamate
1 20-oz. can baked beans or kidney beans
1 28-oz. can tomatoes

Heat shortening; brown onions slightly. Add meat, salt, pepper, chili powder and monosodium glutamate. Stir occasionally until meat is brown. Add beans and tomatoes. Place in 2-quart casserole; bake in preheated 400 degree oven for 45 minutes. Yield: 5 servings.

Mrs. Norman Evenson, Pres.
Bethel LCW
Frontier, Saskatchewan, Canada

CHILI CON CARNE

Salt and pepper to taste
2 lb. ground chuck
1 tbsp. fat or margarine
1 lge. can tomatoes
1 lge. can kidney beans
1 can tomato soup
1 16-oz. jar spaghetti sauce
1 tbsp. chili powder

Brown seasoned meat in fat in deep frying pan. Add remaining ingredients except chili powder. Stir; add chili powder. Bring to a boil, but do not boil. Simmer for 2 hours. Yield: 8 servings.

Mrs. Eva Jane Conge
Hope LWML
Pompano Beach, Florida

CHILI CON CARNE

¼ c. olive oil
2 lb. lean beef, coarsely chopped
¼ lb. beef suet, coarsely chopped
1 c. chopped onions
1 c. chopped celery
2 cloves of garlic
2 tbsp. chili powder
1 tbsp. paprika
2 tsp. oregano (opt.)
Salt and pepper to taste
2 ½ c. canned tomatoes
2 c. red kidney beans

Heat olive oil; add meat and suet. Cook until meat is brown. Add onions, celery and garlic;

cook for 5 minutes, stirring constantly. Add seasonings and tomatoes. Simmer for 2 hours. Add kidney beans just before serving. Yield: 8 servings.

Mrs. Olga Aegard, Pres.
Salem LCW
Pass Lake, Ontario, Canada

COWBOY STEW

1 lb. stew beef
2 c. water
½ onion, sliced
1 tsp. salt
½ tsp. sugar
¼ tsp. pepper
½ tsp. Worcestershire sauce
1 tsp. lemon juice
¼ c. chopped celery
2 tomatoes, quartered
3 carrots, quartered
3 potatoes, quartered
3 sm. onions, quartered

Brown meat in own fat. Drain off excess fat. Add water, sliced onion, salt, sugar, pepper, Worcestershire sauce and lemon juice. Bring to a boil; reduce heat and simmer for 2 hours. Add celery, tomatoes and carrots. Simmer for 30 minutes. Add potatoes and quartered onions. Simmer for 30 minutes longer. Yield: 4 servings.

June M. Schraer, Pres.
Zion LWML
Pevely, Missouri

DINNER PARTY STEW

1 lb. lean beef chuck, cut into small cubes
3 tbsp. flour
Salt
Pepper
3 med. onions, sliced
3 tbsp. fat
½ c. tomato juice
1 ¾ c. meat stock
1 tsp. sugar
½ c. sour cream
1 sm. can mushrooms (opt.)

Roll beef cubes in flour mixed with 1/2 teaspoonful salt and dash of pepper. Brown meat and onions in hot fat for 10 to 15 minutes. Add tomato juice, meat stock and sugar. Bring to a boil; reduce heat. Cover and simmer gently for 1 hour and 30 minutes or until tender. Blend in sour cream and mushrooms; bring to a boil, stirring. Add salt and pepper to taste. Serve in rice ring or on cooked rice, if desired. Yield: 4 servings.

Mrs. Robert O. Kunkel, Pres.
First Lutheran Church LWML
Birmingham, Alabama

EASY OVEN BEEF STEW

1 ½ lb. stew meat
2 med. to lge. potatoes, peeled and sliced
    ½-in. thick
4 med. to lge. size carrots, cut up
3 stalks celery, chopped
½ lge. onion, sliced
1 can tomato soup
1 c. water

Place stew meat in lightly greased 3-quart baking dish. Layer vegetables over meat. Pour mixture of soup and water over all. Cover and bake at 275 degrees for 5 hours. Yield: 4 servings.

Mrs. Alvin Olson
Our Savior's LCW
Great Falls, Montana

EASY OVEN STEW

2 lb. round steak
2 tbsp. flour
1 tsp. salt
⅛ tsp. pepper
⅛ tsp. paprika
2 tbsp. vegetable oil
4 to 6 sm. onions
1 c. sliced celery
4 sm. potatoes, cubed
4 sm. carrots
1 c. water
1 or 2 8-oz. cans tomato sauce

Cut steak into 1/2-inch cubes. Combine flour, salt, pepper and paprika; roll beef in seasoned flour. Toss meat with oil in 3-quart casserole. Bake at 400 degrees for 30 minutes, stirring once. Add vegetables; toss with meat and meat juices. Add water and additional salt and pepper to taste. Pour tomato sauce over all; mix well. Cover and bake at 350 degrees for 1 hour and 45 minutes to 2 hours or to desired doneness. Yield: 4-6 servings.

Mrs. W. J. Docherty, Sec.-Treas.
St. Timothy LCW
Regina, Saskatchewan, Canada

FIVE-HOUR STEW

2 lb. lean stew meat, cubed
1 can peas
1 c. sliced carrots
2 med. onions, chopped
1 lge. potato, cubed
1 tsp. salt
Dash of pepper
1 can tomato soup
½ soup can water

Place ingredients in large casserole; cover. Bake at 275 degrees for 5 hours. Yield: 5-6 servings.

Mrs. Don Haussler, Chmn.
Bethel LWML
Kansas City, Kansas

HAMBURGER STEW

1 lb. hamburger
4 carrots, sliced
3 stalks celery, chopped
1 white onion, sliced
2 tomatoes, cut up
2 potatoes, sliced
1 No. 2 can kidney beans
1 tsp. salt
Pepper to taste

Brown hamburger; add remaining ingredients. Cover with water and simmer for 1 hour or until vegetables are tender. Yield: 4 servings.

Beth Zurell
Bethlehem Lutheran Church
Bristol, Connecticut

HAMBURGER STEW WITH NOODLE CURLS

3 onions, chopped
4 tbsp. shortening
1 lb. hamburger
2 qt. water
4 carrots, diced
4 stalks celery, diced
1 No. 2 can tomatoes
3 ½ tsp. salt
½ tsp. pepper
2 eggs
¾ c. flour
5 tbsp. milk

Place onions in shortening; fry until browned. Add hamburger and toss with fork until lightly browned. Add 1 quart boiling water; simmer for 10 minutes. Place carrots, celery, tomatoes, 1 tablespoonful salt, pepper and 1 quart cold water in large kettle. Bring to a boil. Add meat mixture; simmer until vegetables are tender. Combine eggs, flour, milk and remaining salt. Bring stew to a boil; place a colander on top of kettle. Quickly rub batter through colander with spatula into stew. Cook for 5 minutes. Serve at once. Yield: 6-8 servings.

Mrs. Charistel E. Guiles, Pres.
Trinity LCW
Farwell, Minnesota

HAMBURGER-VEGETABLE SOUP

1 lb. ground beef
1 c. diced onions
1 c. diced potatoes
1 c. sliced carrots
1 c. sliced celery
2 to 4 c. tomatoes
¼ c. uncooked rice
3 c. water
3 tsp. salt or to taste
1 bay leaf (opt.)
2 tbsp. sugar (opt.)
¼ tsp. basil
¼ tsp. thyme (opt.)

Brown meat and onions in a small amount of cooking oil until lightly browned; drain off excess fat. Combine meat mixture with remaining ingredients in a large kettle. Simmer, covered, for 1 hour. Yield: 6 servings.

Lena Krekeler
St. Paul's Serv. Guild
Leavenworth, Kansas
Mrs. Ray Lenz, Christian Growth Chmn.
Trinity Ladies Aid
Boonville, Missouri

2 tsp. salt
¼ c. uncooked rice, washed
⅛ tsp. pepper
¼ c. barley, washed (opt.)
1 ½ to 2 qt. water

Brown meat and onion lightly in fat. Combine all ingredients except water in large kettle. Add water. Simmer slowly for 45 minutes to 1 hour. Yield: 4-6 servings.

Mrs. Stephen Hurnyak
St. John's LCW
Charleroi, Pennsylvania
Mrs. Herbert Imgarten, Pres.
Salem Ladies Aid
Salisbury, Missouri

ITALIAN BEEF STEW

1 lb. stew beef
2 tbsp. olive oil
1 4-oz. can mushrooms
1 8-oz. can tomato sauce
½ tsp. Tabasco sauce
1 tsp. salt
¼ tsp. thyme
1 bay leaf
½ c. green pepper
1 clove of garlic, minced

Brown beef in olive oil. Place in small roasting pan. Add remaining ingredients. Cover; bake at 350 degrees for 2 hours and 30 minutes to 3 hours. Serve with rice. Yield: 5 servings.

Mrs. William R. Thomson, Pres.
Grace LCW
Santa Barbara, California

HAMBURGER-VEGETABLE SOUP

1 lb. hamburger
½ c. chopped onion
2 tbsp. fat or drippings
2 c. canned tomatoes
2 c. cubed potatoes
2 carrots, diced
½ c. diced celery

IRISH STEW

2 lb. stew meat
¼ c. cooking oil
1 lge. onion, cut up
2 tsp. salt
¼ tsp. pepper
1 ½ c. cubed carrots
1 c. peas
½ c. chopped celery
1 c. cubed parsnips
2 med. potatoes, cut into small pieces
1 sm. can tomato soup

(Continued on next page)

Brown meat in large fry pan, using cooking oil. Place in 4-quart pot. Add onion, salt, pepper and enough hot water to cover meat. Cook over low heat for 1 hour and 30 minutes, adding additional water if needed. Add vegetables, tomato soup and 2 cups water. Simmer for 1 hour and 30 minutes. Yield: 6 servings.

Mrs. Elsie Weisenburger, Pres.
Trinity Ladies Aid
Torrington, Alberta, Canada

MEAT STEW

1 ½ lb. beef chuck, lamb or Veal shoulder,
  cut into 1-in. cubes
¼ c. flour
3 tbsp. fat
2 ½ c. water
1 tbsp. Worcestershire sauce
1 tbsp. salt
¼ tsp. pepper
6 med. carrots, halved
6 med. potatoes, halved
6 med. onions

Dredge meat with flour. Heat fat in 6-quart pan; add meat and brown on all sides. Add water, Worcestershire sauce, salt and pepper. Cover and bring to a boil. Cook for 1 hour and 30 minutes. Add carrots, potatoes and onions to mixture. Cook over low heat for 30 to 40 minutes. Yield: 6 servings.

Edna M. Mannie, Pres.
Immanuel LWML
Stockton, California

MEAT BALL SOUP

1 lb. ground chuck
1 tsp. salt
1 egg
Shortening
1 pkg. dry onion soup mix
2 c. diced potatoes
2 c. sliced carrots
4 c. water
1 pkg. frozen peas

Combine chuck, salt and egg. Form into small meat balls about the size of walnuts. Brown in small amount of shortening. Drain off excess shortening. Combine remaining ingredients

except peas; add to meat balls. Simmer for 25 minutes. Add peas; cook only until peas are tender. Yield: 6 servings.

Bernadette Fabin, Sec.
First Lutheran Church Guild
Phillipsburg, Kansas

MEAT BALL STEW

1 10-oz. pkg. frozen mixed vegetables
3 med. potatoes, diced
1 med. onion, chopped
2 stalks celery, chopped
1 No. 303 can tomatoes
¼ c. water
1 lb. ground beef
1 tbsp. (heaping) flour
Salt and pepper to taste

Place vegetables and salt in large saucepan; add water. Bring to a boil. Mix beef, egg, flour and seasonings. Form into 12 meat balls; drop into boiling vegetable mixture. Reduce heat; cook to desired consistency.

Mrs. Kenneth O. Sanborn, Pres.
Emanuel Evangelical LCW
Evansville, Indiana

MINESTRONE

1 lb. beef shank
2 ½ qt. cold water
3 tbsp. salt
1 c. dried white or red beans
1 tbsp. olive or salad oil
2 cloves of garlic or ¼ tsp. garlic salt
½ c. minced onion
½ c. minced parsley
⅛ tsp. pepper
1 c. frozen green beans
2 med. potatoes, diced
¾ c. diced celery
⅔ c. frozen peas
2 c. finely shredded cabbage
1 c. diced carrots
1 c. chopped canned tomatoes
¾ c. shell macaroni
Grated Parmesan cheese

Place meat in deep cooker; add water, 2 table-spoonfuls salt and beans. Cover and bring to a boil; skim. Cover and simmer for 4 hours. Heat oil in skillet and brown garlic; remove garlic. Saute onion and parsley until tender; do not brown. Chop meat; remove fat and gristle. Add remaining ingredients except meat, macaroni

(Continued on next page)

and cheese. Cover and simmer for 30 minutes. Add macaroni and meat, cooking until macaroni is tender. Serve with cheese. Yield: 10 servings.

Mrs. Luana Larson, Pres.
Pinole LWML
San Pablo, California

sour cream. Bake, uncovered, at 325 degrees for 1 hour and 30 minutes. Serve over rice or noodles. Yield: 6 servings.

Mrs. Alfred Christiansen, Chmn.
Peace Ladies' Guild
Saginaw, Michigan

PAPA'S HAMBURGER STEW

3 c. diced potatoes
2 c. sliced carrots
1 lge. onion, chopped
4 tbsp. vegetable oil
1 20-oz. can tomatoes
1 ¼ c. water
3 tbsp. flour
1 ½ lb. ground beef
1 tsp. monosodium glutamate
1 tsp. salt
¼ tsp. ground pepper

Boil potatoes and carrots in water to cover until almost tender; drain. Saute onion lightly in large skillet in 2 tablespoonfuls oil. Add tomatoes and 1 cup water. Blend flour and remaining water. Add to tomato mixture. Cook, stirring constantly, until thickened. Combine tomato mixture with potatoes and carrots. Turn into 2-quart casserole. Blend meat with seasonings. Shape into balls. Brown in remaining oil in skillet. Place in casserole. Bake at 350 degrees for 20 to 25 minutes. Yield: 6 servings.

Sandra Aasheim
Holy Shepherd WOC
Lakewood, Colorado

OVEN STEW

1 ½ lb. beef stew meat
Shortening
1 onion, chopped
2 tbsp. flour
1 tsp. salt
2 cans tomato sauce
1 c. water
1 sm. can mushroom pieces
1 tsp. Worcestershire sauce
½ c. chopped celery
1 c. sour cream

Brown meat in a small amount of shortening; add onion while turning. Sprinkle with flour and salt; cook for a few minutes. Add remaining ingredients except sour cream; slowly stir in

PETE'S STEW

⅓ c. flour
¼ tsp. pepper
½ tsp. celery salt
1 ¾ lb. boned chuck or bottom round, cut into 1 ½-in. cubes
¼ c. fat or salad oil
¼ c. minced onion
1 clove of garlic, minced
3 ¾ c. boiling water
4 tsp. meat extract paste or 4 beef bouillon cubes
½ tsp. salt
½ tsp. Worcestershire sauce
12 sm. white onions
12 sm. carrots, whole or halved lengthwise
½ pkg. frozen peas

Combine flour, pepper and celery salt. Drop in meat a few pieces at a time; toss until coated. Reserve left-over flour. Heat fat in Dutch oven; slowly brown floured meat for 15 to 20 minutes or until browned on all sides. Remove meat. Place minced onion and garlic in meat drippings; simmer until just tender. Stir in reserved flour until blended. Slowly stir in boiling water, meat extract paste, salt and Worcestershire sauce. Add meat; simmer, covered, for 2 hours or until meat is fork tender. Add onions and carrots; simmer, covered, for 15 minutes. Add peas; simmer, covered, for 5 minutes or until vegetables are tender. Serve dumplings on top of stew, if desired.

Mrs. Helene B. James, Pres.
St. Mark's Ladies Aid
Lackawaxen, Pennsylvania

QUICKIE BEEF STEW

1 lb. beef stew meat, cubed
2 potatoes, chopped
2 carrots, chopped
1 med. onion, chopped
1 can cream of celery soup
1 soup can water
Salt and pepper to taste

Place all ingredients in 2-quart casserole; mix thoroughly. Cover; bake at 300 degrees for 2

(Continued on next page)

hours or longer. More liquid may be added, if necessary. Yield: 4 servings.

Mrs. A. Byron Holderby, Jr., Pres.
St. John Evangelical LCW
Roanoke, Virginia

STAY-A-BED STEW

2 lb. beef stew meat
5 med. potatoes, cut into chunks
5 med. carrots, cut into pieces
3 med. onions, minced
3 stalks celery, cut up
1 can peas
1 can tomato soup
1 soup can water
Salt and pepper to taste

Combine all ingredients in roasting pan. Bake at 270 degrees for 4 hours. Yield: 8-10 servings.

Carrie Nabakowski
Resurrection LCW
Hialeah, Florida

STAY-A-BED STEW

1 can tomato soup
½ soup can water
2 lb. stew meat
1 c. sliced carrots
2 chopped onions
1 tsp. salt
Dash of pepper
2 potatoes, cubed

Dilute soup with water. Combine all ingredients in casserole. Cover tightly and bake at 275 degrees for 5 hours. NOTE: Cream of mushroom or celery soup may be substituted for tomato soup.

Mrs. Kenneth J. Hollmann
Mt. Calvary LWML
Galesburg, Illinois

BRUNSWICK STEW

Butter
1 c. lima or white beans
1 onion, finely chopped
1 can tomatoes
1 4-lb. chicken, cut up
Flour
4 c. water
Salt and pepper to taste

Place a lump of butter, beans, onion and tomatoes in large kettle. Dip chicken into flour; place in kettle. Add water, salt and pepper. Cover and simmer for 2 hours. Before serving, rub 3 tablespoonfuls butter into 2 tablespoonfuls flour; add to stew. Cook gently for a few minutes. Add more water if needed. Dumplings or potatoes may be added, if desired. Yield: 6-8 servings.

Mrs. Agnes M. Lodoen
Central LCW
Provost, Alberta, Canada

CHICKEN-CORN SOUP

1 stewing chicken
8 c. whole kernel corn
Chopped hard-cooked eggs
½ c. parsley

Cook chicken in water until tender; reserve broth. Remove bones from chicken; cut chicken into cubes. Set aside. Add corn, eggs and parsley to broth. Simmer for a few minutes or until corn is tender.

RIVELS:

1 egg
1 c. flour
1 tsp. salt

Combine all ingredients to make a stiff dough. Drop small bits of dough into broth; cook for 5 minutes. Add chicken. NOTE: Two cups noodles may be substituted for rivels. Yield: 8 servings.

Mrs. Helen R. Shiffer, Sec.
St. Mark's LCW
Waterford, Pennsylvania

QUICK CHICKEN SOUP

1 3 to 4-lb. chicken
1 lge. onion, diced
1 carrot, diced
2 pieces celery
½ pkg. shell macaroni
1 12-oz. can chili sauce
Salt and pepper to taste

(Continued on next page)

Cook chicken until tender; add onion, carrot and celery. Cook until tender. Remove chicken from broth; bone and dice. Add enough water to broth to make 8 cups; bring to a boil. Add macaroni, chili sauce, chicken, salt and pepper. Cook for 15 minutes over medium heat. Add more water if too thick. Yield: 6 servings.

Mrs. George Kinsel, Pres.
Trinity Ladies Aid
Lafayette, Louisiana

Cook salt pork until crisp. Add onions to fat. Cook until pale golden. Add potatoes to onions. Cover with water. Cook, covered, until potatoes are tender, but not mushy. Add clams to potato-onion mixture; simmer for a few minutes. Melt butter; blend in flour, salt, pepper and sugar. Gradually add milk. Cook until thickened, stirring constantly. Add to clam mixture. Cool. Add evaporated milk; simmer very gently for 10 minutes. Cool and chill for one to two days. Heat to serving temperature. Add additional butter.

Mrs. John Charles, Pres.
Trinity Ladies Aid Soc.
Ashaway, Rhode Island

MOLLE

1 chicken
2 qt. water
2 cans tomato paste
1 sm. onion, chopped
¼ tsp. basil
¼ tsp. thyme
¼ tsp. marjoram
1 clove of garlic, minced
¼ tsp. cumin
1 bay leaf
½ c. flour
2 tsp. chili powder

Boil chicken in water for 1 hour to 1 hour and 30 minutes or until done. Remove chicken. Add remaining ingredients except flour and chili powder to broth. Bring to a boil. Combine flour, chili powder and water to make paste. Blend into soup. Add diced chicken; simmer for 30 minutes. Serve hot. Yield: 8 servings.

Margie Houtman, Pres.
Mt. Zion Ladies League
Denver, Colorado

CAPE COD CLAM CHOWDER

¼ lb. bacon
1 c. water
1 bottle clam juice
4 med. potatoes, cubed
1 med. onion, chopped
1 can minced clams
2 c. milk
1 tbsp. margarine
Salt and pepper to taste

Fry bacon until crisp. Remove from pan. Add water, clam juice, potatoes and onion to fat. Cook for 15 minutes or until potatoes are tender. Add clams; cook for 5 minutes. Add milk and margarine. Heat thoroughly, but do not boil. Add crumbled bacon and seasonings to taste. Serve immediately. Yield: 4 servings.

Mrs. June Jaquish, Sec.
First Good Shepherd Ladies Aid
Las Vegas, Nevada

CAPE COD CLAM CHOWDER

¼ lb. fat salt pork, diced
3 lge. onions, chopped
4 med. potatoes, cubed
2 c. water
1 qt. fresh clams or 2 tall cans minced clams
¼ c. butter
¼ c. flour
1 ½ tsp. salt
¼ tsp. pepper
1 tsp. sugar
4 c. milk
1 14-oz. can evaporated milk

CLAM CHOWDER

1 lge. slice bacon, minced
1 med. onion, diced
1 7-oz. can minced clams
1 c. sliced potatoes
Milk
Butter
Seasonings to taste

Fry bacon and onion. Place in pan. Drain clams, reserving juice. Add juice to bacon with potatoes. Add enough water to cover. Cook until potatoes are tender. Add clams, milk, one pat of butter and seasonings. Serve hot. Yield: 4-5 servings.

Amy J. Smith, Pres.
Bethlehem LCW
Billings, Montana

CLAM CHOWDER

3 strips bacon, finely chopped
1 sm. onion, chopped
2 med. potatoes, cubed
½ c. water
1 7 ½-oz. can minced clams
3 c. milk
Salt and pepper to taste

Brown bacon and onion. Place bacon, onion and drippings in pan. Add potatoes and water. Boil gently until potatoes are tender. Add undrained clams, milk and seasonings. Heat and serve. Do not boil. Yield: 4 servings.

Mrs. Ross Burnham, Pres.
Bethany Ladies Guild
Port Orchard, Washington

CLAM CHOWDER

6 lge. potatoes, diced
1 sm. onion, diced
1 tbsp. salt
2 tbsp. butter
1 can clams
1 15-oz. can evaporated milk

Cook potatoes for 30 minutes or until soft. Add onion, salt and butter; remove from heat. Add clams and milk. Heat for 15 minutes. Serve hot. Yield: 6 servings.

Mrs. Dennis Aulenback, Pres.
St. Stephens LCW
Lunenburg County, Nova Scotia, Canada

CRAB BISQUE

1 10 ¾-oz. can tomato soup
1 10 ¾-oz. can pea soup
2 c. beef broth
½ lb. crab meat, flaked
½ c. cream
Salt and pepper
2 tbsp. Sherry (opt.)

Mix soups and broth; bring almost to a boil. Add crab meat and cream. Season with salt, pepper and Sherry. Serve at once or keep hot over low heat. Yield: 6 servings.

Mrs. Edgar Webb
Eagle Rock Ladies Aid
Los Angeles, California

CRAB GUMBO

6 slices bacon, cut up
3 onions, chopped
2 cans tomatoes
1 can tomato sauce or paste
1 can tomatoes with green chilies
1 lb. okra, cut up
3 c. water
½ green pepper
1 tsp. salt
1 tsp. celery salt
2 tbsp. flour
6 c. flaked crab meat

Brown bacon and onions. Add tomatoes, tomato sauce, tomatoes with chilies, okra, water, green pepper, salt, celery salt and flour. Cook at 325 degrees for 1 hour and 30 minutes. Add crab meat and simmer for 1 hour. Serve over rice. Yield: 10 servings.

Mrs. Arnold Kasper, Pres.
Holy Cross Ladies Aid
Warda, Texas

NEW ENGLAND FISH CHOWDER

1 lb. fish fillets
¼ c. chopped bacon
Onions
2 c. hot water
¾ c. diced celery
2 c. diced potatoes
3 c. milk
1 tsp. salt
Dash of pepper
2 tbsp. butter
Parsley

Cut fish into 1-inch cubes. Fry bacon until browned; add onions and brown slightly. Add water, celery and potatoes; cook for 5 minutes or until potatoes are partially tender. Add fish and cook until fish flakes easily. Add milk and seasonings; heat. Sprinkle with parsley. Yield: 6-8 servings.

Mrs. Gilbert Klatt
St. Paul's Church
Vergas, Minnesota

FISH CHOWDER

2 1-lb. pkg. frozen perch, halibut or haddock
1 c. diced potatoes
1 c. sliced carrots
½ c. diced celery
1 ½ tsp. salt
1 c. water
2 tbsp. butter or margarine
1 med. onion, thinly sliced
1 tsp. Worcestershire sauce
¼ tsp. pepper
2 ½ c. milk
Paprika

Thaw fish slightly; cut into 1-inch pieces. Place potatoes, carrots, celery and 1/2 teaspoonful salt in water. Cover and cook until vegetables are almost tender. Melt butter in large saucepan; add onion and cook over low heat until tender, but not brown. Add fish, Worcestershire sauce and cooked vegetable mixture. Simmer for 10 minutes. Add remaining salt, pepper and milk. Heat slowly. Serve in bowls with sprinkle of paprika. NOTE: If desired, thicken with mixture of 2 tablespoonfuls each butter and flour. Yield: 6-8 servings.

Mrs. Richard W. Loop, VP
Grace LCW
Anaheim, California

PENNSYLVANIA PRETZEL SOUP

1 7 ½-oz. can minced clams
2 c. canned clam juice
2 c. milk
½ tsp. dried thyme
½ tsp. salt
1 tsp. garlic salt
¼ tsp. pepper
2 tbsp. minced onion
2 tbsp. dried parsley flakes
¼ c. butter or margarine
2 tbsp. flour
½ c. heavy or light cream
Paprika
Pretzels

Drain clams, reserving liquid. Combine reserved clam liquid, clam juice, milk, thyme, salt, garlic salt, pepper and parsley in saucepan. Simmer for 5 minutes. Melt 2 tablespoonfuls butter; stir in flour. Remove from heat. Gradually add small portion of seasoned milk to flour mixture; add to remaining milk mixture. Heat, stirring, until slightly thickened. Add clams, cream and remaining butter. Heat. Sprinkle with paprika and float large pretzels on top. Yield: 6 servings.

Mrs. Elizabeth Conaway, Pres.
Zion LCW
Glen Rock, Pennsylvania

TUNA CHILI

2 tbsp. salad oil
1 lge. onion, sliced
½ c. diced green pepper
1 c. diced celery
2 7-oz. cans tuna, drained and broken into chunks
4 oz. noodles
1 15-oz. can kidney beans
1 28-oz. can tomatoes
1 10-oz. can whole mushrooms, undrained
2 tsp. salt
1 tsp. chili powder
⅛ tsp. pepper

Heat oil in skillet. Cook onion, green pepper and celery until onion is yellow. Add remaining ingredients. Cover and simmer for 20 minutes. Uncover and cook over high heat for 10 minutes or until sauce has thickened. Yield: 6 servings.

Mrs. J. Wildgrube
Christ the King Lutheran Church
Edmonton, Alberta, Canada

GLORIOUS LAMB STEW

2 tbsp. fat
Salt and pepper
2 lb. lamb, cut into pieces
1 clove of garlic, crushed
2 tbsp. flour
2 c. water
2 tbsp. tomato paste
2 slices onion
1 carrot, chopped
Leaves of 2 or 3 stalks of celery
1 bay leaf
Few sprigs of parsley
4 med. mushrooms, sliced
3 med. carrots, quartered
10 sm. onions
1 tsp. sugar
5 med. potatoes, quartered
3 tbsp. Sherry wine
1 c. cooked peas

Heat fat until very hot in heavy skillet. Add seasoned meat and brown evenly on all sides. Drain and reserve fat. Reduce heat; add garlic. Sprinkle flour over lamb. Cook gently until flour has been absorbed. Stir in water and tomato paste; bring to a boil. Pour into a 3-quart casserole. Tie onion slices, chopped carrot, celery leaves, bay leaf and parsley in cloth bag. Add to casserole. Cover and bake at 325 degrees for 30 minutes; remove bag. Heat reserved fat in skillet; cook mushrooms gently for 3 minutes. Remove from skillet. Add carrots and onions to skillet; sprinkle sugar over vegetables. Cook only until glazed. Add mushrooms, glazed vegetables and potatoes to meat. Cover and bake in preheated 325 degree oven for 1 hour or until lamb and vegetables are tender when pierced with a fork. Just before serving, pour in wine

341

(Continued on next page)

and peas. Serve with a sprinkling of parsley. Yield: 6 servings.

Mrs. John Schellpfeffer, League Sponser
Church of the Master LCW
Perrysburg, Ohio

Melt butter in large skillet; when hot add lamb. Brown for 3 minutes; add onions. Add paprika, water, celery, salt and rutabaga. Cover and simmer for 2 hours and 30 minutes. Add remaining ingredients; simmer for 1 hour longer. NOTE: If gravy is too thin, thicken with cornstarch. Yield: 6-8 servings.

Mrs. Elinor Nock
Edgebrook LCW
Lincolnwood, Illinois

LAMB STEW

2 lb. lamb
Seasoned flour
Fat
1 pt. sm. onions
1 qt. potato cubes
1 pt. quartered carrots
¼ tsp. pepper
½ tsp. paprika
2 tbsp. chopped parsley
1 c. tomatoes

Cut meat into small pieces; roll in seasoned flour. Brown in hot fat. Cover with boiling water. Cook slowly for 1 hour and 30 minutes. Add onions, potatoes, carrots, seasonings and tomatoes. Cook for 30 minutes longer or until tender.

DUMPLINGS:

1 c. flour
2 tsp. baking powder
½ tsp. salt
½ c. milk
2 eggs

Combine flour, baking powder and salt. Add milk and eggs. Stir and drop by spoonfuls into stew. Cover; cook for 10 minutes longer. Remove stew to hot platter. Surround with dumplings. Sprinkle with parsley, if desired. Yield.; 6 servings.

Mrs. Clarence McIntire, Chmn.
St. Paul's LWML
Leola, South Dakota

CHILI

½ lb. pinto beans
5 c. canned tomatoes
1 lb. chopped green peppers
1 ½ tbsp. salad oil
1 ½ lb. onions, chopped
2 cloves of garlic, crushed
½ c. chopped parsley
2 ½ lb. ground chuck
1 lb. lean ground pork
½ c. butter
⅓ c. chili powder
2 tbsp. salt
1 ½ tsp. pepper
1 ½ tsp. cumin
1 ½ tsp. monsodium glutamate

Wash beans; soak overnight in water. Cover; simmer until tender. Add tomatoes; simmer for 5 minutes. Saute green pepper in salad oil for 5 minutes. Add onions; cook until tender, stirring often. Add garlic and parsley. Saute meat in butter for 15 minutes; add meat to onion mixture. Stir in chili powder; cook for 10 minutes. Add to beans with seasonings. Cover; simmer for 1 hour. Cook, uncovered, for 30 minutes. Skim fat from top. Yield: 12 servings.

Elsie Salmon
Grace LWML
Pittsburg, California

SPRING LAMB STEW

4 tbsp. butter
3 lb. lamb shoulder, cut into 2-in. pieces
2 med. onions, sliced
1 tsp. paprika
¼ c. water
5 lge. celery stalks and leaves, chopped
3 tsp. salt
1 sm. rutabaga
1 bunch carrots, quartered
4 med. potatoes, quartered
½ lb. fresh mushrooms
½ lb. green beans

MY MOTHER'S CHILI AND CHEESE

1 ½ lb. ground meat
1 med. onion, chopped
1 clove of garlic, chopped, or ½ tsp. garlic
   salt
1 tbsp. cumin seeds
4 tbsp. chili powder
1 can tomato sauce
2 soup cans water
Salt and pepper to taste
1 can pinto beans or 1 c. cooked pintos
1 lb. cheese, grated

Place meat in pot. Simmer until meat crumbles, stirring often. Add onion, garlic, cumin seeds and chili powder. Cook until onion is soft. Add tomato sauce, water, salt, pepper and beans. Simmer for 1 to 2 hours. Add cheese. Serve with crackers. Yield: 4 servings.

> Mrs. Gilbert H. Meyer, Comm. Chmn.
> Trinity LWML
> Alice, Texas

OXTAIL SOUP

1 ½ lb. oxtail, cut into 2-in. pieces
Fat
1 ½ qt. water
1 tbsp. salt
½ c. diced onion
¾ c. diced carrots
½ c. diced celery
2 tbsp. rice
1 c. cooked tomatoes

Brown oxtail in a small amount of hot fat in kettle. Add water and salt. Cover; simmer for 3 hours and 15 minutes. Remove meat from bones. Return meat to soup. Add onion, carrots, celery and rice. Cover; simmer for 30 minutes. Skim off fat. Add tomatoes. Yield: 6 servings.

> Mrs. Paul Gollin, Chmn.
> St. James LWML
> Munger, Michigan

VENISON STEW WITH DUMPLINGS

3 lb. venison neck meat, shoulder meat or
   shoulder chops
2 tsp. Accent
1 ½ tsp. salt
1 tsp. paprika
⅛ tsp. pepper
⅓ c. flour
¼ c. bacon drippings or shortening
3 ½ c. water

1 med. onion, sliced
Marrow bones (opt.)
1 bay leaf
4 parsley sprigs
2 celery stalks with leaves
12 sm. white onions, peeled
6 med. carrots, scraped and halved
3 med. potatoes, pared and halved
2 tsp. Worcestershire sauce
¼ tsp. dry mustard
¼ tsp. celery salt
¼ tsp. poultry seasoning

Trim all tallow, cartilege and sinew from meat; cut meat into 1 1/2-inch pieces. Sprinkle meat with 1 1/2 teaspoonfuls monosodium glutamate. Blend 1 teaspoonful salt, paprika and pepper with flour; roll meat in flour mixture. Melt bacon drippings in large, deep kettle. Add meat and brown on all sides. Add water, sliced onion, marrow bones, bay leaf, parsley and celery. Cover and simmer for 2 hours or until meat is tender. Refrigerate overnight for several hours. Carefully remove all solidified tallow from stew, blotting around edges of kettle with paper toweling. Remove marrow bones, bay leaf, parsley and celery. Add remaining monosodium glutamate and remaining ingredients; heat to serving temperature.

DUMPLINGS:

2 c. sifted flour
3 tsp. baking powder
1 tsp. salt
2 tbsp. shortening
1 c. milk

Sift together dry ingredients. Cut in shortening to resemble coarse corn meal. Add milk; mix just enough to combine all ingredients. Drop by spoonfuls on top of pieces of meat or vegetables. Simmer, uncovered, for 10 minutes. Cover tightly and cook for 10 minutes longer. Yield: 6 servings.

Photograph for this recipe on page 329.

CHICKEN MULLIGAN

13 stewing chickens
12 lb. ground beef
30 lb. potatoes, ground
8 lb. cabbage, ground
8 lb. onions, ground
7 lb. carrots, chopped
8 1-lb. cans peas
4 qt. cut string beans
12 qt. canned tomatoes, strained
8 1-lb. cans corn
5 bunches celery, chopped
8 1-lb. cans butter beans
Salt and pepper to taste

(Continued on next page)

Cook chicken until tender; remove bones and grind meat. Reserve chicken broth. Simmer ground beef until done. Combine all ingredients except salt and pepper in 50-gallon iron kettle. Cover with water; add salt and pepper to taste. Cook outside over a fire for 3 hours. Add water when needed. Yield: 300 servings.

Mrs. Harry Fisher, Pres.
St. Peter's Ladies Aid Soc.
New Memphis, Illinois

VEAL MEAT BALLS IN WHITE CABBAGE SOUP

½ lb. veal, ground
½ lb. pork, ground
4 tbsp. bread crumbs
1 tbsp. salt
White pepper
1 tbsp. grated onion
½ c. cream
1 qt. plus ½ c. water

Mix meats and crumbs; add 1 1/2 teaspoonfuls salt, pepper, onion and cream. Add 1/2 cup water gradually, stirring. Shape into small balls. Boil a few balls in remaining water with salt for 3 to 5 minutes. Test for consistency. If meat balls are hard, add more water to mixture. Boil remaining balls.

WHITE CABBAGE SOUP:

1 sm. white cabbage
2 tbsp. fat or butter
¾ tbsp. molasses or brown sugar
2 qt. pork or other stock
6 whole allspice
6 white peppercorns
Salt

Trim cabbage and cube, discarding core and tough portions. Place cabbage in fat in kettle; cook until browned. Add molasses. Continue to brown for a few minutes, stirring constantly. Bring stock to a boil; add to cabbage. Add seasonings. Simmer cabbage for 30 minutes. Add veal meatballs. Yield: 8 servings.

Mrs. Erik Ekberg, Pres.
Bethany LCW
Minneapolis, Minnesota

Quick and Easy Favorites

RECIPE FOR WHITE-CAPPED BURGERS ON PAGE 351

BARBECUED HAMBURGERS

2 lb. ground beef
1 tsp. salt
Dash of pepper
¼ c. sweet pickle relish
1 tbsp. brown sugar
1 tbsp. Worcestershire sauce
1 can tomato soup
¼ c. chopped onion
1 tbsp. vinegar

Mix beef, salt and pepper. Form into eight patties. Brown in skillet. Pour off fat. Combine relish, sugar, Worcestershire sauce, soup, onion and vinegar. Pour over burgers. Simmer for 20 minutes or until done, stirring occasionally. Yield: 8 servings.

Marilyn Matzke, Pres.
Our Saviors Ruth Guild
Henderson, Nevada

BARBECUES OR SLOPPY JOES

1 ½ to 2 lb. hamburger
½ c. diced onion
2 tbsp. flour
1 tsp. dry mustard
2 tbsp. sugar
1 tsp. chili powder
1 tsp. salt
2 tsp. vinegar
1 10 ½-oz. can tomato soup
½ c. water

Brown hamburger and onion lightly. Mix flour, mustard, sugar, chili powder and salt; add to browned hamburger. Add vinegar, soup and water. Simmer slowly for at least 30 minutes. Yield: 12 servings.

Mrs. Russell Ringdahl
Milnor LCW
Milnor, North Dakota

BEEF PATTIES

1 ½ lb. ground beef
½ c. soft bread crumbs
¾ tsp. salt
⅛ tsp. pepper
1 egg, beaten
1 ½ tbsp. prepared mustard
6 slices onion
6 slices American cheese
¾ c. tomato soup

Combine meat, bread crumbs, salt, pepper and egg. Shape into six patties. Place in shallow baking pan. Spread each pattie with mustard. Place 1 slice onion and 1 slice cheese on each pattie. Add soup. Bake at 400 degrees for 35 to 40 minutes. Yield: 6 servings.

Mrs. Wilbert Reisenbichler, Pres.
Zion Ladies Aid
Pocahontas, Missouri

BEEF STROGANOFF

1 lb. round steak
⅔ c. water
1 3-oz. can mushrooms, undrained
1 pkg. dry onion soup mix
½ pt. sour cream
2 tbsp. flour

Brown meat. Add water and mushrooms. Stir in soup mix. Heat to a boil; simmer for 30 minutes. Mix sour cream with flour; add to meat. Cook, stirring until thickened. Serve over rice or noodles. Yield: 6 servings.

Mrs. Ronald Archer, Pres.
St. Andrew's LCW
New Orleans, Louisiana

BEEF STROGANOFF CASSEROLE

1 lb. hamburger
¼ sm. onion, chopped
1 pkg. Noodles Romanoff
1 can cream of mushroom soup
Wheaties

Brown hamburger and onion. Cook Noodles Romanoff according to package directions. Add hamburger, onion and soup. Pour into a 2-quart casserole; bake at 350 degrees for 25 minutes. Sprinkle a small amount Wheaties over top. Bake for 5 minutes longer. Yield: 12 servings.

Mrs. Carl Luett, VP
Evangelical Ladies Friendship Soc.
Bouton, Iowa

BURGER CHILI AND CHIPS

1 lb. ground beef
½ c. chopped onion
¼ c. chopped celery
1 tsp. salt
¼ tsp. pepper
1 1-lb. can chili
1 c. corn chips
1 c. diced American cheese

Brown ground beef; add onion and celery. Cook until tender. Season with salt and pepper. Add chili; mix. Place a layer of corn chips in greased 1 1/2-quart casserole. Alternate layers of chili mixture, with corn chips and cheese, ending with corn chips. Bake at 350 degrees for 30 minutes. Yield: 6 servings.

Mrs. Victor Steege, Pres.
Hope LCW
Maynard, Iowa

CABBAGE ROLLS

8 lge. cabbage leaves
1 lb. chopped beef
1 tsp. salt
¼ tsp. pepper
2 tbsp. chopped onion
1 c. cooked rice
1 egg, beaten
1 can tomato soup

Pour boiling water over cabbage leaves; let stand for 5 minutes. Season meat with salt and pepper; add onion, rice and egg. Place a small amount of meat mixture in each cabbage leaf. Secure ends with toothpicks. Place cabbage rolls in pressure cooker. Pour soup and 1 cup water over rolls. Cover; cook at 10 pounds pressure for 15 minutes. Yield: 4 servings.

Mrs. Ray Hoffman, Pres.
Grace Lutheran Church
Grace City, North Dakota

CHILETTI

1 med. onion, finely cut
Shortening or oil
1 lb. ground beef
1 can chili beans
1 can spaghetti with tomato sauce
Salt and pepper to taste

Brown onion in small amount of shortening until golden. Add ground beef; saute until browned. Add chili beans, spaghetti sauce, salt and pepper, stirring until mixed well. Simmer for 15 minutes. Serve with tossed salad. NOTE: May be placed in casserole and baked at 375 degrees for 30 minutes. Yield: 4 servings.

Lydia D. Thornsby, Pres.
Nativity Womens Group
Adams City, Colorado

CHILI KENOS

1 lb. ground beef
1 tbsp. wine vinegar
1 tsp. salt
½ tsp. pepper
1 tsp. cumin
½ tsp. oregano
2 tbsp. flour
3 tbsp. chili powder
1 c. water
1 can tomato sauce
1 sm. can black pitted olives
¼ lb. cubed cheese
1 bunch green onions
1 sm. can kidney beans
Corn chips

Brown ground beef. Add vinegar, salt, pepper, cumin and oregano. Sprinkle flour over meat mixture; stir. Add chili powder and water. Combine tomato sauce, olives, cheese, onions and kidney beans in bowl. Mix; add to meat mixture. Heat just enough to melt the cheese. Sprinkle corn chips over meat mixture. Yield: 5 servings.

Mrs. James L. Lanter, Pres.
Women of Holy Cross
Concord, California

CREOLE BEEF

2 onions, finely chopped
1 lb. ground beef
2 tbsp. butter
1 10-oz. can spaghetti with tomato sauce
½ can tomato soup
¼ lb. grated cheese
½ tsp. salt
½ c. buttered bread crumbs

Brown onion with beef in butter in frying pan. Drain off excess fat. Add spaghetti sauce, soup, cheese and salt. Place in baking dish; cover with bread crumbs. Bake at 375 degrees for 30 minutes. Yield: 4 servings.

Mrs. Bernard Niemann
Our Redeemer LWML
Staplehurst, Nebraska

CHILI-SIRLOIN CASSEROLE

1 lb. ground sirloin
2 cans chili con carne with beans
1 c. chopped onions
1 ½ c. grated American cheese
2 c. crushed corn chips

Brown sirloin, stirring frequently. Mix sirloin with chili con carne in a 1 1/2-quart casserole. Layer onions on top of meat mixture. Sprinkle with cheese. Top with corn chips. Bake at 350 degrees for 30 minutes. Yield: 4 servings.

Mrs. Eugene P. DeAngelis, Pres.
Shepherd of the Hills
Tujunga, California

HAMBURGER-BEAN CASSEROLE

1 lb. hamburger
2 tbsp. fat
Salt and pepper to taste
2 tbsp. finely chopped onion
1 No. 303 can tomatoes
1 No. 303 can pork and beans
2 tbsp. brown sugar
2 slices bacon

Brown hamburger in fat; add salt and pepper. Drain. Add onion, tomato, beans and sugar. Cook slightly, stirring often. Pour into casserole. Top with bacon. Bake at 350 degrees for 25 to 30 minutes. Yield: 6 servings.

Mrs. C. M. Mundt, Pres.
Zion Women's League
Pittsburg, Kansas

HAMBURGER CASSEROLE

1 ½ lb. hamburger
2 sm. onions, chopped
1 4-oz. can mushrooms, drained
½ c. stuffed olives, sliced
½ lb. American cheese, grated
1 c. cream of mushroom soup
1 ½ c. milk
1 8-oz. pkg. noodles, cooked and drained
1 c. chow mein noodles

Brown hamburger and onions in skillet. Combine all ingredients except chow mein noodles. Place in 9 x 12 x 2-inch pan. Bake at 375 degrees for 25 minutes. Top with chow mein noodles; bake for 15 minutes longer. Yield: 12 servings.

Mrs. George Herdt, Pres.
Zion LCW
WaKeeney, Kansas

HAMBURGER CASSEROLE

1 lb. ground beef
Fat
1 c. sliced onions
1 tsp. salt
¼ tsp. pepper
2 c. cooked sliced potatoes
1 20-oz. can whole kernel corn
1 10-oz. can tomato soup
½ c. milk

Brown meat in small amount of fat; push to one side of pan. Brown onions lightly. Add salt and pepper. Arrange layers of meat, onions, potatoes and corn in greased 2-quart casserole. Add soup diluted with milk. Bake at 375 degrees for 20 minutes. Yield: 6 servings.

Mrs. Charles E. Hayes, Sec.
Mt. Olivet LCW
Lunenburg County, Nova Scotia, Canada

HAMBURGER CASSEROLE

1 lb. ground beef
1 med. onion, diced
2 stalks celery, diced
Fat
2 c. cooked rice
2 cans cream of chicken soup
1 c. water
2 tbsp. soy sauce
1 can chow mein noodles

Brown ground beef, onion and celery in fat. Add remaining ingredients except noodles. Blend well. Pour mixture into shallow baking dish; top with noodles. Bake at 350 degrees for 20 to 25 minutes or until noodles are browned. Yield: 6-8 servings.

Mrs. Ed Mullins
Hanover Ladies Aid
Cape Girardeau, Missouri

HAMBURGER STROGANOFF

½ c. finely minced onion
1 clove of garlic, minced
¼ c. butter
1 lb. ground beef
2 tbsp. flour
1 tsp. salt
¼ tsp. pepper
1 8-oz. can sliced mushrooms
½ can cream of chicken soup
1 c. sour cream
2 tbsp. minced parsley

Cook onion and garlic in butter; add meat. Cook and stir until meat is browned. Add flour, salt, pepper and mushrooms; cook for 5 minutes. Add soup; simmer for 10 minutes. Add sour cream; heat. Top with parsley. Yield: 4-5 servings.

Mrs. C. M. Luckey, Pres.
First Lutheran Church LCW
Cedar Rapids, Iowa

JOHNNIE BIGETTI

Chopped onion
Chopped green pepper
1 lb. ground beef
½ lb. cheese
Mushrooms (opt.)
1 sm. can tomato juice
Blanched almonds (opt.)
1 can tomato soup
1 pkg. broad noodles, cooked
Ground buttered corn flakes

Saute onion and pepper; brown meat. Add remaining ingredients except noodles and corn flakes. Mix with noodles; place in casserole. Cover with corn flakes. Bake at 350 degrees for 30 minutes. Yield: 10 servings.

Mrs. F. W. Rabe, Pres.
First United LCW
Dallas, Texas

KING MIDAS HAMBURGERS

2 lb. ground round steak
½ stick butter
2 med. onions, chopped
¼ lb. mushrooms, cut up
½ tsp. salt
¼ tsp. thyme
¼ tsp. pepper
⅛ tsp. rosemary
½ c. Sherry wine
½ c. water

Shape meat into six patties. Broil until brown on each side, turning once. Melt butter in small skillet; add remaining ingredients except Sherry and water. Simmer until onions and mushrooms are golden brown. Add Sherry and water. Bring to a boil; simmer for 2 to 3 minutes. Serve over hamburgers. Yield: 6 servings.

Mrs. Arlene Tschirhart
Mt. Olive Willing Workers
San Antonio, Texas

MEAT BALLS

1 lb. hamburger
½ c. Rice Krispies
½ c. milk
1 onion, chopped
2 eggs, beaten
1 tsp. salt
Pepper to taste
Flour
Fat
1 can consomme

Combine hamburger, Rice Krispies, milk, onion, eggs, salt and pepper. Shape into small balls.

Roll in flour; brown in fat. Add consomme and enough water to make gravy. Simmer for 30 minutes; thicken gravy as desired. Yield: 6-7 servings.

Mrs. Atto Uecker, Pres.
St. John's Miss'y Aid
Grey Eagle, Minnesota

MEAT BALLS IN MUSHROOM GRAVY

1 ½ lb. ground beef
2 slices dry bread, broken into pieces
1 sm. onion, finely chopped
1 lge. egg, beaten
1 tsp. salt
1 tsp. sugar
⅛ tsp. pepper
1 can cream of mushroom soup
1 soup can milk

Combine beef, bread crumbs, onion, egg, salt, sugar and pepper. Shape into small balls. Brown in shortening in 10-inch skillet. Pour off excess grease; dilute soup with milk. Pour over meat balls. Simmer for 30 minutes or until meat balls are done. Yield: 6 servings.

Mrs. Henry Grishkowsky
St. Paul LCW
Hanover, Illinois

MEATZA PIE

1 lb. ground beef
⅔ c. evaporated milk
½ c. bread crumbs
1 tsp. garlic salt
⅓ c. catsup
1 2-oz. can sliced mushrooms, drained
1 c. shredded sharp Cheddar cheese
¼ tsp. oregano
2 tbsp. grated Parmesan cheese
Sliced ripe olives (opt.)

Mix ground beef with milk, bread crumbs and salt. Place in a 9-inch pie plate. Spread catsup over meat. Arrange mushrooms and Cheddar cheese evenly over meat mixture. Add oregano and Parmesan cheese. Top with olives. Bake at 375 degrees for 25 minutes. Cut into wedges. Yield: 6 servings.

Mrs. R. D. Gubanc, Pres.
Euclid LCW
Euclid, Ohio

MEAT PUFFS WITH MUSHROOM SAUCE

1 ½ lb. lean ground beef
1 ½ med. onions, grated
1 ½ c. soft bread crumbs
2 eggs, well beaten
¾ tsp. salt
¼ tsp. pepper
¼ c. flour
¼ c. fat
1 to 2 No. 1 cans cream of mushroom soup

Combine meat, onions, bread crumbs, eggs and seasoning. Form into small balls; roll in flour. Brown meat balls in fat. Dilute soup with water. Pour over meat balls. Cover; simmer for 20 minutes. Yield: 6 servings.

Mrs. Arthur Kaestner
Holy Cross Ladies Aid Soc.
Renault, Illinois

MINUTE MEAT LOAVES

1 lb. hamburger
½ sm. onion, finely chopped
1 tsp. salt
½ c. fresh bread crumbs
1 can vegetable soup

Combine all ingredients; mix lightly with fork. Spoon into twelve 2-inch cupcake cups. Bake in preheated 450 degree oven for 15 minutes. Yield: 12 servings.

Mrs. Olga Barr, Sec.
Concordia LWML
Geneseo, Illinois

ONE-APIECE MEAT LOAVES

4 eggs, lightly beaten
4 lb. ground chuck
4 c. fresh bread crumbs
1 ½ c. minced onions, grated
¼ c. horseradish
2 tbsp. salt
2 tsp. dry mustard
½ c. milk
½ c. catsup

Lightly toss eggs with meat, crumbs and onions with two-tined fork. Add horseradish, salt, mustard, milk and catsup. Combine lightly, but well. Shape meat into eight individual oval loaves; place in greased shallow pan. Spread top of each loaf with additional catsup. Refrigerate for several hours. Bake at 400 degrees for 30 to 35 minutes or until done. Yield: 8 servings.

Mrs. Lolis Johnson, Hist.
Grace LCW
Pittsburg, California

POLYNESIAN MEAT BALLS

1 lb. ground round steak
1 egg, beaten
Salt and pepper to taste
1 ½ tbsp. finely chopped onion
2 tbsp. flour
1 c. chicken stock
1 tbsp. oil
4 slices pineapple, cut into cubes
3 green peppers, cut into large pieces
3 tbsp. cornstarch
2 tsp. soy sauce
½ c. vinegar
½ c. sugar

Mix meat with egg, salt, pepper and onion. Shape into balls; roll in flour. Brown lightly. Add 1/3 cup chicken stock, oil, pineapple and green peppers. Simmer for few minutes. Mix cornstarch with soy sauce, vinegar, sugar and remaining chicken stock. Add to meat balls. Heat thoroughly. Yield: 6 servings.

Phyllis Merriman, Pres.
Epiphany Woman's Guild
Bothell, Washington

QUICK CHILI BAKE

1   49-cent pkg. corn chips
2 cans chili
1 can hominy
1 can water
1 c. grated cheese

Alternate layers of corn chips, chili and hominy, beginning and ending with corn chips in casserole. Pour water over layers. Add cheese. Bake at 350 degrees for 40 minutes. Yield: 6 servings.

Jean Keller, Pres.
LCW
Inspiration, Arizona

QUICK EGG FOO YUNG

½ c. chopped green pepper
½ c. chopped onion
½ c. chopped celery
3 eggs, beaten
1 c. cooked slivered beef, pork or chicken
1 tsp. Oriental sauce
¼ tsp. salt
1 med. can bean sprouts
Cooking oil or margarine

Parboil green pepper, onion and celery. Drain add to eggs and remaining ingredients. Fry in oil like pancakes.

Mrs. William J. Schulz, Pres.
Holy Trinity Evangelical LCW
St. Clair Shores, Michigan

QUICK FARMER'S CASSEROLE

1 ½ lb. beef
1 c. sliced celery
½ c. chopped onion
½ c. chopped green pepper
¾ c. water
¾ c. tomato paste
1 tsp. salt
1 tsp. paprika
1 1-lb. can pork and beans
1 1-lb. can lima beans
1 biscuit recipe or 1 can refrigerated
    biscuits

Combine beef, celery, onion and green pepper in large skillet. Cook until vegetables are tender. Add water, tomato paste, salt, paprika, pork and beans and lima beans. Simmer while preparing biscuits. Place beef mixture in 12 x 8-inch baking dish; top with bixcuits. Bake at 425 degrees for 25 to 30 minutes or until browned. Yield: 6-8 servings.

Mrs. Walter A. Monter
St. Peter's Ladies Miss'y Aid
Center, Colorado

QUICK STROGANOFF

1 lb. ground beef
1 sm. onion, minced
1 tsp. salt
1 can cream of mushroom soup
1 can cream of chicken soup
½ c. sour cream
1 4 oz. can mushrooms, drained (opt.)

Brown ground beef and onion in skillet. Drain off excess fat. Add remaining ingredients; heat through. Serve over rice or noodles. Yield: 6 servings.

Mrs. David Meyer
St. Paul Priscilla Guild
Mt. Vernon, Iowa

TACOS

1 c. chopped celery
½ green pepper, chopped
1 lb. ground beef
2 tbsp. vegetable oil
1 tsp. salt
1 tsp. chili powder (opt.)
1 6-oz. can tomato sauce
1 4-oz. can taco sauce
1 8-oz. can enchilada sauce
Corn chips
Shredded lettuce
Shredded cheese
Black olives

Saute celery, green pepper and ground beef in oil in large frying pan. Add seasonings and sauces. Simmer for 30 minutes. Place meat sauce on bed of corn chips; top with a large amount of lettuce, cheese and black olives. Yield: 6 servings.

Mrs. Bert A. Wells, Pres.
Grace LWML
Eugene, Oregon

TAMALE LOAF

1 lge. can tomatoes
3 eggs, beaten
1 can cream-style corn
Garlic to taste
12 ripe olives
1 onion, finely chopped
1 c. milk
2 c. corn meal
1 tsp. salt
2 tbsp. olive oil
1 tbsp. pepper
1 lb. hamburger, cooked
½ c. stock or water

Combine all ingredients except meat and stock. Cook until thickened, stirring constantly. Add hamburger and stock. Pour into a greased baking dish and bake at 350 degrees for 30 minutes. Yield: 12 servings.

Mrs. Martha Griesner
St. John's LWML
Valley Home, California

WHITE-CAPPED BURGERS

1 tsp. Accent
1 lb. ground beef
½ c. evaporated milk
1 c. soft bread crumbs
1 egg
1 tsp. salt
1 tsp. dry mustard
¼ tsp. pepper
¼ tsp. thyme
⅓ c. minced onion
4 slices sharp American cheese
1 envelope instant mashed potatoes

Sprinkle Accent over beef in mixing bowl. Add remaining ingredients except cheese and potatoes; mix with fork until blended. Shape beef mixture into four patties; place in well-greased preheated 300 degree electric skillet. Cook for 6 minutes on one side; turn and cook for 6 minutes longer. Cover each pattie with one slice of cheese during last 3 minutes. Prepare potatoes according to package directions. Swirl potatoes on top of cheese. Yield: 4 servings.

Photograph for this recipe on page 345.

CHICKEN PAPRIKA

2 tbsp. shortening
1 tsp. paprika
1 lge. onion, chopped
1 chicken, cut into serving pieces
Salt and pepper to taste
3 tbsp. flour
½ pt. sour cream

Melt shortening; add paprika and onion. Brown. Add chicken, salt and pepper; cover with water. Stew for 1 hour or until chicken is tender. Remove chicken. Thicken broth with flour and water paste. Remove from heat; blend in sour cream. Pour over chicken. Serve with dumplings, wide noodles or rice, if desired.

Mrs. J. Luoncek
St. John's Evangelical Lutheran Church
Kenosha, Wisconsin

HOT CHICKEN SALAD

2 c. diced cooked chicken
2 c. diced celery
½ tsp. salt
⅛ tsp. pepper
½ c. chopped almonds
1 tsp. grated onion
1 c. salad dressing
3 tbsp. lemon juice
½ c. grated sharp Cheddar cheese
1 c. crushed potato chips

Mix all ingredients except cheese and potato chips. Place in oblong baking dish. Cover with cheese and potato chips. Bake at 450 degrees for 10 minutes. NOTE: Two cups light tuna, washed and drained may be substituted for chicken. Yield: 10-12 servings.

Margie Theimer
University Womens' Guild
Norman, Oklahoma

QUICK CHICKEN CASSEROLE

1 ½ c. chopped cold chicken
1 can cream of chicken soup
1 can green beans
1 can French-fried onions

Mix chicken, soup and green beans in casserole. Cover and bake at 350 degrees for 20 minutes or until bubbly. Sprinkle onions on top. Bake, uncovered, until onions are lightly browned. Yield: 4 servings.

Mrs. Harold H. Wood, Pres.
Church of the Ascension LCW
Clarkston, Michigan

CRAB MEAT CASSEROLE

½ c. chopped green pepper
2 tbsp. butter
1 10-oz. can frozen cream of potato soup
¼ c. milk
1 c. flaked cooked crab meat
1 tbsp. Sherry
¼ tsp. curry powder
¼ c. shredded Cheddar process cheese

Cook green pepper in butter until tender; add soup and milk. Heat until soup is thawed, stirring often. Add flaked crab meat, Sherry and curry powder. Pour into a 1-quart casserole. Sprinkle with cheese. Bake at 375 degrees for about 15 minutes. Yield: 4 servings.

Mrs. A. W. Hellenberg
St. Peter's Ladies Aid
Mishawaka, Indiana

QUICK AND EASY CRAB CAKES

1 1-lb. can crab meat
Salt and pepper to taste
⅓ tsp. nutmeg
½ c. chopped parsley
3 tbsp. (heaping) mayonnaise
1 egg, beaten
2 tbsp. milk
Cracker meal

Combine crab meat, salt, pepper, nutmeg, parsley and mayonnaise. Form into cakes. Combine egg and milk. Dip cakes into egg and milk mixture and then into cracker meal. Fry in hot deep fat, turning once. Yield: 4 servings.

Mrs. H. M. Leonard
LCW
Blain, Pennsylvania

FISH BATTER

1 c. flour
2 tbsp. baking powder
Salt
1 egg, separated
½ c. lukewarm water
1 tbsp. melted fat
2 lb. boneless halibut

Sift flour, baking powder and salt into bowl. Drop egg yolk in center; add water and fat. Mix well. Fold in beaten egg white. Dip fish into batter. Fry at 365 degrees for 4 to 6 minutes.

Mrs. Marvin Groth
Grace Lutheran Church
Longview, Washington

OYSTER PIE

1 qt. oysters
1 pkg. prepared stuffing mix
1 stick butter
Pepper to taste
½ pt. cream

Drain oysters, reserving juice. Cover bottom of buttered baking dish with a layer of oysters; top with a layer of stuffing mix. Dot with butter; sprinkle with pepper. Repeat until all ingredients are used, ending with stuffing mix. Pour oyster juice and enough cream over the pie to bring liquids up even with top layer. Dot with butter. Bake at 350 degrees for 25 minutes. Yield: 6 servings.

Mrs. John C. Schweers, Pres.
St. Paul's LCW
Mt. Pleasant, South Carolina

SALMON WITH NOODLES

3 tbsp. butter
3 tbsp. flour
1 tsp. salt
½ tsp. pepper
½ c. pea stock
1 ½ c. milk
1 ½ c. peas
¼ c. chopped pimento
3 c. cooked noodles
1 lge. can salmon
3 tbsp. buttered crumbs

Melt butter; blend in flour and seasoning. Gradually add stock and milk; cook until thick. Stir in peas and pimento. Arrange noodles and salmon in alternate layers in buttered casserole. Top with buttered crumbs. Bake at 350 degrees for 30 minutes. Yield: 8 servings.

Mrs. Conrad Anderson, Pres.
Tabor LCW
Kane, Pennsylvania

SCALLOPED OYSTERS AND CORN

1 10-oz. can frozen oyster stew
1 ½ c. slightly crumbled saltine crackers
1 can corn, drained
Butter or margarine

Heat stew until thawed, stirring often. Arrange alternate layers of crackers, corn and oyster stew in a buttered casserole, adding milk if needed. Dot with butter or margarine. Bake at 400 degrees for 20 minutes. Yield: 4 servings.

Jean Gerrish, Pres.
Immanuel LCW
Bellevue, Nebraska

SHRIMP AND CELERY

2 tbsp. flour
2 tbsp. melted butter
Salt and pepper to taste
Celery salt to taste
Onion juice to taste
Chopped parsley to taste
1 ½ c. milk
1 can shrimp
1 c. cooked celery
Buttered crumbs

Stir flour into butter; add seasonings, onion juice and parsley. Gradually add milk. Cook until thickened, stirring constantly. Add shrimp and celery. Place in baking dish; cover with buttered crumbs. Bake at 350 degrees until browned. Yield: 4 servings.

Mrs. Rudolf Wallin
Moe-Concordia Mary-Martha LWML
Margo, Saskatchewan, Canada

SALMON SUPPER

½ c. diced celery
2 tbsp. butter
1 can cream of celery soup
½ c. milk
3 tbsp. sliced stuffed olives
1 tbsp. lemon juice
1 c. drained flaked salmon

Cook celery in butter until tender; add remaining ingredients. Heat until warmed throughly. Serve over rice if desired. Yield: 4 servings.

Mrs. Shirley Koehler
Cross of Christ Altar Guild
Cudahy, Wisconsin

SHRIMP CREOLE

½ c. chopped green peppers
¼ c. chopped onion
¼ c. olive oil or shortening
2 c. strained tomatoes
½ c. sliced mushrooms
1 tsp. salt
Dash of cayenne pepper
2 c. cooked shrimp
2 tbsp. flour
¼ c. water
2 tbsp. minced parsley

(Continued on next page)

Brown green pepper and onion lightly in oil. Add tomatoes, mushrooms, salt and cayenne pepper. Cover and cook over medium heat for 15 minutes. Add shrimp; cook 15 minutes longer. Make a paste of flour and water. Stir into sauce. Cook for 2 to 3 minutes or until smooth. Sprinkle with parsley. Serve on hot cooked rice if desired. Yield: 4 servings.

Mrs. Conrad Biederman, Pres.
Redeemer LWML
Garson, Ontario, Canada

SHRIMP HURRY CURRY

2 lge. onions, diced
3 tbsp. oil
2 tbsp. flour
1 tsp. curry powder
¾ tsp. salt
Dash of pepper
1 c. water
½ c. raisins
2 cloves
Grated rind and juice of 1 lemon
1 lb. cleaned shrimp

Cook onions in oil for 5 minutes. Stir in flour, curry powder, salt, pepper, water, raisins and cloves; cook until thick. Add lemon juice, rind and shrimp. Cover; simmer for 20 to 25 minutes or until shrimp are pink. Serve over hot rice, if desired. Yield: 4 servings.

Mrs. Harold S. Edwards
Zion LWML
Abilene, Texas

SHRIMP NEWBURG WITH RICE

2 tbsp. butter
1 ¾ tbsp. flour
1 c. heavy cream
3 tbsp. catsup
¾ tbsp. Worcestershire sauce
1 lb. cooked shrimp
Dash of salt
2 tbsp. cooking Sherry
1 c. instant rice, cooked

Melt butter in skillet; stir in flour. Gradually stir in cream; cook until thick. Stir in catsup and Worcestershire sauce. Add shrimp and salt. Add Sherry just before serving. Serve over rice. Yield: 4 servings.

Elizabeth Koster, Pres.
St. Mathews Evangelical Ladies Aid Soc.
Secaucus, New Jersey

BIG CATCH CASSEROLE

1 10 ½-oz. can cream of celery soup
½ c. salad dressing
¼ c. milk
¼ c. shredded Parmesan cheese
2 6 ½-oz. cans chunk tuna
1 10-oz. pkg. frozen peas, cooked and drained
1 4-oz. pkg. noodles, cooked and drained
1 tbsp. chopped onion

Combine soup, salad dressing, milk and cheese; blend well. Stir in tuna, peas, noodles and onion. Pour into a 1 1/2-quart casserole. Bake at 350 degrees for 25 minutes. Yield: 8-10 servings.

Mrs. Marvin Erdal
Bethany Womens Guild
Leesburg, Florida

MAC-O-TUNA CASSEROLE

1 7-oz. pkg. macaroni, cooked and drained
2 cans tuna
1 can cream of mushroom soup
½ c. milk
1 c. grated cheese
1 tomato, sliced
Potato chips

Combine macaroni, tuna, soup, milk and cheese; pour into 1 1/2-quart casserole. Garnish with tomato and crushed potato chips. Bake at 375 degrees for 20 minutes. Yield: 4-6 servings.

Mrs. James E. Hassold, Pres.
Gethsemane LCW
San Antonio, Texas

TUNA CASSEROLE

¼ to ½ lb. noodles, cooked
1 can cream of mushroom soup
1 can tuna
⅓ to ½ c. milk
1 can peas (opt.)
Potato chips (opt.)

Combine all ingredients except potato chips. Stir slightly; pour into greased casserole. Place a few potato chips on top. Bake at 350 degrees for 25 minutes. Yild: 10 servings.

Mrs. Gunard Heikkila
LWML
Manitouwadge, Ontario, Canada
Mrs. Elfred Detmer, Pres.
St. Paul's Mary and Martha Cir.
Chapin, Illinois
Mrs. Ruby Belle Denter, Pres.
Salem LCW
Spragueville, Iowa

QUICK TUNA DISH

1 10 ½-oz. can cream of mushroom soup
1 10 ½-oz. can chicken-noodle soup
1 8-oz. can chow mein noodles
1 sm. can evaporated milk
1 6 ½-oz. can tuna
Crushed potato chips

Combine all ingredients except potato chips. Place in buttered casserole. Top with crushed potato chips. Bake at 350 degrees for 35 minutes or until bubbly. Yield: 6 servings.

Esther Wagner
St. John's Ladies Aid
Sanborn, Iowa

TUNA CASSEROLE

1 can cream of chicken or celery soup
½ c. milk
1 7-oz. can tuna, drained and flaked
1 c. drained cooked peas
1 c. crushed potato chips

Combine soup, milk, tuna, peas and potato chips. Garnish with additional potato chips. Bake at 375 degrees for 25 minutes. Yield: 4 servings.

Mrs. Doyle K. Reid, Christian Chmn.
St. Paul's LCW
Newville, Pennsylvania

TUNA CASSEROLE

1 5-oz. pkg. potato chips, crushed
2 c. chow mein noodles
2 sm. cans tuna
1 ½ c. milk
1 10 ½-oz. can cream of chicken soup
Salt and pepper to taste

Alternate layers of potato chips, noodles and tuna in casserole, beginning with potato chips. Combine milk, soup, slat and pepper; heat. Pour over layers in casserole. Top with layer of remaining potato chips. Bake at 350 degrees for 15 minutes. Yield: 6 servings.

Mrs. Roy Frank
First Lutheran Church
Rice Lake, Wisconsin

TUNA CASSEROLE

1 c. chopped cashews
1 ½ c. diced celery
1 can cream of chicken soup
1 can tuna
1 can chow mein noodles

Combine all ingredients; place in casserole. Bake at 350 degrees for 30 minutes. Garnish with Mandarin orange welges, if desired. Yield: 4 servings.

Barbara Ann Lange, Sec.
LWML
Fort Wayne, Indiana

TUNA-MUSHROOM CASSEROLE

1 can cream of mushroom soup
⅓ soup can water
1 can chunk tuna
1 can or ½ c. fresh mushrooms
2 c. crushed potato chips

Dilute soup with water. Alternate layers of tuna, soup, mushrooms and potato chips in casserole, ending with potato chips. Bake at 350 degrees for 45 minutes. Yield: 4 servings.

Marilyn Koehlert
Immanuel Ladies Aid
Dundee, Illinois

TUNA AND NOODLE CASSEROLE

3 c. raw noodles, cooked
1 can tuna
Salt to taste
1 can cream of mushroom soup
1 soup can water
6 to 8 crackers, crushed
Melted butter

Place one-half of noodles in greased casserole; cover with tuna. Add remaining noodles; sprinkle with salt. Pour mixture of soup and water over noodles. Combine cracker crumbs and butter; sprinkle over casserole. Bake at 350 degrees for 35 to 45 minutes. Yield: 6 servings.

Mrs. Vicotr Dumler
Immanuel Ladies Aid Soc.
Russell, Kansas

SWEET-SOUR TUNA

1 No. 2 can pineapple chunks
2 tbsp. butter or margarine
2 c. green pepper strips
2 tbsp. cornstarch
1 chicken bouillon cube
1 c. boiling water
2 tsp. soy sauce
2 tbsp. vinegar
⅓ c. sugar
2 7-oz. cans tuna, drained and flaked
½ tsp. salt
Dash of pepper
2 3 ¾-oz. cans chow mein noodles

(Continued on next page)

Drain pineapple, reserving 2/3 cup syrup. Cook pineapple in butter for 3 minutes. Add 1/3 cup pineapple syrup and green pepper strips. Cover and simmer for 10 minutes. Mix cornstarch with remaining syrup. Dissolve bouillon cube in boiling water. Add to pineapple; stir in cornstarch mixture. Add soy sauce, vinegar and sugar. Cook, stirring constantly, until thick. Add tuna, salt and pepper and heat thoroughly. Serve over noodles. Yield: 6-8 servings.

Mrs. Harry Amburn
Messiah Ladies Aid Soc.
Wolcottville, Indiana

BROILED PORK CHOPS

Salt and pepper
8 pork chops

Salt and pepper pork chops. Place in broiler; cook for 10 minutes on each side. Yield: 4 servings.

Dolores Eickmeyer, Pres.
Holy Cross Ladies Aid
Livingston, Illinois

CREAMED HAM WITH OLIVES

3 tbsp. margarine
3 tbsp. flour
1 ½ c. milk
2 c. cubed cured ham
1 tbsp. chopped parsley
1 tsp. Worcestershire sauce
¼ c. chopped stuffed olives

Melt margarine; blend in flour. Gradually add milk. Cook over low heat until thickened. Add remaining ingredients. Cook until heated. Serve on corn bread, if desired. Yield: 4-5 servings.

Enid Schwab, Pres.
St. Mark's Von Bora Group
Albion, Indiana

HAM LOGS WITH RAISIN SAUCE

1 lb. ground ham
½ lb. ground pork
¾ c. milk
½ c. oats
1 egg
2 tsp. horseradish
½ tsp. salt
Dash of pepper
1 tbsp. cornstarch
¾ c. cold water
2 tbsp. lemon juice
2 tbsp. vinegar
½ c. brown sugar
½ c. seedless raisins

Combine meats, milk, oats, egg, horseradish, salt and pepper. Shape into six or seven logs. Place in baking dish. Blend cornstarch and water; add remaining ingredients. Cook, stirring constantly, until mixture bubbles. Pour over ham logs. Bake at 350 degrees for 35 to 40 minutes. Yield: 6-7 servings.

Mrs. Dave Rumel
St. Timothy's LCW
Dayton, Ohio

HAM AND RICE

5 c. cooked rice
1 lb. chopped ham
4 green onions and tops
1 sm. can mushrooms
4 eggs, beaten
4 tbsp. butter
Soy sauce

Mix rice, ham, onions and mushrooms. Pour eggs over ham and rice mixture. Fry in butter; pour soy sauce over mixture while frying. Yield: 15 servings.

Mrs. Milton Gingerich, Pres.
St. John's Ladies Aid Soc.
Stuttgar, Arkansas

POTATO HAMBURGER

¾ lb. ground beef
¼ lb. ground pork
1 ½ c. coarsely grated potatoes
½ c. chopped onion
¼ c. chopped green pepper
2 tbsp. salt
¼ tsp. pepper
1 tbsp. sugar
⅓ c. catsup
¼ tsp. celery salt
⅛ tsp. Tabasco sauce

Combine all ingredients except catsup, celery salt and Tabasco sauce. Shape into patties. Fry until brown on both sides. Combine catsup, celery salt and Tabasco sauce. Pour over patties. Simmer for 10 minutes. Yield: 8 servings.

Mrs. Gene Hall, Pres.
Trinity of Freistadt Ladies Aid
Mequon, Wisconsin

Foreign Favorites

RECIPE FOR HOT POT (ENGLAND) ON PAGE 363

ADRIATIC PORK (ALBANIA)

1 ½ lb. boned pork shoulder
1 lge. onion, sliced
1 med. green pepper, cut into strips
1 clove of garlic, finely chopped
1 med. apple, chopped
2 tbsp. cooking oil
2 8-oz. cans tomato sauce
2 c. water
1 tbsp. sugar
Salt and pepper
1 lge. can sauerkraut

Cook pork, onion, green pepper, garlic and apple in oil until pork is lightly browned. Add tomato sauce and water. Cook, covered, over low heat for 1 hour or until pork is tender. Add sugar, salt and pepper. Mix well. Heat sauerkraut to serving temperature. Drain; arrange on platter. Top with tomato and meat mixture. Yield: 6 servings.

Mrs. John Gemmer, Christian Growth Chmn.
Redeemer LWML
Cushing, Oklahoma

POT ROAST (BAVARIA)

1 5-lb. chuck rump or sirloin tip roast
2 tbsp. fat
2 tsp. ginger
1 tbsp. cinnamon
2 tbsp. sugar
1 tbsp. vinegar
1 ½ c. water
1 ½ c. beef
1 c. tomato sauce
⅔ c. chopped onions
1 lge. bay leaf
1 ½ tsp. salt
Flour (opt.)
Sliced mushrooms (opt.)

Brown meat on all sides in fat in Dutch oven. Combine remaining ingredients except flour and mushrooms; pour over meat. Cover; simmer for 3 hours or until meat is tender. Thicken gravy with flour if desired. Add mushrooms. Yield: 8 servings.

Mrs. Warren Rundles, Treas.
Trinity Ladies Aid
El Paso, Illinois

CHICKEN CURRY (BURMA)

1 fryer chicken, cut into 1-in. chunks including
  bones
1 ½ c. fresh tomatoes, diced
1 ½ med. onions, diced
1 clove of garlic, finely chopped
½ tsp. turmeric
1 ¼ tsp. salt
3 ½ tbsp. soy sauce
¼ c. fat

Place all ingredients in 3-quart skillet or saucepan. Cook slowly until chicken is tender and sauce is thickened. Add a small amount of water if sauce cooks too fast. Yield: 2-3 servings.

Mrs. Leona M. Uchtmann, Pres.
St. John's LCW
Chester, Illinois

CHICKEN CHOW MEIN (CHINA)

¼ lb. lean veal, diced
¼ lb. lean pork, diced
Butter
1 med. chicken
4 lge. bunches celery, cut into 1-in. pieces
4 lge. onions, diced
4 tbsp. flour
6 cans mushrooms
¾ bottle soy sauce
3 tbsp. molasses
Salt and pepper

Fry veal and pork in butter. Cook chicken, reserving broth; dice. Simmer celery and onions in strained chicken broth until tender. Combine flour and 3/4 cup butter; add to onion mixture. Add remaining ingredients. Simmer for 30 minutes. Serve hot topped with canned noodles. Yield: 12-18 servings.

Mrs. Stan Mays
St. Peter's Women's Mission Cir.
Estevan, Saskatchewan, Canada

CHINESE RICE (CHINA)

½ lb. cubed pork
⅓ c. fat
½ c. chopped celery
1 onion, sliced
1 tsp. salt
1 tbsp. soy sauce
3 c. chicken broth
1 c. rice
¼ c. sliced ripe olives
¼ c. sliced stuffed olives
¼ c. almonds
½ c. cooked chicken

Brown pork in fat in electric frying pan. Add celery and onion; saute. Add salt, soy sauce, chicken broth and rice. Simmer for 25 minutes. Add olives and nuts just before serving. Garnish with chicken. Yield: 4 servings.

Mrs. William Sweetman
Timothy Ladies Guild
Council Bluffs, Iowa

CHING-TOU-HSIA-JEN--SAUTED GREEN
     PEAS AND SHRIMP (CHINA)

⅔ lb. shrimp
4 tbp. lard
1 tbsp. chopped onion

(Continued on next page)

2 lb. green peas
6 tbsp. of desired soup
1 tsp. salt
⅓ tsp. monosodium glutamate
½ egg white
Cornstarch

Shell and devein shrimp. Wash well and drain. Heat 2 tablespoonfuls lard in heated pan. Saute onion; fry shrimp. Clean pan; reheat with remaining lard. Saute green peas slightly. Add shrimp, soup, salt and monosodium glutamate; simmer. Combine egg white, salt and a small amount of cornstarch; add a small amount of water. Add to shrimp mixture to thicken. Yield: 5 servings.

Mrs. Juanita J. Buss, Sec.
LWML
Mt. Home AFB, Idaho

CHOPPED BEEF AND RICE ORIENTAL (CHINA)

1 ¼ c. instant rice
1 lb. ground beef
2 med. onions, sliced
1 1-lb. can bean sprouts, drained
1 box frozen cut green beans
1 10 ½-oz. can beef bouillon
⅓ c. soy sauce
½ c. water
½ tsp. ground ginger

Combine all ingredients in 2-quart casserole. Mix lightly with fork. Cover. Bake at 425 degrees for 40 minutes or until rice is tender. Yield: 4-6 servings.

Mrs. Lorraine Smith
Faith Women's Guild
Greenville, Mississippi

CHOY (CHINA)

½ lb. lean round pork
2 tbsp. salad oil
¼ c. diced carrots
¼ c. diced celery
2 cloves, minced
2 cloves of garlic, minced
1 tbsp. chopped onion
2 ¼ c. chicken bouillon
1 tsp. sugar
3 tbsp. cornstarch
2 tbsp. soy sauce
¼ c. cold water
1 lb. medium shrimp, cooked shelled and deveined

Saute pork in salad oil in large skillet. Add remaining ingredients except cornstarch, soy sauce, water and shrimp. Cover; simmer for 10 minutes. Blend cornstarch, soy sauce and water until creamy smooth. Add mixture to skillet; cook and stir until thick and clear. Add shrimp;

simmer until thoroughly heated. Yield: 6 servings.

L. Diane Shaffstall, Com. Chmn.
Trinity Ruth Cir.
Pasco, Washington

EGG FOO YONG (CHINA)

6 to 8 eggs
1 can bean sprouts, drained
1 c. cooked veal, finely chopped
½ tsp. salt
¼ tsp. pepper
½ c. finely chopped onion
1 tsp. fat

Beat eggs for 1 minute, using rotary beater. Add bean sprouts, meat, salt, pepper and onion. Mix together lightly. Place fat in hot 6-inch skillet. Pour one-half cup of mixture into skillet. Cook quickly over high heat until set and brown on edges. Turn and brown on other side.

CHINESE BROWN GRAVY:

6 tbsp. shortening
4 tbsp. flour
1 beef bouillon cube
2 tbsp. soy sauce
1 tsp. brown gravy sauce
1 tsp. salt
Dash of pepper
½ c. cold water
1 ½ c. hot water or mushroom juice

Melt shortening; add flour. Add remaining ingredients except hot water. Mix thoroughly. Add hot water. Stir well; cook until smooth. Serve with Egg Foo Yong. NOTE: Any variety of meat may be used. Yield: 4 servings.

Mrs. C. C. Yoquelet
St. John's Mission Soc.
Calumet City, Illinois

FIRE MEAT (CHINA)

2 lb. sirloin tip roast, thinly sliced and cubed
¼ c. sesame oil
1 or 2 chopped green onions
½ c. soy sauce, Japanese sweet type
2 tsp. sugar
Dash of pepper
Garlic powder to taste

Coat meat with sesame oil; add onions. Combine remaining ingredients; pour over meat. Marinate in shallow flat container for 6 to 8 hours. Remove meat from sauce. Broil for 5 to 7 minutes on each side. Serve immediately with rice. Yield: 6-8 servings.

Mrs. Arthur Stenstrom, Pres.
Christ the King LCW
New Brighton, Minnesota

ONE-DISH MEAL (CHINA)

1 c. peas, fresh or canned
1 can bean sprouts, drained
1 lb. left-over roast
2 med. onions, chopped
1 c. chopped celery
3 tbsp. fat
¾ c. uncooked rice
1 can cream of mushroom soup
4 tbsp. soy sauce
½ tsp. salt
¼ tsp. pepper

Drain peas and bean sprouts reserving liquids. Add remaining ingredients. Add enough water to vegetable liquids to measure 2 cups; pour into mixture. Place in large casserole. Cover; bake at 325 degrees for 1 hour and 30 minutes. Yield: 6 servings.

Mrs. Carl Peltzer, Pres.
Tabor LCW
Pueblo, Colorado

PORK AND STRING BEANS (CHINA)

¼ c. oil
2 cloves of garlic, chopped
2 lb. fresh pork, cubed
2 lge. onions, chopped
1 bunch celery, chopped
2 lb. fresh string beans or 2 cans whole
    string beans
6 tbsp. soy sauce
1 can mushrooms
2 tbsp. cornstarch

Heat oil in 8-quart pan. Add garlic; brown lightly. Add pork; brown lightly. Cover; cook for 15 minutes. Add onions and celery; cover and cook for 10 minutes. Add string beans and 4 tablespoonfuls soy sauce. Cover and cook until beans are tender. Add mushrooms. Mix 2 tablespoonfuls soy sauce, cornstarch and a small amount of water; add to pork mixture to thicken. NOTE: Cook mixture 10 minutes longer before adding beans, if canned beans are used. Yield: 10 servings.

Matilda Reimels, Financial Sec.
Bethany Women's Aux.
New York City, New York

STUFFED MUSHROOMS (CHINA)

1 sm. clove of garlic, finely minced
½ lb. pork sausage
Dash of soy sauce
1 pt. medium mushrooms, stemmed

Add garlic to pork. Add soy sauce; mix well. Fill caps of mushrooms with pork mixture. Set mushrooms, sausage-side up, in baking dish. Steam, uncovered, for 2 hours.

Mrs. Ray Hohman, Pres.
Holy Comforter LCW
Treasure Island, Florida

SWEET-SOUR SPARERIBS (CHINA)

2 No. 211 cans chunk pineapple
Ribs
1 c. brown sugar
3 tbsp. cornstarch
¾ c. white vinegar
½ tsp. salt
1 tsp. soy sauce
1 lge. green pepper, chopped

Drain pineapple, reserving 1 cup juice. Boil ribs in salt water until tender. Place in long shallow baking dish. Combine brown sugar and cornstarch; add reserved pineapple juice. Add vinegar, salt and soy sauce. Cook over low heat, stirring constantly, until clear and thickened. Add pineapple chunks; pour over ribs. Bake at 350 degrees for 1 hour. Turn ribs 10 minutes before serving; add green pepper. Return to oven until glazed. Yield: 4-6 servings.

Mrs. Marlyn Else, Sec.
Couples Club
Schleswig, Iowa

SWEET AND SOUR SPARERIBS (CHINA)

1 ½ lb. pork spareribs
2 eggs, beaten
Flour
1 c. water
½ c. vinegar
½ c. brown sugar
⅓ c. catsup
1 tsp. soy sauce
2 tbsp. cornstarch

Cut spareribs into 1-inch pieces. Boil for 10 minutes. Cool. Dip into eggs and then into flour. Fry in deep fat for 10 minutes or until crisp. Combine water, vinegar, brown sugar, catsup and soy sauce; bring to a boil. Thicken with cornstarch. Serve with spareribs. Yield: 4 servings.

Mrs. R. Nygaard
Schreiber LWML
Schreiber, Ontario, Canada

SWEET AND SOUR SPARERIBS (CHINA)

3 eggs, beaten
3 tbsp. flour
3 lb. spareribs, cut into small pieces
3 tbsp. oil or shortening
1 ⅓ c. brown sugar
⅔ c. vinegar
⅔ c. catsup
½ c. chopped sweet pickles

Combine eggs and flour; dip ribs into batter. Fry in oil until brown. Combine remaining ingredients; pour over ribs. Simmer for 2 to 3 hours. Let stand in sauce for several hours. Reheat to serve. Yield: 6 servings.

Mrs. Anna Elman, Pres.
St. Matthew's LWML
Milk River, Alberta, Canada

SWEET AND SOUR SPARERIBS (CHINA)

2 lb. spareribs, cut into bite-sized pieces
Red food coloring
2 tsp. monosodium glutamate
1 tsp. white sugar
½ tsp. pepper
6 tsp. soy sauce
Flour
1 ½ c. brown sugar
¾ c. vinegar
1 ¼ c. water
1 tbsp. cornstarch
Sesame seed

Sprinkle ribs with food coloring. Combine monosodium glutamate, white sugar, pepper and soy sauce. Pour over ribs. Let stand for 15 to 20 minutes. Shake ribs in paper bag with flour to coat. Combine brown sugar, vinegar and water; heat until sugar is dissolved. Pour over ribs. Bake at 350 degrees for 30 minutes. Thicken liquid with cornstarch. Sprinkle with sesame seed. Yield: 4-5 servings.

Shirley A. Lutz, Pres.
Gethsemane LWML
Edmonton, Alberta, Canada

TERIYAKI (CHINA)

¼ c. soy sauce
1 tbsp. sugar
Dash of salt
1 clove of garlic, minced
1 tsp. ginger
1 lb. beef, cut into 2 ½ x ½-in. strips
¼ c. salad oil
1 c. string beans, fresh or frozen
1 c. carrots, chopped
1 c. diagonally sliced celery
1 tbsp. cornstarch
1 c. water

Combine soy sauce, sugar, salt, garlic and ginger; add meat. Marinate for 1 hour. Heat oil in electric fry pan; add vegetables. Steam for 3 to 4 minutes; remove vegetables. Add meat to hot pan; fry for 2 to 3 minutes. Add vegetables and marinade. Mix cornstarch and water; add to mixture. Cook until thickened. Yield: 4 servings.

Mrs. Carl Opgrand, Treas.
Halstad LCW
Halstad, Minnesota

FRIKADELLER--MEAT BALLS (DENMARK)

1 lge. onion, chopped
Butter
¾ c. bread crumbs
1 ¾ c. milk
1 lb. ground beef
2 eggs
1 ½ tsp. salt
¼ tsp. pepper
1 ½ c. beef broth (opt.)
1 c. sour cream (opt.)

Cook onion in 1 tablespoonful butter until soft. Soak bread crumbs in 3/4 cup milk; mix with onion, meat, eggs, salt and pepper. Beat 1 cup milk into mixture with electric mixer. Form into 12 meat balls. Brown meat balls in 4 tablespoonfuls butter. Simmer for 5 minutes on each side or until done. Add beef broth to browned meat balls; simmer until done. Add sour cream; heat. Yield: 6 servings.

Grete Konsgaard, Pres.
St. Paul's LCW
Glen Burnie, Maryland

FRIKADELLER (DENMARK)

½ lb. ground lean beef
½ lb. ground lean pork
1 c. flour
1 egg
2 tsp. salt
¼ tsp. pepper
2 tsp. grated onion
1 ½ c. milk
Butter

Mix ground meats with flour, egg, salt, pepper and grated onion. Add milk, while stirring. Blend well. Form into meat balls with a tablespoon dipped in browned butter. Place in a buttered skillet. Cook over medium heat for 10 to 15 minutes. Turn meat frequently. Remove meat balls from skillet.

MUSHROOM SAUCE:

1 can chopped mushrooms
Milk
2 tbsp. flour
Salt and pepper to taste

Drain mushrooms, reserving liquid. Add enough milk to mushroom liquid to make 2 cups liquid. Blend flour into drippings in skillet. Gradually add milk mixture. Cook until bubbly. Add mushrooms and salt and pepper to taste. Yield: 6 servings.

Mrs. Walter Moeller
Nicolai Ladies Aid Soc.
Porter, Minnesota

LEVERPOSTEJ (DENMARK)

1 to 1 ½ lb. liver
½ lb. pork fat
1 med. onion
2 tbsp. butter
2 tbsp. flour
2 c. milk
2 eggs
¾ tsp. pepper
1 tbsp. salt
½ tsp. allspice
¼ tsp. cloves
2 tbsp. flour

(Continued on next page)

Place liver, fat and onion in meat grinder. Grind five times. Melt butter; add flour and milk. Cook; add cream mixture to liver, stirring well. Add eggs, seasonings, spices and flour. Beat well. Place in loaf pan; set in pan of shallow water. Bake at 350 degrees for 1 hour and 15 minutes. Serve as a sandwich spread.

Mrs. Arol Hansen, Pres.
Bethlehem LCW
Askov, Minnesota

FRIKADELLER (DENMARK)

2 lb. lean ground pork
½ lb. ground beef
2 tsp. salt
2 tbsp. flour
2 eggs
½ tsp. allspice
½ c. milk
Shortening

Combine all ingredients except shortening. Mix well. Melt shortening in heavy skillet; drop in meat mixture from tablespoon and form into oblong rolls with back of spoon. Brown on both sides; cook slowly for 35 minutes. Yield: 7-8 servings.

Mrs. Harry Jensen
United LCW
Shelby, Iowa

LEVERPOSTEJ-- LIVER PASTE (DENMARK)

1 lge. onion
1 pt. ground liver
2 qt. ground heart, tongue and head meat
1 c. milk
4 eggs
2 tsp. pepper
3 tsp. allspice
½ tsp. poultry seasoning
1 tbsp. salt
½ c. (scant) flour
Bacon strips

Combine all ingredients except bacon and mix well. Place in loaf pans; top with bacon strips. Set in pan of water in over. Bake at 350 degrees for 1 hour and 30 minutes to 2 hours. NOTE: Mixture may be processed in pint jars for 1 hour and 10 minutes at 15 pounds pressure. Yield: 4-5 loaves.

Mrs. Howard Johnson, Pres.
Bethesda LCW
Moorhead, Iowa

RIBBENSTEJ MED FRIKADELLER (DENMARK)

1 side of ribs
Salt and pepper
4 apples, peeled and quartered
6 to 8 prunes

Have butcher crack rib bones in middle. Do not cut through. Salt and pepper to taste. Cover with layer of apples. Add prunes that have been soaked and pitted. Fold bones together; tie with a cord. Cover; roast ribs at 350 degrees.

FRICADELLER:

½ c. bread crumbs
1 c. milk
¾ lb. ground beef
¼ lb. sausage
1 med. onion
1 tsp. salt
¼ tsp. pepper
½ tsp. allspice

Soak bread crumbs in milk; add remaining ingredients. Form into balls and brown. Place in roaster when spareribs begin to brown and finish cooking, 45 minutes or longer. Yield: 6-8 servings.

Mrs. Leslie Andersen, Pres.
Nathanael LCW
Reserve, Montana

CORNISH PASTIES (ENGLAND)

1 c. lard
4 c. flour
1 tsp. salt
¾ c. cold water
3 med. potatoes, diced
1 ½ lb. round steak, cut into small pieces
½ lb. pork steak, cut into small pieces
2 med. onions, chopped
Small piece of suet, chopped
Butter

Cut lard into flour and salt. Add water; mix lightly. Divide into six parts. Roll each part out to size of plate. Place layer of potatoes, beef, pork and onions on one-half each portion of dough. Dot with suet and butter. Fold dough over meat mixture; seal edges. Bake at 400 degrees for 10 minutes; reduce temperature to 350 degrees and bake for 50 minutes longer. Yield: 6 servings.

Mrs. Fred Anderson, Pres.
First Lutheran LCW
Iron Mountain, Michigan

OLD ENGLISH SUET PUDDING

3 c. ground suet
5 c. flour
4 to 5 lb. round steak, cut into 1-in. pieces
Salt and pepper to taste
Onion

Combine suet and flour; mix well. Add enough water to make dough into ball. Roll out on floured board. Place remaining ingredients in center; bring edges together. Place on dish towel; tie edges securely. Place in container on rack.

(Continued on next page)

Cover with water; boil for 3 to 4 hours. Yield: 12-14 servings.

Theressa Markworth
First Lutheran Church
Palmdale, California

HOT POT (ENGLAND)

2 lb. beef chuck, cut into 1-in. cubes
3 tsp. salt
½ c. water
6 med. potatoes, sliced
4 med. onions, sliced
6 carrots, sliced
½ tsp. Tabasco sauce
1 1-lb. can tomatoes

Sprinkle beef with salt; brown thoroughly in small amount fat in skillet. Remove beef. Add water to drippings. Cook, stirring constantly, scraping brown particles. Remove from heat; set aside. Layer beef, potatoes, onions and carrots in large casserole. Sprinkle each layer with salt. Combine Tabasco sauce, tomatoes and reserved gravy; pour into casserole. Bake at 350 degrees for 2 hours. Yield: 6-8 servings.

Photograph for this recipe on page 357

DORA WAT (ETHIOPIA)

2 c. finely chopped red onions
1 to 1 ½ c. butter or margarine
3 tbsp. red pepper
5 to 6 c. warm water
3 tbsp. canned tomatoes or tomato sauce
1 chicken, washed and cut up
1 ½ tbsp. salt
1 tsp. pepper
½ tsp. cardamom
½ tsp. cinnamon
½ tsp. cloves
6 to 12 hard-cooked eggs

Saute onions in 1 cup butter until brown. Add remaining butter and red pepper. Cook for 30 minutes, adding a small amount of water, stirring occasionally. Add tomatoes and chicken. Cook for 30 minutes longer, adding salt and water. Remove from fire; stir in spices. Serve over rice; garnish with eggs. Yield: 6-12 servings.

Mrs. Frank J. Schmitt
Immanuel LCW
Escanaba, Michigan

PICKLED HERRING--ETIKKASILKAT (FINLAND)

4 salt herring
1 ½ c. vinegar
¼ c. sugar
2 tbsp. pickling spices
3 onions, sliced
2 bay leaves

Wash herring thoroughly; place in bowl with enough water to cover. Soak for 24 hours, changing water, frequently. Drain; cut off heads. Cut each herring into 4 pieces. Place in jar. Combine 1/2 cup hot water, vinegar, sugar, pickling spices, onions and bay leaves. Stir until sugar is dissolved. Pour over herring. Cover; marinate in refrigerator for 24 hours. Yield: 12 servings.

Sylvia M. Fredrickson, Pres.
St. Matthew's LWML
Sonora, California

KALA LAATIKKO--SALMON SCALLOPED WITH POTATOES (FINLAND)

1 1-lb. can salmon
6 to 7 lge. potatoes, sliced
Butter
Minched onion
Salt and pepper
Cracker crumbs
2 c. milk

Remove skin and bones from salmon. Alternate layers of potatoes and salmon in greased casserole. Season each layer with dots of butter, onion and salt and pepper to taste. Top with cracker crumbs and additional dots of butter. Add milk; bake at 400 degrees for 40 to 50 minutes. Yield: 6-7 servings.

Mrs. Einar Lakso, Church Treas.
St. Paul's Ladies Aid
Iron River, Michigan

PAS-TEES--PASTIES (FINLAND)

3 c. sifted flour
1 tsp. salt
1 c. lard or vegetable shortening
½ c. cold water
2 lb. chuck or steak, cut into small pieces
Small piece suet
3 med. potatoes, thinly sliced
2 med. onions, thinly sliced
1 carrot, thinly sliced
Salt and pepper

Mix flour with salt; cut in shortening. Add water. Refrigerate while preparing filling. Combine meat and suet. Divide pastry, meat and vegetables into six parts. Roll each piece of dough the size of a medium pie plate. Place on portion of meat into each piece of dough. Add salt, pepper and vegetables. Bring edges together; crimp to seal. Prick pastry. Place on baking sheet; bake at 350 degrees for 1 hour. Serve with catsup and dill pickles. Yield: 6 servings.

Mrs. Peter M. Juntunen, Pres.
St. John's LCW
L'Anse, Michigan

SEVEN-HOUR BAKED FISH (FINLAND)
Flour
Sliced dressed Suckers or Rainbow trout
Salt and pepper
Butter

Flour fish; place a layer of fish, salt, pepper and pats of butter into buttered earthen crock. Repeat layers until crock is filled to 1 inch from top. Cover; bake at 350 degrees for 1 hour. Reduce temperature to 300 degrees; bake for 6 hours.

Mrs. Wilho Laurila, Pres.
First Lutheran Church Guild
Trenary, Michigan

VASIKANHYYTELO--JELLIED VEAL (FINLAND)
2 lb. side, shoulder or breast of veal
8 whole allspice
1 ½ tbsp. salt
1 bay leaf
1 tbsp. vinegar
2 sm. carrots, diced
1 egg, beaten
Parsley

Wipe meat; cut into large pieces. Add to boiling water seasoned with allspice, salt and bay leaf. Cook, uncovered, for a few minutes, removing scum from surface of stock. Cover; cook for 40 minutes or until meat is tender. Remove meat; cool. Cut into small cubes. Drain and reserve small amount of stock. Season meat with vinegar. Add salt if desired. Pour small amount of reserved stock in baking mold. Refrigerate until jelled. Add carrots, egg and parsley. Add meat; top with remaining stock. Let stand in cold place overnight. Turn out onto platter.

Mrs. Wayne L. Johnson, Treas.
Zion Cir.
Amasa, Michigan

BEEF BOURGUIGNON (FRANCE)
6 slices bacon
4 lb. lean sirloin or round steak, cut into ¼ x
    4-in. pieces
2 cloves of garlic, crushed
2 lb. fresh mushrooms, sliced or 2 lge. cans
    sliced mushrooms
2 bay leaves, crushed
2 tbsp. chopped parsley
1 tsp. salt
1 tsp. thyme
⅛ tsp. pepper
½ c. butter
¼ c. plus 1 tbsp. flour
2 10 ½ - oz. cans beef consomme
½ c. Burgundy wine

Cut bacon into small pieces; fry in Dutch oven. Remove from pan. Saute meat in pan drippings. Add garlic and mushrooms. Season with bay leaves, parsley, salt, thyme and pepper. Add bacon and remove from heat. In another pan make a roux of butter and flour. Cook, stirring constantly, until butter turns a light tan. Add the consomme and wine. Stir and cook until slightly thickened. Add to beef mixture. Cover; simmer for 1 hour and 30 minutes or until beef is tender. Serve with cooked noodles or rice, if desired. Yield: 8-10 servings.

Mrs. Thomas E. Whalen
Ascension Ladies Guild
Casselberry, Florida

BOEUF BOURGUIGNON (FRANCE)
6-oz. bacon, cut into thin strips
1 ½ qt. water
1 tbsp. olive oil or cooking oil
3 lb. lean stew beef, cut into 2-in. cubes
1 carrot, sliced
1 onion, sliced
1 tsp. salt
½ tsp. pepper
2 tbsp. flour
3 c. red wine
2 to 3 c. brown beef stock or bouillon
1 tbsp. tomato paste
2 cloves or garlic, mashed
½ tsp. thyme
1 bay leaf, crushed
18 to 24 sm. white onions, braised
2 to 3 cans mushrooms, sauted

Simmer bacon in water. Drain and pat dry. Saute bacon in oil. Remove with slotted spoon. Place drippings in 9 or 10-inch deep casserole. Saute beef in the drippings. Add beef to bacon. Saute carrot and onion. Return beef and bacon to casserole; drain off fat. Sprinkle meat with seasonings and flour; toss to coat. Bake in preheated 450 degree oven for 4 minutes. Toss again. Reduce heat to 325 degrees. Stir in remaining ingredients. Cover; bake for 3 to 4 hours. Drain and serve in casserole. Yield: 6 servings.

Mrs. Ivan G. Althouse, Jr.
Christ Lutheran Church Mary-Martha Guild
Lynch, Nebraska

CHICKEN A LA VALLEE D'AUGE (FRANCE)
4 to 5 chicken breasts, split
¼ c. butter or margarine
1 tsp. salt
¼ tsp. pepper
2 shallots or small onions, minced
1 tbsp. chopped parsley
¼ tsp. dried thyme
¼ tsp. rosemary
¾ c. cider
½ c. heavy cream

Brown chicken breasts in butter over low heat for 20 minutes. Add remaining ingredients except cream; blend well. Cover and simmer for 15 minutes or until tender. Add cream; stir and heat, but do not boil. Serve sauce over chicken. Yield: 8-10 servings.

Mrs. Dorina Ruff, Pres.
Immanuel Ladies Aid
Waterloo, Illinois

COUNTRY CHICKEN (FRANCE)

2 fryers
½ c. salad oil
½ lb. smoked ham, cut into strips
1 c. chopped onion
1 green pepper, cut into strips
½ lb. mushrooms
2 tsp. salt
⅛ tsp. pepper
4 c. water
5 cloves of garlic
2 sprigs of parsley
1 bay leaf
½ tsp. dried thyme
4 tomatoes, cut into wedges
Lemon juice to taste
2 tbsp. flour
6 tbsp. soft butter

Disjoint chickens, dividing backs and breasts into halves. Disjoint wings. Brown in hot oil in 4-quart heavy kettle. Remove chicken; set aside. Cook ham, onion, green pepper and mushrooms in pan drippings; add chicken, salt, pepper and water. Tie garlic, parsley, bay leaf and thyme in cheesecloth; add to kettle. Cover; simmer for 30 minutes or until chicken is tender. Remove herbs. Add tomatoes and lemon juice. Blend flour into butter with a fork; stir in enough chicken broth to make a thin sauce. Cook, stirring, until thickened. Serve chicken on platter over noodles or mashed potatoes, if desired. Spoon sauce over top. Yield: 6-8 servings.

Mrs. Milton Muller, Pres.
Peace LWML
Warden, Washington

PAUPIETTES DE VEAU (FRANCE)

3 pieces bacon
3 oz. Swiss cheese
1 c. sausage
6 veal cutlets
Salt and pepper
1 c. butter
1 onion, chopped
1 carrot, sliced
1 glass white wine
1 tbsp. flour

Place 1/2 piece of bacon, strip of cheese and a small amount of sausage on each slice of veal. Salt and pepper to taste; roll and tie. Place butter, onion and sliced carrot in pan; add meat roll. Brown well. Add wine and flour; cook slowly for 45 minutes. NOTE: Best made a day in advance and reheated. Yield: 6 servings.

Florence Butterfass, Pres.
St. Paul's LWML
Chicago Park, California

POULET EN PIE (FRANCE)

3 c. sifted flour
Salt
¼ c. butter
¾ c. shortening
½ c. cold water
1 egg, separated
2 tbsp. cream
2 ½ c. chopped cooked chicken
¼ c. diced bread crumbs
2 tbsp. chopped parsley
6 slices boiled or baked ham

Sift flour with 1 teaspoonful salt into mixing bowl. Cut in butter and shortening until particles are the size of small peas. Sprinkle with cold water, a small amount at a time, tossing and stirring lightly with a fork. Add additional water to driest particles, pushing lumps to side, until dough is moist enough to hold together. Form into ball. Place in floured pastry cloth; flatten to 1/2-inch thickness. Roll to 21 x 14-inch rectangle. Cut into six 7-inch squares. Combine slightly beaten egg yolk, cream, 1 cup chopped chicken, bread crumbs, parsley and seasoning to taste. Stir to combine. Place ham on pastry squares. Top with 2 tablespoonfuls chicken mixture on each square. Place remaining chicken, cut into large pieces, on stuffing. Moisten pastry edges; bring corners to center. Press edges to seal. Cut slits; brush with beaten egg white or additional cream. Place on ungreased baking sheet. Bake at 375 degrees for 25 to 30 minutes or until golden brown.

CHICKEN SAUCE:

⅓ c. butter
⅓ c. flour
1 c. chicken broth
1 c. light cream
Salt and pepper to taste

Melt butter in top of double boiler over hot water. Remove from heat; blend in flour. Add broth and cream. Cook over boiling water until thickened, stirring occasionally. Season to taste. Cover and place over hot water until ready to serve. Serve hot with chicken pies. Yield: 6 servings.

Mrs. Don Linser
Zion LCW
Morris, Minnesota

SALMON SOUFFLE

3 tbsp. butter
3 tbsp. flour
½ tsp. salt
½ c. milk
3 eggs, separated
1 c. salmon
½ c. cooked peas

Melt butter; blend in flour and salt. Gradually add milk; cook, stirring until smooth and thick. Add egg yolks; beat well. Add salmon and peas. Fold in beaten egg whites. Pour into greased casserole; place casserole in pan of hot water. Bake

(Continued on next page)

in moderate oven until knife inserted in center comes out clean. Yield: 5 servings.

Mrs. Gerald Wilkinson, Pres.
Kingsville LWML
Kingsville, Ontario, Canada

BEROAKS (GERMANY)

½ lb. ground beef
3 c. chopped cabbage
1 c. chopped onions
Salt and pepper to taste
Yeast dough

Brown ground beef in skillet for about 4 minutes; add cabbage and onions. Cover and cook slowly for 15 minutes longer, stirring often. Add salt and pepper. Prepare dough and let rise. Roll dough 1/4-inch thick; cut into squares. Place some of the filling on each square; pinch corners together. Place upside-down on greased baking sheet. Let rise for 20 minutes. Bake at 350 degrees for 20 minutes. Yield: 10 servings.

Mrs. Lauren Brunner, Pres.
Trinity Ladies Soc.
Ramona, Kansas

FLEISCH KUCHEN--MEAT CAKES (GERMANY)
DOUGH:

4 c. flour
2 or 3 eggs
2 tsp. salt
Buttermilk or water

Combine all ingredients. Work dough well. Shape dough into two loaves. Place on floured board for 30 minutes.

FILLING:

Ground pork
Dash of pepper
1 onion, finely chopped
¼ c. cold water

Combine all ingredients; mix well. Cut dough into pieces 1-inch thick. Roll each into thin oval or round shapes. Place 1 tablespoonful meat mixture on one-half of one piece of dough. Fold; press edges firmly together. Fry in deep fat.

Mrs. A. Herrmann, Sec.
Zion LWML
Bismarck, North Dakota

HASENPFEFFER (GERMANY)

1 rabbit, cut in serving pieces
1 c. vinegar
2 c. water
1 ½ c. flour
1 tsp. salt
½ tsp. pepper
3 tbsp. shortening
1 lb. prunes
½ lb. gingersnaps

Soak rabbit overnight in vinegar and 1 cup water. Roll in flour seasoned with salt and pepper; brown in shortening. Cover with remaining water; add prunes. Cook for 1 hour to 1 hour and 30 minutes or until done. Thicken gravy with gingersnaps. Yield: 6 servings.

Mrs. Raymond Schubert, Pres.
Hope Women's League
Granite City, Illinois

HASENPFEFFER (GERMANY)

1 rabbit, cut into serving pieces
2 c. wine vinegar
1 c. water
1 lge. onion, sliced
1 bay leaf
2 tsp. salt
½ tsp. allspice
1 tsp. pepper
Flour
1 c. sour cream

Wash and dry rabbit. Combine remaining ingredients except flour and sour cream. Add rabbit; let stand for 12 to 24 hours. Remove meat; strain marinade. Brown meat on all sides in heavy skillet. Add 1 cup marinade or more if needed; simmer for 1 hour or until meat is tender. Place meat on platter. Thicken gravy with a small amount of flour; add sour cream.

Mrs. Arline B. Boehm, Pres.
Trinity Ladies Aid
Millstadt, Illinois

HASENPFEFFER-- MARINATED RABBIT STEW (GERMANY)
MARINADE:

3 c. red wine vinegar
3 c. water
½ c. sugar
1 med. onion, sliced
2 carrots, pared and sliced
1 tbsp. salt
1 tsp. pickling spices
¼ tsp. pepper

Combine all ingredients; mix well.

STEW:

1 2 ½ to 3-lb. rabbit
Flour
1 tsp. salt
½ tsp. monosodium glutamate
¼ tsp. pepper
3 tbsp. fat

Wipe rabbit with damp cloth; cut into serving pieces. Place in deep bowl; cover with marinade. Refrigerate for 2 to 3 days, turning often. Drain, reserving marinade. Mix 1/3 cup flour with seasonings; coat rabbit with mixture. Brown rabbit slowly in fat, turning to brown evenly. Remove from heat. Gradually add 2 cups of marinade.

(Continued on next page)

Cover and simmer for 45 minutes to 1 hour, or until rabbit is tender. Pour 1/2 cup of reserved marinade into a screw top jar. Sprinkle 1/4 cup flour on the liquid and close lid tightly; shake until mixture is well blended. Slowly pour one-half of mixture into cooking liquid. Stirring constantly, bring to a boil. Gradually add only what is needed of remaining mixture for consistency desired. Bring to a boil after each addition. After final addition, cook 3 to 5 minutes. Arrange rabbit on a platter. Pour some of the gravy over the rabbit and serve with remaining gravy. Yield: 6 servings.

Mrs. Glenn B. Welker, Pres.
St. Luke's LCW
Union Bridge, Maryland

HOLLIPSE (GERMANY)

1 med. cabbage
2 c. half-cooked rice
2 lb. hamburger
Salt and pepper to taste
2 tbsp. shortening
1 No. 2 ½ can tomatoes or tomato juice

Separate cabbage leaves. Let stand in hot water until wilted; drain. Place 1 tablespoonful rice on each cabbage leaf. Season hamburger; place 1 tablespoonful hamburger mixture on rice. Roll the cabbage leaves; fasten each with a toothpick. Arrange in a kettle with melted shortening; add tomatoes. Season to taste with salt and pepper. Cover tightly and cook slowly for 2 hours. Yield: 8 servings.

Mrs. Joan Koenig, Sec.
St. John's Ladies Aid
Tyndall, South Dakota

KARUE (GERMANY)

1 bacon square
1 sm. onion, chopped
¼ c. chopped celery
1 lge. cabbage, cut into eighths
1 can cream-style corn
1 can string beans
1 can tomatoes

Simmer bacon square in enough water to cover for 1 hour. Add onion, celery and cabbage; simmer for 1 hour. Add corn, beans and tomatoes; simmer for 30 minutes. Yield: 4 servings.

Mrs. Charles Talmage
Salem Mission
Orange, California

KLEINE KLOESCHEN (GERMANY)

1 ¼ c. flour
1 egg
Salt to taste
Soup broth

Sift flour into a bowl; break egg into flour. Sprinkle with salt. Work egg into flour until the mixture is a crumbly mass of pieces not larger than a navy bean. Drop into boiling soup broth; cook for 10 minutes before serving. NOTE: To store, spread on a board and dry for several days.

Mrs. Lorinz Pyahn, Pres.
Carver County Lutheran High School
Norwood, Minnesota

ROLADEN (GERMANY)

1 slice round steak
½ tsp. salt
¼ tsp. pepper
2 slices bacon
1 onion, sliced
2 tbsp. flour
3 tsp. butter

Trim fat from steak; cut into four to six pieces. Sprinkle with salt and pepper. Top each slice with slice of bacon and slice of onion. Roll up; secure with toothpick. Sprinkle with flour; fry in butter until brown. Simmer, covered, for 1 hour, adding water if necessary. Remove from casserole; make gravy. Yield: 4 servings.

Mrs. Richard Hirt
Redeemer Lutheran Church
Mountain Home, Arkansas

ROLADEN--BEEF ROLLS (GERMANY)

2 lb. chip steak, thin beef slices or tenderized steak
Salt and pepper to taste
½ lb. bacon, finely chopped
1 c. finely chopped onions
½ c. finely chopped parsley
4 tbsp. flour
3 c. water
1 tsp. tomato paste

Rub steaks with salt and pepper. Saute bacon with onions and parsley. Spread filling on beef slices. Roll tightly. Fasten with toothpicks. Brown in same skillet that filling was made in. Add small amount of shortening if needed. Remove from skillet and place in pot. Make gravy with drippings in skillet, adding flour, water and tomato paste. Pour gravy over rolls. Cover and simmer until soft, about 30 to 45 minutes. Add water if needed. Yield: 8 servings.

Mrs. Emma Raschka, Pres.
Christ Lutheran Church Ladies Aid
Dundalk, Maryland

ROLADEN (GERMANY)

2 lb. round steak
Salt and pepper
Bacon
Onion slices

367

(Continued on next page)

Cut steak into small serving portions. Lay out flat and season. On each piece of steak lay a quarter slice of bacon. Top with onion. Roll up each piece separately; tie with a string to form a small roll. Place in skillet and brown on all sides. Add water; simmer for 1 hour and 30 minutes or until tender. Remove from pan and remove strings. Make gravy from drippings; pour over meat before serving. Yield: 6 servings.

Mrs. John W. Meyer
St. Paul's Ladies Aid Soc.
Mattoon, Illinois

ROLADEN--MEAT ROLLS (GERMANY)

4 slices round steak, cut ¼-in. thick
Salt and pepper
Meat tenderizer
Mustard
¼ lb. lean back bacon, finely chopped
1 sm. onion, finely chopped
1 c. lard or vegetable oil
1 tbsp. cornstarch

Sprinkle meat with salt, pepper and tenderizer. Spread large amount of mustard on one side of meat. Mix bacon with onion. Spread on mustard-side of meat. Roll up lengthwise; wrap with thread. Heat lard in pan in preheated 250 degree oven. Add meat rolls; brown lightly. Add boiling water; cook, covered, for 2 hours to 2 hours and 30 minutes. Add water as needed. Remove meat rolls; thicken gravy with cornstarch. Season to taste. Yield: 4 servings.

Mrs. Irma Machmer, Sec.
Peace LWML
Spring Valley, Saskatchewan, Canada

SAUERBRATEN--MARINATED MEAT (GERMANY)

1 ½ c. vinegar
1 c. water
2 tbsp. sugar
2 tsp. Salt
2 tbsp. mixed pickling spices
4 onions, sliced
½ c. red wine
1 4-lb. rump or chuck pot roast
¼ c. flour
Pepper
2 tbsp. fat
⅓ c. gingersnap crumbs
½ c. sour cream (opt.)

Combine vinegar, water, sugar, 2 teaspoonfuls salt and spice in a saucepan. Bring to a boil. Place 3 sliced onions in a large bowl or enamelware pan. Pour hot mixture over onions; cool. Stir in wine. Add meat. Cover; refrigerate for two or three days, turning each day. Remove meat. Strain pickling liquor and reserve. Dry meat on paper toweling. Coat meat with flour. Sprinkle with salt and pepper. Brown meat well in fat for 12 to 15 minutes, turning. Add 1 cup strained pickling liquor and place remaining sliced onion on top. Cover; simmer for 2 hours and 30 minutes or until tender. Remove meat to

a hot platter. Dip off all excess fat from drippings. Stir in gingersnap crumbs and 1 1/2 cups water. Cook, stirring until thickened. Stir in sour cream; heat, but do not boil. Add additional seasonings if desired. Serve gravy with meat. Yield: 8 servings.

Marie Brach, Pres.
First Lutheran Church Thimble Guild
Pasadena, California

SAUERBRATEN (GERMANY)

5 lb. chuck or bottom round
Salt and pepper
Monosodium glutamate
1 clove of garlic, slivered
1 lge. onion, sliced
4 c. water
1 pt. wine vinegar
3 lemon slices
2 tbsp. mixed pickling spices

Rub meat with salt, pepper and monosodium glutamate. Score in 3 or 4 places; insert garlic. Place in large bowl. Top with onion. Heat water with vinegar, lemon and pickling spices. Pour over meat. Cover; let stand for two to three days in refrigerator, turning meat occasionally. Yield: 6-8 servings.

Mrs. Albert J. Krause
St. John's Ladies Aid Soc.
Flushing, New York

SAUERBRATEN (GERMANY)

4 lge. onions
8 stalks celery
2 lge. carrots
3 qt. cold water
1 ½ c. white vinegar
1 c. wine vinegar
½ c. sugar
2 med. bay leaves
3 tbsp. salt
2 tbsp. mixed pickling spices
8 whole cloves
1 5 ½ to 6-lb. bottom round beef
18 to 24 gingersnaps

Slice onions, celery and carrots; place in a large pot with cold water, vinegars, sugar, bay leaves, salt, pickling spices and cloves. Boil for 5 minutes. Place meat in a stone crock; pour boiling stock over meat. Refrigerate for 5 days. Remove meat; dry with towel. Heat a heavy Dutch oven for ten minutes. Place meat in Dutch oven; brown for 30 minutes on all sides, turning frequently. Strain stock; drain onions, carrots and celery on a paper towel. Place over meat. Reduce heat to medium; pour stock over meat, stirring well. Increase heat until stock is boiling; reduce heat; cover and let cook for 2 hours to 2 hours and 30 minutes. Add gingersnaps; cook and stir for 4 minutes. Remove from heat; let stand, covered, for a few minutes before serving.

(Continued on next page)

Strain gravy and serve over sliced meat. Yield: 8 servings.

Mrs. Emmy Cruse
Grace Ladies Aid Soc.
Mastic Beach, Long Island, New York

SAUERBRATEN (GERMANY)

1 3 to 4 lb. chuck roast
¾ c. vinegar
¾ c. water
2 onions, sliced
1 green pepper, sliced
2 bay leaves
2 tbsp. whole allspice
1 tbsp. mustard seed
Flour
Pan drippings
2 tbsp. sugar
1 c. sour cream

Place roast in large bowl. Heat vinegar, water, onions, green pepper, bay leaves, allspice and mustard; pour over roast. Let stand in refrigerator to marinate for 4 days, turning daily. Cook meat in liquid until tender. Brown flour in pan drippings; add meat liquid. Cook until thick; stir in sugar. Just before removing from heat; add sour cream. Serve with roast. Yield: 10 servings.

Mrs. Forrest R. Bevington, Pres.
St. Mark's LCW
St. Joe, Indiana

SAUERBRATEN WITH RAISINS (GERMANY)

1 3 to 4-lb. chuck roast
Salt
2 tbsp. lard, melted
2 med. onions, sliced
1 bay leaf
¼ c. water
¼ c. vinegar
1 tbsp. brown sugar
⅛ tsp. cinnamon
¼ tsp. allspice
⅛ tsp. ground cloves
¼ c. raisins
Flour

Sprinkle roast with salt; brown in lard in Dutch oven. Top with onions and bay leaf. Combine water and vinegar; dissolve brown sugar. Add seasonings; pour over meat. Cover; cook over low heat for 2 hours or until meat is almost tender. Add water as needed. Turn meat; top with raisins. Cover; cook for 45 minutes to 1 hour or until meat is tender. Place roast on serving platter. Spoon off excess fat from broth. Thicken with flour; dilute with a small amount of water if necessary. Season to taste. Yield: 6 servings.

Mrs. Robert S. Todd, Pres.
Beautiful Savior Ladies Guild
Broomfield, Colorado

SAUERBRATEN--MARINATED BEEF (GERMANY)

3 to 3 ½ lb. beef round or rump, thickly cut
1 tsp. salt
½ tsp. pepper
4 bay leaves
½ tsp. peppercorns
8 whole cloves
2 med. onions, sliced
1 sm. carrot, minced
1 stalk celery, chopped
1 ½ c. red wine vinegar
2 ½ c. water
½ c. butter

Rub meat with salt and pepper. Place in deep earthenware crock or ovenware glass bowl with all spices and vegetables. Heat vinegar and water to boiling; pour over meat. Let cool. Cover bowl well; refrigerate. Marinate for 48 hours, turning meat twice a day. Remove meat from marinade. Melt butter in Dutch oven or kettle; brown meat. Strain marinade; pour over meat. Cover; simmer slowly for 2 hours and 30 minutes to 3 hours or until fork tender. Remove meat to warmed serving platter.

GINGERSNAP GRAVY:

2 tbsp. sugar
1 ½ c. hot marinade
⅔ c. gingersnap crumbs
Salt to taste
½ c. sour craem (opt.)

Melt sugar, stirring until golden brown. Gradually stir in marinade and water. Add gingersnaps; cook until thickened. Add salt and sour cream. Serve with sauerbraten. Yield: 6 servings.

Mrs. Fred Meyer
Our Redeemer Ladies Aid
Overland, Missouri

SPARERIBS AND SAUERKRAUT (GERMANY)

4 lb. spareribs
3 tbsp. pork fat
2 tsp. salt
1 tsp. pepper
1 qt. sauerkraut
½ c. thinly sliced onion

Brown spareribs in pork fat; season with salt and pepper. Place a layer of sauerkraut in a 6-quart casserole; place spareribs over sauerkraut. Cover with remaining sauerkraut; top with onion. Cover ingredients with boiling water. Cover closely. Bake at 350 degrees for 2 hours or until spareribs are done. Yield: 8 servings.

Mrs. Gust. Brummund, Pres.
St. John's Ladies Aid
Northfield, Minnesota

MAUSSAKA (GREECE)

1 med. onion, finely chopped
½ lb. butter
1 lb. hamburger

(Continued on next page)

Thyme to taste
Salt and pepper to taste
1 clove of garlic, pressed
2 lge. eggplants
2 eggs, well beaten
½ c. bread crumbs

Brown onion in 2 tablespoonfuls butter; add hamburger. Season with thyme, salt, p e p p e r and garlic. Peel eggplant; parboil for 5 minutes in salted water. Drain; slice coarsely. Fry slices in remaining butter. Place layers of eggplant and hamburger, ending with eggplant, in greased casserole. Pour eggs over top; sprinkle with bread crumbs. Place casserole in pan of warm water. Bake at 350 degrees for 45 to 50 minutes. Yield: 4 servings.

Mrs. A. G. Price
Trinity Evangelical LWML
Toronto, Ontario, Canada

STAMPPOT (HOLLAND)

1 med. cabbage
½ to 1 lb. cubed ham
5 to 6 med. potatoes, cubed
½ tsp. salt
⅛ tsp. pepper
1 ½ c. water
1 to 2 bay leaves (opt.)

Remove core from cabbage; cut cabbage into bite-sized p i e c e s. Place ham, p o t a t o e s and cabbage in 3-quart sauce pan. Add remaining ingredients; bring to a boil. Reduce temperature; simmer for 1 hour or until potatoes are mushy. Simmer for 10 to 15 minutes l o n g e r. Yield: 4 servings.

Mrs. Wolfgang E. Beckman, Pres.
Mt. Calvary LWML
Galesburg, Illinois

CHICKEN PAPRIKAS (HUNGARY)

1 clove of garlic (opt.)
1 tbsp. shortening
2 fryers, cut up
1 lge. onion, minced
Salt and pepper to taste
1 tsp. paprika
Water
1 tbsp. flour
1 ½ pt. sour cream

Brown onions and garlic in 4-quart Dutch oven in hot fat until golden. Add chicken; brown well. Sprinkle with salt, pepper and paprika during last few minutes of browning. Add 1 cup water; simmer for 45 minutes to 1 hour or until chicken is tender. Bring to a boil. Blend flour and 1/4 cup water into paste; add slowly to chicken, stirring constantly, until smooth. Boil for 1 minute. Remove from heat; add sour cream slowly, stirring constantly. Serve with buttered noodles or tiny egg dumplings. Yield: 6 servings.

Mrs. Louis B. Nagy
Martin Luther LWML
Savannah, Georgia

FISH IN WINE (HUNGARY)

1 carrot, sliced
1 stalk celery, sliced
1 kohlrabi, diced
1 onion, sliced
1 sprig parsley, chopped
2 tbsp. butter
2 lb. fish, cut into serving pieces
1 c. white wine
1 tsp. salt
⅛ tsp. pepper

Simmer v e g e t a b l e s, covered, in butter until nearly done. Arrange fish over vegetables. Pour wine over fish; sprinkle with salt and pepper. Cook, covered, over low heat for 15 minutes or until fish is t e n d e r and sauce is slightly thickened. Yield: 6 servings.

Mrs. H. Hufnagel, Sec.
Grace Lutheran Church
Toronto, Ontario, Canada

ROLLED LAMB (ICELAND)

2 sides lamb or veal breast or beef
    flank
2 tbsp. minced parsley
Salt
1 tbsp. grated onion
½ tsp. pepper
¼ tsp. cloves
¼ tsp. allspice
1 tsp. saltpeter
¼ c. sugar
2 ½ qt. water

Remove bones and sinews from meat; wash thoroughly. Sew pieces of meat together to form large squares or rectangle. Flatten out; sprinkle with parsley, 1 tablespoonful salt, o n i o n, pepper, cloves, allspice and 1/2 teaspoonful saltpeter. Roll t i g h t l y; hold meat with meat fork while sewing ends and sides. Tie with cord. Bring 1 pound salt and remaining ingredients to a boil until dissolved. Chill. P l a c e meat in brine. Remove from brine after 5 days. Cover with boiling water; boil slowly for 2 hours. Place meat in press until cold. Slice thinly; serve on openfaced sandwiches.

Mrs. Ivan Utoft, Pres.
Darebod LCW
Tyler, Minnesota

RULLUPYLSA (ICELAND)

Lamb flank
¼ tsp. saltpeter
2 tbsp. salt
½ tsp. pepper
1 lge. onion, chopped

Remove bones from flanks. Mix saltpeter, salt, pepper and o n i o n; spread on l a m b. Roll up tightly; sew outside edges with string. Wind twine around the roll and tie tightly.

(Continued on next page)

BRINE:

4 qt. water
1 c. salt
½ c. brown sugar
½ tsp. saltpeter

Combine all ingredients; boil for several minutes. Cool. Soak Rullupylsa in brine for three to four days. Drain off brine; cover with water. Boil for 2 hours and 30 minutes or until tender. Remove from water; put under weight to cool. Slice thinly and serve on buttered brown bread, if desired.

Mrs. Gudrun McInnis, Pres.
Grace LCW
Langruth, Manitoba, Canada

MULLIG ATAWNY SOUP--CURRY SOUP (INDIA)

1 med. onion, sliced
¼ c. butter
1 med. carrot, diced
1 stalk celery, diced
1 green pepper, diced
1 med. apple, pared and sliced
1 c. diced cooked chicken
⅓ c. flour
1 tsp. curry powder
⅛ tsp. mace
2 whole cloves
1 sprig parsley, minced
2 c. consomme
1 c. cooked tomatoes
Salt and pepper to taste

Saute onion in butter in deep kettle or Dutch oven. Add carrot, celery, green pepper, apple and chicken. Stir in remaining ingredients gradually. Simmer, covered, for 30 minutes. Serve hot. Yield: 6 servings.

Mrs. William Spring, Pres.
St. James LCW
Kansas City, Missouri

RICE AND CURRY (INDIA)

1 med. onion, finely chopped
Fat
1 lb. beef chuck
Flour
1 ½ tsp. curry powder
1 tsp. salt
½ tsp. pepper
1 No. 2 can tomatoes
2 c. raw rice, cooked

Fry onion until browned in small amount of fat. Cut beef into bite-sized pieces; roll in flour. Fry until browned on all sides. Remove meat and onion from fry pan. Mix curry powder, salt, pepper and 2 tablespoonfuls flour; add enough water to make a thin paste. Pour curry paste into fry pan, adding more water until of gravy consistency. Cook and stir for 5 minutes. Add meat mixture and tomatoes. Cook over low heat for 45 minutes or until meat is tender. Serve over cooked rice. Yield: 6 servings.

Ruth L. Turner, Pres.
Rocky Boy Mission Lutheran Women
Box Elder, Montana

SHRIMP WITH RICE (INDIA)

2 lb. long grain rice
3 to 4 whole cardamom, broken
2 to 3 sticks cinnamon, cut into small pieces
½ c. raisins
1 tbsp. sugar
10 to 12 whole cloves
1 stick butter
3 lb. cleaned shrimp
½ c. chopped onion
1 tsp. ground cumin
1 tsp. salt
¼ tsp. pepper
¼ tsp. ground ginger
½ c. Spanish-style tomato sauce
½ c. buttermilk
1 c. green peas

Soak rice for 5 minutes; dry. Add cardamom, cinnamon, raisins, sugar and cloves to rice; mix well. Heat butter; fry rice slightly. Fry shrimps until brown. Fry onions with shrimp. Add remaining ingredients except peas. Add 4 cups water; boil for 10 minutes. Add rice mixture to shrimp; boil for 15 minutes longer or until rice is almost done. Add peas; simmer for 10 minutes longer. Serve immediately. Yield: 8 servings.

Billie June Rood, VP
Good Shepherd Ladies Guild
Leadville, Colorado

SATES--SKEWERED BROILED PORK (INDONESIA)

4 med. onions, chopped
2 cloves of garlic, minced
4 tsp. crushed coriander seed
1 tbsp. salt
1 tsp. black pepper
Dash of cayenne pepper
3 tbsp. lemon juice
2 tbsp. brown sugar
¼ c. soy sauce
1 ½ lb. boned pork shoulder, trimmed and cut into ½-in. cubes

Toss onions, garlic, coriander seed, salt, pepper and cayenne into large bowl. Add lemon juice, brown sugar and soy sauce; toss. Add pork to onion and soy sauce mixture. Let stand at room temperature for 1 hour. Place nine pork cubes on each 9-inch skewer. Broil for 8 minutes per side or until done. Serve with rice. Yield: 6-8 servings.

Mrs. Ludwik Rucki, Pres.
Christ Lutheran Church LWML
Timmins, Ontario, Canada

LASAGNA (ITALY)

1 lge. and 1 sm. onion, chopped
1 clove of garlic, chopped
6 sprigs parsley, chopped
¼ c. salad oil
1 1-lb. 12-oz. can tomatoes
1 4-oz. can tomato paste
2 bay leaves
Salt
¼ tsp. pepper
½ c. water
1 lb. ground beef
4 tbsp. butter or margarine
3 tbsp. flour
¾ c. grated Parmesan cheese
2 c. milk
2 egg yolks
1 1-lb. pkg. lasagna noodles

Combine large onion, garlic and parsley; fry slightly in hot salad oil. Add tomatoes, tomato paste, bay leaves, 1 teaspoonful salt, pepper and water. Stir until well mixed. Toss in ground beef, breaking up into little pieces. Cover and cook over low heat for 45 minutes, stirring occasionally. Cook small onion in melted butter for 1 to 2 minutes. Mix in flour smoothly. Add grated cheese and a dash of salt. Gradually stir in milk. Cook over low heat, stirring constantly, until sauce is as thick as heavy cream. Beat egg yolks slightly; slowly mix in small amount of hot cheese mixture. Mix all cheese mixture and yolks. Cook over low heat for 10 minutes longer. Remove from heat. Cook lasagna noodles as directed on package until tender. Drain. Grease 9 x 13 x 2 1/2-inch baking dish. Place 1 layer of noodles on bottom of baking dish; pour over enough tomato sauce to cover noodles and add some of cheese sauce. Continue layering until ingredients are all used. Cover with cheese sauce. Bake at 325 degrees for 20 minutes; broil until surface is a bubbly gold. Yield: 12 servings.

Mrs. Harold Gloystein. Rep.
Peace Women's Guild
Arvada, Colorado

CHICKEN TETRAZZINI (ITALY)

1 ½ lb. spaghetti
Chicken broth
1 ½ c. chopped celery
3 lge. green peppers, chopped
3 tbsp. butter
1 6-lb. chicken, cooked and cubed
2 cans cream of mushroom soup
1 can evaporated milk
Salt and pepper to taste
1 ½ lb. American cheese, grated

Cook spaghetti in broth. Saute celery and green peppers in butter. Combine all ingredients except a small amount of cheese. Turn into casserole. Sprinkle top with remaining cheese. Bake at 350 degrees for 45 minutes. Yield: 30 serving.

Mrs. Ken Degler, Pres.
St. John's LWML
Mattoon, Illinois

CHICKEN TETRAZZINI (ITALY)

1 3-lb. chicken
2 c. hot water
¼ lb. wide egg noodles or 1 recipe
   homemade noodles
Butter
⅓ c. flour
Salt
2 c. light cream
1 c. chicken stock
2 tbsp. Sauterne wine
6 tbsp. grated Parmesan cheese
½ lb. fresh mushrooms, sliced
Pepper to taste
Garlic to taste

Cook chicken in hot water until tender; remove meat from bones. Cook noodles in unsalted water for 10 minutes; blanch. Melt 1/4 cup butter; blend in flour and 1 1/2 teaspoonful salt. Gradually stir in cream, chicken stock and wine. Cook until thick. Add 1 cup of sauce to noodles with 2 tablespoonfuls butter and cheese. Saute mushrooms in 2 tablespoonfuls butter for 5 minutes. Add 1/2 teaspoonful salt, pepper and garlic. Cook for 5 minutes. Add to noodle mixture. Place in shallow baking dish. Cover with remaining cheese. Bake at 350 degrees for 30 minutes. Broil for 5 minutes to brown. Yield: 6 servings.

Mrs. Eugene Klemp
Zion LWML
Springfield, Minnesota

SPAGHETTI SAUCE (ITALY)

1 lb. hamburger
1 lge. onion, chopped
1 sm. green pepper, chopped
1 tsp. salt
½ tsp. pepper
1 can tomato sauce
1 can whole tomatoes
¼ c. Chianti wine, plain wine or wine vinegar
1 bay leaf
¼ tsp. oregano
1 tsp. garlic salt or 1 sm. clove of garlic
1 tsp. Italian seasoning
2 to 3 c. water
Cooked spaghetti
Parmesan cheese

Brown hamburger, onion and green pepper in large skillet or Dutch oven with tight-fitting lid. Add all remaining ingredients and simmer for 3 hours, adding water occasionally as needed. Cook down to a thick sauce. Mix cooked spaghetti with sauce and let stand for a while before serving with grated Parmesan cheese. Yield: 6-8 servings.

Mrs. Warren Freeman
Grace Ladies Guild
Victoria, Texas

VEAL PARMIGIANA (ITALY)

½ c. chopped onion
1 clove of garlic, mashed
Cooking oil
2 8-oz. cans tomato sauce

(Continued on next page)

¼ c. water
1 tsp. crushed oregano
½ tsp. pepper
1 tbsp. parsley
½ c. plus 2 tbsp. grated Parmesan cheese
½ c. fine dry seasoned bread crumbs
6 slices veal, ¼-in. thick
1 egg, slightly beaten
1 8-oz. pkg. Mozzarella cheese

Saute onion and garlic in 3 tablespoonfuls oil until golden; stir in tomato sauce, water, oregano, pepper and parsley; cover and simmer for 10 minutes. Combine 1/2 cup Parmesan cheese and bread crumbs. Dip veal into egg and then into cheese-crumb mixture. Heat 2 tablespoonfuls oil in skillet; saute veal, two or three pieces at a time, until golden, turning only once. Repeat with remaining veal and 2 tablespoonfuls oil. Pour one-half of tomato sauce into baking dish. Cut Mozzarella cheese into six thick slices; alternate with veal slices in baking dish. Pour over remaining sauce in dish. Sprinkle with remaining Parmesan cheese. Bake at 350 degrees for 25 minutes or until sauce is bubble and cheese melts. Yield: 6 servings.

Mable Lipell
St. Paul's LWML
Woodland, California

VEAL SCALLOPINI (ITALY)

1 ½ lb. veal cutlet, ½-in. thick
¼ c. seasoned flour
¼ c. salad oil
1 clove of garlic
½ c. white wine
1 tbsp. lemon juice
¼ c. water
1 med. onion, sliced
Small piece of bay leaf
1 tsp. salt
¼ tsp. pepper
½ c. mushrooms (opt.)

Rub meat with seasoned flour. Heat in oil in heavy skillet; add veal and garlic. Cook until meat is browned; remove garlic. Add remaining ingredients. Cover; simmer for 45 to 55 minutes or until tender. Yield: 6 servings.

Mrs. Marjorie Boltz
Trinity LWML
Walnut Creek, California

RUMAKI (JAPAN)

⅓ c. soy sauce
2 tbsp. dry Sherry
1 clove of garlic, minced
⅛ tsp. pepper
⅛ tsp. monosodium glutamate
½ lb. chicken livers, cleaned and cut into
   halves
1 5-oz. can water chestnuts, drained
½ lb. bacon

Combine soy sauce, Sherry, garlic, pepper and monosodium glutamate; pour over chicken livers and marinate for 30 minutes. Cut each water chestnut into three crosswise slices. Cut bacon slices into halves. Wrap a chicken liver and water chestnut piece in bacon, securing with one or two toothpicks. Grill over charcoal, turning occasionally, until bacon is crisp or bake at 400 degrees for 20 minutes; do not turn.

Mrs. James G. Krestensen, Pres.
First Lutheran Church LWML
Natchez, Mississippi

SUKIYAKI (JAPAN)

½ lb. large mushrooms, sliced lengthwise
½ lb. fresh spinach, parboiled and drained
2 bunches fresh scallions, cut into 2-in.
   pieces
2 bamboo shoots, sliced diagonally
½ lb. soy bean curd, cut into 1-in. squares
1 tbsp. margarine, melted
1 tsp. sugar
¼ c. water
¼ c. soy sauce
1 lb. boneless rib roast, thinly sliced

Saute vegetables in margarine in large skillet over medium heat for 3 minutes. Stir constantly. Add sugar, water and soy sauce. Push vegetables to one side of skillet; add beef. Cook, stirring and turning for 1 minute. Mix beef with vegetables; cook for 3 minutes or until vegetables are tender. Serve with rice. Yield: 4-6 servings.

Mrs. E. F. Schinnerer, Pres.
Long Beach, California LWML
Compton, California

YASAIITAMAE (JAPAN)

2 lb. sirloin steak, thinly sliced into 1-in.
   pieces
1 tbsp. cooking oil
1 tsp. monosodium glutamate
¼ tsp. salt
¼ tsp. pepper
1 sm. cabbage, coarsely chopped
4 carrots, thinly sliced
1 green pepper, chopped
1 med. onion, chopped

Brown meat in large skillet in cooking oil over medium high heat. Add monosodium glutamate, salt and pepper; stir well. Add vegetables and cook until heated through, but not wilted. Serve at once. Yield: 6 servings.

Mrs. Donald Dannenber
Holy Cross Guild
Kearney, Nebraska

CHILI ENCHILADAS (MEXICO)

½ lge. onion, chopped
½ lb. ground beef
1 tsp. shortening
1 can chili without beans

373

(Continued on next page)

¼ tsp. salt
⅛ tsp. pepper
¼ tsp. crushed red pepper seed
8 tortillas
Butter, melted
½ lb. Longhorn cheese, grated

Saute 2 tablespoonfuls onion and beef in shortening. Add chili, salt, pepper and pepper seed. Simmer, covered, for 10 minutes. Brush tortillas on both sides with melted butter. Place in center of each tortilla, 1 tablespoonful chili mixture, 1 teaspoonful onion and 1 teaspoonful cheese. Roll up tortilla and place in 13 x 9 x 2-inch baking pan. Spoon remaining chili mixture over tortillas, being careful to cover each tortilla. Sprinkle remaining cheese on top. Bake at 250 degrees for 15 minutes. Serve immediately. Yield: 4 servings.

Mrs. Ella Meieroff
Salem Ladies Aid
St. Louis, Missouri

GREEN ENCHILADAS (MEXICO)

12 corn tortillas
Salad oil or shortening
1 can cream of chicken soup
1 soup can water or milk
1 4-oz. can roasted, peeled chopped green chilies
¼ lb. milk Cheddar cheese, grated
1 med. onion, grated

Fry tortillas in a small amount of salad oil until brown and crisp on each side. Drain. Combine soup, water and green chilies in a saucepan; bring to a boil. Place 1 tortilla in greased 2 or 2 1/2-quart casserole; sprinkle with cheese and onion. Cover with sauce. Repeat layers until there are 12, ending with sauce. Cover and bake at 350 degrees for 20 minutes. Serve hot. Yield: 8 servings.

Mrs. Oscan Knudson, Treas.
Immanuel LWML
Carlsbad, New Mexico

POLLO DE HACIENDA--CHICKEN, COUNTRY-STYLE

6 ot 8 pieces chicken
Flour
Salt and pepper
Paprika
Oil
4 strips bacon, cut up
1 can peeled green chilies, cut into strips
3 carrots, sliced
1 tbsp. finely chopped parsley
1 sm. bay leaf
1 sm. sprig thyme
1 lemon, thinly sliced
2 c. tomato juice

Dredge chicken thoroughly in mixture of flour, salt, pepper and paprika. Reserve flour. Fry in hot oil until golden brown. Place chicken in large casserole or baking dish. Add bacon, chilies, carrots, parsley, bay leaf, thyme and remaining seasoned flour. Place lemon slices on top of chicken; add tomato juice. Cover and bake at 350 degrees for 1 hour or until chicken is tender. Yield: 6-8 servings.

Ehria J. Espinoza, Sec.
Trinidad Willing Workers
San Antonio, Texas

CHICKEN TAMALES (MEXICO)

50 long corn shuck leaves
1 3-lb. stewing chicken
1 lge. onion, chopped
2 cloves of garlic, chopped
Salt
3 c. chicken broth
4 tbsp. chili powder
2 tbsp. flour
4 c. masa meal or 6 c. corn meal
1 c. chicken fat or shortening
4 tsp. baking powder

Select leaves 6 to 7 inches long and 4 inches wide. Wash leaves thoroughly; soak in warm water for 1 hour. Shake water from leaf; cut off tip and torn edges. Cook chicken in 6 cups water with onion, garlic and 1 tablespoonful salt until tender. Reserve broth. Remove bones form chicken; run meat through fine meat grinder. Place meat in saucepan; add 1 cup of broth, one-half of chili powder and salt to taste. Mix well. Cook for 10 minutes. Thicken with flour blended with 1/4 cup water. Cool. Combine meal, fat, remaining chili powder, 1 tablespoonful salt and 2 cups boiling chicken broth. Blend well. Add 4 teaspoonfuls baking powder; knead until smooth. Place leaf on bread board. Starting about 1 1/2 inches from base of shuck, spread 1/8-inch thick layer of prepared masa on leaf; masa layer should be about 2 x 4 inches in size. Place 1 heaping teaspoonful of chicken mixture lengthwise along center; roll up, starting with long side. Fold back base end of shuck; place on tray until all tamales are made. Line roaster with leaves, making a ridge with shuck trimmings down center of roaster. Stack tamales closely against ridge with folded end down. Place pot over fire. Pour 2 pints boiling water over tamale. Cover tightly and steam for 1 hour and 30 minutes to 2 hours. Pour additional hot water around edge if needed. Drain; cover and let stand in warm place until ready to serve. Yield: 8 servings.

Mrs. Helma K. Hawk
Immanuel Mary Martha Guild
Mercedes, Texas

TACOS (MEXICO)

1 med. potato, finely shredded
1 tsp. thyme
1 sm. clove of garlic, cut into small pieces
Salt and pepper to taste
1 lb. ground beef
12 frozen tortillas
1 lb. Velveeta cheese, shredded
3 med. tomatoes, peeled and thinly sliced
1 sm. onion, thinly sliced
1 med. head lettuce, thinly sliced
Hot sauce (opt.)

374

(Continued on next page)

Mix potato, thyme, garlic, salt, pepper and meat in 1-quart saucepan. Add 2 tablespoonfuls water. Place over low heat; cook, stirring often, until potatoes are well done. Cover and keep warm. Fry tortillas in skillet for 1 minute on both sides or until crisp. Drain. Place meat mixture on tortillas; add cheese, tomatoes, onion and lettuce. Hot sauce may be used if desired. Yield: 12 tacos.

Mrs. Hugh A. Wright, Pres.
Zion LWML
Independence, Kansas

BENLOSE FUGLER (NORWAY)

1 ½ lb. round steak, cut into 4-in. squares
Bacon
Chopped onion
Salt and pepper to taste
1 tbsp. flour
2 tbsp. butter
1 pt. water

Pound round steak. Place strip of bacon and 1 teaspoonful onion on each square; sprinkle with salt and pepper. Roll and fasten with toothpick. Dredge in flour; brown in butter. Add water. Cover and simmer for 2 hours. NOTE: Spread thin layer of prepared mustard on meat before rolling, if desired. Yield: 4 servings.

Carol Williamson, Pres.
Grace LCW
Kingman, Arizona

LUTEFISK (NORWAY)

3 lb. fresh or frozen lutefisk
3 qt. boiling water
3 tbsp. salt
Melted butter
Lingonberries or whole cranberry sauce (opt.)

Thaw frozen lutefisk. Soak in cold water in a covered container in refrigerator for 24 hours; drain. Skin fish; cut into 2-inch pieces. Wrap fish loosely in cheesecloth. Place in boiling salted water. Cover; simmer for 5 to 10 minutes or until fish flakes easily when tested with a fork. Drain and serve with melted butter and lingonberries. Yield: 6 servings.

Mrs. Woodrow Thompson
Bethlehem Ladies Aid Soc.
Herman, Minnesota
Mrs. Carl E. Carlson
Redeemer Ladies Aid
Saint Cloud, Minnesota

LUTEFISK PUDDING (NORWAY)

½ c. rice
1 c. salted water
2 eggs
1 c. milk
2 c. cooked lutefisk, flaked
2 tbsp. butter

Cook rice in salted water until tender. Beat eggs; add milk. Pour over the rice, lutefisk and butter. Place in buttered baking dish. Bake at 375 degrees for 30 minutes. Yield: 10 servings.

Pat Smeback, Pres.
Peace LWML
Selah, Washington

MEAT BALLS (NORWAY)

2 lb. ground beef
1 lb. ground pork
¾ c. bread crumbs
½ c. cream
1 egg, slightly beaten
1 tbsp. minced onion (opt.)
2 tsp. salt
¼ tsp. pepper
⅛ tsp. ginger
¼ to ½ c. butter
1 c. hot water

Grind beef and pork together three times. Add bread crumbs and cream; mix lightly. Add egg, onion, salt, pepper and ginger. Roll into balls slightly smaller than a golf ball. Brown in butter. Remove meat balls; add water to remaining butter in pan. Return meat balls to pan; simmer for 1 hour and 30 minutes. Add more water if needed. Yield: 16 servings.

Mrs. Eldon Bulman, Pres.
Waterville Ladies Aid
Harpers Ferry, Iowa

ROLLE PULSE (NORWAY)

Veal slices
Pork slices
1 mutton side, cut into 9 x 7-in. pieces
Chopped onions
Chopped green peppers
Ginger
Salt
Salt peter (opt.)
¼ lb. sugar
1 gal. water

Place small veal and pork slices on mutton pieces. Sprinkle with onions, peppers, ginger, salt and salt peter. Roll into oblong rolls and sew together. Combine 1 pound salt and sugar in water; bring to a boil. Pour over rolls; let set for a few days to one month. Remove from solution; boil in fresh water until tender. Place in a press overnight. Cut in thin slices for sandwiches.

Mrs. Emmanuel Caba, Pres.
Trinity LCW
Nampa, Idaho

STUFFED SLICED HAM (NORWAY)

1 ½ lb. thinly sliced boiled or baked ham
1 c. dry red wine
¼ c. butter

375

(Continued on next page)

1 ⅓ c. chopped walnuts
⅓ c. chopped green onions and tops
2 c. grated sharp cheese
1 c. heavy cream

Marinate ham slices in wine overnight. Heat butter. Add walnuts and green onions. Saute slightly. Remove from heat; add 1 1/2 cups grated cheese. Toss to mix. Place 1 spoonful of stuffing on each slice of ham. Roll up; fasten with a toothpick. Grease a shallow baking dish. Place layer of stuffed ham rolls in greased shallow baking dish; add heavy cream and remaining cheese. Bake at 300 degrees for 30 minutes. Garnish with additional chopped green onion. Yield: 12 servings.

Bonnie Scheffler, Sec.
Peace LCW
Lompoc, California

PORK ADOBO (PHILIPPINES)

2 lb. pork, cut into small pieces
¾ c. vinegar
1 ½ c. water
½ c. soy sauce
2 or 3 cloves of garlic, minced
½ tbsp. peppercorns
1 tbsp. salt
Dash of pepper
1 bay leaf

Combine all ingredients; boil for 45 minutes. Remove liquid; set aside. Brown meat in a small amount of fat. Add liquid; simmer for a few minutes. Serve hot over boiled rice. NOTE: One chicken, cut up, may be substituted for pork. Yield: 6-8 servings.

Mrs. Louis C. Castens, Pres.
Trinity Ladies Aid
Riesel, Texas

POLYNESIAN HAM CUBES

1 11-oz. can Mandarin orange segments
1 13 ½-oz. can pineapple chunks
Water
2 tbsp. cornstarch
¼ tsp. cinnamon
2 tsp. soy sauce
¼ tsp. ground ginger
2 tsp. chopped onion
2 tbsp. chopped green pepper
1 lb. cooked smoked ham, cut into ¾-in. cubes
1 c. sliced cooked celery
3 c. cooked rice

Drain orange segments and pineapple chunks, reserving liquids; add enough water to fruit liquids to equal 2 cups. Combine cornstarch and cinnamon in saucepan; add fruit liquid, soy sauce, ginger, onion and green pepper. Cook, stirring constantly, until thickened. Add ham, fruits and celery. Cook until heated through. Serve over rice. Yield: 6-8 servings.

Mrs. Ortha Kling, Pres.
Berea LCW
Hilmar, California

PORTUGUESE SPARERIBS (PORTUGAL)

1 onion, chopped
2 tbsp. butter
⅓ c. water
⅓ c. chili sauce
⅓ c. vinegar
⅓ c. brown sugar
3 tbsp. horseradish
¼ c. Worcestershire sauce
1 clove of garlic, chopped
1 tsp. soy sauce
⅓ c. red wine (opt.)
6 lb. spareribs

Brown onion in butter; add water, chili sauce, vinegar, brown sugar, horseradish, Worcestershire sauce, garlic and soy sauce. Simmer for 5 to 10 minutes. Add wine. Place ribs in shallow pan. Bake at 450 degrees for 1 hour. Reduce heat to 350 degrees; bake for 30 minutes. Pour sauce over ribs; bake for 30 minutes longer, basting once. Yield: 6-8 servings.

Mrs. Eugene Graham, Treas.
Resurrection LCW
Dublin, California

BEEF STROGANOFF (RUSSIA)

2 lb. lean beef, shredded
Juice of 1 lemon
1 onion, chopped
¼ c. butter
½ lb. sliced mushrooms
¼ c. flour
½ c. tomato juice
½ c. stock
Salt and pepper to taste
2 tbsp. Sherry
½ c. sour cream

Sprinkle beef with lemon juice. Saute onion in butter until soft. Remove from pan; saute mushrooms. Remove mushrooms; brown lightly floured beef. Cook for 5 minutes; add remaining ingredients except sour cream. Cook for 5 minutes longer. Stir in sour cream; heat through. Serve over rice or noodles. Yield: 4 servings.

Mrs. James D. DeMart, Pres.
Concordia Ladies Aid Soc.
Pittsburgh, Pennsylvania

CHICKEN KIEV (RUSSIA)

⅛ tsp. salt
⅛ tsp. pepper
½ lb. unsalted butter, softened
4 chicken breasts, halved
1 egg, slightly beaten
2 tbsp. milk
1 ½ c. cracker crumbs

Blend salt and pepper into butter; chill until butter is firm but not hard. Remove skins from breasts; flatten each breast to 1/4-inch thick. Divide butter into eight portions; shape each portion into roll 3/4-inch thick. Place lengthwise

(Continued on next page)

in each breast half. Roll to enclose butter. Wrap in waxed paper or aluminum foil; chill for 1 to 2 hours. Combine egg and milk in bowl. Roll each breast in cracker crumbs. Dip into egg mixture; roll in cracker crumbs. Let stand for 5 to 10 minutes to seal. Deep fry chicken breasts, 2 at a time, in deep saucepan. Fry for 5 to 6 minutes or until golden brown. Turn once during frying time; drain. Place breasts in baking dish; bake at 350 degrees for 10 minutes or until tender. Serve over wild rice. Yield: 4 servings.

Mildred Sundberg
Our Redeemer LCW
St. Paul, Minnesota

FLEISCHKUCHLE (RUSSIA)

1 med. onion, chopped
3 tbsp. melted shortening
Salt
2 tbsp. sugar
1 c. milk
2 eggs, beaten
4 c. flour
1 lb. hamburger
Pepper to taste

Soak onion in 1/2 cup water. Add shortening, 1 tablespoonful salt, sugar and milk to eggs. Add 2 cups flour; mix well. Add remaining flour; mix. Knead dough for 10 minutes or until surface is smooth when cut with sharp knife. Divide dough into two parts. Roll one-half of dough 1/8-inch thick. Mix undrained onion and meat; season to taste. Drop 1 heaping teaspoonful meat at 2-inch intervals onto one-half of rolled dough. Cover with remaining one-half; press firmly between each meat pattie. Cut around each pattie; seal firmly and set aside. Repeat with remaining dough. Deep fry at 370 degrees until deep golden brown. Yield: 25-30 servings.

Mrs. Betty Haar, Pres.
St. Paul's Ladies Aid
Freeman, South Dakota

VEAL PAPRIKAS (SLAVIC)

1 lge. onion, chopped
2 tbsp. fat
2 lb. veal, cubed
Salt and pepper to taste
3 tsp. paprika
1 c. hot water
2 tbsp. flour
1 c. sour cream

Saute onion in fat until light brown. Add veal; brown. Season with salt, pepper and paprika. Add water; cover. Bring to a boil; reduce temperature. Simmer for 1 hour or until meat is tender. Add more water if necessary. Mix flour with sour cream; add to meat. Bring to a boil; mix well until thickened. Serve over dumplings or mashed potatoes.

Mrs. Paul Junas, Pres.
St. John's Lydia Soc.
Hazleton, Pennsylvania

BABOTEE (SOUTH AFRICA)

2 onions, finely chopped
1 tbsp. cooking oil
1 lb. ground beef
2 tbsp. vinegar
2 tbsp. brown sugar
1 tsp. salt
1 tbsp. curry powder
2 thick slices bread
2 c. milk
2 eggs, beaten

Saute onions in oil in medium frying pan. Add ground beef to onions; cook until browned. Add vinegar, brown sugar, salt and curry powder. Soak bread in milk; squeeze out, reserving milk. Add bread to meat; mix well. Place in 8 1/2 x 1 3/4-inch round or square greased casserole. Add remaining milk to eggs; pour over meat. Bake at 375 degrees for 1 hour or until custard is set. Yield: 6 servings.

Mrs. Merritt Vossler, Pres.
Trinity LWML
Wellsville, New York

CHICKEN AND YELLOW RICE (SPAIN)

2 2½-lb. fryers, cleaned and cut into serving
   pieces
Seasoned meat tenderizer
1 c. chopped onions
½ c. olive oil
1 tbsp. vinegar
3 cloves of garlic, crushed
1 green pepper, chopped
1 c. chopped celery
1 c. canned tomatoes, drained
1 lge. bay leaf
Tomato juice
1½ tsp. salt
Pepper (opt.)
½ tsp. powdered saffron
2 c. uncooked rice
1 pkg. frozen peas
2 pimentos, cut into strips

Season meat with seasoned meat tenderizer. Broil chicken on lower rack of oven until browned. Fry onions in oil in large kettle until golden. Add vinegar, garlic, green pepper, celery, tomatoes and bay leaf. Remove chicken; add enough water and tomato juice to pan drippings to make 4 cups. Add salt and pepper. Add to onion mixture. Boil for 5 minutes. Add saffron. Add rice, stirring well; bring to a boil. Add chicken. Simmer for 25 minutes. Cook peas according to package directions. Place rice in center of hot platter. Arrange chicken around rice. Top with peas. Garnish with pimentos. Yield: 8 servings.

Mrs. James Barcellona, Pres.
Good Shepard LCW
Tampa, Florida

PAELLA (SPAIN)

2 c. uncooked rice
½ c. oil
1 broiler chicken, cut into serving pieces

(Continued on next page)

2 cans or 1 ½ lb. fresh shrimp
1 lge. onion, chopped
2 cloves of garlic
1 can tomato sauce
1 can chicken consomme
1 can or 8 artichoke hearts
1 jar pimento strips
¼ c. minced parsley
½ tsp. powdered saffron
1 pkg. frozen peas

Brown rice in 3 tablespoonfuls oil in heavy skillet. Remove rice; brown chicken in remaining oil. Remove chicken; fry shrimp lightly in same oil. Add chicken, onion, garlic, tomato sauce and consomme. Cover; simmer until chicken is tender. Add rice, shrimp and remaining ingredients. Simmer until rice is done. Yield: 8 servings.

Mrs. L. W. Hoener
Trinity LWML
Brownsville, Texas

DILL KOTT (SWEDEN)

3 lb. breast of veal or lean lamb
6 tbsp. chopped dill
Salt and pepper
2 tbsp. flour
2 tbsp. butter, melted
1 tsp. sugar
2 tbsp. white vinegar

Barely cover meat with boiling water. Add 3 tablespoonfuls dill, 1 tablespoonful salt and 1/4 teaspoonful pepper. Simmer for 1 hour and 30 minutes to 2 hours or until meat is done. Reserve 2 cups broth. Add flour to butter in saucepan. Add 1 cup reserved broth; mix to a smooth paste. Add remaining broth, mixing well. Add salt and pepper to taste and remaining ingredients. Simmer until thickened. Serve with meat. Yield: 4-5 servings.

Mrs. Sally E. Burgeson
St. Matthew's Priscilla Guild
New Milford, New Jersey

JELLIED VEAL (SWEDEN)

2 lb. lean side pork
2 lb. veal shank
1 ½ qt. water
2 tbsp. salt
10 whole allspice
2 or 3 bay leaves
4 to 6 cloves
1 lge. onion, cut up
Pepper to taste
1 tbsp. unflavored gelatin

Combine all ingredients except gelatin in kettle. Bring to a boil; simmer for 1 hour and 30 minutes. Skim; cool. Remove veal from bone. Cut veal and pork into small pieces or grind. Return veal shank to stock; cook for 30 minutes. Strain stock; return to kettle. Add meats. Dissolve gelatin in small amount of cold water. Add to meats; cook for 15 minutes. Pour into loaf pans; chill.

Mrs. Bessie Larson
Grace Lutheran Church
Largo, Florida

POTATO SAUSAGE (SWEDEN)

2 lb. lean pork butt
2 lb. potatoes
1 sm. onion
3 tbsp. salt
½ tsp. pepper
¼ c. water
¼ c. casings

Grind meat with potatoes and onion. Add salt, pepper and water. Mix well; stuff into casings. Boil slowly, uncovered, in salted water for 1 hour.

Mrs. Carl L. Nelson, Pres.
Bethlehem Evangelical Lutheran LCW
Chesterton, Indiana

SYLTA (SWEDEN)

8 lb. pork butts
2 veal shanks
Salt
Allspice

Cook pork and veal seperately until done. Remove meats; cool. Reserve veal broth. Place cloth in bowl. Cut meats into small pieces. Alternate layers of pork with veal in cloth. Add salt and allspice to each layer. Tie cloth tightly. Add veal juice. Place plate on top of meat; press with heavy weights. Let stand for one and one half days. Remove cloth; slice. Serve with mustard.

Bernice Olson, Sec.
Bethany LCW
Batavia, Illinois

LUBEE (SYRIA)

1 ½ lb. lamb, cut into chunks
Butter
1 onion, diced
2 lb. fresh green beans, cut into halves
1 tbsp. salt
1 sm. can tomato sauce
Pepper
Allspice

Brown meat lightly in butter. Add onion; simmer. Add green beans and salt. Cover; steam over low heat for 45 minutes. Add tomato sauce; add enough water to almost cover green beans. Sprinkle pepper and allspice to taste. Cook for 15 minutes or until tender. Serve with rice. Yield: 6 servings.

Mrs. Phil Schroeder
University Lutheran Chapel
Columbus, Ohio

INDEX

Order Forms For
FAVORITE RECIPES OF LUTHERAN LADIES, INC.

These order forms not for use by Ladies Aid Societies - see below

ORDER FORM

Send____copies of FAVORITE RECIPES OF LUTHERAN LADIES, "Traditional Meats."

TO:_____

_____

_____

All prices include mailing charges:

☐ $3.45 per book, payment enclosed.

☐ $2.95 each for 3 or more, payment enclosed.

☐ Bill me at $3.95 each.

FAVORITE RECIPES OF LUTHERAN LADIES, INC.
Box 3376, Montgomery, Ala. 36109

ORDER FORM

Send____copies of FAVORITE RECIPES OF LUTHERAN LADIES, "Traditional Meats."

TO:_____

_____

_____

All prices include mailing charges:

☐ $3.45 per book, payment enclosed.

☐ $2.95 each for 3 or more, payment enclosed.

☐ Bill me at $3.95 each.

FAVORITE RECIPES OF LUTHERAN LADIES, INC.
Box 3376, Montgomery, Ala. 36109

GIFT ORDER

Send____copies of FAVORITE RECIPES OF LUTHERAN LADIES, "Traditional Meats" edition.

TO:_____
Name of Person to Receive Book

_____
Address

City   State   Zip Code

My Name

_____
Address

City   State   Zip Code

☐ $3.45 each enclosed   ☐ $2.95 each for 3 or more   ☐ Bill me at $3.95 each

FAVORITE RECIPES OF LUTHERAN LADIES, INC./BOX 3376/MONTGOMERY, ALABAMA 36109

LADIES AID SOCIETY ORDER FOR FUND RAISING

Send____copies of FAVORITE RECIPES OF LUTHERAN LADIES, "Traditional Meats," @ $1.95 each. We will sell books for $2.95 each and make $1.00 profit on each book sold.

LADIES AID SOCIETY TERMS

All books are sent on trial. Unsold books may be returned for credit. Minimum order is 12 books. Postage and handling charges paid on orders for 24 or more books. Offer open only to Ladies Aid Societies.

TO:_____
Name

_____
Name of Organization

_____
Address

City   State   Zip Code

FAVORITE RECIPES OF LUTHERAN LADIES, INC./BOX 3376/ MONTGOMERY, ALABAMA 36109